tinder-box
Criminal
aggression

NEUROPSYCHOLOGY
DEMOGRAPHY
PHENOMENOLOGY

tinder-box Criminal aggression

Nathaniel J. Pallone
& James J. Hennessy

TRANSACTION PUBLISHERS
NEW BRUNSWICK (U.S.A.) AND LONDON (U.K.)

Library of Congress Catalog Number: 96-4403
ISBN: 1-56000-253-0
Printed in the United States of America

Library of Congress Cataloging-in-Publication Data

Pallone, Nathaniel J.
    Tinder-box criminal aggression : neuropsychology, demography, phenomenology / Nathaniel J. Pallone and James J. Hennessy.
        p. cm.
    Includes bibliographical references and index.
    ISBN 1-56000-253-0 (alk. paper)
    1. Criminal behavior. 2. Crimes of passion. 3. Aggressiveness.
4. Criminal anthropology. I. Hennessy, James, 1942–   . II. Title.
HV6115.P35   1996
364.2'4—dc20   96-4403
                                                                    CIP

Contents

FIGURES AND TABLES

PREFACE

This volume undertakes to amplify and extend the conceptual model for what we termed tinder-box criminal aggression which we introduced in *Criminal Behavior: A Process Psychology Analysis.* In particular, proceeding from the proposition that all behavior is the product of bio-psycho-social generators interacting with each other, we have endeavored in the present volume to anchor that model very firmly in research evidence from the neurosciences that links impulsive aggressive violence to neurological and neuropsychological dysfunction, to analyze the ways in which neurological dysfunction is potentiated socially and experienced phenomenologically, and to discern whether (and how) psychometrically-identifiable "traits" represent manifestations of neuropsychological organization.

Though this work is intended primarily for the practitioner and student of the behavioral sciences, it addresses matters that are also of substantial import to the working professional in criminal justice, corrections, and the law, especially in relation to societal standards for criminal culpability and to customary modes of correctional rehabilitation.

Only two names appear on the title page, but any volume that aims at comprehensiveness owes huge debts to many minds and hands. Raymond B. Cattell, that giant of contemporary psychological theory upon whose shoulders we stand, dwarfed, continues as a dominant and inspirational influence, even in his advanced years. We can never repay our debts to Willard Heckel, late dean of the School of Law at Rutgers' Newark campus, a senior academic statesman in legal education and one of the founders of "advocacy law," or to Don Gottfredson, founding dean of the Graduate School of Criminal Justice at Rutgers, who has been both sequentially and simultaneously mentor, colleague, friend. In the interpretation of data from the neurosciences, we have continued to benefit from consultation with Robert Pandina of the Center for Alcohol Studies at Rutgers in New Brunswick, Kirtley Thornton of New Jersey's Center for Health Psychology, and Eugene Loveless of St. Joseph's Hospital in Westchester County, New York. In the criminologic community, no one has been more supportive of our efforts to integrate theory and research from the neurosciences and from process psychology with "real-world" data on aggressive crime as it is committed than Gerhard Mueller of Rutgers and C. Ray Jeffrey of Florida State University.

We continue to be indebted to Phyllis Schulze of the National Council on Crime and Delinquency Library at the Newhouse Center for Law and Justice on the Newark campus and Adeline Tallau of the Library of Science and Medicine on the New Brunswick campus, both at Rutgers. Our work has been facilitated, aided, and abetted in ways too varied to enumerate at Rutgers by Cindy Nahabedian, Kirk Hansen, Ray Collins, and, most particularly, Eric Workowski, who has given new mearning to the term research associate; by Ketrin Saud, Kristin Schaefer, and Peg Aarnowski at Fordham; by the younger James J. Hennessy of Shared Medical Systems, Elisabeth Hennessy Koke, Joanne Hennessy, and David Blische, members of the respective family circles; and by Larry Mintz and Scott Bramson at Transaction Publishers. To Letty and Teri, our gratitude continues for their unwavering support through every day's most quiet need.

Nathaniel J. Pallone & James J. Hennessy

1 CRIMINAL BEHAVIOR AND ITS BIO-PSYCHO-SOCIAL DETERMINANTS

IN THIS CHAPTER, WE REVIEW BRIEFLY THE STATUS OF THE SEARCH FOR THE bio-psycho-social determinants of criminal behavior as reflected in the principal paradigms advanced in scientific psychology, then introduce the pivotal components in a process psychology paradigm for understanding criminal behavior. We conclude with an outline for a conceptual model of process dynamics discernible in aggressive criminal violence under "tinder-box" circumstances that is developed and articulated in succeeding chapters.

EVOLUTION IN THE PSYCHOLOGICAL ANALYSIS OF CRIMINAL BEHAVIOR

For reasons that may have more to do with the vagaries of a criminal justice system in which a mere 15% of all reported crimes result in apprehension and conviction of offenders than with judgments about the corrosive character of crime both societally and individually [NOTE 1], the analysis of criminal behavior has rarely occupied a centrifugal position of priority within the enterprise of scientific psychology. Until recently, analytic models rooted in psychology not surprisingly sought the engines for criminal behavior primarily or exclusively in such "traditional" intra-psychic determinants as formal mental disorder or habitual traits and characteristics of personality. In essence, these models argue that criminal behavior springs from the inside out, with psychological predispositions as the controlling determinants.

In some sharp contrast, analytic models rooted in sociology and in sociologically-anchored criminology site those engines primarily or exclusively in extra-psychic determinants. In essence, these models argue that criminal behavior springs from the outside in, with social conditions (such as poverty, marginality, the sociocultural experience of "anomie," encapsulation in subcultures that foster or tolerate deviant behavior, or, in the most recent variant, those characteristics of external stimuli [NOTE 2] held to be "magnetizing" or "behavior-impelling") as the controlling determinants.

Only within the quite recent past has there evolved a synthesis that accounts both intra-psychic and extra-psychic (or "stimulus") determinants in a comprehensive psychologically-anchored analytic model of criminal behavior, itself rooted in a overarching conceptualization that posits that all behavior is a function of bio-psycho-social variables interacting with each other. Because paradigm shifts within the enterprise of scientific psychology radiate outward toward (as well as inward from) adjacent behavior science disciplines rather slowly, there obtains a palpable "paradigm lag" between analytic models of criminal behavior anchored in contemporary scientific psychology and those anchored in sociology and criminology. Likely, such paradigm lags approximate at least one evolutionary stage in conceptualization.

For their part, criminologists tend to react (sometimes dismissively, often derisively) to what they perceive to be an exclusive preoccupation with intra-psychic variables among psychologists to the detriment of serious scientific attention to extra-psychic variables. But that dismissive posture ignores the prospective contributions to be made to an understanding of criminal behavior from the vast world of psychological inquiry beyond personality and psychopathology, ranging from investigations of stimulation of the lateral hypothalamus in infrahuman species to the effects of negative modeling on the behavior of children.

Attributing criminal behavior to psychopathology

Historically, the earliest psychologically-anchored analytic model attributes criminal behavior to endogenous psychopathology, and, at least implicitly, tends to equate criminal deviance with psychological deviance. To borrow the terms popularized by Melitta Schmidberg (1968) and Michel Foucault (1978), this school of thought regards "badness" as essentially coincident with "madness." That rather narrow stance characterizes such classic works as *The Criminal, the Judge, and the Public* by the distinguished psychiatrist Franz Alexander (1931) and the *Handbook of Correctional Psychology* (1949) by Robert Lindner (originator of the term "the fifty-minute hour" to denominate the typical psychotherapeutic interview), both of which are unabashedly psychoanalytic in their orientation, and perhaps finds its apotheosis in *The Criminal Personality* by clinical psychiatrists Samuel Yochelson and Stanton Samenow (1976).

Doubtless the "badness = madness" model had its origins in the clinical experiences of mental health professionals who were called upon to render judgments as to the psychological stability of putative offenders, often in connection with forensic proceedings to determine guilt or innocence. In the willingness to extrapolate from individual case study data to universal models of behavior that prototypically mars psychoanalytic theorizing in particular and the clinical mental health sciences more generally, the severe limitations imposed on generalizability by implicit and explicit selection criteria and processes which had led to contact between clinician and offender were apparently overlooked.

We should not be surprised that those whose experience with accused or adjudicated offenders issues primarily from the examination of defendants whose behavior or history (criminal or psychosocial) has led either prosecutor, defense counsel, or judge to wonder about psychological normalcy or deviance conclude to active psychopathology in a majority of the clinical cases they examine. Almost invariably such mental health evaluations focus only on defendants accused of crimes of egregious violence directed against persons and rarely on those accused of such "property" crimes as theft, fraud, or embezzlement, although the latter category of offenses statistically exceeds the former at a ratio of at least 5:1. Thus, the "badness = madness" model may have been virtually dictated by the selection processes which brought (and continue to bring) putative offenders to the clinical attention of mental health professionals.

According to the "badness = madness" model, if Mental Disorders X, Y, and Z have been shown to be related to Criminal Behavior Q, and if both Person A and Person B suffer from Mental Disorders X, Y, and Z, we can expect both A and B to commit Crime Q. Put differently: If criminal behavior were singularly a function of mental disorder, we should expect all mentally disordered persons (or at least those mentally disordered in ways X, Y, and Z) to behave criminally.

But that formulation finds little large-scale empirical support. Stated most economically, large-scale studies of both accused and convicted offenders have found criminal offenders arrayed across types of crimes, especially when inflected by relative frequency of their occurrence, to display no singular patterns of formal mental disorder uniquely associated with the crimes they have committed, whether in explanatory or in exculpatory fashion. Moreover, such patterns of disorder as are observed in high incidence in offender populations are also found in relative profusion among subjects in the community who have not been convicted of crime [NOTE 3].

Whether pursuing a "fine screen" or a "gross screen" methodology, research in psychiatric epidemiology over the span of nearly 60 years has consistently indicated that clear symptoms of serious mental illness — defined approximately to coincide with the disabling psychoses, including those of organic origin; the more severe neuroses; significant mental retardation; and certain personality pattern disturbances that incline the individual toward an "explosive temperament," usually resultant in aggressive behavior, with the aggregate set requiring professional mental health attention — are found in the general population in a relative frequency ranging from 11% to 37% [NOTE 4]. The ratios reflect, but do not appear to be governed by, the fineness of the "mesh" in the screening devices.

Simultaneously, these studies have rather consistently identified a portion of the general population to be entirely symptom-free and a mid-range group that exhibits symptoms of "mild" mental illness. Among "gross screen" studies, the median ratio is 30%, while in the more conservative "fine screen" studies the median ratio is 19%. If we apply the latter, "more conservative" figure to the current national population, the extrapolation suggests an aggregate incidence of 47.5 million persons who can be considered "mad." That number exceeds by several-fold the aggregate number of criminal offenses of all kinds committed in the nation in a year (Maguire & Pastore, 1994, 246). The contrast indicates rather clearly that criminal deviance is not coextensive with psychiatric deviance.

That is not at all to deny that some psychopathologically-disordered persons sometimes behave criminally, but rather to assert that the "bad = mad" formulation has shown itself to be insufficient as an analytic model widely applicable to the explanation of criminal behavior across the spectrum of crimes of different sorts [NOTE 5]. Implicitly, the "bad = mad" model proposes a 1:1 correspondence between mental illness and criminal behavior. A more defensible view, which we develop later in this volume, is that mental disorder — and particularly that sort of mental disorder that results from neurological dysfunction — may be contributory to aggressive criminal violence, though likely not to non-aggressive crime. Formal mental disorder, especially when neurogenic, more frequently constitutes an explanatory than an exculpatory condition.

Attributing criminal behavior to measurable differences in personality

Emerging in consonance with the ascendance of psychometric methods in scientific psychology and their use with large pools of subjects, a second and more elaborate analytic model attributes criminal behavior to measurable differences in personality and is perhaps most elegantly epitomized in Hans Eysenck's (1964, 1977) *Crime and Personality* and by Eysenck & Gudjunsson (1989) in *Causes and Cures of Criminality.*

In Eysenck's formulation, criminal behavior is posited as a function of three durable personality characteristics (psychoticism, neuroticism, extraversion), while a fourth dimension, roughly encapsulated as the extent to which an individual seeks to appear "normal" either to all others or to selected others, is posited as contributory. Each of these dimensions can be measured on an instrument alternately called the Maudsley or the Eysenck Personality Inventory. A considerable body of subsequent research (which we review in Chapter 5) has both led to further refinements in Eysenck's original formulation and indicated the limitations of its applicability.

Similarly, although the overt intent had been to develop psychometric methods on which to base decisions about the level of custodial security required by prisoners incarcerated in Federal institutions in the United States, the monumental work utilizing the Minnesota Multiphasic Personality Inventory initiated by

Edwin Megargee and his colleagues (Megargee, 1977, 1982, 1984, 1986; Megargee & Bohn, 1977, 1979; Megargee & Carbonell, 1985), also reviewed in Chapter 5, has contributed to an understanding of how measurable personality characteristics are linked to certain types of criminal behavior but not to others and in some offenders but not in others.

Like those rooted in psychopathology, analytic models which attribute criminal behavior to measurable personality traits or characteristics hold that the engines for criminal behavior are internal. According to the differential psychology model, if Traits X, Y, and Z have been shown to be related to Criminal Behavior Q, and if both Person A and Person B possess the same "quantity" of Traits X, Y, and Z, it is equally probable that both A and B will commit Crime Q.

As in the psychopathology-anchored model, there are limitations inherent in the analytic model anchored in differential psychology and psychometric methodology. Conceptually, a principal set of considerations pivot around what sociologist Kai Erikson and psychologists Jerry Wiggins and Herbert Quay have identified as the "taxonomic trap," in which one reasons backwards rather than forwards. "Forward reasoning" would suggest that anyone who displays those measurable psychological characteristics found uniquely or in singular profusion among convicted offenders is predictably destined to commit similar crimes. "Backward reasoning" starts with the fact of conviction, then seeks to identify measurable psychological characteristics that those similar to each other in respect of the crimes they have committed also share in common.

But, as sociologist Kai Erikson (1966, p. 6) has observed, "Deviance is not a property *inherent* in any particular kind of behavior; it is a property *conferred upon* that behavior by the people who come into contact with it." The first fault line leading to the taxonomic trap is the (relatively uncritical) belief that the same behavior (e.g., buying a Nissan Sentra rather than a Cadillac Seville) is triggered by the same variables in all who so behave; the second is setting out in an attempt to find commonalties among members of the "class" so defined, an enterprise that, especially within the realm of criminal behavior, has usually yielded dispiriting results.

In Quay's (1987, p. 118) formulation: "Juvenile delinquency is a legal construct. Thus, the label 'delinquent' cannot automatically be considered to carry with it any information about the behavior of the individual beyond [his or her] having committed some act(s) which have violated the law. Put another way, since delinquency is not a psychological construct . . . the label does not imply that those who carry it are behaviorally or psychologically homogeneous." There are substantial clinical implications: "Clearly, fever is caused by many different infections, and these different infections are susceptible to different interventions." Or, as Wiggins (1973, 88-89) put it:

> Although members of a criterion group are homogeneous with respect to the defining characteristic of the criterion class . . . the critical condition for being assigned membership in a deviant group is *not* a psychological condition of the individual but the circumstances that led to labeling on the part of society. Hence, when we study "murderers," we are studying not a psychologically homogeneous group of individuals but rather a group of individuals who have been convicted of the crime of murder by one jury or another.

Operationally, a second consideration is that most large-scale studies of adjudicated offenders arrayed by type of offense are conducted with subjects who have been incarcerated or placed on probation after trial. As a function of the widespread practice of plea-bargaining, however, in which offenses of greater severity are "down-graded" to offenses of lesser severity in return for the entry of a plea of guilt (Schlesigner, 1995), the offense recorded in official records may bear little resemblance to the offense actually committed. With scandalous frequency, for example, the adult male who has cajoled or threatened a 9-year-old of either gender into sexual intercourse (but has not used a weapon to force compliance) is convicted, after plea-bargaining, not of statutory rape (an offense that carries a sentence of 30 years in most jurisdictions) but instead of "impairing the morals of a minor" (an offense that typically carries a sentence of 5 to 7 years). The expenses of a trial have been "cost-avoided," and the victim has been spared the trauma of testimony; but "impairing the morals of a minor" customarily connotes such behavior as providing triple-X-rated films to children in the family, light years away from statutory rape. Thus, the process of adjudication frequently places the offender in a wildly misleading taxonomic compartment.

The criminologist will, of course, be quick to add that whether a person who has committed a patently illegal (not to say, immoral and/or socially opprobrious) act is apprehended, prosecuted, and convicted thereof is a consequence of such a set of unpredictable vagaries in the functioning of the criminal justice system (from the decision of the victim whether to report, through apprehension, prosecution, plea-bargaining, and the assessment of penalty) that one may as well invoke "chance" as no less valid an explanatory construct than any other. And the psychologist who is familiar with the criminal justice system might further speculate that it may be easier to predict with accuracy whether a person will *commit a*n act of aggression, hostility, or greed than that he or she will be *convicted of* a criminal violation for committing that act.

For all these reasons, it is a fair assessment that thus far even the elegant research methods of differential psychology have failed to produce instruments capable of reliably identifying, on the basis of differentially measurable psychological traits or characteristics alone, those who have been (or will be) adjudicated as guilty of formally criminal behavior across traditionally-syllabicated categories of crime (i.e., crimes of violence or personal victimization vs.

property crimes, crimes of aggression vs. greed) from the population at large. Megargee's (1970) trenchant observation of a quarter century ago — that no psychometric method or instrument has yet "been developed which will acceptably *post-dict,* let alone predict" criminal behavior — appears still to apply.

A CONTEMPORARY PSYCHOLOGICAL FORMULATION: BEHAVIOR AS BIO-PSYCHO-SOCIAL

In scientific psychology, abetted to be sure by the monumental advances in the neurosciences of the past three decades, it is now an essentially unexceptionable proposition that all behavior results from the interactive effects of bio-psycho-social engines. Implicitly, such a proposition holds that, in any "unit" of behavior (whether that unit be inflected as "cognitive," "emotional," "physiological," "antisocial," or any other such denominator), there are discernible biological, psychological, and social components and antecedents. An explicit corollary assigns primacy in the biological components of behavior to the functioning of the brain and the central nervous system (Hassan & Ward, 1991). That overarching conceptualization is robust enough to account both intra-psychic and extra-psychic variables and also to accommodate (1) the burgeoning evidence from the neurosciences that has produced massive, detailed information about the role of disordered neurology in violent and impulsive behavior and (2) evidence from criminology and sociology on the role of social stimuli in eliciting criminal behavior.

The neurogenesis of violence

It is a fair assessment to say that, from the perspective of scientific psychology and psychiatry, the principal advance in criminologic theory during the past quarter century has been the marshaling of hard evidence that leads persuasively (if not yet quite compellingly) to the proposition that impulsive violence is attributable to neurogenic sources in a preponderance (perhaps even an overwhelming preponderance) of cases.

It is only within the relatively recent past that major technological advances in the neurosciences have made it possible to record brain activity and later to map that activity through technologically powerful imaging devices (Rosse, Owen & Morisha, 1987; Volkow & Tancredi, 1991; Hayman & Hinck, 1992; Andreasen, O'Leary & Arndt, 1993; Garza-Trevino, 1994). Concomitantly, an explosion of knowledge in psychopharmacology and psychoendocrinology has yielded new understandings of a panoply of interactions between brain morphology and functioning, neurochemistry, and emotional and behavioral disorder. According to distinguished neuropsychiatrist Joseph Coyle (1988, 23-24) of Harvard, the "nearly logarithmic growth in neuroscience research" has yielded a major paradigm shift in the mental health sciences, producing in the process "new methods for diagnosing psychiatric disorders, clarifying their pathophysiology, and developing more specific and effective therapies." As the eminent Dutch neuropsychiatrist Herman Van Praag (1988) put it, the net effect has been to re-unite psychiatry and psychology with biology as their governing discipline.

Opportunity-based criminogenesis

From a sociological perspective no less than that of the policy sciences, however, the principal advance in criminologic theory during the same period has surely been the formulation and elaboration of rational choice theory (Clarke, 1984, 1985; Clarke & Cornish, 1985; Cornish & Clarke, 1986; Clarke & Weisburd, 1990; Clarke & Felson, 1993; Cornish, 1993), with its strong emphasis on the *opportunity to behave* as a principal "stimulus determinant" of behavior.

According to Clarke (1987), an adequate understanding of the genesis of criminal behavior requires attention to "the circumstances and conditions under which different forms of crime take place" and "a deeper knowledge of the decision-making processes of people at the point of [criminal] offending." In Clarke's view, whether to commit an offense or not becomes a matter of "rational choice" that is dependent largely on interaction between stimulus determinants and on the capacity to appraise the costs, risks, and benefits of a particular prospective criminal act fairly realistically, a position in consonance with the proposition advanced by Gottfredson & Hirschi (1994, 39) that "aggressive or violent acts are explicable as acts that produce immediate benefits and entail long-term social costs."

But Clarke does not understand "opportunity" to inhere merely in such physical characteristics as lighting in a parking lot or the relative isolation of a dwelling or the availability of an unguarded physical or vulnerable human target. Instead, according to Clarke (1984, 80-81),

> Opportunity is not merely the necessary condition for [criminal] offending, but it can provoke crime and can also be sought and created by those with the necessary motivation . . . opportunity is a rather more complex concept than implied by simple counts of available targets. Whether opportunities are acted upon depends upon their ease and attractiveness, and these qualities must be subjectively perceived and evaluated. Moreover, these subjective processes are affected by motivation as well as knowledge and experience, which explains why opportunities may not only provide the cue for offending in those with an established propensity (as when an untended handbag tempts the sneak thief), but may also provoke crime in the previously law-abiding (as when an accounting loop-hole proves to be the bank clerk's downfall). In addition, opportunities are not merely presented and perceived, but can also be sought or created or "planned." An understanding of how these situational contingencies achieve their effect is in turn likely to demand a deeper knowledge of the decision-making processes of people at the point of offending.

Parameters for an adequate synthesis

Clearly, any analytic model that aspires to comprehensiveness should synthesize psychology's current, overarching proposition that all behavior issues from bio-psycho-social engines both with the burgeoning body of evidence in the neurosciences on the neurogenesis of impulsive behavior and the criminologic evidence on opportunity as criminogenic.

Perhaps heralding more contemporary formulations in consonance with the guiding conceptualization in scientific psychology that sees all behavior in relation to bio-psycho-social antecedents, broader-gauged psychological models that take into account both intra-psychic and extra-psychic factors were essayed in Hans Toch's (1979) *Psychology of Crime and Criminal Justice,* with its strong emphasis on the applicability of social learning theory to criminal offending, and the less than modestly subtitled *Crime and Human Nature: The Definitive Study of the Causes of Crime* by public policy analyst James Q. Wilson and the late, distinguished psychologist Richard J. Herrnstein (1985). Walters (1992), Bartol (1991), Blackburn (1992), and Raine (1993) similarly avoid exclusive reliance on the now rather dated analytic models derived from psychopathology or differential psychology.

An interactionist paradigm

In earlier works (Pallone & Hennessy, 1992, 1993), we proposed an analytic model for understanding the dynamics of criminal behavior which pivots on the overarching conceptualization that behavior of any sort is determined *interactively* among and between bio-psycho-social variables and takes into account the burgeoning evidence on both the neurogenesis of violence and on the characteristics of stimuli and environments that yield the opportunity for behavior. Though he couches his argument in what he calls "the fundamental formula of genetics . . . that the total phenotypical variance is the sum of the genetic and the environmental variance," Eysenck (1995, 210) has argued that "one cannot study either side alone; if we wish to address the problem of crime on a scientific basis, we must look at both sides [biological, psychological, social or environmental] equally, particularly at the way they may interact. Nothing less will do, and attempts to disregard either set of factors takes us right out of science into ideology and politics."

Essentially a *person-x-environment* (or *self-x-situation*) interactionist paradigm (Lewin, 1951; Mischel, 1973; Thibaut & Kelly, 1978), the model we proposed pivots largely on the "process psychology" of pre-eminent theoretician Raymond B. Cattell (1963, 1980, 1985) that conceptually models the "process" whereby an internal "trait" (understood as a relatively stable and enduring predisposition to behave toward a class or category of behavioral objects) is transformed into a "state" (the readiness to behave in a particular way toward a particular behavioral object) as a function of interaction between the behaver and the environment (including characteristics of particular stimuli as well as social influences). The model thus proposes that criminal behavior is understandable as a function of (1) intrapersonal variables (2) *interacting with* (3) stimulus characteristics and (4) social and (5) situational variables — in short, as a function of *biological* determinants interacting with *psychological* and *social and stimulus* determinants.

Biological determinants

- NEUROLOGIC AND NEUROPSYCHOLOGICAL DYSFUNCTION, especially those dysfunctions which affect the capacity to construe the costs, risks, and benefits of behavior and the capacity to inhibit impulsive behavior.
- MOOD-ALTERING CHEMICAL SUBSTANCES, especially those which stimulate or accelerate neurological processes.
- OFFENSE-SPECIFIC PHYSICAL CHARACTERISTICS (e.g., the physical agility required to enter second-story windows on the part of those who wish to specialize in burglary or the skills needed to operate an automobile on the part of those who wish to specialize in motor vehicle theft).

Psychological determinants

- COGNITIVE CAPACITY, particularly in respect of the capacity to conceptualize, to resolve conflict through verbal exchange, and to engage in planful behavior.
- HABITUAL WAYS OF BEHAVING toward varied objects of behavior (the so-called traits or characteristics of personality).
- PAST LEARNING HISTORY, including sensitization to particular objects, stimuli, and social and cultural environments, and the dynamics which govern the *self-selection* of particular sociocultural environments with high or low tolerance for certain kinds of behavior.
- ENDOGENOUS PSYCHOPATHOLOGY, which possibly itself is biologically determined.

Social and stimulus determinants

- SOCIAL LEARNING and VICARIOUS CONDITIONING, including the learning of avoidance behavior (deterrence).
- HABITUATION TO SUBCULTURES of violence and/or (putatively; but usually simply *or*) greed.
- CHARACTERISTICS OF STIMULUS SITUATIONS, including the availability of targets of behavior and the extent of surveillance.
- A panoply of ENVIRONMENTAL CONTINGENCIES (including such oddities as the relative concentration of air-borne lithium in the municipal water supply, even at non-toxic levels, and the frequency of thunderstorms), which, upon close inspection, often turn out to potentiate biological determinants.

Interaction

The model proposes that these determinants interact with each other in any unit of behavior, but that the "weights" associated with each determinant vary not only between different behavers with respect to the same (or similar) objects of behavior but may also vary within the same behaver from one unit of behavior toward a particular class of objects on one occasion and another unit of behavior toward the same class of objects on another occasion. We propose that the overall analytic model is sufficiently robust to apply across a vast array of different sorts of criminal behavior and, in our earlier work, applied the model to homicide and to larceny as offenses of widely varying character.

We can conceive that biological, psychological, and social-stimulus determinants together constitute 100% of the "variance" in criminal behavior. Following Cattell's lead, statistical purists would wish as the next step to specify the precise portion of the total variance that each set of determinants contributes and finally to identify the precise mathematical relationships (for example, additive, multiplicative, or exponential) that obtains between each set. Thus far, those refinements have proved elusive. We must at this point content ourselves with the statement that each set displays a weight (that is, accounts for some portion of the variance), however small or large, and the belief that such weights are likely not ordered additively.

It is not difficult to contrast, for example, (1) the "professional" car thief who undertakes to equip himself with sophisticated tools before he selects a likely prospect parked in the far corner of a public lot after the close of the business day with (2) the intoxicated (and therefore putatively relatively less inhibited than usual) youth who chances upon an unattended late-model sports car, its key in the ignition and its motor running while its owner has dashed from the curb into the corner store or (3) the bank employee who coolly and deliberately devises a scheme to skim by sophisticated tampering with computer programs small amounts each day from each of many accounts with (4) the bank clerk who steals $100 in cash from a mail deposit envelope when the depositor has failed to include a deposit slip.

In the first and third cases, intrapersonal (biological, psychological) variables seem to be paramount, though obviously social and stimulus determinants are contributory, while, in the second and fourth cases, the relative contributions made by social and stimulus determinants appear to be paramount. We are inclined to believe (though we cannot as yet demonstrate with even a pretense to mathematical precision) that social and stimulus determinants "potentiate" biological and psychological determinants non-linearly.

AGGRESSIVE CRIMINAL VIOLENCE UNDER TINDER-BOX CIRCUMSTANCES

As a corollary, pursuing a construct initially advanced in an analysis of the dynamics of criminal sexual aggression (Pallone, 1990), we also sketched an interactive model for what we termed "tinder-box" criminal violence, which we posited as applicable to most episodes of aggressively violent crime. That model pivots on three fundamental propositions:

- A substantial proportion of the episodes of aggressive criminal violence (homicide, assault, sexual assault) that occur in this country each year are of the "tinder-box" variety: They occur between people known to each other and interacting in what social psychologists term "mutually familiar social environments," in which victims and offenders are similar to each other in a variety of characteristics; and whether one emerges as one sort of statistic rather than another (that is, as offender rather than as victim) in some cases represents virtually a matter of "chance." In contrast, neither stranger-to-stranger and/or "random" acts nor instrumental acts of aggressive criminal violence are so preponderant as the sound- and sight-bites of print and electronic journalism suggest [NOTE 6].

- There is now very sound scientific reason to believe that neurologic or neuropsychological dysfunction frequently underlies impulsivity and that such impulsivity constitutes a significant contributing factor in tinder-box violence.

- There is reason to believe that actors with a high taste for risk, which may itself be construed as the product of neurogenic impulsivity, *self-select* those psychosocial environments that are peopled by like-minded (and likely also neurogenically impulsive) "others" in mutually-familiar social environments which exhibit high tolerance for risky behavior. Such self-selection constitutes what may, in the circumstance, be construed as "conscious choice" on the part of such actors that functions so as to create the proximate opportunity for aggressive criminal violence. And that self-selection is most assuredly experienced phenomenologically as a "rational choice" on the part of the actor, for it is experienced as ego-syntonic and quite in consonance with what are experienced as internal imperatives.

Drawing upon research evidence from the neurosciences, developmental psychology, personality and social psychology, and the psychology of learning, and from criminologic data on the perpetrators, victims, and situational conditions implicated in aggressive criminal violence, we essayed a stepwise progression from what we called neurogenic impulsivity to violent criminal behavior, including the relative contributions made by

- Such apparently INTRA-PSYCHIC CHARACTERISTICS as the neurologically-based need for serial stimulation, impairment in foresight and planfulness, and the acquisition of a taste for risk on the one hand; and

- Such INTERACTIVELY-LINKED EXTRA-PSYCHIC CHARACTERISTICS as child-rearing practices, vicarious conditioning, subcultures of violence, and the availability of mood-altering chemical substances.

The present work amplifies that adumbration by developing a broad conceptual model which addresses the neuropsychology, demography, and phenomenology associated with impulsive, aggressive criminal violence. We do not presume that the model will fit the universe of criminal violence but offer it instead as an explanatory construct for that portion of episodes of *aggressive* violence that occur under tinder-box conditions.

Aggressive vs. instrumental violence

A distinction should be made conceptually, as it is operationally, between *aggressive* and *instrumental* violence. The latter grouping includes those acts of criminal violence that occur *secondary to* another crime, with some motive (generally, greed) other than aggression as paramount — as when the pickpocket struggles with his or her victim in an episode of criminal behavior that commences as theft but eventuates as assault.

Quite specifically, we posit the tinder-box model as applicable to the major proportion of cases of *aggressive* criminal violence but only incidentally to episodes of instrumental violence. For example: Although robbery is typically included as a subcategory in the usual lexicon of "crimes of personal victimization" (a term frequently used in the criminologic literature interchangeably with "crimes of violence"), we regard that offense as pivoting essentially on greed rather than aggression and thus do not include it under the rubric "aggressive violence." If a robber is armed, or should the victim be injured during a robbery — each a circumstance that suggests that aggression as well as greed may have motivated the offense — the putative offender is customarily charged with assault or aggravated assault as well as robbery. But, in real-world terms, since something on the order of 90% of all convictions result from the entry of pleas of guilty (likely as the result of plea-bargaining), it will be the "leading offense" of greatest severity (i.e., assault) that constitutes the "offense of record" (Pallone & Hennessy, 1992, 81-83, 87-89). Hence, our taxonomic decision is congruent with real-world practices in the criminal justice processing of offenders.

On the basis of evidence from both the neurosciences and from psychometric investigations, we shall argue that neuropathology infrequently contributes to instrumental violence.

Sadistic aggression

A further distinction should be made concerning *sadistic* aggression. While instrumental violence may pivot on greed rather than aggression, sadistic criminal behavior represents at the opposite polarity aggression undertaken essentially for its own sake with little or no instrumental value (Pallone, 1996).

In criminology and in the criminal justice processing of offenders, sadism carries very different connotations from those with which it is traditionally associated in the mental health sciences. In both the *Diagnostic and Statistical Manual of Mental Disorders, Fourth Edition* (DSM-IV), the American Psychiatric Association's (1994) current nosological lexicon, and in its international counterpart, the World Health Organization's (1992) *International Classification of Diseases, Tenth Edition* (ICD-10), "sadism" is identified exclusively as a sexual paraphilia, the defining characteristic of which is the derivation of pleasure from inflicting either physical or psychological pain or humiliation upon either a willing or an unwilling partner during the course of sexual activity. In the quaint prose of DSM-IV, redolent of the Marquis himself or even *The Story of O,* "Sadistic fantasies or acts may involve forcing the victim to crawl or keeping the victim in a cage . . . restraint, blindfolding, paddling, spanking, whipping, pinching, beating, burning, electrical shocks [or] cutting, stabbing, strangulation, torture, mutilation." The key elements are that the inflictor requires that the "partner" undergo pain either to stimulate his/her own sexual arousal or to intensify his/her own sexual gratification. Implicitly, the partner who is "willing" nominates himself/herself for diagnosis for the obverse companion disorder, sexual masochism.

In contrast, save when the clanking of chains or the lashing of whips disturbs the peace of the neighborhood, the criminal justice community (law enforcement officials, prosecutors, the courts, collectively the agents representing societal response to crime) takes little interest in consensual activity between adult parties, despite the pain or humiliation that may be inflicted on a "willing" partner through "bondage and discipline" practices. Similarly, "psychological" pain or humiliation that is not induced physically is customarily not the business of law enforcement, whether the partner is "willing" or not. Such pain or humiliation may be adequate cause for dissolution of a marriage, or even for the assessment of liability in a civil court action (as in cases in which "psychological suffering" is alleged as a result of a pattern of harassment or abuse, not necessarily sexual), but it will not trigger criminal prosecution. At base, the criminal justice community is concerned only with those situations in which one person *victimizes* another in an act that is specifically not consensual. Hence, the inflicting of physical pain, whether by the means litanized in DSM-IV or by any other means, or restraining the freedom of another (whether by "keeping the victim in a cage" or locked in an attic or cellar) upon an unwilling "partner" is the concern of the criminal law, whether during the course of sexual activity or not and whether or not the inflictor or restrainer is sexually motivated or derives sexual gratification therefrom.

In the mental health sciences, as exemplified by DSM-IV and ICD-10, "sadism" customarily appears as a noun, denoting a mental state liable to formal diagnosis as a mental disorder. But it is the corresponding adjective (or sometimes the adverbial form) that one encounters in the criminal justice community, where the goal is more often to describe behavior rather than to diagnose the mental condition which underlies that behavior. In criminologic terms, the descriptor "sadistic" typically bears two connotations: (1) The use of physical force or aggression with disregard of the consequences, even in a situation in which deterrence may technically be justified, as in defense of the self or property, and (2) the use of physical force or aggression substantially beyond that which is required to effect a criminal act, whether that act is even remotely sexual in nature or not. In one prototypical scenario, the householder who riddles with buckshot the face, chest, and knees of an unarmed intruder, continuing to fire after the intruder has been incapacitated, will be said to have behaved sadistically, even though he/she may have been entitled to deter and to protect. In another, the armed robber who nonetheless pistol-whips a store clerk who has acceded, without resistance, to the demand that all the cash on hand be surrendered is said to have committed a "sadistic" robbery. In neither case will the criminal justice community be in the least concerned with whether the most modest level of covert, channelized, or symbolized sexual excitation or gratification is involved.

Hence, in the criminological literature, one finds among the offenses discussed under the rubric "sadistic" such crimes as homicide with dismemberment and/or mutilation and robbery with atrocious assault and grievous bodily harm, especially when no resistance has been offered by the victim. Though alternate terminology (e.g., "wanton and reckless disregard," "inhumane treatment") may be used, sadistic elements in a crime of any sort constitute "aggravating factors" that, upon conviction of the perpetrator, may trigger either assignment of the maximum penalty permitted by law or, in some states, a specific "penalty enhancement" through selective incapacitation or other means.

Neither DSM-IV nor ICD-10 estimates the relative prevalence of sexual sadism as a formal mental disorder. Although that massive compendium of criminologic data of all sorts, the *Sourcebook of Criminal Justice Statistics* (Maguire & Pastore, 1994, 288-291) enumerates the number of episodes of rape reported to law enforcement authorities annually, it does not report the proportion of rape victims who suffer injury (whether sadistically or not). But Quinsey & Upfold (1985) found that approximately half (49%) the rape victims they studied suffered injury of some sort (including 11% who were "seriously injured" and another 1.5% who were murdered) in addition to the degradation and humiliation of the sexual assault itself. *Sourcebook* data indicate that some 138,000 rapes (lone- and multiple-offender victimizations aggregated) were reported in the year under review; extrapolation of the Quinsey & Upfold rates suggests that injuries ensued in some 67,000 cases, with 15,000 of those injuries "serious." (If the sexual assault ended in the murder of the victim, owing to the peculiarities which guide the Federal data reporting mechanisms upon which the *Sourcebook* is based, the offense is enumerated only as "homicide.") To place the matter in context, the *Sourcebook* estimates that nearly 410,000 victims of robbery were "seriously" injured during the same year. If the operational meaning of "serious injury" generalizes between Quinsey & Upfold and the Federal crime reporting system (a questionable assumption), and again bracketing aside issues like victim resistance, it may be that more than 27 times as many robbery as rape victims suffered serious, perhaps sadistically-motivated, physical injuries. Moreover, there is some fragmentary evidence that deliberately-inflicted serious injuries are statistically more frequently associated with robbery, "bias" crimes, and gang-to-gang assaults than with other criminal offenses, including sexual offenses. In contrast to instrumental violence, we shall argue that neuropathology constitutes a principal determinant in the perpetration of sadistic criminal aggression.

Toward an interactive paradigm

In succeeding chapters, we review the evidence from contemporary research in the neurosciences bearing upon neuropsychological dysfunction with a particular focus on neurogenic impulsivity, from neurochemical and criminologic research on the contribution to aggressive violence made by mood-altering biochemical substances, from criminologic research on the demography of criminal violence, and from psychometric and developmental psychology and the psychology of learning in both human and infra-human species that bears upon aggression and especially upon the phenomenology of risk-taking behavior, culminating in a broad-gauged model that portrays the prototypical interactive and developmental sequence that leads from neuropsychological anomaly or dysfunction through the acquisition of a high taste for risk to involvement in impulsively violent behavior. Finally, we draw inferences that issue from a contemporary understanding of the role of neurogenic impulsivity in aggressive criminal violence for traditional concepts of culpability and for offender rehabilitation.

NOTES

1. Elsewhere (Pallone & Hennessy, 1992, 74-87), we have reviewed in some detail data bearing upon the sequelae to formal reports of crime from such official Federal sources as the annual *Sourcebook of Criminal Justice Statistics,* occasional reports of the Federal Bureau of Justice Statistics, and reports of the National Center for State Courts. In the aggregate, these data reveal that, for every 1000 crimes reported in a year to law enforcement authorities, 154 convictions result, leading to 95 sentences to probation and 59 sentences to incarceration. These "rates" vary substantially by type of crime, however. In the case of homicide (which accounts for only 0.2% of all episodes of crime reported in a year), there are 430 convictions for every 1000 crimes reported, while, at the other extreme, in the case of motor vehicle theft (which accounts for approximately 11% of all episodes of crime reported in a year), there are but 80 convictions for every 1000 crimes reported. For larceny (the most frequently reported crime, accounting for fully 55% of all episodes of crime reported in a year), there are 140 convictions for each 1000 crimes reported. Moreover, on the basis of data of less than universal scope, we estimated that 90% of all criminal convictions result from entry of a plea of guilty, likely as the result of "plea-bargaining" in which the offense as committed is substantially euphemized. That proportion differs only marginally from the figures cited by Brian Forst (1995, 167), who reported that 84.4% of all such convictions (27 of every 32) result from guilty pleas.

Since undetected, unapprehended, unprosecuted, or unconvicted offenders are rarely (for all the obvious reasons) available as subjects in behavioral science research focused on criminal behavior, one is left to wonder whether the relatively small subset of convicted offenders who are available for study may constitute an atypical sample not reflective of their unapprehended and unconvicted counterparts.

Further, these data account only for episodes of crime formally reported to law enforcement authorities. The annual victimization surveys conducted by the Bureau of the Census for the Federal Bureau of Justice Statistics through in-person interviews in a random, stratified sample of American households routinely inquire whether respondents have been victimized, whether the offense was reported, and, if not, why not. Rates of not reporting vary enormously by type of crime: 50% in the case of sexual assault, 65% in the case of larceny. If one uses as a baseline data on victimization rather than data on formal reports of crime, the ratio between crimes committed and crimes for which convictions are obtained recedes further. As further detailed in Chapter 4, Hennessy & Kepecs-Schlussel (1992) analyzed rates of victimization by category of offense in the 76 largest cities in the U.S. in relation to a variety of socioeconomic and demographic variables.

2. The proposition that behavior can be attributed solely to the properties of stimuli, sometimes termed by sociologists "radical behaviorism," represents a significant misreading both of Pavlovian and of Skinnerian (i.e., of "classical" and of "operant" conditioning conceptualizations. In both cases, what may be construed as factors or forces internal to the behaving organism are recognized as important contributors to the shaping of behavioral responses to stimuli.

The simplest experiments in each paradigm focus on behavioral responses to food — but within an organism that has been deprived of food for some period of time, with the precise measure of the extent of food deprivation sometimes regarded as the operational measure of "drive strength." For the Pavlovian, salivation may represent a primal response, while the Skinnerian is more typically attuned to exploratory behavior preparatory to acquisition of whatever substance constitutes the stimulus that is capable of relieving food deprivation. The Skinnerian will assiduously avoid invoking an anthropomorphic construct like "hunger" to describe the internal state of a food-deprived organism while nonetheless recognizing the reality of that state; the Pavlovian typically shows less reluctance toward anthropomorphism. More advanced formulations of the Skinnerian paradigm in particular also account the contribution made by the learning history and physical capacities (e.g., prehensility in the rat) of the individual organism, other variables that may be regarded as "internal" rather than external.

3. A review of epidemiological studies of mental illness among convicted and imprisoned offenders is found in Pallone (1991, 13-56). Although the incidence of formal mental disorder of one or another sort among imprisoned offenders is found to exceed that among non-offenders, the relationship between mental disorder and crime appears to be not only not exculpatory but not even convincingly explanatory (as, for example, the child who with a broken arm may contract influenza, but it is not assumed that one condition "causes" the other).

Moreover, there is evidence that the "Penrose Effect" continues in full force. More than half a century ago, British psychologist Lionel Penrose (1939) reported a neatly inverse relationship between the number of prison beds and the number of mental hospital beds across the nations of Europe in the 1930s. A reading of contemporary data suggests that the "Penrose Effect" is alive and well in the United States. Data on the high frequency with which those who are declared to be criminally deviant are also found to be psychiatrically deviant, albeit not in ways that exculpate criminal wrong-doing, is remarkable fodder for theories of social deviance. According to data from the National Institutes of Health, the number of beds in public and private mental hospitals declined nationally from 451,000 in 1965 to 177,000 in 1985. According to Bureau of Justice Statistics data, during roughly the same period the number of convicted offenders confined in state and Federal prisons increased from 210,000 in 1965 to 420,000 in 1983, not including in either case those confined in jails or on probation or parole. In an exhaustive review of the then-current research literature, Teplin (1983), although complaining about methodological flaws, concluded that "the research literature offers . . . support for the contention that the mentally ill are being processed through the criminal justice system." In part on the basis of his own earlier research (Lamb & Grant, 1982), distinguished psychiatrist H. Richard Lamb (1988, p. 1147) of the University of Southern California attributes the process whereby mental illness is criminalized to the confluence of a variety of psychological, social, and economic factors: "As a result of deinstitutionalization [i.e., discharge from mental hospitals after brief periods, during which patients are not treated psychotherapeutically but merely stabilized on psychotropic medication], there are now large numbers of mentally ill persons in the community. At the same time, there is a limited amount of community psychiatric resources, including hospital beds. Society has a limited tolerance of mentally disordered behavior, and the result is pressure to institutionalize persons who need 24-hour care wherever there is room, including jail. [The result is] a criminalization of mentally disordered behavior — a shunting of mentally ill persons in need of treatment into the criminal justice system." That process leads to a cadre of "revolving door clientele" (Pallone & Hennessy, 1977) in jail facilities especially, whose crimes are relatively minor and who are generally released at trial, with their sentences reduced to "time served," after which they return to the same social circumstances from whence they came prior to their incarceration, so that, as Adler (1986) put it, "jails [become] a repository for former mental patients." Scull (1984) has put the case even more pungently: "The shift away from a social control apparatus placing heaviest emphasis on segregating deviants into institutions like asylums [has had] its usefulness as ideological camouflage, allowing economy to masquerade as benevolence and neglect as tolerance . . . for many ex-inmates and potential inmates, the alternative to the institution has been to be herded into newly emerging deviant ghettos, sewers of human misery and what is conventionally defined as social pathology, within which society's refuse may be repressively tolerated."

In an inventive study at the Kline Institute at NYU, Martell (1991) analyzed the "instant offense" which had triggered referral of patients who were both homeless (typically, after discharge from in-patient psychiatric treatment) and had been arrested on criminal charges to a forensic psychiatric hospital in relation to charges lodged against a control group. Martell found a significantly higher incidence of charges of assault and of burglary (but not of homicide, robbery, sex offenses, weapons offenses, larceny, or drug offenses) among the homeless mentally ill. Similarly, Mulvey (1994) has proposed an "increased risk for violence" among those "dually diagnosed" as mentally ill and addicted to mood-altering substances. Torrey, a leading critic of the "deinstitutionalization" movement (1988), amplifies the "dually diagnosed" dyad: "A history of violent behavior, noncompliance with medications, and substance abuse are important predictors of violent behavior" (1994), although, importantly, "the vast majority of individuals with serious mental illness are no more dangerous than members of the general population." Such evidence may be relevant to the matter of the relative incidence of the "bad" among a subset of the "mad," but it fails to support the correlative contention that mental illness is in itself criminogenic.

4. The history of psychiatric epidemiology and attendant issues in measurement are discussed by Mechanic (1980) in general and by Pallone (1991, 13-56) in relation to offender populations. Early studies relied on "gross screen" questionnaires containing "symptom questions chosen to represent the manifest currents of behavioral disturbance that generally reflect the emotional substrate underlying most of the many narrowly circumscribed patient syndromes to which psychiatrists try to attach a specific diagnostic tag . . . the sample of symptoms covered [is] intended not for the impossible task of discriminating among those numerous syndromes (especially in cases falling outside the clinical range of full blown pathology, as most do), but to mark, as does a physician's thermometer, progressive grades of deviation in emotional 'fever' and disability, from an asymptomatic state of presumptive wellness" (Srole & Fischer, 1986, 83-84). But Weissman, Myers & Harding (1978, 459) complained that the "gross screen" approach is not discerning enough to produce useful data and further reveals a rather too simplistic conceptualization of a common etiology for disorders of varying shapes and sizes: "Psychiatric epidemiology in the United States has been dominated for the past 30 years by the view that mental illness is unitary and [that] various diagnostic [categories] represent different manifestations of the same underlying defect in mental functioning . . . . Community surveys have assessed frequency of overall impairment . . . rather than rates of specific psychiatric disorders." To remedy that situation, Weissman and her colleagues at Yale devised a more discerning approach to the construction of mental health census screening instruments with a finer mesh, more closely approximating a clinical interview in mental health practice, and, not incidentally and somewhat surprisingly, yielding ratios of mental illness in the general population generally negatively discrepant with those produced by the earlier gross screen methodology. The currently accepted methodology, adopted for use by the National Institutes of Mental Health (NIMH), rests on the approach pioneered by Weissman and her group and by a research group at Washington University, St. Louis, led by Lee Robins (1985), a principal architect of the Diagnostic Interview Schedule (DIS) developed at NIMH to reflect specific diagnostic criteria for the major groups of mental disorders contained in the American Psychiatric

Association's *Diagnostic and Statistical Manual*; the DIS has been incorporated into the diagnostic process in routine clinical practice, so that a "running census" of patients, at least in Federally funded mental health installations, is now possible. Nonetheless, it is noteworthy that, in his inimitably incisive prose, Schofield (1986, 13) proposed that "The total incidence of mental illness in the population is greater during those periods in the national economy which support the expense of mental health census-taking than during economic periods that do not support such surveys" and, as a corollary, that "The greater the number of psychiatrists, psychologists, and other trained mental health experts in the population, the higher the incidence of mental illness."

5. The "badness = madness" model originated at a time when psychiatric deviance was by and large attributed to "functional" anomalies in psychosocial development and patterns of interaction, long before the explosion in knowledge in the neurosciences led to reformulation of traditional notions of the etiology of mental illness. A more contemporary view undergirds Raine's (1993) central contention that criminal behavior is virtually universally attributable to psychopathology, with an emphasis on neurogenic psychopathology, and itself constitutes a "clinical disorder." While our perspectives on aggressive crime are highly congruent with Raine's position, we are not so persuaded as he that *non-aggressive* crime motivated by greed pivots on psychopathology rather than on sociopathy nor that neurogenic disorder plays so paramount a role therein.

Until publication of the fourth edition of the American Psychiatric Association's (1994) *Diagnostic and Statistical Manual of Mental Disorders* (DSM), *organic mental disorder* was formally included in the lexicon of recognized disorders. But that term has disappeared, to be replaced by the omnibus, non-specific term *mental disorder due to a general medical condition,* a "catch-all" category that is intended to encompass a wide array of symptoms ranging from delirium to amnesia to sexual dysfunction without specifying the organic root or "cause," which might range from the effect of medical disease itself (e.g., high fever related to delirium, hypoxia resulting from respiratory infection leading to anxiety) or represent the side-effect of pharmaceutical therapy for medical illness. It is important to note that the diagnostic criteria now require that the "medical condition" to which psychological symptoms are attributed must be independently verified; one presumes that one purpose of the "new" and non-specific category is to preclude implicit medical diagnosis on the part of psychiatrists, psychologists, and other mental health professionals who routinely rely on the DSM system. One can read into that situation the triumph of the position long taken by maverick psychiatrist Thomas Szasz (1987, 1993, 1994), who has insisted that, if psychological consequences predictably follow a medical (or neurological) disorder, there is no basis on which to diagnose a "mental" disorder that is in any real sense distinct from the underlying medical disorder of which psychological and behavioral "symptoms" are manifestations.

6. Belatedly, both formal reporting agencies and the press have come to understand that a large proportion of acts of aggressive criminal violence "happen" rather than "are planned" or elected with deliberation. Hence, Nelson (1996), in an account of a report on homicide by a public health body, reports that although "most [perpetrators] and victims knoew one another . . . 55 percent of the shootingw were unplanned" — or, in our terms, occurred under tinder-box circumstances.

NEUROLOGIC INVITATIONS TO AGGRESSIVE VIOLENCE

IN THIS CHAPTER, WE REVIEW EVIDENCE FROM THE NEUROSCIENCES BEARING ON aggressive violence, which may arise from naturally-occurring (typically, congenital) or induced (as the result of injury or accident) dyfsunctions or anomalies in brain morphology and/or brain biochemistry. Before we turn to that body of evidence at the molar and molecular level, however, it may prove useful to consider a broad paradigm that links neurology with aggression from the very wide perspectives of evolutionary biology — and does so in a manner that is rather engaging poetically.

AN ETHOLOGIST'S PARADIGM: AGGRESSION AS THE INEVITABLE CONSEQUENCE OF NEUROLOGY

The propositions that (1) aggression represents the very purpose of neurology and that (2) therefore *aggression is an inevitable consequence of the mere fact of neurology* (and not only, or even primarily, of disordered neurology) anchor the conceptual formulations on the biological bases of aggressive behavior by French physician and ethologist Henri-Marie Laborit (1977) in his remarkable *Decoding the Human Message.*

Much of Laborit's clinical experience in medicine came from service as a physician under combat conditions in the French Navy during World War II and included service as chief of the Naval Medical Corps from 1948 to 1960, a period that saw armed conflict in several French colonies in Africa and Asia (including what was then French Indochina and later became Vietnam) seeking their independence, and his research on the phenothiazines (a group of powerful medications intended to offset the florid symptoms of psychosis) earned the Lasker Medal of the American Public Health Association. Clinical experience under conditions of armed conflict between a European colonial power and the "oppressed peoples" of third-world nations on two continents surely provides unique vantage points from which to study aggression.

Laborit's paradigm starts with the premise that the preservation of existence is the primordial imperative for any organism. The preservation of existence requires that the organism derive and transform energy from the sun, the only independent source of energy in our universe. Through the process of photosynthesis, the simpler plant organisms derive energy directly from the sun; these organisms are thus not required (that is to say, have no existential need) to locomote [NOTE 1].

But animals have no such capacity to transform energy directly; instead, in order to continue to exist, they "need" to locomote in order to forage for sustenance. Thus, according to Laborit, *aggression is endemic to any form of animal life*. To survive, animals (including the human species) must move from place to place to procure, by foraging, the nutrients produced by plants and thus to ingest the solar energy those plants have transformed; the alternative is death, so such an "existential need" is quite primordial. To make such movement possible, the process of evolution has yielded the brain and the central nervous system, along with a skeleton and musculature.

Endowed with a brain (in which memories of pleasure and pain can be recorded) and a central nervous system (capable of directing movement of the skeleton and musculature) and compelled to sustain life, any animal (no matter how primitive) inevitably seeks first to aggress against simpler organisms, then to establish dominance over a more-or-less defensible "territory" in which it can forage (or, where humans can cultivate) in relative freedom from predatory attack. By contrast, with the exception of such species as the Venus fly-trap, which are capable of destroying some varieties of predatory insects (in what some observers regard as a variety of "defensive aggression"), plants do not "aggress."

To establish and defend such dominance requires aggressive behavior — in the first instance, against the plant life (and, among many animal species and in the human species, against animal life as well) that must be consumed if even the simplest organism is to sustain its own life; and, in the second, against competitors who "covet" the same territory for the same life-sustaining purposes [NOTE 2]. In the human species, a variety of social controls, including both general societal norms and those role models which have been promulgated by the society in which one lives as generally positive and/or those which one has chosen ipsatively for emulation or imitation, may constrain and channel aggression in ways that are more or less socially acceptable. In infra-human species, the outer limits of aggression are set by competition with more powerful organisms; generally, those whose position in the evolutionary schema has yielded more highly developed central nervous systems and more efficient brains are destined to prevail in such competition. Among humans, as Desmond Morris (1969) observed, the sense of dominance may extend to include a variety of symbolic representations of "territoriality," both animate and inanimate (e.g., one's spouse, one's automobile).

Aggression itself is, in this conceptualization, construable as quite an inevitable consequence of neurology itself—not to say also, as essential to life at a very primitive level in all animal species, including the human. The question, then, becomes not whether humans will behave aggressively, but rather whether such aggressive behavior as constitute the inevitable consequence of the sheer fact of neurology (the purpose of which is to permit locomotion and which therefore inevitably dictates aggression) will be sufficiently and appropriately socialized and channelized so as not to unduly impede the welfare of other organisms. As Lore & Schultz (1993, 16) observed, "all organisms have coevolved . . . potent inhibitory mechanisms that enable them . . . to suppress aggression when it is in their interests to do so," so that "humans are exquisitely sensitive to subtle social controls" to modulate, direct, or inhibit aggression.

Though not part of Laborit's paradigm, the extension in the human species of the primitive urge toward territorial dominance (Heinsohn & Packer, 1995) — rooted in evolutionary biology and pivoting on the existential need in all animal species to forage for life-sustaining nutrients — toward mere self-aggrandizement unrelated to survival issues seems but a few poetic steps.

KNOWLEDGE EXPLOSION IN THE NEUROSCIENCES

Medicine is the praxeological science par excellence. Its history displays clearly an evolution from clinical observation derived from attention to the remediation of disease entities, replete with hunches, speculations, and leaps of faith that are perhaps more frequently today associated with folk art than with science, to more systematic, scientifically-anchored specification of conditions antecedent to discernible pathology, today supported by a panoply of technologically-sophisticated measuring devices that differ from those of even the 19th century as radically as the sledge differs from the automobile. In the mix, medicine has also developed a strong experimental tradition, through which clinical observations are put to laboratory test, often on infra-human subjects.

Deriving initially from neurology as a branch of medicine, the aggregate neurosciences have undergone a roughly parallel evolution. Physicians originally had no option but to base their speculations on clinical observations of behavior in relation to what they more or less presumed to be disorder in the brain, often following an obvious injury to the skull. Once the West overcame its resistance to study of corpses, the excision of the brain, during autopsy or in the laboratory, became available as a vehicle to test clinical hypotheses about disordered neurological processes that had been speculatively linked to disordered behavior (Engel, 1989; Kandel, Schwartz & Jessell, 1991).

Experimentation with infra-human animal species, especially those whose brains and central nervous systems are recognizably similar to the human, provided during the 18th and 19th centuries another avenue for investigation, resulting in reasoning by analogy from one species to another. In the early part of the 20th century, neurohormones were first identified and study of the process whereby "signals" are biochemically transmitted to and from the brain began in earnest (Feldman & Quenzer, 1984, 97-99), while physicians like Kurt Goldstein and Karl Lashley and psychologists like Ward Halstead and Ralph Reitan [NOTE 3] developed psychological tests capable of reliably differentiating the cognitive functioning of patients with medically-verified neurologic disorders from "normal" subjects, so that neuropsychological tests could be used as at least "gross" screening devices for brain dysfunction (Franzen & Lovell, 1987). Simultaneously, invention of the electroencephalograph made it possible by the 1930s to measure with some precision bioelectrical activity within the brain utilizing electrodes placed in standardized positions on the scalp (Rosse, Owen & Morisha, 1987). Similarly, advances in biochemistry made it possible to assess, at least at a gross level, the concentration and distribution of neurochemical substances through such surgical procedures as lumbar puncture (Hyman & Nestler, 1993).

But it is only during the last half of this century that monumental advances have been achieved in the neurosciences, based largely on the adaptation to the study of brain and central nervous system (CNS) processes of highly sophisticated, electronically-advanced imaging techniques initially designed to aid in the diagnosis of physical pathology. Use of these techniques has made it possible to study brain and CNS "events" as they actually occur within patients or in subjects in research laboratories. In the virtual alphabet soup of advanced imaging, these techniques include computerized tomography (CT) or computerized axial tomography (CAT), magnetic resonance imaging (MRI) and functional magnetic resonance imaging (fMRI), positron emission tomography (PET), regional cerebral blood flow (rCBF) analysis, brain electrical activity mapping (BEAM), single photon emission tomography (SPECT), and the superconducting quantum interference device (SQUID). Contemporaneously, major technological advances have improved the accuracy and sophistication of the electroencephalograph (Quantitative EEG, or QEEG) through computerization (Rosse, Owen & Morisha, 1987, 22-29; Valciukas, 1991, 140-149; Andreasen, Cohen, Harris, Cizadlo et al., 1992; Daniel, Zigun & Weinberger, 1992; Neyland, Reynolds & Kupfer, 1992; Andreasen, O'Leary & Arndt, 1993; Hyman & Nestler, 1993, 207-209; Kosslyn, 1994; Mills & Raine, 1994, 146-147; Thornton, 1995). Valciukas (1995) provides lucid, non-technical descriptions of the physics and biochemistry of each of the principal brain-imaging techniques. More detailed, but highly technical, descriptions can be found in Hayman & Hinch's (1992) *Clinical Brain Imaging.*

Because, collectively, these techniques have made it possible to identify with relative precision the sites and the rates at which various neurohormones are metabolized in the brain in relation to neurochemical and behavioral sequelae (Woods, Brennan, Yurgelun-Todd, Young & Panzarino, 1995), perhaps the most significant advances based on neuroimaging technology have occurred in neuro-psychopharmacology, enabling pharmaceutical researchers to design neuro-chemical substances targeted on specific receptor sites and intended to produce particular behavioral sequelae with a level of accuracy that could only have been dreamed of but a few decades ago. For neuropsychologists who focus on the relationship between "events" in the brain and behavior, the impact has been no less revolutionary. Once forced to content themselves with correlational data (usually from psychometric instruments) about changes in cognitive or emo-tional functioning as a consequence of damage to brain tissue following injury or following ingestion of neuroactive chemical substances, because they permit precise identification of "where in the brain activity occurs while one performs a specific task" (or responds to emotionally-relevant stimuli), as the distinguished Harvard researcher Stephen Kosslyn (1994, 47) has observed, the new technolo-gies make it possible to "observe neural activity in an awake, behaving human being . . . and avoid the difficulties of studying effects of brain damage."

Indeed, in the second edition of the American Psychiatric Association's (semi-official) *Textbook of Neuropsychiatry,* as an index to the monumental growth of knowledge about behavior attributable to the knowledge explosion in the neurosciences Yudofsky & Hales (1992) observed that "95% of what we know about the brain as it relates to behavior has been discovered since 1983." From the perspective of the sciences of behavior, doubtless the principal benefit has been the development of the capacity to relate behavior, attitudes, and emotional states to neurological events observable through advanced, techno-logically-sophisticated devices with relative scientific precision as those events are actually occurring. To that extent, scientific psychology can no longer afford to stand apart from the neurosciences if it intends to provide coherent accounts of human behavior, however that behavior may be inflected.

A GLIMPSE INTO THE WORLD OF THE NEUROSCIENCES

Key terms in the lexicon of neuroscience

To begin to understand research from the neurosciences relevant to the psychological study of criminal violence, it will be useful to glance at least briefly at the vocabulary of the several disciplines principally implicated. Among the recurrent terms we encounter:

- BRAIN STRUCTURES [Brain Morphology]. A term that refers collectively to the principal anatomical structures of the brain. In what she calls "the modal brain," according to Liederman (1988, 375-376), the *right hemisphere* "is more important for the synthesis of stimuli over space and time into configurational gestalts," so that the "perception of three-dimensional space, visuospatial patterns, and musical chords is mediated primarily by the right hemisphere," while the *left hemisphere* is concerned with verbal stimuli and "is more important for the analysis of stimuli as discrete, finely timed events," so that "behaviors such as speech, speech-sound discrimination . . . and syntactic comprehension are mediated primarily by the left hemisphere." The frontal lobes are generally held to be the "seat" of such mental functions as cognition; the parietal lobes, of such functions as the integration of sensory signals and of motor activity; the temporal lobes, of such functions as memory, pattern recognition, and visual-motor coordination; and the occipital lobes, of vision. The various lobes are linked through complex networks of neural pathways, across the synapses or junctions of which signals are transmitted bioelectrically and biochemically, via a wide array of neurotransmitting enzymes and agents. (A simplified diagram of the brain, illustrating particular morphological structures relevant to violence and aggression, appears later in this chapter.)

- CENTRAL NERVOUS SYSTEM. In the *Glossary* of the American Psychiatric Association (Stone, 1988, 31), "the brain and the spinal cord." In a more expansive definition, Valciukas (1995) includes the brain, brainstem, spinal cord, and nerves. According to Ferster & Spruston (1995, 756), "to control behavior, the central nervous system employs approximately one trillion (10^{12}) neurons, all connected in networks of unfathomable complexity." The *autonomic nervous system* (Stone, 1988, 20) is that "part of the nervous system that innervates [activates] the cardiovascular, digestive, reproductive, and respiratory organs. It operates outside of consciousness and controls basic life-sustaining functions such as heart rate, digestion, and breathing. It includes the sympathetic nervous system and the parasympathetic nervous system." In turn, the sympathetic nervous system (163) is identified as "the part of the autonomic nervous system that responds to dangerous or threatening situations by preparing a person physiologically for fight or flight," while the parasympathetic nervous system is identified as "The part of the autonomic nervous system that controls the life-sustaining organs of the body under normal, danger-free conditions."

- EPILEPSY. In the *Glossary* of the American Psychiatric Association (Stone, 1988, 63), "a neurologic disorder characterized by motor or sensory seizures and accompanied by abnormal electrical discharge which may be shown by electroencephalogram." *Temporal lobe epilepsy,* or complex partial seizures, originate in the temporal lobe and have often been associated with unprovoked aggressive behavior, although many authorities believe the link is mediated by the sense of disorientation experienced by patients during seizures (Berkow & Fletcher, 1992, 1438). According to Stevenson & King (1987, 209), "seizure activity results from an abnormal electro-physiological discharge [which is] secondary to neurochemical alterations." Clinically, epilepsy is classified according to the frequency and severity of seizure activity as grand mal, petit mal, sub-clinical, and pre-clinical.

- FRONTAL LOBE SYNDROME. According to the U.S. Public Health Service version of the 9th edition of the *International Classification of Diseases* (1989, 1093; hereinafter, ICD-9), frontal lobe syndrome is a condition characterized by "changes in behavior following damage to the frontal areas of the brain," including "a general diminution of self-control, foresight, creativity, and spontaneity, which may be manifest as increased irritability, selfishness, restlessness, and lack of concern for others . . . measurable deterioration of intellect or memory is not necessarily present . . . particularly in persons previously energetic, restless, or aggressive, there may be a change toward impulsiveness, boastfulness, temper outbursts," since, as Berkow & Fletcher (1992, 1394) put it, "The frontal lobes influence . . . the planning and organizing of future expressive behavior." Magnetic resonance imaging studies have confirmed "abnormal frontal lobe development and function" in relation to impulsivity and hyperactivity among in childhood (Giedd, Castellanos, Casey et al., 1994). But, in the 10th edition (ICD-10), published by the World Health Organization in 1992 but still not in general use in the United States, frontal lobe syndrome has been subsumed into an "umbrella" category termed *organic personality disorder* [NOTE 4], to the considerable chagrin of a sizable fraction of the neuropsychiatric community (Malloy & Richardson, 1994; Mindux, Rasmussen & Lindquist, 1994; Salloway, 1994).

- HEMISPHERE (or CEREBRAL HEMISPHERE). Either of the rounded halves of the cerebrum connected by the corpus callosum; frequently referred to as the "left brain" or "right brain." Most authorities hold that the hemispheres are "specialized" in the human brain, with the right hemisphere the seat for processing of spatial stimuli and the left the seat for verbal, analytic, and cognitive functions. Hemispheric "dominance" is generally held to be linked to the preferential use of one or the other side of the body (as in right-handedness or left-handedness), with the contralateral hemisphere identified as dominant.

- HYPOTHALAMUS. In the *Glossary* of the American Psychiatric Association (Stone, 1988, 80), "the principal center in the forebrain for integration of visceral functions involving the autonomic nervous system." According to Berkow & Fletcher (1987, 1017-1020), the hypothalamus is thus "the master gland . . . the final common pathway directing input [which] receives input from virtually all other areas of the central nervous system." Among the neurohormones modulated by the hypothalamus are dopamine, a ubiquitous and powerful neurotransmitter in the brain which is related biochemically to the equally powerful neurotransmitter norepinephrine, and a hormone labeled TSH, which stimulates the activity of the thyroid gland, itself a modulator of hormonal activity throughout the endocrine system. Over-production in thyroid secretions (hyperthyroidism) is associated with behavior that is characteristically hyperactive, while under-production (hypothyroidism) is associated with lethargy.

- IMPULSIVITY. As used in this volume, the "habit" of acting, or propensity to act, upon urges (often vaguely defined or understood by the actor) without due consideration to the costs, risks, and benefits associated with behavior. Such urges may have their origins in neurologic dysfunctions or anomalies that either or both create the experience of restlessness in the prospective actor and/or sensitize him or her to particular targets of behavior. In rather an archaic fashion, the *Glossary* of the American Psychiatric Association (Stone, 1988, 82) defines impulse as "a psychic striving; usually refers to an instinctual urge," then goes on, equally archaically, to define an "instinct" (85) as "an inborn drive," identifying "the primary human instincts [as] self-preservation, sexuality, and, according to some proponents, aggression." But impulse [control] disorders are appropriately identified (83) as "a varied group of non-psychotic disorders in which impulse control is weak [such that] the impulsive behavior is usually pleasurable, irresistible, and ego-syntonic." When a prospective actor is simultaneously subject to a variety of impulsive urges to behave, he or she may be said to be in a state of mania, a condition identified by the *Glossary* (95) as "A mood disorder characterized by excessive elation, hyperactivity, agitation, and accelerated thinking and speaking. Sometimes manifested as flight of ideas. Mania is seen in mood disorders and in certain organic mental disorders" and is further a dependable consequence of central nervous system stimulants. Mania (or some aspects thereof) is measurable through the Ma scale of the Minnesota Multiphasic Personality Inventory, which may also represent a gauge to the respondent's typical level of impulsivity. In an interactionist paradigm, *impulsivity* is the antonym of planfulness, which in its turn is an essential ingredient to mature judgment.

- LESION. In most medical dictionaries (e.g., *Steadman's, Random House*), defined as a localized and usually well-defined area of diseased or injured tissue; hence, "a wound or injury or a localized pathological change in a bodily organ or tissue." In brain pathology, the term applies to tumors and hematomas as well (Stevenson & King, 1987, 231). Because, unlike cells on the surface of the body, brain cells do not regenerate but remain "permanently" damaged after injury, the term generally connotes inoperative cells when applied to brain pathology.

- METABOLISM. According to Hinsie & Campbell (1970, 468), "the bio-physiological processes by which the living cells and tissue systems of an organism undergo continuous chemical changes in order to build up new living matter and to supply the energy necessary for the life of an individual." Thus, the process by which material ingested by an organism is transformed by that organism (through the action of enzymes produced by the endocrine system) and hence rendered usable by that organism. Within the present context, particularly applicable to those substances the ingestion of which is related to the process of neurotransmission. The transformed substance usable by the organism that emerges from such a process of metabolism is termed a *metabolite*. According to Rafuls, Extein, Gold & Goggans (1987, 323), dysfunctions in metabolism (which are typically attributable to the body's over- or under-production of the enzymes principally involved in neural regulation, called neuroendocrines) may account for mental disturbances of various sorts, including delirium, dementia, anxiety, apathy, depression, irritability, euphoria, aggressivity, and psychosis.

- NEUROHORMONE. In the *Glossary* of the American Psychiatric Association (Stone, 1988, 107), "A chemical messenger usually produced within the hypothalamus, carried to the pituitary and then to other cells within the central nervous system. Neurohormones are similar to neurotransmitters, except that they interact with a variety of cells, whereas neurotransmitters interact only with other neurons."

- NEUROPSYCHOLOGY. According to Hartlage (1987, 4), "a body of scientific knowledge related to brain-behavior relationships that uses measurement procedures developed on the basis of psychological research for the description and diagnosis of behaviors mediated by the central nervous system." Clinical neuropsychology, according to Hartlage, "involves the professional application of psychological tests, modified neurological assessment procedures, clinical observation, and anamnestic [case history] data toward the formulation of diagnostic and treatment conclusions related to the functional status of the central nervous system" (9).

- NEURORECEPTOR. According to Berkow & Fletcher (1987, 2475), "a small binding or recognition site (possessing a specific molecular configuration) on a cell surface that causes a physiological response upon stimulation by a neurotransmitter or other chemical, such as a drug or toxin. Some receptors cause inhibitory (e.g., relaxation of a muscle) or excitatory (e.g., contraction of a muscle) physiological responses."

- NEUROTOXIN. According to Valciukas (1991, 153-154), a substance "capable of producing a deleterious effect on the nervous system at the structural (macroscopic or molecular) or functional (behavioral or psychological) level" and thus "any substance that occurs naturally in the environment, or is produced by living organisms, which is capable of producing a [negative] biological effect on the nervous system." Neurotoxins are capable of "producing temporary or permanent change in nervous system function." Among the more common neurotoxins, Valciukas enumerates naturally-occurring or synthesized chemical compounds developed for therapeutic purposes to alleviate medical conditions, chemical compounds used to arrest the progress of neurological disease, chemical substances that cause behavioral changes (including both psychotropic medications and the so-called "street" drugs), and chemical compounds initially developed for industrial (e.g., soluble lead as a paint additive) or agricultural (e.g., dioxin, pesticides such as DDT) uses, the accidental ingestion of which lead to demonstrably negative neurological consequences.

- NEUROTRANSMITTER. According to Feldman & Quenzer (1984, 444), "a chemical substance that is released [within the central nervous system] and stimulates or inhibits adjacent neurons or stimulates effector organs such as muscles and glands." According to Berkow & Fletcher (1992, 2650), the process of *neurotransmission* follows these sequential steps: *Synthesis* (chemically, usually from chemical substances that are metabolized by the action of enzymes from what are typically called "precursor" substances to yield the neurotransmitting substance) and storage of the neurotransmitter in a nerve structure that is "prejunctional" (or chemically adjacent) to the nerve terminal at which transmission will occur; *release* of the neurotransmitter from the nerve terminal; *interaction* of the neurotransmitter with the receptor nerve; *rapid termination* of the interaction between the neurotransmitter and the receptor nerve; and *destruction* of the neurotransmitter or re-uptake into the terminal. Among the major neurotransmitters (sometimes called the "ubiquitous" neurotransmitters because they act at a variety of receptor sites), Berkow & Fletcher include *acetycholine, dopamine, norepinephrine, serotonin, gamma-amino-butyric acid* (or GABA, termed "the major inhibitory neurotransmitter in the central nervous system"), *beta-endorphin*, and *vasopresin.* Dopamine is frequently cited in accounts of the neurogenesis of severe mental disorder. Dopamine, norepinepherine, and serotonin interact with the enzyme monoamine oxidase, the chemical inhibition of which is pivotal to the action of a variety of anti-depressant pharmaceutical agents. Berkow & Fletcher (1987, 2477) apply the term pathology of neurotransmission to the aggregate "defects in the process of neurotransmitter storage, release, synthesis, degradation [chemical decomposition] and changes in receptor activity ... that lead to faulty transmission resulting in clinical disorders." Such defects might occur as the consequence of neurochemical dysfunctions or of damage to (or destruction of) brain morphological structures that function as transmitter or receptor sites.
- NEUROTROPIC. According to Valciukas (1995), a descriptive term applied to "chemical compounds that display affinity for the nervous system." In practical terms, equivalent to the descriptor *neuroactive.*
- PHARMACOKINETICS. That branch of pharmacology that studies the pathways and rates of absorption, distribution, and elimination of drugs within the organism, with particular attention to "target" organs and other organs and physiological, biochemical, and/or neurological systems affected; thus, according to Berkow & Fletcher (1992, 2610) "The study of the time course of a drug and its metabolites in the body following drug administration by any route." Usually distinguished from PHARMACODYNAMICS: "The pharmacologic response observed relative to the concentration at the active site depends upon the *pharmacodynamics* of the drug, while the attainment and maintenance of the appropriate concentration are a function of the *pharmacokinetics* of the drug. The former is concerned with how a drug acts on the body; the latter deals with how the body acts on a drug."

- POST-CONCUSSION SYNDROME. In ICD-10, the 10th edition of the *International Classification of Diseases* (World Health Organization, 1992, 67-68), a state that "occurs following head trauma (usually sufficiently severe to result in loss of consciousness) and includes a number of disparate symptoms such as headache, dizziness, fatigue, irritability, difficulty in concentrating and performing mental tasks, impairment of memory, insomnia, and reduced tolerance to stress, emotional excitement, or alcohol. These symptoms may be accompanied by feelings of depressing or anxiety . . . Such feelings enhance the original symptoms and a vicious circle results." The ICD-9 (U.S. Public Health Service, 1989, 1110) description observed also that "the symptom picture may resemble that of frontal lobe syndrome" and that "This syndrome is particularly associated with the closed type of head injury [i.e., without skull fracture] when signs of localized brain damage are slight or absent." Some experts (e.g., Bockar, 1976, 8) are quite insistent that the syndrome may readily arise following a blow to the head that does not result in loss of consciousness and that the symptom picture may not develop for some time following an injury, so that "the patient may not make the connection between a minor accident and his sudden development of symptoms." Persons who suffer repeated concussions (e.g., amateur and professional athletes who routinely sustain blows to the head) are said to experience *cumulative concussion syndrome.*
- PSYCHOENDOCRINOLOGY. The study of the effects of the functioning of the endocrine system upon behavior and emotion, as mediated by the central nervous system. According to Rafuls, Extein, Gold & Goggans (1987, 308), "Psychiatric disorders are often seen in patients with primary disorders of the neuroendocrine system . . . Of those endocrine disorders causing psychiatric symptoms, hypothyroidism has been found to be responsible for a large percentage . . . The next most frequent are disorders of glucose regulation, with the most common being diabetes mellitus." *Hypoglycemia* and *hyperglycemia* are also disorders in glucose regulation.
- SYNAPSE. According to Feldman & Quenzer (1984, 448), "the junction usually between the axon terminals of one neuron and the dendrites or soma of an adjacent neuron. Nerve impulses in the axon cause a release of neurotransmitters at the synapse that act upon the adjacent neuron either to excite or inhibit it."

Principal sources of neurologic dysfunction

At the expense of radical oversimplification of enormously complex processes, we can say that neurologic dysfunction customarily arises from two highly interactive sources which are only conceptually separable: *Morphological* anomalies in the brain (or, less frequently, in the brainstem, the spinal cord, or one or more nerve pathways leading to the brain), and *biochemical* anomalies in the production and/or metabolism of neurotransmitters. Bioelectrical anomalies and/or seizures of varying levels of severity (including sub-clinical and pre-clinical) represent the manifestations of biochemical anomalies, which in turn may result from morphological anomalies or dysfunctions.

Brain morphology

Morphological anomalies may arise pre-natally as a result of chromosomal abnormality, injury to the fetus, or exposure to neurotoxins ingested by the mother during pregnancy (e.g., fetal alcohol syndrome). More often, such anomalies result from injury to brain tissue following head trauma (including mechanical injury to the brain during birth, industrial accident, auto accident, falls from heights, blows to the head), with or without skull fracture or coma. Because, unlike tissue on the perimeter of the body, brain tissue does not regenerate following injury, neurotransmission is directly affected by morphological anomaly, dysfunction, or damage [NOTE 5].

It is widely held that neurotransmitters are metabolized at (relatively) specific "sites" (neuroreceptors, or bundles of nerves synaptically linked) in the brain. When a neurotransmitter "reaches" a receptor site that has been damaged or no longer functions, it cannot be absorbed and metabolized in the "usual" way and instead may "spill over" to adjacent sites, where it may innervate (activate) bundles of nerves associated with functions other than (and perhaps quite different from) those controlled by the damaged receptor site. At those alternate "landing places," they may interact with other neurotransmitters in "abnormal" ways to produce successor metabolites not usually associated with the action of the "misguided" neurotransmitter. If, for example, the receptor site in the brain that "decodes" neurochemical transmission typically associated with sexual excitation has been damaged and if adjacent receptor sites control aggressive behavior, aggressive rather than sexual excitatory behavior may ensue. In human terms, the consequence may be that a victim is sadistically mutilated rather than seduced.

In acute or traumatic injury diffused over large areas of the brain, a variety of receptor sites may be rendered temporarily (through edema) or permanently inoperative, triggering widespread dysfunction in neurotransmission and consequently in cognitive, emotional, and behavioral functioning.

Brain biochemistry

Biochemical anomalies may arise in consequence either of naturally-occurring or externally-induced over-production or under-production of neurotransmitters. If naturally-occurring, such anomalies are typically rather clearly linked to morphological anomalies. But the ingestion of a wide array of neurotoxic substances, ranging from caffeine and nicotine through industrial solvents or seafood infected with mercury to the deliberate use of "street drugs," may interfere with the body's rate of production of particular neurotransmitters to morphological anomalies. But the ingestion of a wide array of neurotoxic substances, ranging from caffeine and nicotine through industrial solvents or seafood infected with mercury to the deliberate use of "street drugs," may interfere with the body's rate of production of particular neurotransmitters (typically, by altering the composition of successor metabolites) and/or with the rate of neurochemical or bioelectrical transmission.

Cocaine, for example, interferes with the rate at which norepinepherine is metabolized (technically, with the "re-uptake" of a successor metabolite). Among other functions, norepinepherine is implicated in vasoconstriction and bronchodilation (and is sometimes used in medical emergencies to increase blood pressure). It is by inhibiting the "normal" metabolism of norepinepherine that cocaine induces euphoriant and stimulant effects (Feldman & Quenzer, 1984, 178-179). Of course, simultaneous ingestion (or sequential ingestion in rapid sequence) of neurotoxins with antagonistic biochemical properties (e.g., a central nervous stimulant such as cocaine or the amphetamines along with a central nervous system depressant such as alcohol) wreaks havoc with brain processes.

Although it has been customary to speak of "bioelectrical transmission" in the brain and central nervous system, this intellectual shorthand is less than precise (Engel, 1989, 53). Instead, it is the case that, as neurotransmitters pass across synaptic junctions, that chemical reaction or interaction itself generates bioelectricity. *Bioelectrical anomalies* are more appropriately regarded as the consequence of morphological and/or biochemical anomalies that accelerate or decelerate the rate of neurotransmission. Such anomalies are readily detectable (via the EEG and its variants) as indices to the specific biochemical and/or morphological anomalies of which they are manifestations.

A simplified visual guide to brain structures

In their review of research on abnormal patterns of lateralization between hemispheres of the brain in relation to aggression, Hillbrand, Langlan, Nelson, Clark & Dion (1994, 81-82) provided succinct descriptions that will serve us well as a guide to the primary functions associated with the principal areas of the brain [NOTE 6]:

The human brain is structured according to four levels of organization. The brain stem, phylogenetically the oldest part of the brain, is the first level of organization. It is a structure we share with reptiles, hence the metaphor "the reptilian brain." It handles essential body functions such as alertness, breathing, and heart rate. Anatomically' immediately above the brain stem and its companion, the cerebellum (responsible for posture and muscle coordination), is the limbic system. It is a brain structure most highly developed in mammals and is often called "the mammalian brain." It plays an essential role in regulating many body functions such as temperature, blood pressure, heart beat, and blood sugar level, and is often described as being mainly responsible

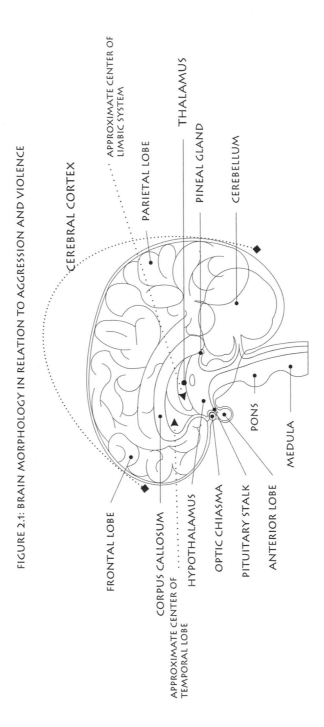

FIGURE 2.1: BRAIN MORPHOLOGY IN RELATION TO AGGRESSION AND VIOLENCE

for the "four F's" (feeding, flight, fight, and sex). Above that structure rests the cerebrum and its outer layer, the cerebral cortex. An uniquely human structure, the cerebrum is responsible for most activities that set us apart from other animals, such as thought and language. The fourth level of brain organization consists of the lateralized structure of the cerebrum. Although anatomically roughly symmetrical (as are the brain stem and the limbic system), the cerebrum is organized in such a way that each half (hemisphere) plays a relatively specialized role. The left hemisphere is more active when we process verbal material, whereas the right hemisphere is more active when we process spatial material.

On the opposite page, we offer a simplified diagram of the principal structures in the brain with particular attention to those structures known, or believed to be, implicated in violent and aggressive behavior in the human species. The legend which follows should be read counter-clockwise:

- FRONTAL LOBE. Regarded as the locus of control for movement, production of speech, "planfulness." Dysfunction correlated with *impulsivity*. Injuries or dysfunction associated with emotional control, motivation, inhibition, intolerance for frustration, easily-provoked aggression, promiscuity, lethargy. Cognitive impairment associated with frontal lobe lesions ("frontal lobe syndrome") includes memory disorder, attention-deficit disorder, impairment in ability to initiate cognitive activity and goal-directed behavior, abstract reasoning (and hence, impairment in planfulness), but not necessarily mental retardation. Impairment in motor functions, especially those sequenced to a purposive goal (apraxia) and production of speech (aphasia), misperception of social cues, loss of ability to read and write (agraphia), sometimes without impairment of speech, are associated with lesions; in severe cases, misperception leads to confabulation.

- CORPUS CALLOSUM. A thick band of nerve fibers connecting cerebral (left, right) hemispheres. In severe injury (or surgery) involving disconnection, resulting in inability or impairment in communication between hemispheres, patient is unable to control movements associated with the contralateral hemisphere; whence, such phenomena as "alien hand syndrome."

- TEMPORAL LOBE. Associated with hearing and interpreting language, music. Dysfunction results in defects in vision, speech, hearing, "dreamy states," gustatory and olfactory hallucinations. Site of one form of epileptic disorder. Injuries may result in *unprovoked, abrupt aggression,* may also cause impairment in memory, thus affecting ability to re-learn appropriate behavior.

- HYPOTHALAMUS. Receives sensory information and relays it to the cortex. The center of the forebrain, its functions include metabolism of carbohydrates, regulation of body heat, sexual activity. Contains many receptor sites (also found in the cortex) for the neurohormone norepinephrine, which is implicated in alertness, depression, anxiety. Above the hypothalamus lies the THALAMUS, which processes sensory information and relays it to the cerebral cortex. Abnormally high biochemical activity (measured bioelectrically) in a circuit that links the frontal cortex to the thalamus has been associated with *obsessions and compulsions.*

- OPTIC CHIASMA. Site at the base of the forebrain where the inner half of the fibers of the right and left optic nerves cross to the opposite hemisphere. Above the optic chiasma lies a structure called the nucleus accumbens, thought to be the principal center for decoding sensations of pleasure.
- PITUITARY STALK. Site of a "master" endocrine gland at the base of the brain affecting all hormonal and neurohormonal functions.
- ANTERIOR LOBE. Primarily concerned with olfactory functions; hence, also called the "olfactory lobe."
- PONS. Connects the midbrain and the BRAINSTEM, the junction between brain and spine that controls "automatic" body functions like breathing. Above the pons lies the MIDBRAIN (mesencephalon), which contains the substantia nigra at its center and the tegmentum as its "roof." Lesions are associated with paralysis of various sorts; experimental destruction of portions of the tegmentum in infra-human species produces a state that mimics catatonia. MIDBRAIN contains the HIPPOCAMPUS, which consolidates recently acquired information and is implicated in the transformation of short-term to long-term memory, and the LIMBIC SYSTEM (the "visceral brain," dysfunctions in which result in explosive rage), including the AMYGDALA (implicated in both violence and sexual arousal).
- MEDULA (Medula Oblongata). Portion of the BRAINSTEM connecting the pons and the spinal cord. Site of the vagus nerve, central to swallowing, heart rate, respiration, digestion, speech, and of the "spinal accessory nerves." Also called "the bulb," whence: "bulbar syndromes."
- CEREBELLUM. Governs muscle coordination, controls movement, posture, balance and is implicated in the learning of rote movements. Lesions result in ataxia, discoordinated movement, dysarthria, uncoordinated eye movement, "cerebellar fits."
- PINEAL GLAND. Located in the forebrain, secretes melatonin and is one of the principal sites for the secretion of *serotonin* and norepinephrene; involved in biorhythyms, gonadal development. The AMYGDALA lies nearby.
- PARIETAL LOBE. Receives and processes data from the senses. Directly affects taste. Lesions are associated with impairment in conception of arrangement of body parts, leading to *disorientation.*
- LIMBIC SYSTEM (also called the "visceral brain"). Includes the THALAMUS and AMYGDALA (a principal structure in controlling heart rate and perspiration, two of the principal physiological correlates of anxiety, and is generally implicated in the generation of emotions resultant from perception and thought), parts of the brainstem, and adjacent region of the cerebral cortex. Limbic system functions deal primarily with emotions and behavior. Limbic system injury distorts emotions and physical desires; *impulsive sexual behavior* and/or hypersexuality may result, especially in association with temporal

lobe dysfunction. Some neuropsychiatrists hold that *distorted perceptions, hypervigilance,* and perhaps *paranoia* result from an over-production of the neurohormone *dopamine* in the limbic system, coupled with an under-production in the cerebral cortex.

- CEREBRAL CORTEX. A thin covering over the four lobes (frontal, temporal, patietal, occipital) that comprise the right and left hemispheres of the brain and constitutes the "site" for a panoply of critical neuronal circuits. The processing of sensory information, including the decoding and integration of visual stimuli (Maunsell, 1995), the control of motor behavior, and certain learning and memory functions have been "sited" in regions of the cortex (Ungerleider, 1995). Circuits that link neurons in the cortex are held to be "susceptible to experience-dependent [and use-dependent] modifications during development but . . . become fixed in the adult" (Singer, 1995, 758). Diffuse injuries to the cortex which involve the shearing of axons, especially at the connections between the cortex and brainstem, impair the brain's ability to process emotions and behavior. Abnormally high bioelectrical activity in a circuit that links the frontal cortex to the thalamus deep inside the brain has been associated with obsessions and compulsions.

SCHIZOPHRENIA: RESULT OF FAULTY PARENT-CHILD INTERACTION — OR BRAIN DISORDER?

There can perhaps be no more dramatic example of the impact of the revolution in the neurosciences on the mental health sciences than the radical changes in conceptions of the genesis of that package of disorders in perceiving, thinking, and feeling we group under the label "schizophrenia" and regard as the most insidious, pernicious, and disabling of the mental disorders.

Three decades ago, in what were still (relatively speaking) the "dark ages" of neuroscience research, there abounded a variety of what can now only be regarded as rather fanciful (and generally psychodynamically-inclined) conceptual models about the origins of schizophrenia in faulty parent-child interaction during the early years of life. Gregory Bateson and his colleagues (Bateson et al., 1956; Bateson, 1972, 1978), for example, attributed schizophrenia in adulthood to a pattern of communication between mother and child such that the mother consistently gave conflicting messages to the child, in which what might be termed cognitive content failed to replicate emotional content, within a pattern of interaction in which the "victim" is prohibited from "escaping," so that he or she has no option but to endure exposure to inherently indecipherable communications and thus finds himself/herself in a "double-bind."

For the child thus victimized, so the model suggests, the world becomes indecipherable. Perduring into adulthood, the expectation that such double-bind communications will continue triggers a retreat from reality into fantasy, thus impairing the capacity of the victim to contact and appraise the "real world" accurately.

While there remains disagreement about the specific neurochemical and/or anatomical brain anomalies that yield schizophrenia, the terms of discussion in the 1990s are radically different (Zuckerman, 1995). Illustrative of contemporary research which has revolutionized earlier conceptualizations are such studies as these:

- British researchers Brown, Colter, Corsellis, Crow et al. (1986) found evidence at autopsy of structural brain changes particularly involving the temporal lobe among schizophrenic patients.

- Harvard neuropsychiatrists Cohen, Buonanno, Keck, Finklestein & Benes (1988) identified through computerized tomography (CT) scans and magnetic resonance imaging (MRI) techniques consistent neuroanatomical anomalies in schizophrenic patients, even though "standard" (i.e., office-based and conducted without the use of imaging devices) neurological examinations had failed to detect these abnormalities in nearly two-thirds of the cases.

- At the Neurosciences Laboratory of the National Institute of Mental Health, Luxenberg, Swedo, Flament and their associates (1988) identified through CT scans consistent neuroanatomical abnormality in patients diagnosed as obsessive-compulsive schizophrenics.

Indeed, the evidence on the neurogenesis of schizophrenia is now so solid that most neuropsychiatrists regard schizophrenia as primarily a brain disease. In a major review of that evidence, University of Maryland neuropsychiatrists Heinrichs & Buchanan (1988, 16-17) conclude that:

> the evidence for a higher rate of neurological abnormalities in schizophrenia is consistent and compelling. These signs are not random but are concentrated in the functional domains of sensory integration, coordination, and sequential motor acts. There is some suggestion that these functional systems are impaired at the level of subcortical structures such as the limbic system. Furthermore, there are indications that neurological signs are more prominent among those with thought disorder and cognitive impairments, as well as those with chronic forms of the illness. In addition, there is significant reason to believe that neurological abnormalities characterize a portion of the relatives of schizophrenic patients and predate the onset of the schizophrenic illness.

Though Heinrichs & Buchanan hold that schizophrenia is neurogenic in origin, they do not specify which neurologic dysfunctions (chemical or anatomical) may constitute its sources. Other investigators have shown less reluctance. Thus, in a detailed review of studies published between 1963-1990, Davis, Kahn, Ko & Davidson (1991) of the Mount Sinai School of Medicine in New York analyzed the research evidence linking dysfunctions in the metabolism of the neurotransmitter dopamine to the genesis of schizophrenia (Snyder, 1988), including studies done at autopsy and analyses of the contents of cerebrospinal develop a complex and interactive model for dysfunctions in the metabolism of dopamine at several receptor sites in the brain, including the frontal lobes.

Similarly, Bracha, Livingston, Clothier, Linington & Karson (1993) attributed the severity of delusions among psychotic patients to deficiencies in the metabolism of dopamine. Indeed, in an inter-generational study of schizophrenic patients and their families, Sabaté, Campion, d'Amato, and their associates (1994) have reported efforts to locate a specific dysfunctional receptor site for dopamine and to determine whether such dysfunction is related to a specific gene. Pharmacologically, Wetzel, Hillert, Gründer & Benkert (1994) demonstrated biochemical methods through which the "negative symptoms" of schizophrenia could be altered by means of interfering with dopamine receptor sites in the brain.

Alternately, in another major review, Albert Einstein College of Medicine neuropsychiatrists Javitt & Zubin (1991) proposed that schizophrenia may result from a naturally-occurring neurochemical dysfunction at a specific binding site in the brain that serves as a receptor for a particular amino acid (NMDA, or, chemically, N-methyl-D-aspartate). These investigators observe that such dysfunction results in irregularities in the cognitive, emotional, and behavioral functions associated with the frontal lobes. Partially confirmatory evidence is provided in a study of the recovery of disordered cognitive functions among former users of the street drug phencyclidine (PCP, or "Angel Dust"), the metabolites of which bind at the same frontal lobe site (Cosgrove & Newell, 1991).

In addition, that receptor site "may play a key role in learning and memory and in neurodegeneration and stroke-related brain death" (Hoffman, 1991). Hyman & Nestler (1993, 67-69) link disruptions in NMDA metabolism to hypoglycemia as well. According to Hoffman, psychopharmacology researchers have successfully "cloned" the principal NMDA receptor site, so that it becomes possible to synthesize artificial successor metabolites, which may well become the basis for future medication not only in the treatment of schizophrenia but also in learning and memory disorders. Similarly, Tong, Shepherd & Jahr (1995) have been successful in mediating NMDA metabolism pharmacologically.

However conceptually elegant, intellectually engaging, and useful a contribution to understanding what social psychologists call "family systems" (Rieber, 1990), Bateson's "double-bind" theory may be, it seems light years away from what is now known (and in "hard science," rather than social science, terms) about the neurogenesis of schizophrenic disorder. Nor, for that matter, have we been able to identify studies of patterns of communication between parents and children in whom there are frontal lobe dysfunctions or naturally-occurring dysfunctions in the metabolism of dopamine or NMDA, whether intergenerationally (genetically) transmitted or not.

A SCHEMATIC FOR NEUROGENIC AGGRESSION
DERIVED FROM RESEARCH ON INFRA-HUMAN SPECIES

The obvious and major advantage to studying neurologic anomalies and dysfunctions in animals is that (even under the strictures imposed by the Federal Animal Welfare Act of 1981) such dysfunctions can be *experimentally* induced and a priori conditions can be specified with a high degree of precision. In such research, the effects of neurotoxins on previously intact or "healthy" brains of animal subjects and brain dysfunction consequent to deliberate and specific injury to specific areas of the animal brain can be studied. With the exception of Germany under the Third Reich (Loew, 1981), no civilized nation could possibly countenance similar experimentation on human subjects. Instead, scientific investigations of neurologic conditions in relation to aggressive behavior can be conducted only after the human subject has behaved violently, perhaps criminally (and perhaps mutilated or murdered another human in the process) or at autopsy, after a violent offender has been killed by police or executed by the state [NOTE 7].

Clearly, there can be no direct translation to the analysis of aggressive behavior in humans of findings from laboratory studies of rats, mice, cats, pigeons, or even apes and chimpanzees in which brain morphology or brain biochemistry has been deliberately altered. Nonetheless, it proves instructive to contrast information from animal studies (Lewandowski & Forsstrom-Cohen, 1986) conducted under precisely controlled laboratory conditions with *post-hoc* investigations of human violence.

After reviewing studies on the neurogenesis of aggressive behavior among infra-human species, most conducted under controlled laboratory conditions (in which, for example, brain dysfunction is deliberately induced in "experimental" but not in "control" animals), Feldman & Quenzer (1984, 248-252), following the lead of Moyer (1968), offer a classificatory schematic for neurogenic aggression in animals that may prove generally applicable to human aggression as well:

- PREDATORY AGGRESSION, exemplified by "an attack on an object of prey."

- INTERMALE AGGRESSION, typified by "fighting to establish dominance in mating functions."

- FEAR-INDUCED AGGRESSION, in reaction to threat or danger.

- IRRITABLE AGGRESSION, induced by such stimuli as isolation, deprivation, or pain and "directed to any of a number of available objects."

- TERRITORIAL DEFENSE, represented by attacks on intruders.

- MATERNAL AGGRESSION, represented by defense of the young against predators.

- INSTRUMENTAL AGGRESSION, represented by attacks on objects "associated with fear or injury."

According to Feldman & Quenzer, accumulated research evidence supports the proposition that "each form of aggression has a particular anatomical and endocrine basis" and that "experimental manipulation will differentially affect the various types" of aggressive behavior.

Morphologically, the structures of the brain found recurrently to be associated with aggressive behavior in infra-human species are the *frontal lobe* and the *hypothalamus*. Biochemically, the ubiquitous neurotransmitters *dopamine, norepinephrine,* and *serotonin* emerge as important mediators (or modulators) of aggressive behavior, even in the absence of dysmorphologies in brain structure. The rate at which which dopamine is metabolized accelerates and the rate at which norepinepherine is metabolized decelerates when laboratory animals are induced (by such situational variables as isolation or deliberate provocation) to behave aggressively, while biochemical blocking of the usual route for the metabolism of serotonin suppresses intraspecies aggression (Cases, Seif, Grimsby, Gaspar et al., 1995).

Among human subjects, the same substances are major factors in brain biochemistry. The over-production of dopamine plays a primary role in the genesis of psychosis and has sometimes been linked to antisocial behavior generally (Gabel, Stadler, Bjorn et al., 1995) and to criminal violence in particular (Tiihonen, Kuikka, Bergstrom et al., 1995), while the over-production of norepinephrine plays a primary role in the genesis of manic states and its under-production a primary role in certain depressive states, and serotonin is regarded as a major contributor to the psychobiology of depression (Stone, 1988, 53, 112, 154).

Reasoning by analogy across species

It proves instructive to consider whether similar or analogous brain morphological anomalies and/or biochemical dysfunctions are associated in post-hoc fashion with violent behavior among human subjects. Should studies of experimentally-controlled (and/or -induced) aggression in infra-human species and investigations of neurologic functions among humans who have committed violent crimes prove concordant rather than discordant, there may emerge corroborative evidence on the neurogenesis of violence (Lore & Schultz, 1993).

The evidence we find most persuasive is that which (1) remains congruent between clinical and laboratory observations within the human species and (2) simultaneously congruent *across* species. If the clinical observations of neurologists and neuropsychiatrists say that Behavior A is related to Neurological Condition B *and* if empirical data from human studies seem to corroborate that association in a wide array of subjects (thus seeming to control for the selective perception endemic to clinical observation) *and* if research in comparative behavioral psychobiology yields the finding that a behavior analogous to A on the part of laboratory animals is associated with neurological condition B in those animals *and* if there is evidence of essentially similar neurodevelopment across species (Finaly & Darlington, 1995), how much skepticism is it reasonable to maintain about an association between A and B that may perdure even across species?

Frontal lobe lesions in mice and men

Let us take as a case in point the evidence that links damage or dysfunction in the frontal lobes of the brain to impulsive violence both among humans and in laboratory animals. The frontal lobes in the human brain are generally held to be the "seat" of such mental functions as cognition, memory, abstraction, concentration, and judgment. Both clinical (Cicerone & Wood, 1987; Joseph, 1990; Wood, 1987) and empirical evidence (Gorenstein, 1982; Linz, Hooper, Hind, Isaac & Gibson, 1990) linking impulsive violence to frontal lobe dysfunction (whether as the result of injury or of congenital anomaly) among humans is, as we have seen, sufficient to warrant the inclusion of *frontal lobe syndrome* as a distinct organic mental disorder in ICD-9 (U.S. Public Health Service, 1989).

As we noted earlier, at least when engendered by an identifiable injury to the brain (so that baseline data can be inspected for purposes of contrast), the "principal manifestations" of the disorder include impairment in self-control, foresight, creativity, and spontaneity, behaviorally observable "as increased irritability, selfishness, restlessness, and lack of concern for others" and including, importantly, "a change toward impulsiveness, boastfulness, temper outbursts," even in the absence of "measurable deterioration of intellect or memory." Such a litany is not unfamiliar in a recitation of the antecedents to criminal violence, and many social scientists will recognize in that litany precisely those characteristics which have been held, at least from Cleckley's (1941) "mask of sanity" onward, to be the distinguishing attributes of persons labeled psychopathically deviant (Blackburn & Maybury, 1985).

In consonance with the ICD-9 description, British neuropsychologist Rodger Llewellyn Wood (1987, 21-22) attributes human aggressiveness to dysfunction in the frontal lobes of the brain as a principal cause. Aggressive episodes are said to result from "some paroxysmal electrical event," so that "once started, the patient seems to have little or no control over the course of behaviour." Moreover, "Diminished insight is an almost inevitable consequence of severe frontal lobe injury" (25).

Now, let's consider some evidence from infra-human species. The naturally-occurring rate of generational maturation in such laboratory species as the white rat, coupled with the wide availability and relatively low cost of videotape equipment, enables animal experimenters to record virtually every moment of the life of a laboratory animal, including the animal's learning history (or, if one insists on anthropomorphism, "pattern of socialization" to reinforcers and contingency conditions of various sorts) from birth onward (or at least until the point of an experimental intervention) — a set of conditions under which the usual academic debate about nature vs. nurture essentially evaporates. Rather, it is possible to specify with high precision those conditions under which a laboratory animal has been trained or "nurtured" — for example, to behave aggressively or peaceably in response to intrusion or attack by another animal; and the very character of the laboratory itself permits the induction of a "target" dysfunction in ways that are simply not possible in research on human subjects.

Under these conditions, we can determine what happens when we deliberately damage the frontal lobes of the brain in laboratory rats who have been reared to respond peaceably or aggressively. According to distinguished neuropsychopharmacologists Robert Feldman and Linda Quenzer (1984, 248-252), the consequences are uniform, whether the animals had been "socialized" to respond aggressively or non-aggressively to intrusion or attack. Not only do the deliberately brain-damaged animals respond with lethal aggression when another animal "intruded" into the experimental space, but with a particularly virulent form thereof:

> . . . the topography of the killing is different in that . . . [animals] with frontal lobe lesions are particularly vicious and ferocious, biting the [victim] again and again even though the victim is dead.

There seems but a short analogical step between that description and a scene-of-the-crime report on sadistic murder with mutilation. It is hardly surprising, then, that Feldman & Quenzer conclude that "each form of aggression has a particular anatomical and endocrine basis." Nor is there, in the situation just described, much tolerance for the customary chicken-and-egg discussion about what preceded what or which is the "causative" and which the resultant variable [NOTE 8].

HISTORICAL SIGNPOSTS LINKING HUMAN VIOLENCE TO DISORDERED NEUROLOGY

Physicians have long made the clinical observation that disordered neurologic processes are associated, whether causally or correlatively, with disordered behavior. As Engel (1989, 22-25) observes, even in ancient times, Hippocrates noted that injuries to the head could cause sensory and motor disorders, and Galen included head injuries among the major causes of mental disorders. But highly specific medical accounts of systematic observation of the linkage between neurologic disorder and violent behavior can be traced only to the late 18th century.

Hadfield's neurogenic treason

Perhaps the earliest clearly documented evidence linking disordered neurology to criminal violence arises in the celebrated Hadfield trial of 1799, as a result of which the British Parliament enacted the Trial of Lunatics Act a year later. In that case, the first historically-documented "expert witness" in an English court (or perhaps in any court anywhere) to offer scientifically-anchored testimony on the mental condition of a defendant in a case of attempted murder relied on grounds that were frankly neurological and neuropsychological. In his resourceful monograph *Crime and Insanity in England: The Historical Perspective,* distinguished Oxford criminologist Nigel Walker (1968) recounts that Hadfield had fired a pistol at George III as the King entered the Royal Box at the Drury Lane Theatre. Though the shot went a foot wide of its mark and landed harmlessly in the orchestra pit, the event amounted to attempted homicide; but even an *unsuccessful* attempt to assassinate the monarch itself constitutes treason, then as now a capital offense.

For that reason, Hadfield was permitted greater latitude in the preparation and presentation of a defense than was the custom in ordinary criminal matters. A jurist named Erskine, whom Walker describes as "at the peak of his career" and as having "mastered the literature of his subject," appeared for the defense. To examine the defendant, Erskine engaged "Sir Alexander Crichton, whose recently published *Inquiry into the Nature and Origin of Mental Derangement* included discussions of insane motives for murder" and who later become personal physician to Czar Alexander I and, in that position, organized the first department of health for Imperial Russia. According to Walker, those physicians who had testified in earlier trials [NOTE 9] had typically known the defendant personally for some time, either as patient or as a member of the community whose "peculiarities" had become common knowledge. But Crichton did not meet or examine Hadfield until well after the attempt on the king's life, so that Walker construes his activity as the precursor for the role and function of today's "expert witness" in mental health.

But the capital issue is that — and, as a consequence of the knowledge explosion in the neurosciences of the past three decades, this point is more significant today than it was when Walker composed his treatise — the pivot for Hadfield's madness was not primarily psychological, but rather neuropsychological, since Hadfield

> had obvious and disfiguring wounds in the head, acquired in the service of his King in action against the French six years before. One of these had penetrated the skull, so that Erskine was able to invite the jury to inspect the membrane of the brain itself [and] The regimental surgeon [testified] how he had been compelled to have Hadfield tied to a bed for a fortnight . . . incoherent, with "manifest symptoms of derangement."

Crichton's evidence was to the effect that the prisoner's madness was probably the result of his wounds (76-77).

Both the jury and the Lord High Justices were persuaded by Crichton's testimony, which had very clearly designated a neurological basis for Hadfield's mental condition, and thus surely stands as the birthdate for forensic neuropsychiatry. But Hadfield had made an attempt at the life of the monarch, an act that might have gained him popularity among the American colonists who had fought a revolution against the same monarch; and, from Crichton's testimony, it was clear that Hadfield might, at any moment and without warning, emit what we might today describe as impulsive neurogenic violence [NOTE 10]. Yet the state of the law at that time contained no provision for the confinement even of patently dangerous persons who had been found not culpable on mental grounds. Very likely because the object of Hadfield's attack had been the monarch rather than a lesser personage,

> a hastily drafted Bill was . . . passed by Parliament in order to provide a clear-cut and foolproof procedure for such cases . . . Whether the [Trial of Lunatics] Act of 1800 "for the safe custody of insane persons charged with offences" would have been drafted and passed with such urgency if Hadfield's target had not been a royal one . . . is doubtful (Walker, 78).

The Act of 1800 made formal provision for the confinement in mental institutions of defendants found not guilty on the ground of insanity and further provided that "the only possible verdict in cases in which the jury was satisfied that the accused was insane at the time of his crime was to be the special verdict [and] that the acquittal was on the ground of insanity; the alternative of plain acquittal was no longer open to them." Upon such acquittal, the defendant was "to be kept in strict custody, until His Majesty's pleasure be known." In the Hadfield case, it pleased His Majesty that the defendant should be confined in the hospital named for St. Mary of Bethlehem, the notorious Bedlam of history and legend, where inmates were with some frequency caged and chained well into the 19th century. The Act provided the same disposition for persons found "not competent to stand trial." Apparently, the Act was held to apply only when the putative offense carried the death penalty, but at a time when "the penalty for all felonies was capital" (80).

Phineas Gage's crowbar-impaled brain

In the United States, the attribution of violent behavior to identifiable neurologic and neuropsychological precursors in a relatively systematic manner is traditionally dated to the case of Phineas Gage, foreman of a railroad construction crew who suffered massive brain injury in 1848 when, as the result of an accidental explosion, an iron tamping rod resembling a crowbar, some 42 incehnces in length and an inch and a quarter in diameter, passed through his skull and entered the brain (Stevens, 1971, 34-35). As Fedoroff, Starkstein, Forrester et al. (1992, 918) observe, "one of the best-known and earliest examples of behavioral and emotional changes associated with traumatic [brain] injury is Phineas Gage [whose] penetrating frontal lobe injury, caused by a railroad spike, led to a variety of emotional and personality changes, including disinhibition, apathy, loss of appropriate social behavior, and lability of mood."

The extent of Gage's injuries (replete with sketches illustrating the point of entry followed by the spike and the site of its lodging in the brain), the process of recovery, and the emotional, cognitive, and behavioral sequelae were recorded by the treating physician, John H. Harlow (1868), in a paper roughly contemporaneous with the injury and in a retrospective after Gage's death, exhumation of the body, and detachment of the skull. Although he appeared to recover physically, wholesale behavioral changes ensued, so that Gage became "fitful, irreverent, indulged in the grossest profanity," and, generally, impulsively violent. Dr. Harlow observed that, although his memory showed no major impairment, the "balance between his intellectual faculties and animal propensities seems to have been destroyed."

As neurologists Damasio, Grabowski, Frank et al. (1994) put it in their report of the specific injuries to the frontal lobe regions derived from their "reconstruction" of the projectile's trajectory as it traveled through Gage's brain based on contemporary neuroimaging techniques, the major significance of the case lay in the carefully documented recognition that there obtains "a neural basis for moral reasoning and social behavior."

No longer able to work at his former occupation, Gage apparently became a moderately well-known "freak attraction" in the taverns of New England towns and later in California. Although he apparently frequently became embroiled, in violently impulsive ways, in assaultive behavior in the rough-and-tumble of the tavern ethos (during which, for that matter, he doubtless found himself often on the receiving end of further blows to the head, in a clear precursor to what is today called "cumulative concussion syndrome"), he was apparently not arrested or prosecuted, presumably because law enforcement officers understood that "the man with the crow-bar brain" could not be regarded as accountable for his actions.

That situation both reflects the early Anglo-Saxon practices described by Nigel Walker and anticipates the contemporary practice of non-prosecution for violent behavior when there is documented medical evidence of recent brain trauma to which sudden and unexpected alterations in behavior (especially unprovoked aggressive outbursts) are to be attributed. Instead, such cases are essentially exculpated extra-judicially (i.e., before the matter is subject to formal processes of adjudication), provided that the offense has not resulted in death or serious injury and that the neurologically-disordered putative offender undertakes, or returns to, competent medical care.

There are accounts (perhaps folkloric) that Gage joined a traveling circus and for a number of years earned his living as a side-show attraction, into the indentation in whose skull circus-goers could place their fingers at a penny a pop. Gage died in 1861 in California, with epilepsy recorded as the proximate cause of death. After his death, the body was exhumed at the request of Dr. Harlow. Later, "the skull and the tamping iron, alongside which Gage had been buried, [became] part of the Warren Anatomic Medical Museum at Harvard University" (Damasio, Grabowski, Frank et al., 1994).

Contemporary clinical evidence: The Texas tower sniper's walnut-sized brain tumor

Current clinical literature in neuropsychology and neuropsychiatry especially is replete with dramatic examples of neurogenic violence. In his work on behavioral neurology, for example, Rhawn Joseph (1990, 102) summarizes the case of Charles Whitman, the "Texas Tower" sniper who killed 14 people and wounded 38 others on the University of Texas campus during a 90-minute shooting spree in 1966. Long before his murders, Whitman had consulted a psychiatrist with complaints of "periodic and uncontrollable violent impulses," achieving neither relief nor even an accurate diagnosis. Before embarking on his killing spree, Whitman had penned a note specifically asking that, at his death, an autopsy be performed to learn "if there's something wrong with my brain." At that autopsy, there was revealed in Whitman's brain a "multiform tumor the size of a walnut compressing the amygdaloid nucleus."

Joseph (Ibid., 96-103) thus attributes aggressivity to dysfunctions in limbic system structures in the brain, particularly the hypothalamus and the amygdala, citing experimental evidence on both animal and human subjects of the effects of electrical stimulation of these structures in producing violent behavior. Clinical support for Joseph's position was offered by Tonkonogy & Geller (1993), who found that episodes of what the official lexicon of the American Psychiatric Association terms "intermittent explosive disorder" developed in patients with cancerous tumors in the region of the hypothalamus, concluding that "hypothalamic lesions played a major role in the development of aggressive behavior."

CURRENT FORMULATIONS ON THE NEUROGENESIS OF AGGRESSIVE BEHAVIOR AMONG HUMANS

Neuropsychiatric researchers who have analyzed the cumulative evidence are united in the view that sudden-onset violent behavior (i.e., that which we would term "impulsive" violence) derives from neurologic dysfunction, although there obtains little consensus about whether the specific dysfunction(s) implicated are neurochemical or morphological, or, as Wood (1987) proposes, bioelectrical. It should be observed that these investigators did not limit their inquiries to those who had committed and/or been convicted of criminal violence. Rather, they considered aggressive and violent behavior, whether formally criminal or not — i.e., whether or such behavior had been adjudicated as criminal and been met with formal sanctions. As in the case of the hapless Phineas Gage, impulsively violent behavior may not always eventuate in prosecution or formal criminal sanction.

Brain injury and disordered neurochemistry

Mount Sinai School of Medicine neuropsychiatrists Larry Siever and Kenneth Davis (1991, 1656) favor the neurochemical position. They hold that "Impulsivity/aggression is a *genetically-transmitted* dimension associated with reductions in serotonergic activity" — that is, in an inherited incapacity to metabolize properly the powerful neurotransmitter *serotonin.* Substantial implications follow for treatment of impulsive aggression through neurochemical agents capable of "correcting" faulty metabolism of serotonin. Similarly, Siever & Davis attribute disorganization in cognition and perception — which may underlie the habitual mis-construing of costs, benefits, and risks associated with deviant behavior in general — to dysfunction in metabolizing the neurotransmitter *dopamine,* and, once again, there are implications for treatment by means of psychopharmacology.

In a report in *Neuropsychiatry & Clinical Neurosciences,* Brown, Fann & Grant (1994) indicate that "2 million [adult] persons in the United States suffer closed head injuries annually" and that "of these injuries, 500,000 are serious enough to require hospitalization," urging that "postconcussional disorders may represent one of the most common etiologies of neurobehavioral disorder, especially in younger persons." Silver, Hales & Yudofsky (1987, 179-180) estimate that "as many as 5 million children sustain head injury per year," with approximately 200,000 requiring hospitalization and further observe that the incidence of brain injury in the U.S. is 150% that of schizophrenia.

While the exterior of the skull at maturity is smooth and hard, the interior is relatively craggy, with many bony structures protruding. A blow to the head sufficient to shift brain cells (themselves rather gelatinous in texture) within the skull may thus cause edema (swelling), with consequent "temporary" rearrangement of spatial relationships among and between brain cells, or direct damage to cells, most of which do not regenerate, with consequent "loss" of function that may be associated with damaged cells.

Among infants and very young children, in whom the skull remains relatively malleable, falls from cribs, sofas, or chairs represent a leading source of closed head injury. Among older children and adolescents, the leading sources are falls from heights, sports and play injuries, and injuries sustained in auto accidents. To these sources, among adults are added industrial accidents. Obviously, deliberate blows to the head sustained at any age — whether as the result of child abuse, domestic violence, or adult-to-adult physical assault or confrontation — will similarly result in closed head injury.

Current leading scientific opinion in neuropsychiatry relates head trauma, often unreported and untreated, to a variety of consequent mental disorders, including "confusion, intellectual changes, affective lability, or psychosis . . . substance abuse, impulse disorders, and characterologic disorders, such as antisocial, borderline, and narcissistic personality disorders," although and very significantly, "the cognitive functions of the patient are preserved" (Silver, Yudofsky & Hales, 1987, 180).

Similarly, head trauma resultant in even sub-clinical epilepsy or epileptiform disorder (that is, dysfunctions in brain bioelectrical activity that cannot be detected by electroencephalographic devices, estimated to be some 15% of all cases), is said to perpetuate as *organic personality syndrome*, further differentiated into categories labeled "*pseudo-psychopathic* (characterized by emotional lability, impulsivity, socially inappropriate behavior, and hostility) and *pseudo-depressive* (characterized by apathy, indifference, and social disconnectedness)," with both syndromes "marked by indifference for the consequences of behavior and an inability to perceive appropriately the effects of such behavior on others" (Stoudemire, 1987, 134-135). The latter characteristics (i.e., indifference to the consequences of behavior, disregard of the social impact of one's own behavior), indeed, are virtually the defining traits embedded in classic conceptions of psychopathy (Hare, 1985; Heilbrun & Heilbrun, 1985; Meloy, 1988).

In a study that provided further confirmation of Stoudemire's (1987) view that closed head injury perpetuates as organic personality disorder either of the "pseudo-depressive" or "pseudo-psychopathic" variety, Fletcher, Ewing-Cobbs, Miner, Levin & Eisenberg (1990) followed for a year a group of children aged between 3 and 15 who had sustained closed head injuries and had been treated in the children's pediatric neurosurgery service at the University of Texas' Houston medical campus. Data collected by means of structured checklists completed by parents (the Vineland Adaptive Behavior Scales, the Child Behavior Checklist) indicated that negative behavioral effects associated with the head injuries persisted throughout the follow-up period; those effects ranged from "quiet withdrawal to hyperactive, aggressive behavior" (97).

Moreover, persons who have suffered past head trauma frequently fail to link such trauma to current disorders (Silver, Yudofsky & Hales, 1987, 180):

> Prototypic examples of brain damage in which the patient, while providing a [psychiatric] history may fail to associate [current symptoms] with the traumatic event include the alcoholic who is amnestic for a fall that occurred while inebriated; the 10-year-old boy whose head was hit while falling from his bicycle, but who fails to inform his

parents; or the wife who was beaten by her husband, but who is either fearful or ashamed to report the injury to her family physician. Such trauma may be associated with confusion, intellectual changes, affective lability, or psychosis; and the patient may first present [these latter symptoms] to the psychiatrist for evaluation and treatment.

Victims of head trauma, particularly that which has been undetected, diagnosed imprecisely, or minimized, are "prone to the taking of risks," so that a vicious circle develops, since risk-takers are attracted to activities that entail a high probability for further head trauma (Ibid., 180-181). Hence, victims of head trauma are at risk for risk-taking behavior which further increases the probability of future, additional head trauma, and which, in its turn, increases the likelihood of future risk-taking behavior, approximating what has been called the "cumulative concussion syndrome." That circle indeed begins to sound very like the tinder-box circumstances that surround a high proportion of the episodes of criminal violence in this country.

In his review of the research on traumatic brain injury in relation to aggression, Miller (1994, 96) has put the matter briefly but dramatically:

> . . . pre-existing impulsive traits or behavioral difficulties [may] go unnoticed or are glossed over until after a brain injury. It is quite possible for someone to get away with marginally antisocial behavior as long as he/she is able to use what barely functional neurocognitive abilities and coping skills he/she possesses to keep from crossing the line into really deep trouble. Then the brain injury occurs which diminishes even these rudimentary adaptive skills. What remain are the impulsivity, aggressiveness, egocentric childishness, and poor frustration tolerance without any real measure of compensatory judgment or restraint. Thus, to the extent that head injuries tend to happen preferentially to people with premorbidly impulsive and often aggressive lifestyles, it is hardly surprising that superimposed injury to the brain would serve to intensify and exacerbate this pattern, whether through frontal [lobe] disinhibition or lowered threshold to paroxysmal brain activity, or both. A vicious circle if ever there was one — those most prone to sustain a brain injury are those most likely to have the worst reaction to it.

Although the criminologic literature is replete with representations that victimization in child abuse is a frequent precursor to criminal offending in adulthood, the matter of the character and effect of the injuries sustained by abused children is rarely indicated. Ito, Teicher, Glod, and their associates (1993) studied neurological abnormalities in abused children, finding a prevalence in electrophysiologically-measured brain abnormalities in abused subjects precisely twice as great (54.4% vs. 26.9%,) as in non-abused subjects. These abnormalities were found "predominantly in the left side of the frontal, temporal, or anterior region." The investigators concluded that their findings "support the hypothesis that early abuse alters brain development, particularly limbic structures." Similar findings from the same research group were reported by Teicher, Glod, Surrey & Swett (1993).

Since minimally 90% of adults are right-handed (Satz, Soper & Orsini, 1988), injuries to the left hemisphere are consistent with blows to the head of a facing person delivered by a right-handed abuser, whether by fist, open hand, or blunt instrument (e.g., baseball bat, broom handle). As we shall see in later in this chapter, left hemisphere dysfunctions have associated with criminal aggression with some frequency.

Although they did not inquire into the nature of the injuries sustained, in their review of the research evidence on the victimization of children, Finkelhor & Dzuiba-Leatherman (1994, 180) reported the relative incidence of physical abuse annually is 3.59 per 1000 and that 84% of all victims of physical abuse sustain physical injury. In the 1990 Census, persons aged 17 and under constituted 27% of the U.S. population, for an aggregate of some 67 million. Extrapolation of the Finkelhor & Dzuiba-Leatherman ratio suggests some 234,000 episodes of physical abuse annually, with 196,000 injuries. If the proportion resulting in injury to the brain discerned in the studies by the Ito-Glod research group generalizes, the total number of children who sustain such injury annually as a result of physical abuse by parents, siblings, or caregivers is no less than staggering.

Attributions to multiple neurologic sources

Neuropsychiatrist David Bear of Vanderbilt University (1989, 88) puts it categorically that repetitive aggression arises in neurologic dysfunction, which may be either morphological or neurochemical in character: "Overly frequent or aimless aggression . . . in humans reflects structural or chemical dysfunction of neuronal circuits [so that] unpredicted or even unpredictable aggressive acts . . . become understandable — and in an important sense, predictable — when viewed as a breakdown of specific neuronal systems regulating aggression at multiple levels within the human brain." According to Bear (1987, 1989), the hypothalamus, the amygdala, and the frontal cortex are the "specific neuronal systems" dysfunctions in which are most often implicated in aggressive behavior.

More expansively, Cornell Medical College neuropsychiatrist Kenneth Tardiff (1988, 1042) has summarized the accumulated evidence that links violent behavior with a burgeoning array of neurological anomalies or dysfunctions:

A number of organic disorders are associated with violent behavior, including substance abuse, central nervous system disorders, systemic disorders, and seizure disorders. Central nervous system disorders which have been associated with violent behavior include traumatic brain injuries, including birth injury as well as trauma as an adult acutely and in the post-concussion syndrome; intracranial infections; cerebrovascular disorders; Alzheimer's disease [a degenerative brain disorder primarily affecting the cerebral cortex]; Wilson's disease [a disorder of liver functioning]; multiple sclerosis. Systemic disorders affecting the central nervous system include metabolic disorders such as hypoglycemia, vitamin deficiencies, electrolyte imbalances, hypoxia [a pulmonary disorder resulting in oxygen deficiency], uremia, Cushing's anemia [a disorder of the adrenal glands, yielding excessive production of certain corticosteroids in the body], systemic infections . . . and industrial poisons such as lead.

NEUROPATHOLOGY AMONG VIOLENT OFFENDERS

Because disordered brain and neurochemical processes often eventuate in violent behavior, and because subjects with a history of violence are to be found in great profusion in prison populations, many studies of the relationship between neurological disorder and violence have been conducted within correctional settings, with offenders convicted of violent crimes as subjects. These studies have contributed directly to the emerging picture of the neurogenesis of violence.

A relatively large number of studies has investigated the incidence of brain morphological and biochemical anomalies among samples of incarcerated criminal offenders, usually by means of technologically sophisticated medical instruments but sometimes by means of complex neuropsychological test batteries that have been concurrently well validated against such "hands on" technology (Franzen & Lovell, 1987). However, because these studies have invariably involved either extensive laboratory equipment (e.g., technologically sophisticated equipment for computerized imaging) or surgical procedures (e.g., many studies of the metabolism of neural transmitting enzymes require samples of spinal fluid, available only through lumbar puncture), and, particularly in those cases in which data have been gathered through advanced imaging techniques, the samples in these studies tend to be rather small, so that the resultant conclusions can be generalized only with caution. But, at the conceptual level, a persuasive (if not yet quite compelling) case can now be made linking dysfunction, anomaly, or abnormality in the neurological substratum especially to impulsive displays of violence and/or aggression (Prentky, 1985; Valzelli, 1981; Garza-Trevino, 1994). Statistical data on aggressive violent crime reveals a high incidence of "tinder-box" situations (in contrast to those acts of criminal violence that are carefully deliberated and could hardly be denominated as "impulsive" events); thus, such a linkage holds promise for understanding variables at work in some large proportion of episodes of criminal aggression..

Brain anomalies

Head trauma and epilepsy

According to distinguished University of Chicago psychiatrist Carl Bell (1986), the incidence of undetected and untreated closed head trauma, likely indicative of brain dysfunction of at least a sub-clinical level of severity, is nearly four times greater than the norm among members of lower socioeconomic status groups and among Blacks, two groups among whom crimes of violence also show high prevalence (as we shall see in detail in Chapter 4). Closed head trauma is frequently followed by epilepsy or epileptiform disorder, often at the sub-clinical or pre-clinical level. Such traumata have been found to result in increased aggression, behavioral dyscontrol, impaired insight, and aberrant sexuality of various sorts (Wood, 1987, 17-25). According to Forrest (1987, 394), increases in sex drive typically follow injuries to the brain that result in temporal lobe epilepsy, even of sub-clinical severity, such that

> sexual behavior . . . is usually marked by loss of specificity as to objects or forms of excitation [of such severity that] It is often helpful to make it clear to the family that the patient is not a "sex maniac" when the patient's drives appear to become amplified due to brain injury.

In a clinical study, Fornazzari, Farcnik, Smith et al. (1992, 42) reviewed the histories of psychiatric patients "from different racial, social, and economic backgrounds" who were each afflicted with "hallucinatory threatening scenes, violent, aggressive, and sometimes horrifying," concluding that "violent, brief hallucinations with no other epileptic sign may be manifestations of frontal lobe seizures" of sub-clinical severity.

Yeudall, Fedora & Fromm (1987) reviewed data on the incidence of head injury *prior to* offending among alcoholic psychopaths (77%), homicide offenders (75%), rapists (21%), and offenders who had committed a single episode of physical assault (25%). British psychologist Cedric Hart (1987) essentially confirmed these results in an investigation of neuropsychological impairment in two groups of homicide offenders, one of which was comprised of persistent violent offenders with previous convictions as well as a conviction for homicide and the other of which was comprised of "one-time aggressive" offenders without prior convictions. Hart's findings pointed toward greater impairment among persistent offenders. Similarly, although they did not analyze characteristic patterns of criminal behavior prior to incarceration, Merbitz, Jain, Good & Jain (1995) found a significant difference in mean number of disciplinary infractions resultant from aggressive behavior *during* incarceration among felony offenders whose medical histories included reports of traumatic head injury (likely resultant in injury to the brain) prior to incarceration and "otherwise similar" prisoners without documented histories of such injuries.

The incidence of epilepsy among prisoners incarcerated for criminal behavior of all sorts significantly exceeds that of control subjects matched for age (Wettstein, 1987, 458). In a study of all new adult male admissions to the Illinois state prisons utilizing comprehensive neurological examinations, including electroencephalograph (EEG) readings, Whitman, Coleman, Patmon, Desai, Cohen & King (1984) found the rate of epilepsy among prisoners to be four times higher than the incidence in a comparably aged group of non-prisoners and further opined on the basis of case history data that head trauma likely accounted for epilepsy in 45% of the cases detected. A variety of reports, many clinical in character, also link epilepsy to homicidal violence (Hindler, 1989). Similarly, at the Medical College of Ohio, Lesco (1989) attributed a murder-suicide by a 67-year-old male with no history of mental illness, violent behavior, or substance abuse to rapid-onset paroxysms in brain-bioelectrical activity associated with Alzheimer's disease.

Dysfunctions measured by EEG

British neuropsychiatrist Denis Williams (1969) summarized data linking bioelectrical anomalies to aggressive crime in some 1250 prisoners he had examined over two decades. Among those whose criminal histories classified them as "habitual aggressives," he found that 65% displayed such anomalies, as measured by abnormal EEG readings; among those who had committed a "solitary major crime" of an aggressive nature, only 12% had abnormal EEG readings. Moreover, "The areas of abnormality [i.e., those areas of the brain in which EEG findings indicated abnormality] were indeed the same as those most often involved in temporal lobe epilepsy" (514). Remarkably congruent findings were reported by Geiger (1960) in an analysis of some 650 Wisconsin juvenile offenders whose crimes represented "impulsive, violent, and destructive behavior," with neuropathology detected in 74% of the cases (93% of the time via EEG abnormality and 7% of the time by means of clinical indices). Clinical reports by Bonkalo (1967) and Gunn (1978) have also linked brain anomalies measured by EEG specifically to homicide.

Similarly, Blackburn (1975, 1979) found EEG evidence of abnormally high cortical arousal among prisoners diagnosed as "primary psychopaths." These subjects also scored significantly higher than controls on psychometric measures of "sensation seeking" and susceptibility to boredom, so that Blackburn's results support at a basic physiological level Hare's (1970) view that hyperarousability is a distinguishing characteristic of psychopaths.

Howard (1984) took EEG readings of consecutive admissions to a prison hospital in Britain, with the finding that atypical brain activity was recorded in 60% of the cases. Howard further observed that particular anomalies in brain functioning were prevalent in subjects who had committed crimes of violence against strangers rather than against friends or acquaintances. His finding is corroborated in a clinical study by Martinius (1983) of criminal homicide and partially corroborated among juvenile homicide offenders under the age of 13 examined at the NYU Medical Center by Lewis, Shanok, Grant & Ritvo (1983).

EEG abnormality in relation to schizophrenia and psychopathy

Gorenstein (1982) reported evidence of dysfunction in the frontal lobe of the brain, the seat of such psychological functions as foresight, planning, and the regulation of impulses among subjects classified as psychopaths according to behavioral and psychometric criteria.

Parallel findings were reported by Krakowski, Convit, Jaeger & Lin (1989) in studies of schizophrenics with a history of criminal violence, verified by EEG readings, leading these investigators to conclude that "violence as well as neurological and neuropsychological deficits characterize a more severe form of schizophrenia." Raine & Venables (1988) similarly reported anomalies in parietal lobe functioning as measured by EEG among inmates diagnosed as psychopathic.

Neuropathology and inventoriable psychopathology

In a study that compared EEG readings, CT scans of the brain, and results of the Luria-Nebraska Neuropsychological test battery, Langevin, Ben-Aron, Wortzman & Dickey (1987), found "a consistent trend toward more neuropathology" in violent and assaultive offenders than in offenders who were guilty of property crimes. But, perhaps in a manner that explains weak statistical associations between inventoried personality traits and criminal violence, these differences in neuropathology were not matched by differences in subjects' psychometric profiles on the Minnesota Multiphasic Personality Inventory (MMPI).

Contrary data on the relationship between neuropathology as verified by advanced imaging techniques and MMPI scores were reported by Ball, Archer, Struve & Hunter (1987) of Eastern Virginia Medical College, who found that abnormal EEG patterns were matched on several MMPI scales, including that for psychopathic deviation, among adolescent psychiatric inpatients. Similarly, Cullum & Bigler (1988) reported that clinically significant elevations on certain MMPI scales invariably followed head injury which had resulted in lateralized cerebral dysfunction (verified by CT scan) among patients who were treated at the Health Sciences Center of the University of California, San Diego. The question of whether paper-and-pencil instruments like the MMPI can detect psychological sequelae to neuropathology thus remains moot.

Brain dysfunction among sex offenders

Several studies have focused specifically on sex offenders. On a "gross" neuropsychological screening test, DeWolfe & Ryan (1984) found "signs" of left hemisphere dysfunction in 87% of the sexual assaulters (rapists) they examined. In a more extensive investigation that involved both administration of a comprehensive neuropsychological test battery, measures of penile tumescence in response to erotic stimuli of varying character (male/female, adult/child), and CT scans, Hucker, Langevin, Wortzman & Bain (1986) found a high incidence of neuropathology involving the left temporo-parietal region of the brain among subjects whose criminal histories classified them as focused pedophiles. In another investigation, Langevin, Wortzman, Dickey et al. (1988) reported a 30%

incidence of neuropathology (primarily in temporal lobe disorders as measured by CT) among incest offenders. And, in a summary review of evidence derived from varied measurement techniques (e.g., neurological and neuropsychological), Langevin, Marentette & Rosati (1995) put the incidence at 67% among "sexual aggressives" (e.g., rapists) and at 42% among incest offenders.

At the Kessler Institute for Rehabilitation Medicine, Galski, Thornton & Shumsky (1990) found evidence of brain damage, or of significant neuropsychological dysfunction, in 77% of the incarcerated criminal sexual psychopaths they examined on the Luria Nebraska Neuropsychological Battery, discovering as well so strong an association between neuropsychological impairment and the degree of violence associated with the most recent sex offense that they were led to conclude that "the organic brain impairment discovered . . . in this sample through neuropsychological examination establishes the link between brain dysfunction and aberrant sexual behavior [since] violent sexual offenses seem to be linked with more severe neuropsychological dysfunction, specifically associated with left hemisphere functioning," a finding that parallels that of DeWolfe & Ryan (1984).

At the University of Alberta Medical Center, Flor-Henry, Lang, Koles & Frenzel (1991) examined brain anomalies among pedophiles utilizing the QEEG and the plethysmograph among pedophiles, incest offenders, and control subjects. Among those classified as "true" pedophiles in consequence of penile tumescence responses to deviant sexual stimuli depicting children ranging in age from 6 to 11, the investigators observed distinct abnormalities in frontal lobe functioning and impairment in communication between the left and right hemispheres. Similar anomalies were not found among incest offenders or controls. These anomalies parallel those found among exhibitionists in an earlier study by the Flor-Henry research group (1988).

Cerebral lateralization and asymmetry

Hillbrand, Langlan, Nelson, Clark & Dion (1994) trace the proposition that criminal aggressivity is related to asymmetry between the right and left hemispheres of the brain to the work of Lombroso in the late 19th century, based largely on clinical observation of facial asymmetries. Particularly since research in the neurosciences has reasonably well established that differential mental functions depend primarily on one or another hemisphere, interest in studying hemispheric "dominance" and morphological asymmetry between hemispheres among offenders has re-emerged, along with a panoply of technologically advanced methods for assessment.

Although he is perhaps best known for construction, validation, and refinement of scales to measure psychopathy (Hare, Harpur, Hakstian & Forth, 1990; Hare, 1991), Robert Hare of the University of British Columbia, undoubtedly the leading authority worldwide on psychopathic deviation, has also researched the relationship between psychopathy and cerebral function intensively (Hare, 1979, 1982). Rather early on, Hare (1970) had posited hyperarousability is a distinguishing characteristic of psychopaths. Later investigations confirmed that view.

Hare & McPherson (1984) found "asymmetric left-hemisphere arousal" patterns in a study that involved administration of a dichotic listening task requiring activation of lateralized brain functions to inmates who had been classified as high or low in psychopathy (psychometrically as well as behaviorally) and to control subjects who were presumably crime-free. Jutai, Hare & Connolly (1987) also found asymmetric left-hemisphere arousal among subjects who had been identified through Hare's methodology as psychopathic.

These results were replicated and amplified in studies by Raine, O'Brien, Smiley & Scerbo (1990). Nonetheless, in a study which utilized an impressive array of neuropsychological (rather than neurological) measures, Hare (1984, 139) concluded that "psychopaths are less likely to display gross symptoms of neurological impairment or dysfunction than are individuals who exhibit some of the features of psychopathy but who fall short of fitting the complete clinical syndrome." That description sounds very like Stoudemire's (1987, 135-135) characterization of *organic personality disorder, pseudopsychopathic type.*

Most studies have investigated aggression retrospectively (e.g., from case records and/or criminal history) rather than prospectively or predictively. To that extent, such studies have attempted to *post*-dict aggression, an activity of considerable conceptual significance. But the prediction of aggressive behavior is vastly important at the operational level in the management (and patient and staff safety) of such closed institutions as mental hospitals, as well as jails and prisons, especially since the case records of the inmates and patients thereof customarily display relatively high baseline rates for aggressive behavior.

At Connecticut's Whiting Forensic Institute, Hillbrand and his colleagues conducted a genuinely predictive study of cerebral lateralization in relation not to past, but to future, aggression. Observing that "Most recent studies have found that individuals with abnormal patterns of lateralization are over-represented among violent individuals," Hillbrand, Langlan, Nelson, Clark & Dion (1994) tracked in-hospital aggressive behavior over a six-month period among court-committed patients. Cerebral lateralization was measured through neuropsychological examination rather than through neuroimaging, and aggressive behaviors (as recorded by medical and nursing staff) were differentially classified according to type (physical vs. verbal), object (self vs. others vs. physical objects), and level of severity, including as well the character and frequency of intervention by professional medical staff in aggressive episodes. Their findings:

> Patients with severely abnormal lateralization engaged in more frequent as well as more severe acts of physical aggression [and] more severe (though not more frequent)

acts of verbal aggression . . . The order of magnitude of these differences was notable [so that] patients with severely abnormal lateralization had engaged in an average of 13.2 incidents of aggression during the six-month period, whereas subjects with normal lateralization had engaged in an average of 1.50 incidents of aggression. Further analyses revealed that age, race, head trauma, brain damage, or psychiatric diagnoses could not explain the pattern of results.

However, Hillbrand's research group also found severe abnormal lateralization to be statistically associated with low scores on a measure of intelligence, "suggesting the possibility that this factor accounted for the differences in aggression." They thus concluded that "The answer to the question . . . 'Is there an association between cerebral lateralization and aggression?' may be, 'Yes, but not necessarily a causal link.'"

Differential incidence of neuropathology across offense categories

Most tellingly, Yeudall & Fromm-Auch (1979) found evidence of neuropathology through administration of a comprehensive neuropsychological battery in 94% of the homicide offenders, 96% of the sex offenders, 89% of the assaulters, and 86% of the juvenile offenders they examined, with these findings confirmed by subsequent EEG readings.

Congruent findings were reported by Spellacy (1978), who also reported that neuropsychological assessment discriminated between violent and non-violent prisoners more effectively than did results of the MMPI. Similarly, though they employed only clinical neuropsychological test measures rather than medical neurological assessment devices, Bryant, Scott, Tori & Golden (1984) found consistent associations between neuropsychological deficit or dysfunction and a history of violent criminal behavior.

Basing their analyses on the substantially more powerful techniques of neuroimaging, Mills & Raine (1994) reviewed studies of offenders utilizing CT, MRI, PET, or rCBF techniques published from 1981 onwards, with subject samples that included murderers, rapists, incest offenders, pedophiles, exhibitionists, and property offenders as well as presumably non-offending "normal" control subjects. Collectively, Mills & Raine concluded, the discerning evidence they reviewed lends support to the propositions that

Frontal lobe dysfunction may be associated with violent offending while temporal lobe dysfunction may be associated with sexual offending and fronto-temporal dysfunction may be associated with violent sexual offending. Anterior brain dysfunction may represent a general predisposition to offending irrespective of location of the dysfunction such that dysfunction to frontal or temporal areas may predispose to offending, with the type of offending (e.g., violent, sexual, or violent and sexual) determined . . . by non-biological factors (146).

Figure 2.2: Relative incidence of inventoried neuropathology [% of cases] reported in studies utilizing varied neurological and neuropsychological measurement techniques — among aggressive offenders arrayed by offense, among juvenile offenders, and among victims of child abuse

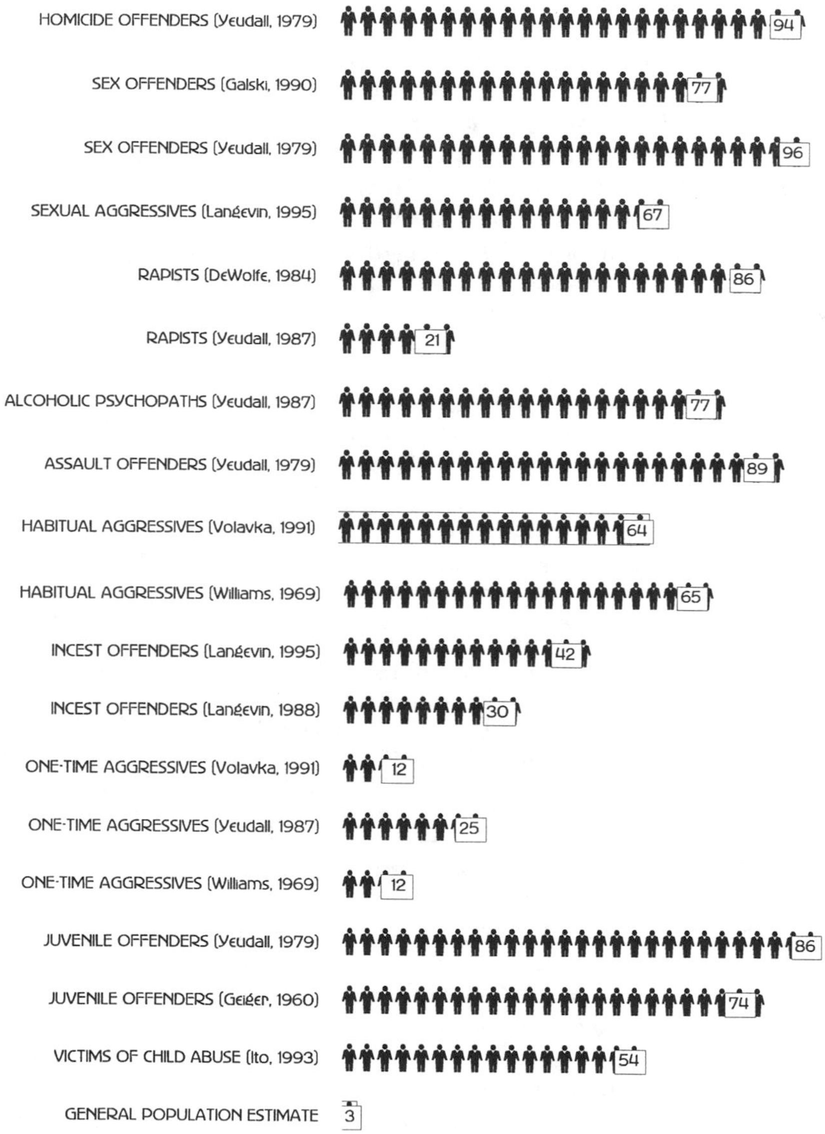

HOMICIDE OFFENDERS (Yeudall, 1979)	94
SEX OFFENDERS (Galski, 1990)	77
SEX OFFENDERS (Yeudall, 1979)	96
SEXUAL AGGRESSIVES (Langevin, 1995)	67
RAPISTS (DeWolfe, 1984)	86
RAPISTS (Yeudall, 1987)	21
ALCOHOLIC PSYCHOPATHS (Yeudall, 1987)	77
ASSAULT OFFENDERS (Yeudall, 1979)	89
HABITUAL AGGRESSIVES (Volavka, 1991)	64
HABITUAL AGGRESSIVES (Williams, 1969)	65
INCEST OFFENDERS (Langevin, 1995)	42
INCEST OFFENDERS (Langevin, 1988)	30
ONE-TIME AGGRESSIVES (Volavka, 1991)	12
ONE-TIME AGGRESSIVES (Yeudall, 1987)	25
ONE-TIME AGGRESSIVES (Williams, 1969)	12
JUVENILE OFFENDERS (Yeudall, 1979)	86
JUVENILE OFFENDERS (Geiger, 1960)	74
VICTIMS OF CHILD ABUSE (Ito, 1993)	54
GENERAL POPULATION ESTIMATE	3

Longitudinal studies

A small number of studies have presented longitudinal evidence linking brain dysfunction measured (or uncovered diagnostically) prior to offending to later criminal behavior. Virkkunen, Nuutila & Huusko (1976) followed a sample of brain-injured World War II veterans for nearly 30 years, concluding that the incidence of later criminality was associated with injury to the fronto-temporal region; importantly, they found that "the criminal acts very often happened only after several decades following the head injury." In a rare instance in which longitudinal data were available on a large birth cohort, Petersen, Matousek, Mednick et al. (1982) reported that "previous EEG abnormalities" detected in childhood or early adolescence were associated with later criminal behavior.

Similarly, Volavka (1991) reported that early indices of "a light slowing of the EEG frequency predicts later development of crime" and further observed that "The incidence of EEG abnormality was particularly high among those offenders who murdered without apparent motive." In a summary of data from several studies in addition to his own, Volavka (250-251) commented:

> . . . 333 offenders who committed violent crimes underwent EEG. The principal and unique advantage of this study is the separation of the offender sample into two subgroups: Those who were habitually aggressive and those who had committed a single violent crime. Sixty-four percent of the habitually aggressive offenders had an abnormal EEG compared with only 24% of single [episode] offenders. When offenders with mental retardation, epilepsy, or a history of major head trauma were removed from analysis, EEG remained abnormal in 57% of the habitual aggressors but in only 12% of those who had committed a single violent crime. The pattern of EEG abnormalities remained similar to that observed for the complete sample. Thus, this study demonstrated that it is persistent aggressivity that is associated with EEG abnormalities . . . relationships between violent crime and EEG findings sometimes emerge only after certain biochemical changes impinging on brain activity are introduced. Such changes may be elicited, for example, by administering certain drugs that activate EEG abnormalities in violent offenders . . . These findings, together with other neuropsychiatric abnormalities (such as psychomotor signs and symptoms, multiple neurologic soft signs, and impairments on [varied measures of neuropsychological functions] . . . have raised the possibility that the degree of brain dysfunction (particularly epilepsy) in the violent offender has been seriously underestimated by most investigators, as well as by the criminal justice system.

Incidence of inventoried neuropathology arrayed by offense
— and among victims of child abuse

To the extent that direct proportional comparison of the relative incidence of neuropathology is possible in light of varying modes of assessment (i.e., neurologic, neuropsychological, electrophysiological, and neuroimaging techniques), we have amalgamated data from studies on samples of aggressive criminal offenders reviewed earlier and display these data graphically in Figure 2.2. Though, technically, "juvenile offenders" cannot readily be uniformly classified as aggressive offenders, data from studies by Geiger (1960) and by the

Yeudall research group (1979) are included, for, as we shall see in Chapter 5, the matter of whether criminal aggression during adolescence perpetuates in what Moffitt (1993) calls "life-course-persistent" aggression may well hinge precisely on neuropathology. In most jurisdictions, any offense committed by a person aged 14 and under is recorded and prosecuted only as "delinquency," including homicide, rape, and aggravated assault. In other jurisdictions, a juvenile may be processed and sanctioned as an adult for the more virulent offenses, but typically not before the age of 15. These distinctions are discussed at length by Musick (1995, 23-46). With respect to the genesis of the neuropathology, it is important to recall data from the studies by Ito's research group (1993), which puts the incidence of neuropathology among victims of child abuse at 54%; that datum is also included in the graphic representation.

To place these massed data in context, it is useful to recall that Brown, Fann & Grant (1994) report an annual incidence of 2,000,000 closed head injuries among adults, with 500,00 "serious enough to require hospitalization" and that Silver, Hales & Yudofsky (1987, 179-180) estimate that "as many as 5 million children sustain head injury per year," an aggregate that equates to the *induction* of neuropathology in approximately 3% of the total national population, albeit on an annual basis. As a further point of comparison, Manderscheid, Witkin, Rosenstein et al. (1985) reported that organic mental disorders of all sorts accounted for but 5.3% of the diagnoses at admission for the nearly 400,000 patients entering the nation's public hospitals annually. While direct comparisons are not warranted, the differences in proportions in relation to those found in the studies among offenders represented in this graph are quite remarkable. In the aggregate the relative incidence of neuropathology in the general population is (relatively conservatively) estimated at 3%.

When massed in this fashion, data from disparate studies of offenders require little interpretation. In all, 17 offender groups are represented in Figure 2.2. With the single exception of the rapists in the 1987 study by the Yeudall research group (which focused on a history of head injury prior to offending), whether measured neurologically or inferred from neuropsychological assessment, neuropathology is found in very high incidence among seriously and persistently aggressive offenders, as well as among juvenile offenders.

At the extremes, the relative incidence of neuropathology among the sex offenders in Yeudall's 1979 study (96%) exceeds the estimated incidence in the general population (3%) at a ratio of 32:1 — or, phrased differently, the incidence of neuropatholgy among the sex offenders studied in that investigation exceeds the estimated incidence in the general population by 3200%. Among the habitually aggressive offenders studied by Williams (1969) and by Volavka (1991), the incidence of neuropathology exceeds that in the general population by some 2130%.

In contrast to other offender groups, the relative incidence is markedly lower among incest offenders (30% in Langevin's 1988 study, 42% in his 1995 study) and among the three groups representing "one-time aggressives" (12% in Williams' 1969 study and in Volavka's 1991 sample, 25% in Yeudall's 1987 investigation) who, as we shall see in Chapter 5, may be regarded as having behaved aggressively as a consequence of what Megargee, Cook, & Mendelsohn (1967) call "over-controlled hostility." As we shall note in that chapter, these relative incidences are quite congruent with psychometric research which distinguishes "persistent" from "one-time" aggressive offenders by means of scales derived from the Minnesota Multiphasic Personality Inventory. Yet an incidence of 12% exceeds, in relative terms, the incidence estimated in the general population by 400%, and an incidence of 25% exceeds that in the general population incidence by 833%.

Statistical purists may wish to calculate with precision the significance of the difference between such proportions. But the data speak rather loudly for themselves — and argue rather forcefully that the relationship between neuropathology and aggressive criminal offending is hardly merely "accidental" or correlative.

Neurochemical anomalies

A wide range of psychopharmacological and psychoendocrinologic research on offender groups has been reported, much of it undertaken in Scandinavian countries, and, because of the extensive laboratory protocols necessarily involved (e.g., studies of the metabolism of neural transmitting enzymes that require samples of spinal fluid), typically limited to small groups of subjects. Relevant studies yield evidence that coalesces to produce a picture that is indicative but not yet definitive. Nonetheless, the relevant data suggest relationships between specific anomalies in neurochemistry and criminally aggressive behavior.

Monoamine oxidase

Monoamine oxidase (MAO) is an important neural transmitter involved in the catabolism of dopamine and norepinepherine that is believed to regulate mood; its deliberate biochemical inhibition constitutes the biochemical basis for a class of antidepressant psychotropic medications, called monoamine oxidase inhibitors, including such familiar pharmaceutical preparations as Nardil® and Parnate® (Schatzberg & Cole, 1986, 46-54),

In studies of violent and aggressive offenders, Boulton, Davis, Yu et al. (1983), Lidberg (1985), and Virkkunen, Nuutila, Goodwin & Linnoila (1987) have found evidence of the abnormal metabolism of monoamine oxidase, concluding to an enduring relationship between impaired impulse control and naturally occurring anomalies in the body's regulation of neurochemical transmission.

In a multidimensional study that suggests the interaction of extrinsic forces and intrinsic neurochemical factors in the generation of violent behavior that extended Virkkunen's (1979) earlier work on the effects of alcohol on violence in subjects who had been diagnosed with antisocial personality disorder, Virkkunen, Nuutila, Goodwin & Linnoila (1987) observed a high rate of alcoholism among violent offenders in whom they had also observed anomalies in regulation of neural transmitters and opined that, because ingestion of alcohol represents a temporary corrective to abnormal metabolism of monoamine oxidase, "alcohol abuse in these individuals . . . may represent an effort to self-medicate," even though "alcohol only makes the situation worse by further impairing impulse control."

Nonetheless, it will patently be the case that, whether at the scene of a crime or in later studies which rely only on social history variables, violent behavior will be attributed to alcohol ingestion; the issue of why it seems to a particular abuser of alcohol that he or she "feels better" when drinking (i.e., the issue of whether alcohol use or abuse is itself an effort to self-medicate and thus secondary to a naturally occurring neurologic anomaly) will scarcely be raised.

Serotonin

Serotonin is a powerful neurotransmitter directly related to the psychobiology of depression and, in the view of many authorities (Siever, Steinberg, Trestman & Intrator, 1994), of aggression as well. Some authorities hold that schizophrenia itself results from the under-production of serotonin in the brain, coupled with the over-production of dopamine. Lithium achieves its antidepressant effect by stimulating the release of serotonin in the brain.

At Eastern Pennsylvania Psychiatric Institute, Coccaro, Siever, Klar & Maurer (1989) reported abnormal metabolism of serotonin among subjects with a history of impulsive aggression who had been independently diagnosed as psychopathic. In an experiment which involved pharmacological alterations in the way in which serotonin is metabolized, Halperin, Sharma, Siever et al. (1994) studied aggressive and non-aggressive children diagnosed with "attention-deficit hyperactivity disorder," finding significant differences in neurochemical processing among aggressive subjects. Similar results have been reported by Virkkunen & Narvanen (1987) in a more complex study that also traced the interactive effects between insulin, tryptophan, and serotonin and by Virkkunnen & Linnoila (1993) in relation to impulsive violence among alcoholics.

In animal studies, abnormalities in the regulation of serotonin have also been linked to aggressive behavior (Feldman & Quenzer, 1984, 248). Among monkeys, those with abnormally low naturally-occurring levels of serotonin production were found both to exhibit greater impulsive violence and risk-taking behavior and to occupy lower positions in a "male social hierarchy" (Mehlman, Higley, Faucher, Lilly et al., 1994; Wright, 1995).

Stein, Hollander & Liebowitz (1993) reviewed the accumulated research evidence on anomalies in serotonin metabolism in relation to impulsivity, concluding that "The concept that impulsivity is a failure in serotonergically mediated behavioral inhibition has proved remarkably fertile" and that "there has been notable convergence on the conclusion that impulsive aggression and auto-aggression correlate with serotonergic hypofunction and respond to treatment with serotonin reuptake blockers."

Similarly, in their review of the accumulated research literature on both animal and human subjects, Albert Einstein College of Medicine neuropsychiatrists Brown, Botsis & Van Praag (1994) concluded that "Decreased serotonin function has consistently been shown to be highly correlated with impulsive aggression across a number of different experimental paradigms," including the experimental manipulation of serotonin concentration and metabolism. They further note that "such lowered serotonergic indices appear to correlate with the dimension of aggression dyscontrol and/or impulsivity rather than with psychiatric diagnostic categories per se." Brown and her colleagues also observe that "recent research has shown that a new class of drugs, the serenics, specifically cause the inhibition of antagonistic behavior, without causing sedation" in infra-human experiments and may be expected to produce similar effects in human subjects. Alternately, some pharmaceutical preparations designed to inhibit the normal process by which serotonin is metabolized (the "serotonin re-uptake inhibitors," including Prozac®) have clinically been linked to impulsive criminal violence [NOTE 11].

Glucose

Deficits in the body's capacity to metabolize glucose resulting in abnormally low levels of glucose in the blood yield the pathophysiological condition *hypoglycemia*, "a syndrome characterized by symptoms of sympathetic nervous system stimulation or of CNS dysfunction" (Berkow & Fletcher, 1992, 1126). Rafuls, Extein, Gold & Goggans (1987, 308-309) further identify as a subtype "cerebral hypoglycemia," the principal symptoms of which are "mental disturbances of slow cerebration, aggressiveness, and impairment of speech and gait [along with] altered states of consciousness, perseverative thoughts and speech patterns, and confusion" sometimes of psychotic severity, so that "The behavior pattern is somewhat like that of an alcoholic." Hypoglycemia is frequently secondary to diabetes, which in its turn may be caused by chronic alcoholism, and is frequently linked to "acting out" psychopathological conditions (Messer, Morris & Gross, 1990), whether expressed in formally criminal behavior or not.

Though their subjects had no particular history of criminal behavior, Gur, Resnick, Gur et al. (1987) found anomalies in the metabolism of cerebral glucose, especially in the left hemisphere of the brain, among schizophrenic patients (but not among non-schizophrenic controls) studied at the University of Pennsylvania's Brain-Behavior Laboratory using positron emission tomography (PET). In another study, Gur, Mozley, Mozley et al. (1995) investigated both the concentration and site of glucose metabolism among healthy men and women "in a state of restful wakefulness" using both PET and MRI imaging techniques and cytogenic analysis (analysis of cell structures). After observing that "men are more likely to express affect instrumentally, such as through physical aggression, whereas women use symbolic mediation, such as vocal means," these investigators reported that, although no differences were found in overall quantity of glucose metabolized in the brain between men and women, consistent gender differences were found in the specific brain sites where such metabolism occurred. They interpreted their findings as supporting "a neurobiologic explanation of . . . sex-related differences in behavioral dimensions," including aggression.

In studies of violent offenders across types of crime, Matti Virkkunen (1982-a-b, 1983-a, 1984, 1985, 1986, 1987, 1989, 1994) and his colleagues at the University of Helsinki have found evidence for the abnormal metabolism of glucose, an imbalance in which can produce "manic" states, especially among those diagnosed with antisocial personality disorder, with the effect observed among violent offenders, arsonists, and alcoholics but not among non-offending, non-alcoholic control subjects.

In their review of the relevant research on hypoglycemia in relation to criminal behavior, Fishbein & Pease (1994) observed:

> The behavioral symptoms associated with the rapid decline in blood sugar are of particular interest to criminologists. These symptoms include fatigue, irritability, nervousness, depression, vertigo, faintness, insomnia, confusion, inability to concentrate, anxiety, dysperceptions, destructive outbursts, headaches, heart palpitations, blurred vision, lack of sex drive in women, impotency in men, and difficulty in performing simple physical or mental tasks [so that] Individuals experiencing these symptoms may have difficulty in coping with the normal stresses of life, concentrating and making rational decisions, and may be at risk for engaging in antisocial or irrational behaviors.

Testosterone

Several investigators (Bradford & McLean, 1984; Dabbs, Frady, Carr & Besch, 1987; Rada & Kellner, 1976; Rada, Kellner, Stivastava & Peake, 1983; Virkkunen, 1985; Virkkunnen, Kallio, Rawlings et al. 1994) have reported abnormally high concentrations of testosterone among inmates with a history of violent crime, whether these were sexually focused or not. In his massive review of the research evidence, including studies in which testosterone levels were experimentally manipulated, British neuropsychologist John Archer (1994, 3-5) concluded to "a strong association between testosterone and aggressiveness" especially when exacerbated by "influences from the social environment, particularly those related to status and anger" and further observes that "aggressiveness changes when testosterone levels are manipulated" pharmacologically.

In what may stand as the definitive study, Dabbs, Carr, Frady & Riad (1995) measured testosterone levels among nearly 700 male prisoners in relation both to offense history prior to incarceration and to behavior during incarceration. Higher levels were found to be associated with rape, child molestation, murder, assault, and armed robbery in the offense history and with such offenses as assault, atrocious assault, and participation in riots or disburbances during incarceration; lower levels were associated with burglary, theft, and drug offenses in the criminal history and with damage to property and unauthorized absence from work assignments during incarceration. Nonetheless, some clinical investigators have reported a converse effect, such that excess testosterone is hypothesized to exert a "calming" effect — at least among subjects who have putatively never been convicted of crime (Angier, 1995).

There is some evidence that excess testosterone activates aggression even among mice (Gandelman, 1980), while, according to Feldman & Quenzer (1984, 248), in animal studies excess testosterone triggers intermale aggression. Pertinently to correctional treatment or crime control considerations, testosterone levels are amenable to biochemical manipulation through hormone-suppressing agents. As Archer (1994, 19) put it, "medically-based intervention is possible for those unable to control their violent impulses, just as it is for those unable to control their sexual impulses." Whether testosterone excess operates in a similar fashion among girls and women is unclear, although clinical reports on the secondary behavioral effects of one form of estrogen replacement therapy (i.e., "challenge" therapy, which proceeds by means of the artificial pharmacological introduction of testosterone so as to "challenge" the body to produce estrogen through the introduction of the male hormone, against which the woman's body "rebels") among post-menopausal women suggest an increase in irascibility and sometimes aggressivity (Berkow & Fletcher, 1992, 1794-1795), though rarely resulting in criminal violence. Instead, Fishbein (1992) holds it more likely that aggressive criminal violence among women may result from dysfunctions in the production of the thyroid enzyme, which functions interactively with a variety of neurotransmitting enzymes and is sometimes termed the "pack mule" of the neuroendocrine system on that account.

Prostacyclin

At a primitive molecular level, Virkkunen, Horrobin, Jenkins & Manku (1987), through analysis of cereberospinal fluid among violent offenders diagnosed with antisocial personality disorder, found anomalies in the production of prostacyclin, an ubiquitous metabolite of unsaturated fatty acids that in turn directly affects the metabolism of the powerful neurotransmitter norepinephrine and itself directly influences the perception of pain.

Related biopsychological issues

Cranial capacity

In his monumental work on *Race, Evolution, and Behavior,* Rushton (1995-a, 1995-b) adduced evidence linking cranial capacity to race membership in the first instance and, in the second, demonstrating differential rates of crime between races, with a neat hierarchy in each case indicating that, on average, the largest cranial capacity and lowest rate of crime is to be found among members of Oriental races and the smallest cranial capacity on average and highest rate of crime among Blacks. Whites occupy the intermediate position.

Drawing on concepts from evolutionary biology, Rushton further related cranial capacity to "reproductive strategies" that had developed within races over evolutionary eons and that affected both birth (or propagation) rates and cranial capacity. Briefly, the line of reasoning argues that, in physical and climatological conditions in which survival needs could easily be met by foraging in abundant vegetation without the evolutionary imperative to develop careful methods of cultivation (and domestication of animals for farm and food purposes), there evolved a reproductive strategy that produced large numbers of children; but, since survival presented few major challenges, there was no evolutionary imperative to increase cranial capacity to devise those techniques and strategies required for survival. In conditions in which survival needs could be met only by careful attention to cultivation and domestication, however, diametric evolutionary imperatives were encountered.

Implicit in Rushton's argument is the proposition that cranial capacity is itself related to crime, with intelligence the likely nexus [NOTE 12]. While the criminologic indices he assembles unassailably demonstrate that indeed the incidence of crime varies between racial groups (at least in North America), it is not at all clear (as we shall see in Chapter 5) that intelligence is strongly predictive of criminal behavior.

Although the proposition that cranial capacity determines the capacity to "learn" adaptive behavior *across* species (Finlay & Darlington, 1995) is unexceptionable, the relationship between cranial capacity and intelligence *within* the human species has been found to be relatively weak. Andreasen, Flaum, Swayze, et al. (1993) employed magnetic resonance imaging scans to measure cranial capacity (the volume of the intracranial cavity, cerebral hemispheres, lateral ventricles, temporal lobes, hippocampus, cerebellum, and cerebrospinal fluid) in relation to verbal, performance, and full-scale scores on the Wechsler Adult

Intelligence Scale, Revised. Though some coefficients did not differ significantly from zero, most fell in the range .30-.40. The highest coefficient reported, at $r = .56$, was calculated between volume of the right temporal lobe and full-scale IQ score among women; among men, the corresponding coefficient was calculated at .39. Since the coefficient squared (multiplied by 100) represents the commonly accepted estimate of proportional common variance, even the highest coefficient reported *fails* to account for 69% of variance in intelligence. Thus, even if it were the case that criminal behavior is a direct function of intelligence, it is not evident that intelligence is a direct function of cranial capacity.

Physique and the XYY chromosomal pattern

Based perhaps on the commonplace observation that "bullies" tend to be relatively tall in stature, muscular, often laconic and perhaps slow in thought, and frequently bordering on corpulence, early conceptualizations linked body type to violent and/or criminal behavior (Hall & Lindzey, 1970, 338-377; Wilson & Herrnstein, 1985, 72-103). In criminology, the leading advocate for a perspective that in fact attributed criminal violence causally to body type was the 19th century Italian physician, penal reformer, and prison superintendent Cesare Lombroso; in psychology, the principal spokesperson has been the late William Sheldon of Harvard.

Both Sheldon (1949) and Sheldon and Eleanor Glueck (1956) carried out extensive studies of juvenile delinquents, finding the mesomorphic physique prevalent in their samples, with that body type described as "strong, tough, resistant to injury, and generally equipped for strenuous and exacting physical demands." Associated psychological characteristics were said to include aggressiveness, assertiveness, a need for dominance, high energy, a taste for risk, and particular reactivity to alcohol (Sheldon, 1942). As Herrnstein (1990, 12) has observed, "just such a combination of personality traits has been directly associated with criminal tendencies."

Later investigators linked the mesomorphic physique to the presence of an additional "male" chromosome (the "XYY chromosome abnormality") in the genetic endowment, so that it was hypothesized that a propensity for violent and/or criminal behavior is indeed transmitted genetically, perhaps as a result of the over-production of testosterone attributable to the double Y chromosome. Medical reports indicate that the incidence is sporadic, approximating 1:800 live births (a frequency of 0.125%), and the anomaly is reported to occur only in males. (Klinefelter's Syndrome, sometimes termed a "reciprocal" abnormality, occurs when the male carries an extra X chromosome, with an incidence of 1:900 live births, often in the children of older mothers, and is linked to increased frequency of sterility, hypogonadism, and mental retardation.)

Detailed cytogenic (cell structure) analyses of large samples of imprisoned offenders have revealed the XYY chromosomal pattern in slightly under 1% of the cases (Finley, McDanal, Finley & Rosecrans, 1973). In Denmark, Close, Goonetilleke, Jacobs & Price (1968) followed a birth cohort of all males born in Copenhagen from 1944 through 1947, finding "little or no recorded evidence" of criminal violence among men with the XYY pattern. Witkin, Mednick, Schulsinger et al. (1976) also studied a Danish cohort, finding criminality represented no more often than chance would predict among either XYY men or among those with Klinefelter's Syndrome. Similarly, in a study in Sweden, Akesson & Wahlstrom (1977) found no relationship between the XYY pattern and criminality, while British researchers Harrison & Tennent (1977), in a study of offenders and matched controls, found no differences in neurologic function attributable to the XYY anomaly. Mednick & Volavka (1980), although they found no evidence of a pattern of violent criminality, discovered EEG abnormalities among Danish men with the XYY pattern.

Nonetheless, the incidence among prisoners reported by Finley, McDanal, Finley & Rosecrans (1973) is on the order of 800% the prevalence among live births, a relative incidence that is almost certainly not an artifact of chance. Yet, as the late, distinguished Harvard psychologist Richard Herrnstein (1990, 12) has put it:

> The extra Y chromosome turns up unpredictably in any social class or ethnic group or family setting. Such men are taller than average and have other minor physical characteristics [in common]. They also have a 10 to 20 times greater tendency to break the law than do genetically normal men from comparable populations. Even with their elevated criminal tendencies [however], there are too few XYY men to affect overall crime rates much.

But, as Herrnstein (1995, 45) also observed, it may be that "the correlation between physique and personality is itself sociological," for it remains a commonplace observation that "bullies" tend to cluster in certain shapes and sizes, while others who may be internally disposed toward bullying but who lack the requisite physique either opt for other ways to assert themselves into dominance (e.g., verbal cajolery, intimidation) — or perhaps opt for the use of weapons that equalize differences in physique. Moreover, physique seems likely intimately linked to learning history.

If the genetic endowment with which A is born dictates that, at age 18, he will stand 6'5" and weigh on the order of 270 pounds, in the situation in which A wants what B has, B is unlikely to demur from the mere assertion — unless, of course, B is similarly genetically endowed. But if C's genetic endowment is such that, at age 18, he will stand 5'3" and weigh but 140, such an assertion will avail nothing. Instead, C will experience an imperative to develop those skills of ratiocination and persuasion that will lead C to accede "voluntarily" to his statement of want. Nonetheless, it is a reasonable assessment to say that there remains little interest in the pursuit of a genetic-physiological substratum for aggressively violent behavior, but the "why" of that situation is rather more difficult to discern. Surely the state of the evidence, though fragmentary, suggests the utility of continued investigation (Mednick & Christiansen, 1977; Livesley, Jang, Jackson & Vernon, 1993).

In consequence of the massive explosion in research in the neurosciences on the substratum for violence, it may be that an interest in physique has been subsumed into a focus on neuropsychological functioning. Or, considering the prospective political and cultural consequences to inquiry into genetic determinants and limitations, self-censorship on the part of researchers may be as valid an explanation as any [NOTE 13]. The widespread (and sometimes mindless) antagonism toward Rushton's views on cranial capacity in relation to gender (Fausto-Sterling, 1993) or in relation to race and crime constitutes a case in point (Horowitz, 1995).

Genetic "factors" and criminal predisposition

Distinguished researchers Sarnoff Mednick and his colleagues (Mednick & Christiansen, 1977; Mednick & Volavka, 1980; Mednick, Gabrielli & Hutchings, 1984; Mednick, Cannon, Barr et al., 1991; Fogel, Mednick & Michelsen 1985; Gabrielli, Mednick & Volavka, 1982; Buikhuisen & Mednick, 1988; Moffitt & Mednick, 1988; Moffitt, Mednick & Gabrielli, 1989; Cannon, Mednick, Parnas, Schulsinger, Praestholm & Vestergaard, 1994) have long espoused the view that genetic "factors" predispose toward criminal behavior. In their many investigations, they have studied rates of criminal behavior (and of mental illness) among parents and offspring in intact families, among biological parents and children raised in adoptive families, among adults who had suffered one or another physical trauma pre-natally or during birth, and among adults who suffer "minor physical anomalies" (e.g., facial malformations, "low-seated" ears) as a result of such traumata. Their findings of high concordance between rates of criminal behavior between biological parents and their offspring raised in adoptive families in particular support the proposition that a disposition to behave criminally can be transmitted genetically, with the effect more potent for property crime than for violent crime and further potentiated when biological parents also had histories of substance abuse. Eysenck & Gudjunsson (1989), Raine (1993), Rushton (1994, 47-58), and Rutter (1996) generally follow Mednick and his associates. Livesey, Jang, Jackson & Vernon (1993) have adopted an alternate approach that seeks the interactive effects of genetic and environmental influences in the heritability of personality disorders.

In many of these studies (especially those undertaken before the explosion of knowledge in the neurosciences), the likely agents of genetic transmission of such "predisposition" were not clearly identified, so that the term "genetic factors" became a short of intellectual shorthand. But Moffitt, Mednick & Gabrielli (1989, 31) have interpreted "these findings [as] highly consonant with repeated reports of a high incidence of brain dysfunction in violent offenders" and further opined, in regard to congenital or birth issues, that "obstetrical complications may subtly compromise brain function, reducing the ability of some individuals to inhibit violent impulses," in such fashion that "The consequent long-standing violent response style ultimately culminates in violent criminal offending."

A reading of the Mednick corpus in light of current knowledge and opinion in the neurosciences might incline toward the interpretation not (or perhaps not only) that there exists a set of chromosomal patterns or "genes" for criminality, aggressivity, or violence but rather that there obtain directly genetic influences on brain morphology and brain biochemistry, dysfunctions in which (in relation to social influences) may "predispose" to criminal behavior, as well (as we proposed in relation to the XYY chromosomal pattern) on such variables as adult height and weight and, more controversially, on intelligence. As Sir Michael Rutter (1996) of London's Maudsley Institute put it: "There can be no such thing as a gene for crime. That is not how genes operate. Rather, genes affect (along with other factors) how people behave and how they respond to stress." Or, as Zuckerman (1995, 331) put it:

> We do not inherit personality traits or even behavior mechanisms as such. What is inherited are chemical templates that produce and regulate proteins involved in building the structure of nervous systems and the neurotransmitters, enzymes, and hormones that regulate them.

Two studies conducted at Children's Hospital in Denver may prove illustrative of the distinction. Gabel & Shindledecker (1993) initially confirmed a relationship between "severe aggression and antisocial/destructive behavior" in children and adolescents and substance abuse in their parents, with the effect more severe for drugs than for alcohol and when the father rather than the mother had been drug-addicted. These findings might be attributed alternately to non-specific "genetic factors" or, in the case of intact families, to the effect to negative sociobehavioral modeling. In a later investigation, Gabel, Stadler, Bjorn et al. (1995) analyzed blood samples among boys aged 6 and 15 who were or were not diagnosed behaviorally with "conduct disorder" problems sufficient to warrant admission to a residential treatment facility and whose fathers themselves did or did not have a history (past or present) of substance abuse. Gabel and his associates found evidence of abnormally accelerated activity in the metabolism of monoamine oxidase (as we saw earlier in this chapter, a neurotransmitter involved in the catabolism both of dopamine and norepinepherine) among subjects classified with conduct disorders whose fathers had a history of substance abuse, but not in other pairings (sons with conduct disorders with non-abusing fathers, sons without conduct disorder but with abusing fathers).

As we also have seen, dysfunctions in the regulation of dopamine and monoamine oxidase have been linked both to schizophrenia and to antisocial behavior generally. The same neurologic dysfunction, transmitted intergenerationally literally through the genetic endowment, may thus account for substance abuse in fathers and conduct disorders in their sons; and, of course, conduct disorders in the sons may themselves prefigure later substance abuse disorders.

DISORDERED NEUROLOGY AS AN INVITATION, NOT AN IMPERATIVE

In this chapter, we have reviewed evidence on brain dysmorphology and brain biochemistry anomalies in relation to aggressive and violent behavior. We have seen that there are strong associations between neuropathology and aggressively violent behavior and that the cumulative evidence suggests a high incidence of neuropathology across most categories of violent crime. As a matter of intellectual shorthand (and at the expense of prescinding from such issues as the rate of biochemical absorption, biotransformation, depletion, and secretion), we use the term *neurogenic impulsivity* to encompass a state of *consistent hyperarousal*, along with concomitant impairment in foresight, planfulness, the capacity to consider consequences and to construe alternatives, and sometimes in cognition that is often the legacy of brain dysfunction and/or anomaly (frequently, but not always, involving the frontal lobes or the left hemisphere) and that eventuates characteristically in precipitate and frequently in aggressive behavior, whether its source lies in brain dysmorphology, biochemical anomaly, neuroendocrine disorder, or in some combination thereof. If a more or less formal definition seems useful, we can rely on that provided by Oxford neurophysiologist Susan Greenfield (1995, 6-7, 125):

> Arousal is best thought of, physiologically, as some form of generalized activation of brain cells caused by certain chemical pulsing through the brain . . . In extreme examples, arousal can be conspicuous by its low levels (sedation) as well as by its high levels . . . Fighting and fleeing are extreme forms of arousal . . . Arousal for a physiologist occurs when electrical activity in the cortex of the brain, as recorded by surface electrodes on the scalp, reveals that the active neurons are not in synchrony, but are each active in different ways and times, producing a desynchronized EEG. The ultimate source of this increased activity is about as far away from the cortex as possible, deep down in the brain . . . . Evolutionarily, this is the most basic part of the brain, called the brainstem.

Though its weight argues strongly toward at least a correlative relationship between morphologic or neurochemical anomalies and violent criminal behavior, the state of the evidence is not yet robust enough to predicate "cause and effect" relationships. Such predication would require, as Heinrichs & Buchanan (1988) have observed in regard to the evidence on the neurogenesis of schizophrenia, clear indication that neurophysiological dysfunction not only "predates" but compels criminal violence. We have seen that, thus far, there are but few longitudinal studies that bear on well-documented neurologic and neuropsychological antecedents to later violent behavior.

With the increased availability of advanced neurologic measuring devices and, frankly, a new awareness in the medical community about the pre-clinical and sub-clinical signs of neurologic disorder early in childhood, it may be that more precise data will become available in a relatively short period of time — unless, of course, the burgeoning body of knowledge that links even sub-clinical neurological disorder to aberrant behavior in later life renders clinical interventions to obviate possible and probable consequences substantially more widely available and more generally prescribed. Though they provide useful points of comparison and permit us to reason by analogy, inferences from experimental studies on infra-human species are suggestive and instructive but do not convincingly fill the void.

The issue of the directionality of the relationship is complicated by the relative insensitivity of even highly sophisticated measuring devices to the time of onset of brain dysfunction, except perhaps in cases of very recent head trauma, typically independently verifiable from physical evidence of contusion, fracture, concussion, or coma. Though many knowledgeable commentators would regard most neurochemical anomalies as constitutional or congenital rather than acquired through accident or injury, the regulation of neurotransmitters may be affected by brain dysmorphologies consequent to injury sustained during violent behavior; thus, the issue of directionality applies as well to anomalies in neurochemical processing.

There is also the viciously circular matter of the interaction between brain dysfunction, substance abuse, and violence, as Virkkunen, Nuutila, Goodwin & Linnoila (1987) and Miller (1994) have suggested. People with brain dysfunctions are often differentially susceptible to the abuse of alcohol or drugs; people who abuse alcohol or drugs tend to find themselves in violence-prone situations; people in violence-prone situations are susceptible to head injury, whether from confrontations with others who are also precipitate in their behavior, or brain-impaired, or intoxicated, or all three, or from injuries attendant on arrest.

Even without a corpus of longitudinal and directional data, however, the evidence for a palpable neurogenic contribution to aggressive and violent behavior is persuasive; we do not set it forth as compelling. Allegiance to the overarching conceptualization that all behavior pivots on bio-psycho-social roots aside, to hold that disordered neurology, even abetted by the ingestion of neuroactive substances, represents an imperative toward violence is to careen precipitously toward the taxonomic trap that has marred psychological analyses of criminal behavior which rest on the perspectives of differential psychology.

Moreover, such an insistence would founder on empirical grounds alone, for it is clear that the annual incidence of 7 million episodes of severe head trauma reported by Brown, Fann & Grant (1994) and Silver, Hales & Yudofsky (1987) exceeds the aggregate number of acts of criminal violence by more than five-fold, to say nothing of the incidence of congenital brain anomalies, brain-biochemistry dysfunctions, or neuroendocrine anomalies. For us, neurologic and neuropsychological dysfunction, whether or not lubricated by the ingestion of neuroactive chemical substances, constitutes an invitation, not an imperative. As we shall see in later chapters, that invitation is redeemed all too enthusiastically in those subcultural contexts in which heedless, precipitate behavior is both the norm and normative.

It is the neurogenic invitation to behave in precipitate ways that the behaver carries about in his or her more-or-less "permanent" psychobehavioral baggage; the *opportunity* to behave in precipitate ways is provided by the sociocultural context (prototypically, self-selected, with the self-selection itself a function of neurogenic impulsivity); and it is both the construing of, and the organismic ways of experiencing, both the invitation and the opportunity as normative that yield the phenomenology of violent behavior. These factors meld to constitute the tinder-box.

NOTES

1. Though they acknowledge no intellectual debt to Laborit, similar paradigms are sketched in *Biobehavioral Aspects of Aggression* by David Hamburg and Michelle Trudeau (1981) and by the distinguished American psychologist Theodore Millon (1990) in *Toward a New Personology.*

2. Rather explicitly, Laborit's paradigm reflects a hierarchical conceptualization that places the human species at the upper end of a spectrum and implicitly subordinates other animal and plant species. Particularly among "animal rights" activists, such an hierarchical ordering is no longer acceptable. Pursuing a non-hierarchical line of reasoning, those persuaded differently object not only to what Laborit would see as the inevitability of aggression by humans against other animal species for food (and clothing, whether in the form of fur coats or leather shoes), but, at the extreme, to scientific experimentation on animals.

In part because of the notoriety surrounding well-publicized "raids" on laboratories conducting research in the neurosciences involving apes and chimpanzees (in which the brains of the animals were deliberately damaged in studies which sought to determine the effects of dysfunction in certain morphological structures or the alternate pathways for the metabolism of certain neurohormones when the customary receptor sites had been rendered inoperative, as might happen in the human species as a result of automobile or industrial accident), the Federal Congress adopted the Animal Welfare Act of 1981, laying down strictures governing animal research. Subsequent court decisions have brought a variety of animal species not enumerated in the original legislation under the purview of the Act.

Francione (1995) details both the social and legislative history of animals rights legislation in the U.S., the net effect of which has been to constrain neuroscientific research using animals in a variety of ways.

3. Failure to include David Wechsler in this litany may seem an oversight, particularly since the several Wechsler scales continue to be widely used as screening devices for brain impairment. Yet the accuracy of the methodology proposed by Wechsler of "sieving" scores on the subtests which comprise each instrument in order to derive a "deterioration quotient" remains a matter of controversy. In their review of the literature, Berg, Franzen & Wedding (1987, 94-97, 175-178) categorically conclude that the Wechsler instruments can be currently regarded as no more than the grossest of "gross" screening devices for organicity, with unacceptably high rates of both false positives and false negatives. Instead, to determine whether cognitive deficit, problematic behavior, or "soft signs" of neuropsychological dysfunction have a genuinely neurogenic basis, they recommend "fine screening" by means of comprehensive medically-anchored neuropsychiatric examination (including, in today's technologically advanced world, advanced scanning or imaging techniques). Nonetheless, Howeison & Lezak (1992) continue to regard the discrepancy between "performance scale" IQ and "verbal scale" IQ as a reasonable first approximation to a gross index of brain disorder. The matter is discussed more fully in Chapter 5, with particular focus on criminal offenders.

4. The decision by the World Health Organization to eliminate *frontal lobe syndrome* as a distinct diagnostic category in its taxonomic lexicon met rather a negative reception in the United States, to the extent that the *Journal of Neuropsychiatry & Clinical Neurosciences* devoted virtually the entire contents of its Fall 1994 issue to the topic. Particularly pertinent are the contributions of Ames, Cummings, Wirshing, Quinn & Mahler (1994) on repetitive and compulsive behavior associated with frontal lobe degeneration: Duffy & Campbell (1994) on the theoretical and clinical bases for distinguishing not one but three frontal lobe syndromes, which they term the "dysexecutive, disinhibited, and apathetic types"; and Fogel (1994) on the significance of recognition of frontal lobe dysfunctions in mental health policy and practice.

5. The overarching (and thus far unrealized) goal in brain injury rehabilitation can be said to "transfer" the executive functions for both physiological and psychological processes from (permanently) damaged to intact, but otherwise apparently "unused," cells in the brain. Although clinical reports in individual cases (e.g., that of the Central Park jogger multiply-raped, brutally beaten, brain-injured and left for dead in 1990, who, after considerable inpatient treatment in a rehabilitation hospital specializing in brain injury, was able to return to a demanding executive job), the specific molecular processes remain conjectural. Some specialists in neurotherapy and cognitive rehabilitation point toward "plasticity," a phenomenon presently understood primarily in relation to neurodevelopment in early and mid-childhood. As Berkow & Fletcher (1992, 1394) observe, "plasticity is most prominent in the developing brain; e.g., if severe damage strikes the dominant left hemisphere language areas before age 8, the right hemisphere can assume near normal language capacities."

6. Research in the neurosciences continues to confirm with precision hypotheses about "localization" of executive functions within the brain and about brain capacities in relation to specific behavioral capacities. Thus, at Heinrich-Heine University in Germany, Schlaug, Jäncke, Huang & Steinmetz (1995) examined musicians identified as having "perfect pitch," musicians without perfect pitch, and non-musicians by means of PET scans to measure regional cerebral blood flow and metabolism during the processing of verbal and non-verbal stimuli. As expected, their study revealed left hemisphere asymmetries in musicians with perfect pitch.

7. In testimony before Congressional committees considering pending legislation on animal experimentation in scientific research, Dr. Franklin Loew (1981), dean of veterinary medicine at Tufts, rather archly noted that Nazi Germany could well afford what appeared to the outside world as a total ban because it had substituted human for animal subjects.

8. Criminologists are sometimes not only skeptical but downright dismissive. Indeed, both attitudes are likely to greet the psychobiologist who recites to an audience of criminologists, say, the research evidence accumulated over nearly 60 years and across species, including the human, in the literature of experimental and comparative psychology, neuropsychology, neuropsychiatry, and neurosurgery that links frontal lobe anomalies to unbridled human aggression. We have been asked whether it is not the case that the majority of studies that speak specifically to that aggression which has been declared formally criminal have been conducted among prisoners serving long-term sentences. When we answer in the affirmative, the response is often to the effect that "If you'd been in stir for a long time, your brain would look pretty peculiar too" — as if to imply that such brain anomalies obtained consequent to, and resultant from, rather than antecedent to and perhaps causally related to, that formally criminal behavior which had led to incarceration.

9. Walker traces the remote antecedents for the principles governing an insanity pleading announced at Daniel M'Naghten's trial of 1843 to Saxon jurisprudence, well before the Norman conquest — and, indeed, opines that even earlier sources may be found in the laws of Rome applied during the Roman occupation of Britain in the first century.

Certain provisions of the Roman code, Walker believes, were preserved orally and were thus incorporated into the first written laws for what was to become modern Britain. Thus, Walker observes (16-20), the "Penitentials" of Egbert, the eighth-century Saxon archbishop of York, contained provisions for exculpation for murder for "a man who hath fallen out of his senses or wits, and it come to pass that he kill someone." According to Frantzen (1983, 83), the same archbishop had insisted upon rather "public penance for murder, fornication, worship of idols, and other serious sins" at a time before the systematic use of incarceration as a form of punishment, so that Egbert's willingness to exculpate on the basis of mental disorder stood in sharp contrast to a generally harshly punitive stance. Similarly, the laws of the Saxon king Ethelred in the eleventh century prescribed leniency (but not exculpation) "if anyone does anything unintentionally" or "when a man is an involuntary agent [because] he acted as he did from compulsion" (Walker, Idem). Walker (67) cites some 222 trials at one British court alone — albeit, London's central criminal court (the celebrated "Old Bailey") — in the century preceding M'Naghten at which either the matter of the accused's mental state at the time of the criminal act or his or her mental fitness to stand trial was raised.

By Walker's count, the pleading of incompetence to stand prevailed in 83% of the cases in which it was raised, while what amounts to an insanity defense prevailed in 45% of the cases in which it was raised. For the United Kingdom as a whole, there were perhaps four times as many insanity defenses during that period (72). Thus, Walker contends (74), "Successful defences of insanity had been a regular feature of Old

Bailey trials" well before the M'Naghten case, including even the empaneling of physicians to offer what we would today call "expert witness" testimony as to the defendant's state of mind at the time of his or her allegedly criminal behavior.

10. To the extent that Walker is correct in his facts and interpretations, it seems entirely clear that forensic neuropsychiatry and forensic neuropsycholgy long predate forensic psychiatry and forensic psychology.

11. An alternate view of the role of serotonin in aggression rather controversially links its metabolism to dominance vs. non-dominance among crayfish (Barinaga, 1996; Yeh, Fricke & Edwards, 1996). Neurobiologists at Emory and Georgia State studied the metabolism of serotonin among crayfish who establish territorial dominance vs. those who are subordinated in such contests, concluding to "a neuron . . . whose response to the neurotransmitter serotonin differs dramatically depending on the animal's social status. In dominant animals, serotonin make the neuron more likely to fire, while in subordinate animals serotonin suppresses firing." Whether the metabolism of serotonin in dominant animals observed after the establishment of dominance pre-existed "violent combat [in which contending crayfish] try to tear each other limb from limb," with "the winner of that clash . . . strutting his stuff confidently through the territory, while the loser skulks about, trying to stay out of his rival's way" was not ascertained in these studies, however.

12. Realization that homicide had become the leading cause of death among young Black men and that more Black Americans were killed by other Black Americans in a single year than had died under enemy fire during the entire nine years of the U.S. misadventure in Vietnam (when a system of deferments from conscription tilted sharply, if not frankly, in the direction of the white upper and middle classes and thus ensured that inner city Black youth would yield the major contribution to cannon fodder) prompted officials at the Federal Alcohol, Drug Abuse, and Mental Health Administration (ADAMHA) to convene a special conference on homicide in the black community. The year for which these data are relevant was 1977, and the conference went forward as scheduled in 1980. Nor was there particularly strong negative comment in the public press, and barely a beep was heard on Capitol Hill.

How very different things were in the spring and summer of 1992. Dr. Frederick C. Goodwin, a distinguished neuropsychiatrist then serving as director of ADAMHA, declared research on violence to be a "number one" priority for his agency, citing the by-now familiar data that ADAMHA had first publicized 15 years earlier. In the aftermath of strong protest from members of Congress, Goodwin resigned his position. When the press learned that the National Institute of Health had provided financial support for a conference on possible links between genetic and racial factors and violent crime to be held at the University of Maryland in the fall, the voices on the Hill became even louder and more outraged. NIH found a self-serving quasi-scientific reason to withdraw its support — but the message was clear: It is not "politically correct" to investigate race as a factor in violence. Indeed, to do so might burden us with "inconvenient knowledge." And that inconvenient knowledge might cause us to re-examine conditions of life in a caste-riven society in ways that disturb the frugal comforts of the white middle class.

That no such consequence ensued in the wake of ADAMHA's 1980 conference barely warrants rehearsal. To be politically correct is a marvelous new pathway through which to avoid the burden of inconvenient knowledge. Do we really want to know — or care? Or ought we to admit that, so long as Black-initiated violence constitutes a convenient scapegoating mechanism, it serves our purposes well — especially if it can be reasonably well containerized within the Black community?

The 1980 ADAMHA Symposium on Homicidal Violence among Black Males is summarized in *Public Health Reports,* 1980, 96, 6, 549-561. Especially germane are the reports therein by Dorothy Rice, National Center for Health Statistics; Lawrence Gary, Institute for Urban Affairs & Research, Howard University; Philip Bowman, Institute for Social Research, University of Michigan; Ruth Dennis, Department of Psychiatry, Meharry Medical College; and Bertha Holliday, Vanderbilt University. Hammond & Yung (1993) and Brinson (1994) reprise more contemporary data on the same set of issues.

Three years after the massive public protest that canceled the University of Maryland's planned conference, a meeting with a similar theme took place at the Aspen Institute in Maryland in Fall 1995. According to press reports (Montgomery, 1995), speakers "down-played" the "gene-crime link," hewing to a moderate — and less politically incorrect — view that "social injustice ranks far higher than chemical disturbances on the scale of things that create criminals."

13. There are also attendant unsettled scientific matters. At maturity, the human brain contains literally hundreds of millions of cells the functions of which remain unknown, even through advanced research in the neurosciences. Indeed, some neuroscientists hold the view that the function of some "excess" cells may be merely to "occupy space" in the brain in ways that may facilitate the activity of those cells whose specific functions are known.

In an historical commentary on studies of cranial capacity from 1849 onward, Anne Fausto-Sterling (1993) of the medical faculty at Brown makes the capital point that the brain "is swaddled in connective tissues and fluid-filled cushion" (the meninges), so that "cranial capacity could reflect differences in the brain's protective coverings" rather than differences in brain mass. She goes on to remark somewhat caustically that "whenever scientists have correlated brain size with achievement they found that scientists had the largest brains."

3 NEUROCHEMICAL CONTRIBUTIONS TO AGGRESSIVE VIOLENCE

THIS CHAPTER CONSIDERS EVIDENCE BEARING ON CONTRIBUTIONS TO AGGRESsive violence attributable to the ingestion of neurotoxins, including alcohol and other neuroactive chemical substances, even in the absence of brain dysmorphology or anomalies in brain biochemistry.

BIOCHEMICAL SUBSTANCES CLASSIFIED ON THE BASIS OF CHARACTERISTIC NEUROLOGIC EFFECTS

Customarily, substances which trigger alterations in pre-ingestion mood are grouped according to their typical effects on neurologic functioning. Each group contains both naturally-occurring substances and pharmaceutical preparations synthesized to alleviate medical or psychiatric conditions:

- CENTRAL NERVOUS SYSTEM DEPRESSANTS, so-named because they decelerate neurologic processes (e.g., marijuana, barbiturates). These substances "depress activity in all parts of the central nervous system and, in sufficient doses, cause death from respiratory depression" (Hofmann & Hofmann, 1975, 17). The group includes pharmaceutical preparations intended to control clinically significant mania, agitation, or hyperactivity (the "major tranquilizers," e.g., the phenothiazines). Alcohol (ethanol) is typically included in this group, although its behavioral effects are relatively atypical and dose-dependent, as we shall see shortly.

- CENTRAL NERVOUS SYSTEM STIMULANTS, with obverse effects, so-named because they accelerate neurologic processes (e.g., cocaine, amphetamine).

- NARCOTICS, so-named because of their ability to induce sleep (from the Latin) and, by extension, to produce analgesia for pain. Depending on dose, these substances may induce stupor and coma. Technically, only such substances as the opiates (morphine, heroin), codeine, and synthetic agents, many of which have been developed for medical use (e.g., such standard pharmacologic agents to treat insomnia as Halcion[®] and Restoril[®]) are included. However, the term is often imprecisely used to refer to "street drugs" or "controlled dangerous substances" without regard to their biochemical properties or neurologic effects.

- HALLUCINOGENS, so-named because they produce effects which mimic hallucinatory states. Hofmann & Hofmann (1975, 20-21) regard this grouping as relatively arbitrary and somewhat misleading: "This category of drugs is both ill-named and ill-defined, largely out of ignorance. We speak of these drugs as hallucinogens, though they appear to elicit true hallucinations only infrequently . . . We speak of them as 'psychotogenic' or 'psychotomimetic,' as if they were capable of producing a state identical with or substantially similar to a psychosis [but] these terms are applicable only with substantive qualification." Perhaps for these reasons, Feldman & Quenzer (1984) prefer the term "phantasticants." Despite these demurrers, this group customarily includes such "psychedelics" as lysergic acid diethylamide (LSD), peyote, phencyclidine (PCP, or "Angel Dust"), and mescaline. Hallucinatory effects have sometimes been reported with the use of potent medically-prescribed analgesic pharmaceuticals at high doses (e.g., Darvon®, Percoset®) and with the ingestion at relatively high doses of such diverse substances as nutmeg, a common spice, or the seeds of the morning glory plant (Seymour & Smith, 1987, 106-109). Acute effects of some powerful psychotomimetic substances are linked in the clinical literature to the elicitation of lethal violence by some persons for whom such violence seemed out of character and otherwise unpredictable.

Neurochemical mechanisms

The specific biochemical properties of the various substances enumerated (as well as others that are typically classified into one or another of these groups), as well as the specific biochemical pathways through which similar neurologic and neuropsychological effects are produced, differ from each other not only across groups, but even within groups. Although it is far beyond the scope of this volume to explore the relevant neurochemical processes in detail, it may be useful to illustrate the major variants briefly.

Among the CNS depressants, marijuana interferes with the customary metabolism of *serotonin* (Feldman & Quenzer, 1984, 231), while the barbiturates affect the metabolism of *gamma-Aminobutyric acid,* or GABA (Hyman & Nestler, 1993, 226). As we have noted, among the central nervous system stimulants, cocaine interferes with the metabolism of *norepinepherine*; the amphetamines alter the metabolism of both *dopamine* and *norepinephrine* (Feldman & Quenzer, 1984, 183). Not surprisingly, since morphine is derived from opium and heroin from morphine, the major narcotic substances display relatively similar neurochemical dynamics in interfering with the metabolism of *Beta-Endorphin* (Hyman & Nestler, 1993, 231). Among the hallucinogens, LSD interferes with the metabolism of *serotonin* (Feldman & Quenzer, 1984, 226-227), while PCP interferes with the metabolism of NMDA (Hyman & Nestler, 1993, 70). There was growing consensus among neuropharmacologists by mid-1995 that synthetic substances based on the amphetamines and constructed to mimic the effects of LSD (the methoxylated amphetamines, of which the street drug "Ecstasy" is the prime exemplar) actually destroy some brain cells responsible for the production of serotonin. A comprehensive, biochemically detailed overview of the specific ways in which the principal drugs of abuse affect normal processes of neurotransmission is provided by Berkow & Fletcher (1992, 520-521).

Drug interaction

Use of two (or more) substances simultaneously or in relatively rapid succession creates a set of biochemical interactions in which one substance may potentiate (if it is a biochemical agonist to the other substance or substances) or engender conflicting effects (if it is a biochemical antagonist to the other substance or substances).

Particularly among chronic substance abusers, as Seymour & Smith (1987, 129-130) observe, drugs of one type (e.g., CNS stimulants) are sometimes used to mediate the effects of drugs of another type (e.g., CNS depressants). Virtually every clinician who treats drug users/abusers and/or alcoholics has learned that it has become the fashion to ingest substances from different groups, often with antagonistic chemical properties, in serial fashion, becoming rather like neurobiochemical ping-pong balls in the process. With some frequency, the person whose substance-of-choice is a CNS stimulant such as cocaine or amphetamine, after spending five sleepless, hyperactive days, will use a CNS depressant such as alcohol to induce sleep, or a confirmed alcoholic will seek a CNS stimulant to rouse him/her from days of stupor. Such behavior is often defended as quite rational (indeed, as a "rational choice") and perhaps necessary in order to meet job or other demands. But death is often the consequence — not as the result of an overdose with a single substance, but as the result of the rapid, serial ingestion of substances with antagonistic biochemical effects.

In addition, some street drugs are deliberately amalgamated from substances with antagonistic biochemical properties (e.g., the "speedball," concocted of cocaine spiced with heroin). Similarly, the so-called "designer drugs" fabricated of non-controlled and often commonly-available chemicals (e.g., formaldehyde) as "clones" or "work-alikes" to naturally-occurring or to synthesized controlled dangerous substances in a frank effort to circumvent the law relatively frequently contain trace elements of compounds that coalesce to produce wildly unpredictable results.

Drug interactions occur with some frequency between prescription medications, especially when the prescriptions have been written by different medical specialists and when the patient fails to reveal to each practitioner that he/she is taking other medications for other purposes. For example: Prednisone and hydrocortisone, generic corticosteroids, are widely prescribed by physicians who specialize in diseases of the joints for such conditions as arthritis and rheumatism. There have been reports of depression and even hallucination as an infrequent side effect of these medications when taken alone (Perry, 1987). But, among some patients, these substances interact with commonly-prescribed sedatives or sleep-inducing preparations (such as Halcion® or Restoril®) to produce relatively florid symptomatology. There is, moreover, the prospect for drug interactions in mixing over-the-counter (OTC) pharmaceutical preparations even as mild as aspirin or cold remedies, and there have been clinical reports of negative interactions even with vitamin compounds (McCance-Katz & Price, 1992).

An attendant problem both biochemically and behavioral is the matter of "escalating thresholds" among regular and addicted users of virtually any neuroactive substance, so that dosages must be periodically increased if the user is to obtain the desired effects.

Alcohol and drug use during pregnancy: Effects on fetal neurodevelopment

Depending on dosage, frequency, and duration, use of alcohol or drugs by women during pregnancy may lead to *fetal alcohol syndrome* or to *fetal drug syndrome* in the newborn infant. High and consistent dosages either of alcohol or drugs throughout pregnancy typically result in what medical specialists rather euphemistically term the "intrauterine demise" of the fetus. According to Berkow & Fletcher (1992, 1857, 1860, 2009), the predictable consequences to fetal alcohol syndrome include retardation of prenatal growth, especially in neurodevelopment, and consequent mental deficiency; post-natal metabolic deficits are also sometimes observed. These effects are observed with the consistent ingestion of as little as three ounces of ethanol daily, or the equivalent of three drinks.

Germane to our interests, it is particularly important to note that the frontal lobes begin to develop within 20 weeks of conception (Hayman & Hinch, 1992), so that continued use of alcohol (or drugs) by the mother may lead to direct brain dysmorphologies in the newborn in the very area in which foresight, planfulness, and impulse control are sited. There are no reliable overall estimates of the relative incidence of fetal alcohol syndrome, but Bracha, Torrey, Gottesman et al. (1992) reported high levels in monozygotic twins of alcoholic mothers and Westermeyer (1993) observed a high incidence American Indians.

The term "fetal drug syndrome" has been applied to cases in which addiction to any drug is congenital in the newborn infant, but the most troubling cases arise from the mother's use of cocaine and its derivatives (e.g., "crack-addicted babies"), the opiates, and barbiturates. According to Berkow & Fletcher (1992,

2009-2010), the infant may display signs of withdrawal from addiction even at birth, and "sudden infant death syndrome" follows in an alarmingly high proportion of cases. If the infant survives, a "variety of neurobehavioral effects" may be expected to ensue. Again, there are no reliable overall estimates of the relative incidence of fetal drug syndrome, but it has been estimated that at least 150,000 "crack-addicted babies" have been born since 1980. Psychiatric researcher Marc Schuckit (1994), perhaps the leading epidemiologist of alcohol abuse, has convincingly demonstrated that early tolerance to high dosages of alcohol among young adults is predictive of the development of florid alcoholism in later life. It is not yet known whether *congenital* addiction to alcohol or to drugs functions in parallel fashion.

Typical and paradoxical drug effects in relation to neurologic dysfunction

As a matter of intellectual shorthand, we have spoken of consistent hyperarousal in CNS functions born of neurologic dysfunction as *neurogenic impulsivity* and its obverse as *neurogenic lethargy*, whether those states arise in consequence of morphologic or biochemical anomalies. Implicitly, these terms take as their reference point a "normal" state of arousal in the non-injured, non-biochemically-anomalous brain. Ingestion of neuroactive substances affects the "normal" state of affairs in the intact brain in characteristic ways, but their ingestion by the brain-disordered or biochemically anomalous yields variant effects.

In the dysmorphologic or biochemically-anomalous brain, the biochemical effects of ingestion of neuroactive substances can produce interactive results which vary considerably from the effects to be expected when those substances are metabolized in the "normal" brain. For example, if a neruogenically impulsive person ingests a CNS stimulant or hallucinogen, the net interactive effect is likely to be an enhanced or potentiated state of hyperarousal. But if he or she ingests a CNS depressant or narcotic, the net interactive effect may yield a regression toward the norm.

Reverse mirror-image effects can be expected to eventuate among neurogenically lethargic persons. When a person who is notably neurogenically impulsive or lethargic "selects" as a drug-of-choice for consistent use/abuse a substance that enhances or potentiates his or her habitual mood state, it can be inferred that he/she is making an effort to maintain that level of CNS arousal that he/she construes as phenomenologically "normal," but when he or she selects a substance with effects characteristically antagonistic to the habitual mood state uninfluenced by the ingestion of mood-altering substances, following the lead of Virkkunen and his associates (1983-a, 1986, 1994), it may be that he/she is seeking a means to alter the habitual state so that it more nearly approximates the norm.

There are myriad issues that arise from the precise nature of brain dysmorphology or biochemical anomaly in relation to the ingestion of substances with relatively specific biochemical properties. We have noted that cocaine achieves its stimulant effects by interfering with the metabolism of norepinepherine. When cocaine is ingested by a person with pre-existing anomalies in the routes and mechanisms for norepinephrine metabolism, the net effect can be radically unpredictable.

Finally, medications which have been designed to treat specific medical disorders may produce unexpected (and sometimes quite positive) psychobehavioral effects. For example, imipramine is a medication originally developed as a pharmacological treatment for orthostatic hypotension, a cardiovascular disorder, that was found to alleviate depression among patients without such disorder and is now widely prescribed as an antidepressant (Berkow & Fletcher, 1992, 434-436). Further, such not-deliberately-intended effects may vary differentially among neurologically-disordered patients. Thus, amantadine hydrochloride is a pharmaceutical preparation developed in the 1950s to treat or prevent infections of the respiratory tract caused by virus (specifically by slowing its growth) and is also used to treat symptoms of Parkinson's disease (by increasing the naturally-occuring rate of production of dopamine). But the preparation has been found, rather unexpectedly, also to reduce agitation, disinhibition, and aggressive behavior among subjects with frontotemporal impairment resultant from closed head injury (Gualtieri, Chandler, Coons & Brown, 1989).

Biochemically-induced moods relevant to aggression

Before turning to the research evidence on the incidence of substance abuse among criminal offenders, it will be useful to review those biochemically-induced mood states that are particularly relevant to the analysis of violent and aggressive behavior which psychopharmacologists and medical experts agree typically follow ingestion of substances of various sorts. Most such litanies start with a substance or group of substances and proceed to enumerate the varied likely consequences in mood alteration.

For our purposes, it is more useful to relate each mood state which may be implicated in violent and aggressive behavior to the varied substances known to produce that state. Thus, from the definitive compendia provided by Hofmann & Hofmann (1975), Schatzberg & Cole (1986), Frances & Franklin (1987), Perry (1987), Seymour & Smith (1987), Hartman (1988), and Hyman & Nestler (1993), we have melded and re-arrayed information concerning the predictable psychobehavioral effects associated with various groups of substances according to effect rather than in the usual litany.

- AGITATION: Primarily associated with CNS stimulants and with alcohol ingestion during early phases of metabolism. Also follows overdoses of some anti-depressant prescription medications and sometimes occurs as a paradoxical effect (i.e., an infrequent effect that is contrary to usual clinical experience and counter to the intended medical effect and which exacerbates rather than relieves symptoms) of certain medications (e.g., tranquilizers) intended to control mania, agitation, or hyperactivity. May follow over-dose with monamine oxidase inhibitors.

- AGGRESSION: Primarily associated with CNS stimulants and with acute alcohol intoxication (in a state technically termed "alcohol idiosyncratic intoxication" in the third edition of the *Diagnostic & Statistical Manual of Mental Disorders* of the American Psychiatric Association, but curiously absent from the fourth edition).

- COGNITIVE IMPAIRMENT: Primarily associated with alcohol ingestion at high doses and in chronic states of alcoholism, and to CNS stimulants, hallucinogens, marijuana, narcotics, opiates (morphine, heroin).

- CONCENTRATION IMPAIRMENT: Associated with acute intoxication with virtually any neuro-active substance, with withdrawal from alcohol intoxication, and with overdoses of anti-depressant medication (e.g., lithium).

- DELIRIUM: Primarily associated with hallucinogens and withdrawal from alcohol intoxication. Also attributable to CNS depressants, monamine oxidase inhibitors, and steroids.

- DEPERSONALIZATION: Primarily associated with acute hallucinogenic intoxication, but also occurs with heavy, chronic marijuana use.

- DISINHIBITION: Primarily associated with acute alcohol intoxication and with CNS stimulants.

- DYSPHORIA: Associated with narcotics, CNS depressants, opiates, and rapid withdrawal from virtually any neuroactive substance, especially CNS stimulants.

- EMOTIONAL LABILITY: Associated with acute (high dosage) use of, or habituation to, virtually any CNS-active substance and with withdrawal from medically-prescribed CNS depressants. Also linked to high dose usage of steroids.

- EXCITEMENT, EUPHORIA: Primarily associated with CNS stimulants. May follow (as a paradoxical effect) medications intended to control mania, agitation, or hyperactivity.

- HALLUCINATION: Primarily associated with hallucinogens and with acute alcohol intoxication ("alcohol hallucinosis"), often auditory in character. Also attributable to high dosage use of CNS stimulants.

- HYPERACTIVITY, IMPULSIVITY: Attributable primarily to CNS stimulants. Also associated with withdrawal states from acute alcohol intoxication.

- IMPOTENCE: Primarily associated with acute and chronic alcohol use. Also attributable to chronic use of CNS depressants or stimulants at high doses. Occasionally follows use of monoamine oxidase inhibitors.
- INSOMNIA: Attributable primarily to CNS stimulants, steroids.
- IRASCIBILITY: Primarily associated with chronic or acute use of alcohol and CNS stimulants. May emerge as a result of withdrawal from virtually any habit-forming CNS-active substance.
- JUDGMENT IMPAIRMENT: Associated with active intoxication with any neuroactive substance and especially prominent as an effect of CNS stimulants.
- MEMORY IMPAIRMENT: Primarily associated with chronic alcoholism or marijuana use, but may follow chronic use of virtually any CNS-active substance in sustained and high dosages.
- MISPERCEPTION: Associated with hallucinogens, high dosages of CNS stimulants, and acute alcohol intoxication.
- PARANOIA: Primarily associated with CNS stimulants, hallucinogens, and marijuana and with withdrawal from alcohol.
- SELF-DESTRUCTIVE BEHAVIOR: Associated primarily with hallucinogens and high dosages of CNS stimulants.
- STUPOR: Primarily associated with advanced stages of acute alcohol and narcotic intoxication.

It should be emphasized that the altered states included in this litany are those which can be expected to ensue among substance users whose brain biochemistry functions normally. When alcohol or other neuroactive substances are ingested by people with brain dysmorphologies or neurochemical dysfunctions or anomalies, paradoxical and/or heightened effects are to be expected, so that the results of substance use by the brain-disordered are wildly unpredictable.

ALCOHOL AND SUBSTANCE USE AND ABUSE AS CRIMINAL

As a nation, we are apparently obsessed by the use and abuse of psychoactive substances. As the table on the next page indicates, in a typical year, on the order of 27% of all arrests made for all offenses combined are made for offenses *exclusively* related to the sale, manufacture, processing, or possession of "controlled dangerous substances" (opium, cocaine, marijuana, or synthetics) or to alcohol (e.g., driving under the influence, public drunkenness, and other violations of liquor laws, such as sale to minors) and not related to felony crime of any sort.

Similarly, only 20% of all arrests are made for felony crimes, with the remainder largely for "public nuisance" offenses and misdemeanors. In different terms: The aggregate total of arrests made for offenses *exclusively* related to alcohol and drug use/abuse offenses but *not* related to felony crime exceeds the aggregate total of arrests made in all jurisdictions for all crimes of violence combined by 161%. Nor is that obsession a phenomenon of recent origin. In his study of police activity in American cities during the 19th century, legal scholar Sidney Harring (1983) found that felonies accounted for a mere 15% of all criminal arrests, with "most [other] arrests related to drinking."

Table 3.1: Gross annual data on arrests in the U.S. for alcohol & drug offenses in relation to all arrest activity

All arrests for all offenses, all U.S. jurisdictions		14,075,100 [100.0%]
• Arrests for violent crime felonies	742,130 [5.2%]	
• Arrests for property crime felonies	2,146,000 [15.2%]	
Arrests specifically for drug offenses		920,424 [6.5%]
• Heroin, cocaine + derivatives	487,824 [1.2%]	
• Marijuana	64,429 [3.4%]	
• Synthetic or manufactured drug	17,408 [0.1%]	
• Other "dangerous controlled substance"	119,655 [0.9%]	
Arrests specifically for alcohol offenses		2,929,300 [20.7%]
• Driving under the influence	1,624,500 [11.5%]	
• Liquor laws	541,700 [3.8%]	
• Public drunkenness	753,100 [5.4%]	

→ **SOURCE**: Data extracted from *Sourcebook of Criminal Justice Statistics* (Maguire & Pastore, 1994, 418, 448).

It may not be entirely coincidental that some 40% of the specific pathological conditions, both those regarded as "functional" and those regarded as neuropsychiatric, cataloged in the current edition of the *Diagnostic and Statistical Manual of Mental Disorders* of the American Psychiatric Association (1994) as constituting the universe of mental disorders are associated with the use or abuse of alcohol or other substances. Such disorders cover a vast range, from essentially self-limiting conditions like intoxication through longer-term delirium or hallucinosis to relatively permanent neuropsychiatric conditions induced by the effects of particularly virulent substances on the biochemistry and even the morphology of the brain, which perpetuate as dementia, organic psychosis, or organic personality syndrome (Perry, 1987). With respect to alcohol and each class of "abusable substance," the associated psychological disorders include patterns of abuse, dependence syndromes, intoxication and withdrawal states, delusional disorders, and dementia.

Offenses in which alcohol or drugs are implicated can be categorized as those which are legislatively defined as *criminal in themselves* (e.g., driving under the influence, possession of a controlled dangerous substance, whether for personal use or in sufficient quantity to suggest an intent to distribute) and those that are *criminogenic*, in the sense that alcohol or drugs contribute in a substantive manner to the commission of a felony offense. Though the topic is vastly engaging in social policy terms, we are not here concerned with the analysis of, or the exploration of alternate approaches to deal with (e.g., decriminalization), substance use or abuse as criminal in and of itself. Instead, our interest lies in substance use as criminogenic, with particular attention to crimes of aggressive violence.

ALCOHOL AND SUBSTANCE USE AND ABUSE AS CRIMINOGENIC

Intoxication and habituation to neuroactive substances of a variety of sorts (not limited to alcohol and those illicit drugs that have been legislatively declared "controlled dangerous substances" but including medicants available by prescription as well and such common household items as glue, spices, and flower seeds) biochemically trigger neuropsychological states that are relatively substance-specific, each with predictable behavioral consequences. Some substances trigger (or perhaps potentiate, or both) aggressivity and impulsivity that find expression in behavior that is formally criminal. It should not be surprising, then, to find a linkage between alcohol and substance use and/or abuse and aggressive criminal violence.

CNS-active substances as engine, lubricant, or motive

A particularly troublesome lacuna in the criminologic research literature has been the absence of careful consideration of the typical biochemically-determined neuropsychological sequelae to the use and abuse of alcohol, controlled dangerous substances of various sorts, and indeed of pharmaceutical preparations. As we have seen, each of the major classes of "usable" and/or "abusable" CNS-active substances possesses rather specific biochemical properties that produce predictable neuropsychological effects, ranging from euphoria, aggressivity, and overwhelming impulsivity (as in the case of psychotomimetic CNS stimulants, such as cocaine and the amphetamines) through disinhibition of customary behavior control (alcohol) to persistent passivity and withdrawal (as in the case of narcoleptic CNS sedatives and depressants). It seems likely that substances with variant biochemical properties may be *differentially* criminogenic in relation to criminal behavior of one sort, but not of other sorts — i.e., that the use or abuse of drugs with particular properties which produce predictable, but very particular, neuropsychological effects accelerates or contributes to particular types of criminal activity, but not to other types.

Conceptually, in a manner not unlike the model advanced by Moss & Tarter (1993), we might construe the use or abuse of alcohol and other psychoactive substances, whether "controlled" and "dangerous" or not and whether obtained illegally or through medical prescription, as prospectively associated with felony crime in several ways:

- As *engine,* functioning so as to induce a person "under the influence" to commit a criminal act of which he/she might otherwise seem incapable when not actively intoxicated.
- As *lubricant,* functioning so as to facilitate or potentiate what, at least post-hoc, appears to be a predisposition to criminal behavior, with the felony committed either "under the influence" or not.
- As *motive,* functioning as the goal to which criminal activity is directed, with the felony committed typically while the offender is not "under the influence."

The *engine* and *lubricant* functions correspond to what the late William McGlothlin (1985, 155) of UCLA has called the "direct pharmacological effects" of drug or alcohol use, among which he catalogs

> drug-induced disinhibition resulting in impulsive actions, crimes of negligence such as those resulting from driver-impaired performance, and the occasionally reported use of drugs . . . as a means of fortifying [oneself] to engage in criminal activities.

It is biochemically credible to suppose that the use or abuse of CNS stimulants (and perhaps of hallucinogens) accelerates crimes of violence and personal victimization. Among the property crimes, it seems likely that burglary alone might be accelerated by stimulants. Conversely, it is likely that the CNS depressants retard violent behavior of all sorts. These speculations, however, do not necessarily point to substance use or abuse as the primary engine for crime; instead, such use or abuse might more convincingly be regarded as a lubricant which potentiates other predisposing factors, both intra- and extra-personal. And almost certainly it is the "profit crimes" of burglary and robbery that are implicated when the acquisition of abusable substances functions as motive. In McGlothlin's (1985, 154-155) formulation:

> . . . drug use contributes to crime directly by potentiating impulsive and violent behavior . . . Alcohol is the only drug for which there is sufficient statistical data to establish a causal connection: the evidence clearly shows a relationship between acute effects and crimes of both violence and negligence . . . barbiturates have been found to potentiate assaultiveness [and] amphetamines and cocaine in high doses can produce paranoid reactions resulting in violence . . . Marijuana and the stronger hallucinogens are also capable of producing psychotic reactions, and there are occasional references [in the research literature] to violent behavior during these episodes [but] marijuana typically decreases both expressed and experienced hostility . . . there is growing evidence that the pseudohallucinogen phencyclidine [i.e., PCP], has a fairly high potential for producing combative and violent behavior . . . Opiates produce a reliable sedating reaction without the increased emotional lability and aggressiveness accompanying alcohol and barbiturate use. Thus, the pharmacological properties of opiates would be expected to decrease rather than potentiate criminal behavior, and this is generally consistent with the available evidence . . . Finally, and perhaps this is the issue of major concern, there is the question of income-generating crime among individuals with expensive drug habits [and] commission of acquisitive crimes during a period of withdrawal.

Alcohol and aggression: Paradoxical neuropsychological effects and social constraints

Alcohol is something of a special case because of the relatively paradoxical effects typically observed at low and at high levels of consumption. At high levels of consumption, alcohol produces the pattern of psychomotor retardation associated with CNS depressants. But at low levels of consumption (during what many experienced drinkers call the "rush" at first ingestion), alcohol produces what is commonly referred to as "disinhibition" of impulse control accompanied by a sense of exhilaration, a state of affairs conducive to aggressivity and assaultiveness (Frances & Franklin, 1987, 141-143). Indeed, Valciukas (1995) identifies "disinhibition syndrome" as "the lessening of cortical control of impulsive . . . function due to drugs and/or alcohol." In the disinhibition account, biochemically it seems more likely that alcohol will prove criminogenic during the early (or "rush") phases of ingestion than after prolonged ingestion. In a study based on PET scans, Tiihonen, Kuikka, Hakola, Paanila et al. (1994) found changes in regional blood flow in the prefrontal cortex following acute alcohol ingestion and thus attribute euphoric feelings to abnormally accelerated activation of that area of the brain. As Levin (1987, 19) has described the process:

> The sedative-hypnotics, including alcohol, initially depress the inhibitory synapses of the brain. Since the negation of a negative is a positive, the depression of the inhibitory synapses is excitatory. It is for this reason that alcohol is sometimes misclassified as a stimulant, although it is a depressant. Behaviorally, this disinhibition may manifest itself in high spirits and a devil-may-care attitude which may subjectively be experienced as euphoria. Anxiety is concomitantly reduced . . . Excitatory synapses are soon also depressed, however, and the behavioral and experiential effects of alcohol catch up with its pharmacological effect, which has been depressive all along.

An alternate explanation incorporates hypoglycemia (a rapid decrease in blood glucose level) as a modulator in the link between alcohol and violence. As Pernanen (1981, 19) puts it: "Hypoglycemia has been [reported] as a factor responsible for violent behavior. Alcohol is known to cause hypoglycemia in individuals who are under-nourished. Since much excessive alcohol use is associated with poor nutritional habits, this condition could be a factor in explaining the association between prolonged alcohol use and violent crime." According to Berkow & Fletcher (1987, 1084), alcohol-induced hypoglycemia results both from nutritional deficiency and impairment in the capacity of the liver to metabolize glucose, with the impairment itself perhaps due to heavy alcohol usage (870). Yet another hypothesis holds that withdrawal from alcohol among those dependent on the substance triggers a neuronally-dictated state of hyperarousal in the limbic system (Adinoff, O'Neill & Ballender, 1995).

From the pioneering studies of premier criminologist Marvin Wolfgang (1958) onward, a considerable body of research evidence, much of it summarized by Collins (1981) and Roizen (1981), has pointed toward a consistent link between alcohol and violent crime. Because of ubiquity and ease of access (at least since repeal of the Volstead Act 60 years ago), alcohol is apparently infrequently implicated as motive in profit crimes. After reviewing the then-current studies, Blum (1981, 115-116) proposed that the criminogenic character of alcohol consumption in relation to criminal violence is modulated by a number of impinging variables:

> Under no circumstances will alcohol be a sole "cause" of violence. Alcohol may alter perceptions, cognitive performance, moods/emotions, and response capabilities and preferences. Less adaptive solutions, such as violence . . . occur with decrements in judgment. Violence may also be adaptive, or perceived as such. One expects that violence will occur when both preexisting and situational factors stimulate, facilitate, or permit it. Violence in association with alcohol may vary with dosage and, in turn, with pharmacologically specific effects including arousal levels, cognitive deficits, and psychological reactions to such changes (e.g., anxiety).

Quite similar conclusions were reached by Swedish psychologist Roland Gustafson (1994), one of the world leaders in studying alcohol and aggression, in a summary of his own research over the space of a decade (much of it involving the experimental manipulation of both dosage and type of alcohol, or a placebo, and of situational factors that invite or discourage aggressive responses) and after reviewing related studies by other investigators from the 1960s onward [NOTE 1]. Underscoring the interaction between biochemical factors and situational cues and norms and also highlighting the differential effects of alcohol that has been prepared for consumption through variant methods (brewing, fermenting, distilling), Gustafson concluded that

> Theoretically, no traditional model fully explains how the changes in intoxicated aggressive behavior are mediated . . . From experimental studies that use human subjects it is concluded that a moderate dose of alcohol does not increase aggression if subjects are unprovoked. Under provocative conditions aggression is increased as a function of alcohol intoxication provided that subjects are restricted to an aggressive response. If subjects also have access to a non-aggressive response, no increase in aggression is observed. Beer and wine do not increase aggression under any conditions . . . Most likely, both psychological and pharmacological mechanisms play important roles in the control of alcohol-related aggression . . . a moderate dose of alcohol facilitates aggressive responding with the provision that the subject is provoked and that the number of response alternatives is restricted. A provoked intoxicated subject having access to only an aggressive response alternative will definitely be more aggressive than a sober subject under the same conditions . . . If, however, the subject has access to a non-aggressive response alternative subjectively experienced as equally effective in affecting the opponent in a desired way, the intoxicated and provoked subject is no more aggressive than the sober and provoked subject.

Since a considerable proportion of overindulgence in alcohol occurs precisely under conditions in which non-aggressive responding is non-normative (e.g., taverns, "sports bars" during the telecasts of body-contact games), Gustafson suggested that efforts to control alcohol-related aggression be focused on situational variables and behavioral repertoires:

> It is possible to propose a number of preventive measures. The most drastic one is to restrict the availability of liquor by controlling, for example, where liquor can be bought and the number of outlets . . . all measures aiming at the reduction of individual and collective frustration and other forms of provocations would reduce the level of alcohol-related aggression. It is also possible to train alternative behavioral strategies so that non-aggressive alternatives would be equally strong or stronger than aggressive alternatives in the behavioral hierarchy.

But a variant hypothesis implicates the rate of biotranformation of dopamine among alcoholics in violent behavior. On the basis of data collected from single photon emission tomography (SPECT) scans on habitually violent alcoholics, non-violent alcoholics, and non-violent non-alcoholics in Finland, Tiihonen, Kuikka, Bergstrom et al. (1995) discerned differences in the rates at which dopamine is metabolized among alcoholic subjects in relation to "healthy controls." But, in relation to control subjects, such biotransformation occurs more rapidly in violent alcoholics (95% with extensive histories of impulsively violent criminal offenses) and markedly less rapidly in non-violent alcoholics. Were differences in rate of dopamine biotransformation merely artifacts of ingestion of, or habituation to, alcohol, we might expect that alcoholics would differ from non-drinkers but not that violent alcoholics would differ from non-violent alcoholics. Instead, these results point in the direction of a neuro-chemical basis for differential susceptibility to the violence-inducing characteristics of alcohol among some heavy drinkers but not among others.

ALCOHOL AND SUBSTANCE USE/ABUSE AND VIOLENT CRIME

Despite what is generally conceded to be an "epidemic" in the use of "controlled dangerous substances" since the 1950s and the consequent and widespread belief that substance abuse similarly represents a major (or even the major) contributory factor in felony crime, little systematic research effort has attempted to establish precise and biochemically credible linkages. Such studies as have been reported have prototypically relied on data from self-reports, often of the offender but sometimes of the victim, as the standard index of crimino-genic alcohol or substance use or abuse, with but few inquiries based on independent observations and yet fewer based on laboratory assessments of whether alcohol or drugs (licit or illicit) can be detected in the physical system of an accused (or witnessed) offender.

Independent observations (most often, by arresting police officers, sometimes armed with relatively unsophisticated devices for estimating blood alcohol levels through samples of respiratory air, or, far less frequently, by knowledgeable witnesses) tend to vary, but essentially only marginally, from self-reports of victim or offender. Only relatively recently have sophisticated laboratory assay methods been employed in this arena of inquiry; and then, given the relative infrequency of instant apprehension, typically only at the point of arrest, often long after the allegedly criminal event.

Variant methods of inquiry

Contemporary studies of the relationship between substance use or abuse and felony crime can be categorized by method of inquiry into those which utilize self-report data and those which employ laboratory assay methods. Among self-report studies, there is a further distinction between those investigations that inquire into the criminal behavior patterns of known alcohol or substance users and those that inquire into the alcohol and/or substance use or abuse habits of known offenders.

Among the laboratory assay studies, there is also a further distinction, predicated on the "sensitivity" of the specific methodology (Wish, 1990) used to detect metabolites which biochemically succeed the ingestion of "controlled dangerous substances" or to determine blood alcohol content, typically among samples of arrestees, usually long after the criminal event. From the perspective of criminogenesis, to interpret appropriately studies utilizing either self-report or laboratory assay methods, it is often necessary to regroup the data reported so as to eliminate those cases in which the offenses-of-record are related exclusively to substance abuse or alcohol laws.

Self-report data

Incidence of crime self-reported by drug users

A number of investigations, both in this country (Newcomb & Bentler, 1988), in Britain (Hammersley & Morrison, 1987, 1988), and in Sweden (Torstensson, 1987) have addressed criminal activity among known substance abusers. In some cases, data were collected from retrospective interviews with persons currently identified as drug or alcohol abusers. In others, more elaborate research designs collected longitudinal data on subjects who had applied for (and/or completed) treatment in drug rehabilitation facilities operated by mental health authorities. That subjects in the latter studies in particular were at liberty in the community, whether under probation or under the provisions of pre-trial diversion or not, and thus in a position to seek outpatient treatment might well lead us to expect to find a relatively low incidence of violent offenses, merely as an artifact of implicit selection criteria.

Some studies, particularly those which rely on the retrospective self-reports of known abusers, have produced such astounding data that distinguished criminologist James Inciardi (1982) was led to severe criticism of certain research designs as likely conducive to eliciting inaccurate information. While that may be too harsh a reading, even if one presumes their *willingness* to reveal the truth, there is ample reason to question the *accuracy* of memory of subjects who are either self-identified or who have been otherwise formally designated as addicted to substances known to affect memory.

As a case in point: Ball, Rosen, Flueck & Nurco (1982) reported that their sample of 243 subjects had been responsible for 473,000 "serious felony crimes" over a period of eleven years, or 1946 crimes per person, 177 crimes per person per year, or one serious felony crime every two days. Not incidentally, that annual rate of offending stands in stark contrast to figures cited by Greenwood (1995, 258) in his analysis of the deterrent effects of "selective incapacitation" of high risk offenders, viz., "between 2 and 3.5 offenses per year for robbery; 6 or 7 offenses per year for burglary; and 3 to 3.5 offenses per year for auto theft." Current, relatively conservative, estimates suggest something on the order of 500,000 "hard-core" drug addicts nationwide, as distinct from "drug abusers" or "part-time recreational users." If one uses the annualized rate for the subjects in the Ball, Rosen et al. study as a basis and multiplies that rate by the (conservatively) estimated number of addicts, one would expect that the drug addicts of the nation are responsible for some 88,000,000 serious felonies per year — a figure that exceeds the total number of felony crimes reported to all law enforcement agencies in the U.S. in a year by some 700%.

In what may well stand as the definitive concurrent study of the relationship between drug use and criminal behavior among adolescents, Inciardi, Horowitz & Pottieger (1993) examined in detail the annual incidence self-reported by subjects in Miami. If we look only at aggregate data, the numbers reach astronomical proportions. The 611 subjects interviewed by the Inciardi team (1993, 175-177) reported a total of 429,136 criminal offenses, or a mean of 702 per subject, or approximately two offenses daily. But some 60% of these offenses concerned "drug business" (buying or selling of controlled dangerous substances), another 30% were offenses (property crimes, burglaries, robberies, motor vehicle thefts) likely related to the purchase of drugs, and another 10% reflected "commercialized vice" (prostitution, procuring), likely also related to the purchase of drugs. Among the astronomical total of 429,136 offenses, there were only 721 assaults (0.16%) reported, with no homicides or sexual assaults.

Among the most carefully designed and executed longitudinal investigations, McGlothlin's (1985) is a prime exemplar. His subjects were self-identified male narcotics users with a mean age of 25 admitted to a treatment program in California who were followed for a decade after admission through periodic interviews and collection of police arrest records. Data concerning arrests for drug and other offenses, extent of drug dealing activity, employment, number of crimes self-reported annually, the number of person-days per year during which each subject self-reported as engaged in criminal activity, and a variety of other variables were arrayed in several ways.

Of the several arrays, the most pertinent is that which contrasts subjects who used narcotics on a daily basis (and could thus be classified according to any lexical scheme as "addicts") with those who used narcotics less frequently. In this contrast, the addicts were arrested significantly more frequently each year for felony property offenses and for drug offenses, but not for violent felonies; more frequently self-reported as engaged in drug dealing (58% vs. 16%); and self-reported a significantly higher number of property crimes per year (47 vs. 17), a higher level of income from crime ($9100 vs. $1700), and a significantly smaller proportion of person-days per year during which they were not engaged in criminal activity (53% vs. 83%).

Considering his own data and data from some 45 other studies that investigated the criminal behavior of known drug abusers over long periods of time, McGlothlin (1985, 166-167) reached what he called "unequivocal conclusions" that

> during periods of addiction, individuals are more likely to be arrested . . . to commit more crime, and to acquire more money from property crimes.

Since the crimes committed by these known-addict subjects are predominantly property crimes (with the crimes of violence observed virtually invariably themselves associated with "drug deals gone sour"), McGlothlin's results (as do those of Inciardi and his associates) argue that drug use functions criminogenically primarily as motive rather than as engine.

Incidence of crime among alcoholics

Curiously, despite the substantially greater period of time during which careful scientific study of the behavioral effects of alcohol use has progressed, few studies of known alcoholics (or "problem drinkers") have reached the clarity and precision of McGlothlin's or Inciardi's among drug abusers. Perhaps the ubiquity and ease of legal access to alcohol have encouraged fewer of those who overuse this substance to seek treatment than those whose use of other substances de facto violates the law and for whom participation in community-based treatment (perhaps through pre-trial diversion) may even represent an alternative to prosecution. The stringent confidentiality maintained by Alcoholics Anonymous, without question the principal source of treatment nationwide and likely worldwide (Nathan & Skinstead, 1987), may further discourage detailed investigation (McCrady & Miller, 1993; Nowinski, 1993; Maisto, 1995).

Hence, in his summary of the studies relevant to criminal behavior among known alcoholics, Collins (1981-a, 164-166) cites data that suggest that only between 3% and 10% of self- identified "problem drinkers" arrayed by age in five-year intervals between 21 and 59 reported "police problems" during the immediately preceding thirty-six months. But the character of these "problems" is not specified and may range the spectrum from warnings for boisterousness through traffic charges to arrest (or conviction) for violent felony. In her review of studies of alcoholics admitted voluntarily for inpatient or outpatient treatment, Greenberg (1981) cites 11.5% as the median rate for subjects in these groups who self-reported that they had been arrested or convicted for a criminal offense, whether a violent or property crime, unrelated to alcohol use.

Incidence of alcohol and drug use among convicted offenders

Several major studies of inmates of jails and prisons have been completed by the U.S. Bureau of the Census for the Bureau of Justice Statistics (BJS), based on interviews with inmates conducted according to standard schedules by trained Census interviewers. In the most recent survey (Beck, Gilliard, Greenfeld et al., 1993) among convicted felons incarcerated in state prisons, interviews were conducted with a random, stratified sample of inmates (96% male; 49.7% white) carefully selected to represent accurately the total population. Some 47% had been convicted of crimes of violence (homicide, kidnapping, rape, sexual assault, robbery, assault), 25% of property offenses (burglary, larceny or theft, arson, fraud), 21% of drug offenses (possession, trafficking), and 7% of "public order" offenses (weapons possession, prostitution, and violation of probation or parole).

Prisoners were asked to indicate whether they had been "under the influence" of alcohol or drugs at the time of the instant offense, although data are not reported on the character of the particular drug group (i.e., CNS stimulants, depressants, narcotics, hallucinogens) whose influence they acknowledged. Resultant self-assessment data (Ibid., 18, 26) are recapitulated graphically on the opposite page. Inspection of these data yield some surprises. Cumulatively, 47% of the prisoners serving sentences for homicide, 44% of those incarcerated for sexual assault, 52% of those incarcerated for robbery, and 49% of those incarcerated for assault reported that they had been "under the influence" of one or another substance, or combination of substances, during the criminal act for which they were incarcerated. But among *property* offenders, the comparable cumulative proportion in the prisoner survey data rises to some 61%. While the cumulative proportions suggest a palpable contribution to crime *across* categories, these self-report data reveal few *differential* contributions made by the offender's use of alcohol, drugs, or alcohol and drugs together to offenses inflected by character or category in a manner consistent with biochemical credibility.

Biochemical credibility suggests that, if alcohol and/or substance use functions as engine, we should expect a substantially higher proportion of violent than of property offenders in particular to self-report alcohol and/or drug influence as contributory to offense behavior. But that is not the case: Instead, the figures suggest that proportionally more property than violent (or drug and public order) offenders committed their crimes "under the influence." That conclusion is at variance with what biochemistry would predict but reasonably congruent with the finding of Franklin, Allison & Sutton (1992) that drug or alcohol intoxication was not differentially related to offense category in a study of all offenders committed to the prisons of North Carolina during the year 1988, with data from smaller scale studies (Welte & Miller, 1987) on incarcerated offenders, and with findings reported by Gottlieb, Gabrielsen & Kramp (1988) in a study of Danish offenders over a 25-year-period. In the aggregate, then, these prisoner self-report data suggest a generalized contribution to criminal behavior issuing from alcohol and substance abuse that is not inflected differentially by major offense category.

To parallel Hillbrand and his associates (1994) in regard to cerebral lateralization, to judge from the self-reports of offenders, there may be a link between

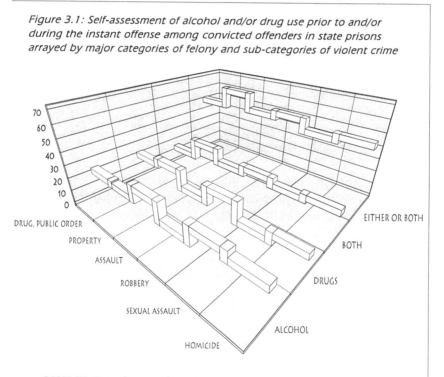

Figure 3.1: Self-assessment of alcohol and/or drug use prior to and/or during the instant offense among convicted offenders in state prisons arrayed by major categories of felony and sub-categories of violent crime

→ **SOURCE:** Data from Beck et al., *Survey of State Prison Inmates* (Bureau of Justice Statistics, 1993). Data on drug and public order offenders collapsed.

alcohol and substance abuse and violent crime, but that link cannot be predicated as more than contributory — that is to say, that alcohol and substance use appears to function essentially as "lubricant" rather than as "engine" across offenses of quite disparate character.

Drug abuse as motive

Further data from the same survey of convicted and imprisoned offenders (Beck, Gilliard, Greenfeld et al., 1993, 22) indicate that 26% of the property offenders and 27% of the robbery offenders self-reported that they had commit-ted their offenses "to get money to buy drugs." These rates surely portray illicit drugs as a powerful and pervasive *motive*. If we extrapolate those rates to the overall incidence of property crime (approximately 12 million) and of robberies (approximately 640,000), it would appear that funding the abuse of controlled dangerous drugs motivates something approximating 3,100,000 property of-fenses and 173,000 robberies, or a total of some 3,250,000 or so felony offenses annually, accounting for roughly 25% of all episodes of reported felony crime.

Analysis of social policy on alcohol and substance use and abuse is beyond the scope of this volume [NOTE 2]. But, when one looks at the data in this way, one cannot but be arrested by the position taken by those who propose decriminaliza-tion of substance abuse, indeed perhaps in a model that resembles the British experiment (Royal College of Psychiatrists, 1987) in providing drugs without charge to registered addicts, thus removing "money to buy drugs" as a motive for crime.

A responsible social policy toward decriminalization, however, should also eliminate drug addiction as a "mitigating factor" in the assessment of sanctions for criminal offenses, whether for a first or subsequent offense. Decriminaliza-tion should not be expected to affect the incidence of those violent crimes in which substance abuse functions as engine or lubricant, however — but perhaps elimination of drug addiction as a mitigating factor in assigning penalties (thus mollifying the effects of "voluntary misconduct") might be expected to have some deterrent effect.

Laboratory assay data

Self-reports among convicted offenders may be the only viable route to determining whether substance use is perceived phenomenologically to function biochemically as "engine" or "lubricant" in criminal behavior. But, particularly among habitual alcohol and/or substance abusers, the extent to which biopsy-chosocial functioning is influenced by the presence of neuroactive substances may be radically underestimated. Thus, other investigators have utilized sophis-ticated laboratory assay methodologies to detect the presence of alcohol or drugs in the physical systems of arrestees for crimes of one or another sort (Wish & O'Neil, 1989; Wish, 1990). These studies have usually found alcohol-positive and/or drug-positive rates vastly in excess of those found by self-report methodology, whether in studies of known abusers or of known offenders.

There are some problematic issues, however. While the scientific evidence for the presence or absence of neuroactive substances of various sorts is incontrovertible at the point of apprehension, it is fallacious to assume guilt on the basis of arrest. Moreover, except for the rare situation in which an alleged offender is apprehended almost immediately after a criminal act as a result of "hot pursuit," that a suspect is under the influence of a neuroactive substance at the time of arrest may tell us little about his or her condition at the time the criminal event occurred, if indeed he or she committed the criminal act.

Yet utilization of laboratory assay techniques to determine the presence of alcohol and neuroactive substances (technically, more frequently their successor metabolites) within the physical system of an examinee should provide more reliable data than self-reports. Since it is rare that apprehension for a violent or any other crime occurs under "hot pursuit" circumstances, such technology can be brought into play only at the point of arrest, usually long after the criminal event itself. Moreover, laboratory assays are substantially more expensive to conduct than are self-report surveys; and, since laboratory assay technology always involves the collection of physical specimens, the matter of the rights of the accused in respect of self-incrimination enters the picture.

Finally, there are issues concerning "bandwidth fidelity" in the accuracy of "more" and "less" sensitive assay methodologies (Wish, 1990), since, in general, such techniques can detect some substances with greater accuracy than others (Pallone, 1990-c). Among the most ambitious large-scale investigations have been those conducted by Creative Socio-Medics, Narcotic Addiction and Research, Inc., and the Toborg Group The data they have yielded contrast markedly with self-reports from convicted offenders, indicating substantially higher laboratory-assayed drug-positive rates among arrestees than self-reported among prisoners virtually across all categories of crime.

TLC methodology: National CJDASS study

In the pilot program for the National Criminal Justice Drug Alert Surveillance System, thin-layer chromatography (TLC) was utilized as the laboratory assay methodology by Creative Socio-Medics Corporation (Richardson, Morein & Phin, 1978) in a study which analyzed the urine specimens of 1816 arrestees (90.7% male; 49.2% white; 85.3% of all those arrested for all misdemeanors or felonies) in four "representative" U.S. counties (Dade, in Florida; Erie, in New York; King, in Washington; Maricopa, in Arizona) over a two-month period.

Specimens collected at the point of admission to county jail, immediately after arrest, whether under "hot pursuit" or more normal circumstances, were assayed for the presence of a wide variety of "controlled dangerous substances" with both CNS-stimulant (e.g., amphetamine, ampitriptyline, cocaine, phenetzrine), -depressant (e.g., barbiturate, diphenhydramine, hydroxyzine, meperidine, phenothiazine), or narcotic (e.g., codeine, methadone, morphine, pentazocine, propoxyphene) properties and their metabolites. Alcohol use was not assayed.

Drug positive rate among arrestees for crimes of violence		13.6%
• Arrested for criminal homicide	45.4%	
• Arrested for assault	11.9%	
• Arrested for rape	16.6%	
• Arrested for robbery	18.0%	
• Arrested for other violent crimes	7.5%	
Drug positive rate among arrestees for property crimes		16.6%
• Arrested for burglary	14.1%	
• Arrested for forgery or fraud	15.5%	
• Arrested for larceny	19.0%	
• Arrested for other property crimes	17.7%	

When arrestees for suspected felony offenses are arrayed by type of offense (as above), the "positive" rates found in TLC laboratory analyses yield some remarkable contrasts with the self-report data for convicted felons just reviewed. Although the positive rate among arrestees for crimes of violence in the aggregate essentially matches the rate self-reported by prisoners, as do the rates among those arrested for assault and for robbery, the laboratory-assayed drug positive rate for those arrested for homicide in this sample exceeds the self-reported rate by a ratio of 450%, while the rate for those arrested for rape exceeds that self-reported by more than 300%.

EMIT methodology

"Enzyme multiplied immune urine tests" (EMIT), a laboratory methodology that is "more sensitive for identifying recent drug use" than thin-layer gas chromatography (TLC), such that "Estimates of drug use based on TLC (are) one half to two thirds lower than the estimates from EMIT tests" (Wish, Brady & Cuadrado, 1986), has been utilized in large-scale studies in New York City and in the District of Columbia.

NADRI Manhattan Study. In a study of arrestees in New York County (Manhattan) by Narcotic and Drug Research, Inc., urine specimens for 5571 arrestees (97% male; 84% of all those arrested for felony or misdemeanor during a seven-month period; no racial data indicated) for the presence of cocaine, methadone, morphine, and phencyclidine (PCP) through EMIT methodology (Wish, Brady & Cuadrado, 1986). Once again, alcohol use was not assayed. Specimens were collected in Manhattan Central Booking before subjects were sent to court for arraignment. Results are re-arrayed and tabularized on the next page. When arrestees for suspected felony offenses (64% of all arrestees) are arrayed by type of offense charged, the "positive" rates found by EMIT laboratory analysis are remarkably high, exceeding both those found by self-report inquiry among convicted felons and those found in the Creative Socio-Medics study by very substantial margins.

Drug positive rate among arrestees for crimes of violence   53%
- Arrested for criminal homicide   56%
- Arrested for assault   37%
- Arrested for rape   41%
- Arrested for robbery   54%
- Arrested for other violent crimes   53%

Drug positive rate among arrestees for property crimes   57%
- Arrested for burglary   59%
- Arrested for forgery or fraud   48%
- Arrested for larceny   56%
- Arrested for other property crimes   61%

NADRI Cocaine Study. In another study (Wish, 1986), the same research group focused on a single substance, viz., cocaine. Under similar circumstances, urine specimens for 429 arrestees (71% of all those arrested for felony or misdemeanor during a three-month period; no race or gender data indicated) for the presence of cocaine, either through EMIT or through TLC. In this sample, only four felony charges are represented.

When arrestees for these four suspected felony offenses (47% of all arrestees) are arrayed by type of offense charged (indicated below), the "positive" rates found for cocaine by the "more sensitive" EMIT procedures or the "less sensitive" TLC method are incredibly high, generally exceeding the already markedly high rates found in the first NADRI study (which had tested for a variety of substances, using the "more sensitive" EMIT procedures) by nearly 50% on average.

Cocaine positive rate among arrestees . . .
- Arrested for assault   53%
- Arrested for robbery   83%

Cocaine positive rate among arrestees . . .
- Arrested for burglary   77%
- Arrested for larceny   56%

Toborg-District of Columbia Study. The "more sensitive" EMIT laboratory methodology was also utilized in a study of arrestees in the District of Columbia by Toborg & Bellassai (1987). Urine specimens for 6160 arrestees (82% male; apparently an indeterminate proportion of all those arrested for felony or misdemeanor between June 1984 and January 1985; 83% black; 34% charged with misdemeanors only; 41% with prior convictions for either felony or misdemeanor) for the presence of amphetamines, cocaine, heroin, methadone, and phencyclidine (PCP). In the District, arrestees for misdemeanors may be released by precinct police authorities after booking, following a telephone interview with a member of the Pretrial Services Agency; those not so released are held in a Superior Court lock-up facility. Specimens were collected in this facility by a Pretrial Services Agency technician and analyzed on-site before subjects were sent to court for arraignment.

Drug positive rate among arrestees for crimes of violence   41%

- Arrested for criminal homicide   None represented
- Arrested for assault   33%
- Arrested for rape   None represented
- Arrested for robbery   53%
- Arrested for other violent crimes   42%

Drug positive rate among arrestees for property crimes   45%

- Arrested for burglary   42%
- Arrested for forgery or fraud   None represented
- Arrested for larceny   47%
- Arrested for other property crimes   45%

When arrestees for suspected felony offenses (66% of all arrestees) are arrayed (as above) according to standard nomenclature by type of offense charged (with some curious gaps noted, especially among violent crime categories), the "positive" rates found by EMIT laboratory analysis tend to exceed those by self-report inquiry among convicted felons and those found in by TLC methodology in the Creative Socio-Medics study but to be lower than those reported by NADRI.

NIJ Drug Use Forecasting Studies. Wish & O'Neil (1989) consolidated data from the National Institute of Justice's "drug use forecasting" studies in 13 cities, through which "voluntary and anonymous" urine specimens of samples of arrestees were analyzed through EMIT technology for the metabolites of eight controlled dangerous drugs and two pharmacological preparations (Darvon® and Valium®) that have become subject to abuse.

Among male arrestees, the proportions found drug-positive range from 50% in Indianapolis to 85% in San Diego; among females, the proportions range from 44% in Dallas to 87% in the District of Columbia. The presentation of source data in the Wish & O'Neil report does not permit segregation of arrestees for felony crime from those arrested for other offenses (including drug offenses), nor arraying drug positive rates by offense charge. Similarly, in a study of adjudicated delinquents (70% male, 62% white) aged 16 and under judicially ordered into a "secure detention" facility in Florida, Dembo, Washburn, Wish, Schmeidler et al. (1987) found 39% to be the median drug-positive rate at admission, as assayed by EMIT methodology. The investigators further reported, rather unexpectedly, high congruence between self-reports of drug use and laboratory results among their subjects.

Perceptions of victims on offender drug and alcohol use

For more than two decades, the National Crime Victimization Survey has conducted interviews with representative samples of U.S. households to determine principally whether victims have reported episodes of criminal behavior ("attempted" or "completed") to law enforcement authorities — and if not, why not.

In the most recent survey (Bureau of Justice Statistics, 1994, iii), some 110,000 respondents in 66,000 households were interviewed concerning their victimization in rape, robbery, assault, theft, burglary, larceny, or motor vehicle theft, with the finding that only 50% in the aggregate were formally reported and that the most frequently cited reasons for not reporting (Ibid., 7, 110-111) were that the attempt had not been successful (25% of the time) or that the episode had been reported "to another official" (15% of the time). Crimes which occurred in commercial settings (e.g., shoplifting) were not surveyed, nor was homicide.

Table 3.2: *Proportion of victims reporting that offender(s) had been "under the influence" during crimes of* . . .

• Homicide	*None represented*
• Rape (47% of episodes not reported to police)	39%
• Robbery (49% of episodes not reported to police)	35%
• Aggravated assault (38% of episodes not reported to police)	32%
• Simple assault (57% of episodes not reported to police)	31%

Among a vast array of inquiries, interviewers questioned respondents who had been victimized in violent offenses concerning their perceptions as to whether the offenders by whom they had been victimized were "under the influence" of alcohol or drugs during the criminal episode(s). The relevant data (Ibid., 7, 58) for crimes of violence are reported here. Although the survey questionnaire (Ibid., 120-140) contains some 90 questions eliciting a vast array of information about the alleged offense in which the respondent had been victimized, inquiry was not made as to whether the *victim* had been "under the influence" during the victimization.

Alcohol and drug use among victims as perceived by offenders in crimes of violence

But, as we shall emphasize in the next chapter, the offender is only part of the equation in a crime of personal victimization. Although the National Crime Victimization Survey makes no such inquiry, a number of investigators have studied drug or alcohol toxicity among victims of criminal violence.

Thus, Budd (1982), of the Los Angeles Coroner's office, reported that toxic levels of alcohol were found at autopsy in the blood samples of 61% of murder victims. Similar findings were reported in investigations of homicide victims in Erie County, New York over a period of a dozen years by Abel (1986, 1987), who reported toxic alcohol levels in 45% of these victims, with drugs detected in another 4%. Abel (1988) further reported that the victims of homicide by means of stabbing more frequently displayed such toxic levels than did those who had died as a result of gunshot wounds. In a more discerning analysis, Welte & Abel (1989) found significant correlates between the victim's blood alcohol level and other variables, so that higher levels were found in young male adults, among victims killed in warmer months, among victims killed at night, among black victims, and among victims killed on weekends. As an historical apostrophe, we might also note findings reported by Waller (1972) that concentrations of alcohol sufficient to render them legally inebriated were found in 61% of the *pedestrians* victimized in fatal traffic accidents over a seven-year period in two California counties.

Table 3.3: Perceptions of convicted and imprisoned offenders on whether they, their victims, or both were "under the influence" of alcohol and/or drugs during the instant offense

In crimes of homicide . . .
- Offender under the influence   52%
- Victim under the influence   46%
- Either/both offender or victim under the influence   70%

In crimes of sexual assault . . .
- Offender under the influence   42%
- Victim under the influence   19%
- Either/both offender or victim under the influence   47%

In crimes of assault . . .
- Offender under the influence   50%
- Victim under the influence   42%
- Either/both offender or victim under the influence   68%

In crimes of robbery . . .
- Offender under the influence   52%
- Victim under the influence   19%
- Either/both offender or victim under the influence   61%

Although the National Criminal Victimization Survey does not inquire into alcohol or drug use among victims, the BJS study of prisoners (Beck, Gilliard, Greenfeld et al., 1993, 18) inquired into the perception of offenders convicted of offenses in the group customarily labeled as crimes of violence or personal victimization (including robbery) as to whether their victims were "under the influence" of alcohol or drugs or both at the time of the instant offense. Among all violent offenders, some 30% reported that their victims had been so influenced; when the data are extrapolated, these investigators reported that either the victim or the offender had been under the influence of alcohol or drugs or both in some 61% of the cases. These data are re-arrayed according to offense category in the table on this page.

If one judges whether neuroactive substance use/abuse lubricates violent crime on the basis of these data, rather clear conclusions emerge: As perceived by convicted offenders, neuroactive substance use by *either* the victim *or* the offender or both contributes to 70% of the cases of homicide, 47% of the cases of sexual assault, 61% of the cases of robbery, and 68% of the cases of assault. Moreover, to the extent that they reflect particular vulnerability on the part of victims to which offenders are sensitized and upon which they readily seize, these data quite readily fit the interpretive framework suggested by Gottfredson

Figure 3.2: Variant data on alcohol and substance use/abuse in relation to aggressive criminal violence by method of assessment: Perceptions of offenders and victims vs. laboratory assay data

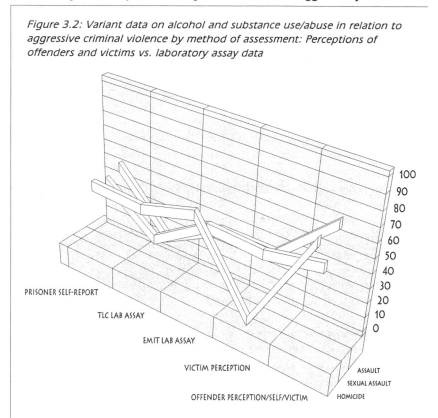

→ **LEGEND**: Offender self-assessment of themselves and their victims from survey of prisoners in state institutions (Beck et al., 1993) cover both alcohol and drugs. TLC (Richardson, 1978) and EMIT (Wish, 1986) laboratory assay data cover drug but not alcohol use among arrestees. Victim perception data from the National Crime Victimization Survey (Bureau of Justice Statistics, 1994) cover both alcohol and drug use by offenders, but not by victims; NCVS data on "aggravated" and "simple" assault extrapolated and collapsed. Data on offender perceptions of drug or alcohol influence in victim or in either/both victim and/or offender from Bureau of Justice Statistics survey of convicted offenders (Beck et al, 1993).

& Hirschi (1994), which sees criminal behavior as essentially predatory, opportunistic, and hedonistic.

In the next chapter, which focuses on the social envelope that surrounds criminal violence, we shall inspect at closer range data on victimization in violent crime and on social contexts which elicit, foster, or encourage aggressive behavior. For our present purposes, it suffices to observe that these data accord with biochemical credibility in portraying neuroactive substance use as a lubricating factor in criminal violence — but not only among offenders, not in isolation from other factors, and not rectilinearly. Indeed, we shall later propose that mutual use of neuroactive substance constitutes a standard feature of those tinder-box environments in which violent behavior is both the norm and normative.

Alcohol and/or drug use as lubricants in aggressive criminal violence

Though data from studies with variant modes of inquiry fail to differentially identify the contribution made by alcohol or by drugs of various sorts to criminal offenses arrayed by category, there is reasonable coherence with respect to aggressive crimes of violence (homicide, sexual assault, assault). In Figure 3.2, we have assembled the relevant data drawn from self-report studies of prisoners concerning their own use of drugs and/or alcohol, from laboratory assay studies concerning drug-positive rates among violent crime arrestees, from National Crime Victimization Survey information on the perceptions of victims on whether their assailants were "under the influence," and from prisoners' perceptions of the relative incidence at which drugs or alcohol influenced either or both themselves or their victims.

To be optimally useful to a theory of the genesis of crime, research on drug use or abuse among offenders should first establish *whether* substance use functions as engine, lubricant, or motive, and, optimally, *in relation to which crimes*. The relevant data do not permit such inflected inferences. Indeed, the acquisition of controlled dangerous substances through the proceeds of robbery or of property crime more convincingly portrays drugs as "motive" than as "engine" in respect of those offenses.

But, in the aggregate, the data suggest that alcohol or substance abuse by the offender contributes to violent crime across subcategories and that the situation in which both victim and offender are "under the influence" is reported by offenders to be modal in virtually every subcategory. We may conclude that the presence of biochemical substances with mood-altering properties in the physical system of *either or both* the offender or the victim lubricates criminal violence with relatively high incidence — as indeed apparently all criminal behavior regardless of inflection.

Alcohol and drug abuse in the general population

In an extensive review of the survey research conducted with stratified samples representative of the adult population of the nation (and relying on self-reports supplied by respondents), Polich & Kaelber (1985, 61) concluded that 75% of the adult men and 60% of the adult women in the nation consume beverage alcohol. Of these, a "high level of alcohol-related problems" (i.e., adverse psychosocial consequences) is found among 15% of the male consumers and 4% of the female consumers. Kolb & Gunderson (1985) estimate that approximately 20% of alcohol users can be expected to develop other serious mental disorders concomitantly with, or as the result of, such use.

On the basis of the Polich & Kaelber figures, a base rate for "psychosocial problems" associated with alcohol use among the general population can be calculated by syllabicating proportions. Thus, the base rate is projected at 11.25% (i.e., 15% of the 75% of adult males who use alcohol) among men and at 2.4% (4% of the 60% of adult females who use alcohol) among women. If one applies the estimates of Kolb & Gunderson (1985), the base rate among men would be calculated at 15% (i.e., 20% of 75%) and among women at 12% (i.e., 20% of 60%). On the basis of similar calculations, Hartman (1988, 160) estimates that there are 9,000,000 "problem drinkers" in the United States.

The proportions that result from these calculations, however, substantially exceed that in the National Institute of Mental Health Epidemiological Catchment Area studies, in which Burke & Regier (1988, 82) reported that 4.7% of the nearly 19,000 subjects surveyed by means of the NIMH Diagnostic Interview Schedule were categorized as suffering from "alcohol abuse/dependence" disorders.

The consumption of controlled dangerous substances itself constitutes criminal behavior, so that self-reports of the use of such substances itself constitutes an admission of illegality (Burke & Regier, 1988, 88). Nonetheless, a National Household Survey on Drug Abuse conducted by the National Institute on Drug Abuse (1987, 10-25, 30-33, 46-49), based on a stratified sample of households representative of those in the nation, reports that 33% of respondents over the age of 12 admitted to the use of marijuana at least once in their lives, 12% to the use of cocaine, 7% to the use of hallucinogens, 9% to the use of stimulants, and 86% to the use of alcohol, with these categories not mutually exclusive. There is no strong basis for an estimate regarding perpetuation of drug use (or, in the case of these surveys, perhaps only "experimentation") into serious drug-induced mental disorders, but, if anything, the effects of psychotomimetic substances like cocaine on brain functioning are physically more devastating than those of alcohol.

In a review of the relatively small number of studies that have followed longitudinally subjects who reported use of controlled dangerous substances at least once, Croughan (1985, 97) reports that "dependence" followed such use at ratios ranging from 2% to 10%. If we apply the higher ratio reported by Croughan to the proportion of the population that admitted to "ever" having used marijuana, the most frequently used of the several substances covered in the NIDA survey (and, in the process, make the rather questionable assumption that equally serious sequelae follow experimentation with any controlled dangerous substance, regard-less of biochemistry), one projects that, at most, the incidence of drug-induced mental disorders in the general population is 3%. That proportion is very close to the figure in the National Institute of Mental Health Epidemiological Catchment Area studies, in which Burke & Regier (1988, 82) reported that some 2% were categorized as suffering "drug abuse/dependence" disorders.

In studies of the epidemiology of drug and alcohol use in the general population, mere "involvement" with the police or the courts on whatever charge (including possession of controlled dangerous substances, driving while intoxicated, etc.) is held to be indicative of "serious" problems associated with substance use. By that standard, commission of a crime (no less than apprehension and prosecution therefor) not associated with substance use while "under the influence" is most assuredly indicative of "serious'" problems consequent to such use. When applied to offenders:

- According to extrapolations from national data concerning alcohol consumption and the likelihood of serious problems attendant thereupon, the incidence of serious problems attendant upon alcohol consumption can be expected to vary among males in the range between 11.25% and 15%. Applying the same standard to correctional populations, the Bureau of Justice Statistics self-report data (Beck et al., 1993) on convicted offenders recapitulated earlier suggest an incidence among convicted violent offenders between one and a half and two times as great as that in the general population.
- According to extrapolations from national data concerning drug use and the likelihood of serious problems consequent thereto, the incidence of consequent serious problems can be expected to approximate 3%. Applying the same standard to offender populations, Bureau of Justice Statistics self-report data suggest an incidence among convicted violent offenders approximately four times that to be expected in the general population, and laboratory assay studies suggest an incidence among arrestees for violent offenses between 15 and 20 time as great as that found in the general population.

Withal, there are both biochemical and statistical-epidemiological reasons to believe that alcohol and/or substance abuse is contributory to violent crime, though it seems equally clear that criminal violence cannot be attributed to alcohol or drugs without considering a variety of modulating factors. And it is equally clear that, biochemical credibility notwithstanding, substance use/abuse is related to criminal behavior virtually generically rather than differentially.

NEUROTOXINS AND NEUROACTIVE INFLUENCES IN THE ENVIRONMENT

Beyond alcohol and those drugs which have been formally denominated "controlled dangerous substances," a number of other biochemical substances have been linked, sometimes in clinical reports and sometimes in carefully designed experimental studies, to the emission of violent behavior, or, in some cases, to the inhibition of violent behavior. In the main, the relevant studies suggest that these substances potentiate extant neurologic and neuropsychological dysfunctions.

Anabolic steroids

The clinical literature contains many reports of impulsive rage leading to murder attributable either to freely available over-the-counter substances the sales of which are not regulated or to combinations of controlled and uncontrolled substances. Thus, Pope & Katz (1990) recounted three cases examined at Boston's McLean Hospital "who impulsively committed violent crimes, including murder, while taking anabolic steroids," substances then freely available at health food stores as "body-building" dietary supplements. According to the investigators, all had "benign premorbid psychiatric histories, no evidence of antisocial personality disorder, and no history of violence."

Conacher & Workman (1989) similarly reported cases of homicide in which the use of anabolic steroids by the young adult perpetrators "played a necessary, if not primary, role in the etiology of the violent behavior." In each case, there was no history of criminal violence, nor of antisocial personality disorder; the crimes were committed impulsively. Moss, Panzak & Tarter (1992) administered a series of psychometric instruments to male body builders who did or did not use anabolic steroids, reporting that "current users scored higher than nonusers only on psychometric scales measuring hostility [and] aggression." It is reasonable to conclude that the aggression-inducing effects of steroids are dose-dependent and relatively readily reversible.

Until Spring 1991, when the defense of "roid [i.e., steroid-induced] rage" became a favorite topic for the tabloid television programs that specialize in the "re-enactment" of lurid criminal violence, anabolic steroids were freely available at health food stores as dietary supplements to stimulate weight gain and had become especially popular among gymnasts concerned with "body building" and, although not permitted by most codes of competition, by both amateur and professional athletes. These substances also have legitimate medical uses in the treatment of underweight children. But they achieve their effect precisely by altering naturally-occurring endocrinological processes, so that whatever propensity for violence is unleashed by their use is to be attributed to deliberately-induced (though perhaps unintended) neurochemical anomaly. Anabolic steroids have now been placed on the roster of "controlled substances" by the Federal Food and Drug Administration.

Formaldehyde

Formaldehyde is a chemical compound used in manufacturing fertilizers, dyes, and embalming fluids. Among workers for whom formaldehyde exposure is an occupational risk, the neuropsychological sequelae include dizziness, loss of balance, impairment and concentration, and memory deficit (Hartman, 1988, 258-259). In aqueous solutions, formaldehyde is used as a preservative and disinfectant and is widely available from housewares and garden supply outlets.

Among the "designer drugs" constructed of commonly-available ingredients whose sale or purchase is not regulated but which are deliberately intended to mimic the effect of controlled dangerous substances, formaldehyde-soaked cigarette tobacco had become by 1990 commonplace. It is ingested by inhalation of smoke from a formaldehyde-soaked home-rolled cigarette (typically called "Love Boat") and produces an intense, psychotomimetic "high" resembling the effect of cocaine inhalation, but of much briefer duration. Once ingested by smoking, the substance emerges as aldehyde dehyrogenase or aldehyde reducatase, metabolites which interfere with the catabolism of the ubiquitous neurotransmitter norepinepherine. There have been clinical reports of aggressive violence attributable to Love Boat, including cases of attempted murder.

Industrial toxins

Hall (1989) found evidence at autopsy both of cadmium and lead, powerful neurotoxins, in a mass murderer who killed himself but who had previously been a rather quiet and law-abiding citizen, leading to the conclusion that "immunotoxic biochemical pathology due to heavy metal poisoning affected inhibitory control mechanisms."

Ingestion of lead through skin absorption or through breathing represents an occupational hazard for many workers, associated with symptoms such as agitation, anger, depression, and cognitive impairment (Hartman, 1988, 70-85), all of which individually or in interaction may be implicated in specific cases of aggressive violence.

For a time in the early 1980s, lead (often ingested by infants in the form of paint chips flaking from the ceilings of uncared for apartment buildings in urban ghettoes) was posited as a principal factor in later mental deficiency (Needleman, 1983, 1989), as a result of which the Federal Centers for Disease Control decreased the established standards for "safe" (non-toxic) levels of exposure to lead. But, as a result of challenges to the initial research, the matter remains unsettled.

Valciukas (1991) discusses at length a large variety of other chemicals used in industrial and manufacturing processes, including pesticides, which, alone or in combination with other substances, may be implicated in violent behavior, along with technical matters relating to exposure, dosage, metabolism, biotransformation, and secretion (i.e., the pharmacodynamics and pharmacokinetics of these substances).

Lithium transported by air

Lithium is a naturally-occurring (rather than synthesized) chemical element (a "light metal") used industrially in the manufacture of certain lubricants, special glasses, and ceramic glazes. Lithium's psychoactive properties have been known since the 1870s (Olfson, 1987). It produces a variety of effects which tend to calm or tranquilize manic or impulsive behavior. In precise chemical interaction with carbon dioxide, it has become (as the compound lithium carbonate) the medication-of-choice in the treatment of manic-depressive schizophrenia (Feldman & Quenzer, 1984, 395-397).

As a light metal, lithium is frequently released into the atmosphere during mining operations, and it is transportable through natural means, such as wind and rain. It is often found in minor concentrations in shale and can be released into the atmosphere in "trace" amounts through such processes as oil exploration. Once released, it can be transported to far distant locations, where it may settle into unsuspected receptor substances.

Because lithium may have toxic effects at high concentrations should it settle in drinking water supplies, some states in which the incidence of oil exploration or other mining operations is high have adopted legislatively or administratively the requirement that levels of lithium concentration (as well as the concentration of other air-borne substances that may yield toxic effects) be monitored on a regular basis. Should concentrations reach toxic levels, the responsible municipal authority is required to purify the water supply and/or to maintain a non-toxic alternate supply.

Thus, Dawson, Moore & McGanity (1972) studied the concentration of lithium in the water supplies of 200 Texas counties (induced ''naturally'' through rainfall coincident with its release into the atmosphere as a by-product of oil exploration, rather than added artificially in the manner of fluoridation) at levels below the toxic threshold in relation to state psychiatric hospital admissions, suicides, and homicides. They found that the higher the rate of naturally-transported lithium in the water supply, the lower the rate of homicide as well as of suicide, of violent behavior generally, and of psychiatric hospital admissions;

and, in what must surely be interpreted as an Orwellian proposal, recommended that "any community should derive prophylactic benefit from lithium ingestion with respect to . . . homicidal tendencies."

Adoption of such a proposal carries some downside risks, however, for later research demonstrated that heavy concentrations of lithium (or what might be called "overdoses") induce a variety of organically-based psychiatric disorders (Dubovsky, 1987; Perry, 1987; Hartman, 1988, 210-211). Just such a scenario (involving both the addition of a lithium-like substance to the municipal water supply in a Southern town and an epidemic of florid psychotic symptoms) undergirds *The Thanatos Syndrome* (1987), the final work of fiction by the late psychiatrist Walker Percy [NOTE 3].

Schrauzer & Shreshta (1990) replicated and extended the investigation on a smaller sample of Texas counties. Analyzing data over a nine-year period for 27 counties, they found an inverse relationship between lithium concentration levels (again, well below the toxic threshold) and the rates of homicide, suicide, and sexual assault; over a five-year period, they found the same inverse relationship between lithium concentration levels and the incidence of arrests for possession of opium, cocaine, and related illicit drugs. These investigators were also able to identify the concentration levels (between 70 and 170 micrograms per liter) at which lithium is associated with decreases in criminal aggression.

Nicotine

Nicotine is a central nervous system stimulant that enhances concentration, attention, and short-term memory and, at high dosages, to elicit or increase anxiety in both human and animal subjects (McGehee, Heath, Gelber, Devay & Role, 1995). There is some, but not definitive, evidence that it stimulates central nervous system arousal ("readiness to fight") states (Feldman & Quenzer, 1984, 146-148), likely by accelerating the transmission of "excitatory" neural transmission.

In a short paper that does not essay the neuropsychopharmacology implicated, Lester (1977) found that, among a wide array of variables investigated in a multivariate analysis of correlates of homicide in a sample of 18 industrialized nations, per capita cigarette consumption was a potent predictor of homicide rate among women (but not among men). Nonetheless, McGehee and his colleagues (loc. cit.) doubt that the concentrations of nicotine in the central nervous system that are attributable to even very high consumption of tobacco products via cigarette smoking are sufficient to account for major alterations in arousal level. But it may be the case that nicotine is consumed simultaneously with other CNS-active substances, whether other stimulants (e.g., caffeine) or depressants (e.g., alcohol), also at high dosages.

"Tobacco dependence" was included among substance abuse disorders in the Third Edition of the American Psychiatric Association's *Diagnostic and Statistical Manual of Mental Disorders* published in 1980; in subsequent editions, the term "nicotine dependence" has been substituted, while the ICD classification employs the more benign term "harmful use of tobacco." In December 1994, the American Psychiatric Association issued a position paper on nicotine dependence that focuses on the medical sequelae to the consumption of tobacco rather than on the behavioral consequences associated with the psychoactive effects of nicotine.

Over-the-counter pharmaceuticals

Strauss (1989) reported the case of a man aged 27 who had "used both cocaine and an over-the-counter cold preparation. The combination of drugs resulted in a psychosis that led to the homicide of a close friend . . . [the offender] had no psychiatric history and only minor legal difficulties." Such a case presents many interesting legal challenges; doubtless the psychological state induced by drug interaction constituted a brief psychotic reaction, rather than the induction of psychosis itself, or perhaps what Anneliese Pontius of the Harvard Medical School (1987, 1989) terms "psychotic trigger reaction" attributable to "seizure-like episodes" in the limbic system.

Refined sugar

Schoenthaler (1982, 1983-a-d) has argued forcefully that aggressive behavior can be reduced among institutionalized juvenile delinquents, including repetitive violent offenders, as a direct result of the simple dietary manipulation of reducing intake in refined sugar — primarily by substituting unsweetened orange juice for sugar-laden soda and/or fruit for heavily processed snack foods. If such results occur under confinement or under highly controlled conditions, it may be the case that violent behavior can be deterred through dietary manipulation.

In a study that examined the obverse hypothesis, Rosen, Booth, Bender, McGrath, Sorrell & Drabman (1988) added small amounts of sugar to the diet of preschool and elementary children, reporting "small increases in the children's activity level" (and decrements in cognitive performance among girls) among experimental subjects in relation to controls fed a sugar substitute. Similarly, Kruesi, Rapoport, Cummings & Berg (1987) reported that "duration of aggression against property" was significantly associated with ingestion of sugar, but not of a sugar substitute, among preschool children.

On the basis of studies such as these, it was proposed during the 1980s that either the intake of refined sugar or dysfunctions in its abnormal metabolism (hypoglycemia or hyperglycemia) underlay most cases of hyperactivity in childhood. However, in their massive review of the relevant research, Fishbein &

Pease (1994) concluded that "It appears that some children, both hyperactive and nonhyperactive will exhibit an unusual reaction to some food, including sugar... However, the majority of subjects tested to date are not drastically affected by the presence of sucrose in their diets."

Thunderstorms and nitrogen narcosis

In a study of a wide range of variables in relation to rate of criminal homicide in 18 industrialized nations, Lester (1977) reported that the number of thunderstorm-days per year emerged as the second most potent predictor (after per-capita cigarette consumption) in a multivariate equation. Though he essayed no causative linkage, it is likely that the nexus is neurochemical.

Thunderstorms release vast quantities of nitrogen into the atmosphere; it is not unreasonable to conjecture that such rapid infusion may well trigger episodes of nitrogen narcosis, "a condition resembling acute alcohol intoxication" (Berkow & Fletcher, 1992, 2528). Nitrogen narcosis is an occupational health hazard among persons whose work subjects them to rapid changes in atmospheric pressure (e.g., pilots of high-altitude aircraft, deep sea divers). Moreover, an extraordinary number of "conversions" during or immediately after thunderstorms have been recorded in the history of religion, and it may be that nitrogen narcosis constitutes an underlying neurochemical mechanism for such quasi-hallucinatory experiences (Pallone & Hennessy, 1994-95).

In a remarkable experiment at the behaviorial neuroendocrinology laboratory at Johns Hopkins, Nelson, Demas, Huang et al. (1995) artificially suppressed the brain mechanisms in mice that regulate the production of nitric oxide, a compound composed of equal parts of nitrogen and oxygen that functions as a neurotransmitter in certain regions of the brain particularly concerned with agression and sexual behavior. In analyses of "inter-male aggression in an intruder-resident model," the experimenters reported an increase in "offensive attack, biting, wrestling, and chasing," along with brutally aggressive sexual behavior toward females, that ranged from four-fold to six-fold in comparison both with laboratory-raised and with "wild" mice with normal capacities to produce and metabolize nitric oxide, such that "the [altered] animals display a marked increase in inappropriate aggressive and sexual behaviour reflected in persistent fighting and mounting behaviour despite obvious signals of surrender or disinterest, respectively." Nelson and his coworkers opine that nitric oxide "may be a major mediator of sexual and aggressive behaviours relevant for studies of their biological determination in humans and well as mice."

Nitrous oxide is a compound of two parts nitrogen and one part oxygen originally synthesized in the early 19th century which, when inhaled, produces both euphoria and intoxication. Familiar as "laughing gas," it is used as a mild anesthetic in dentistry and surgery and also is used in the production of such pressurized foods as "instant" whipped cream. Sold in cannisters under pressure in gourmet food stores, the compound has become a substance of abuse, particularly among adolescents seeking a chemically-induced state of euphoria.

Data from the social sciences produce correlative evidence of a linkage between a naturally-occurring phenomenon (thurnderstorms) and behavioral consequences. Data from the neurosciences suggest that dysfunctions in the capacity to process atmospheric nitrogen may constitute the underlying bio-chemical explanation. The situation constitutes a principal exemplar of why social science data alone constitute an insufficient basis for the understanding of aggressive behavior.

Tryptophan

Tryptophan is an amino acid that affects the metabolism of brain serontinin, a powerful neurotransmitter and neural regulator. Until 1990, when its sale came under the control of the Federal Food & Drug Administration, tryptophan was freely available as a dietary substance in health food stores, where it was billed as "nature's tranquilizer." As we have seen, one current hypothesis on the genesis of disorders of affect attributes their source to functional deficiencies in the metabolism of a tryptophan by-product (Martin, Owen & Morisha, 1987). Tryptophan ingestion affects the body's production of dietary niacin; niacin deficiency produces such behavioral sequelae as "malaise, poor concentration, nervousness, irritability, emotional lability, and depression" (Gross, 1987). The substance is found in corn, so that "dietary niacin deficiency is common in areas of the world where corn is a dietary staple."

Thus, Mawson & Jacobs (1978) studied the relationship between annual consumption of corn, measured in bushels per capita, and homicide rates across 45 nations of the world; consumption and homicide were found to vary inversely. Kitahara (1986) replicated the Mawson & Jacobs study, with essentially simi-larly findings of linkages between low levels of tryptophan consumption and high homicide rates when socioeconomic variables were used to equate a sample of 18 nations in Western and Southern Europe.

As if to provide a clinical extension, Morand, Young & Ervin (1983) adminis-tered oral tryptophan (or a placebo) to a sample of male schizophrenics who had been convicted of violent crimes — with the expected tranquilizing results, but without inquiry into the etiology of the violent behavior of which their subjects had been convicted. Even in infra-human studies (Feldman & Quenzer, 1984, 249), a metabolite of tryptophan has been linked to *intra-species* aggression. In a carefully controlled experimental study at McGill University, Benkelfat, Ellen-bogen, Dean, Palmour & Young (1994) artificially depleted plasma tryptophan among male subjects in the 18-30 age range, observing a virtually uniform depression of mood to clinically significant levels. At the University of London's

Institute of Psychiatry, Cleare & Bond (1994) essentially replicated the experimental procedure, observing a virtually uniform increase in aggressivity, with the effect particularly strong among subjects with "pre-existing aggressive traits."

NEUROCHEMICAL LUBRICANTS OF AGGRESSIVE VIOLENCE

There is ample evidence of linkages between the use or abuse of alcohol and other mood-altering substances and aggressive violence. Acute effects of some powerful psychotomimetic substances are linked in the clinical literature, indeed, to the *elicitation* of violence by some behavers for whom such violence seems out of character and otherwise unpredictable. A vast array of empirical data suggests a potentiating effect even in cases in which elicitation is not in question. In particular, nearly half the convicted offenders confined in state prisons for sexual assault and 60% to 70% of those confined for homicide, assault, or robbery reported the influence of neuroactive substances as a contributing factor in their offenses. Given such data, the continuing wide availability of alcohol quite legally (Dull & Giacopassi, 1988) and of controlled dangerous substances despite more than half a century of recurrent "wars on drugs" may itself constitute an element of the social environment that favors violence.

Though the biochemistry of alcohol and the several classes of neuroactive substances in relation to aggressive behavior is well understood scientifically, the cumulative research evidence does not permit the inflection of differential contributions to violent and non-violent crime by category or by biochemical properties of specific substances. Nonetheless, the aggregate data suggest that alcohol and/or substance use (or abuse) lubricates a large proportion of aggressive violent crime in each subcategory (homicide, sexual assault, assault) — but not rectilinearly, not in isolation, and most potently when both victim and offender are "under the influence," or perceived by the offender to be so. The demographic and cultural characteristics of social contexts which, by favoring or fostering the latter conditions, contribute to tinder-box situations are discussed in the next chapter.

NOTES

1. In addition to psychotherapeutic and self-help (Alcoholics Anonymous) treatment for excessive alcohol consumption, pharmacological treatment has been limited until recently to the use of Disulfarim (Antabuse®), a chemical antagonist to alcohol which, when ingested while alcohol is still present in the bloodstream, produces intense physical discomfort. As Berkow & Fletcher (1992, 1554-1555) describe both the pharmacology and the phenomenology, "Disulfiram interferes with the metabolism of acetaldehyde (an intermediary product in the oxidation of alcohol) so that acetaldehyde accumulates, producing toxic symptoms and great discomfort. Drinking alcohol within 12 h after taking disulfiram produces facial flushing in 5 to 15 min, then intense vasodilation of the face and neck with suffusion of the conjunctivae, throbbing headache, tachycardia, hyperpnea, and sweating. Nausea and vomiting follow in 30 to 60 min and may be so intense as to lead to hypotension, dizziness, and sometimes fainting and collapse. The reaction lasts 1 to 3 h. Discomfort is so intense that few patients will risk taking alcohol as long as they are taking disulfiram." Clearly, this method of pharmacologic treatment constitutes an "aversive" regimen. During the early 1990s, a pharmacotherapeutic regimen based on Naltrexone hydrochloride, a substance originally used as a chemical antagonist for opioids in the treatment of "hard core" narcotics addiction, has been used successfully as an alternate (O'Malley, Jaffe, Chang, Shottenfeld et al., 1992; Volpicelli, Alterman, Hayashida & O'Brien, 1992; Swift, Whelihan, Kuznetsov, Buongiorno & Hsuing, 1994).

2. Skog & Waahlberg's (1989) *Alcohol and Drugs: The Norwegian Experience* contains several instructive papers detailing that nation's social control policies from the Middle Ages onward. Among the varied options that relatively small (in population) and geographically compact nation has attempted in this century to control alcohol use and abuse are prohibition, government monopoly, and dissuasive pricing that virtually converts to a system of rationing. In contrast to data from the U.S. (Combs-Orme, 1983), relatively strong correlations are reported between the annual incidence of episodes of aggressive criminal violence and alcohol consumption per capita over the half-century between 1930 and 1980. The net outcome of these rather stringent policies has been to increase "black market" production and consumption.

In a similar vein, Mark Moore of the Kennedy School of Government at Harvard has argued (1995, 194) that, in the U.S., "current drug control policies *increase* rather than reduce crime . . . Because current policies outlaw the manufacture, distribution, possession and use of various drugs, they create criminal offenses where none previously existed. And because a black market . . . has arisen, some violence has been created by our control policies. In effect, we could reduce crime by *decreasing* rather than increasing the stringency of controls . . ."

3. A scenario in which lithium (or a substance very like it) is introduced into the water supply without the knowledge or consent of the citizenry became the nub of Walker Percy's 1987 *The Thanatos Syndrome*, a marvel of irony and comic genius that takes as its theme no less than the conflict between the heavily biological means of mood alteration and behavior control emphasized in the mental health professions today and yesterday's emphasis on the gentle art of "the talking cure."

In Percy's rendition, those responsible are high-level Federal scientists — acting quite beyond their warrants, however. Moreover, though the substance produces the anticipated decrease in aggressive behavior, it also elicits retrogressive tendencies, with macabrely picaresque consequences, including the wholesale sexual molestation of children. Into this morass to save the day and restore the community to its usual, aggressive, but relatively more predictable, self returns Percy's hero — an alcoholic psychiatrist recently released from prison after serving a term for defrauding health insurance companies.

4 SOCIAL AND DEMOGRAPHIC POTENTIATORS OF CRIMINAL AGGRESSION

THIS CHAPTER FOCUSES ON SOCIAL VARIABLES THAT POTENTIATE NEUROLOGIC dysfunctions in the equation that yields aggressive criminal violence: the demography of victimization and of offending and their mutual social context, with special emphasis on the determinants of a pervasive subculture of violence that elicits, encourages, or reinforces behavioral pathogens that drive aggression.

APPLYING THE TECHNIQUES OF EPIDEMIOLOGY

In their report on the work of a National Academy of Sciences' panel on the control of violent behavior, Reiss & Roth (1993) highlighted the identification of "risk factors" as a necessary step in improving "causal understanding and preventive interventions." Application of the techniques of medical and psychiatric epidemiology to the broadest sets of relevant data depicting offenses as they are actually committed should permit us to determine with tolerable accuracy who is "at risk" for victimization and for offending in aggressive criminal violence.

Expressed somewhat simplistically, the overarching twin goals in medical epidemiology are to determine the means by which the pathogens responsible for physical disease (or illness) are transmitted and to identify those groups who are particularly "at risk" to contract "target" diseases, most frequently by contrasting the relative incidence with which the target disease is found in a group differentiated according to demographic (or sometimes behavioral) characteristics and in the population at large. In the first case, medical epidemiology relies on the investigative methods of the biological sciences and, in the second, on those of the social sciences. Such epidemiological investigations are generally preparatory to the energizing of public health efforts to control the spread of illness or disease, through what is usually called "preventive medicine," in which focus is frequently placed on convincing those "at risk" to avoid pathogens, contaminants, or other agents that favor the spread of a target disease.

At the level of the control of illness or disease, the development of a statistical portrait of members of those groups empirically determined to be at particular risk for (or, in the more familiar terminology associated with infectious medical disorders, "susceptible to") particular diseases is paramount, with risk determined largely by the over-representation of one or another group with identifiable characteristics among those infected. "Risk markers" may be found to inhere in genetic or constitutional predisposition, environmental influences (e.g., exposure to toxins), and/or "lifestyle" variables [NOTE 1]. Especially in the case of infectious disease, particular attention is given to environmental variables that either give rise to, or support the spread of, the pathogens responsible for the target disease. Medical epidemiology is also concerned with why some people are resistant (or "auto-immune") to the spread of infectious disease, while others are particularly at risk, or are *differentially* at risk, for one sort of illness but not another.

A current example which has engaged both medical epidemiologists and public health officials, no less than energized the public, is the control of acquired immune deficiency syndrome, both by stemming its spread in the population (largely through efforts to convince members of "at risk" groups to alter their behavior) and by developing pharmacologic agents which will eradicate pathogens in the environment and/or alter the course of the disease once contracted.

Analogously, the goal in psychiatric epidemiology has been to identify those groups statistically at greatest risk for mental and emotional disorders of various sorts (Srole et al., 1962, 1986; Mechanic, 1980, 54-72; Pallone, 1991, 13-56) in relation to a variety of external stressors and/or other predictive factors, including genetic markers and neurologic and neuropsychological dysfunctions and anomalies. A current example is the effort to identify those persons who are at risk interfamilily and/or intergenerationally for alcoholism and, again, the preventive measures pivot largely on efforts to convince "at risk" groups to alter their behavior and to avoid "exposure" to behavioral contagion by foregoing participation in social contexts which favor alcohol consumption, perhaps most economically expressed in the pivotal injunction in the Alcoholics Anonymous credo to "change people, places, and things."

Methodologically, the earliest epidemiologic investigations in mental health and illness typically merely enumerated the diagnoses assigned to successive admittees to psychiatric hospitals or to other mental health service facilities (Lemaku, 1961), with the obvious limitations in respect of non-patients. Such an investigative approach is perhaps analogous, in the present context, to an enumeration of offenses reported by "known" victims. Other investigators (e.g., Pasamanick, 1962) selected random, stratified samples representative of the community, then undertook careful, professional diagnostic evaluations of subjects, in effect replicating the formal differential diagnostic process.

Today, however, largely as a result of the efforts of the National Institute of Mental Health in standardizing practices in what is increasingly termed "mental health census taking," psychiatric epidemiologic studies are conducted in the community at large (often on a door-to-door basis) by trained interviewers utilizing interview schedules comprised of questions about symptoms of mental illness and relying principally or exclusively on self-reports of respondents. The resulting data lack the specificity of formal diagnoses, even when responses are screened post-hoc by trained clinicians, but this method has the enormous advantage of uncovering previously "undetected" cases of mental disorder (Shrout, Lyons, Dohrenwend et al., 1988; Weissman, Myers & Ross, 1986). Such efforts are directed primarily toward the identification of "at risk" groups; identification of the pathogens responsible for the disorders enumerated in census-taking, however, may pivot largely on fundamental research in the basic neurosciences and in personality and social psychology.

TOWARD AN EPIDEMIOLOGY OF VICTIMIZATION

Victimology, the study of characteristics of victims of crime, has become a recognized specialty in sociology and criminology (Karmen, 1990; Fattah, 1991, 1993), although, like the early studies in psychiatric epidemiology which investigated the characteristics of persons "known" to be mentally disordered because they were patients in treatment, many studies have investigated only "known" victims. Only rarely have the techniques developed and refined in the census-taking function in medical and psychiatric epidemiology been frankly applied to the analysis of the incidence of criminal offending and victimization by seeking to discern the characteristics of those persons who are "at risk" for criminal violence (Jason, 1984; Farrington, 1987; Pallone & Hennessy, 1992, 133-135), whether as victim or offender. Application of these techniques can be expected to illuminate the demography of aggressive criminal violence.

Census-taking: The National Criminal Victimization Surveys

In essence, the National Criminal Victimization Surveys (NCVS) conducted by the Bureau of Justice Statistics since 1973 constitute an ongoing "census" of criminal victimization, in a manner parallel to the household surveys in psychiatric epidemiology. Collectively, they represent the studies of largest scale in victimology [NOTE 2].

As we observed earlier, the NCVS report published in 1994 covered a sample of 110,000 respondents aged 12 and older in 66,000 households in the nation selected to reflect the principal characteristics of the national population. Because of that scale and the exhaustive, enumerative character of the NCVS interview schedule, the resultant data provide a comprehensive foundation for an epidemiologic portrait of the victim of aggressive criminal violence.

Some caveats are in order as we inspect the data. Particularly because of the vast imbalance in the national population between the races [NOTE 3] and because we necessarily focus on proportions rather than absolute numbers, it is easy to misconstrue the data unless we bear in mind that, during the period under review, whites comprised 85% of the population aged 12 and over (approximately 176 million persons), Blacks 11% (nearly 24 million), and members of "other" racial groups 4% (some 7 million). In the general population, then, whites outnumbered Blacks at a ratio of more than 7:1 and members of "other" racial groups at 25:1, while Blacks outnumbered "others" at more than 3:1. Similarly, women and girls constituted 51% of the population in the 1990 Census. If victimization (or offending) were gender- or race-neutral, one would expect to find an incidence in each approximating the distribution of the races and genders in the general population.

Moreover, respondents asserted that they had been victimized in some 6.9 million episodes of violent crime (in this case, sexual assault, assault, and robbery, but excluding homicide); during the same period, according to Uniform Crime Report data (Maguire & Pastore, 1994, 431), only 1.76 million episodes of violent crime (including homicide) had been reported to law enforcement authorities. Overall, NCVS data indicate that 50% of the crimes of violence covered in the survey had been reported (with but few differences between victims by race or gender), for an aggregate of some 3.5 million episodes.

But that proportion leaves a discrepancy between victims' assertions and Uniform Crime Report (UCR) data on the order of 1.75 million. It may be, of course, that offenses independently enumerated in the NCVS data (e.g., assault resulting in robbery, enumerated as two separate offenses) were collapsed into a single offense when formally reported and are thus represented only under the latter category in UCR data. Alternately, offenses enumerated under one rubric (e.g., verbal abuse categorized as "assault") in NCVS data may have been "down-graded" from "felony" to "misdemeanor" status (e.g., an episode of verbal abuse recorded as "harassment" rather than "assault") when reported to police. Or it may merely mean that NCVS operational definitions are substantially more elastic than those from which UCR data are derived; or all of the above may be operative. Such not insignificant considerations aside, as extrapolated and compressed, the massive NCVS data (Bureau of Justice Statistics, 1994) on victimization seem to suggest that:

- *Race is a potent marker in victimization in violent crime.* Blacks are at greater risk than whites or members of "other" racial groups by a ratio approximating nearly 2:1. The overall rate of victimization per 1000 of the population aged 12 and over for Blacks is 50.4 vs. 29.8 for whites and 23.7 for "others" (Ibid., 24). That rate is inflected by type of specific violent offense, with the ratio climbing to 3:1 in the case of sexual assault, where the rate is 15.6 among Blacks, 4.7 among whites, and 5.1 among "others."

- *Risk is inflected by gender as well as by race.* The rate of victimization in criminal violence among Black men is 63.0 per 1000 of the population vs. 36.2 among white men; among Black women, the rate is 40.0 and among white women 24.1 (Ibid., 25). Thus, Black men are at greater risk than white men by a ratio of 3.5:2 and Black women at a ratio of 3.3:1.

- *Victimization varies substantially with age and race.* The highest rate, 158.1 per 1000 of the population, is found among Black men aged 16-19, with the second highest, at 131.2 per 1000, among Black men aged 20-24. Contrasting rates for white men in the same age groups are 88.6 and 83.8, respectively, so that the Black-white ratio approximates 2:1 in the first case and 3:2 in the second (Ibid., 29). After peaking in late adolescence and early adulthood, rates of victimization decline rather sharply with age both among Blacks and whites and among men and women. In the 25-34 age group, for example, the rate among white men is 38.7, less than half that for the 20-24 age group, and among Black men, the rate is 55.7, approximately 40% that for their counterparts aged 20-24 (but still 140% that among same-aged white men). The lowest rates for victimization are found in respondents above the age of 65, but the Black-white differential continues at a ratio approximating 2:1 among men across races and at a ratio of 3:1 among women.

- *Socioeconomic status is a powerful determinant of victimization.* At the polar contrasts, the rate of victimization is 64.4 per 1000 of the population among persons with family incomes of less than $7500 per year, while the comparable figure among those with family incomes of $50,000 or more is 21.2, for a ratio of 3:1 (Ibid., 33). Similarly, formal educational attainment is related to victimization, with the racial differential once again in evidence. The highest rate, at 78.4 per 1000, is found among Blacks with three or fewer years of high school education; for whites the comparable figure is 41.5, so that the ratio approximates 2:1. At an orthogonal contrast, the rate of victimization among whites with college degrees is 20.1, or half that among whites with three or fewer years of high school, but the comparable figure among similarly college-educated Blacks is 41.8 (again, approximately half that for those with less than a high school education), so that the 2:1 ratio differential again holds (Ibid., 36). Victimization also varies in relation to stability in personal residence (Ibid., 42), sometimes considered an index to socioeconomic status. At the polar contrasts, the rate is 18.5 per 1000 of the population for those who have lived in the same residence for five or more years, rising to 94.5 for those who have lived in their residences for six or fewer months (and may perhaps be regarded as "transients" on that account), at a ratio of 5:1.

- *Victimization is highest in large center cities, lowest in their suburbs, and varies by region of the country.* Among center city residents in major metropolitan areas, the rate of victimization is 39.7 per 1000 of the population, declining to 22.4 in the suburban area of the same cities, at a ratio of

1.75:1 (Ibid., 38-39). The confounds between race, educational attainment, and urban vs. suburban residence are so clear as to require no comment. Rates are highest in the Western states, at 44.4 per 1000, and lowest in the Northeastern states, at 23.3, at a ratio of nearly 2:1.

• *Prototypically, victimizations occur in physical spaces and environments that can be construed as "home turf" for the victim.* Overall 32% of victimizations in violent crime occur in, at, or near the victim's home or that of a friend or neighbor, with another 12% inside a school building or on school property, and 5% in parks or playgrounds (Ibid., 75). Collectively, these familiar environments are the sites for 49% of violent victimizations. Nearly half the remainder (24%) occur "on the street," but not near the victim's own home or that of a friend or relative, in what might be construed as "unfamiliar" environments. Geographically, 52% of all victimizations occur within a mile of the victim's home (Ibid., 81). Slightly more than half the episodes of violence against teachers or students within school buildings or on school grounds are committed by intruders rather than by members of the academic community associated with those schools (Toby, 1986, 1995).

Substance use/abuse by victims

We have already noted that the NCVS survey does not inquire into the state of sobriety of the victim during the victimization episode. But the studies of Budd (1982), Abel (1986, 1987, 1988), and Welte & Abel (1989), and most particularly the data from the Bureau of Justice Statistics study of prisoners in state correctional facilities, reviewed in Chapter 3, provide sufficient information to warrant the surmise that:

• *Substance use/abuse on the part of the victim may be differentially contributory to certain crimes of aggressive violence.* We have seen that 46% of the offenders imprisoned for homicide and 42% of those imprisoned for assault, but only 19% of those imprisoned for sexual assault, perceived their victims as "under the influence" of alcohol or drugs or both during the instant offense. Perhaps as pertinent are the perceptions of 70% of the homicide offenders, 68% of the assault offenders, and 47% of the sexual assault offenders that *either* their victims *or* they themselves *or both* were "under the influence." In some large measure, as we suggested earlier, it may be the *perception* on the part of the offender of the victim's insobriety (rendering him/her putatively more vulnerable) that constitutes the relevant variable.

Neuropathology among victims

There are no relevant large-scale data sets that speak to the relative incidence of neuropathology among *victims* of aggressive criminal violence. In the absence of specifically responsive data, there is no particular reason to believe that such incidence varies from that in the community at large (Chapter 2). However, we have seen that victimization varies with socioeconomic status, with residence in large center cities, and with race. These are the circumstances in which distinguished University of Chicago psychiatrist Carl Bell (1986) found the incidence of undetected and untreated head trauma to be substantially higher than in the population at large.

Also instructive is a major study conducted at Semmelweiss University, Budapest, that produced evidence of neurogenic impairment in the capacity to inhibit violent behavioral responses among homicide victims. In postmortem examinations of the brains of victims and of control subjects, Demeter, Tekes, Majorossy & Palkovitz (1988, 1989), found consistent morphological anomalies in brain structures involved in the metabolism of *serotonin*, so that the behavior-inhibiting effect of that substance was compromised among *victims*. That finding is particularly pertinent when juxtaposed to data on the incidence of neuropathology among offenders reviewed in Chapter 2.

The "victimization quotient"

Typically, studies by social statisticians and victimologists have been primarily descriptive, with little examination of the extent to which data on offending or victimization covary with even gross social indices relevant to the structural characteristics of locales, cities, regions, or subcultural and even ethnic envelopes. Descriptive data are often reported in uninflected, aggregate terms. For example, during "scare" campaigns, local law enforcement agencies may sponsor public service announcements which proclaim that "The crime of assault [or rape or burglary] occurs every X minutes in this jurisdiction," whether a specific city, county, or the nation.

What is omitted in this approach is the relative ratio between the actual *occurrences* and the *opportunities* for crime victimization to occur. In a city of 200,000, for example, there may occur annually 300 robberies — so that 0.15% of that city's population is victimized by robbery (providing, of course, that no citizen is victimized twice in the same year). With the proper extrapolations and the knowledge that a 365-day year contains 8760 hours, those figures can be interpreted to mean that one robbery occurs each 29 hours. But, in a city of 1,000,000, there may occur annually 900 robberies. In this case, only 0.09% of the population is victimized, even though the absolute number of robberies is three time greater than in the city of 200,000 and even though a robbery occurs ever 9.7 hours. The comparisons grow even more tenuous when very large cities, such as New York or Los Angeles, are compared with such smaller municipalities as, say, Colorado Springs or San Jose.

In a monographic analysis of these phenomena which avoids inconsistencies and misleading conclusions, Hennessy & Kepecs-Schlussel (1992) applied a psychometric methodology used widely in intelligence test scaling to data from the Uniform Crime Reports compiled by the Federal Bureau of Investigation concerning the number of crimes reported in each of the several subcategories for the 76 largest cities in the US — in effect, all cities whose populations exceeded 200,000 and which had participated in the UCR reporting program — with an aggregate population of some 48 million. In order to better understand the relative incidence of reported crime in jurisdictions whose populations vary substantially, these investigators devised a scale that effectively reduces disparate numbers to comparable units of measurement. Such a "transformation" procedure has routinely been employed in test development, particularly in aptitude and achievement measures, and is perhaps best exemplified by the several Wechsler scales for the measurement of intelligence.

In the first step, Hennessy & Kepecs-Schlussel computed the ratios between crimes reported in each major category (i.e., crimes of violence, further syllabicated as murder, rape, assault, robbery, arson, and property crimes, further syllabicated as larceny, burglary, motor vehicle theft) and population within the reporting jurisdiction. Ratios were also computed between the FBI's *crime index. total* and population.

Those ratios (one for each city for each category of crime and one for the total crime index for each city) were then converted to standard z score transformations, values which indicate the deviation of each ratio from the mean value for its category. By their nature, z distributions have a mean of zero and a standard deviation of +/-1.0. Thus, the transformation of each ratio to a z distribution allows for direct calculations of the relative differences and/or similarities in reported incidences across categories of crime and between cities. While virtually all statistical analyses operate at the level of z score analysis, these values may be difficult to interpret because of negative algebraic signs. Hence, it has become customary to further transform z scores to more "user-friendly" integers, typically through addition or multiplication by a constant. Hennessy & Kepecs-Schlussel transformed the z scores for each of their ratios into a scale score system comparable to that used to report subtest performance on the Wechsler intelligence measures — that is, scales that have means of 10 and standard deviation of 3. They also computed "quotients" for aggregated scale scores for crimes of violence, for property crimes, and for total crimes.

In their analysis (Ibid., 40-41), "quotients" indicating an incidence of crimes of violence greater than the mean by a full standard deviation or more were earned by Atlanta, Detroit, Dallas, Kansas City (Missouri), St. Louis, Cleveland, Newark (New Jersey), and Miami (in that order), while "quotients" indicative of an incidence less than the mean by a full standard deviation or more were earned by Virginia Beach, Mesa (Arizona), Honolulu, Colorado Springs, Arlington (Texas), Anchorage, San Jose (California), and Lexington (Kentucky). Quotients for crimes of violence and for property crimes were found to correlate at $r = +.64$ across the nation's 65 largest cities (Ibid., 60).

City structural characteristics and victimization in violent crime

Against these quotients, the investigators correlated Bureau of the Census data reflecting per capita expenditures in each city for all municipal services, per capita expenditures for police services, population density in number of residents per square mile, and proportion of minority (Black and Hispanic) residents in the population of each city (Ibid., 64-68).

The latter variable emerged as the most potent correlate of the overall "violence quotient," as well as of quotients for homicide, assault, and robbery and the overall quotient for property crimes, with r significant beyond p = .01 in each case. According to Bureau of the Census data, among the eight "most dangerous" cities in this study, the median proportion of racial minority population is 48%, while among the seven "safest" cities, the median proportion of racial minority population is 10%. Population density correlated significantly only with the quotient for robbery. Total expenditures for municipal services failed to correlate significantly with any index of crime victimization.

Determinants of police presence: Incidence of crime vs. the phenomenology of fear

In a finding that has major implications for crime control, and quite contrary to expectation, expenditures for police services covaried with quotients for homicide and for robbery (as well as for motor vehicle theft) — that is, the higher the expenditures for police services, the higher the quotients of victimization for these offenses. The initial analysis did not inquire into the relationship between expenditures for police services, the number of officers represented by such expenditures, or how officers are deployed (e.g., whether on patrol, in vehicles, on foot, or otherwise engaged).

Among the cities identified in the Hennessy & Kepecs-Schlussel monograph as having the highest quotients for crimes of violence, the mean number of police officers, according to Federal data (Infomerica, 1995), is 331 per 100,000 of the population; conversely, among the cities with the lowest quotients, the mean number of officers is 163, for a ratio of 2:1. One might expect higher crime rates to require some municipalities to maintain larger police forces, but that ratio suggests that the relative size of the police force apparently does not appreciably deter violent crime. For comparative purposes, we might note that the range varies from a low equated to 14 officers per 100,000 of the population (in the small, rural town of Goshen, New York) to a high of 1119 over the same conventional metric (in Atlantic City, trailed by Washington, D.C., with 756 for that metric).

In an effort to understand the apparent lack of deterrent effect, we correlated data represented by the same metric (number of officers per 100,000 of the population) for each of the 76 cities in the Hennessy & Kepecs-Schlussel sample with quotients these investigators reported for each subcategory of violent crime, for violent crimes in the aggregate, for property crimes in the aggregate, and with population density and the proportion of the population that is comprised by minority groups.

We might expect to find a converse relationship between the size of the police force, particularly when calibrated for population size, and the incidence of crime (Tauchen, Witte & Griesinger, 1994). Indeed just such an expectation underlay the principal component in the Federal crime control legislation of 1994. Instead, we found small-to-moderate but statistically significant relationships between the calibrated size of the force (using data for 1993) and the aggregate incidence of violent crime (at .38) and in three subcategories (at .52 for homicide, .29 for assault, .47 for robbery) and at .28 with the overall index of victimization, whether in property or violent crime. Overall, the data suggest that those cities which have lower rates of violent crime have smaller, not larger, police forces as calibrated in relation to population of the city. The correlation with indices for property crime and for sexual assault failed of significance. However, the correlation with population density (at .41) and with proportion of the population represented by minority groups (at .55) also reached significance.

Table 4.1: Stepwise multiple regression: Size of police force calibrated by population in the 76 largest cities in the U.S.

Variable	Multiple r	F	p
• Minority population proportion	.55	31.1	.001
• Population density per square mile	.64	24.5	.001
• Quotient for homicide	.67	18.2	.001

Superfluous/Redundant Variables

- Quotient for sexual assault
- Quotient for assault
- Quotient for robbery
- Quotient for aggregate violent crime
- Quotient for aggregate property crime

When we entered the same variables into a stepwise multiple regression analysis against calibrated police force size, the first variables to emerge were those representing minority population proportion and population density, in that order, followed by the quotient representing the rate of homicide; all other variables proved either redundant or superfluous. Results are indicated tabularly in Table 4.1. Were the incidence of crime the governing variable which drives the relative size of police agencies, we would expect the several quotients which reflect such incidence to emerge as potent variables in this analysis. Instead, the major contributor is the minority proportion of the population, followed by the density of the population; the only index of crime to be represented makes a rather minuscule contribution to variance. A jaundiced interpreter might conclude that, since the size of the police force apparently hinges upon whether a city has a high proportion of its minority citizens crammed into a densely populated geographic area, the driving force is the phenomenology of fear rather than the demography of victimization.

However that may be, the inference seems warranted that the relative size of the police force does not materially deter violent crime across the major population centers of the country. Thus, findings from the Hennessy & Kepecs-Schlussel study and further analyses add to the epidemiologic portrait of victimization by suggesting that:

- *Victimization in aggressive violence varies directly in relation to the racial composition of city of residence across the spectrum of crimes of violence.*
- *Victimization in violent crime is apparently not deterred by expenditures for police protection nor by a higher incidence of police officers in relation to total population.*

TOWARD AN EPIDEMIOLOGY OF AGGRESSIVE CRIMINAL OFFENDING

There is no source that mimics an enumerative census-taking function in respect of criminal offending in a manner analogous to the Federal victimization surveys. Indeed, given Constitutional guarantees against self-incrimination, a household survey on self-reported offending is virtually unthinkable. Instead, we must turn for very rough approximations to data on the characteristics of arrests as distilled from the FBI's Uniform Crime Reports and reported in the Bureau of Justice Statistics' *Sourcebook of Criminal Justice Statistics* (Maguire & Pastore, 1994), perceptions of victims recorded in NCVS reports (Bureau of Justice Statistics, 1993), and the self-reports of convicted offenders (Beck, Gilliard, Greenfeld et al., 1993) in the Bureau's survey of state prison inmates.

Gross data on violent crime

For purposes of perspective, we have assembled tabularly *Sourcebook* data (Maguire & Pastore, 1994, 363, 451) bearing upon the total number of crimes reported in each subcategory of offense classified under UCR rubrics as "violent" (including robbery, which we regard as a crime of greed rather than aggression), indicating the proportion of the total number of violent offenses and the total number of all (violent plus property) offenses represented by each category, along with the proportion in each category "cleared by arrest."

Violent crime represents only a quite minor proportion of all felony crime reported in a year. According to UCR reports, some 1.7 million episodes of violent crime are reported, constituting approximately 13% of all felony crime reported to law enforcement agencies. Overall, some 45% of the aggregate episodes of violent crime are "cleared by arrest," sharply inflected by category.

But arrest is not necessarily indicative of guilt, and the vagaries consequent upon arrest do not predict conviction. Hence, in the same year in which 1.7

million episodes of violent crime were reported and some 765,000 of these episodes were "cleared by arrest," there were only some 160,000 convictions for crimes of violence (Ibid., 536). The overall annualized ratio between formal reports, arrests, and convictions is thus on the order of 23.2. Moreover, since only 54% of the convictions for violent offenses result in prison sentences (Ibid., 537), the annualized ratio between reports of violent crime and imprisonment for the commission of violent crime is on the order of 22:1.

Table 4.2: Annualized incidence of violent crime

Subcategory	Episodes	% All Violent Crime	% All Crime Reported	% Cleared by Arrest
• Homicide	23,250	1.4%	0.2%	66.6%
• Forcible sexual assault	93,804	5.5%	0.7%	52.6%
• Assault (aggravated)	1,018,917	59.9%	7.7%	59.7%
• Robbery	653,628	38.2%	4.9%	26.7%

Finally, since NCVS data indicate that only half the victimizations in violent offenses are reported to law enforcement authorities (Bureau of Justice Statistics, 1994, 7), the annualized ratio between victimizations and sentences to prison in violent crime is thus on the order of 44:1. Such considerations urge the utmost caution in generalizing from data on victimization which may not result in reporting, prosecution, or imprisonment; from data on arrests, which may not result in conviction; or from the self-reports of imprisoned offenders who rather clearly constitute only a subset who may not mirror unreported, undetected, unprosecuted, and unconvicted offenders.

Convergence and divergence in racial caste across subcategories of aggressive violence

Politically correct or not, and particularly in view of the Hennessy & Kepecs-Schlussel report on minority population proportion as a potent contributor to the aggregate quotient for violent crime, it is not possible to ignore race as a variable in aggressive criminal violence. In the table on the next page, we have assembled data from several sources bearing on racial convergence and divergence between victim and offender across subcategories in single-offender aggressive violence. Overall, 78% of all episodes represent same-race pairings between victim and offender, a figure that almost precisely replicates those reported by Klaus, Rand & Taylor (1983) and Palley & Robinson (1988). But, as Wilbanks (1985) first observed, closer inspection of the data reveals a substantial paradox.

When viewed from the perspective of the victim, aggressive criminal violence appears to be tightly bound with the two principal racial "castes," with most whites victimized by other whites and most Blacks victimized by other Blacks. But a different picture emerges when the same data are assembled from the perspective of the offender. While white offenders overwhelmingly have "cho-

Table 4.3: Racial caste convergence and divergence in single-offender aggressive violence: Homicide, assault, sexual assault

→ VICTIMIZATION DATA: *Most whites are victimized by whites and most Blacks are victimized by Blacks — The probability that a white victim has been attacked by another white exceeds the probability of attack by a Black by 5:1 — The probability that a Black victim has been attacked by another Black exceeds the probability of attack by a white by 7:1*

When the **victim** is white . . .

in this number and proportion of cases the **offender** is . . . . . . for this proportion
of all cases

• White	2,536,000	77%	65%
• Black	505,000	15%	13%
• Member of "other" groups	267,000	8%	7%

When the **victim** is Black, . . .

in this number and proportion of cases the **offender** is . . .

• Black	502,000	82%	13%
• White	72,000	12%	2%
• Member of "other" groups	40,000	7%	1%

→ DATA ON OFFENDING: *White offenders rarely cross caste lines, but Black offenders are equally likely to attack whites as Blacks — The probability that a white offender has attacked a white victim exceeds the probability of attack against a Black victim by 32:1 — The probability that a Black offender has attacked a white victim exceeds the probability that a white offender has attacked a Black victim by 17:1*

When the **offender** is white . . .

in this number and proportion of cases the **victim** is . . .   . . . for this proportion
of all cases

• White	2,536,000	97%	70%
• Black	72,000	3%	2%

When the **offender** is Black . . .

in this number and proportion of cases the **victim** is . . .

• Black	502,000	50%	13%
• White	505,000	50%	13%

→ SOURCES. Data on homicide [cases reported to law enforcement authorities] from *Sourcebook of Criminal Justice Statistics* (Maguire & Pastore, 1994, 389). Data on sexual assault and assault [simple and aggravated and attempted vs. completed collapsed] from National Crime Victimization Survey Report (Bureau of Justice Statistics, 1994, 55, 61-62). Data have been rounded to the nearest 1000. Data on offending do not include offenses against members of "other" racial groups by whites or Blacks and thus do not total 100%.

sen" other whites as their victims, the probability that Black offenders have attacked white victims is as great as the probability that they have attacked Black victims.

Thus, aggressive violence appears to be containerized among whites but crosses caste lines among Blacks. To interpret these data properly, especially because whites outnumber Blacks in the general population at a ratio of 6.67:1, it is important to attend both to proportions and to absolute numbers of cases. Though the number of Black-on-white episodes nearly approximates the number of Black-on-Black episodes, each accounts for only 13% of the aggregate total.

Yet it is the Black-on-white episodes that prototypically engage media attention; as this is written, the nation is obsessed with the just-concluded trial of football star O.J. Simpson for the murder of his former wife and a male friend (or companion), both white; that of Colin Ferguson, a serial killer who murdered whites on a Long Island commuter railroad, concluded six months earlier, with similar media attention. Disproportional attention in the media readily elicits the misperception that aggressive violence is virtually exclusively a matter of Black predators and white victims; thus is the phenomenology of fear born, nurtured, and reinforced.

Nonetheless, it should be underscored that distinguished Black psychiatrist Carl Bell of the University of Chicago, whose work on the incidence of neuropathology in the urban ghetto we reviewed in Chapter 2, has estimated that, by the age of 11, 80% of urban Black children will have witnessed a beating, stabbing, or shooting (Bell, 1990; Meharry Medical College, 1991).

Were racial caste not a factor in aggressive criminal violence, we might expect both victims and offenders to be "distributed" in consonance with their representation in the population. These data indicate that whites are victims in 80% of all cases of aggressive violence, in an almost precisely congruent 1:1 ratio. Alternately, Blacks are over-represented at a ratio of 4:3. Blacks are also over-represented among offenders at a ratio of slightly more than 2:1, while whites are under-represented at a ratio of 9:10. Thus:

- When read in juxtaposition with data on victimization, the conclusion is inescapable that *Blacks are at greater risk both for offending and for victimization in aggressive violence than are whites. Moreover, Blacks are at substantially greater risk for cross-race offending.*

That generalization, of course, begs the question of the inextricable confounds between race and socioeconomic status and its correlates (level of education, stability of employment, character of residence) in the society. It may be that the latter variables constitute the driving forces for both offending and victimization as well as the visible indicia of centuries of profound exploitation. So long as the confounds remain, however, it is not possible to syllabicate components and concomitants.

Gender divergence

In the national population, women and girls (in the currently-accepted non-sexist terminology, members of the female gender) outnumber members of the male gender at a ratio of 51:49. But males are radically over-represented as offenders in each category of aggressive violence and as victims in assault and homicide [NOTE 4]. Clearly reflecting the incidence of male-to-male homosexual rape and child abuse, males are under-represented among victims of sexual assault but only at a ratio of 5:6. The relevant data (Maguire & Pastore, 1994, 271, 272, 389; Bureau of Justice Statistics, 1994, 590) are extrapolated and presented tabularly on this page.

In the aggregate, members of the male gender are over-represented not only as offenders (at a ratio of 1.75:1) but also as victims (at a ratio of 1.3:1). Girls and women are under-represented not only as offenders (at a ratio of 2:7) but also as victims, at a ratio of approximately 3:4. Only in the case of sexual assault are member of the female gender over-represented, at even then at the surprising ratio of 1.15:1.

The data on assault and homicide suggest that a substantial portion of aggressive criminal violence corresponds to the pattern Feldman & Quenzer (1984, 248-252), on the basis of studies on infra-human species, identified as "intermale aggression."

Table 4.4: Gender discrepancy in aggressive crimes of violence

	Victim	Offender
Assault		
• Male	64.6%	84.1%
• Female	35.4%	14.8%
Sexual assault		
• Male	41.0%	96.4%
• Female	58.9%	3.6%
Homicide		
• Male	78.0%	88.4%
• Female	21.9%	11.5%

- Collectively, these data rather convincingly indicate that, *with the exception of sexual assault, aggressive violence is largely a male-to-male transaction.* In the aggregate, male-to-male transactions account for 85% of all episodes of aggressive criminal violence. Aggressive violence is far from gender-neutral. Males are at substantially greater risk for offending at ratios of 1.7:1 in assault, very nearly 2:1 in sexual assault, and 1.8:1 in homicide,

Aggressive offending inflected by age

Since estimates by victims may prove inaccurate, data from police records on the age of arrestees for aggressive violent crimes yield the most reliable large-scale information on age in relation to offending. We have arrayed UCR data on

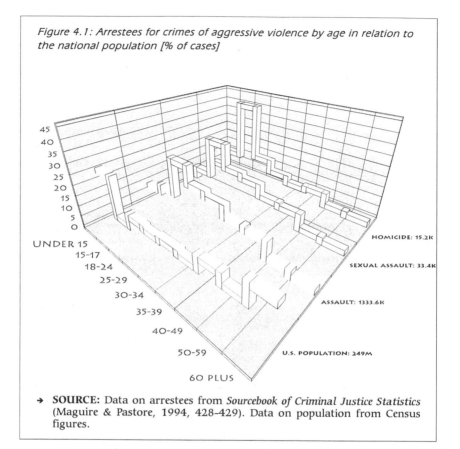

Figure 4.1: Arrestees for crimes of aggressive violence by age in relation to the national population [% of cases]

→ **SOURCE:** Data on arrestees from *Sourcebook of Criminal Justice Statistics* (Maguire & Pastore, 1994, 428–429). Data on population from Census figures.

the age of arrestees for crimes of aggressive violence in relation to Census data for the national population in the graph on this page.

Quite clear associations are seen between age and risk for aggressive offending, at least to the extent that arrest is a reasonable index thereof. Persons in the young adult age group (18-24) represent 9% of the national population but 41% of the arrestees for homicide at a ratio of 9:2, 28% of the arrestees for sexual assault at a ratio of slightly more than 3:1, and 26% of the arrestees for assault (aggravated and simple collapsed), also at a ratio that approximates 3:1. Those in the late adolescent (15-17) group represent 4% of the population but 13% of the arrestees for homicide at a ratio of 3.25:1, 10% of the arrestees for sexual assault at a ratio of 5:2, and 9% of the arrestees for assault at a ratio of slightly more than 2:1 [NOTE 5]. In the adjacent cell, those in the 25-29 age group account for 8% of the population but are represented among arrestees for homicide, sexual assault, and assault at ratios of slightly more than 2:1. There is, moreover, evidence that early initiation into aggressive criminal offending perpetuates into early adult-hood. In a 9-year follow-up of males who had been released from juvenile institutions, Lewis, Yeager, Lovely et al. (1994) reported that 94% had continued (though not necessarily escalated) their offense patterns.

Collectively, persons aged 15-29 constitute 21% of the population but 69% of those arrested for homicide, 55% of those arrested for sexual assault, and 53% of those arrested for assault; in the aggregate, they represent 54% of all arrestees for all crimes of aggressive violence. There seems to be little question that aggressive violence "centers" in this age range. Alternately, those aged 40 and over are under-represented among arrestees, at ratios ranging from 1:17 (in the case of persons aged 60+ for assault) to 3:5 (in the case of those aged 40-49 arrested for homicide). From these data, we can conclude that

- *Risk for aggressive criminal offending is sharply inflected by age.* Young adults aged 18-24 are at risk at ratios ranging from 3:1 to 9:2, late adolescents aged 15-17 are at risk at ratios ranging from 4:1 to 2:1, and persons aged 25-29 at ratios of 2:1. The greatest risk levels for aggressive criminal offending center in the 15-29 age range.

Relationship between victim and offender

Another important component of the phenomenology of fear is the portrayal of random, stranger-to-stranger aggressive violence as normative, especially when coupled with racial caste differences between victim and offender. Cases such as that of Colin Ferguson are prime exemplars claiming major media attention, further reinforced by accounts of "drive-by" shoot-outs between drug-dealing "posses" in the urban ghettoes in which children connected with neither of the conflicting parties are randomly killed or injured. But such events are statistically atypical.

Data on the relationship between victim and offender extrapolated from UCR reports on arrestees in the case of homicide and from NCVS data in the case of assault and sexual assault are displayed graphically on the next page. Homicide data include only those cases in which the relationship is known (some 61% of all reported homicides). One might speculate with virtually equal cogency that a large proportion of homicides in which the relationship is unknown (typically, because the offenses has not been "cleared by arrest") are perpetrated by strangers (as in situations in which a homicide is committed to facilitate robbery or perhaps to silence a victim after sexual assault) or, alternately, that the distribution of the "unknown" cases follows the pattern observed in the "known" cases. It is not uncommon that an arrest of a friend or relative of the victim, and less frequently of an offender previously unknown to the victim, is made long after the homicide itself. Rather than pursue either speculation to prospectively erroneous conclusions, we have confined the analysis to "known" cases only.

In the aggregate, the data indicate that 29% of the episodes of aggressive criminal violence are committed by strangers, 13% by relatives (or ex-relatives, most particularly ex-spouses), and 58% by friends or acquaintances. In each subcategory, the risk of victimization by a relative, friend, or acquaintance far outweighs the risk of victimization by a stranger. By subcategory, strangers are responsible for 19% of the homicides and 31% of the assaults and sexual assaults, respectively. The data do not readily conform to the pattern Feldman & Quenzer (1984, 248-252), drawn from animal studies, term "predatory aggression." Instead, collectively, the data suggest that

- *Aggressive criminal victimization is, modally, not random. Instead, risk for offending varies with offender-victim relationship,* such that friends, acquaintances, relatives, and ex-relatives are more likely to aggress criminally than

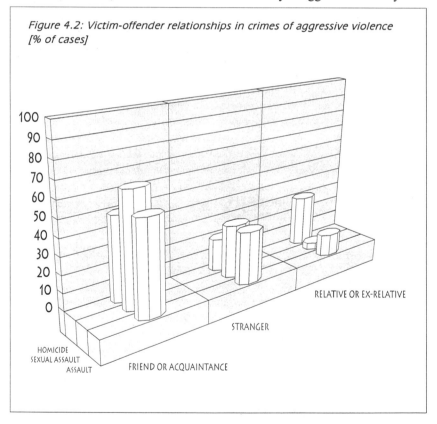

Figure 4.2: Victim-offender relationships in crimes of aggressive violence [% of cases]

→ **SOURCES.** Data on victim–offender relationships in cases of homicide from UCR reports (Maguire & Pastore, 1994, 380-381) include only cases in which relationships are known. Data on relationships in assault and sexual assault from victim perceptions (Bureau of Justice Statistics, 1994, 55, 63, 94).

are strangers at ratios of 4:1 in the case of homicide and 2:1 in the cases of assault and sexual assault.

Use of weapons by offenders

That crimes of aggressive violence are prototypically perpetrated with the aid of a lethal weapon represents a further element in the phenomenology of fear. In the table below, we array UCR data (Maguire & Pastore, 1994, 366) on the use of weapons in homicide and NCVS data (Bureau of Justice Statistics, 1994, 83) on weapons in sexual assault and assault (aggravated and simple collapsed).

Weapons are differentially related to subcategories of aggressive violence. In homicide, a firearm is modal but in sexual assault, in assault, and in the aggregate, the absence of a weapon is the norm, with the offender relying instead on intimidation, direct physical confrontation, and/or the use of fists, hands, and feet Indeed, it may be the case that the availability of a lethal weapon is the pivot that turns the transaction from assault to homicide — and perhaps also determines who shall emerge from the transaction as offender and who as victim.

Table 4.5: Proportion of crimes of aggressive violence in which weapons other than intimidation or physical confrontation (fists, hands, feet) were utilized by offenders

Subcategory	Firearm	Knife, Club
• Homicide	68%	15%
• Sexual Assault	9%	13%
• Assault	13%	13%
• Aggregate aggressive violence	13%	13%

- On the basis of these data, *we offer the quasi-tautological generalization that access to a lethal weapon constitutes a clear risk marker for homicide. Almost tautologically, the willingness to employ intimidation and/or physical confrontation potentiates assault and sexual assault.* The availability of weapons, and the legislative control thereof, is discussed in some detail later in this chapter.

Socioeconomic status

There are no large-scale data sets that discerningly address the socioeconomic status of offenders inflected by type of offense. In its survey of state prison inmates, the Bureau of Justice Statistics (1993, 9) reports that 43% of all respondents had been raised in single-parent households, that 26% reported parental alcohol abuse and 4% parental drug abuse, and that 37% reported that at least one family member had been incarcerated for felony crime. To that relatively grim picture might be added the conclusion reached by Allen & Simonsen (1975) that, whatever the social, academic, or economic yardstick applied, prison inmates can appropriately be described as the "chronic losers" in a society, a finding more recently confirmed by Kepecs-Schlussel & Hennessy (1995).

In his study of inmates in New York State prisons who aggress against other inmates while in prison, Kevin Wright (1991) observes that a majority of all inmates not only come from lower socioeconomic origins but indeed have been "state-raised" under the auspices of child protective agencies, to which guardianship had been assigned as a result of abuse or neglect. With some frequency, such children have been the objects of neglect by substance-abusing parents or single mothers. Children under such protection are usually shunted from one foster home to another, with inadequate socialization as one of several deleterious long-term effects. That, surely, is a formula for a headstart toward becoming a "chronic loser." Thus, Wright (5) comments that "Prison populations are composed of predominantly poor, lower-class segments of society who differentiate themselves along ethnic lines and are generally hostile to one another [and represent] the worst of society's rejects." While these generalizations apply to convicted offenders across categories and may thus support a generalization concerning socioeconomic status and family structure as risk markers in felony crime generally, there is not sufficient evidence to link these variables differentially to aggressive offending.

Neuropathology

In Chapter 2, we reviewed in some detail findings from the neurosciences bearing upon aggressive criminal violence, and we saw indeed strong differential associations. Based on the accumulated evidence as displayed graphically earlier, we may generalize that

- *Neuropathology in the offender constitutes a potent risk marker for homicide, for sexual offenses, and in persistent assaultive offending. Neuropathology is essentially not predictive of isolated, one-time episodes of assault.*

Substance use or abuse by the offender

In Chapter 3, we reviewed findings from several sources on the contribution made to criminal offending by use or abuse of neuroactive substances by offenders and by the perception by the offender of similar use/abuse on the part of the victim. Based on evidence accumulated from laboratory assay studies, the perceptions of victims, and the self-reports of imprisoned offenders as displayed graphically earlier, it is reasonable to generalize that

- *Substance use or abuse by the offender constitutes a risk marker in aggressive criminal offending, with risk potentiated if the victim is, or is perceived by the offender to be, also under the influence of neuroactive substances.*

THE SHARED WORLD OF OFFENDER AND VICTIM

In a study which compared a large sample of Black women who had committed homicide with their victims on a number of social characteristics, Paula McClain (1982) concluded that victims and offenders inhabit a mutual world, observing that "Victims and offenders are of [the same] socioeconomic status backgrounds and exhibit essentially similar behavior patterns that increase their probability of involvement in homicide." McClain's generalization may have applicability considerably beyond the two groups she studied.

Our review of very broad data sets has indicated that risk markers for victimization in aggressive criminal violence inhere in race, gender, age, socioeconomic status, residence in center cities, remaining within familiar physical environments, and the perception that one is "under the influence" of alcohol or drugs, and that these risk markers operate essentially independently of the relative incidence of police presence; about the relative incidence of neuropathology among victims, there are no reliable data.

When we considered risk markers for offending, many of the same variables were indicated. We saw that Blacks were at greater risk for both victimization and for offending at a ratio of 2:1, that persons aged 16-24 were at the greatest risk for either victimization or offending, and that, to the extent that the comparison can be reasonably calibrated, victims and offenders likely inhabit similar socioeconomic strata. Among offenders, there is rather clear evidence that neuropathology constitutes a palpable risk marker, and the self-reports of convicted offenders indicate that risk for offending is potentiated by substance use or abuse.

We also saw that, prototypically, aggressive criminal violence is a transaction between relatives or between friends and acquaintances — and quintessentially between young males in a pattern of intermale aggression that perdures across species. That degree of relationship supports the speculation that victims and offenders share mutually familiar physical and social environments. In those circumstances, who emerges from a specific behavioral interaction as the victim and who as the offender may essentially be a matter of the luck of the draw.

A PERVASIVE CULTURE OF VIOLENCE?

Premier criminologist Marvin Wolfgang and the late Italian psychiatrist Franco Ferracuti (1967) coined (or perhaps re-invented) the term subculture of violence in their work on lawlessness in Sardinia, the troubled Italian dependency which even in the 1980s lay claim to the dubious title "kidnapping capital of the world" (Marongiu & Clarke, 1993). However apt the term may have been within its context, it appears to apply equally well to American society in general.

Political and cultural historians have long attributed a major role in the shaping of the American ethos to the myths and realities of the taming of the frontier. Though they may have held royal patents, the European-born colonists who settled New England and the mid-Atlantic in essence purchased their land from Native Americans, albeit usually at exploitatively advantageous terms. In contrast, the Spanish *conquistadores* who invaded what is now Florida and the southwest and those primarily American-born pioneers who tamed the ever-shifting western frontier from Kentucky to Colorado merely seized their lands from Native Americans by force of arms. Though the older settlements of the East sought to emulate the lawfully ordered life of European cities, the settlements of the frontier were governed principally by threat of violence.

Commentators from Frederick Jackson Turner (1893) and Edwin Lawrence Godkin (1898, 25-31) to Vernon Louis Parrington (1930, 159-165) hold that, in forcing individuals to rely on themselves rather than on a social order controlled by a moneyed elite (witness the limitation that the privilege of voting in elections extended only to those who owned property), the taming of the frontier immeasurably catalyzed the development of "true" participative democracy in this country.

That may be the positive side. On the negative, there is no question that the process of Western expansion left in its wake the popular image of the frontiersman and his successor, the two-fisted gunman, ready to risk all in pursuit of his wants or needs, celebrated in legends ranging from Daniel Boone to Billy the Kid — and perpetuated today not only in the cinematic exploits of "good guy" rogue-heroes like "Dirty Harry" Callahan, Rambo, and even Sam Anderson, the FBI agent in *Mississippi Burning* who scruples not in the least to use the tactics of terror in order to combat terrorism, but even in the ubiquitous video games that grace the arcades of shopping centers, and, in the latest adaptation of high technology to cultural imperatives, the home computer and the information super-highway. To paraphrase Aldous Huxley (1956), we are properly outraged when violence or the threat of violence is used as a means to a patently "evil" end; we should be equally outraged when violence or the threat of violence is used as a means to a patently "good" end.

Quite clearly, the ethos of the frontier embodied the normative expectation of violence; we should not be surprised, then, to find empirical evidence from the behavioral sciences that confirms that the normative expectation of violence represents a central thrust in a variety of American subcultures, or perhaps in the culture as a whole — a situation historians discerned more than a century ago.

Determinants of a culture of violence

Confluence of deaths by violence

A significant and growing body of research, both in the United States and cross-nationally, seems to confirm that a relatively high coincidence of deaths by violence (homicide, suicide, traffic fatalities, and other accidents) comprise the indicia either of a culture of violence or at least of general societal acceptance of (or perhaps indifference to) violence. The "confluence phenomenon" appears to be pervasive in the United States and perhaps in other nations.

Hirsch, Rushforth, Ford & Adelson (1973) early observed a confluence in the rate of homicide and suicide in single midwestern county in the U.S. In a study of the 50 states and the District of Columbia, Sivak (1983) reported a high congruence between the homicide rate and the rate of traffic fatalities in a single year. Those findings were largely replicated by Lester (1988).

Wilbanks (1980) found both a high congruence between suicide rate and accident rate and a positive correlation between suicide and homicide rates in a sample of 181 regions in the U.S., again in a single year. In another study, Wilbanks (1982) concluded that these relationships varied "among subgroups of the population [in] so complex a pattern of correlations" that no unilinear theoretical explanation seemed applicable. Hollinger (1980) confirmed Wilbanks' initial findings on the confluence of death by violent means, with particular emphasis on mortality among young adults. In a study which analyzed mortality rates from suicide, homicide, and accident throughout the nation between 1900 and 1975, Hollinger & Klemen (1982) found that these rates "tend to be parallel over time," a finding they interpreted as "reflecting self-destructive tendencies."

Such self-destructive tendencies were further underscored by Sorensen (1994) in an analysis of motor vehicle accidents (not necessarily leading to fatalities) which contrasted the characteristics of accident-free drivers with those of drivers repeatedly involved in accidents, finding remarkable differences between the two groups in their past involvements with the criminal justice system, social service agencies, debt collection agencies, and even clinics for the treatment of sexually transmitted diseases. Sorenson further demonstrates dramatically that the relative incidence of auto accidents inflected by age is essentially identical with the relative incidence of arrests for criminal offending similarly inflected. As we shall see in the next chapter, those rates also precisely match what appears to be a naturally-occurring decline in psychometrically-inventoried impulsivity as a general personality characteristic.

Internationally, Day (1984) found a high correlation between homicide and suicide over a 30-year-period in some 40 nations, a finding confirmed by Zahav & Riv (1988) in a study of 19 industrialized nations, and by de Castro, Albino & Martins (1986) in an analysis of the congruence of homicide and suicide rates in Portugal over a 12-year-period.

Regionalization hypotheses. The South vs. the West

In an investigation of the confluence of suicide, homicide, and violent crime in the several regions of the nation, Gastil (1971) proposed that a "subculture of violence" inheres primarily in the American South. Generally confirmatory data were adduced by several other investigators (Loftin & Hill, 1974; Doerner, 1975; Bailey, 1976-a; Franke, Thomas & Queenen, 1977; Humphrey & Kupferer 1977; Huff-Corzine, Corzine & Moore, 1986; Lester, 1988-a), while O'Carroll & Mercy (1989) claimed that the American West rather than the South constitutes the pre-eminent subculture of violence. As we have seen in our review of NCVS data earlier in this chapter, the rate of victimization is highest in the Western states, lending support to the O'Carroll & Mercy nomination.

If one adds to the litany of distinguishing regional characteristics the matter of judicially-ordered executions, however, there is simply no question that the American South far and away leads the nation. Executions under current statutes, revised following the ruling of the U.S. Supreme Court in Furman v. Georgia in 1972, resumed in 1976. According to Amnesty International (1987, 54-64, 192-193), three states (Texas, Florida, and Georgia) collectively carried out 63% of all the executions in the nation in the decade following restoration of the death penalty. In the aggregate, those three states accounted for only 14% of the nation's population in the 1990 Census. During 1993, according to Bureau of Justice Statistics data (Stephan & Brien, 1994), five Southern states (Florida, Georgia, Louisiana, Virginia) accounted for 74% of the nation's executions; collectively, those states accounted for 19% of the nation's population.

Prevalence of violent death inflected by age

Wynne & Hess (1986) identified a particularly strong relationship between homicide and suicide among youth aged 18 and under, attributing both phenomena to "long-term trends in the conduct of typical adolescents," which includes as well "premarital sex, out-of-wedlock births, substance abuse, and delinquency." In a discerning analysis, Hollinger, Offer & Ostrov (1987) studied suicide and homicide rates over five decades in the United States in relation to the age of those who kill themselves or others. Their results show significant positive correlations between suicide and homicide rates among those who are between 15 and 24 years old over the entire 50-year-period, as well as significant negative correlations between those rates among adults ranging in age from 35 to 64 years.

In a comprehensive investigation at the Netherlands Institute for the Study of Criminality, Marianne Junger (1994) reviewed the accumulated research evidence on the incidence of delinquency and of mortality by motor vehicle accident, drowning, and fire among children aged 14 and under in Europe and North America in relation to a wide range of coincident variables, including gender, ethnicity, social disadvantage, health and psychiatric problems, family composition and socialization practices, and hyperactivity (without, however, inquiring into its genesis in neuropathology or social learning). She concluded that (104-105) "children involved in accidents are more difficult to handle than nonaccident children and more often display aggressive behavior," that "delinquent children are involved in accidents more often than nondelinquents," and, most tellingly, that the correlative variables she investigation "are related to accident liability and in the same way to crime." On the basis of these findings among adolescents and young adults, one might reasonably conclude that the confluence in violent deaths is a phenomenon inflected sharply by age, a conclusion consistent with our analysis of risk markers in aggressive criminal offending and victimization.

Poverty, racial inequality, and violent death

In a systematic analysis of nearly 500 standard metropolitan statistical areas (SMSAs) in the U.S., Messner (1982, 1983-a, 1983-b) studied the rates of death by violence of all sorts (i.e., homicide, suicide, traffic fatalities, household accidents, industrial accidents) per 100,000 of the population, finding that these were highest in the South. While racial composition of the SMSA and proportion of the population below the poverty level were related to homicide rate outside the South, no such relationships obtained within that region; Messner thus concluded that the propensity for violent death appears to pervade the region, regardless of race or economic deprivation.

Nonetheless, Lalli & Turner (1968) and Hawkins (1989) hold that social class constitutes the pivotally important mediator in the confluence between suicide and homicide, whatever the region of the country. Similarly, Williams (1984) adduced evidence that poverty and racial inequality are potent predictors of homicide rate across a sample of 125 SMSAs across the nation. In a slight variation, McDowall (1986) used time-series analyses to study the link between the proportion of families at or below the poverty level in a single city (Detroit) over the period of half a century and the rate of criminal homicide, finding that the two varied together. McGahey (1990) has opined that poverty level, as measured by joblessness at least, may differentially affect crime rates in accordance with offense category — e.g., minor drug offenses might actually increase in incidence during times of general economic affluence. But, in a "macrodynamic time series analysis," Rattner (1990) found consistent positive relationships between level of unemployment and rate of homicide; the intervening variable may be the abiding sense of frustration and futility generally experienced in times of economic hardship, termed anomie and often invoked as a principal pivot for both criminal violence and political revolution in sociological accounts.

With particular pertinence for a period in the nation's economic history marked by wholesale "downsizing" of the labor force, Catalano, Dooley, Novaco et al. (1993) found significant relationships between job termination through "layoff" or "reduction in force" and violent behavior among subjects interviewed longitudinally through the NIMH Epidemological Catchment Area surveys, even when controlling for pre-existing psychiatric disorder.

Suicide and homicide in the Black community

Lalli & Turner (1968) early observed that the rate of suicide among American Blacks is only about half that among whites. Since the genesis of suicide is sometimes held to inhere in anomie, or a pervasive feeling of hopelessness and helplessness (Clarke & Lester, 1989), that observation is striking when read in conjunction with data that demonstrate that criminally aggressive violence perpetrated by Blacks is equally directed into and out from the Black community. Observing that "Black homicide rates are 7-8 times those of Whites [but] that Blacks have a rate of poverty only 4 to 5 times that of Whites," Poussaint (1983), a distinguished Black psychiatrist at Harvard, concludes that

> Blacks — for both environmental and political reasons — are likely to reflect emotional predispositions that allow them to more readily become a homicide [than a suicide] statistic. Projected self-hatred facilitates blind rage and gives the perpetrator of a violent attack a sense of legitimacy and justification. In addition, Blacks have been indoctrinated by a criminal justice system that places higher value on a White life than on a Black life.

However that may be for the adult population, Shaffer, Gould & Hicks (1994) analyzed suicide rates among adolescents arrayed by race over the past three decades, finding a sharp convergence between Blacks and whites beginning about 1985. Their gloomy conclusion that "The perception that young Blacks are at much lower risk for suicide than whites requires conviction" is the more striking when read in juxtaposition to the epidemiological data earlier reviewed on race and age as risk factors for both victimization and offending in crimes of aggressive violence.

The encapsulation of victimization in aggressive criminal violence largely within racial "castes" in the U.S. finds few consistent parallels in comparative data on an international scale, perhaps because few nations are as ethnically diverse as ours. Thus, Hansmann & Quigley (1982) studied the relationship between homicide rate and measures of ethnic, religious, linguistic, and economic heterogeneity in some 40 nations of the world, concluding that heterogeneity is associated with higher rates of homicide, a finding that would indeed suggest that aggressive violence rather readily crosses what we (following Dollard, 1937, as indicated in NOTE 3) have called "caste" lines. Lester (1989) contrasted the homicide and suicide rates in the U.S. (where whites are both more numerous and, generally, more ascendant) and South Africa (where Blacks are more numerous but whites are more ascendant), inflected by race and by gender, over a six-year period, concluding that similar patterns obtained, with higher rates of suicide among whites and higher rates of homicide among Blacks in each nation. Moreover, in her study of those nations of the world which have traditionally reported the lowest rates of crime within their regions, Adler (1983) found *synomie* (the diametric contrary to anomie) an important determinant. To the extent to which synomie within a population is facilitated by racial similarity, there are implications for intra-caste vs. extra-caste criminal aggression probabilities.

Violent death, traditional family values, and family structure

Prolific researcher David Lester and his colleagues have conducted a series of inquiries that link lethal violence to what can be construed as a variety of traditionalist social values. Lester has reported that the rate of both suicide and homicide in the various U.S. states varied inversely with the extent of regular church attendance (1987-b) and with marital status (1987-c), corroborated the relationship between homicide rate and the participation of women in the labor force (1988-b) in a cross-national study of 18 industrialized nations, and reported (1986-a) that homicides and suicides in the 48 coterminous U.S. States covary with the divorce rate, certainly an index to abrogation of traditionalist values. In a study of the relationship between suicide and homicide in the various states of the union, Yang & Lester (1988-b) reported higher rates in states in which a greater proportion of women were employed outside the home on a full-time basis, a factor they interpreted as indicative of the disintegration of traditionalist social values.

But contrasting findings have been reported (Straus, 1979, 1990; Straus & Gelles, 1990) from a major series of studies at the Family Violence Research Institute of the University of New Hampshire. Thus, Gelles & Hargreaves (1990) found no significant differences in prevalence of episodes of child abuse between mothers who were employed full-time, those employed part-time, and those not employed outside the home; but they reported a significantly lower rate of family violence in those families in which the mother was employed full-time. In this detailed investigation, prevalence of episodes was found to vary according to the age of the child-victim and according to the interaction between the child's age and the mother's employment status. In a companion investigation, Kalmuss & Straus (1990) measured both "subjective" and "objective" dependency among married women and related these measures to episodes of wife abuse. Their unequivocal conclusions argue in a manner directly contrary to prototypical notions of "traditional" family structures:

> The rate of severe violence is almost three times higher among women high than among those very low in objective dependency. The increment in severe violence between the parallel levels of subjective dependency is only twofold.

A factor analytic approach to pervasive violence

These analyses more convincingly argue toward "pockets" of violence or violence-proneness inflected in various ways than to a pervasive culture of violence throughout the society. Data in the Hennessy & Kepecs-Schlussel

(1992) monograph on rates of criminal offending and victimization provide a convenient starting point from which to gauge whether there obtains a "cultural set" toward violence that is not inflected by geographic or regional peculiarities, family structure, or age but instead pervades the society.

Table 4.6: A nationwide culture of violence: Convergence between violent crimes and violent deaths by suicide, motor vehicle accident, and household or industrial accident across the 76 major population centers of the U.S.

Intercorrelations between causes of violent death

	Suicide	Motor Vehicle Accident	Other Accident
• Suicide		.95	.91
• Death resulting from Motor Vehicle accident	.95		.87
• Death resulting from "other" [household, industrial] accident	.91	.87	

Correlations between non-homicidal causes of violent death and incidence of violent crime

	Suicide	Motor Vehicle Accident	Other Accident
• Homicide	.71	.72	.84
• Sexual Assault	.73	.73	.82
• Assault	.72	.73	.83
• Robbery	.61	.62	.79

Culture of Violence Factor loadings

• Homicides	.951
• Sexual assaults	.939
• Robberies	.912
• Suicides	.873
• Deaths from Motor Vehicle accidents	.869
• Deaths from "other" accidents	.940

→ **SOURCES:** Data on incidence of crime from Hennessy & Kepecs-Schlussel (1992, 20-21), derived from Uniform Crime Reports. Data on death by suicide or as the result of motor vehicle or "other" (household or industrial) accident from National Center for Health Statistics (1992), Centers for Disease Control, U.S. Public Health Service, *Vital Statistics of the United States. Volume II, Mortality, Part B (490-527)*. Each correlations reported reaches statistical significance at or beyond p = .01. Factor 1 accounts for 84.6% of the common variance.

From data supplied by the Center for Health Statistics of the U.S. Public Health Service (1992), we extracted information on the number of deaths by suicide and resulting from motor vehicle accidents or household or industrial accidents in each of the 76 cities studied by Hennessy & Kepecs-Schlussel. These variables were found to correlate substantively among and between themselves and also to correlate highly with indices for each subcategory of violent crime. In view of such high correlations, we factor-analyzed data representing both subcategories of violent crime and subcategories of violent death. The results of these analyses are reported tabularly on the opposite page.

But one factor emerged, with very high loadings for each index of violent death. That factor is clearly to be denominated a pervasive and generic "culture of violence" factor which accounts for episodes both of willfully aggressive, criminal, self-inflicted, and "accidental" violence across urban configurations, regions of the country, cities with variant proportions of majority and minority population, with high or low rates of violent, aggressive, or property crime, with high and low proportions of younger and older population, and with radically variant expenditures for public services and relative ratios of police power.

To the extent that there is high correlative incidence of death by one or another violent means in the psychosocial environment, we might expect such a phenomenon to function in such a way as to lead the individual behaver to believe that violence constitutes a universally acceptable, normative facet of social interaction. To that extent, we might expect a culture of violence to potentiate other variables inclining a behaver toward violence.

Individuals in our society are relatively free to self-select their own sociocultural environments. Hence, we might expect that those persons who are internally disposed toward violence will, with some degree of deliberation, elect to place themselves into those sociocultural situations which are readily receptive to aggressive violence as a normatively acceptable facet of social interaction. In turn, their presence within such a sociocultural situation serves further to reinforce the normative expectation governing the acceptability of (or indifference toward) aggressively violent behavior.

Intergenerational transmission of patterns of violence

We should expect those sociocultural factors that accept, favor, or tolerate violence to be reflected, modeled, and learned intrafamilially. In particular, we should expect something approaching a pattern of the intergenerational transmission of propensity toward violent behavior as parents function as pervasive role models for their children (Gessner, O'Connor, Mumford, Clifton & Smith, 1995; Hirschi, 1995). There is a rather rich clinical literature that suggests that such is precisely the case, with weaker empirical support, although the matter of the specific mechanisms of transmission and the relationships through which such propensities are transmitted (e.g., whether transmission occurs more potently between parents and children of the same gender) and the precise magnitude of the intergenerational effect remain recondite.

Effects of childhood victimization

Typical of clinical reports is Sorrells' (1977) study of juveniles who had been charged with homicide or attempted homicide over an 18-month period in California, reporting what he termed "clear evidence" of intergenerational transmission of violence in family histories that were prototypically violent and chaotic and revealed high rates of crime and substance abuse by parents. Similar results linking childhood victimization with later criminal behavior were reported by Shoham, Rahav, Markowski & Chard (1987) in an investigation of violent vs. non-violent adult offenders. Alternately, Pollock, Briere, Schneider & Knop (1990) found no significant differences in incidence of antisocial behavior among young adult males aged 18-21 as a function either of paternal alcoholism or of victimization in child abuse perpetrated by their fathers. Feldman, Mallouh & Lewis (1986) conducted detailed clinical interviews with close relatives of adults who had been convicted of murder, 87% of whom had suffered extreme physical and/or sexual abuse as children and 53% had been the victims of attempted filicide. Data from interviews with relatives were supplemented by psychiatric evaluations and Army, prison, school, and juvenile court records on assailants. According to these investigators, "The mechanisms whereby such abuse and parental behavior may contribute to subsequent violence include modeling, organic consequences of abuse, lack of parental attachment, and displaced rage."

However, in his review of some 60 relatively carefully designed empirical studies in the United States and Britain, Oliver (1993,1315) reached much more modest conclusions:

> The crude rates of intrgenerational transmission of child abuse . . . are as follows: One-third of child victims grow up to continue a pattern of seriously inept, neglectful, or abusive rearing as parents. One-third do not. The other one-third remain vulnerable to the effects of social stress on the likelihood of their becoming abusive parents . . . There is no justification for any extremist advocacy in apportioning responsibility between the "sins of the parents" and the failings of society. The contention that clinical research on abuse is inferior to, and must give way to, large-scale or statistically-balanced surveys is plausible, popular, convincing, and wrong.

Based largely on self-reported data supplied by offenders, there is similarly a widespread belief that personal sexual victimization in childhood, often at the hands of a parent or sibling, is frequently linked to criminal sexual psychopathy in adult life (Burgess, Hartman & McCormick, 1987; Davis & Leitenberg, 1987; Pierce & Pierce, 1987; Prendergast, 1991, 1993). Langevin, Wright & Handy (1989) reported a 42% incidence of (self-reported) childhood sexual victimization among adult pedophiles, with that rate escalating to 53% among uninflected sex offenders studied by Lang & Langevin (1991). Those levels are massively in excess of the rate of childhood victimization in either sexual or physical abuse estimated by Knutson (1995) and by Zaidi, Knutson & Mehm (1989) at between 1% and 2% in the general and putatively non-offending population. Such data support the belief that childhood sexual victimization may be *differentially* associated with sexual offending in adulthood, whether against children or not.

There is also some reason to believe that victimization not of a sexual nature similarly perpetuates; the evidence amassed by Straus & Gelles (1990) on the intergenerational transmission of patterns of intrafamilial physical abuse argues in that direction. Similarly, Barsky, Wool, Barnett & Cleary (1994) confirmed that both physical and sexual abuse in childhood perpetuate into adulthood in the form of formal psychiatric disorder, especially hypochondriasis.

Widom's studies on the "cycle of violence"

But the most precisely discerning studies of what she terms the "cycle of violence" have been conducted by Cathy Spatz Widom and her colleagues. Widom (1989, 140-141) reviewed the body of research literature linking the experience of abuse or neglect in childhood to violent criminal behavior in adulthood, concluding to a relative incidence of 15% to 20% and further opining that "It may, in fact, be that neglected children show higher levels of subsequent violent behavior than those who are abused." Alternately, in a longitudinal study of the long-term consequences of childhood victimization, Widom & Ames (1994) found "no support for a direct relationship [between] child sex abuse, arrests for running away in adolescence, and adult arrests for prostitution."

In her most ambitious report on what she termed the "criminal consequences" of childhood victimization, Widom (1995) calculated the rate of arrest for juvenile and/or adult offenses among a large sample (908) subjects who had been the victims of sexual or physical abuse or of neglect as children (with such episodes documented in official court records rather than detected by retrospective self-report) between 1967-1971 in contrast to a sample of control subjects who had not been so abused. Widom's reporting of detail (Ibid., 5) is sufficient to permit regrouping of data in such fashion as to highlight the net increment in arrest rates prospectively attributable to childhood victimization, as indicated in the table on the next page.

The proportions reported as "increments" (or, in one case, as a "decrement") in relation to baseline rates may be construed as constituting specific "risk enhancement" factors for juvenile and adult offending putatively attributable to childhood victimization, at least to the extent to which the sheer fact of arrest constitutes a gross index to such offending.

Perhaps most significantly, Widom's data indicate that far less than a majority of victims of either abuse or neglect offend criminally, whether as juveniles or as adults. But, consistent with much of Widom's earlier research, clear patterns are evident. Overall, the most potent increases in risk for offending are associated

Table 4.7: Widom's "cycle of violence": Risk enhancement for juvenile and adult arrest and for alcohol abuse as a function of childhood victimization

		Juvenile arrest rate	*Net risk enhancement*
Baseline:	Control subjects, no documented history of abuse or neglect	16.8%	
Sexual abuse:	Victimization in childhood sexual abuse	22.2%	Baseline + 32.0%
Physical abuse:	Victimization in childhood physical abuse	19.9%	Baseline + 18.5%
Neglect:	Victimization in neglect	28.4%	Baseline + 69.0%
		Adult arrest rate	
Baseline:	Control subjects, no documented history of abuse or neglect	21.0%	
Sexual abuse:	Victimization in childhood sexual abuse	20.3%	Baseline - .03.3%
Physical abuse:	Victimization in childhood physical abuse	27.4%	Baseline + 30.4%
Neglect:	Victimization in neglect	30.7%	Baseline + 46.2%
		Lifetime alcohol abuse prevalence rate	*Net risk enhancement*
Women			
Baseline:	Control subjects, no documented history of abuse or neglect	21.8%	
Sexual abuse:	Victimization in childhood sexual abuse	29.4%	Baseline + 34.8%
Physical abuse:	Victimization in childhood physical abuse	26.7%	Baseline + 22.4%
Neglect:	Victimization in neglect	32.0%	Baseline + 46.7%
Men			
Baseline:	Control subjects, no documented history of abuse or neglect	54.0%	
Sexual abuse:	Victimization in childhood sexual abuse	52.9%	Baseline - 02.0%
Physical abuse:	Victimization in childhood physical abuse	54.4%	Baseline - 00.2%
Neglect:	Victimization in neglect	51.4%	Baseline - 04.8%

→ **SOURCES**: Data on arrest rate adapted from Widom, 1995. Data on alcohol abuse symptomatology adapted from Widom, Ireland & Glynn, 1995.

with victimization in neglect rather than abuse, in a manner that suggests that impaired socialization in the neglecting parents may be intergenerationally transmitted to the neglected child. Moreover, as we noted earlier and shall see at closer range in Chapter 6, a formal judicial finding that a child has been the victim of neglect is frequently followed by placement in foster care, often with negative consequences compounded.

For the sexually abused and for the neglected child, victimization effect appears more potently to accelerate juvenile offending than adult offending, while the obverse obtains for the physically abused. Perhaps most surprisingly, and certainly in sharp contradiction to widely held clinical views (as well as the conventional wisdom), the effect of childhood sexual abuse wanes in adulthood, so that the rate of adult offending among victims of such abuse is slightly lower than the comparable rate among control subjects with no documented history of abuse or neglect. As Widom (Ibid., 1) put it in a summary statement:

> Of all types of childhood maltreatment, physical abuse was the most likely to be associated with arrest for a violent crime later in life. The group next most likely to be arrested for a violent offense were those who had experienced neglect in childhood . . . Though a more "passive" form of maltreatment, neglect has been associated with an array of developmental problems . . . A childhood history of physical abuse predisposes the survivor to violence in later years . . . Victims of neglect are more likely to engage in later violent criminal behavior as well.

Widom's results were confirmed in a study of what they termed the "abuse-to-abuser hypothesis for the genesis of pedophilia" by Fedoroff & Pinkus (1996) at the Clarke Institute of Psychiatry, Toronto, who found few significant differences between child sex abusers who had or had not been sexually abused as children themselves — save that those who had themselves been the victims of abuse were more likely to reveal a long-standing sexual interest in children. Our psychoanalytic colleagues are likely to interpret that finding as indicative of fixation at an early stage of psychosexual development triggered by traumatization.

In a companion 25-year follow-up of children victimized in substantiated cases of abuse or neglect in childhood, Widom, Ireland & Glynn (1995) found evidence of a relationship between victimization in child abuse or neglect and subsequent alcohol abuse problems among women but rather surprisingly not among men. Among men subjects, they found instead that alcohol abuse problems in adulthood were associated with substance abuse problems in either parent during childhood, so that negative role models (a topic to which we turn shortly) appeared to have a more discernible effect among men, while personal victimization (whether in physical or sexual abuse) or neglect appeared to have a direct effect among women. Once again, data are reported in sufficient detail as to permit regrouping that indicates increments to base rates found among control subjects attributable to childhood victimization, as indicated tabularly in Table

4.7. What is perhaps most surprising in these data is the finding that a majority of men demonstrate symptoms of alcohol abuse at some point during the 25-year follow-up period, whether abused or neglected or not.

Family dysfunction without abuse

Cornell, Benedek & Benedek (1987-a, 1987-b, 1989) examined case records over an eight-year period for subjects between 12 and 18 who had been charged with homicide and for a control group of adolescents who had been charged with larceny. The investigators garnered information on some 52 variables reflecting family dysfunction, school adjustment, childhood problems, history of violence, delinquent behavior, substance abuse, psychiatric problems, and stressful life events. Yet their gloomy conclusion is surprising. "Subjects charged with larceny scored higher [i.e., had more problems] on composite measures of school adjustment, childhood symptoms, criminal activity, and psychiatric history" than did those charged with homicide. That conclusion seems to argue more convincingly for the intergenerational transmission of a proneness for antisocial behavior motivated by greed than for aggressive behavior among children of dysfunctional families who were, however, not themselves the victims of abuse.

Mathew, Wilson, Blazer & George (1993) investigated the prevalence of both psychiatric disorder, antisocial behavior, and substance abuse among adult children of alcoholic parents who had participated in the NIMH Epidemiologic Catchment Area survey. In comparison to participants whose parents were not alcoholic, indices of both antisocial behavior and substance abuse were significantly greater among adult children of alcoholics, with the effect further inflected by gender, with rates among male children higher; similar relationships were found for depression, anxiety, and phobia.

Mechanisms of transmission

One might (perhaps naively) expect that, if a child has suffered neglect or violence at the hands of a parent or neglect as a result of parental alcoholism, he or she would undertake ever greater controls over his or her own behavior as an adult so as not to inflict similar experiences upon others. As Widom and her colleagues have demonstrated, among the survivors of abuse the risk for criminal offending is only modestly enhanced as a function of childhood victimization. Yet there remains little debate about *whether* an inclination toward violence is transmitted from one generation to another. Rather, there remain questions only about the *how* of transmission. The psychoanalytically-inclined may appeal to the notion of "identification with the aggressor" as an explanatory mechanism.

Though he did not assay the relationship between neuropathology and impulsivity either in parents or children, in his examination of juvenile offenders who had committed homicide ("kids who kill"), Sorrells (1977, 320) concluded to the social learning of impulsivity as the principal agent, originating in the family and supported by the media.

> If a youngster has little impulse control and his current life is miserable and gives little hope of anything better in the future, he is susceptible to the most fleeting of impulses and seldom stops to exercise judgment . . . Every young person learns or fails to learn impulse control from the combined influence of the peer group, the media, and the family. Many of [these] youngsters had parents who were unable to control their own violence . . . Children undoubtedly learn more from what they observe than from what they are told. These children observed their parents get drunk, assault each other, and, in general, operate from impulse rather than from purposeful direction. They learned from their parents that to feel is to act and that being out of control is the expected state of affairs. If a child fails to get models of integrity and nonviolence in his home, he is certainly unlikely to get them from the media . . . violence on television is portrayed as both romantic and exciting and the victims die cleanly. One youngster who had stabbed a man to death commented that he didn't expect his victim to writhe and gasp while dying — people don't die like that on TV . . . Violence is a cheap form of excitement, and excitement is a cheap form of gratification. For these youngsters, the adults in their families and the adults in popular entertainment usually chose violence over long-term gratification. So did they.

After reviewing a wide array of investigations essentially from a social learning perspective, Kaufman & Zigler (1987) concluded that

> The best estimates of the rate of intergenerational transmission suggest that approximately 30% of all individuals who were physically or sexually abused or extremely neglected will subject their offspring to one of these forms of maltreatment . . . Being maltreated as a child puts one at risk for becoming abusive, but the path between these points is far from direct or inevitable.

That relative proportion is endorsed by Dembo, Dertke, LaVoie & Borders (1987) with particular attention to risk for drug abuse. And, in a substantial review of a wide array of empirical studies, Widom (1989-a-d) concluded to the dependability of intergenerational transmission but attributed the phenomenon to complex interaction among psychosocial variables. DiLalla & Gottesman (1991) amplified Widom's conclusions by underscoring the role of biogenetic and physiological variables: "There is clear evidence for a genetic role in criminality and for a physiological basis for violent behavior. The inclusion of such genetic and biological evidence is necessary for an understanding of the transmission of violence from one generation to another."

Neuropathology as a vehicle for transmission

To the extent to which Cloninger, Reich & Guze (1975) were correct in proposing that psychopathy is intergenerationally transmitted and further compounded by a process they identify as "associative mating" (whereby individuals choose spouses not very different from themselves, or, more simply "birds of a feather flock together"), it may be that harsh child rearing practices in a subculture that condones violence (Erlanger, 1974-a-b; Laybourn, 1986) constitutes an important intervening bio-psycho-social variable.

One would expect that child rearing practices in such a subculture would favor (or at least condone) physical punishment as a means of behavior control. Indeed, Wauchope & Straus (1990, 142) reported that the incidence of physical violence directed against children in "blue collar" families was nearly twice that in "white collar" families, and similar levels are observed in families in which one or both parents are themselves alcoholics or drug addicts (Tarter, Blackson, Martin et al., 1993; Blackson, Tarter, Martin & Moss, 1994). Especially in light of Bell's (1986) findings on the incidence of head trauma in relation to social class and those of Ito, Teicher, Glod, and their associates (1993) on the incidence of neuropathology resultant from physical abuse of children, the prospect that such class-linked child rearing practices may yield a higher incidence of "accidental" head injury (and thus also of consequent neuropsychological dysfunction) must be weighed carefully.

Support for such an interpretation emerges from studies by Tarter, Hegedus, Winsten & Alterman (1984) on neuropsychological impairment among juvenile delinquents who had themselves been the victims of parental physical abuse; by Wolfe, Fairbank, Kelly & Bradlyn (1983) on autonomic arousal levels in relation to videotaped depictions of even non-stressful interactions between parents and children on the part of physically abusive mothers; and by Rohrbeck & Twenty-man (1986) on neuro-psychological deficits among abusive mothers. There is, moreover, as we saw in Chapter 2, some indication that neurologic dysfunctions specifically related to deviant behavior may be genetically determined from the studies of Gabel, Stadler, Bjorn et al. (1995) on anomalies in the metabolism of monoamine oxidase among boys with diagnoses of conduct disorder whose fathers had histories of antisocial behavior.

In her summary of studies at the NYU Medical Center that traced the further criminal behavior of subjects who had been incarcerated for violent crimes as juveniles, distinguished psychiatrist Dorothy Otnow Lewis (1990) linked neuro-pathology, personal victimization, and violent role models interactively.

> In our follow-up study of formerly incarcerated delinquents . . . we found that a constellation of neurological, psychiatric, cognitive, and experiential variables was associated with increasing degrees of adult violence. Subjects with . . . evidence of serious neuropsychiatric impairment and a history of growing up in violent, abusive families tended to become violent criminals. The biopsychosocial constellation we have described [is comprised of] recurrent aggressive behaviors in the context of neurological impairment, cognitive dysfunction, episodic psychotic symptoms, and abusive family violence . . .
>
> How might these biopsychosocial variables interact to engender violence? . . . the effects of central nervous system injury are usually diffuse, affecting the frontal lobes, the limbic system, and, in essence, all parts of the brain concerned with adaptation.

These kinds of injuries impair judgment and reality testing and increase impulsivity [so that] The cognitive impairment that is often a consequence of diffuse brain injury diminishes the ability to appreciate the subtle meanings of human interactions, to pick up cues, to plan logically, and to anticipate the consequences of behaviors. Injury to the limbic system may contribute further to the intensity of emotions, including rage. Paranoid misperceptions and misinterpretations, whether caused genetically, psychodynamically, or as a result of brain injury, contribute further to the tendency to lash out in response to real or imagined provocations . . .

When children with these kinds of neuropsychiatric and cognitive vulnerabilities are raised in violent abusive households, adding, as it were, insult to injury, violent behaviors are generated in the following ways. First, physical abuse itself often injures the brain, thus increasing emotional lability, impairing cognition, and diminishing impulse control. Second, violent irrational parental behaviors engender rage in the helpless child, a rage more often than not displaced onto individuals other than the abusers. Finally, parental violence and abusiveness act as models for behavior.

Whatever the relative contribution of psychosocial, cultural, genetic, and neurobiological factors, there appears to be little dispute as to the fact of the transmission of patterns of violence between generations, nor about the interaction between a pervasive culture of violence, violent role models in the family, and the elicitation of violent behavior in the individual.

Social imitation and vicarious conditioning

In general, conceptual models for the process of learning among humans or in infra-human species from Tolman to Guthrie to Skinner have focused on how learning occurs in an individual, typically in a one-to-one situation in which an individual learner stands in a singular relationship with an individual instructor (or experimenter). Yet it is patently the case that most human learning occurs not in one-to-one situations in which an individual learner is socially isolated from other learners. Rather, from the time a child enters a classroom (in today's world, as a function of high rates of participation in the labor force on the part of mothers, perhaps modally at the age of 3) until he or she leaves school, learning occurs in a social context, and much of what is learned is acquired through methods of instruction that quite deliberately capitalize on social factors. Outside school and throughout post-school life, we continually are the targets of communications through the media, from neighbors and co-workers, from the pulpits, that more or less consciously rely on the process of social learning to achieve effect. Yet so universal and so ubiquitous a process as social learning has been studied formally for little more than half a century.

Following Miller & Dollard (1950), Bandura and his associates established with scientific precision that learning most frequently occurs not through immediate and direct reinforcement of Learner A's behavior but because Learner A has observed Learner B behave and has observed and vicariously experienced the reinforcement (positive or aversive) that follows B's behavior, so that A learns to behave through social imitation and is reinforced vicariously (Bandura, 1962, 1965; Bandura & McDonald, 1963; Bandura & Rosenthal, 1966; Bandura, Ross & Ross, 1963). Reciprocally, that Learner A's behavior can be extinguished vicariously — whether through observation and vicarious experiencing of lack of positive reinforcement or of directly aversive (punitive) reinforcement — has also been very amply demonstrated (Bandura, Grusec & Menlove, 1967).

Imitative learning in infra-human species

Nor is behavioral learning through imitation limited to humans. In a remarkable monograph, Wanda Wyrwicka (1995) of the UCLA School of Medicine has summarized research on imitative learning in infra-human species from the early 1920s onward, including what might (anthromorphically) be termed "positive" (or biologically appropriate) and "negative" (biologically inappropriate) behaviors. As early as 1921, for example, it was known that the presence of another animal engaged in feeding stimulated food consumption even among food-satiated chicks, who continued to eat well beyond their physical needs or capacities. Similarly, weanling kittens have learned to imitate their mother's feeding behavior even when biologically inappropriate, harmful, or overtly noxious food substances were presented, and rats have learned to avoid electric shocks in a T-maze by "following the leader." Wyrwicka also traces imitative learning in both human and infra-human species to similar (or at least analogous) brain mechanisms. Some comparative psychologists equate (perhaps anthropomorphically) the capacity to learn, whether through direct or vicarious reinforcement, with cognition at a primitive level (Zentall, 1993), at least in the sense of the ability to perceive relationships between "ends" and "means."

Role models and aggressive behavior

The case can readily be made that, at some pre-scientific level, the pivots for the process which has guided the construction of the heroic myths and the transmission of the normative values in every society designed to elicit and maintain pro-social behavior are to be found in the principles of social learning by means of vicarious conditioning. Thus, we tell children the fable of George Washington, the cherry tree, and the inability to tell a lie, while simultaneously conveying the high regard in which Washington is held, in order to persuade the young to conform their behavior to that of an idealized, widely socially-approbated behavioral model. But the case can also be made that the very process of social learning and teaching that holds forth the positive behavioral models of which society-at-large approves must perforce portray the reciprocal — that is, in order to depict what is right and proper, it is also necessary to portray what is wrong and improper (Pallone, 1986, pp. 64-69), so that implicitly or explicitly every positive behavioral model conjures a reciprocal negative model. And that process occurs even when the intent is to convey positive behavioral images, let alone when the intent is what Wilson & O'Leary (1980, p. 210) have called "unhealthy persuasion."

In their rich array of investigations, Bandura and his colleagues conducted many inquiries on behavior that is aggressive in nature, but without particular regard as to whether such behavior could reasonably be construed as formally criminal. In his touchstone *Principles of Behavior Modification*, Bandura (1969) underscored the relationship between social models and the expectation of relative impunity in the genesis of aggressive behavior:

> There is a substantial body of research evidence that [even] novel modes of aggressive behavior are readily acquired through observation of aggressive models. Findings of these controlled investigations lend support to field studies demonstrating the crucial role of modeling in the genesis of antisocial aggressive behavior and in the cultural transmission of aggressive response patterns. Modeling influences continue to regulate aggressive responsiveness to some extent even after the behavior has been acquired. The behavior of models continually exerts selective control over the types of responses exhibited by others in any given situation. Moreover, seeing individuals behaving aggressively without adverse consequences reduces restraints in observers, thereby increasing both the frequency with which they engage in aggressive activities and the harshness with which they treat others.

And, in a summary statement covering nearly three decades of research on learning by social imitation, Bandura (1979) more expansively situates aggressive behavior in relation to a variety of antecedents, whether functioning alone or in interaction with each other, and to external reinforcers or mechanisms of reward [NOTE 6]:

> Social learning theory holds that . . . the [sources] of aggression are found in structural determinants, observational learning and reinforced performance. Mechanisms that give rise to acts of aggression include the following. aversive instigators (physical assaults, verbal threats and insults, adverse reductions in conditions of life, thwarting of goal-directed behavior); incentive instigators (the expectation that aggressive behavior will bring benefits); modeling instigators (the disinhibitory, facilitative, arousing, or stimulus-enhancing influence of other people's behavior); instructional instigators (aggression as obedience); and delusional instigators (the influence of bizarre beliefs, e.g., a divine mandate to assassinate the president) . . . The following conditions sustain or regulate aggressive responses. external reinforcement (tangible rewards, social and status rewards, expressions of injury, alleviation of aversive treatment); punishment (inhibitory or informative); vicarious reinforcement through observed reward and observed punishment; and self-reinforcement, including self-reward, self-punishment, and strategies for neutralizing self-punishment (moral justification, palliative comparison, euphemistic labeling, displacement of responsibility, diffusion of responsibility, dehumanization of victims, attribution of blame to victims, misrepresentation of consequences).

Research evidence on what Wilson & O'Leary (1980, 210) term "unhealthy persuasion," or the conscious and deliberate modeling of aggressive behavior, is perhaps best exemplified in Stanley Milgram's (1963, 1965, 1974) investigations of "mandates for evil." In these laboratory analogue studies, subjects were teamed in dyadic working groups with experimental "confederates." The task was so arranged as to make it appear that the confederate could either impede or accelerate the subject's own performance; moreover, the subject was told that, if he/she believed the confederate's performance to be inadequate, he/she could "punish" the confederate via the delivery of an electric shock. In actuality, the device through which the shock was to be delivered was electrically inert. Subjects were also advised in general terms at what levels such "shocks" could be considered mild, moderate, or severe. Left to themselves, subjects (typically, undergraduate students) showed little inclination to "punish" the confederate with whom they had been paired. But, when prodded by the experimenter, many subjects delivered "shocks" at the "severe" level; for their parts, the confederates mimicked pain and distress. Even when the confederate appeared on the verge of collapse, subjects urged to do so continued to administer electric shock.

In a curious turn of events, substantial negative reaction in the public press followed publication of Milgram's initial results, and testimony before Congressional committees considering Federal legislation to ensure the safety of human subjects in medical research referred with some frequency to Milgram's studies. Whether on that basis or not, behavioral science research was included in the package of legislation customarily called the "protection of human subjects" legislation, which pointedly precludes experimentation which involves either or both noxious stimuli or deception. That Milgram had demonstrated how it might have come to pass that six million people were killed in an organized program of genocide in the Germany of the Third Reich barely entered the discussion.

Primitive reinforcers, shared symbols, and deviant behavioral models

The process by which elemental forms of reinforcement are transformed into symbolic substitutes — a process that antecedes and underlies the process of social learning — itself constitutes a fascinating exercise in the psychology of positive and negative socialization. Most of us would not dispute that even very simple organisms experience what we might, with self-conscious anthropocentrism, describe as "pleasure" or as "pain."

At the most primitive level, consumption and elimination are held to be pleasurable, while pressure and confinement are held to be painful. That even the most primitive organism behaves so as to sustain pleasurable sensations and to avoid painful ones is foundational to every conceptual schemata for the process of learning. Not only in the human species but among a wide array of infra-human species as well, a variety of symbols come to elicit the responses associated with pleasure-giving or pain-provoking stimuli; not only the human infant but also the family's pet dog responds to mother's verbal injunction "It's dinner time" and/or to the rattling of food boxes. That much might be explained through the mechanism called associative learning, whereby the pairing of a neutral stimulus (e.g., the mother's voice intoning certain words) with a "natural" or "unconditioned" stimulus (e.g., a bowl of porridge) yields a "conditioned response" (whereby the child comes to respond to the mother's voice alone with great whoops of glee, salivation, or what have you).

But, in the normal course of events, it might be anticipated that the so-called "neutral" stimuli to which natural responses are conditioned might be highly variable from learner to learner. In addressing Fido, for example, one pet owner intones "Chow down," another "Feeding time," a third *Mangere,* while a fourth whistles in imitation of a canary. Indeed, one of Skinner's (1938) earliest and most dramatic illustrations consisted in demonstrating that the "accidental" temporal pairing of a neutral with a natural stimulus results in the learning of what he termed "superstitious behavior." In such circumstances, those symbolic, indirect reinforcers which come to substitute for primitive, direct reinforcers in eliciting and maintaining behavior vary substantially between the learning repertoires of individual behavers.

Yet social learning situations depend to some very large measure on the extent to which the meaning of the same symbolic reinforcer is shared between individual learners. In social learning, A learns behavior X not because A behaves in way X and is reinforced (positively or aversively, directly or symbolically) therefor, but rather because A observes B behave in way X and obtain reinforcement therefor; so also, observers $C, D,$ and E may learn behavior X in the same way, and at the same time, as A. For learning to occur in that manner, it is minimally necessary that A (and C, D, E as well) in some way identify with B, or have been previously socialized in the same way as B, to the extent that he or she finds the same symbolic mechanisms of reinforcement (praise, punishment, scolding, etc., etc.) to have a similar effect on him or her as on B. But, in the face of what are likely quite different learning histories, how does it happen that such mechanisms as a teacher's praise or scolding, or a warning or pat on the back from an officer of the law for that matter, come to be experienced symbolically in much the same way as rather primitive and elemental forms of physical punishment or means of physical gratification?

Sociologists and criminologists frequently attribute the genesis of criminal behavior to "identification with a deviant subculture." If such identification has pervaded the social learning history, we can readily expect that symbolic substitutes for primitive reinforcers widely-shared by others who have been positively socialized to non-deviant subcultures will exert little control over the behavior of a person who has been "positively" socialized to a "deviant" subculture.

That perverse pattern of "positive deviant" socialization is highlighted in a study by Gessner, O'Connor, Mumford, Clifton & Smith (1995), who found negative adult role models, membership in "dysfunctional" families, and general alienation for the values and mores of the larger culture to be potent predictors of the willingness to engage in destructive behavior. Hence, reinforcers which most of us perceive as "negative" (e.g., punishment, incarceration, even execution) may function symbolically as "positive" rewards for the deviantly socialized. Nor should we dismiss as untenable the hypothesis that, for one young man of 17, a sentence to an adult prison may carry the same reinforcing value that admission to a select Ivy League university holds for another.

Sociocultural reinforcers: Violence and the media

Vicarious conditioning need not be limited only to those situations in which a behaver is physically present while another is conditioned. Instead that social learning can occur through "long-distance" vicarious conditioning, as the individual interacts with those sources that inform (or appear to inform) him or her of the world beyond his/her immediate psychosocial environment. Thus, journalistic and entertainment media are the prototypical vehicles for long-distance vicarious conditioning. Moreover, when those media confirm a behavior, belief, attitude, or value that the individual already holds (technically, has already acquired), the tenacity with which that behavior (or belief or attitude or value) will be held in the future may increase in a geometric progression (Stern & Pallone, 1971). Or, to put the matter more technically: Behaviors that are maintained through random or intermittent schedules of reinforcement become highly resistant to extinction (Skinner, 1974). Long-distance vicarious conditioning provides either random or intermittent reinforcement. When such reinforcement supports a previously acquired behavior, especially when that behavior is also endorsed by the subculture to which one belongs (or has self-selected), that behavior (or belief or attitude or value) becomes enormously difficult to change.

Violence elicited or facilitated by the media

Prior to the adoption of Federal legislation severely restricting both biomedical and social science research which involves deceiving subjects (the "human subjects" regulations of 1968), personality and social psychologists had conducted a panoply of in vitro studies, typically using college students as subjects, on whether exposure to violence via films elicits or facilitates aggressive behavior in laboratory analogue situations. Summarizing their own studies and a range of others, Geen & Berkowitz (1969, 107) generalized that "aggressive tendencies elicited by film violence . . . lead to the strongest attacks on persons who are associated with the victims of the observed aggression." Similar results were reported by Stern & Pallone (1971) in a study of racial attitudes following exposure to news reports depicting racial aggression vs. harmony.

Both in consequence of (relatively well-advised) Federal restrictions and because, as Duckitt (1992) has forcefully argued, studies in analogous situations among college students generalize only weakly to "real time" behaviors, more recent studies have been conducted in vivo. A number of investigators, many of them from the fields of communication and information sciences, have studied what we have called such long-distance conditioning in eliciting or extinguishing the emission of aggressive criminal violence in "real time." In virtually all cases, both the stimuli and the responses represent cases of intermale aggression. Among studies that focused directly on the influence of the journalistic or entertainment media in relation to criminal aggression, positive associations have been reported by a number of investigators:

- Lester (1981), in a study homicide rates in nations with a free press vs. those with a controlled or censored press.

- Phillips (1983), in an investigation of the impact of heavily publicized prize fights in relation to subsequent homicides, measured through a sophisticated time-series regression analysis.

- Harry (1983), in a study of changes in the rate of assaultive episodes among patients in a maximum security hospital for mentally disordered offenders following the exhibition of excitatory or pacifying motion pictures.

- Hennigan (1982), in an assessment of the impact of the introduction of regular television broadcasting into isolated and previously television-less cities in the Canadian Rockies on crime rates.

- Heath, Kruttschnitt & Ward (1986), who reported that an interactive effect between exposure to violence by means of television in childhood plus victimization in child abuse was succeeded by an expectation of violence as normal in adult life.

- Wass, Raup, Cerullo & Martel (1989) on the effects of a preference for music celebrating themes of homicide, Satanism, and suicide on dispositions toward murder and suicide among adolescents.

- Zillman & Bryant (1983) and Linz, Donnerstein & Penrod (1984), in studies of the effect of exposure to filmed or televised violence against women in relation to sex offenses.

- Wahl & Lefkowits (1989), on the effects of a made-for-television film about a psychotic killer, as judged by the attitudinal reactions of college students in a laboratory analogue situation, who expressed the belief that mentally ill persons are rather uniformly dangerously aggressive, despite a filmed "trailer" to the contrary.

- White (1989), on the relative incidence of homicides in SMSAs whose professional football teams were participating in televised NFL playoffs, with the finding that a greater number of killings was reported in cities with losing than with winning teams consistently over a six-year period.

- Stack (1989), in an assessment of the effect of the publicizing of mass murders and murder-suicides by means of network television news reports on suicide and homicide rates over a 12-year-period, with a particularly strong effect observed for "gangland" mass murders.

There is also evidence that the effects of exposure to violence through the media are accelerated differentially by intrapersonal variables within the individual and by social influences during exposure. Thus:

- In a major review of the research evidence on the extent to which violence in the media elicit or contribute to aggressive behavior among viewers, Wood, Yong & Chachere (1991) concluded that the effect was particularly strong among children and stronger yet among children previously diagnosed as emotionally disturbed.

- In a retrospective analysis of two decades of research on "trait arousability," Mehrabian (1995, 18) summarized studies that link enjoyment of violence as depicted in motion pictures to arousability, posited as an enduring intrapersonal characteristic and related to what he termed "weak nervous systems." Subjects who watched 10-minutes excerpts from films depicting "highly violent scenes" and who had also scored high on trait arousability as measured by Mehrabian's scale both found the depictions "more enjoyable" and thereafter experienced a larger "number of violent thoughts (e.g., killing, stabbing, wounding, striking" than subjects low in arousability. Mehrabian interpreted these findings to mean that "more hostile or aggressive persons experience more violent thoughts and show greater enjoyment of violent entertainment."

Echoing Milgram's (1974) investigations of the "mandates for evil," there is evidence that the interactive effect between susceptibility to social influence as an intrapersonal variable ("other-directedness") and direct social reinforcement or modeling is particularly potent. In a study in Canada in which subjects watched a videotape of a "fight-filled ice hockey" game in the presence of an experimental confederate with either "deplored, watched passively, or supported" violent behavior, Russell & Pigat (1991) concluded that "endorsement of violence is mediated by the social dependency needs" brought to the situation by subjects in conjunction with the extent to which "others" in a social interaction situation express approval or disapproval of the violence depicted. In this experimental situation (which, since it involved the use of deliberate deception, counters Federal policy on research and human subjects and thus could not have been conducted in the U.S.), direct and immediate (through the presence of the experimental confederate who conveyed to the subject a belief that violence is normal and normative) social reinforcement coalesced with more remote or long-distance (through the videotape depiction itself) social conditioning to deliver the same set of attitudes toward violence.

That situation, in which "mandates" for violence (usually unwarranted, often sadistic) are mutually and simultaneously communicated at short- and long-distance, is surely replicated hundreds of thousands of times weekly. As Marolla & Scully (1986) have demonstrated, we can readily infer such an interactive effect in the nub of gang-perpetrated violence. As we shall see in Chapter 6, criminological studies analyzing the circumstances under which crimes of aggressive violence are actually committed confirm that the presence of third parties serves to potentiate both aggression and brutality.

Depictions of violence and sexual assault

A wide and impressive array of studies has confirmed exposure to violence and/or violent pornography (Comstock, 1986; Donnerstein & Linz, 1986; Goleman, 1985; Heath, Kruttschnitt & Ward, 1986; Linz, Donnerstein & Penrod, 1984; Malamuth & Briere, 1986; Malamuth & Ceniti, 1986; Sommers & Check, 1987; Smeaton & Byrne, 1987), often in laboratory analogue situations, as a determinant either of negative attitudes toward women or of prospective sexual violence. Indeed, that effect is now so well established that criminal sexual aggression is often held to result from the acceptability of violent male behavior toward women, supported by frequent depictions of their victimization in the mass and entertainment media (Briere, Malamuth & Check, 1985; Malamuth, 1986, 1988; Malamuth & Check, 1985; Marolla & Scully, 1986).

A large number of investigations has rather convincingly demonstrated abnormal psychophysiological reactivity and sexual arousal, as measured by penile tumescence (and/or by such other indicators as electrodermal activity and vasoconstriction, generally accepted as manifestations of anxiety and tension respectively), among sex offenders when exposed in vitro to aberrant sexual stimuli of various sorts (Lalumiere & Quinsey, 1994).

Indeed, Quinsey, Chaplin & Upfold (1984, 656), utilizing penile tumescence calibrated by means of the plethysmograph as the dependent measure, found strong evidence that rapists differ markedly from offenders convicted of non-sex crimes not only in their responses to sexual stimuli but also to stimuli which depict non-sexual violence, such that (with added emphases).

> [Stimuli] that involve vicious attacks and victim injury differentiate rapists from nonrapists . . . Rapists [are] differentiable from nonrapists on the basis of their relative responsiveness to rape cues and consenting sex cues . . . rapists respond more to rape stimuli than to consenting sex stimuli . . . rapists respond to nonsexual violence involving female but not male victims . . . non-sex-offenders' sexual arousal is inhibited by victim pain, whereas rapists' arousal is not . . . [the sexual responses of] non-sex-offenders are inhibited by descriptions of violence and victim injury, whereas [those of] rapists are not.

Nor is it inconsequential that depictions of sexual violence in the guise of entertainment appear to appeal equally across genders. Novelist Sara Paretsky (1991) reviewed data on the preferences of women in the purchase of works of fiction, in motion picture attendance, and in the purchase of records, with an emphasis on "heavy metal." She was led to wonder:

> why ... women are paying to read about a man flaying women alive and stripping off their skins? Or a man releasing starving rats inside a woman's vagina? That's what we're doing. And we're doing it enough to make *The Silence of the Lambs* and *American Psycho* best sellers ... If we feel shame for being weak enough to be abused, we may find a perverse release in reading about someone else's torment ... we women loathe ourselves so much for our weakness that we start identifying with those who torment us ... [Through our book and record purchases and movie attendance] we fund an industry of torment against ourselves.

High-tech pornography

Investigations of the effects of pornography on behavior have typically been conducted utilizing print and pictorial media of the variety we now call "low-tech" — the proverbial "little book in a brown paper wrapper," triple-X-rated motion pictures, or videotapes made for "private" sale and circulation. By summer 1995, however, the much-heralded information super-highway capable of linking via communications satellite anyone with a home computer (reportedly installed in 30% of all U.S. households) to vast storehouses of information held electronically in large-array super-computers seemed just around the corner.

Particularly virulent versions of "virtual reality" games of violence had been widely advertised [NOTE 7] , and already there had been journalistic accounts of the distribution of child pornography (replete with sound, and sometimes interactive features, so that the computer-user could alter the sequence of events or the pairing of parties) by means of the InterNet, and Federal legislators were busy drafting bills to prohibit the down-loading of such material even when it had been "posted" to electronic addresses from nations that have no prohibitory laws governing the manufacture or distribution of violent or pornographic stimuli, whether they involved adults or children. Interesting Constitutional issues were raised thereby (Mann, 1995). In addition, there were journalistic reports of pedophiliac seduction by means of electronic communication via "E-mail living rooms," through which (primarily homosexual) adults enticed adolescents who felt drawn either to the gay lifestyle or to a lifestyle characterized by sexual freedom to abscond from their "condemnatory" homes and families (Peyser, Murr & French, 1995).

Even without access to the InterNet, however, the computer user could avail himself or herself of seven compact discs called "The Lucky 7 Bundle" offered by an organization called CD Express, consisting of seven interactive "full nudity" films plus "7777 full-screen computer photos by the immortal erotic photographer J. Stephen Hicks." The advertising material promised "the steamiest sexxxisest [sic] interactive computer movies every made. These great looking full-motion videos have dozens of fantasy girls doing anything and everything your heart desires. So hot you won't believe your eyes!" The disc titles included Private Pleasures, Girls with Girls, Campus Girls, Bad Girls, and Satin, Leather & Lace. Strangely missing from the "Bundle" were interactive films devoted to Men with Men or Boys with Boys.

The price for the "Lucky 7 Bundle" was advertised as $69.95, with a toll-free telephone number provided for ease of ordering, and, for a modest extra charge, the "Bundle" could reach the "end-user" via overnight delivery. Technical requirements were listed as, at minimum, a personal computer with a 386DX central processing unit, 4 megabytes each of random access memory and of hard disk space, a monitor with video graphics array display, a dual speed compact disc drive, a sound card (apparently the better to interpret grunts and groans), Microsoft's Windows Version 3.1, and (in order to communicate "anything and everything your heart desires" to this array of hardware and software), a "Windows compatible mouse." Pointedly, the advertising material indicated that the package "does not work on a Macintosh." It was not indicated whether the availability of greater random access memory permitted the implementation of more fanciful "heart desires" about who does what with or to whom, but pornography seemed to have come a very long way from the proverbial Skid Row theaters devoted to "skin flicks."

To date, we have found no empirical studies of the effects of such computer-based stimuli. We incline to believe that those effects may be rather more intense than the effects of exposure to violence and violent pornography derived from research on "low-tech" and, importantly, non-interactive stimuli, in which the viewer had to content himself or herself with the fantasies of writer and director rather than indulge "anything and everything your heart desires."

Exporting of a taste for violence via American "cultural imperialism"

At a time when the nation's economy is troubled over export-import imbalances, it has been a source of satisfaction that revenues from the exportation of American-made motion pictures and television programs (and the worldwide broadcast of U.S.-based cable television channels via communications satellite) have continued to grow at exponential rates, so that, by 1995, "entertainment" had become our second-ranked export product, trailing only the diverse and sometimes quite deadly products of the aerospace industry. Social commentators and literary scholars worldwide have expressed misgivings about such American "cultural imperialism," and some nations have made (generally ineffective) efforts to limit accessibility, typically tied to quasi-pornographic content.

We have not been able to locate careful scientific studies which assess the impact of American-made entertainment vehicles which portray violence on the behavior or attitudes of audiences in other nations. However, on the eve of the Academy Award festivities for 1995, journalist Dick Polman (1995, A1, A19) conducted interviews around the world in an impressionistic assessment. Among the interviewees were the members of the Hill family, who reside in the village of Amersham in the "outer ring" of exurban communities southwest of London and quite near the Cotswolds, with their quaint thatch-roofed cottages. Except for the presence of a modern Safeway supermarket near the town square at palpable incongruity with the 400-to-500-year-old timbered "character houses" that comprise the village, Amersham so resembles a sleepy early Victorian town that the BBC frequently films its "period" works there. Among the members of the family interviewed by Polman was the eldest son:

> Tom Hill, who is 10, prowls the little parlor, decked out in American sweatpants, speed-rapping his love for American films. "Awesome! There's a lot more action in 'em! In a British film, you got people just walking around; they'd be afraid to use their guns; they give you maybe one murder. In America, they'd be blowing everybody's guts out, and they don't even care!" . . . Not only does he want to be American, he wants to live there. And here's why. "Americans have more fun. They have more stuff, drive-ins, guns."

Tom's father, who is employed by the BBC, seems to share his son's enthusiasms. "William Shakespeare lived 400 years ago. How boring. He can't compete with Arnold Schwarzenegger."

The images of the United States which flow into Victorian Amersham are not limited, of course, to motion pictures and television fare, whether drama or "action" cartoons; they include the quite congruent and mutually reinforcing news reports of the murder of British tourists leaving a car rental agency near Miami's airport by teen-age car-jackers. Perhaps the American car-jackers were as influenced by pervasive images depicting a normative culture of violence in which "everybody's blowing everybody's guts out" as young Tom Hill has been.

Social and cultural beliefs supportive of sexual violence

The agency of conditioning in these investigations appears to be behavioral modeling. But there are other variations, in which the agency for influence is not modeling but rather the relatively more indirect transmission of norms and values. Thus, some investigators have considered how more pervasive social and cultural beliefs and norms influence criminal behavior. Davidovich (1990, 28-30) has illustrated how injunctions in the Koran on the relationship between men and their wives "have perpetuated violence against women in many of the Middle Eastern countries." Similarly, Hull & Burke (1991) have identified supports for the tolerance of sexual abuse in the attitudes toward women fostered by the "religious right" in the U.S.

Effect on legal proceedings

As Surette (1992) has demonstrated, media depictions of criminal court proceedings, whether through entertainment vehicles or live coverage of actual cases, have elicited widely variant public "images" that frequently do not conform to reality. But there is also evidence of a long distance vicarious conditioning effect on the behavior of prosecutors in criminal proceedings. In a remarkable inquiry conducted at the School of Journalism at Indiana University, Pritchard (1986) found that the level of press attention to murder cases, as determined by average length of newspaper reports, emerged as the most potent single predictor of whether prosecutors offered plea-bargains in subsequent cases.

The defensive posture of the entertainment industry

Violence on television has twice been the focus of reports commissioned by the National Institute of Mental Health. The first (Surgeon General's Scientific Advisory Committee on Television and Social Behavior, 1972) reached the rather non-specific conclusion that television programming "is correlated" with violent behavior. But the second (Pearl, Bouthilet & Lazar, 1982) with less equivocation reported that

> the consensus among most of the research community is that violence on television does lead to aggressive behavior by children and teenagers who watch the programs [and that] In magnitude, television violence is as strongly correlated with aggressive behavior as any other behavioral variable that has been measured.

Though it issued no formal report, similar sentiments were widely shared by the scholars and researchers who attended the 1994 International Conference on Violence in the Media (Storm, 1994, A1, A10), during which it was estimated that the typical American child with "typical" televiewing habits will have witnessed some 18,000 episodes of homicide portrayed as entertainment before he or she reaches the age of 18. Not incidentally, that figure derives from investigations undertaken before the advent of the "information super-highway," which promises inter alia to deliver violence-on-demand, since the televiewer will no longer be confined to pre-selections determined by network programming.

Understandably enough, the entertainment media have periodically launched counterattacks on the scientific community. Thus, Milavsky (1990), a researcher at the National Broadcasting Company, contended that "the scientific evidence does not support such definite conclusions" about the linkage between television violence and crime — indeed, in a study financed by the Federal National Institute of Justice during a period in which a media star sat in the White House, Milavsky, inter alia, criticized the massive experimental evidence on the social learning of aggression among children by complaining that "Most of the experiments deal with mild forms of aggressive behavior directed at toys . . . Serious interpersonal aggression [has not been] studied because the constraints of research ethics do not allow placing people in real jeopardy."

Indeed so — but apparently no such ethical constraints guide the entertainment industry, despite what comes close to standing as incontrovertible evidence. Milavsky did not advance the usual, and largely unexceptionable, market-place arguments that drive the entertainment industry. The contours of that argument veer in the direction that far fewer viewers, whether adults or children, are interested in depictions of pacific than of aggressive themes. Support is to be found in the periodic indices of volume of viewership, which routinely demonstrate that action-adventure programming outdraws "family-oriented" situation comedies among adults and that, once they gain control over the television dial, children seem to prefer action-oriented cartoons with violent themes to the simple pastorality of Barney or Sesame Street. Once the competition for viewership accelerates through additional cable channels and the information super-highway, one might well expect, since "violence sells," an escalation in violence on the airwaves.

The world as a dangerous place: Televiewing habits and viewer vulnerabilities

In a detailed review of the then-current research and forensic evidence, Army psychiatrist Raymond Lande (1993) of Washington's Walter Reed Hospital observed that "Although many instances of children and adults imitating video violence have been documented, no court has imposed liability for harm allegedly resulting from a video program, an indication that considerable doubt still exists about the role of video violence in stimulating human aggression." Lande opined that "a small group of vulnerable viewers are probably more impressionable and therefore more likely to suffer deleterious effects from violent programming" and that "research on video violence [should] be narrowed to identifying and describing the vulnerable viewer."

Results of three studies in Britain by Anne Sheppard (1994) suggest that nearly all young children could be numbered among "vulnerable viewers." Sheppard asked subjects aged 6 to 9 to watch episodes of a children's cartoon program "with clear heroes and villains" which "presents a 'moral' with each story" and of a "British soap-like police drama," then measured their memory for crucial elements of plot, understanding of motives, and evaluation of characters portrayed. She reported that "The extent of misconstruing was a surprise finding," so that "variable recall, poor comprehension in terms of being able to relate motives to consequences, and confused character evaluation when the heroes and villains were not clearly discriminated" resulted. What the children perceived in these video depictions differed considerably from what adults perceived — and perhaps differed also from what the producers intended (133):

> Many of the children . . . tried to make sense of what was going on by evolving their own stories and interpreting screen events in ways other than those intended by the programme makers. Children . . . May strive to interpret subsequent events within the framework of the (wrong) working hypothesis. Inappropriate inferences may lead to

further inappropriate inferences and serious misconstruing and, in turn, affect character evaluation and the child's growing working knowledge.

As we have seen, Wood, Yong & Chachere (1991) would likely number children who already suffer emotional disturbance among "vulnerable viewers" and NYU neuropsychiatrist Dorothy Otnow Lewis (1990) would likely enumerate "children with . . . neuropsychiatric and cognitive vulnerabilities" issuing both from brain dysfunction and from harsh child-rearing practices. As we noted a few pages ago, Mehrabian (1995) has reported that "more hostile or aggressive persons experience more violent thoughts and show greater enjoyment of violent entertainment." Enduring hostility and/or aggressivity surely suggest themselves as components of the "particular vulnerabilities" to which Lande refers. But that begs the question of the genesis of such hostility and aggressivity; and it is a reasonable surmise that, whatever their origins, such traits are socially reinforced through continued exposure to violence in the form of entertainment media. And Russell & Pigat (1991) might nominate "social dependency needs," akin to susceptibility to social influence, for inclusion in the litany of "vulnerabilities."

We might well add the neurogenically impulsive (and, as we shall see in the next chapter, those generally deficient in the capacity to mediate the data of experience through verbal cognition) to the litany of "vulnerable viewers" particularly susceptible to video violence. Nonetheless, Lande's opinion seems unexceptionable as a design for the study of the phenomenology of aggression. Indeed, in the next chapter, we essay to identify those internal predispositions, including the neuropathologic, that render the individual the more "vulnerable" to social influences which either elicit or tolerate violent behavior. That roster may respond to the matter of who is represented among the particularly vulnerable.

If we focus on the matter of how those vulnerabilities are activated, there seems little mystery as to the mechanism whereby the phenomenology of fear is widely reinforced and maintained. In a remarkable set of studies that surely encapsulates the relationship between mere exposure to the entertainment media and the pervasiveness of the expectation of violence as normal and normative, a research team at the University of Pennsylvania's Annenberg School of Communications led by George Gerbner (Gerbner, 1993, 1995; Gerbner, Morgan & Signorielli, 1991; Seplow, 1994) has measured continuously for a quarter century both the viewing habits and the social attitudes of adults in most major U.S. cities.

Respondents are categorized as "heavy" television watchers (those who averaged four or more hours daily) or as "light" watchers (averaging less than two hours daily). Heavy watchers perceive the world as a dangerous place, with aggressive violence lurking around every corner and behind every tree; accordingly, they do not venture from their homes after dark, refuse to acknowledge the presence of strangers they happened to pass in the street even in broad daylight, sometimes arm themselves defensively when driving alone, and the like. Quite the reverse is true for light televiewers. Most importantly, these behavioral consequences obtain without regard to the content of televiewing — that is, whether the heavy viewers spend their time before the tube gazing at Barney, Sesame Street, Marcus Welby, Lucy, or re-runs of Leave It to Beaver, or whether the light viewers prefer X-rated depictions of sexual violence on premium cable channels. Those results have been independently confirmed by Wakshlag, Vial & Tamborini (1983).

Sociologist Steven Messner (1986) offers an alternative explanation of similar phenomena. Messner correlated viewership ratings of violent television programs with UCR data on the rate of violent crime in the same locales, finding an inverse relationship. But, since viewership of violent programs correlates highly with overall television viewership, Messner concluded: "If everybody's home watching TV, they aren't out there where they can get raped, robbed, assaulted, or murdered. And, since they're home making noise, they're discouraging burglars." Yet the same effect apparently does not obtain when people are at home watching reruns of Father Knows Best or Snow White. In Messner's view, then, the phenomenology of fear keeps people at home and glued to the television; in Gerbner's view, remaining glued to the television is what elicits the expectation of violence. That, indeed, is quite a circular vicious circle.

Vicariously-conditioned and internalized racial-ethnic stereotypes

Sociologists and social psychologists demonstrated nearly half a century ago that racial and ethnic stereotypes are at the least reinforced through media for mass information and entertainment; it may well be that the images of one or another ethnic group that one derives from newspapers, magazines, motion pictures, and television in fact shape one's perceptions and expectations of that group at least as effectively a personal encounters with members of that group; and it may be either that the images derived from the media precede and thus shape personal encounters *or* that personal encounters are reinforced via the images contained in the media. In turn, those perceptions and expectations lead one to "assign" members of that group to certain roles, but not to others. Such role "assignments" function as behavioral prescriptions, in the sense that they define and constrain the sort of behavior members of the majority anticipate — and/or will tolerate — from members of a minority group and similarly define and prescribe the behavior of the majority in relation to the minority. Moreover, since the group in question is subjected to the same stereotypical images of itself from the same sources of mass communication, the affected group tends to *internalize* the "popular" image of itself. That, surely, is an ample paradigm for long-distance vicarious conditioning.

In what is probably the landmark inquiry, Berelson & Salter (1946) studied the manner in which members of the white majority (and most particularly, those of Anglo-Saxon or Nordic ancestry) and members of several other racial and ethnic minority groups were portrayed in magazine fiction — at a time when reading weekly magazines like *Collier's* and the *Saturday Evening Post* constituted a principal means of entertainment. Both in this study and in a panoply of successors, the results were as anticipated. Members of the majority were typically portrayed in the roles of hero and heroine, as good-looking, bright, courageous, trustworthy, successful, well-employed, etc., etc. But members of minority groups were portrayed (if at all) in minor and clearly stereotypic roles, with Italians as gangsters, Blacks as shoe shine "boys" or servants, Jews as aggressively money-grabbing, the Irish as jovially dim-witted, American Indians as treacherous and prone to alcoholism. Frequently, derogatory "nicknames" were used to describe minority characters; even so sensitive a writer as Graham Greene, in a 1939 short story, speaks of "a Dago in a purple suit" ogling the wares on display in a shop window on the "forever tawdry" Tottenham Court Road in central London. Those stereotypes were largely transferred — at least until the civil rights explosion socially and legislatively during the 1960s — to motion pictures and television, as reflected in the portrayal of such characters as Amos 'n Andy, Mrs. Goldberg, and Frank Nitti of The Untouchables.

After nearly three decades of such research, Berelson & Steiner (1964, 502-505) concluded to a clearly interactive and mutually reinforcing set of stereotypes which, if not directly elicited, were strongly reinforced through the mechanism we have called long-distance vicarious conditioning, with mass communications media as the principal channels.

> The common stereotypes of the society tend to be copied . . . in the mass media of communication . . . People prejudiced against one ethnic group tend to be prejudiced against others . . . The stereotyping of ethnic groups tends to be quite similar across the society, among various social groups, and often within the stereotyped group itself.

And, in richly detailed counterpoint, the distinguished forensic psychiatrist Carl Malmquist and his equally distinguished University of Minnesota colleague psychologist Paul Meehl (1978), perhaps the leading international authority in actuarial assessment, recount the clinical dynamics through which a film portrayal of Barrabbas (the "bad thief" of the New Testament, whom the crowds urged that Pilate free even as the Christ was led to crucifixion) stimulated one viewer to homicidal rage.

Jean Genet's (1960) *The Blacks: A Clown Show* illustrates with ultimate irony both that art "copies" stereotypes from the larger society and that the stereotype is often internalized by members of the minority group in question. The play centers around a rag-tag company of Black actors and actresses who are called upon (for reasons Genet never fully explicates) to entertain an audience of affluent whites. After considerable discussion about what the audience will find pleasing, the company decides to enact that which whites will find most credible — the violent rape of an elderly white woman by a young Black man.

Stereotypes in advertising

So much for the entertainment media. We might expect that the information media, whose avowed role is merely to report facts, might be less tainted by stereotypes. Nonetheless, in a remarkable decision for a court whose member-ship by that time had been assessed as strongly conservative, the U.S. Supreme Court in essence affirmed the effect of information media on the eliciting and reinforcing of racial stereotypes in October 1991 in a decision in a case against the nation's leading daily newspaper that focused on the content of its advertising pages.

In a suit brought by civil rights groups, plaintiffs charged that the *New York Times* had violated those provisions of the Federal Civil Rights Act of 1964 concerning non-discrimination in housing because it had not, over a period of 20 years, insisted that those firms that placed real estate advertising in its pages consciously and deliberately portray racial and ethnic mixtures among the frolicking and gamboling families depicted in photographs of the house and apartment developments placed on offer. Over the course of that period, a disproportionately small number of models (in comparison to the racial compo-sition of society at large) had been members of minority groups.

Hence, plaintiffs asserted, the net effect of those advertisements had been to communicate to members of the white majority that the residences offered were intended for "people like us," while members of minority groups had by the same set of tokens been led to feel that such residences were not intended for "people like us," despite disclaimers in small print that the developer adhered rigidly to Federal equal opportunity and/or affirmative action guidelines. The Court found no merit in the *Times'* argument that it merely printed advertising copy as submitted by its paying customers. Instead, the court seemed to say, the *Times,* as the closest we have to a national journal of record and as a principal influence on public opinion, has a positive obligation to break the interactive chain.

It is of more than passing interest that, in spring and summer 1995, the investment banking firm Dean Witter undertook a major advertising campaign to recruit candidates for "a career as a Dean Witter account executive." Rather than place the customary block of small gray type in the classified section of newspapers, however, the firm placed full page advertisements in such mass circulation national newsweeklies as *Time* and *Newsweek*, featuring, above a caption that read "We're looking for people who understand the power of a dream, like Gwen Cohen," a large photograph of an (dare we say, without courting accusations of both racism and genderism?) attractive Black woman. The non-verbalized messages seemed clear at several levels: That Dean Witter sought actively to communicate that it welcomed "people like you" both among its employees and among its investors. Implicitly, there may also have been communicated a message of exclusion.

Highly publicized drug use/abuse among celebrities

In a celebrity-conscious society, few behaviors among such figures as sports stars, visible actors and actresses, and popular musicians escape public notice. In the last quarter-century, which marks the energizing of the successive "wars on drugs," figures as varied as "mainstream" motion picture actors Tony Curtis and Stacy Keach, baseball star Darrell Strawberry, and singer Mick Jagger have undergone highly publicized encounters with controlled dangerous substances — and not to the detriment of their careers. That fact alone suggests the growing acceptability of drug use in the society at large; more positively, the absence of negative consequence may be interpreted as an index to the strength of the theme of redemption in a society that numbers years with explicit reference to that theme. (More darkly, comedian John Belushi and singer Kurt Cobain met untimely ends as a result of drug overdose.) During the same period, "gangster rap" emerged as a new art form, with an explicit message that counters what are presumed to be societal norms both on drug use and on adherence to the law more generally and further appears to suggest that no intrusive negative consequence are likely to follow from disregard of those norms; today, it is rivaled by "skinhead rap," with similar refrains extolling violence as normative.

Over the same period, there has been a 53% increase in the proportion of college freshmen who favor decriminalization of drug use (Astin, Korn & Riggs, 1993, 61). It is improbable that the phenomena are not related, nor that the mechanisms underlying long-distance vicarious conditioning are not involved. Similar observations likely apply to other indices of social change, including the acceptability of non-marital sexual relationships, divorce, and the recognition of the rights of gay men and women.

Deterrence: Learning "avoidance" behavior?

Constructs like learning, conditioning, aversive reinforcement, and extinction are ubiquitous in the lexicon of learning and social learning. Among those concerned with the prevention of crime especially, the construct deterrence conveys powerful meaning. What psychological realities (if any) might that term denote? Military psychologist Thomas Milburn (1963) provided what has perhaps become the classic definition:

> Deterrence can be considered to cover the processes through which one influences the choices, the alternatives and their nature, that decision makers [or behavers] perceive

as available to them. Usually deterrents are considered negative incentives employed to dissuade [a behaver] from aggression or violence. The idea of deterrence does not rule out the coordinate application of positive incentives to persuade the [behaver who is the object of the effort to deter] to act, behave, or operate in other directions or with other means (conceivably specific ones) than dangerous, violent means . . . Deterrence is a process in that its success is related to several conditions that change over time. It is an influence process in that one seeks, through employing various combinations of incentives, to induce conformity to some code of action or avoidance of some specific classes of behavior . . .

In our context, deterrence seems to suggest a situation in which a criminal behavior has not been emitted — or, interpreted psychologically, a situation in which a criminal behavior has not been "acquired" for inclusion in the behavioral repertoire. That is not quite the same thing as extinction, which conveys the notion of "unlearning," or the extirpation from the actor's repertoire of a behavior which has already been learned. Similarly, inhibition suggests that a behavior that is an element in the repertoire is not emitted (perhaps because of strongly aversive situational contingencies, to be sure), but there is no suggestion that the behavior that is inhibited is thereby removed from the repertoire, so that, at some future time and under variant situational contingencies, it will no longer be available as a behavioral alternative.

Perhaps the notion in the lexicon of social learning theory that most nearly equates to deterrence is rather more complex — viz., the *learning of avoidance behavior*. The psychology of learning is replete with ample evidence that subjects, both animal and human, learn to avoid emitting behaviors that are associated with noxious or aversive reinforcements. In experiments with children, Bandura, Grusec & Menlove (1967) demonstrated conclusively that avoidance behavior can be learned (and extinguished) vicariously as well as directly; and Church (1959) holds that the phenomenon can be observed even among rats, so long as the aversive reinforcers produce a sufficiently powerful (indeed, painful) and observable effect on those subjects to whom they are directly applied. From a criminologic perspective, it may be that "extinction" of a criminal behavior already acquired is a construct that properly belongs within the realm of corrections, while "deterrence," in the sense of learning to avoid criminal behavior in the first instance, is a construct that properly belongs within the realm of crime prevention as a function of the agencies of positive socialization.

Long-distance vicarious deterrence

Research evidence on what we might call "vicarious deterrence" tends to be somewhat tangential. But a study by Phillips & Hensley (1984) seems to provide support for the proposition that knowledge of sanctions imposed on others through long-distance vicarious conditioning either elicits or deters similar criminal behavior. After reviewing all relevant studies, these investigators conclude that attention given in the information media to "stories in which violence is rewarded or unpunished" is followed by "imitative increases in fatal violence," including homicides, suicides, and deaths by auto. Alternately, "the number of homicides significantly decreases [after] the broadcasting of a punishment story."

In a carefully designed study at the University of Michigan's Institute for Social Research, Kessler, Downey, Milavasky & Stipp (1988) investigated the rate of teenage suicides subsequent to television newscasts concerning suicide over an eleven-year period. During the period between 1973-80, the rate of suicides increased after such broadcasts. Following substantial attention to the problem of adolescent suicide by major political and entertainment figures resulting in a (short-lived, it must be admitted) anti-suicide campaign at the break of the decade, adolescent suicides were found to decrease following newscasts with similar content. Though the investigators were skeptical about applying the constructs of imitative learning to either phenomenon, less cautious commentators might point to the putative effects of behavioral models presented negatively in contrast to those presented positively or even neutrally.

In a related context, however, in her study of crime rates in cities which previously had no access to television following the introduction of TV broadcasting in those locales in the 1950s, Hennigan (1982) found that "the introduction of television was consistently associated with increases in larceny," but not with increases in violent crime. Attributing this finding to the content of television programming in that era, during which "the advertising of consumption goods was high, upper- and middle-class lifestyles were overwhelmingly portrayed, and larceny was portrayed much less often than crimes of violence," Hennigan concluded that the observed increases in larceny were not associated with "the social learning of larceny through viewing it on TV," but rather with "viewing high levels of consumption, relative deprivation, and frustration."

Legislatively-prescribed vs. judicially-imposed sanction

Formal sanctions are intended both to punish wrong-doing by those who have behaved criminally and to deter wrong-doing by those who have not yet behaved criminally but may contemplate so doing. Formal sanctions attached to each subcategory of felony (and misdemeanor) are determined by the legislatures of the fifty states and by the U.S. Congress for the limited number of offenses that fall under the Federal criminal code. Capital punishment is, as of this writing, an option for certain types of homicides in 38 states and in the Federal judicial system. For homicides that do not rise to the capital level and for all other subcategories of crime, violent and property, formal sanctions are expressed through the type and length of sentence following conviction. In most jurisdictions, the maximum sentence for non-capital homicide is 30 years or lifetime imprisonment; for sexual assault, 15 to 30 years; for assault, 15 to 25 years; and for robbery, 10 to 15 years.

But those are maxima. The operational decision as to length of sentence, and as to whether the sentence will be served in confinement or on probation, is the responsibility of the presiding judge in the court of jurisdiction. Following adjudication of guilt, the presiding judge (or, in Federal cases and as a result of the Kennedy-Thurmond Act of 1984 in reform of the Federal prison system, a sentencing board; and, in some state jurisdictions, a jury) pronounces sentence. The sentence may dictate incarceration for a fixed or indeterminate term; or may alternately place the offender on probation for a period generally corresponding to the length of incarceration for the offense prescribed by the legislative authority in the relevant criminal code; impose a "community service" alternative to incarceration; order restitution; or order some combination of restitution, probation, and community service.

In the typical circumstance, the decision on sentence is made by the presiding judge after weighing "aggravating" and "mitigating" factors and circumstances and after receiving the report of a probation office responsible to the court concerning the character of the accused, his or her prior involvement with the criminal justice system, economic status, family obligations, and standing in the community, the likelihood of satisfactory completion of probation as an alternative to incarceration, and other factors likely to influence the court's decision in the matter of incarceration vs. probation (Frishtik, 1988). It is not surprising that the sentences actually imposed typically diverge substantially from the maxima prescribed in the legislation.

In most states, offenders sentenced to prison need serve only some 25% to 33% of the recorded sentence before becoming eligible for parole. Unless one is bound and determined to behave fractiously during confinement, therefore, one can reasonably expect to reduce the length of his or her term on the order of 67% to 75% — unless a "mandatory minimum" period of ineligibility for parole has been judicially stipulated. These terms can be further reduced in some states through the practice called "good time," whereby a prisoner receives fractional additional credit (typically, at a rate of 125%) toward eligibility for parole for each day he/she serves without incurring intra-institutional charges for disciplinary infractions. In real world terms, that practice is analogous to compensating a worker for 6.25 days for every five days he or she performs his/her job functions in a satisfactory manner. There is small wonder, then, that prisoners are typically released long before the expiration of their maximum sentences.

In the table on the next page, we have assembled *Sourcebook* data (Maguire & Pastore, 1994, 451, 536-537) on the number of episodes of violent crime in each UCR subcategory reported, the number of convictions, and the proportion of sentences imposed to prison and to probation, respectively, along with the median length of the term of sentence imposed (in months). *Sourcebook* data (650) on releases from prison in the 34 states that participate in the National Corrections Reporting program reflect the median number of months served before release in relation to each subcategory are also included.

Only a proportion of the episodes of violent crime in each subcategory are "cleared by arrest." Further shrinkage occurs after arrest, as the decision to prosecute or to dismiss charges and/or to "down-grade" charges through plea-bargaining are made. The number of offenses reported annually overwhelms the number of sentences imposed annually, whether to prison or probation, by a ratio of 2:1 in the case of homicide, 5:1 in the case of sexual assault, 19:1 in the case of aggravated assault, and 14:1 in the case of robbery. If we consider only the intrusive sanction of incarceration, the ratios become 2.3:1 for homicide, 8:1 for sexual assault, 42:1 for assault, and 19:1 for robbery. To the extent that the latter ratios may be interpreted as representing the probability of incurring the intrusive sanction of incarceration, the prospective offender (even the prospective homicide offender) might construe the "odds" as in his or her favor.

Table 4.8: Annual incidence of violent crime, proportion and median length [months] of sentences imposed to prison and to probation, and median number of months actually served in prison before release

Offense	Episodes	Sentences Imposed	Median Prison Sentence [Months, %]	Median Probation Sentence [Months, %]	Median Months Served in Prison Before Release
• Homicide	23,250	10,895	240 [91%]	60 [05%]	68
• Forcible sexual assault	93,804	18,024	120 [67%]	60 [14%]	44
• Assault (aggravated)	1,018,917	53,661	51 [45%]	36 [28%]	15
• Robbery	653,628	47,446	72 [73%]	48 [10%]	27

→ **SOURCE.** Maguire & Pastore, 1994, 451, 536–537, 650. Proportions do not add to 100% by subcategory because cases in which sentence is reduced to "time served" while awaiting trial are not included.

In the 34 states represented in the National Corrections Reporting program, the homicide offender is released after serving a median of 68 months, the sexual assault offender after serving a median of 44 months, the assault offender after serving a median of 15 months, and the robbery offender after serving a median of 27 months. If we use median figures for time served as the numerator and median for length of sentence imposed for the same offenses as the denominator, the fractional proportion is 28% for homicide, 36% for sexual assault, 29% for assault, 38% for robbery. Or, to put the matter rather more dramatically: The taking of a life (homicide) is, on a statistical basis, likely to cost the offender five years and eight months of his own liberty — if he or she is apprehended, prosecuted, and convicted. But the probability attached to that, on a statistical basis, is only on the order of 40%.

In the next two chapters, we propose that a "taste for risk" is a principal component of the phenomenology of aggressive criminal offending. When one considers the relative improbability of apprehension, prosecution, conviction, and sentence to intrusive sanction and further factors into the equation the probable length of actual incarceration even if sentenced to prison, there is little mystery as to why formal sanctions appear to have minimal deterrent effect for aggressive criminal violence. Indeed, Sherman (1993) has proposed that disparities between legislatively-prescribed and judicially-imposed sanctions may, in effect, render formal sanctions irrelevant as deterrents to criminal behavior and perhaps invite defiance as a response [NOTE 8].

Controversial studies on the deterrent effect of capital punishment

The classic (and surely most controversial) studies to consider vicarious deterrence are those which have focused on the deterrent effects of the death penalty, with sharp and adamant positions taken by "abolitionists" and "retentionists" respectively — often at the expense of adopting an "advocacy scholarship" that is never dispassionate and hardly clothed in objectivity. These studies were undertaken principally during that period in the mid-1970s in which the matter of capital punishment was Constitutionally in limbo, following the decision of the U.S. Supreme Court in *Furman v. Georgia* [NOTE 9], which in effect placed a nationwide moratorium on the imposition of the death penalty (Zimring & Hawkins, 1986; Pallone & Hennessy, 1992, 267-268).

Pioneer criminologist Thorstin Sellin (1959) fired the opening salvo in a study which compared homicide rates between 1920 and 1957 in neighboring U.S. states with similar social and demographic characteristics that were said to differ only in whether they did or did not have death penalty statutes in effect. Sellin concluded that either there were no differences in rates of homicide between neighboring "abolitionist" and "retentionist" states or, where such differences obtained, the rates were lower in "abolitionist" jurisdictions. Utilizing a quite different research methodology (viz., time-series analyses) over a 50-year period in one state, Decker & Kohfeld (1984) concluded that "the death penalty had no deterrent effect on homicides." Put into terms from the lexicon of the psychology of learning: There is little support in the Sellin or Decker & Kohfeld studies for the notion of vicarious deterrence of homicide attached to the death penalty; instead, there is the suggestion in Sellin's study that retention of the death penalty produces a mild but discernibly paradoxical effect — by eliciting rather than extinguishing criminal homicide.

Sellin's position was countered by Isaac Ehrlich (1975-a, 1975-b), a specialist in econometrics, in a study of homicide rates between 1933 and 1967 in neighboring states. Utilizing the methods of economic cost-benefit analysis, Ehrlich reached the conclusion that each death penalty that was not imposed had resulted in the murder of eight victims — or, alternately, that imposition of the death penalty on one offender in one homicide deters other homicides by other offenders at the ratio of 1:8. That is powerful support for vicarious deterrence indeed. Similar, but not quite so powerful, conclusions were reached by Lester (1989) in an analysis of data on the number of executions and murders in California over a ten-year period and by Archer, Gartner & Beittel (1983) in a study of the extent to which homicide rates had declined in 14 nations following abolition of the death penalty. In his turn, Ehrlich was answered (often with criticism of his methodology, admittedly more at home in the field of economics than in criminology) by such luminaries as Daniel Glaser (1979) and William Bailey (1975, 1976-a, 1976-b, 1980, 1989, 1990).

In what it may have conceived as an ultimate effort to resolve the matter at the level of public policy, the National Academy of Sciences commissioned seasoned researchers Lawrence Klein, Brian Forst, and Victor Filatov (1978) to review and distill the empirical evidence. They concluded (351) that "the deterrent effect of capital punishment is definitely not a settled matter, and this is the strongest social scientific conclusion that can be reached at the present time." In an independent review, Arnold Barnett of the Sloan School of Management at MIT (1978, 291) concluded that "no specific evidence has been presented that indicates with any conclusiveness whether executions deter murders," a conclusion repeated by Bailey (1990). On the basis of clinical data derived from murderers awaiting execution, van Wormer (1995) asserts that the death penalty itself may in some cases function as a stimulus to homicide, in what amounts to a convoluted route to suicide.

Clearly, such findings pleased partisans of neither the abolitionist nor the retentionist camp, however much they suggest that, with respect to capital punishment and subsequent homicides, there is as much reason to support as to reject the notion of vicarious deterrence. Hence, the debate continues, at both the empirical and conceptual levels, with McFarland (1983) reporting no pattern of deterrence either nationally nor locally following four well publicized executions in the U.S. and with Archer et al. (1983) reporting a reduction in the homicide rate in some 14 nations of the world following abolition, and with such data variously interpreted (Bailey, 1983-a; Bowers, 1983; Forst, 1983; Yang & Lester, 1988). Congruently, in a study of the effects of re-institution of the death penalty in Oklahoma, Cochran, Chamlin & Seth (1994), found not only no evidence for deterrent effect on rates of felony murder (a category that, because the slaying is related to the furtherance of another felony crime, like robbery or rape, corresponds to "instrumental aggression" in the Feldman-Quenzer schematic) but instead evidence of an increase in the level of brutalization associated with stranger-to-stranger homicides (a category that corresponds to "predatory aggression" in that schematic).

Execution as an infrequently-implemented sanction

Yet what has been omitted in these analyses is consideration of the real-world context in which capital punishment is being, and has historically been, operationally administered in "retentionist" jurisdictions. When the rates at which the death penalty is, and has been, implemented (i.e., legislatively prescribed, judicially imposed, and, after the inevitable or in some state mandatory appeals have been exhausted, actually carried out) at any time in this century are added to the picture, the question of whether homicide rates are higher or lower in "retentionist" or "abolitionist" jurisdictions reduces largely to a straw-man issue.

According to the U.S. Department of Justice's *Report to the Nation on Crime and Justice* in 1983, the number of homicides reported nationwide annually between 1930 and 1935 varied between 10,200 and 12,000. According to Stephan & Brien (1994), the "peak" year for executions in this century (i.e., not for the imposition of the death penalty at trial, but for its actually being implemented) nationwide was 1935, when 199 offenders were executed. If 199 executions in 1935 represents the peak, it seems clear that the death penalty has never been carried out in this country in this century at a ratio greater than 2% of the known cases of murder. In full and appropriate context, the question of deterrence thus becomes whether homicide rates are higher or lower in those states in which the death penalty has not been imposed and implemented in something on the order of 98% of the murders for which it stood as the legislatively prescribed sanction, even during a period many would regard as the most bloodthirsty in our recent history.

There are very many reasons indeed to be found in the psychology of learning to support the hypothesis that a sanction that is infrequently-implemented will have at best a marginal effect on behavior despite its severity. That proposition is substantively related to the well-demonstrated resistance to change of a behavior that is maintained on either a random or intermittent schedule of reinforcement. A more objective analysis of the evidence might conclude that, because the death penalty is and has been an infrequently-implemented sanction in the U.S., even in those jurisdictions in which it is prescribed by law, no statement can be made about its deterrent effect with any pretense to scientific validity.

To settle the question of deterrent effect would seem to require either cross-national comparisons with societies (if any such exist) in which the death penalty is virtually universally imposed and carried out as a sanction for aggressive (or even non-aggressive) crime, with all sorts of adjustments for endemic differences — or a radical and unthinkable change in the frequency of imposition and implementation of the capital sanction in "retentionist" U.S.

states. That such investigations have not been undertaken may be as it should be, however — for, as Lowenstein (1988) argues, the moral issue of whether to retain or abolish capital punishment may be simply too important a policy decision to be left to empirical behavioral science.

Legal scholars Franklin Zimring & Gordon Hawkins (1986) imply a sort of aversive conditioning effect in the arithmetic they use to depict the degree of escalation in annual executions necessary if (1) U.S. courts continue to impose the death penalty at the post-Furman rate and (2) the nation is to reduce the current log-jam phenomenon on death row so as to avoid future court contests claiming that prolonged anticipation of execution in itself constitutes cruel and unusual punishment. To follow their formula: To reduce, even within a ten year period, the 1993 death row population of approximately 2700 (Stephan & Brien, 1994, 7) to a stable group of no more than 300, and assuming continuation of the post-Furman rate of imposition of the death penalty (approximately 300 per year), would require something like 540 executions annually — an increase on the order of 1400% over the rate of execution in 1993, when 38 offenders were liquidated. Thereafter, assuming a constant rate of homicide and of imposition of the death penalty in a burgeoning population, we would need to execute approximately 300 per year.

That, they quite properly contend, would constitute a blood bath of proportions unprecedented in peacetime in any nation at any time in the history of the human species that is likely to prove totally unacceptable to the American public — to say nothing of our relative physical incapacity to execute at that rate even if we wanted to. Clinically, we can attest that most people we know who enjoy rousing violence in the entertainment media are simultaneously aware of the make-believe character thereof — the actor who is drawn and quartered in tonight's offering will be up-and-at-'em tomorrow. Though the research evidence is far from clear, we suspect that what most citizens want is the threat of the death penalty rather than its implementation through executions — just as the television viewer's thirst for make-believe blood reduces to what is no more than a make-believe thirst. If we are correct in that surmise, executions at the rate of two or more for every working day in the calendar year will very likely produce a massively adverse reaction on the part of the citizenry.

The availability of firearms

If either the general society or segments thereof implicitly foster or tolerate a culture of violence, we should expect to find also a high tolerance for the possession of lethal weapons. The data we have reviewed concerning weapons in aggressive criminal violence point with absolute clarity to firearms as the weapon most frequently used in killings; moreover, firearms are also the most frequent means of self-destruction (Wood & Mercy, 1990). Some 14,000 homicides are attributable to firearms each year, along with another 17,000 suicides by firearms, and approximately 4000 accidental deaths resulting from firearms; firearms are thus the weapons of death in some 35,000 killings each year.

These reasons alone might argue in favor of strict control over the possession of such weapons, even though death by firearms, whether through homicide or suicide, represents only a tiny fraction in relation to the known and acknowledged ownership of handguns and long guns. In his remarkable treatise on the Constitutional history of "the right to bear arms" in Britain and the United States, political scientist Wilbur Edel (1995, 141-142) puts the aggregate at "211 million guns in a nation of 250 million." By Edel's reckoning, there are nearly six weapons for every seven members (man, woman, child) of the population. But the number of deaths by firearm of any sort — homicide, suicide, accident — aggregate to no more than 35,000 annually. If Edel's total is accurate, the ratio between firearms acknowledged to be owned and death by such a weapon is of the order of 6029:1. If one assumes a 1:1 correspondence between a single firearm and a single death by firearm and further assumes that each of the 35,000 or so firearms represented in an annual enumeration of death by firearms is also represented in the aggregated acknowledged ownership (both statistically questionable assumptions), legislation which banned the private ownership of firearms altogether would yield a "false positive" rate on the order of 99.834%.

Whenever the matter of legislative control of gun ownership arises, substantial opposition is raised by the National Rifle Association and other membership groups composed of those committed either to blood sports or to "recreational" shooting by means of target practice (or both). Indeed, as Edel (1995, 115-116) demonstrates, the NRA coined the phrase "jack-booted fascists" to describe Federal law enforcement officers charged with implementing such relatively weak legislative control over the sale and purchase of firearms as early as 1981, when the organization had as its executive vice president a person who "at the age of 17 . . . had been convicted of murder for shooting to death a 15-year-old Mexican boy." The phrase was to become infamous in the Spring of 1995 in the wake of the bombing of the Federal building in Oklahoma City; when the NRA continued to use the phrase in its recruiting literature in the aftermath of that event, former President George Bush ceremoniously and very publicly resigned his lifetime membership in the organization.

Virtually invariably, opposition to legislative control of gun ownership is rooted in what is held to be a right to bear arms guaranteed by the Constitution, but prototypically quoted well out of context. In fact, the full text of the Second Amendment reads.

A well-regulated militia being necessary to the security of a free state, the right of the people to keep and bear arms shall not be infringed.

The conditional clause which opens the text is surely susceptible to the interpretation that "the right . . . to keep and bear arms" arises within and is limited to those circumstances under which an organized governmental authority finds it necessary to establish and to equip an armed force — thus, the Armed Forces of the United States and the militia (or, as they are termed today, National Guard units) of the various states. Edel (1995) traces both the Constitutional and case law history (16-18, 25-36) of what he terms (141) "the mistaken but widespread belief that the Second Amendment guarantees every individual" rights of gun ownership. More particularly, the Amendment surely contains no language that suggests that it is the right of every citizen to own an automatic weapon capable of delivering tens, or hundreds, of rounds per minute, especially since such "assault" weapons are barred from use in blood sports in most states. However that may be, it seems clear that opponents of gun control legislation have the statistics on their side.

Gun ownership and violent crime

The relationship between gun ownership and control policies and the rate of violent crime has been studied and debated among social scientists as avidly as in the popular press and in legislative chambers. Yet the empirical data have yielded few unclouded conclusions.

King (1973) underscored a paradox early on by analyzing the extraordinarily liberal gun control legislation and very low rate of violent crime in Switzerland vs. the strict gun control legislation, tradition of unarmed constabulary, but burgeoning rate of violent crime, in Britain. Menninger (1984) offered similar contrasts between the high rate of homicide by firearm in the U.S. with the low rate in Japan, contending that gun ownership in this country is tied to our "pioneer, frontier-conquering heritage," a position essentially supported by Harding (1993) in an analysis of ownership and violence among Australian aborigines in contrast to other nations. Roth (1994) has inventoried varied provisions for the control of firearms, ranging from prohibition of private ownership to heavy sanctions for carrying concealed weapons and "disrupting" black-market sales and trades.

After studying both homicide and suicide cases in a single American city, Danto (1971) concluded that "murderers and suicidal persons are prone to misuse the firearm as they would misuse any potential instrument of destruction" — that is, were a firearm not available, another instrument would be selected to accomplish the lethal task, a view echoed by Lester (1987-d). But it is at some variance with Clarke's (1987) data about the role of opportunity in criminal behavior in general and with Clarke & Lester's (1989) data on the availability of the means to suicide in particular. Indeed, Klein, Reizen, Van Amburg & Walker (1977), in an analysis of all fatalities (whether homicide or suicide) in one state over a five-year period, found that the weapons employed had been acquired primarily for "self protection," rather than for recreational or criminal purposes, a conclusion also drawn by Roth (1994). But ownership of a firearm may itself precipitate what Feldman & Quenzer (1984, 248-252) identified, on the basis of animal studies, as "fear-induced" aggression.

Effects of legislative control of gun ownership

More discerning analyses have studied the effects of tightening or loosening extant gun control legislation on homicide and suicide. Thus, Lester & Murrell (1982) concluded that states in the nation that had enacted tight handgun control laws evinced lower rates of suicide by firearm two years after the introduction of such legislation, but with no sharp decrease in overall suicide rate, so that other means were apparently found once the "weapon-of-choice" became relatively less accessible; but no similar effect was observed on the rate of mortality by homicide through handgun. Lester also (1987) demonstrated that police officers were murdered at higher rates in jurisdictions with lax gun control legislation. In a later study, however, Lester (1988-c, 176) found that "Gun ownership, rather than the strictness of gun control laws, is the strongest correlate of the rates of suicide and homicide." Relatively congruent conclusions were reached by Cook (1982) and Moore (1995).

Several investigators have considered the deterrent effect of strict gun control legislation. Loftin & McDowall (1984) amassed data from Florida during a period in which possession of an unlicensed firearm carried a mandatory three-year prison sentence. They concluded that implementation of that legisla-tion "did not have a measurable effect on violent crime." In a similar study in Michigan, Loftin, Heumann & McDowall (1983) concluded that the introduc-tion of similarly strict legislation, which carried a mandatory two-year sentence, produced no significant deterrent effects on violent crime. Perhaps such findings led to the very loose Florida legislation of the late 1980s (adopted after a publicity campaign on the part of conservative legislators whose rallying cry was "Law-abiding citizens are armed and dangerous"), whereby firearms permits could be issued virtually without examination of such characteristics as psychiatric stability of the applicant or prior criminal history. But, in an investigation of neighboring cities in the United States and Canada with very different local legislation on handgun ownership, Sloan, Kellerman, Reay & Ferris (1989, 1256) unearthed an interesting network of relationships:

> Despite similar overall rates of criminal activity and assault, the relative risk of death from homicide, adjusted for age and sex, was significantly higher in Seattle than in Vancouver. Virtually all of this excess risk was explained by a 4.8-fold higher risk of being murdered with a handgun in Seattle. Rates of homicide by means other than guns were not substantially different in the communities studied.

The central thrust of these studies surely veers in the direction of a linkage between the availability of firearms and criminal violence. But the linkage may not be rectilinear. Two non-rectilinear propositions compete with one other.

- Those who commit homicide, suicide, or aggravated assault short of homicide by means of firearms do so because firearms are rather freely and widely available.

- Because firearms are more readily available than alternate means, those inclined toward lethal violence are likely to commit (or attempt) such violence by means of firearms rather than search out those alternate means.

The second proposition seems to us a sounder conjecture than the first — that is, it seems likely that the availability of firearms potentiates, rather than elicits, a disposition toward violence.

But, if that proposition approximates the reality, Danto (1971) and Clarke & Lester (1989) may well be correct in predicting that, in the absence of a readily available firearm, those inclined (whether neuropathologically, intrapsychically, by means of social learning, through eliciting stimuli, or through some combination of such variables) toward lethal violence will soon enough either deliberately search out or otherwise "happen upon" a substitute weapon. Moreover, we would expect those who are disposed toward violence to self-select those environments in which firearms or other weapons are relatively readily available.

Terrorism on the InterNet

By spring 1995, our respective universities had linked to those "patches" of the information super-highway devoted (though not restricted) to "academic traffic." We spent an hour in our university offices "grazing" the relatively limited arena of the InterNet to which our institutions had provided access to survey what sources of information were readily accessible concerning the availability of weapons. We discovered, within that limited time span and with our limited access, some two dozen "bulletin boards" focused on firearms and containing down-loadable detailed instructions as to what dealers the prospective purchaser should contact, typically through "electronic mail," in rather frank blueprints on how to avoid the impact of Federal legislation on the sale of assault weapons. Moreover (as the news media also discovered in the aftermath of the destruction of the Federal building in Oklahoma City in April 1995), we also found some eighteen bulletin boards providing detailed, down-loadable instructions on how to fabricate explosive devices, ranging from Molotov cocktails to pipe bombs, using materials freely available at most hardware stores.

Anecdotal evidence is a poor substitute for empirical data; to date, however, we have found no studies on the use of telecommunications in marketing weapons of destruction or instructing users on how to manufacture their own. That we were able to access such information effortlessly from the frugal comfort of faculty offices and not in the dingy alleyways where "Saturday Night

Specials" are surreptitiously bought and sold nonetheless serves as a something of a marginal gloss, indicating that electronic technology has already come to serve a pervasive culture of violence.

RACE, SCAPEGOATING, AND THE PHENOMENOLOGY OF FEAR

Especially because Blacks are substantially over-represented as offenders in criminal violence, the invitation to scapegoat is strongly seductive — and only rarely resisted. Indeed, to some large extent, the phenomenology of fear pivots precisely on the scapegoating phenomenon, with its implicit promise of the "too-easy" answer.

As we have seen, Blacks perpetrate 26% of the episodes of (single-offender) criminal violence, whether against Black or white victims, a ratio of slightly more than 2:1 in relation to their representation in the population at large. We have also noted that the relative size of police forces in the major population centers of the nation is driven not primarily by rates of crime but, to some major extent, by minority representation in those centers. When age is added to the mix, the scapegoat image becomes that of the young Black man as the prototypical offender. When we turn to the television, the young Black men we see are prototypically engaged in violent behavior, as readily on the gridiron, the basketball court, or the boxing ring as in the criminal court. Though the packagers of television drama and situation comedy have been careful to avoid casting Blacks in "negative" roles (without demonstrating such reluctance in relation to the role of quaint buffoon), newscasters do not share that reluctance — and, invariably, it is the episode of Black-on-white violence that receives journalistic attention. Black-on-Black violence, though equally frequent, remains largely under-reported, perhaps because it contributes little to "market share."

We learn who we are and what we may become not merely in the immediate psychosocial surround of the home, family, neighborhood, school; instead, we are influenced by the role models that parade before us. It is foolhardy for us to expect a young Black male on the threshold of adolescence, enmeshed in a pervasive culture of violence that delivers uniform images of his prospective future, to perceive his prospects and possibilities otherwise. When we factor into the mix Carl Bell's estimate that, by the age of 11, 80% of urban Black children will have witnessed a beating, stabbing, or shooting (Bell, 1990; Meharry Medical College, 1991), that escape from the pathological vise of pervasive violence is possible at all evokes wonderment.

But scapegoating may tell us more about the scapegoater than about the scapegoatee. As a statistical exercise, suppose that we play "Let's Pretend" with the data on the annual incidence of aggressive criminal violence. Let's pretend that Blacks do not exist in American society, and so are not available to perpetrate

26% of those episodes. Our "Let's Pretend" assumptions reduce the incidence of aggressive criminal violence by 26%. Let's now compare the rate of criminal offending thus reduced to similar rates in other nations of the world.

Table 4.9: Rates of aggressive criminal violence (homicide, sexual assault, assault) per 100,000 of the population in member nations of the European Economic Community, in other selected nations, and in the United States under two conditions

Group	Nation/Condition	Rate per 100,000	Rank order
USA under two conditions			
•	Actual USA: All offenses committed by all offenders	474.7	1
•	"Let's Pretend" USA: Offenses committed by Black offenders omitted	351.3	2
Member nations of the European Economic Community			
•	Belgium	167.6	6
•	Britain (England, Scotland, Wales)	326.3	3
•	Denmark	217.1	5
•	France	130.3	9
•	Germany	170.9	8
•	Greece	81.9	11
•	Ireland	14.1	15
•	Italy	41.4	13
•	Luxembourg	89.6	10
•	Netherlands	212.1	7
•	Portugal	11.4	16
•	Spain	42.4	12
Non-European industrial nations			
•	Canada	256.1	4
•	Japan	16.2	14
The world's most populous nation			
•	People's Republic of China	8.9	17

→ **SOURCE:** Data extrapolated from *International Crime Statistics* (International Criminal Police Organization, 1990).

For convenience, let's select as a primary comparison group the "first world" nations of Europe that have chosen to ally themselves with each other in the European Economic Community (the "European Common Market," whose members in 1990 included Belgium, Britain, Denmark, France, Germany, Greece, Ireland, Italy, Luxembourg, the Netherlands, Portugal, and Spain), most of which are far more culturally and racially homogeneous than we. Comparisons may also be relevant with Canada (because we share the continent), with Japan (our principal rival for worldwide economic supremacy), and with the People's Republic of China (whose 1.2 billion people account for some 25% of the world's population). In Table 4.9, we display INTERPOL data (for the year 1990) for crimes of aggressive violence for those nations and for the United

States, with the latter arrayed under two conditions. as they were actually committed, including those in which Blacks were the offenders, and under the "Let's Pretend" condition which omits offenses committed by Blacks [NOTE 10] In all cases, data are aggregated under the customary metric of incidence per 100,000 of the population. It may be of interest that several large Western hemisphere nations (e.g., Brazil, Mexico, Venezuela) do not report crime data to INTERPOL, nor does India, the nation with the world's second-largest population.

In real numbers, the United States is clearly the hands-down leader among the nations represented. When we reduce the aggregate under the "Let's Pretend" condition in which aggressive offenses committed by Black offenders are eliminated, we are still the world's leader in the incidence of crimes of aggressive violence. The "adjusted" figure for the U.S. with offenses committed by Black offenders eliminated from consideration ranks as the second-highest among these nations; the U.S. is the leader among first-world nations in aggressive crimes of violence whether offenses committed by Blacks are included or when they are excluded. The conclusion seems inescapable that violence inheres in the socioculture of the American nation rather than in its minority population. Some commentators might even propose that the propensity toward violence largely flows (and historically, if one considers the legacy of slavery, has flown) *from* the larger society *into* the minority community rather than the reverse.

A familiar principle in phenomenological psychology holds that a perceptually dominant concern tends to over-organize us with respect to its focus but to under-organize us with respect to everything else. If the phenomenology of fear is wed inextricably to the media-induced or -supported image of the young Black man as prototypical perpetrator in aggressive crimes of violence, we over-organize ourselves individually and societally with respect to Black-initiated aggressive violence but simultaneously under-organize ourselves with respect to white-initiated aggressive violence, in a situation in which the latter outweighs the former at a ratio of 3:1 [NOTE 11]. The phenomenology of fear thus readily leads to an unwarranted sense of security among non-Blacks who flee urban centers with a high proportion of Black population. Those of our colleagues who hew to a Marxist (or economic determinist) interpretation of social data are well advised to wonder, in this situation, "Who benefits? Who pays?"

A phenomenology of fear that rests on statistically unwarranted beliefs about Black-initiated violence implicitly writes behavioral prescriptions that govern cross-race encounters, inclining television-influenced non-Blacks to construe any Black (especially a young male) as a prospective predator, and may even determine whether such encounters will occur. As Elijah Anderson (1990, 209) put it in *Streetwise*, his remarkable analysis of life in an urban ghetto that has become for the 1990s what Frederic Thrasher's *Street Corner Society* and *The Gang* proved to be for the 1930s:

. . . whites and Blacks are skilled in the art of avoidance, using their eyes, ears, and bodies to navigate safely. Although this seems to work . . . it vitiates comity between the races. One class of people is conditioned to see itself as law-abiding and culturally superior while viewing the other as a socially bruised underclass inclined to criminality. This perspective creates social distance and racial stereotyping, to which middle-income Blacks are especially sensitive. Further, it makes even liberal whites vulnerable to . . . racism.

That they are likely to be prejudged as menacing or threatening is not lost among young Black men; and in those mutually distorted perceptions, the phenomenology of fear generates easily — and may even mature into a self-fulfilling prophecy. Anderson recounts an encounter that might readily have matured into a full-fledged confrontation:

> One evening I was walking down the street and this older white lady was at the middle of the block, and I was walking toward her. It was just me and her. Then all of a sudden this young white man runs across the street and just stands between me and this lady. He just kept watching me, and I stared him down, When I passed him, I turned and kept on looking at him. I know he thought I was going to mess with that woman or something.

Nor is the phenomenology of fear a property only of members of the racially dominant caste. DeFrances & Smith (1994, 2) analyzed data from surveys undertaken between 1985 and 1991 by the Federal Department of Housing & Urban Development to identify "neighborhood problems." Their conclusions: "Black households regularly [cited] 'crime' as a neighborhood problem more frequently than white households and have consistently had a higher percentage of violent crime victimization as well as overall victimization." Among these respondents, it is not clear whether same-race or cross-race victimization contributed more heavily to the phenomenology of fear.

CONTOURS OF THE CULTURE OF AGGRESSION

Most members of a society undergo relatively similar social learning experiences. Most of us have heard the same, generally pious, tales of George Washington, Abraham Lincoln, Betsy Ross, Molly Pitcher, Crispus Attucks, Nat Turner, Sojourner Truth, and Martin Luther King. For that matter, most of us view the same televised football games or prize fights or crime drama — or witness in "real-time" mass destruction in the deserts of Iraq and Kuwait (and in Oklahoma City), on a scale unprecedented in the annals of destroying or of witnessing, or in the once-grand cities of the "former Yugoslavia," or the forlorn plains of Somalia.

Some behavioral scientists hold the view that disparate elements in the social learning process congeal (rather than "blend") so as to constitute a relatively pervasive social-cultural environment that delivers relatively homogeneous messages about what is good or bad, acceptable or unacceptable, in ourselves, in others, and in our relations with each other. Once congealed, that environment is itself recycled through the process of social learning, so that mutual reinforcement occurs circularly and constantly.

We are likely to regard that circular process as inevitable — and to applaud when it serves either those ends that we endorse or those values we hold to be required for the maintenance of civilized society, such as a respect for the truth, diligence, honesty, compassion. Indeed, whenever we approach a traffic intersection, we rather trust that social learning and stimulus determinants (such as the color of the light signal) will control the behavior of most other drivers in pro-social ways — that is, that we can proceed confidently when we face the green signal, with reasonable assurance that the behavior of others is being determined by the stimulus value of the red signal.

But, implicitly or explicitly, every positive behavioral model conjures a reciprocal negative model. And that process occurs even when the intent is to convey positive behavioral images. There is some empirical evidence that such reciprocal negative models sometimes exert their own attraction, elicit among some the learning of negative social behavior; and that our societal preoccupation with violence — whether conveyed through news reports, crime drama that idolizes the rogue-hero, professional sports events (with their own quota of idolatry for the rogue-hero), cartoon characters who blast at each other with thermonuclear weapons on the television or the computer monitor, "tabloid" docu-drama reenactments of alienated husbands stalking wives who have found comfort elsewhere, or "gangster rap" or "skinhead rap" — serves to further legitimate violence as an acceptable feature of our society (Daly & Wilson, 1989).

Some commentators, indeed, believe that the process by which violence comes to be perceived as an acceptable behavioral option for the individual through which to resolve conflicts has its genesis in formal public policy that governs the ways in which a society or a nation deals with its citizens and with other societies or nations — and that popular culture merely reflects formal public policy on the acceptability of violence. Thus, King (1978) described the "brutalization effect" that follows publicity about executions and, in his judgment, actually elicits violent behavior in its wake. Or, as Wilkes (1986, 26) put it after reviewing data from some 110 nations, "when a nation does violence to human beings by conducting wars or executing criminals, it incites its citizens to criminal violence" precisely because that nation has itself legitimated violence. One might suspect that it also "incites" the creators of television entertainments and the arbiters of what is portrayed in the news media. As Edel (1995, 157) has put it:

> The remedy — part conceptual, part economic — depends on . . . reversing the perception, fostered by an endless stream of Rambo-type movies and war stories that

focus almost exclusively on the heroics rather than the horror of mass killing, that a nation's values and its greatness spring from the barrel of a gun.

Neither King nor Wilkes addressed the brutalization effect of the race-caste system in the United States, of the legacy of three centuries of bondage and a subsequent century and a quarter of continued and continuing economic exploitation, resulting in substandard education by design, economic marginalization, and encapsulation in the lowest socioeconomic strata in the society, with the aggregate compelling residence in the center cities, in which strata and places of residence the rates of drug trafficking and of aggressive victimization are disproportionately high. But no such reticence stilled the voices of Algerian psychiatrist Frantz Fanon (1965) in *The Wretched of the Earth,* American psychiatrists William Grier and Price Cobbs (1968) in *Black Rage,* novelists Richard Wright (1957) in *White Man, Listen!* and James Baldwin (1963) in *The Fire Next Time,* or legal scholar Lennox Hinds (1978) in *Illusions of Justice.*

When the brutalization effect from the legacy of slavery and economic marginalization is factored into an equation already heavy with the overarching ethos of the frontier that shapes and informs a generalized, virtually universal, culture of violence, that aggression readily overflows the bounds of the caste system among those so brutalized, despite a police presence that is dictated by that system itself, seems not in the least incomprehensible. And, as we observed in Chapter 2, the same brutalization effect issuing from the same legacy also produces an incidence of neuropathology, according to distinguished Black psychiatrist Carl Bell (1986), some four times greater than in the majority community. For their part, the creators of entertainments and the arbiters of the news are wed inextricably to the nurturance of a phenomenology of fear that is not independent of brutalization of the same stamp. That, it appears, is what "market factors" dictate.

The research evidence from studies in social learning for vicarious conditioning and extinction is incontrovertible. The research evidence on the role of long-distance vicarious conditioning in the elicitation and/or facilitation of criminal aggression is somewhat more fragmentary, but the direction is relatively clear, whether the agency of influence is the behavioral model or the relatively less direct transmission of normative attitudes and values.

Similarly, there is evidence that supports the notion of long-distance vicarious deterrence. But the evidence on deterrence of homicide through the ultimate sanction of capital punishment is mixed; there is as much evidence in favor of the effect as in opposition to it. It may be the case that the relative infrequency of the actual carrying out of death sentences even during those periods in which such sentences were rather freely legislatively prescribed and judicially imposed clouds the situation in such a way as to preclude dispassionate conclusions. There is little evidence that legislatively-adopted maximal sanctions carry potent deterrent effect. Certainly, there is strong reason to believe, on the basis of evidence from studies of learning and social learning, that a negative sanction that is infrequently imposed has little aversive value. And the absence of invariant negative sanctions — a situation which carries an implicit promise of impunity — itself supports and sustains a pervasive culture of aggressive violence.

One feature of that culture of violence is that it is estimated that nearly six of every seven men, women, and children in the land, including the roughly 12% of the population aged 9 and under, either own, or have direct in-home access to, a privately-owned firearm. With the ready access to firearms and with messages trumpeting the normative expectation that violent confrontation is an acceptable feature of human interaction whether the role models one selects for emulation are the "good guy" heroes of motion pictures or television or the negative figures of a frankly deviant subculture, the question may not be why there are as many as 35,000 deaths by firearms (or even some fraction of a million episodes of aggravated assault in which firearms are implicated) in the nation in a year — but rather why there are as few.

NOTES

1. Medical epidemiology is traditionally said to have had its birth in the early 19th century, when London physicians traced the genesis of an epidemic of influenza to contaminants in a particular pumping station used to deliver the municipal water supply. Despite more than a century and a half of increasingly sophisticated statistical analyses of illness-inducing variables of all sorts, only recently has there emerged consensus among medical epidemiologists concerning a common metric through which to express the findings resultant from their investigations (Taubes, 1995). The metric currently in favor is the *risk ratio,* which contrasts the prevalence of a "target" disorder in a particular group under study with the prevalence of another group or perhaps with that in the general population.

But even such a ratio remains relatively speculative, for it is often not known, for example, whether the group to which members of the "at risk" pool (typically, in which the target disorder is found more frequently) are compared have in some fashion developed an "immunity" to the target disorder; thus, the matter of whether members of the "at risk" group are "abnormally" or "merely normally" susceptible remains a mater of intense debate in medical epidemiological circles. In our terms, may it be the case (for example) that girls and women are "immunized" from the emission of violent behavior and that boys and men are "merely" normally susceptible to such behavior? Or is it that girls and woman exhibit a baseline for such behavior to which the rates of similar behavior among boys and men demonstrate "enhanced" risk? For such reasons, we have preferred to use the term *risk marker* as indicative of a looser and less definitive association that the term "risk factor" frequently employed in medical epidemiology.

Moreover, even medical epidemiology has yet to agree upon a common set of rubrics through which to express *interaction* between what may or may not be "independent" risk factors (or markers) for physical disorders or infectious diseases. Is it the case, for example, that sustained, heavy cigarette smoking over a long period interacts linearly, curvilinearly, or not at all with exposure to carcinogens transmitted through environmental pollution in the genesis of cancer? As Taubes (1995) has demonstrated, many medical epidemiologists advocate the conservative position that the relative incidence of a disorder in an "at risk" group should exceed that in a comparison group by 200%-300% (i.e., that the risk ratio derived should range between 2:1 or 3:1) before *causative* links are inferred.

2. A substantial redesign of the questionnaire which constitutes the principal instrument utilized in the National Crime Victimization Survey was undertaken in 1993 (Bastian, 1995), with the rather overt purpose of *increasing* the episodes of sexual assault enumerated, largely apparently as a result of lobbying efforts by groups of feminist scholars who have long claimed that sex offenses are radically underestimated, whether through UCR or NCVS data. Thus, "to expand the types of sexual crimes counted . . . Direct questions were added to encourage the victims to report to interviewers incidents that may have been committed by someone known to them." Curiously, the data for the first year in which the redesigned survey instrument was employed demonstrated a *decrease* of more than 20% in the number of sexual victimizations unearthed through NCVS interviews in comparison with the preceding year, accompanied to be sure by a 3% decrease in the number of episodes reflected in UCR data on such offenses reported to law enforcement authorities. While the purpose may have been, intentionally or otherwise, to "criminalize" behavior that had previously been regarded as relatively normal "seduction" activity in various segment of the society, the obverse effect seems to have obtained.

3. By summer 1995, a veritable chorus composed of both biological and social scientists had intoned a chant which holds that "race" is a purely social construct, not a biological reality (Branch, Brook-Gunn, Broughton et al., 1995). Among the reasons for such a position cited both in scholarly journals and in the popular press is the virtual disintegration of the "package" of distinctive racial characteristics in the wake of contemporary research into genomes and genotypes, such that similar eye shape is found among certain tribes in West Africa and Scandinavians, that skin complexion varies as much among those who are said to belong to the "Negroid" race as between members of that race and members of the "Caucasoid" race, that skin color is indistinguishable between many southern Europeans and many Africans, etc., and that all such superficial classificatory differences are construable as evolutionary adaptations to climatological conditions and environmental imperatives. As the distinguished cognitive psychologist Howard Gruber (1995, 98) put it: "In the case of African Americans . . . the original populations — the captured slaves — came from many quarters of Africa; the continent is huge and its human populations exhibit great cultural and biological diversity, by no means a single race."

However that may be, the emergence of the chorus rather curiously followed major public attention to the publication, virtually simultaneously, of *The Bell Curve* by Herrnstein & Murray (1994) and *Race, Evolution, and Behavior* by Rushton (1995-a), both widely (if less than accurately) interpreted as quasi-white supremacist tracts. Perhaps it seemed easier to dismantle the concept of race altogether than to rejoin either or both works on scientific grounds. And, one suspects inevitably, those volumes were soon joined by such works as *The End of Racism* by Dinesh D'Souza (1995), a conveniently distorted history of race relations in the U.S. which broadcasts the outlandish view that both slavery and racial discrimination following Emancipation in fact emanated from a benevolent paternalism on the part of whites who sought to "save" Blacks from such "cultural pathologies and civilizational inferiorities" as results from genetic inferiority in intelligence, including laziness and criminal propensity. While it is tempting to join the chorus of scholars who seek to dismiss the construct on political grounds, we have retained the concept of race because, however well- or ill-founded biologically, it has become a conventional rubric for the reporting of criminologic data. But, for a quarter-century in our own writing, we have preferred to utilize John Dollard's (1937) by-now hoary term racial caste, which underscores the confounded effects of "race" and social class in American society that is itself the inextricably-bound legacy of economic exploitation based on notions of racial superiority.

4. Gender differences in homicide offending in particular have been studied for some time. In an investigation of killing by women in both the U.S. and Britain, Palmer (1981) concluded that "females, if they kill at all, are much more prone to commit suicide than homicide" and that the prototypical victim of the woman who murders is her own child. The latter observation echoes an early finding by Cole, Fisher & Cole (1968) that the victim of a woman killer is generally another member of her immediate family and further corroborated by Steinmetz (1980) and, in a study in Canada, by Husain, Anasseril & Harris (1983). Similarly, Wilbanks (1983), in a study of all homicides in the U.S. during 1980, found that "women are more likely to kill a lover than any other victim/offender category" and that "females almost never kill other females." It is worth observing that, in a review of World Health Organization data on death in the U.S. And 23 other highly developed industrial nations, Christofell & Liu (1983) reported that homicide rates for infants and children aged 1-4 are atypically high in the U.S., with mother as the statistically most frequent slayer.

5. Pallone & Workowski (1994) analyzed UCR data on arrests for 1990 in relation to age, with a focus on youth crime. In all, there were some 96,000 arrests of persons aged 18 and under for violent crimes (homicide, rape, robbery, aggravated assault), representing 17% of all arrestees for these offenses; nearly 564,000 for property crimes (burglary, larceny, auto theft, arson), representing 32% of all arrestees for these offenses;, and nearly 812,000 for "non-index" offenses (i.e., those not litanized in the FBI's roster of "serious crimes"), including non-aggravated assault, vandalism, possession of stolen property, use of controlled dangerous substances, driving under the influence, and such "nuisance" offenses as disorderly conduct, curfew violations, possession of stolen property, etc., representing 14% of all arrestees for these offenses.

Among the entire under 18 age cohort, arrests for "non-index" crimes outnumbered arrests for violent offenses at a ratio of 17:2, while arrests for property crimes outnumbered arrests for violent crimes at a ratio of 9:2. In rank order, the most frequent cause for arrest in this age cohort was larceny, followed by violation of liquor laws (purchasing or consuming under the "legal age"), running away from home, and burglary. Among 19 offenses, aggressive crimes of violence ranked toward the bottom as a cause of arrest, with aggravated assault ranking 11th (after curfew violations), rape ranking 17th (after arson), and homicide ranking 18th. In the 15-17 age group (which, as we have seen, is substantially over-represented among arrestees for crimes of aggressive violence), there were nearly 49,000 arrests for violent offenses, 224,000 for property offenses, and 414,000 for "non-index" offenses. Even in this limited age range, the ratio between arrests for "non-index" crimes in relation to arrests for violent offenses and that for property crimes in relation to violent crimes (at 17:2 and 9:2, respectively) remain constant with similar ratios derived from arrest data for the entire under 18 age cohort.

6. During the past two decades, Bandura (1977, 1986-a-c, 1989-a-b) has expanded and extended his position on social learning theory to incorporate findings from cognitive psychology and an emphasis on the concepts of agency and of the "self" as an active agent in its world.

7. For those not satisfied with the imaginative reconstruction of combat conditions by means of the computer monitor and multi-media sound effects, some enterprising enterpreneurs have organized closer approximations through "paintball combat" camps, wherein by the day or week participants don jungle warfare gear and stalk each other through rugged forests, armed with high-speed rifles which fire paintball pellets at their opponents. The activity is particularly recommended as a "togetherness" exercise for fathers and their adolescent sons. In journalist Marc Schogol's (1995), account, "paintball pellets are little biodegradable latex capsules filled with color gelatin that are fired from air guns and splatter when they hit something solid. Like a rock, a tree — or a peron. This allows you to put on camouflage coveralls, goggles, and face masks, divide up into teams and play some pretty darn realistic war games in some pretty darn realistic terrain." Schogol further comments on the sources of popularity for paintball combat: "The Good Book admonishes us to study war no more, but tell that to teenagers who've been raised on Arnold Schwarzenegger movies."

8. In a detailed analysis of the deterrent effects of legislative policies leading to the "selective incapacitation" of offenders with high risk for re-offending, leading criminological researcher Peter Greenwood (1995, 258) recounts an approximation model that reduces deterrence effect to mathematical precision: " ... The average or expected time served for any one crime is qJS — i.e., the probability of arrest and conviction [represented as q] multiplied by the probability of incarceration [represented by J] and by the average term [represented by S] ... This formula also represents the amount of crime that will occur under sentencing policy q, J, S, measured as a fraction of the crime that would occur if no offenders were incarcerated."

9. Pallone (1988) reviewed both legal and social science developments during the period that evoked the most impassioned of the "advocacy scholarship" studies of the death penalty. Thus, Zimring & Hawkins (1986) declared that they had divined a "stunningly simple" pattern in the social history of those nations which have abolished the death penalty. First, that executions cease, and then laws are changed, so that formal abolition follows informal abolition; second, that public opinion favoring capital punishment changes diametrically soon after formal abolition, since most citizens adhere to the societal norms embodied in formal law.

Yet neither the empirical data nor recent legislative history confirm that Zimring & Hawkins intuit. The Supreme Court seemed to accomplish judicially what we lacked the courage to accomplish legislatively by invalidating the death penalty statutes of the 40 states with such laws on the books in its Furman v. Georgia decision of 1972. But that surcease was to endure only four years. The legislatures of some 38 states rewrote their laws to correct the deficiencies the Court had pointed to in Furman (perhaps, as Zimring & Hawkins believe, in response to a Federal judicial challenge to a traditional state legislative right), by and large limiting the death penalty to pre-meditated murder, separating the determination of guilt from the imposition of sentence in independent trial "phases," providing for automatic judicial and sometimes gubernatorial review of death sentences once imposed, and according the accused all manner of counsel and assistance in the preparation of the defense in both the "guilt" and "penalty" phases of trial.

With those changes, the Court found (in Gregg v. Georgia, 1976) that the newly-revised state statutes no longer constituted that "cruel and unusual" punishment against which the Eighth and Fourteenth Amendments protect us. Most recently, the Congress has added large-scale drug distribution (or "king-pinning") to the litany of Federal offenses for which the death penalty can be imposed, with court challenges sure to follow. In the nearly two decades since Furman, the Court has ruled that mandatory death sentences are unconstitutional (Woodson, 1976); that death is "grossly disproportionate and excessive" as a penalty for rape (Coker, 1977) or for kidnapping which does not result in murder (Eberheart, 1977) or when imposed upon accomplices who are not direct participants in a slaying (Edmund, 1982); that the accused has a right of access at public expense to mental health expertise in the preparation of his/her defense (Ake, 1985); that prosecutors may not peremptorily challenge prospective jurors in a capital case solely on the grounds of race (Batson, 1986); and that states may not execute a person who has become insane since conviction (Ford, 1986). Those decisions seem to fall distinctly on one side of the Zimring & Hawkins equation.

But the same Court has also ruled that prosecutors may challenge for cause prospective jurors who oppose the death penalty in principle (Lockhart, 1983); that a Federal judge need not stay an order to execute in order to permit a condemned prisoner to prepare an appeal to the Federal courts (Barefoot, 1983); that a presiding judge may in effect overrule a jury when it imposes a sanction less than death during the "penalty" phase of a capital trial (Spaziano, 1983); that the right to counsel earlier enunciated in Gideon (1963) does not extend to a right to competent or effective counsel (Strickland, 1984); that it is not necessary that any but very local standards be applied in review of the "proportionality" of the death sentence against non-capital sentences imposed in the same state for similar crimes under similar circumstances (Pulley, 1984); that, although the Federal Food & Drug Administration patently has the authority to determine the safety of drugs used in experiments on human subjects, many of whom are volunteers in the prisons, and on animals, it is justified in declining similar review of the toxins used to execute by lethal injection, since these pose "no threat to public health" (Clancy, 1985); and that, while conceding that the death penalty is more often imposed when the victim is white than when the victim is a member of another race, the "mind set" of the community from which jurors are drawn does not in itself deprive an accused of his/her rights (McClesky, 1987). Those decisions would seem to fall on the other side of the equation.

In the world beyond the courts, the number of executions has risen steadily year by year, and every public opinion poll since Furman to raise the question has revealed strong and sometimes overwhelming support for the death penalty among the electorate.

More ominously, some observers point to an increase in what might be regarded as the "extra-judicial" execution of murder suspects killed by police not under circumstances of "hot pursuit," as in the 1985 case of Alex Mengel, accused of murdering both a police officer and a woman IBM executive in upstate New York, which had not yet re-established capital punishment. Mengel was arrested in Canada while wearing the scalp and hair of his female victim. He was fatally shot "in self defense" when, though manacled, he attempted to disarm one of two state police investigators transporting him from court to a jail facility after arraignment. A grand jury investigation cleared both officers, and state police authorities vowed to "review and upgrade the procedures used when transporting prisoners." The generally liberal press of New York raised no significant cry of police brutality.

For the historically-minded, the analysis of factors related to the abolition of the death penalty and its reinstatement in ten American states between 1897 and the mid-1930s by Galliher, Ray & Cook (1992) will prove highly instructive. Those interested in a discussion of the variant rationales in support of, and opposed to, the death penalty may wish to consult the remarkable editorial entitled "Elephants, Monstrosities, and the Law" by Daniel Koshland (1992) in *Science*.

10. These data are, of course, susceptible to many interpretations. At the extremes, racially and culturally homogeneous nations in Asia (Japan, the People's Republic of China) report rates of aggressive criminal violence that are minuscule in relation to those in every English-speaking Western nation except Ireland. Especially since the Irish Republic insists upon its cultural heterogeneity with Britain despite a common language, and because the relative rates are highest in Britain and its former colonies (the U.S. and Canada), it may be that high rates of violence are associated with Anglo-Saxon cultural hegemony. Alternately, it is of more than passing interest to note that Blackburn (1993, 52-53) reports an over-representation of offenders "of West Indian origin" in the United Kingdom since 1970. Rushton (1995-a, 157-160; 1995-b) also analyzed INTERPOL data (on homicide, rape, and assault) for 1986, with predominant racial group (Mongoloid, Caucasoid, Negroid) as the pivot for syllabicating nations. On that basis, he reaches the conclusion that the incidence of aggressive crimes of violence is 153.3 per 100,000 of the population for 28 Negroid nations vs. 76.4 for 48 Caucasoid nations and 38.4 for Mongoloid nations. Most knowledgeable criminologists (as well as medical epidemiologists) demur at such a classificatory scheme not because of egalitarian motives but rather because the plain fact is that virtually without exception the so-called "Negroid nations" and most "Mongoloid nations" are either third- or fourth-world countries whose data-recording is simply unreliable. Indeed, the general opinion tends toward systematic under-reporting in these nations (and, for that matter, in the People's Republic of China). With the exception of the PRC, the "grab-group" of nations we selected as our principal comparison group (i.e., the members of the European Economic Community, Canada, and Japan) share the communality of advanced industrialization, while the EEC itself is a political economic union formed by decision of its member nations, so that no pre-selectivity on our part is involved. Even so, the differences between the data reflected in our table and Rushton's figures are striking. His mean for "Caucasoid nations" is exceeded not only by the U.S., Britain, and Canada (which may be regarded as "multi-racial," though in varying degrees), but also by Denmark, the Netherlands, and Germany, nations which are certainly "Caucasoid" by any reasonable definition. Denmark and Holland have long histories of tolerating multicultural diversity; Germany has not.

Moreover, our "Let's Pretend" figure for the U.S., with episodes of aggressive criminal violence committed by Blacks omitted, shows an incidence (351.3) that is more than four and a half times as great as Rushton's mean for Caucasoid nations and more than two and a quarter times as great as his mean for Negroid nations. We used INTERPOL data for 1990, but to attribute these differences to real differences in the rates of crime in variant years is to suppose that the incidence of aggressive crime increased rapidly worldwide over a four-year period; if that is so, the phenomenon has utterly escaped either journalistic or scholarly notice. Neither we nor Rushton have focused on weighted means, and to that extent both sets of data bear close inspection. In our case, the data reported indicate the rate per 100,000 of the population on a nation-by-nation basis, with the aggregate population of the nations represented ranging from 1.2 billion in the Peoples' Republic of China (a "Mongoloid nation" in Rushton's schema) to 392,000 in tiny Luxembourg, a "Caucasoid nation" in that schema which has nonetheless chosen to ally itself with the European Economic Community — and it is the latter decision which accounts for its presence in our list.

The booby-traps implicit in groupings according to dominant race can perhaps be illustrated by contrasting the relative populations of nations that are clearly dominated by one or another racial group with those of cities and consolidated metropolitan statistical areas (CMSA) in the U.S. Thus, the aggregate population of the four Scandinavian countries (Norway, Sweden, Finland, Denmark), each of which is clearly "Caucasoid" by any reasonable definition, approximated in 1990 that of the New York CMSA, while the population of Liberia, clearly a "Negroid" nation, at 2.4 million stood only slightly larger than that of the Borough of Brooklyn (2.3 million). Even were the problem of reliable reporting of criminologic (and health and illness) data to be bracketed aside, it is not evident that Rushton's generalizations could be supported by the analysis of weighted means.

11. In a secondary analysis of data from the 1991 survey of state prisons inmates, Bureau of Justice Statistics researchers DeFrances & Smith (1994, 2) reported that 55% of respondents serving sentences for violent offenses and 69% of those serving sentences for property offenses had "committed the crime outside their own neighborhoods." Yet, as we saw earlier in this chapter, according to NCVS data, most victimizations occur with the home neighborhood. If it is simultaneously true that most victimizations occur on "home turf" and that a majority of incarcerated offenders have committed offenses away from that turf, it may be the case that offenses committed "within the neighborhood" have been prosecutorially and judicially processed in such a way that they are regarded as "disputes" worthy only of sentence to probation rather than to prison, while offenses committed outside that "turf" are sufficiently suggestive of predatory intent as to warrant incapacitating sanction.

5 PSYCHOMETRIC DIFFERENTIATION AND THE PHENOMENOLOGY OF VIOLENCE

THIS CHAPTER EXPLORES THE INVENTORIABLE TRAITS THAT DIFFERENTIATE aggressive criminal offenders on psychometric instruments, along with the behavioral and phenomenological patterns usually associated with such traits.

IDENTIFYING CHARACTERISTICS THAT DIFFERENTIATE OR DEFINE: LESSONS FROM THE BIOMEDICAL SCIENCES

If we adopt the reasoning central to the biomedical sciences, for a trait or characteristic of any sort to be regarded as "differentiating," it is necessary to demonstrate both that the characteristic in question is shared widely among members of the "target" group (in the biomedical sciences, nosologically organized around recognized disease entities; in our case, the taxonomic group labeled aggressive criminal offenders) but not among people-in-general. For a trait or characteristic to be regarded as "defining," it is necessary to demonstrate both that it differentiates members of the "target" group from people-in-general and from members of other nosological or taxonomic groups with contrary (though not necessarily contradictory) properties.

In clinical medicine, elevated body temperature (at least beyond a specified threshold) may signify illness of some sort, but before appropriate treatment can be initiated it will be necessary to ascertain whether the patient is suffering from influenza or from the effects of poisoning by means of insect bite. Hence, within the context of clinical medicine in particular, the identification of differentiating and defining characteristics takes on special significance in relation to the rate of "false positives" and "false negatives" associated with the methodology employed in the process of differentiation and definition. The relevant methodologies, respectively, pivot on ascertaining *relative incidence, reference range and threshold value,* or *statistically significant difference.*

We may, for example, wish to differentiate children who develop chronic bronchitis before the age of 5 from children who do not and perhaps also from those who, by the age of 5, display exceptionally healthy respiratory capacity. In the social sciences, we may wish to differentiate adolescents who voluntarily drop out of high school from those who graduate and perhaps also from those who graduate with high academic honors. Some characteristics or traits will be assessed through categorical variables (e.g., history of bronchial ailment in parents, whether or not the high school maintains an organized program of athletics), while others will assessed through more precise and generally continuous measurements (e.g., density of pollutants in the atmosphere near a child's home in relation to duration of exposure, number of siblings who have dropped out, of vs. finished, high school).

Relative incidence

The method most frequent in epidemiologic studies (and that which we pursued in Chapter 4) focuses on the relative incidence of a characteristic (generally reflected in a categorical variable) within a "target" group. Whether the characteristic can be predicated as "differentiating" will depend upon whether the incidence with which it is found in the target group exceeds by a factor greater than chance its incidence in the population at large; whether the characteristic can also be predicated as "uniquely differentiating" or "defining" will depend upon whether the incidence with which it is found in the target group exceeds by a factor greater than chance *both* its incidence in the population at large *and* its incidence in a group with contrary properties.

Suppose, for example, that among a group of persons who divorce after only two years of marriage, the incidence of hazel eyes is 75%, but that the incidence of hazel eyes in the population at large is only 15%. We might conclude, on that basis, that having hazel eyes represents a characteristic of "early" divorcees that differentiates them from the general population. When we encounter a group of early divorcees, we are justified in predicting, sight unseen, that 75% of the members of that group will have hazel eyes, or that the probability of encountering a person with hazel eyes among the members of that group is some five times as great as the probability of encountering a hazel-eyed person in the population at large. Even so, we can in no wise assume or predicate a *causal* relationship between that *differentiating* characteristic and membership in the taxonomic group we have labeled early divorcees.

Suppose, further, that we also learn that, among persons who regard themselves as happily married after 25 years and for whom the prospect of divorce is reliably and validly assessed as quite remote, the incidence of hazel eyes is 5%, while the incidence in the general population remains at 15%. Should we encounter a group of long-and-happily marrieds, we are justified in predicting, sight unseen, that 5% of the members of that group will have hazel eyes, that the probability of encountering a person with hazel eyes in that group is only some 33% the probability of encountering a hazel-eyed person in the population at large, and that we are 15 times more likely to encounter a person with hazel eyes among early divorcees than among the long-and-happily-marrieds. We seem to be justified in pronouncing hazel-eyedness a *defining* characteristic.

But life is rarely so simple. Suppose that the incidence of hazel-eyedness among the long-and-happily-marrieds is not 5%, but instead 60%, while the incidence in the population at large remains at 15% and among early divorcees remains at 75%. We now construe hazel-eyedness a characteristic that differentiates members of *either* taxonomic group from the general population. But clearly that characteristic does *not* uniquely differentiate or define either taxonomic group, since it does not distinguish members in one group from those in the other.

Let us now presume that we encounter a young person with hazel eyes who is contemplating marriage. On the basis of our last set of associative data, what *prediction* is justified as to the longevity of that marriage? Since we can only suppose *either* that he or she will divorce early *or* that he or she will enter a long and happy marriage, it is obvious that *no useful prediction* can be made that would "sort" into one of these two groups. However, we might alternately be justified is predicting that he or she is *unlikely* to enter a long and unhappy marriage. The process whereby we first construct a taxonomic group, then search out the differentiating characteristics of the members of that group, does *not* permit us to predict *from* the differentiating characteristic *to* membership in the group.

If that is so, we might wonder, why bother? Reasonable responses are relatively less difficult to justify if we change the terms of the discussion from the realm of the social sciences to that of the biomedical sciences. If the condition that underlies the taxonomic classification is not "early divorce," but rather "early and fatal heart disease," the effort is no longer a fun-and-games quasi-statistical exercise. The professionally responsible physician is at the least justified in informing (or perhaps even required by the Hippocratic oath to inform) the person who shares one or more of the characteristics of the nosologic group defined by serious medical malady of that commonality. Once such information has been transmitted, both physician and the patient devise stratagems through which to *defeat* an implicit prediction (such as dietary control, a regimen of exercise and regularized periodic examinations, pharmacotherapy, and the like), even though the implicit prediction is, in a technical statistical sense, *not* justified.

To complicate matters further, let us suppose that the same differentiating characteristic is also found in an incidence greater than chance among persons aged 85 and over who are free both of cardiac or other medical disorder. Now our physician is placed in a foolish predicament: pronouncing "risk" for membership *either* in an "early cardiac disorder" or "long-lived with no cardiac disorder" group.

Even though the strict constructionist would argue that no statistically-justified prediction can be made, no responsible physician would maintain his or her own counsel. Instead, he or she would urge upon the patient the same stratagems for the promotion of health, since, *even in a "false positive" situation*, these could be expected to produce beneficial results and since tacit acquiescence in the face of a false negative may have life-threatening results. Obverse implications follow, however, when the stratagems to defeat the implicit prediction involve intrusive or invasive medical procedures which may themselves (e.g., surgical excision of a limb or organ) yield consequences deleterious to health.

Contemporary clinical medicine strives to move beyond the identification of a single trait or characteristic that differentiates the person "at risk" for one or another medical disorder. Instead, the contemporary approach seeks to identify those characteristics which *interactively differentiate* (and thus constitute multivariate risk factors). In the case of early cardiac disorder, the interactive differentiators might include history of cardiac problems in parents and grandparents, past personal medical history, level of stress and tension in the occupation, extent of alcohol consumption, level of marital discord, and the like. Pending compilation of a comprehensive set of interactive differentiators, however, it would professionally irresponsible for the physician not to inform a patient that he or she may be "at risk" even on the basis of a single differentiating characteristic.

Optimally, the biomedical sciences would prefer to identify those multivariate risk factors associated with disease entities with statistical precision, replete with beta weights for each. But in clinical medicine the physician usually bases nosologic decisions (and therefore the design of ameliorative treatments) on the clinical confluence of interactive differentiators without further mathematically precise specification. As the distinguished psychologist Paul Meehl (1995) has intimated, whether such reasoning applies analogically to the search for differentiating and/or defining characteristics of aggressive criminal offenders depends in some large measure on whether we perceive criminal aggression as more similar to an index of social disorganization like early divorce — or to a life-threatening medical disorder like early cardiac disease.

Reference ranges and threshold values

Many of the characteristics which define a medical disorder are not assessed through categorical variables but are instead measured in relatively precise terms. In clinical medicine, for example, hematological analyses rely on precise indices that specify the "quantity" of a given substance (e.g., hemoglobin, potassium, sodium, uric acid, cholesterol) within the blood sample of a patient, with the resultant figure expressed in a common metric that relates relative "concentrations" to a norm. The resultant metric is typically not interpreted in absolute terms, but rather in relation to "reference ranges" that depict "normality" not as a single point but instead as a series of points on a continuum (Berkow & Fletcher, 1992, 2582-2591) above and below "thresholds" that define *clinically significant* medical conditions.

For many diseases, readings beyond the threshold level, whether at the upper or lower terminus of the "normal" range, become the *defining characteristic* that triggers a medical diagnosis. The reference range for normal glucose concentration, for example, is 70 to 110 micrograms per deciliter of blood (under conditions of fasting), with hypoglycemia the prospective diagnosis at the lower threshold and hyperglycemia (perhaps as a precursor to diabetes) the prospective diagnosis at the upper threshold; for iron, the reference range is 50 to 150 micrograms per deciliter, with the lower limit the threshold for a diagnosis of iron deficiency, while a concentration above the upper limit may indicate a flaw in the metabolism or excretion of iron compounds. The capital issue is that, in medicine, it is not an absolute quantity that is regarded as clinically significant, but rather that quantity *in relation to* a normative reference range and to threshold values. Thus, since both levels fall well within the reference range for normality, the person with a glucose concentration of 96 mg/dL is *not* pronounced to be at greater risk for disorders of glucose metabolism than is the person with a concentration of 84 mg/dL.

As complements to the notion of threshold levels, the science of toxicology has added the constructs *no observable effect level* and *no observable adverse effect level*, and an international organization of toxicologists and government health officials has compiled data concerning all three sets of values (threshold of clinical significance, no effect, no observable adverse effect) for a myriad of toxic and potentially toxic substances (Valciukas, 1995, 169-170). As Valciukas (1991, 192-193) remarks, the notion of threshold levels enjoyed considerable currency in scientific psychology during the 19th century, especially in the measurement of reaction times and pain perception by such eminent figures as Wundt and Fechner. It barely survives in clinical and psychometric psychology today, when we encounter the notion of thresholds only in a subset of instruments which key continuous measurements at various levels to qualitatively or clinically significant nosological categories.

Statistically significant differences

In some relatively sharp contrast, contemporary psychological research has come to rely largely on the calculation of statistically significant differences between members of taxonomically- (rather than nosologically-) differentiated groups in precise scores on psychometrically-measured traits. Because they have been so constructed that scores fall along a continuum that replicates the normal density function ("the bell-shaped curve"), and since, by definition, any score within one standard deviation above or below the mean on an instrument so constructed falls within the *statistical norm* (i.e., that range that encompasses 68% of the cases), the psychometric instruments employed to measure such traits implicitly (but generally tacitly) anchor in a reference range. But most instruments make no reference to threshold values, nor to the functional or nosologic meaning of scores above and below the norm.

Prototypically, scores earned by members of one taxonomic group are contrasted statistically with those of members of another group (or of several other groups). Should such scores prove significantly different in a statistical sense, the trait measured is assumed to differentiate members of one group from another, with little attention as to whether either set deviates from the norm and even less as to whether scores in either set bear functional relevance. Moreover, since it is a statistical truism that, if the sizes of the samples are large enough, even quite trivial numerical differences will prove statistically significant, a considerable proportion of the research conducted in this fashion reduces at best to statistical curiosity. As psychological science matures, we may learn to further emulate the biomedical and toxicological sciences by reporting that, in one or another research study, we have found statistically significant differences "with no observable effect" and may instead, as Rosenthal (1987), Dawes (1994), Cohen (1995), and Wilcox (1995) have suggested, learn to attend to effect size and to the relative frequencies and distributions characteristic of functionally relevant measurements.

If that judgment seems harsh, let us return momentarily to the biomedical sciences: Suppose that we analyze glucose concentrations in two groups of subjects, taxonomically-ordered in some fashion (say, those who divorce early and those who remain married, and happily so, for 25 or more years; or those who drop out of high school and those who graduate with honors). In the first group, we find that the mean is 84 mg/dL, in the latter 96 mg/dL. If the samples are large enough, the difference is certain to reach statistical significance. But, since both values fall within the reference range for normality and since neither approaches the threshold level for hypoglycemia at one polarity or for hyperglycemia at the other, the statistically significant difference we have discovered is essentially nosologically and clinically meaningless, and we can draw no conclusion whatever about the relationship between glucose metabolism and marital longevity (or early school leaving).

On the other hand, if it be the case that for 80% of the subjects in the first group, the concentration is uniformly 55 mg/dL (a level beyond the threshold for the clinical diagnosis of hypoglycemia) and for 20% the concentration is uniformly 200 mg/dL (a level beyond the threshold for the diagnosis of hyperglycemia), while the concentration level is uniformly 96 mg/dL for 100% of those in the second group (a set of data that yield mean values of 84 vs. 96, respectively), we are in a position to draw meaningful inferences.

Two sets of instruments that prove exceptions to the general abandonment of reference ranges and threshold values in psychometrics (one suspects, perhaps because they were developed before Wundt and Fechner became distant memories) are the several Wechsler scales to measure intellectual functioning and the Minnesota Multiphasic Personality Inventory, along with their respective successors and imitators. It is not accidental that we shall rely heavily upon these instruments as we attempt to draw out the differentiating characteristics of aggressive criminal offenders.

INTELLIGENCE AND CRIMINAL AGGRESSION

If we accept Wechsler's (1958) classic definition of intelligence as "the global capacity to act purposefully, to think rationally, and to deal effectively with the environment," we might readily hypothesize a difference in intelligence between members of the general population and those who become enmeshed in the circumstances that precede criminal aggression. We would expect that higher levels of the capacity to "think rationally" and to deal effectively with the environment, even an environment which reflects a "culture of violence," might incline one to avoid conflicts or to find resolutions thereto which do not involve the risk of emerging as a statistic in criminal violence, whether as offender or as victim. However appealing the logic that would attribute violent confrontation as an avenue to settling conflicts between pairs of actors to a mutual deficit in the conceptual ability to attempt resolution by non-violent means (or, for that matter, to assess costs, risks, and benefits associated with criminal behavior realistically), studies of the intelligence of aggressive offenders support no such easy general rectilinear linkage.

Nonetheless, distinguished psychologist Richard Herrnstein (1990, 12) generalized that "the impulsive violent crimes and the opportunistic property crimes are most often committed by people in the low normal and borderline retarded range" of intellectual functioning. Herrnstein's generalization makes rather specific reference to the classificatory schematic developed by David Wechsler (1939, 1941, 1944, 1955, 1958, 1971; Matarrazzo, 1972) for the interpretation of scores on the Wechsler-Bellevue Intelligence Scale in 1937 and applicable to its several successor instruments, including the current Wechsler Adult Intelligence Scale, Revised (WAIS-R), and the companion instruments for children aged 5 and older (of which the current version is the Wechsler Intelligence Scale for Children, III, or WISC-III) and for young children (the Wechsler Pre-school and Primary Inventory, or WPPSI).

That schematic (Wechsler, 1958, 42) employs a series of references ranges and threshold values, to which are keyed qualitative descriptors, as indicated tabularly on the next page. On each instrument, the mean is 100 and the standard deviation is 15, and scores follow a symmetric, normal density distribution.

Wechsler's original instrument was developed nearly six decades ago, when the very construct "intelligence quotient" (calculated as the ratio between mental age as determined by a test of intellectual functioning and chronological age) had just celebrated its 25th birthday and before it became prevalent to regard intellectual capacity as graduated along a normally distributed continuum. Nonetheless, both Wechsler's classification schematic and his several instruments have become the standards against which tests developed subsequently have been validated.

Table 5.1: Wechsler's classification schematic for IQ scores

Classification	Range	% Cases
• Retarded	69 –	2.2%
• Borderline	70-79	6.7%
• Dull-normal	80-89	16.1%
• Average	90-109	50.0%
• Bright-normal	100-119	16.1%
• Superior	120-129	6.7%
• Very superior	130 +	2.2

Contemporary studies of criminal offenders quite frequently measure intelligence among their subjects but rarely focus on this variable; instead, measured intelligence is used to "equate" groups that are to be compared to each other (so that prospective subjects at extreme ends of the intelligence spectrum are likely to be excluded) or reported merely descriptively. Data on intelligence must thus often be culled from among the focal variables in such studies, despite easy generalizations that turn on largely impressionistic evidence (Lowenstein, 1989). With these caveats, current studies offer only limited support for Herrnstein's generalization about the relationship between intelligence as measured grossly and aggressive criminal violence.

Wilson & Herrnstein's general threshold level for criminal offending

Wilson & Herrnstein (1985, 148-172) date careful scientific study of the relationship between criminal behavior to 1914, shortly after the advent of the "mental testing" movement with the work of Alfred Binet, Sir Francis Galton, and Lewis Terman. In their review of the research on intelligence and criminal offending (not, however, inflected as violent or non-violent, nor as aggressive or non-aggressive), they concluded that

> Reviews of the literature since the 1940s repeatedly place the average offender IQ at about 91-93. We estimate a 10-point gap between offenders and nonoffenders (154).

While that narrow range derives primarily from studies of adult offenders, it is remarkably congruent with findings reported by Caplan (1965) in an analysis of intelligence scores in what is likely the largest the largest "sample" of juvenile offenders ever assembled. Caplan reported a mean IQ of 89 for more than 35,000 male and of 88 for nearly 17,000 female offenders examined between 1929 and

1963 at the direction of the juvenile courts of Cuyahoga County, Ohio (Cleveland) on a variety of instruments, including both clinically administered measures (with the Stanford-Binet scales representing some 43% of all cases) and group or "actuarial" measures (with the Otis test of intelligence representing another 40% of all cases).

Since the mean IQ in the population at large is 100 by definition, the figure to which Wilson & Herrnstein conclude deviates by -0.6 standard deviation units, a level that differs but marginally from Herrnstein's (1995, 47) estimate of "an average IQ for offenders of 91.5." Doubtless, such a disparity from the population mean of 100 yields statistical significance, although both the numerical values cited and the mean for the population fall within Wechsler's reference range for "normal" intelligence. Nonetheless, those values are useful as an approximation to a "threshold level" for criminal offending in general, against which studies which have focused on aggressive criminal offenders can be compared. Wilson & Herrnstein quite accurately observe that consideration of intelligence as contributory to offending has all but disappeared from the criminologic literature. In some measure, that situation may reflect either the expectation of rectilinearity in such a relationship or an exclusive (if unwarranted) reliance on the methodology of statistically significant differences while ignoring the alternate methodologies which focus on reference ranges, threshold values, and relative incidences obtained through power analyses and obtained through effect size differences.

Studies among aggressive offenders

Aggregate measures of intelligence

Most investigations have concerned themselves with gross or aggregate measures which reflect overall intellectual functioning, usually expressed in IQ terms. On the basis of aggregate measures, it is difficult to draw any inference on the relationship between level of intelligence and aggressive criminal offending, a situation that is tantamount to predicating either that no such relationship obtains or, more cautiously, that no such relationship has yet been convincingly demonstrated.

Differences in the expected direction. Scattered contemporary studies have reported statistically significant differences between those convicted or accused of aggressive crimes and those convicted or accused of non-aggressive offenses. Among the studies which are supportive of Herrnstein's generalization:

- Among *adult homicide offenders*, Langevin (1982) reported lower levels of intelligence as measured by the Clark Vocabulary Scale and the Raven Progressive Matrices than among non-violent offenders or comparison subjects not implicated in criminal activity. But he also found a higher frequency of neurological dysfunction, long held to be significant in intellectual functioning, among homicide offenders.

- Similarly, among *juveniles* who had been *convicted of homicide,* Hays, Solway & Schreiner (1978) found significantly lower scores on the Wechsler Intelligence Scale for Children than among juveniles who had been convicted of "status" offenses.

- Holcomb & Adams (1982) and Holcomb, Adams & Ponder (1984-a) reported significant differences between Black and white *men accused of murder,* and Holcomb, Adams, Ponder & Anderson (1984-b) reported findings of low mean intelligence across races among males accused of murder.

- Congruently, in a study of incarcerated offenders in New York, Kepecs-Schlussel (1994) found significant differences between Black and white offenders across categories of offense.

- In a study in Greece, Kokkevi & Agathonos (1988) found significantly lower levels of intelligence among *mothers convicted of child-battering* than among control subjects; but the same relationship did not obtain among battering fathers.

- In a study that differentiated "death-row" from "life-sentence" murderers, Heilbrun (1990) reported that offenders who had been sentenced to death had more frequently murdered women, and in "especially cruel" ways; their mean IQs were significantly lower than those of murderers sentenced to life. Heilbrun thus concluded that "low IQ is associated with male criminal violence and can discriminate within a group of violent male criminals by level of severity."

Differences, but not in the expected direction. However, in one of the key studies that proved pivotal to the formulation of her "five-factor" model for sexual offending, distinguished researcher Ann Burgess and her colleagues (Burgess, Hartman, Ressler, Douglas et al., 1986) reported, almost incidentally, that 80% of the male sexual murderers they examined "were of average to superior intelligence," a relative incidence ratio in relation to the general population of 8:5 that is substantially at variance with the Wilson-Herrnstein (uninflected) threshold for criminal offending.

Relatively congruently, Kepecs-Schlussel & Hennessy (1995), in a large-sample study of offenders in New York, found that 45% of the offenders who had been convicted of criminally negligent homicide (typically, because they had killed a victim with an automobile while driving under the influence of drugs or alcohol) but only 20% of the offenders who had been convicted of homicide of other sorts (from premeditated murder to unintentional manslaughter) had IQ scores on the Revised Beta above the population mean of 100, a relative incidence of 9:4 between the two groups.

No significant differences. But other studies have failed to discern differences in aggregate measures of intelligence between offenders inflected by type of crime and/or between aggressive offenders and the population mean. Thus, Cavallin (1966) reported a mean IQ of 102 among *incestuous fathers* in Kansas with an average age of 39 who had victimized their pre-teen daughters. That level virtually matches the population mean and exceeds the Wilson-Herrnstein threshold.

Panton (1976) found no significant differences in intelligence as measured by the Revised Beta (a non-verbal, presumably "culture-fair" measure that is the lineal descendant of the Army General Classification Test developed prior to World War I, revised several times since, and frequently employed with prison populations) between a group of capital *offenders convicted of murder or of rape* and the entire non-capital offender population of North Carolina. In another study, Panton (1977) found no significant differences between those incarcerated for drug abuse and those incarcerated for drug trafficking, and Pierce (1979) similarly reported a mean IQ of 101 among incarcerated violent drug abusers. In her monograph on the Biosocial Project which followed a cohort sample of 1000 subjects in Philadelphia from birth to early adulthood, Denno (1990) reported that "previous findings of direct links between crime and intelligence level or mental retardation were not confirmed."

Although they did not syllabicate their data according to offense category, the monograph by Megargee & Bohn (1979, 156-158) reporting their massive study of Federal prisoners that eventuated in the development of a classification system based on offender typology is so richly detailed that it is possible to re-assemble data on IQ as measured by the Revised Beta for 927 offenders in their sample. When IQ scores are re-arrayed in relation to predominant offense pattern, the weighted mean for offenders whose patterns were predominantly or exclusively violent is found to be 101, while the weighted mean for offenders whose patterns were predominantly or exclusively non-violent is found to be 102. Both figures represent very minor variations from the population mean and exceed the Wilson-Herrnstein threshold by approximately +0.67 standard deviation units.

With a particular focus on whether intelligence is differentially associated with delinquency between races, Gordon (1986, 105-106) reviewed correlational studies between 1969 and 1984 which had used a wide array of instruments of different types (Differential Aptitude Test Battery, Mill Hill Vocabulary, Primary Mental Abilities, Raven Progressive Matrices, Wechsler Intelligence Scale for Children with uninflected Full-Scale IQ scores only). The highest coefficient reported in any study was -0.27, and many did not differ significantly from zero. Since the proportion of common variance attributable to the correlate is estimated by squaring the coefficient, even at the upper limit only 7.3% of the variance in delinquency status scores could be attributed to differences in measure of intelligence.

In a study of 1700 offenders incarcerated in the prisons of New York, Kepecs-Schlussel & Hennessy (1995) reported virtual identity between the IQ scores on the Revised Beta of those convicted of homicide (some two-thirds of the sample) and those convicted of larceny. The mean IQ for homicide offenders (in the aggregate, rather than syllabicated according to the circumstances of the offense) was found to be 86.3 and that for larceny offenders 85.9. While these means do not differ from each other, each differs from the population mean by -1.0 standard deviation units, falling at the mid-point of the "dull-normal" reference range on the Wechsler schematic and below the Wilson-Herrnstein threshold by approximately half a standard deviation unit.

Moreover, the means reported by Kepecs-Schlussel & Hennessy are at some substantial variance with data from the Megargee & Bohn study, a discrepancy that might be explained by the variant nature of the offenses which lead to incarceration in Federal vs. state prisons. But Kepecs-Schlussel & Hennessy opined that the rates of incarceration in a state with a shortage of prison beds may explain the discordance of their data from figures typically cited in previous research. That their subjects were disproportionately (in relation the national population and thus also in relation to the standardization samples on which psychometric instruments are normed) non-white may be contributory, since non-whites typically scores below whites on measures of intelligence (Shockley, 1971; Jensen, 1980; Gottfredson, 1994, 1995).

Inflected measures of intelligence

Both early and contemporary research on the character of intelligence veers rather sharply away from the proposition that intellectual capacity is a unitary trait that can adequately be described through a single score on an aggregate or gross measure. Instead, from Charles Spearman (1927) to Guilford (1967) and Cattell (1971), the prevailing view has been that intelligence is a composite both of "general" cognitive ability and a variety of "specific" cognitive abilities through which "general" ability makes contact with the data of experience. Operationally, this distinction is most accessibly exemplified in the several Wechsler instruments, each of which contains subtests which employ primarily verbal or primarily non-verbal stimuli as avenues through which to assess "general" cognitive ability. Scores on the subtests which utilize primarily verbal stimuli are transformed to yield a "Verbal IQ" (VIQ) and on those which utilize primarily non-verbal stimuli to yield a "Performance IQ" (PIQ), with "Full Scale IQ" (FSIQ) derived as an aggregate measure. Such syllabication is not possible on instruments (e.g., the Revised Beta) which report only an "aggregate" index [NOTE 1].

PIQ > VIQ discrepancies as an index to aggressive offending. Early interest in whether such inflected measures of intelligence are capable of differentiating criminal offenders from non-offenders is reflected in Levi's (1943) doctoral research on intelligence levels among adjudicated delinquents at New York University under Wechsler's sponsorship (Weider, Levi & Risch, 1943; Levi, Oppenheim & Wechsler, 1945). Both in that study and in myriad successors, Performance IQ was found to exceed Verbal IQ among both male and female and adolescent and adult subjects who had been adjudicated as offenders, in a pattern that has come to be termed the "verbal deficit" configuration. While retaining the term "sociopath" then in current usage, Wechsler (1958, 160-161, 176-177) generalized:

> A significant Verbal minus Performance constellation (V-P) [is] frequently met with in subjects roughly labeled as "acting-out" individuals . . . This "pattern" was first noted by Levi and this author in the test performance of adolescent psychopaths and has since been reported for [many] other groups . . . Whatever the cause, the Verbal minus Performance differences are sufficiently consistent and significant to be of diagnostic value . . . The most outstanding single feature of the sociopath's test profile is his systematic high score on the Performance as compared to the Verbal part of the scale [so that] A distinction must be made between intellectual understanding and affective acceptance of conventional behavior. Sociopaths generally have a grasp of social situations, but they are inclined to manipulate them to their advantage in an antisocial way . . . One feature relatively common to both male and female adolescent sociopaths is . . . the tendency to disregard those aspects of available knowledge (reality) which do not lead to the satisfaction of immediate needs.

Wechsler himself (Ibid., 160) observed that a difference of 10 points between VIQ and PIQ was to be expected as a normal (or "chance") phenomenon in approximately 32 cases in 100, whatever the subject's criminologic status. But later analyses proved congruent with those early findings of a consistent pattern in the organization of cognitive abilities in which the capacity to mediate the data of experience non-verbally appears to exceed the capacity to mediate those data through verbal means. Matarazzo (1972, 435) reviewed some 29 studies published after 1943, in all but two of which the PIQ > VIQ pattern had been substantiated, although the (unweighted) mean difference in those studies indicates a rather small discrepancy equivalent to approximately 6 IQ points, or 0.40 standard deviation units. Importantly, of the studies reviewed by Matarazzo, only 7% had reported mean FSIQs that fell within the reference range for "borderline" intelligence in the Wechsler schematic, 33% had reported mean FSIQs that fell within the "dull-normal" reference range, and 60% had reported mean FSIQs that fell within the "average" reference range; none fell above the average range. But conclusions based only on aggregate, rather than inflected, measures of intellectual functioning utterly mask what may be important differences in the ways in which adjudicated offenders cognitively contact the world of experience.

Although the magnitude of the discrepancy has varied, the relative "verbal deficit" pattern has also been confirmed in studies by Ollendick (1979), Hubble

& Groff (1980), DeWolfe & Ryan (1984), Grace & Sweeney (1986), Lindgren, Harper, Richman & Stebbens (1986), and Walsh, Beyer & Petee (1987), sometimes demonstrating as well larger absolute discrepancies among non-white subjects, and in a systematic review of conceptual and methodological issues by Quay (1987). Though she observed a "verbal deficit" pattern among some subjects in her study of a birth cohort in New Zealand, however, Moffitt (1988) reported considerable instability in the organization of cognitive abilities over time. Nonetheless, in a study that contrasted adolescents diagnosed with disruptive behavior disorders, with attention deficit disorder (according to Barabasz & Barabasz [1995], clearly attributable to frontal lobe dysfunction), and with dual diagnoses, Aronowitz, Leibowitz, Hollander et al. (1994) reported that "Results are discrepant with previous findings of deficient verbal functioning in delinquent populations."

PIQ > VIQ discrepancies as a gross index to left hemisphere dysfunction. It is of more than passing interest that Matarazzo (1972, 390) also details studies covering 28 groups of subjects categorized not according to criminal offending but rather according to neuropathology or normality. In each of these studies, PIQ > VIQ discrepancy differentiates those subjects with confirmed lesions in the *left hemisphere* (at an unweighted mean difference of 9 IQ points), but not those with diffuse lesions, with lesions in the right hemisphere, or normal controls. In subjects with lesions in the right hemisphere, the obverse VIQ > PIQ discrepancy prevailed, at an unweighted mean difference of 9 IQ points; among those with diffuse neuropathology, the VIQ > PIQ pattern also prevailed, but at an unweighted mean difference of 4 IQ points. Each pattern was observed in precisely half the studies with normal controls, with an unweighted mean difference of only three IQ points. In more recent studies, Rourke & Fisk (1988) pronounced the verbal deficit pattern a relatively reliable indicator of learning disabilities in children, and Feldman, Levin, Lubs, Rabin et al. (1993) observed the same pattern among adults with third-generation familial dyslexia in contrast to non-dyslexic age-matched family members. Howieson & Lezak (1992), in the American Psychiatric Association's semi-official *Textbook of Neuropsychiatry*, regard the pattern as a reasonable first approximation to identifying left hemisphere dysfunction.

It will be recalled from our discussion in Chapter 2 that left hemisphere functioning is associated with verbal mediation of the data of experience, is thought to control such functions as sequential and analytic processing of ideas and concepts (Taylor, Sierles & Abrams, 1987, 4-5) primarily expressed in verbal concepts (Hillbrand et al., 1994), is dominant "for the analysis of stimuli as discrete, finely timed events" (Liederman, 1988, 375-376), and that anomalies in left hemisphere metabolism of certain neurotransmitters differentiates schizophrenic patients (Gur, Resnick, Gur et al., 1987). Moreover, as Berkow & Fletcher (1992, 2101-2102) put it, "[in the] ability to process information, learning preference, and learning disorders, children with reading and generalized learning disabilities tend to have more difficulties with functions controlled by the left hemisphere than the right." It is not difficult to construe a relationship between impairment in left hemisphere functions and criminal offending. That the same discrepancy provides *both* a relatively reliable psychometric marker for persistent criminal "acting-out" behavior, as attested in research extending over half a century, *and* a gross index to prospective left hemisphere dysfunction might or might not constitute something more than an interesting coincidence. We shall see later in this chapter that Hare and his colleagues at the University of British Columbia (1984, 1987) have reported consistent anomalies in left hemisphere functioning among subjects who, psychometrically and by offense history, are reliably classified as psychopaths.

The "verbal deficit" pattern and "predictive" sorting. We have earlier observed that Berg, Franzen & Wedding (1987, 94-97, 175-178) conclude that the Wechsler instruments can be currently regarded as no more than the grossest of "gross" screening devices for neuropathology, with unacceptably high rates of both false positives and false negatives, primarily because the various indices devised (including not only discrepancies between VIQ and PIQ but the relatively complex calculation of "deterioration quotients") fail to differentially identify or to localize brain dysfunctions. Even our very brief discussion of the studies reviewed by Matarazzo would support that conclusion.

But, more pointedly: The conclusion may nonetheless be warranted that the PIQ > VIQ pattern may provide a gross marker *either* to "acting-out" criminal behavior *or* a differentially sensitive gross marker for neuropathology localized in the left hemisphere (but not in the right hemisphere, nor to diffuse neurologic dysfunction) *or* may reflect no more than a normally-occurring "chance" variation reflecting the distribution of inflected intellectual capacity in the population at large. That is most assuredly an unsatisfactory state of affairs in a clinical situation in which the goal is to "sort," by means of what we have earlier termed (Chapter 1) "forward reasoning," an examinee into a specific nosologic group, analogous indeed to the matter of hazel-eyedness in relation to marital longevity in our earlier example.

On this point, with specific reference to the "predictive" validity of the Wechsler verbal deficit pattern, Brody & Brody (1976, 223) have been caustically eloquent: "Since conditions like sociopathy occur infrequently in the population, it is virtually certain that inferences . . . from patterns of verbal and performance IQ will be wrong [since] the probability that an individual who has a higher performance than verbal IQ will be classified as a sociopath [is only] negligibly different than the probability that any individual selected at random will be classified as a sociopath."

But, if we abandon any effort at prediction by means of "forward reasoning" and instead employ "backward reasoning" — or, to borrow the terms used by Robyn Dawes (1993), forego "prediction of the future" in favor of attempting to "understand the past" — in order to discern the characteristics of a taxonomic-nosologic group constructed on independent grounds (in this case, aggressive "acting out" behavior that has been adjudicated as formally criminal), the consistent "verbal deficit" pattern may tell us something of importance in the effort to understand whether, and how, cognitive capacity is related to aggressive criminal offending among those who have *already* so offended.

Intelligence as a moderating variable

Not all investigators have assumed a rectilinear relationship between intelligence and criminal offending. In a study of candidates for parole in Georgia, Heilbrun (1978) found that inventoried intelligence was more closely associated with criminal history than was inventoried psychopathy, such that subjects with low IQ scores had more frequently committed violent crimes. Heilbrun concluded that "IQ is a moderating influence in the prediction of violent behavior."

Similarly, in what they frankly described as a "revisionist" analysis, Hirschi & Hindelang (1978) found a curvilinear relationship between inventoried intelligence and rate of offending among adolescents in California, with the lowest rate found among those in the bottom quintile (with IQ scores below 86), the highest rate in the next quintile (with scores between 87 and 95), and declining rates in each succeeding quintile.

In a carefully designed cohort study in Denmark, Kandel, Mednick, Kirkegard-Sorensen & Hutchings (1988) concluded that higher intelligence constitutes "a protective factor for subjects at high risk for antisocial behavior." These investigators compared men "at high risk for serious crime" in consequence of "severely criminal fathers" who had nonetheless not offended with three other groups: those at similarly high risk who had offended; those at low risk, with noncriminal fathers, who had offended; and those at low risk who had not offended. The principal differentiator was intelligence as measured by the Wechsler instrument for adults, as further related to successful academic performance, so that "Results are interpreted in terms of the reinforcing effect of success in the school system." In Herrnstein's (1995, 47) view, significantly subnormal intelligence may constitute a similar protective barrier since "even the most slapdash crimes usually require some mental competence." Or it may be the case that offenses committed by the mentally retarded are dealt with through societal responses outside the criminal justice system.

Overall, these studies might be interpreted to suggest that people with higher levels of cognitive capacity may be enabled thereby to assess costs, risks, and benefits relatively realistically, or, in Wechsler's terms, not "to disregard those aspects of available knowledge (reality) which do not lead to the satisfaction of immediate needs."

Mental retardation and exculpation

Significant mental retardation of such character as to render the person unable to appreciate the nature of his or her behavior is a prime empirical determinant for exculpation for the responsibility for criminal behavior under the M'Naghten Standard (West & Walk, 1977; Bartol, 1983, 113-136; Rogers, 1986; Baroff, 1990) for "insanity" prevalent in the criminal codes of the various states. In a well-ordered world, in which criminal defendants avail themselves of the defenses open to them, one would expect to find virtually no mental retardates among those formally adjudicated as guilty of criminal offending; instead, one would expect to find the mentally retarded who have nonetheless offended confined in forensic psychiatric institutions.

But, in a survey among prison administrators in 48 states, Denkowski & Denkowski (1985) found that mentally retarded inmates constitute 2% of the prison population, with the operational definition for assessment of mental retardation set as an IQ below 70 on the Wechsler Adult Intelligence Scale, Revised, the standard threshold. Wechsler's schematic for that reference range indicates that 2.2% of the population in general are so classified, so that the prevalence rate for prisoners reported by Denkowski & Denkowski is virtually identical with that for the general population.

We can readily conclude that there is little evidence of an association between mental retardation and rate of criminal offending; and perhaps also that retardation operates less frequently as a basis for exculpation than the relevant legislation would allow. That interpretation is suggested by McAfee & Gural (1988, 7-8), who hold that "Identification of defendants with mental retardation is more than haphazard in most states" and that "defendants with mental retardation who are quiet, cooperative, and 'normal' in appearance may never be assessed" formally.

The state of the evidence

Studies of aggressive criminal offenders based on aggregate measures have yielded little evidence that intelligence when measured grossly represents a distinguishing characteristic for aggressive criminal offenders in anything remotely approaching a rectilinear fashion. On balance, aggressive offenders are not reliably and demonstrably intellectually less able than the population at large, nor can distinctions be made among and between those who offend aggressively in one way rather than another. There is very fragmentary evidence that members of the same taxonomic group (e.g., the homicide offenders in the Kepecs-Schlussel & Hennessy study) differ as greatly among themselves when their offenses are further syllabicated to reflect specific circumstances as, in the aggregate, they differ from non-aggressive offenders.

But, for more than half a century, systematic differences have been consistently observed between "performance and "verbal" scores on the several Wechsler instruments among adolescents and adults offenders described as "acting-out" criminally, even though the discrepancies in absolute magnitude are relatively small and even though the aggregate measure derived from the combination of these independent scores does not depict these offenders as atypical of the population at large. Thus, there is some evidence that the PIQ > VIQ pattern (or what has been called the "verbal deficit" configuration) may constitute a differential marker. But the same pattern has also been found to represent, though less robustly, a differentially sensitive indicator for subjects in whom neuropathology in the left hemisphere has been medically documented; and that pattern is to be expected by chance on the order of 32 times in 100.

Given such a discrepancy in an individual case, we are in a position akin to that of the physician who has detected elevated body temperature in a patient: Is he/she suffering from a common cold or a systemic infection, or is the temperature reading a chance aritfact attributable to physical exertion? For us, the anomalous position is to "sort" into quite disparate taxonomic groups (e.g., "non-offending normals" vs. "aggressive offenders" vs. "left-hemisphere-neuropaths") — or perhaps to wonder about a possible nexus between neuropathology in a specific brain site and a pattern of "acting-out" criminal offending. But more definitive evidence than the PIQ > VIQ marker will be required to confirm such a nexus.

ACTUARIAL MEASURES OF PERSONALITY AND PSYCHOPATHOLOGY

A rather large group of studies has considered the personality traits and/or characteristics of aggressive offenders measurable through psychometric means, whether through the now-fanciful "projective" devices or through actuarial instruments.

The so-called "projective" psychometric instruments are devices of markedly low internal stimulus structure, so designed as to elicit highly variable interpretations or "projections" of their meaning from an examinee. Advocates believe that these interpretations or projections of meaning reveal the examinee's perceptions, beliefs, attitudes, and/or values, and these instruments are invaluable in the initial stages of therapeutic intervention. Chief among the several devices of this sort are the Rorschach Psychodiagnostic Plates, a series of essentially symmetric inkblots devised by Swiss psychiatrist Herman Rorschach in 1921, and the Thematic Apperception Test, a series of reproductions of drawings showing one or more persons about whom the subject is to invent a story, devised in 1938 by Harvard psychologist Henry Murray.

Though a variety of "scoring" systems has been developed for each, the interpretation of the examinee's responses depends essentially on the examiner's acuity and experience, and, as one might expect, is extraordinarily variable (that is to say, unreliable) between examiners. As a corrective, a number of researchers have developed methodologies for the scoring and interpretation of projective protocols that are tantamount to the application of actuarial methodology to the processing of clinical data, with that generated by John Exner (1993) for the Rorschach the most robust. But one still, in fact, hears murmurs about something called "clinical intuition" in the interpretation of projective test data.

Doubtless reflecting the current state of practice in psychology and psychiatry, very few contemporary studies attempt to use projective test data to differentiate offenders, aggressive or otherwise, though these instruments continue to be widely used for forensic and other clinical purposes. But few contemporary psychoclinicians would quarrel with Paul Meehl's (1954, 138) conclusion about the superiority of actuarial over clinical techniques both for clinical and research purposes: "Always, the actuary will have the last word."

In contrast, "actuarial" instruments are devices of markedly high internal stimulus structure, so designed as to severely restrict an examinee's responses (generally, merely *yes/no* to a series of self-relevant statements). The examinee's responses (or pattern of responses) are then compared to those of subjects in a "norm group" of known dimensions whose contemporaneous (or subsequent) behavior (or membership in a taxonomic or even nosologic group) has been determined independently, so that many such instruments claim "concurrent classificatory" validity in addition to their capacity to compare and contrast an examinee with "otherwise similar" subjects.

Because these instruments are objectively scored (today, typically by computer) and because scores are expressed in terms of norms, derivation of scores from the examinee's responses is invariant between examiners. Since many actuarial instruments contain multiple scales to measure several traits simultaneously, it is usually possible to compare an examinee's score profile on these several scales to those of others in several taxonomic or nosologic groups represented in the normative sample.

Some investigations utilizing actuarial measures of psychological characteristics attend to individual traits, relying on absolute scores on the individual scales of the instrument employed, while others focus more heavily on profiles, or aggregate patterns of scores on individual trait scales. Whatever the focus, such investigations frequently seek to differentiate offenders convicted of one sort of crime from those convicted of other sorts. Since such instruments are scored on the basis of norms, comparisons to members of the general population who are putatively non-offenders are relatively easily made, though the statistical significance of such comparative differences is rarely calculated with precision.

Minnesota multiphasic personality inventory

The classic exemplar of actuarial devices of this sort is the *Minnesota Multiphasic Personality Inventory* (MMPI), an instrument developed in 1943 at the University of Minnesota's School of Medicine by psychologist Starke Hathaway and psychiatrist Charnley McKinley which is doubtless the world's most widely used psychometric instrument (Graham, 1987; Parker, Hanson & Hunsley, 1988). The MMPI has been characterized in the American Psychiatric Association's semi-official *Textbook of Psychiatry* as the instrument-of-choice in the actuarially-based differential diagnosis of current mental disorder (Clarkin & Hurt, 1988, 229-231). In addition to its ubiquity in clinical practice, the MMPI is very likely the most widely researched diagnostic instrument in history; by Anastasi's (1988, 526) count, it had been the subject of some 8000 investigations in the half-century following its publication, with additional studies accumulating at the rate of 250 per year. A decade ago, a major restandardization study was undertaken at the Mayo Clinic to provide contemporary norms inflected by age and sex (Colligan, Osborne, Swenson & Offord, 1989), and a revised version (the MMPI-2) was published in 1989 [NOTE 2].

Structurally, the MMPI consists of some 566 statements (567 in the revised version), with a fourth grade reading level, which subjects are instructed to endorse as *True* or *False* in relation to themselves. Because the instrument was developed through a sophisticated psychometric process called "criterion referencing," the pattern of responses given by each subject can be compared to those of members of the standardization sample whose psychiatric diagnoses were established through exhaustive formal diagnostic procedures conducted by mental health professionals (not including results of the instrument under development), so that the resulting "scores" reflect the degree of congruence between a given subject's self-reports and those of members of distinct diagnostic groups whose differential diagnoses had been firmly established by customary intensive professional examination (Anastasi, 1988, 526-530; Graham, 1987, 4-5). In this fashion, it has been possible to establish "threshold levels" on the primary clinical scales that, in fact, have demonstrable *nosologic* relevance.

In an inventive study in which he administered the instrument once again to the same subjects after an interval of 40 years, Greene (1990) found remarkable stability in scores over this substantial time span. That situation sits at a diametric contrast to the customary instability over even short periods of time characteristic of projective assessment methods. Indeed, some who are as persuaded on the clinical-projective side of the ledger as we are on the actuarial might argue that it is by design that projective devices tend to be highly sensitive to nuances that differentiate the psychological state of *this* moment from that of the *next* moment. To that argument, the actuarialist will respond that only knowledge of relatively enduring intrapersonal traits and characteristics, as distinct from momentary and evanescent conditions, will permit even the *post*-diction of behavior (criminal or otherwise) at a reasonable level of accuracy.

Whatever the terms of the conceptual debate, the sort of longitudinal stability in those intrapersonal characteristics measured by the MMPI, as demonstrated by Greene, suggests that such characteristics indeed constitute enduring aspects of personality and behavior; and that, in turn, may even prompt reconsideration of the pre- vs. post-diction debate. If certain intrapersonal characteristics remain stable over a period of four decades that have seen major societal changes on a global scale no less than the usual intrapersonal and interpersonal changes expected over a major part of the adult life span of an individual, the measurement of a characteristic taken *post-hoc* on the MMPI might, under some conditions and with some justification, nonetheless may yield some predictive information.

The MMPI yields scores on three measures of what has been called "test-taking attitude," including dissimulation, and on ten "primary clinical" scales. The measures of "attitude" (often collectively called the "validity" scales) are: *L*, a measure of the extent to which the subject answers certain questions so as to portray himself or herself in a favorable light, and thus considered a "social desirability" index; *F*, a measure of the extent to which a subject endorses a variety of test items rarely endorsed by subjects in the standardization sample found on other grounds to be free of disabling psychiatric symptomatology; *K*, a measure of defensiveness and consistency in responding to test items. The ten *primary clinical scales* are denominated: *Hypochondriasis (Hs)*, or abnormal preoccupation with physical complaints; *Depression (D); Hysteria (Hy)*, or the tendency to translate emotional problems into physical symptoms; *Psychopathic deviation (Pd)*, or the tendency toward disregard of customary social mores; *Masculinity-femininity (Mf)*, or the tendency to endorse traditionally opposite-gender-linked interests and attitudes; *Paranoia (Pa)*, or fearful hypervigilance against external psychological, social, or physical threat; *Psychasthenia (Pt)*, or obsessive rumination coupled with compulsive behavior; *Schizophrenia (Sc)*, or disorientation, apathy, emotional constraint and/or coldness, sometimes coupled with delusion or hallucination (Colligan et al., 1989, 17); *Mania (Ma)*, or elevated mood and accelerated speech and motor activity; and *Social introversion (Si)*, or the tendency to withdraw from social contacts and responsibilities. Over the course of the years, some 132 additional or "derivative" scales have been developed (Graham, 1987, 116-194), in the main also on a criterion-referenced basis (e.g., the MacAndrew *Alcoholism* Scale, the Harris-Lingoes *Inhibition of Aggression* Scale, the Wiggins *Authority Conflict* Scale, the Megargee *Over-controlled Hostility* Scale).

A score equivalent to the 97th percentile (represented by a value of 70 on the normalized T distribution on which scores are reported) constitutes the customary threshold level for assessment of disorder serious enough to warrant formal diagnosis of a mental disorder; this point is usually called the "threshold of clinical significance" and is generally regarded as a reasonable basis for a formal diagnosis of mental disorder, in a manner akin to the process whereby a concentration of glucose greater than 110 micrograms per deciliter of blood is sufficient to justify a diagnosis of hyperglycemia in clinical medicine. A T-value of 60 (equivalent to the 84th percentile) is typically regarded as the "threshold of clinical interest," and its meaning is analogous to that attached to a glucose concentration of 100 micrograms per deciliter, which suggests that a disease entity is not yet florid but that the patient should continue to be monitored medically. In the early days of the instrument's use, index codes representing the two or three highest scales (and often the lowest one or two as well) were employed to describe configural patterns for subjects (Hathaway & Meehl, 1956), but this practice has more recently yielded to computerized scoring and profile interpretation.

Essentially a self-administering, paper-and-pencil device, the MMPI is incapable of directly detecting neurologic disorder, brain syndromes, or mental deficiency except at the most profound (non-reader) level. Nonetheless, the MMPI is sensitive to a number of characteristics (e.g., psychopathic deviation, mania, schizophrenia, psychasthenia, social introversion) which may, in given cases, represent behavioral manifestations secondary to underlying neurologic disorder insofar as they are amenable to psychometric inventory.

Scales and profiles among aggressive offenders

Again reflecting the current state of practice, the MMPI has become the actuarial measure-of-choice in current psychological studies of aggressive offenders, whether of individual traits or of profiles. Among contemporary studies which which have relied on the instrument's primary clinical scales:

- Sutker, Allain & Geyer (1978) compared women homicide offenders to non-violent women offenders, finding that the non-violent group scored significantly higher on Pd and Mf and on a "validity" (rather than clinical) scale which measures denial of psychopathology (K).
- Panton (1976, 1978) found no significant difference on any scale between North Carolina death row inmates who had been convicted of murder vs. those convicted of rape.
- Among an array of characteristics investigated, Langevin (1982) reported that only significantly higher scores on the MMPI scale which measures the tendency to "convert" psychological problems into physical symptoms (Hy)

differentiated the murderers in his sample from non-violent offenders and from comparison subjects not implicated in crime.

- An increasingly sophisticated series of investigations has been reported by Holcomb and his associates. Holcomb & Adams (1982) reported that their sample of Black convicted homicide offenders scored significantly higher than white convicted homicide offenders on an MMPI scale which measures the tendency toward manic behavior (Ma) but lower on the scale measuring social introversion (Si).

- These results were partially replicated in a second study of racial differences (Holcomb, Adams & Ponder, 1984-b), in which a sample of Black accused murderers scored significantly higher on Ma and on a scale which measures deviant ways of responding to the instrument's questions (F). And the results of the latter investigation, in turn, were also partially replicated in a study of accused murders not inflected by race, in which abnormally high scores were observed in a scale (F) which measures test-taking attitude and deviant response set.

- Holcomb & Adams (1985) also contrasted convicted males who had committed murder while alcohol-intoxicated with other convicted offenders who committed murder not in a state of intoxication, with a comparison group of non-violent offenders with no history of significant alcohol problems, and with alcoholics who were not implicated in crime. The investigators reported that the intoxicated offenders had higher scores than the non-intoxicated killers on an MMPI scale which measures the tendency of the examinee to present the self in a favorable light (L) but lower scores on the Mf and Pd scales. As a group, the homicide offenders in the sample, intoxicated or not, had higher scores on the MMPI scale which measures suspiciousness and hypervigilance (Pa) but lower scores on Ma than did the non-violent offenders or the alcoholic non-offenders.

- In an effort to detect "malingered amnesia" for the offense among men accused of murder, Parwatikar, Holcomb & Menninger (1985) reported that the putative amnesiacs had higher scores on Hy and on MMPI scales which measure subjective depression (D) and hypochondriasis, or an obsessive concern with physical health (Hs). In yet a more ambitious investigation, Anderson & Holcomb (1983) employed an advanced statistical procedure called "cluster analysis" to identify five "types" of capital murderers on the basis of MMPI scores.

- Similarly, in a study of convicted homicide offenders in Britain reported by McGurk (1978), cluster analysis of MMPI scores revealed two broad categories of characteristics — labeled respectively the over-controlled and the under-controlled; but whether these two personality "types" are unique to murderers or may be reflected in the broader offender population remained indeterminate.

- However, after an extensive four-way comparison between convicted homicide offenders, offenders guilty of assault, offenders guilty of armed robbery, and non-violent control subjects, Lang, Holden, Langevin & Pugh (1987) concluded that personality indices of any sort were inefficient differentiators. In what reduces to a redundancy of the first magnitude, only the past criminal history of the subject differentiated efficiently.

- In a three-way contrast, Kalichman (1988) compared the MMPI profiles of adult women who had murdered their husbands (or male partners), adult men who had murdered their wives, and adult men who had murdered strangers during the course of another crime. Women scored higher on Pa and on Si than men in either group; men who had committed felony murder scored higher on Ma than men who had committed spousal homicide.

- Cornell, Miller & Benedek (1988) compared the MMPI profiles of adolescent homicide offenders with those of a comparison group of adolescents charged with larceny; the homicide cases were further subgrouped into those who committed homicide secondary to robbery or rape and those who acted in the context of interpersonal conflict with the victim (roughly corresponding to "tinder-box" homicides). No significant differences were found between the homicide and larceny groups; but the "felony crime" killers differed from the "conflict" killers on F, Hs, Hy, and Sc.

- Walters, White & Greene (1988) found serious mental disorder (that is, depression, mania, schizophrenia, schizophreniform disorder) on the basis of non-psychometric assessment (through clinical review of case history and interview material) among 78% of the inmates in a maximum security Federal prison. Their report contains sufficient detail to permit recalculation of mean values on MMPI scales for that portion of the sample found to be disordered on the basis of independent and non-psychometric clinical assessment; such recalculation indicates that the mean values for this group exceeded the threshold of clinical significance on Pd, Pa, and Sc. Hence, the judgments reached on the basis of clinical, non-psychometric assessment are confirmed psychometrically on the MMPI.

- In a study of convicted pedophiles, Davis & Hoffman (1991) found elevations at or beyond the threshold of clinical interest on one validity and eight clinical scales (F. D. Hy, Mf, Pa, Pt, Sc, and Ma) and beyond the threshold of clinical significance on another (Pd).

- Variant results were reported by Mann, Stenning & Borman (1992) in an investigation of the utility of the revised version of the instrument with pedophiles confined in state, Federal, and military prisons. In their aggregate sample, the mean elevation reached the threshold of clinical interest on only one scale (Pd), while the threshold of clinical significance was reached on none. The revised version thus appears to "flatten" the profiles of pedophiles. Somewhat optimistically, the investigators concluded that "past MMPI research with pedophiles appears to be generalizable to MMPI-2 profile interpretations if one remembers to interpret lower scores as clinically significant."

Megargee's over-controlled hostility scale

Among the many derivative scales constructed by identifying unique patterns of responses among members of taxonomic or nosologic groups (a variant form of criterion referencing), that with the most direct relevance for the study of aggressive offenders (and, prospectively, very direct relevance to tinder-box aggression) is the *Over-controlled Hostility* (O-H) scale developed by Megargee and his associates (1967).

In a conceptualization that anticipated that of Hirschi & Gottfredson (1994), who attribute deviant behavior to a lack of (or failure in) self-control, Megargee (1966) proposed that frequent or persistent criminal aggression is committed by an actor who is "under-controlled" in his or her responses to even mildly provocative situations or stimuli; alternately, some acts, particularly acts of extreme aggression on the part of an actor whose responses to provocation have usually been well modulated, may result from an "eruption" of "over-controlled" hostility. Megargee, Cook & Mendelsohn (1967) were able to identity 31 items on the MMPI to which differential responses were reliably given by offenders convicted of brutally assaultive crimes, those convicted of moderately assaultive crimes, those convicted of non-assaultive crimes, and non-offenders; these items constitute the O-H scale. Graham's (1987, 183) description of the overarching conceptual model is reminiscent of the description by Feldman & Quenzer of quite savage aggression by pacifically-raised but experimentally brain-injured rats which we reviewed in Chapter 2:

> Chronically over-controlled persons have very rigid inhibitions against the expression of any form of aggression. Most of the time, the over-controlled individuals do not respond even with aggression appropriate to instigation, but occasionally, when the instigation is great enough, they may act out in an extremely aggressive manner.

The scale has been utilized in a number of investigations, with generally (though not uniformly) supportive results: Thus:

- Arnold, Quinsey & Velner (1977) cross-validated the O-H scale in a study of offenders found not guilty (usually of the charge of homicide) by reason of insanity and committed to a forensic psychiatric hospital. In consonance with the conceptual model, the scale successfully differentiated persistently aggressive offenders from those who were generally free of serious criminal behavior before the instant offense. In a subsequent clinical case study, Arnold, Fleming & Bell (1979) outlined the dynamics which triggered the behavioral expression of under-controlled hostility leading to homicide. Alternately, Mallory & Walker (1972) and Hoppe & Singer (1976) reported that the O-H scale failed to differentiate incarcerated offenders in accordance with offense histories. After observing that aggressivity should not be assessed on the basis of the most recent offense only, Lane & Kling (1979) related both the severity of the instant offense and the chronicity of the prior offense pattern to over-controlled hostility both among prisoners and forensic psychiatric patients.

- Quinsey, Maguire & Varney (1983) reported that the O-H scale effectively differentiated "murderers without previous criminal records from men who have committed less serious assaults and murderers with extensive histories of assault." They also found that offenders with "extensive histories of assault" who scored high on the scale were less assertive in "behavioral role-playing situations." In a partial replication in which the offense histories of prisoners were categorized by "expert" raters, du Toit & Duckitt (1990) found clear differences between those identified on the O-H scale as over-and the under-controlled.

- Race has emerged as a factor in over-controlled hostility in some studies. Fisher (1970) reported consistently higher O-H scores among Blacks than among whites, a finding replicated among forensic psychiatric patients by Hutton, Miner, Blades & Langfeldt (1992), even when controlling for socio-economic status and educational attainment.

- In an ambitious study of all offenders incarcerated in Iceland, Gudjonsson, Petursson, Sigurdardottir & Skulason (1991) investigated the relationship between O-H scores and measures of denial and deception. Results indicated significant relationships between O-H scores and both other- and self-deception.

The O-H scale has thus far proved valuable as a vehicles to differentiate what Volavka (1991) termed "one-time agggressives," corresponding roughly to Megargee's over-controlled group, from "habitual aggressives," corresponding to Megargee's under-controlled group. From Chapter 2, we recall that 64% of Volavka's "habitual aggressives," but only 12% of his "one-time aggressives," were found to display neuropathologic anomalies, at a relative incidence of nearly 5:1, and that these proportions were virtually identical with those reported by Williams (1969) in his cumulative study of offenders in Britain. It may thus be the case that the O-H scale constitutes an indirect index to neuropathology.

The Megargee-Bohn typology study

Without question, the most extensive body of MMPI data about convicted criminal offenders has eventuated from the Megargee-Bohn Typology Study, undertaken in the mid-1970s to develop an actuarially-anchored system on which to base decisions about level of correctional supervision required, determine treatment needs (if any), and assign subjects to rehabilitative regimens while incarcerated.

In that ambitious undertaking, Edwin Megargee of Florida State University (the principal architect of the O-H scale) and Martin Bohn of the Federal prison system analyzed in detail MMPI data on 6350 inmates of the Federal prison, including 1350 who were followed throughout the period of their incarceration and subsequent to release. Extensive analysis yielded a typology of ten distinct offender groups with characteristic MMPI profiles (assigned colorful names derived from military nomenclature, like "Easy" and "Foxtrot"), with which specific patterns of criminal behavior and distinct social history variables were found to be statistically associated (Megargee, 1977; Megargee & Bohn, 1977; Megargee, 1986).

Megargee & Bohn (1979) described both their method of cluster analysis of the MMPI and the derivation of their forensic scales in a seminal monograph. That work reviews varying taxonomic systems for classification of offenders and describes in detail studies undertaken in the Federal prison system with the MMPI over a seven year period, beginning with 2500 youthful offenders in Tallahassee. From the psychometric profiles of these inmates, classificatory rules were devised for 9 profile clusters; further revision yielded 10 groups, and decision rules for classification were computerized. The final revision resulted in the capacity to computer-assign 96% of sample, so that an actuarial method could be employed in the classification of prisoners. An array of attitude, ability, achievement, demographic, family history, and criminal history data were analyzed to determine the defining characteristics of members of the final ten groups. Detailed statistical analysis found differences in behavior, social history, lifestyle, personality pattern, and offense histories.

The Megargee-Bohn typology has been cross-validated in a number of studies, including those by Edinger (1979) on a large sample of prisoners (1291 males, 146 females) in state correctional facilities; by McGurk (1981) on homicide offenders in Britain; by Edinger, Reuterfors & Logue (1982) on adult males in a forensic mental health unit; by Henderson (1983) on non-violent offenders; by Smith, Silber & Karp (1988) on women inmates; by Veneziano & Veneziano (1986) on juvenile offenders; by Walters (1986) on offenders in the armed forces; by Dahlstrom, Panton, Bain & Dahlstrom (1986) on death row inmates; by Mrad, Kabacoff & Duckro (1983) on paroled offenders in halfway houses; by Megargee (1986) on prisoners who had threatened to assassinate the president; and by Greene (1987), who investigated the stability of the ten offender types in relation to ethnic variation. Thus, in a review of the accumulated research evidence, Zager (1988) concluded that "the reliability, validity, and practical utility of the system have been demonstrated." Similarly, Villanueva, Roman & Tuley (1988) reported that the typology accurately post-dicted rehabilitation outcome among offenders in a residential treatment facility.

Indirectly, because their focal interests lay elsewhere (and perhaps inadvertently, since they did not reference the rich Megargee-Bohn literature), Ira Bernstein and his associates have provided data that corroborate the MMPI scale elevations reported in the principal Megargee-Bohn monograph. Prompted by an interest in a factor analytic approach to simplifying the manifold dimensions of the instrument, Bernstein & Garbin (1985) analyzed data from a sample of 2000 Federal inmates, and Bernstein, Teng, Granneman & Garbin (1987) analyzed data from a sample of nearly 17,000. Their mean scale elevations for the inmate sample (1985, 777) are highly congruent with those reported in the principal Megargee-Bohn source document.

Nonetheless, some investigators have found the Megargee-Bohn typology less than optimally applicable to offender populations in such specialized settings as halfway houses (Motiuk, Bonta & Andrews, 1986) and medium security facilities like prison camps (Baum, Hosford & Moss, 1984), or for post-dicting lifetime criminal violence (Moss, Johnson & Hosford, 1984), and Megargee himself has questioned the predictive validity of several derivative

Figure 5.1: Reference range re-assembly: Weighted mean scores [T-values] on MMPI primary clinical scales for Megargee-Bohn groups with predominantly aggressive offense patterns in relation to clinical threshold

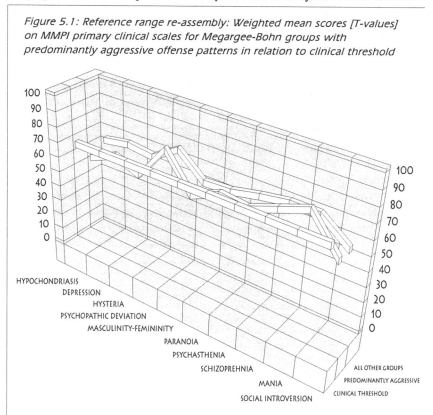

scales concerning prison adjustment constructed from the initial typological data (Megargee & Carbonell, 1985).

Re-assembling the Megargee-Bohn source data

It is important to emphasize that the Megargee-Bohn typology study was not undertaken to link psychological characteristics to type of criminal offense for which an inmate had been sentenced, but instead to provide a sound actuarial basis for decisions for security classification and program assignment. Nonetheless, because their principal monograph is rich in its presentation of source material (Megargee & Bohn, 1979, 107-234), it is possible to reassemble the source data so as to trace such linkages with some degree of precision.

We have re-assembled the data in two ways: (1) graphically in Figure 5.1, with a focus on *reference ranges* in terms of mean T-values on each scale for subjects grouped according to characteristic offense patterns and (2) tabularly in Table 5.2, in an essentially *nosologic re-assembly*, with a focus on the threshold of clinical significance.

Delineating aggressive offenders nosologically by means of threshold values

Traditional behavioral science approaches to the interpretation of the re-assembled Megargee-Bohn data might focus on the determination of statistically significant differences between mean scores for aggressive and non-aggressive offenders, whether or not either set meets or exceeds the standard, nosologically-relevant clinical threshold. An approach which adopts the reasoning of the biomedical sciences, however, would pivot on consideration of relative incidence in relation to threshold values that hold clinical or nosologic significance. From that perspective, some remarkable differences come into focus. As we inspect those differences on a scale-by-scale basis and with emphasis on mean score elevations among the violent offender groups, it is important to recall that the threshold level is a *T*-value equivalent to the 97th percentile; by definition, then, we would expect a score elevation at or above that value in but 3% of the cases in the norm group, which we may regard as an approximation to people-in-general. (Not incidentally, that situation is in remarkable contrast to the incidence in which the "verbal deficit" pattern in inflected intelligence as measured by the Wechsler instrument is found "by chance" in the general population.) We begin the analysis with those clinical scales on which mean elevations for violent offender groups exceed the threshold of clinical significance.

Psychopathic deviation. Each of the four groups (Baker, Charlie, Delta, Foxtrot), representing 100% of the violent offenders in the Megargee-Bohn subject pool, has a mean elevation in excess of the threshold level on the Pd scale. In a loose way, we may say that the relative incidence with which scores of that magnitude are found among violent offenders in relation to the general population is on the order of 33:1. But scores at that level are also found among non-violent offenders in the groups named Able, George, and How, which collectively represent 37% of the total subject pool but 53% of non-violent offenders, so that the relative incidence among non-violent offenders in relation to the general population may be said to be on the order of 18:1.

Table 5.2: A nosologic re-assembly: Mean elevations above the threshold of clinical significance on the primary MMPI scales in relation to characteristic offense patterns among offender groups in the Megargee-Bohn typology study

Group Name	% Total Sample	Scales at/above T = 70	Offense Pattern
• Able	17	Pd	Moderate, median violence, heavy use of marijuana
• Baker	4	Pd	Violent, extensive; heavy alcohol, little drug use
• Charlie	9	F, Pd, Pa, Pt, Sc, Ma	Extensive, violent, heavy drug use
• Delta	19	Pd	Violent, often for excitement; Heavy use of amphetamines
• Easy	7	None	Non-violent
• Foxtrot	8	F, Pd, Sc, Ma	Violent; Heavy use of drugs with antagonistic biochemical properties (i.e., both CNS stimulants and depressants)
• George	7	D, Pd	Drug, liquor offenses
• How	13	F, Hs, D, Hy, Pd, Pa, Pt, Sc	Mixed; More often victim rather than perpetrator in violent crime; Heavy use of LSD
• Item	19	None	Non-violent, draft evasion, drug, liquor
• Jupiter	3	Pt, Sc, Ma	Property offenses

→ **SOURCE:** Data extracted and re-arrayed from Megargee & Bohn, 1979, 107-234.

If we consider these ratios together, we may regard the "trait" of psychopathy as a "threshold" variable for criminal offending across gross offense categories, analogous to the Wilson-Herrnstein threshold for level of intelligence. Such an interpretation is consistent with the criterion-referencing process itself, since the scale was originally developed with convicted offenders (curiously, however, not including homicide offenders) as the criterion reference group (McKinley & Hathaway, 1956).

But if we contrast what we are calling the "relative incidence" *between* groups of aggressive and non-aggressive offenders, we see a *relative ratio* that approximates 5:3 in the direction of the violent groups. We may now be justified in regarding Pd scores as differentiating aggressive offenders *both* from people-in-general and from non-aggressive offenders.

Technically, as the statistical purist will quickly recognize, we are not quite justified in the statements in the last two paragraphs. Instead, because we are discussing (weighted) mean elevations, the technically-justified statement is that, on the basis of these data, we can expect that 100% of the *mean* scores among *groups* of violent offenders and 53% of the *mean* scores among *groups* of non-violent offenders will exceed the threshold value; and that is not quite the same as predicating that 100% or 53% of the *individual* scores among members of those taxonomic groups will exceed that value. But the intellectual shorthand is not overly misinforming or misleading.

Mania. Mean elevations above the threshold on the Ma scale are observed for the groups named Charlie and Foxtrot, representing 56% of violent offenders, at a ratio of 18:1 in relation to the general population. A similar elevation is observed only among members of Jupiter, representing 4% of non-violent offenders, at a ratio of 4:3 in relation to the general population; we would thus expect to find elevated Ma scores among non-violent offenders only negligibly more often than in the population at large. But the *relative* ratio between violent and non-violent offenders in elevated mean Ma scores is on the order of 14:1. Overall, the relative incidence with which clinically elevated scores on Ma are observed among aggressive offenders, non-aggressive offenders, and in the population at large can be expressed as 56:4:3. Ma may thus be clearly be regarded as differentiating aggressive offenders *both* from people-in-general and from non-aggressive offenders.

Schizophrenia. Mean elevations above the threshold on the Sc scale are observed for the groups named Charlie and Foxtrot, representing 56% of violent offenders, at a ratio of 18:1 in relation to the general population. Similar elevations are observed in How and Jupiter, representing 22% of non-violent offenders, at a ratio of 7:1 in relation to the general population. But the relative ratio between violent and non-violent offenders is on the order of 5:2. The overall relative ratio can be expressed as 56:22:3 as between aggressive and non-aggressive offenders and in the population at large. Sc may thus also be regarded as differentiating aggressive offenders *both* from people-in-general and from non-aggressive offenders.

Psychasthenia. A mean elevation above the threshold on the Pt scale is observed for group Charlie, representing 30% of violent offenders, at a ratio of 10:1 in relation to the general population. Similar elevations are observed in How and Jupiter, representing 22% of non-violent offenders, at a ratio of 7:1 in relation to the general population. But the relative ratio between violent and non-violent offenders is on the order of 10:7. The overall relative ratio can be expressed as 30:7:3 as between aggressive and non-aggressive offenders and in the population at large. Pt may thus be regarded as differentiating both aggressive non-aggressive offenders from people-in-general and as differentiating aggressive from non-aggressive offenders, but more weakly than either Ma or Sc.

Paranoia. A mean elevation above the threshold on the Pa scale is observed for group Charlie, representing 30% of violent offenders, at a ratio of 10:1 in relation to the general population. A similar elevation is observed in How. representing 27% of non-violent offenders, at a ratio of 9:1 in relation to the general population. The relative ratio between violent and non-violent offenders is only on the order of 10:9. The overall relative ratio can be expressed as 30:27:3 as between aggressive and non-aggressive offenders and in the population at large. While Pa may differentiate offenders from people-in-general, it does not differentiate aggressive from non-aggressive offenders.

Non-delineating scales. Mean elevations on the remaining scales fail to delineate aggressive offenders either from the general population or from non-aggressive offenders. On Hs and Hy, mean elevations above the clinical threshold are observed only for group How, representing 19% of non-aggressive offenders, at ratios in each case of 6:1 in relation to the general population. On D, mean elevations above the threshold are observed for groups George and How, representing collectively 29% of non-aggressive offenders, at a ratio of 10:1 in relation to the general population. No group of either aggressive or non-aggressive offenders scores above the clinical threshold on Mf or on Si.

The Ma-Pd-Sc interactive trait-set as the "psychometric signature" of aggressive offenders

Consideration of the re-arrayed Megargee-Bohn data on the basis of reference ranges and threshold values quite strongly points to Ma as not merely a differentiating, but as the *pivotal* defining, trait of the aggressive offenders in this subject pool, with Pd and Sc in what we might regard as supporting roles. To borrow Blanchard & Neale's (1994) phrase, clinically elevated scores on Ma-Pd-Sc may represent the "psychometric signature" for aggressive offending. Reverting to our intellectual shorthand, we may say that clinically significant elevations on the Ma scale are 18 times as frequent among aggressive offenders as in the population at large and 14 times as frequent among aggressive offenders as among non-aggressive offenders. Similar elevations on the Pd scale are 33 times as frequent among aggressive offenders as in the population at large but only 1.6 times as frequent among aggressive offenders as among non-aggressive offenders; on the Sc scale, clinically significant elevations are similarly 18 times as frequent among aggressive offenders as in the population at large and 2.5 times as frequent among aggressive offenders as among non-aggressive offenders.

We can approach these data with a focus on the *set* of traits or characteristics represented by simultaneously clinically elevated scores on Ma-Pd-Sc. That *trait-set* is found in groups Charlie and Foxtrot, collectively comprising 56% of the aggressive offenders in the Megargee-Bohn sample but in *none* of the groups comprised of non-aggressive offenders, so that the relative incidence of clinically elevated scores as between aggressive and non-aggressive offenders can be expressed in the ratio 56:0; the statistical purist might say quite correctly that the set is found "infinitely" more often among groups of aggressive than among groups of non-aggressive offenders.

The probability of observing elevated scores on that trait-set in the population at large constrains a rather more technical discussion. Even though each scale had been developed by means of criterion-referencing, McKinley, Hathaway & Meehl (1956, 123) reported slight but significant correlations among and between the traits that comprise this set (at .21 for Ma vs. Sc and .31 for Pd vs. Sc but only .01 for Ma vs. Pd). Although each scale may measure a specific nosologic entity, these entities apparently coexist in the population at large. For that reason, we can expect subject who score high on one scale to score high on the other two, although the magnitude of the correlations does not suggest that clinically elevated scores on one scale in the triad will be accompanied by similarly elevated scores on the other two. But, even were it the case that each of these scales correlated with the other two perfectly and positively (i.e., at $r = +1.00$), at maximum we would expect the find an elevated triad no more frequently than three times in 100 in the population at large. In this situation, the most conservative statement that can be made about the relative incidence of *simultaneous* elevations at or beyond the clinical threshold in the general population is that such elevations are to be expected in not more than 3% of the cases. Following that line of reasoning, we may say that the overall relative ratio for the interactive trait-set can be expressed as 56:0:3 as between aggressive and non-aggressive offenders and the population at large. There seems little need to calculate a measure of statistical significance of the difference between those proportions before pronouncing the interactive Ma-Pd-Sc trait-set *the* defining characteristic of aggressive offender groups, at least in the Megargee-Bohn sample.

Or, to speculate about the matter from quite another perspective: Considering the data in relation to reference ranges and clinical threshold values, it appears to be the case that the readiness to engage in impulsive violence (of the character that current research in the neurosciences attributes to neuropathology) may perpetuate itself in such fashion that it is reflected in clinically elevated scores on the MMPI's mania scale — and that its behavioral expression is aided and abetted by impairments in the capacity to assess "reality" correctly (perhaps most particularly, in the realistic assessment of costs, benefits, and risks associated with prospective lines of behavior), as reflected in clinically elevated scores on the MMPI's psychopathic deviation and schizophrenia scales. Particularly since a high proportion of episodes of aggressive criminal violence occurs under tinder-box circumstances, should we expect that those who perpetrate such violence will display actuarially measurable personal characteristics *different from* impulsivity, psychopathic deviation, and impaired contact with reality?

Mayo Clinic restandardization and age-related decline in Ma, Pd, and Sc scores

A decade ago, a major restandardization study of the MMPI was undertaken at the Mayo Clinic to provide contemporary norms inflected by age and sex (Colligan, Osborne, Swenson & Offord, 1989). Particularly in view of the interactive set which appears to define aggressive offenders, it is germane to consider "incidental" findings reported by Colligan and his associates (44) that negative correlations were found between age and scores on Ma and Pd, respectively, among both male and female subjects in their restandardization sample and on Sc, but among males only. These findings emerged from a restandardization study whose subject pool represented the general population, putatively free of criminal offenders. But they are remarkably congruent with the data on the epidemiology of aggressive criminal offending and victimization and on the confluence of death by violence in late adolescence and early adulthood we reviewed in Chapter 3 and with the general direction of research in "career criminality," so much so that one cannot help but wonder whether the same naturally-occurring psychological phenomenon is not also reflected in decreases in overt criminal behavior, perhaps through a process which has been termed "symptom abandonment" as a function of age (Pallone & Tirman, 1978).

Research on career criminality has generally found that formal criminal behavior (and particularly that behavior reflected in crimes of violence) tends to decrease with age. In what is perhaps the touchstone investigation, Blumstein & Cohen (1987) studied the criminal careers of some 13,000 arrestees in Detroit and the District of Columbia, concluding that participation in crime tends to stabilize in early adulthood. At this point, many who commenced delinquent behavior in adolescence or earlier apparently forsake the criminal lifestyle, but those who do not apparently continue to commit crimes at a relatively constant rate for the remainder of their life-span. These data support Blumstein & Moitra's (1980) earlier contention that a very small proportion of persons (on the order of

6% of all those ever convicted) are responsible for a very large proportion (on the order of 52%) of all criminal activity.

In Moffitt's (1993, 1994) interpretation, there is evidence of two distinct patterns of formally criminal behavior, with the first encompassing "a small group" of offenders (perhaps accounting for 15% of all offenders) who exhibit "life-course persistent antisocial behavior culminating in a pathologic personality" but who may be responsible for a major portion of all offenses, and a second group that exhibits "adolescence-limited antisocial behavior." It is not incidental that, in Moffitt's view, "children's neuropsychological problems interact cumulatively with their criminogenic environments" in the "adolescence-limited" group. Moffitt's "life-course persistent" offenders are reminiscent of those identified as "under-controlled" in the experience and expression of hostility by means of Megargee's O-H scale [NOTE 3].

The accumulated research evidence on "crime specialization" is also pertinent. Although the belief remains widespread (doubtless elicited by journalistic accounts and supported by what are generally interpreted as high rates of recidivism) that an offender progresses inexorably through graduated acts of criminality in approximate concordance with chronological age, that belief is not supported by the accumulated research evidence, which has generally found little evidence for progression but instead some evidence for retrogression. Thus, after reviewing the relevant published research, Loeber (1990) concludes that "Patterns of antisocial behavior tend to change during preadolescence and adolescence: the number of youths who engage in *overt* antisocial acts *declines*."

Among adult male offenders, Holland & McGarvey (1984) found that "there was specialization in nonviolent offenses [but] little tendency toward consistently violent behavior. Seriousness progression from nonviolent to violent misconduct was infrequent; however, there was substantial retrogression from violent to nonviolent offenses." There is also evidence that the phenomenon is international in dimension (Goeppinger, 1975). Buikhuisen's (1982) finding that, as a group, what he called "persistent" offenders tend to suffer more frequently from CNS dysfunctions implicated in learning, and therefore in impaired ability to profit from experience, may offer an undergirding explanation. More pointedly, Hare, McPherson & Forth (1988) analyzed the criminal careers over a 25 year period of Canadian offenders who had been identified in Hare's earlier studies as psychopaths or as nonpsychopaths, reporting that "the criminal activities of nonpsychopaths were relatively constant over the years, whereas those of psychopaths remained high until around age 40, after which they declined dramatically," adding that "The results are consistent with clinical impressions that some psychopaths tend to 'burn out' in middle age."

Neurodevelopment and aggressive "burn out"

If decline in impulsivity and psychopathic deviation, coupled (among men) with improved reality contact resultant in a decrease in the internal imperative to act (or "act out") toward stimuli perhaps influenced by an increased capacity to realistically assess the costs, risks, and benefits of behavior represent reasonable operational approximations to "burn out," those clinical impressions are psychometrically verified through the Mayo Clinic restandardization data base.

In view of the strong congruence between psychological (i.e., the declines in MMPI scores related to aggressive offending observed in the Mayo Clinic restandardization study) and social (i.e., demographic data on aggressive criminal offending) variables that depict violent offending as centered in adolescence and early adulthood and as decreasing thereafter, one is tempted to search for a corresponding neurodevelopmental variable. But there is only fragmentary evidence that systematic changes occur in neurological functioning at roughly the age of 30 that might explain such phenomena.

It is reasonably well accepted that brain electrical activity as measured by EEG changes at approximately age 30 (Duffy, McAnulty & Albert, 1993), and there is some evidence that the metabolism of dopamine (Joseph & Roth, 1983; Murray & Waddington, 1991; Joseph, Villalobos-Molina, Yamagami & Roth, 1995), norepinephrine (Rogers & Bloom, 1985; Christiansen & Grzybowski, 1993), gamma-aminobutyric acid or GABA (Rogers & Bloom, 1985) and acetycholine (Taylor & Griffith, 1993) varies systematically with age, in each case in a direction consistent with both demographic and psychometric data. Some neurologists sometimes speculate about a naturally-occurring process of "hardening" in the myelin sheath that covers the brain, the spinal cord, and the axons of certain (effector) nerves (Berkow & Fletcher, 1992, 1487-1488) and that may, in a very literal sense, decelerate neuronal communication within the central nervous system. (Demylelinization, or the corrosion of the myelin sheath, is a major symptom of multiple sclerosis.) Alternately, some neurologists propose that the *ratio* of excitatory synapses changes in relation to inhibitory synapses during the latter part of the third decade of life.

A neurogenic etiology for psychopathic deviation?

From its probable origins in early Victorian notions of "moral insanity" to its present incarnation as "antisocial personality disorder" in the American Psychiatric Association's (1994) official lexicon of mental disorders, few constructs relevant to the mental health sciences have led so precarious an existence as has "psychopathic deviation." Lykken (1987) argues that the construct is readily divisible into "genus" and "species," identifying four "genera": the dissocial, the neurotic, the organically impulsive, and the sexually explosive. While one could wax eloquent for eons on the topic, suffice it to say that descriptions of the disorder tend toward tautology in the extreme. Yet psychometric measures of psychopathy reliably distinguish offenders from non-offenders and, in many studies, aggressive offenders from non-aggressive offenders (Stevens, 1993, 1994).

Conceptualizing psychopathic deviation under any rubric (whether termed antisocial personality disorder, psychopathy, sociopathy, or even moral insanity) as a trait rather than as a description of behavior constitutes the nub of the tautology, and that is nowhere better illustrated than in the "diagnostic criteria" for antisocial personality disorder specified in the American Psychiatric Association's lexicon (649-650):

[A] There is a pervasive pattern of disregard for and violation of the rights of others occurring since age 15 years, as indicated by three (or more) of the following: (1) failure to conform to social norms with respect to lawful behaviors as indicated by repeatedly performing acts that are grounds for arrest; (2) deceitfulness, as indicated by repeated lying, use of aliases, or conning others for personal profit or pleasure; (3) impulsivity or failure to plan ahead; (4) irritability and aggressiveness, as indicated by repeated physical fights or assaults; (5) reckless disregard for safety of self or others; (6) consistent irresponsibility, as indicated by repeated failure to sustain consistent work behavior or honor financial obligations; (7) lack of remorse, as indicated by being indifferent to or rationalizing having hurt, mistreated, or stolen from another.

[B] The individual is at least age 18 years.

[C] There is evidence of Conduct Disorder . . . with onset before age 15 years. D. The occurrence of antisocial behavior is not exclusively during the course of Schizophrenia or a Manic Episode.

Clearly, these diagnostic criteria are virtually redundant with a description of past behavior; that is to say, "habitual criminality" is itself a principal criterion for the diagnosis — to the extent, indeed, that the clinicians employed in the New York state correctional system surveyed by Stevens (1993) described the process of applying the diagnostic label to offenders as "looking for hay in a haystack." Moreover, construing a "package" of past behaviors as a portable "trait" suggests that the "trait" readily generalizes from one class of behavioral objects to other, dissimilar classes of behavioral objects. As we have seen, the criminologic literature argues otherwise. Moreover, regarding psychopathy as a "trait" or even disorder rather than as a habitual way of behaving (especially in a situation in which the "diagnostic criteria" merely recapitulate a description of behavior patterns) tells us absolutely nothing etiologically.

There is a viable alternative to such tautology. Among many criminal offenders regardless of offense category and especially among aggressive offenders, there is discernible a generalized tendency to *underestimate the costs and risks,* both for the behaver and for others affected by his/her behavior, *and conversely to overestimate the benefits* attached to behaving in formally proscribed ways, a position consistent with that of Hirschi & Gottfredson (1994). This generalized pattern is often *mistakenly* described as a "psychological characteristic" or "personality trait" rather than (more economically and more directly) denominated as a habitual way of behaving (Pichot, 1978). The accumulated research evidence from studies of intellectual functioning among "acting-out" offenders points toward a proximate etiology for such habitual mis-construing of costs, risks, and benefits; and the research evidence from the neurosciences points toward an ultimate substratum in neuropathology, specifically in those morphological structures that control foresight and planfulness, upon which the capacity to accurately construe costs, risks, and benefits rests.

Though fragmentary, there is direct evidence for the proposition that the "characteristic" or "syndrome" variously labeled psychopathic deviation or "antisocial personality disorder" may arise from a neurogenic etiology, whether that characteristic is measured by the familiar Pd scale, by alternate scales of psychopathy, or through clinical devices. Robert Hare of the University of British Columbia, undoubtedly the leading authority worldwide on psychopathic deviation, is best known for construction, validation, and refinement of scales to measure psychopathy (Hare, Harpur, Hakstian & Forth, 1990; Hare, 1991, 1993). But he has also researched the relationship between psychopathy and cerebral function intensively (Hare, 1979, 1982), early (1970) distinguishing *hyperarousability* as a characteristic of psychopaths. Support has been advanced in a number of studies:

- Blackburn (1975, 1979) found evidence of abnormally high cortical arousal, as measured through EEG readings, among prisoners diagnosed as psychopathic, findings that support Hare's view.

- Gorenstein (1982) reported evidence of dysfunction in the *frontal lobe* of the brain, held to govern such functions as foresight, planning, and the regulation of impulses among subjects otherwise diagnosed as psychopathic, with similar (but not parallel) results reported by Linz, Hooper, Hynd, Isaac & Gibson (1990) among juveniles adjudicated as delinquent.

- Hare & McPherson (1984) administered a listening task that required activation of lateralized brain functions to inmates who had been classified as high or low in psychopathy and to control subjects who were presumably crime-free but whose level of psychopathy was not inventoried, finding that "psychopaths are characterized by asymmetric low left-hemisphere arousal."

- Jutai, Hare & Connolly (1987) similarly found "asymmetric left-hemisphere arousal" patterns among subjects who had been identified through Hare's methodology as psychopathic. These results were replicated and amplified by Raine, O'Brien, Smiley & Scerbo (1990).

It is germane to underscore that the findings by Hare and Raine and their associates concerning left hemisphere dysfunction accord with research on the relative "verbal deficit" configuration in inflected Wechsler intelligence test scores reviewed earlier in this chapter and that the same configuration has been found a relatively reliable screen for left hemisphere organicity. Withal, there is reason to suppose both that neurogenic factors underlie what has typically been identified as psychopathic deviation (Stein, Hollander & Leibowitz, 1993) and that the term itself is largely redundant with, and recapitulative of, behavioral history.

Resting on data from the neurosciences rather than from psychometrics, Siever, Steinberg, Trestman & Intrator (1994) evince no reluctance in grounding both psychopathy and impulsivity in disordered brain processes. Instead, reasoning that it is is at least as likely that the so-called "underlying" patterns of behavior (technically, the Axis II disorders in the American Psychiatric Association's DSM nosologic system) as that specific symptom manifestations (the Axis I disorders) result from long-standing brain anomaly, they posit rather categorically a genesis for both impulsivity and psychopathy in impairment in brain biochemistry, specifically in the metabolism of the ubiquitous neurotransmitter serotonin:

> Impulsivity is a central feature of . . . antisocial personality disorder. A relative failure to suppressive aggressive or otherwise risky behaviors with possible negative consequences may underlie the tendency toward fighting, irritability, drug abuse, promiscuity, and self-damaging acts characteristic of these disorders. Emerging evidence implicates biological abnormalities of behavior-inhibiting systems such as the 5-HT [i.e., serotonin-metabolizing] system in the expression of impulsivity.
>
> The individual with antisocial personality disorder displays characteristics of impulsivity . . . "Psychopathy" is another basic characteristic and is defined by glibness and disregard of others' feelings associated with manipulative and exploitative behaviors . . . A growing body of work suggest that psychophysiological correlates include inadequate detection of emotional cues and reduced cortical arousal [i.e., impaired capacity to inhibit behavior] compared with that observed in psychiatrically healthy individuals.

Though his conclusions rest on statistical correlations rather than on data from neuroimaging studies, Eysenck (1995) similarly argues that "conscience is a learned response," so that, obversely, psychopathy at the least represents a failure to learn appropriate or customary values and behavioral norms, or perhaps the learning of contrary values and norms. Most pertinently, however, Eysenck links "evidence from psychophysiological and other biological studies" to "low cortical arousal" attributable to impairment in the production of serotonin. As we noted in Chapter 3, neuropsychiatrists Brown, Botsis & Van Praag (1994) reached similar conclusions with respect to the centrality of serotonin regulation in aggressive violence and further observed that "a new class of drugs, the serenics, specifically cause the inhibition of antagonistic behavior" in infra-human experiments and may be expected to produce similar effects in human subjects.

Even a conservative view currently accounts some role in the emergence of psychopathy as an enduring pattern of behavior to neuropsychological impairment or dysfunction. As Robert Archer (1995, 520) has put it, with particular emphasis on "language-based verbal skills deficits" (i.e., the "verbal deficit pattern" reflected in PIQ > VIQ on the Wechsler instruments) and "deficits in self-control function," such "neuropsychological deficits may initiate a chain of events that culminate in antisocial disorder," since "such neuropsychological problems render children more vulnerable to pathogenic social environments."

Psychopathy: Trait or description of behavior?

We are not alone in our preference for a description of behavior rather than the invoking of a "trait" understood as an enduring and "portable" *potentiality* for behavior, especially psychometric measures of that potentiality are merely redundant with recorded behavior. In particular, criminologists are frequently disdainful of fine conceptual distinctions made in the mental health sciences which have little correspondence to behavioral variegation. Thus, Rachlin, Halpern & Portnow (1984) have argued that psychopathic deviation should be equated with socially deviant behavior rather than mental illness: "There is a tremendous difference between . . . acts that are truly irresistible and those that are merely not resisted."

From a sociological perspective, Wheeler (1976) has argued that the "so-called psychopathic deviate is an individual whose behavior conforms to the standards of his subculture but not to 'normal' social standards [who] often does not show any significant abnormality in behavior outside adherence to non-normative standards and values." In the next chapter, we further explore the process whereby the neurogenically impulsive elects to place himself or herself into a "subculture" whose social standards veer from the "normal."

The California psychological inventory

From its inception, the MMPI was intended to function as a diagnostic instrument, identifying those persons suffering from emotional disorders of one or another sort who were presumably in need of professional mental health treatment. To that extent, the instrument sought to differentiate the "abnormal" from the "normal" — and to differentiate those who are "abnormal" in *this* way from those who are abnormal in *that* way. But the MMPI has never claimed to be able to differentiate particularly efficiently among persons who are *not* disordered in some way. Instead, the task of delineating the various aspects of "normal" personality has been ceded to instruments designed for that purposes, including Cattell's Sixteen Personality Factor Questionnaire (16-PF).

Among the best-known and most widely used of the instruments intended for what is called the "multidimensional assessment of normal persons" is the *California Psychological Inventory* (CPI) developed by Harrison Gough of the University of California at Berkeley, who had also been instrumental in the development of derivative scales on the MMPI that measure dissimulation, dominance, prejudice, and social responsibility. The CPI has been available commercially since 1956. Intended for use with subjects as young as 13, the instrument measures such dimensions of *normal* personality as dominance, flexibility, intellectual efficiency, (need to) achieve by means of conformance or by means of independence, responsibility, sense of well-being, tolerance, sociability. Scores are reported on a normalized *T* distribution, as with the MMPI.

Not surprisingly, the CPI has been employed with some frequency in studies of criminal offenders in situations in which no assumption has been made that such investigations require instruments that focus on psychopathology. Because its lower limit encompasses a significant proportion of juvenile offenders who are adjudicated through the courts (rather than "handled" through the state's child protective agency without formal court intervention), the CPI is especially popular in both clinical and research applications with young offenders. Moreover, though it is difficult to document such a generalization, one suspects that the wide use of the CPI with offender populations is at least in part an abreaction to the failure, prior to the Megargee-Bohn typology study, of the MMPI to post-dict criminal behavior with unquestioned efficiency. Thus, for the differentialist, if the multidimensional assessment of abnormal personalities fails, perhaps the multidimensional assessment of normal personalities will succeed.

According to Laufer, Skoog & Day (1982, 562), who reviewed some 62 studies of offender groups with the CPI, that is precisely the case: "Scales from the [CPI] inventory . . . have proven to be moderately predictive of parole success, assault proneness, prisoner's grades in educational courses, probationer/parolee employment stability, and recidivism."

Moreover, the profiles that emerge from these studies show considerable similarity. In particular, mean scores for samples of offender subjects on the *responsibility* and *socialization* scales are typically quite low, often equivalent to the 2nd percentile. Since the purpose of the instrument is to assess "normal" personalities, the most cautious interpretation of such findings is that, in comparison with persons who are considered to be psychologically normal rather than abnormal, criminal offenders are markedly less responsible and less positively socialized. That is, of course, precisely what one would expect of people who, as a group, tend to score high on the mania and psychopathic deviation scales of the MMPI. Hence, research evidence on the CPI tends to complement that derived from the MMPI.

The Maudsley/Eysenck inventory

In the first edition of his landmark *Crime and Personality,* the distinguished British psychologist Hans Eysenck (1964) of the University of London set forth the proposition that criminal behavior is a function of three personality characteristics — *psychoticism, neuroticism, extraversion* — and that a fourth dimension, roughly encapsulated as the extent to which an individual seeks to appear "normal" either to all others or to selected others, contributes to certain types of criminal behavior. What has been called the "Eysenck theory of criminality" has been further elaborated in the second edition (1977) and by Eysenck & Gudjonsson (1989) in *Causes and Cures of Criminality.*

Each of the three personality dimensions is measurable through an instrument initially named the Maudsley Personality Inventory (after the teaching hospital in London where Eysenck held his faculty appointment and where he pioneered in the development of aversive behavior therapy) or the *Eysenck Personality Inventory* (EPI), the successor instrument, developed largely on the basis of Eysenck's considerable experimental research on brain-behavior relationships. The theoretical rationale that underlies the instrument holds that the characteristics of personality measured by the instrument represent the product not only of psychosocial developmental experiences but also of typical patterns of neuropsychological organization. Thus, neuroticism as a characteristic of the adult personality reflects lability in the autonomic nervous system, while extraversion reflects cortical inhibition (Jensen, 1965) and psychoticism is related to impairment in the production of serotonin (Eysenck, 1995). Scores on the instrument are reported in percentile terms and, because independent norm tables are provided for a variety of subject groups (including criminal offenders), a process approximating the utilization of reference ranges and threshold levels is enabled.

A number of contemporary studies, often conducted by Eysenck and his colleagues at the Maudsley, have focused on the psychological characteristics of violent offenders in particular. In a study that provided further confirmation for the conceptual model but did not seek to differentiate offenders by type of crime, Eysenck & Eysenck (1977) reported by-age comparison of scores on the EPI for 2070 British prisoners and 2442 non-offender control subjects. Prisoners scored significantly higher on the P (Psychoticism) and N (Neuroticism) scales in all age groups, ranging from 16 to 69; on the E (Extraversion) scale, score differences proved not significant until age 30-39, when they fell in the predicted direction. Some 22% of the prisoners and 15% of controls, however, scored at clinically significant thresholds on all three scales, while 5% and 13% respectively scored low. It is worth noting that the characteristic measured by the E scale has much in common with susceptibility to social influence as behaviorally measured in the Milgram (1974) and Russell & Pigat (1991) studies on "mandates for violence," reviewed in Chapter 4.

Scores on all three scales were found to decline with increasing age among both prisoners and controls. Up to age 30, prisoners had higher L (essentially, social desirability) scores than controls, but the reverse situation obtained at higher age levels. Correlations between L, E, P, and N scores were low both among prisoners and among controls, a finding which contributed evidence to the proposition that these are independent traits of personality; thus, scores in combination with each other should provide a sounder basis for a prediction of criminal deviance. Not incidentally, there is remarkable congruence between the findings in this study on age-related decline in EPI scores held to be related to criminal deviance and the similarly age-related decline in scores on the MMPI Pd and Ma scales reported by Colligan and his associates (1989) in the Mayo Clinic restandardization study.

Studies by McGurk & McDougall (1981) and by McGurk & Bolton (1981) on delinquents aged 17-20 in comparison to similarly-aged control subjects and by Putnins (1982) on delinquents aged 15-18 and comparable controls established the applicability of the conceptual model to juvenile offenders, but without providing evidence that EPI scales successfully discriminated according to type of offense. In a cluster analysis of the EPI scores of delinquents aged 14-17, McEwan (1983) was able to post-dict the number of offenses in subjects' prior criminal records but not to discriminate between types of offenses. Gossop & Eysenck (1983) successfully discriminated incarcerated felony offenders from (non-incarcerated) drug addicts, but without differentiation as to type of offense among felons.

Data which support the contention that violent and non-violent offenders can be differentiated on the basis of EPI scores were reported by Eysenck, Rust & Eysenck (1977), however, in a study of adult prisoners in England, and by Singh (1980) in a study of convicted homicide offenders in the Punjab, among whom members of the family had most frequently been the victims. Barack & Widom (1978) similarly demonstrated the utility of the instrument and the applicability of the conceptual model to American women awaiting trial on varied felony charges. In a study which contrasted murderers in India from criminal recidivists who had not been convicted of homicide, Ram (1987) found higher levels of psychoticism in the homicide offenders but higher levels of extraversion and neuroticism among non-homicidal recidivists.

Several investigations have proposed methodological refinements or modifications to the instrument as a device for offender populations. Thus, in an investigation of the validity of the P scale on a sample of patients in a hospital for abnormal offenders who completed both the EPI and the MMPI, Davis (1974) proposed that the EPI psychoticism scale measures a dimension he denominated *emotionality*, a construct that bears a striking resemblance to mania as measured by the MMPI's Ma scale.

Similarly, Saklofske, McKerracher & [Sybil] Eysenck (1978) extracted from the E, N, and P scales those items which had most robustly differentiated adult offenders from control subjects to construct a "second order" scale they denominated criminal propensity, cross-validated on samples of adjudicated delinquents vs. non-delinquent adolescents. Blackburn & Maybury (1985) employed the EPI to determine correlates of that blend of particular reactivity to environmental stimuli, lack of affect, and lack of behavioral control considered by many to constitute the defining characteristics of the psychopathic personality.

The "second-order" scale derived by Saklofske, McKerracher & Eysenck rather closely parallels the Pd scale of the MMPI, while the Blackburn-Maybury blend mirrors those traits measured by both the Ma and Pd scales. Indeed, in their meta-analysis of what they termed "crime-proneness" studies across nations, genders, races, and methods of measurement, Caspi, Moffitt, Silva & Krueger (1994) concluded that indices of "negative emotionality" and "weak constraint" by whatever means measured constituted potent correlates of criminal behavior. Those constructs also mirror what the Ma and Pd scales of the MMPI measure.

VERBAL DEFICIT, IMPULSIVITY, PERCEPTION OF RISK, AND THRILL-SEEKING

This review suggests that two psychological traits reliably and robustly differentiate aggressive offenders: the "verbal deficit" pattern in inflected measures of intelligence and "impulsivity" as variously psychometrically inventoried. We have also seen that the verbal deficit pattern constitutes a gross index to neurologic dysfunction (differentially sensitive to the left hemisphere), that there is sound reason to believe that (as the evidence from the neurosciences we reviewed in Chapter 2 suggests) impulsivity is a frequent consequence of even relatively minor neurologic dysfunction, and (as the evidence from the effects of neuroactive chemical substances we reviewed in Chapter 3 suggests) that impulsivity can be either elicited or escalated by the ingestion of CNS stimulants. There is also evidence (Chapter 4) that suggests that both the "habit" of preferring action to thought (that is, of construing stimuli and of mediating behavior largely non-verbally) and impulsive patterns of behavior can be learned intrafamilially and intergenerationally and are frequently reinforced through long-distance vicarious conditioning. But, to use the familiar terminology of Raymond B. Cattell (1963, 1980), "traits" are not coextensive with behavioral "states." Granted that the "verbal deficit" and impulsivity may constitute differentiating traits of aggressive offenders, in what patterns of behavior do such traits characteristically find expression?

Stimulus-bound cognition, alexithymia, and the discharge of impulse into behavior

As initially formulated by Kelly (1955, 1967, 1970, 1980) and refined by later contributors (Bannister & Fransella, 1971; Maher, 1969; Niemeyer, 1985, 1990; Niemeyer & Niemeyer, 1987), "personal construct psychology" interprets behavior as a function of the way the behaving person "construes" *both* an object of behavior *and* the ways of behaving accessible to him or her in relation to that object. The process of construing is in some large measure cognitive, reflecting the ways in which the person characteristically interprets the data of experience.

For most people, construing an object or other stimulus (including interpersonal stimuli) entails considering and weighing alternative meanings the stimulus may have in and of itself (the *ding an sich* of the Kantians), as well as the behavioral prescriptions for the self that flow from each alternative meaning. That process requires the capacity to differentiate among and between often complex stimuli. In turn, differentiation depends in some measure on the capacity to notice, name, and order variant stimuli and variant aspects of the same stimulus, intellectual operations which typically occur through verbal mediation.

Especially when the difference between verbal and non-verbal intelligence is relatively large (and most particularly when both are subnormal), we may expect that the relative incapacity to mediate the data of experience verbally will result in impairment or constriction in the capacity to differentiate, construe, fantasize, and/or imagine, since these cognitive operations are largely mediated verbally. If that is so, the person whose cognitions are verbally-deficient is likely to suffer impairment in "decoding" the cognitively complex words, gestures, or behavior of other actors. Even in childhood, is the parent who admonishes the child not to reach for the lit burner on the stove "protective" or unreasonably "restrictive," and what prescriptions for the child's own behavior flow from those alternate constructions?

Extrapolated into adolescence and adulthood, the relative incapacity to construe and to interpret the intentions and actions of others so as to consider and weigh alternative meanings may constrain the person to respond to the actions and intentions of others in inappropriately hostile or aggressive ways not warranted by the realities (the *ding an sich*) of interpersonal stimuli.

The person who is limited in the capacity to construe may become, on that account, more *stimulus-bound* than one who is able to construe imaginatively a variety of possible meanings for, or responses to, stimuli or able to construe alternate meanings for the behavior of others. In turn, the capacity to construe alternate meanings for cognitively complex stimuli and to devise (by imaginative and prospective construing) alternate ways of behaving in relation to (not necessarily or even primarily *in response to*) provides a firmer basis for the assessment of costs, risks, and benefits associated with responding to stimuli (including interpersonal stimuli) in *this* way rather than in *that*. The conceptual model for what distinguished psychologist Albert Mehrabian (1995) of UCLA terms "stimulus screening" to describe"the cognitive counterpart of arousability" seems quite applicable. In Mehrabian's formulation (6-7):

> Cognition of any situation tends to be selective; we orient ourselves toward, and attend to, those elements of a situation . . . important to our ongoing activities, while we ignore

less important elements . . . the degree to which individuals habitually and automatically screen less relevant elements of any situation they encounter can be treated as an individual-difference variable.

On the basis of that formulation, Mehrabian constructed nearly two decades ago a measure for "trait stimulus screening" which has demonstrated in subsequent research associative relationships with distractibility, impulsivity, hostility, and aggressivity, as enduring intrapersonal "traits"; to the use of stimulants and hallucinogens and to alcohol consumption; and also (recalling the finding of the Hennessy & Kepecs-Schlussel study reviewed in Chapter 4) "high density residential environments." That litany sounds like a recitation of the social and psychological factors implicated in aggressive criminal offending. Though he specifically labels "stimulus screening" a "cognitive" operation, Mehrabian does not essay the relationship between the organization of general cognitive capacity and the ability to screen stimuli so as to appreciate (or alternately to ignore) their "complexity and novelty." But it is not an unreasonable inference that persons who evince a relative deficit in verbal intelligence — and thus lack the capacity to apprehend fully the "complexity" of stimuli — will on that account experience greater arousability in relation to those stimuli. As Mischel (1979) intimates, unless the perceiver apprehends that complexity, how he or she construes and responds to stimuli cannot avoid being relatively primitive.

Alexithymia is a construct from the canon of psychoanalysis that appears to have fallen from favor. Traditionally, the condition has connoted "difficulty in describing or recognizing one's own emotions, with a limited fantasy life and general constriction in the affective life" (Stone, 1988, 10), and people who display alexithymia are sometimes said to suffer impairment in an "inner life," or, as Miller (1988) has it, to suffer "a deficit in inner speech use." As a result, their behavior seems to be governed primarily by external stimuli, with little or no concern for the consequences of their actions. Alexithymia is typically not posited as an emotional or mental disorder in its own right but rather as indicative or symptomatic of one or another reasonably well-defined psychopathologic condition. Though the term had its origins in the murky world of id, ego, and superego, it seems particularly apt as a description of the stimulus-bound character of cognition among those who display the relative deficit indicated by the PIQ > VIQ configural pattern in the organization of intelligence that has characterized *both* "acting out" aggressive offenders and subjects with left hemisphere dysfunctions over a period of 50 years of research on the Wechsler instruments.

Among the major figures in the pantheon of psychoanalysis, few have been more articulate than Anna Freud (1946) in her classic *The Ego and the Mechanisms of Defense* in urging that, unless hostile impulses can be discharged *safely and imaginatively* through fantasy, there is little option but that they must instead be discharged through hostile behavior. That interpretation is consistent with the conclusions drawn by Raine (1993-a) in a study of the prevalence of "borderline personality" among violent offenders in Britain and by Liisa Keltikangas-Jarvinen (1982) that the responses to projective test devices by violent offenders (but not those of non-violent offenders) uniformly demonstrated an alexithymic inability to fantasize — a deficit akin to the relative incapacity either (or both) to construe alternate responses to stimulus situations or to foresee the consequences of one's behavior.

Moreover, we can expect those who are relatively more alexithymically stimulus-bound to suffer consequent impairment in the capacity to delay gratification, since that capacity in its turn depends upon the capacity to imagine and to order or prioritize alternatives. Such persons are often described as, and describe themselves as, "acting on impulse" rather than on the basis of thought. In fact, the description is largely inaccurate, for "thought" has occurred, but has not been verbalized. An alternate description, that the behavior (and perhaps the thinking) seems "concretistic," may be more appropriate.

We surmise that stimuli that are experienced or interpreted monolithically (that is, for which the experiencer or interpreter is able to construe no alternative meanings) control or determine behavior more directly among alexithymics or those who display the "verbal deficit" pattern in cognition than among those whose capacity to verbally mediate the data of experience demonstrates little or no impairment. If that surmise is not grossly inaccurate, we may also have found a key to understanding the genesis of the "vulnerabilities" that Lande (1993), whose work we reviewed in Chapter 4, claims render some people particularly susceptible to the universal messages proclaiming violence as normative that persistently assault the television viewer, while others are quite capable of relegating those messages to the realm of "safe" fantasy.

Alternate speculations may compete with these surmises. If an actor has suffered a congenital or induced central nervous system dysfunction that has produced a strong and persistent state of hyperarousal but no inventoriable deficit in verbal capacity, he or she may nonetheless experience an internal, neurogenic imperative to act rather than to construe — and he or she may on that account display an alexithymic affinity to undifferentiated stimuli which results in impulsive behavior.

Or may it be the case that the same central nervous system dysfunction yields *both* a relative deficit in the capacity to mediate and construe the data of experience verbally *and* a strong, persistent state of hyperarousal that is experienced phenomenologically as an imperative to act prior to (or in the absence of) mediating and construing?

Risk at the visceral level

Conventionally, impulsivity has been associated with risk-taking behavior, and a substantial if somewhat circular body of empirical literature has developed that relates willingness to take risks in relation to other traits (Jackson, Hournay & Vidmar, 1972; MacCrimmon & Wehrung, 1985; Slovic, 1987) and even identifying risk-taking as a valuable trait among successful corporate leaders (Maccobby, 1976, 1988). Not infrequently, such studies infer impulsivity on the basis of scores on scales designed to assess willingness to take risks and measured *in vitro* in the comparative safety of the laboratory or college class-room, in situations that do not even begin to approximate "virtual reality," let alone "real-time." Thus, subjects might be asked whether they regard hitch-hiking or lending money to a stranger or sneaking out of the house or the dorm after curfew as a "risky" piece of behavior; rather infrequently are subjects asked whether they have engaged in each such behavior.

However, as Boverie, Scheuffele & Raymond (1995) have observed, in many "previous studies of risk-taking, subjects were asked to rate hypothetically 'risky' situations" but "these situations were not based on the real experiences of subjects and may not have been considered 'risky' by subjects." With some frequency, intelligence (typically measured grossly rather than through inflected indices) has been identified as a moderating variable in willingness to take risks, in a manner not incongruent with the conclusions of Heilbrun (1978), Hirschi & Hindelang (1988), and Kandel et al. (1988) on high intelligence as a shield against criminal offending nor with those of such investigators as Loevinger (1976, 161-180) and Gessner, O'Connor, Clifton et al. (1993) on the maturity of moral judgment.

In contrast to generalizations based on questionnaire studies that ask subjects (presumably representative of people-in-general), for example, whether driving carelessly is more risky than mountain-climbing, let's consider how risk is sought in "real-time" — and among people who, demographically, might fit the epidemiologic profiles for aggressive offending or victimization we reviewed in Chapter 4.

In New York City, the practice of riding about on the tops of subway cars has developed into a sport called "subway surfing." At times, its practitioners are not content merely to ride along (whether in a standing, sitting, or reclining position), but instead engage in a wild array of acrobatic stunts — with the train hurtling through an underground tunnel at 45 miles per hour or on elevated tracks several stories above street level at somewhat slower speeds. Quite clearly, this is a dangerous sport, and deaths have resulted from its practice.

According to interviews with two of its practitioners, as reported in the Parkchester Journal (1991) of the *New York Times,* there is substantial overlap between seeking to experience risk through this unusual sport and in other ways:

> Elliott Ortiz, at 22 years old, is an old-timer at the dangerous stunt that he and other young people perform on the roofs of trains across the city, particularly along the elevated tracks in the Bronx. It is called "surfing" or "hang on," and the transit authorities say it is the most perilous of the many games that threaten and occasionally kill young people on New York City's subways . . . . The risk is the lure, Mr. Ortiz, who is unemployed, said . . . "I've got to learn not to be afraid of nothing; rats, cockroaches, a gang from one block to the other," he said. "It's like . . . you are escaping from hell."

Another expert subway surfer echoed those sentiments, conveying clear and explicit perceptions of what, in the next chapter, we shall call the *choreography of the dare*:

> Joseph Araujo, a 17-year-old senior at Harry S. Truman High School in the Bronx, said that he and a few friends surf every day . . . "It's mostly like a dare to see who is who, what you can do," he said. "Some people just do it to see how far they can go — how close they can get to death without really dying." He compared [subway] surfing to proving yourself on the street, where being tough and fearless is often more important than safety. "Sometimes it's scary," he said. "But that's what the street is all about."

It may well be the case that, among those whose phenomenological world is constrained by rats, cockroaches, and gangs and punctuated only by the lure of risk, the process of what the psychology of learning terms "response generalization" occurs rather more readily than among those affluent enough to engage mountain-climbing as a preferential sport.

Thrill-seeking as a behavioral pattern

Distinguished psychologist Frank Farley has long been concerned with "thrill-seeking" as an enduring pattern of behavior. Farley (1986, 45-46) distinguishes those who "are risk-takers and adventurers [and] seek excitement and stimulation wherever they can find or create it" from those who "cling to certainty and predictability, avoiding risks and the unfamiliar," labeling those in the first group as *T-types* (i.e., the *capital T* types) and those in the second as *t-types* (i.e., the *lower-case t* types). Moreover, "thrill-seeking can lead . . . to outstanding creativity . . . but it can [also] lead to extremely destructive, even criminal, behavior." Farley holds that the genesis of thrill-seeking or thrill-avoidance is likely neurophysiological, but is both mediated by, and mediates, social factors:

> . . . we all seek unconsciously to maintain an optimal level of "arousal" or activity in the central nervous system . . . If arousal is too high or too low, we try to adjust it to some middle ground, often by choosing environments and experiences that are either soothing or stimulating. Some of our research and that of others implicates such physiological arousability as the basis for stimulation-seeking, while other research suggests a role for biochemistry (such as monamine oxidase or testosterone). These

interpretations may not be incompatible, but the precise biological bases are not certain at present. Experiences around the time of birth or perhaps early nutrition may also play a role.

Whatever its source, thrill-seeking appears to fluctuate inversely with age:

[thrill-seeking] is most often found among those in the 16-to-24 age range. From then it drops off gradually, as my colleagues and I found in two large studies of people from approximately 10 to 75 years old . . . most people reach their strongest expression of [thrill-seeking behavior] in their late teens to early 20s, with a decline into old age.

Farley's data, then, are highly congruent with those of Colligan and his associates (1989) on age-related decline in scores on the mania and psychopathic deviation scales of the MMPI and of Hare and his colleagues (1988) on the age-related decline in criminal behavior among offenders categorized as psychopaths. Those results are further confirmed by White, Labouvie & Bates (1985) and Bates, White & Labouvie (1994), who found, in longitudinal studies of a large sample of adolescents and young adults, that sensation-seeking as measured psychometrically correctly predicted alcohol and substance abuse over time. For these subjects, involvement in the drug world may have been a major source in satisfying their thrill-seeking behavior; and such involvement (especially with CNS stimulants as the drugs of choice) may further reinforce thrill-seeking as a behavioral pattern.

In summarizing a decade of research on what he has termed the "thrill-seeking" or *Type-T* personality, using a variety of measures (some patterned after scales from the Eysenck Personality Inventory), Farley (1986, 46) has identified four sub-types among habitual thrill-seekers in a schematic that categorizes both what he calls the "criminal mastermind" and those who behave in particularly violent and brutal ways:

- CONSTRUCTIVE T (T +) — MENTAL, a group that encompasses "people who seek stimulation mainly in the mental domain, such as artists, scientists, entertainers."
- CONSTRUCTIVE T (T +) — PHYSICAL, a group that includes "people who seek stimulation mainly in the physical domain, such as adventurers and physical risk-takers.
- DESTRUCTIVE T (T -) — MENTAL, a group that encompasses "people who seek stimulation mainly in the mental domain, such as criminal masterminds, schemers, and con artists."
- DESTRUCTIVE T (T -) — PHYSICAL, a group that includes "people who seek stimulation mainly in the physical domain, such as violent delinquents and criminals."

Positive and negative socialization as mediators

That thrill-seeking is mediated socially is well illustrated in an inventive study by Michael Levenson (1990), who compared and contrasted antisocial, pro-social, and adventurous risk-takers in relation to emotional arousability, conformity, moral reasoning, psychopathy, and proclivity to use or abuse of mood-altering substances. His sample of pro-social risk-takers consisted of police and fire officers who had been decorated for bravery in the line of duty; his adventurous risk-takers consisted of skilled mountain climbers; and his anti-social risk-takers were habitual drug offenders. Levenson found no differences between the three groups in moral development, empathy, or independence vs. conformity. Though we might well expect "heroes" to differ from "villains" on each of these variables, such was not the case. But significant differences were found between the groups on substance abuse proclivity, emotionality, depression, psychopathy, disinhibition, and susceptibility to boredom. Hence, Levenson concluded (1073, 1079) that the three groups

> appear to represent both different psychological types and different forms of risk taking . . . different types of risk taking have very different antecedents and consequences . . . [pro-social risk takers] literally risk their lives in the performance of their duties [but] the reasons for pro-social risk taking may be very different from those for risk or sensation-seeking. It is important to distinguish doing harm to others for personal gratification (anti-social behavior) from the antistructural violation of social norms in the service of positive social change.

The findings of other investigators tend to complement those of Farley and Levenson. In studies of risk-taking in prospective criminal behavior situations among convicted offenders, Stewart & Helmsley (1979, 1984) found that risk-taking correlated with psychoticism as measured by the Eysenck Personality Inventory and with unrealistic "expectancy of gain." Their risk-takers characteristically misconstrued costs and benefits associated with criminal behavior, perhaps as a function of "verbal deficit" or its underlying neuropathology. In their study of firefighters and incarcerated felons, Alexander, Wolfson, Scrams & Rienzi (1995) found that firefighters (prosocials) self-reported significantly fewer episodes of victimization in aggression over the lifespan than did felons (antisocials), a situation that may explain the *direction* of thrill-seeking behavior. But the personal testimony of the two "subway surfers" (who would be classified as "adventurous" risk-takers under Levenson's model or as $T+$ thrill-seekers under Farley's model) whom we met a few pages ago suggests that the categories may not be experienced phenomenologically as quite so distinct as the conceptual schematic suggests.

RISK FOR OFFENDING AND DIFFERENTIATING TRAITS

This chapter has reviewed variables within the offender that can be regarded as part of the "psychological baggage" carried from one behavioral situation to the next. If we return to our epidemiologic portrait of risk for offending in Chapter 4, what traits might we expect to find in the "psychological baggage" of those at risk for offending in aggressively violent ways that contribute to what Megargee (1982) has called the "algebra of aggression"? It seems reasonable to expect that, in contrast to members of the general population, they would:

- Evince high energy, prefer action to thought, display restlessness and an inability to tolerate frustration, and have an exaggerated sense of self-importance — as might be suggested by scores that are high on MMPI Scale Ma (Graham, 1987, 67) — and that expectation is amply supported by Megargee & Bohn (1979), Holcomb & Adams (1982), and Holcomb, Adams & Ponder (1984-b) and further buttressed by Davis' (1974) conclusions on the P scale of the EPI as a measure of emotionality.

- Seek competitive situations, evince a variety of problems in impulse control, and arouse resentment and hostility in others — as might be suggested by scores that are low on MMPI Scale Si (Graham, 1987, 70) — and that expectation is supported, at least tangentially, by Holcomb & Adams (1982).

- Be excessively suspicious of others and hypersensitive to criticism — as might be suggested by scores that are high on MMPI Scale Pa (Graham, 1987, 54- 55) — and, once again, the expectation is supported by Megargee & Bohn (1979) and Holcomb & Adams (1985).

- Tend to act without consideration of the consequences of their behavior — as might be suggested by scores that are high on MMPI scale Pd (Graham, 1987, 46- 49). That expectation is not quite supported in these studies; instead, it may be the case that the aggressive offender is indeed positively rather than negatively socialized, albeit positively socialized to a subculture of violence; or it may be the case that a clinically significant level of inventoriable psychopathy represents a uniform characteristic that is relatively invariable among offenders across specific categories of offenses. However, demographic data on the age distribution of victims of criminal aggression and statistical data on the age, sex, and race similarity of victims and offenders seem entirely congruent with Mayo Clinic data on an age-related decline in Pd scores (Colligan et al., 1989) as well as with the Eysenck & Eysenck data on age-related decline in extraversion, neuroticism, and psychoticism among both offenders and non-offenders.

Evidence from studies of personality traits among aggressive offenders as measured by actuarial instruments is thus not incongruent with expectations derived from an epidemiologic portrait of criminal aggression. Overall, however, the characteristic that differentiates aggressive offenders as a group most reliably is the MMPI mania scale, a measure of impulsivity. Current opinion in the neurosciences clearly attributes persistent impulsivity to neurogenic hyperarousability.

Some investigations have found that offenders convicted of violent crimes frequently display impairment in reality contact. Such impairment may result from a generally schizoid disposition (as might be reflected in a clinically significant score on the MMPI Sc scale) or, with equal cogency, with limitations to mediate the data of experience (e.g., a relative deficit in verbal intelligence). Contrary to expectation, however, they have been found to be only slightly more psychopathically deviant than offenders convicted of other crimes. It may be that an elevated level of psychopathic deviation represents an intrapersonal threshold for criminal behavior of any sort, that the character of that behavior is contingent upon stimulus determinants, and that impairment in the capacity to construe costs, risks, and benefits of behavior flowing from impaired reality contact interact with "portable" mania to incline toward impulsive violence of the character reflected in a majority of cases of criminal aggression.

An epidemiology of aggressive offending permits few expectations concerning the role of intelligence, and studies of aggressive offenders based on aggregate measures yields little evidence that intelligence is a rectilinearly distinguishing characteristic. Aggressive offenders are not uniformly found to be intellectually less able than the population at large, nor can reliable distinctions be made among and between those who offend aggressively in one way rather than another. There is some evidence that aggressive offenders differ among themselves as much as, or more than, as an aggregate, they differ from non-aggressive offenders.

Yet systematic differences have been consistently observed in the "verbal deficit" between "performance" and "verbal" scores on the several Wechsler instruments among adolescents and adults offenders described as "acting-out" criminally; and that difference, which reflects a relative deficit in the verbal mediation of the data of experience, may constitute a differentiating characteristic. The same pattern has also been found to represent, though less robustly, a distinguishing characteristic of subjects in whom neuropathology in the left hemisphere has been medically documented; and, independently, left hemisphere dysfunction has been associated with persistent psychopathy psychometrically and behaviorally. There is also some evidence that relatively high intelligence mediates criminal aggression as a sort of shield that protects *both* offender and victim.

People with normal overall intelligence whose "non-verbal" grasp of situations exceeds their capacity to construe those situations and to construe, largely through verbal mediation, alternate ways of behaving in response to those situations (that is, those in whom the "verbal deficit," or the resultant condition called alexithymia, is found) may have little choice but to "act out" when the situations they encounter demand (or are construed to demand) a relatively immediate behavioral response. The capacity to assess costs, risks, and benefits associated with alternate courses of behavior (the defining behavioral characteristic of psychopathy as a psychological trait) may thus represent a function of the "verbal deficit."

If the surmise that higher levels of intelligence in some way function as a shield against acts of criminal aggression is reasonably accurate, it may be the case that lower levels of intelligence are associated with individual acts. One can readily make the case that the "verbal deficit" resultant in alexithymia plays a role, say, in those cases of homicide in which the offender acts on the basis of rage — a situation that, at bottom, reduces to a bit of intellectual shorthand that means "I couldn't figure out what else to do," or that "There were no behavioral alternatives; I was bound by external stimuli."

But, though we know of no definitive empirical studies, we tend to believe that, to the contrary, higher levels of intelligence may be required for genocide, for murder on a mass scale, than for homicide (Staub, 1989; Smith, 1991). Only those with high levels of cognitive capacity are likely to be able to devise and implement plans for the construction of concentration camps and gas chambers or thermonuclear weapons or guided missiles [NOTE 4]. As the world has seen since the collapse of Tito's dictatorially-ruled people's republic on the Balkan peninsula, it apparently requires training as a physician followed by a psychiatric residency at a distinguished American university to devise and implement a strategy for the wholesale and systematic rape of girls and women as an instrument of "ethnic cleansing."

Withal, the psychometric evidence, whether derived from studies of intellectual capacity or personality traits, may point in the same general direction — toward a link between neuropsychological dysfunction and impulsive violence. Because so large a proportion of aggressive crimes each year occur under "tinder-box" circumstances, there is additional reason to believe that disordered neurology represents a substantial contributing factor. In the next chapter, we consider how such psychometric traits meld with neurologic and demographic characteristics in the tinder-box prior to, and preparatory to, a conflagration.

NOTES

1. Among other instruments which measure inflected intelligence is the Kaufman Brief Intelligence Test (or K-BIT), an instrument which has gained wide use in correctional settings (Klinge & Dorsey, 1993), in some measure because of the relative time economy in administration (approximately 30 minutes). The instrument yields two scores (Verbal or "crystallized" and Non-Verbal or "fluid"), with relatively high correlations with the Wechsler instruments at several age levels (Kaufman & Kaufman, 1993). However, there is not yet a sufficient body of evidence on whether Verbal vs. Non-Verbal differentials on this instrument carry the same implications as the Wechsler "verbal deficit" configuration. But a companion instrument developed by the same research team, called the Kaufman Short Neuropsychological Assessment Procedure (Kaufman & Kaufman, 1994) or K-SNAP yields (among several other scores) an "impairment index" for neuropathology that correctly identified 83% of the adult and 78% of the adolescent subjects in the standardization sample. With that level of accuracy in the companion instrument, the matter of whether K-BIT inflected scores convey the same meanings as inflected scores on the Wechsler instruments may be superfluous.

2. In 1989, a major revision of the MMPI was published as the MMPI-2. Though producing similar score patterns, this version utilizes contemporary language and terminology that, *inter alia*, "eliminated sexist wording and outmoded content" and has been normed on a larger and more demographically representative national sample. In what may be interpreted as a bid for "market share" in relation to the CPI, norms were developed for the adolescent years as well. As of this writing, few studies of offender groups utilizing the MMPI-2 have appeared in the literature either of clinical or of correctional psychology. Indeed, as Bartol (1991, 127) has observed, despite an avalanche of commercial promotion that has confessed the willingness of its publishers to sacrifice an enormous body of research on the MMPI, "there is little evidence that the MMPI-2 will replace the original MMPI and its extensive empirical foundation anytime soon," especially since it is not yet clear whether the massive research literature which has accumulated over half a century is applicable to the revised version (Ben-Porath, Shondrick & Stafford, 1995).

Several technologically sophisticated programs are now available to administer, score, and interpret the MMPI by computer (Butcher, Keller & Bacon, 1985). Some programs merely replace clerical work in providing scores for the various scales, but others offer interpretive summaries as well. The latter programs, as Fowler (1985) put it, attempt to "simulate the expert test interpreter." In his review of available programs, Fowler (1985) assessed his own system, developed at the University of Alabama in the early 1960s, along with others developed at the Mayo Clinic, at the University of Minnesota, and at the University of Kentucky, and those developed for more or less commercial purposes. For correctional settings, the Weathers Report program, developed by Dr. Lawrence Weathers, is eminently useful, since it yields scores on the MMPI's three validity and ten primary clinical scales, on some 132 secondary or derivative scales, and on 20 forensic scales derived from the massive typology study of Federal prisoners by Megargee & Bohn (1979) and from Megargee & Carbonell's (1985) validation studies of correctional scales developed by other researchers. Scores are normed against the Mayo Clinic restandardization data base and reported along with actuarially-derived "proposed" diagnoses from the American Psychiatric Association's nosologic lexicon. Along with other programs of its type, the Weathers Report variation proceeds along the lines of "best statistical fit" in relating presumably clinically relevant statements to configural code type profiles. As of this writing, it is usable only with the original MMPI, not with the revised MMPI-2.

3. Interesting speculations present themselves when we juxtapose the data on risk for offending in aggressive criminal violence in relation to chronological age reflected in formal arrest records (reviewed in Chapter 4) and the data on rank-order of various offenses as the trigger for arrest among youth assembled by Pallone & Workowski (1994) within the interpretive framework proposed by Moffitt. According to the latter set of figures, the greatest discrepancies between representation in the general population and participation in criminal activity leading to arrest occur in the crimes of auto theft, where members of the youth cohort aged 18 and under represent 43% of all arrestees, arson where they represent 37% of all arrestees, larceny where they represent 31% of all arrestees, and burglary where they represent 30% of all arrestees. That the youth cohort is over-represented among putative property crime offenders (as well as among aggressive offenders, though with a smaller margin of discrepancy in relation to their proportional representation in the general population) lends substantial support to Moffitt's "adolescence-limited" model — and further leads to speculation about whether, during adolescence, it may be the case that "progression" operates more potently than "specialization." Such a speculation would find considerable support in research in developmental psychology that holds that adolescence is a time of "exploration." In our arena of interest, it may be that the adolescent who is disposed to behave criminally alternates between crimes of various sorts until he/she finds a type of crime that "fits" and at which he or she can be reasonably successful. Similarly, it may be that the imposition of negative sanctions functions in such a way as to demonstrate beyond question those types of crime at which the adolescent cannot expect to succeed. Specialization may thus follow a period of "exploratory progression."

4. Consider the knowledge of thermodynamics and in particular the physics of combustion at play in the use of incendiary devices, whether dropped from aircraft or guided to their targets by sophisticated electronic devices, in the pattern known as "saturation" or "firestorm" bombing, which aims at mass homicide in a given geographic area, as distinct from "precision" bombing (Sherry, 1995). If we conceive the target to represent a rectangle, "firestorm" bombs are not concentrated but instead aimed at points representing the center and the perimeter. As described by Sayle (1995, 43) "The firestorm is not seen in nature. To achieve the effect, fires need to be started in many places, miles apart. Rising, heated air draws in more air, which soon reaches gale force and links the fires together, killing by asphyxiation, heat, and the collapsing of buildings. As the fire burns inward toward the center, escape becomes all but impossible. Called . . . self-energized dislocation — the target provides the fuel, the attacker only the lighter — the firestorm is the most one-sidely efficient way yet discovered of killing human beings." We doubt that even an aggregate of persons of subnormal intellectual capacity at the level Wilson & Herrnstein posit as the typical threshold for violent offending could master the requisite knowledge to devise such a plan for mass murder, however readily each could kill by means of hands, clubs, firearms, or Molotov cocktails.

6 A PROCESS PARADIGM FOR TINDER-BOX CRIMINAL AGGRESSION

THIS CHAPTER PRESENTS A STEPWISE, INTERACTIVE MODEL FOR A PROCESS psychology of aggressive criminal violence, along with case vignettes and a case study that illustrate the dynamics in that process. Finally, we explore the implications for traditional notions of criminal culpability and for traditional modes of correctional rehabilitation that issue from an understanding of the role of neuropathology in criminal aggression.

PROCESS: TRANSFORMATION FROM INTRAPERSONAL TRAITS TO BEHAVIORAL STATES

During a very long and very distinguished career, preeminent theoretician and empiricist Raymond B. Cattell has insisted that the overarching aim in psychological science should be the specification of conditions under which specific behaviors become comprehensible (Cattell, 1963, 1980, 1985; Cattell & Child, 1975; Smith, 1988). From his first published work nearly 60 years ago, Cattell has decried the propensity to search for "sole and single causes" of behavior, which searches typically prove fruitless anyway, since only quite primitive muscular reflexes (the familiar patellar tendon) seem to be "caused" by single antecedent conditions. Yet even in this domain, as recent analyses of the neurophysiology, neurochemistry, and neurophysics of reflex actions suggest, the apparently simple may prove to be amazingly complex.

Interaction between traits and stimulus determinants

In particular, though he has contributed massively to the precise measurement of the "traits" of personality (through the development and validation of the 16 Personality Factor Questionnaire) and of cognitive capacity (through the Culture-Fair Test of Intelligence), Cattell has asserted that the identification of traits alone cannot serve as a sufficient basis for the construction of comprehensive conceptual models of human behavior.

Instead, for Cattell, the goal in scientific psychology is to identify how and under what conditions enduring traits within individual behavers interact, meld, and congeal *both* with each other *and* with stimulus determinants in the physical and social environment to yield specific behaviors, then to specify the conditions under which specific behaviors are either reinforced, maintained, and perhaps "chained" into patterns, or extinguished.

The goal, in short, is to understand the *process* through which enduring "traits" within an individual actor are transformed into "states" of readiness to behave and/or into actual behavior. In such a conceptualization, identification of intrapersonal traits (whether psychological, biological, or demographic) constitutes only a prelude to a psychology of process, for it is necessary to identify other components as well — ranging from the traits of other actors to the characteristics and demands of social, psychological, and physical environments — that may interactively blend and congeal to produce the behavior under study. Implicit in Cattell's thought is a preference for multivariate over univariate explanations for behavior; indeed, Cattell has contributed substantively to the techniques and research methodology of multivariate analysis.

Multivariate explanations of behavior

Expressed somewhat simplistically, a univariate explanation satisfies itself that a particular behavior results from a single, specific antecedent variable (that is, from *this* and/or from this alone), while a multivariate explanation seeks the engines for the same behavior in mixtures or blends of several antecedent variables, each of which may make a differentially-weighted contribution.

Suppose, for example, that we have access to a body of research evidence bearing on the mastery of the Chinese language by people who were born and bred in the United States and who, further, monolingually spoke and read English in their family homes. Suppose that body of evidence tells us that bright people (assessed through intelligence, an intrapersonal variable) score higher on a measure of mastery of Chinese after a year of instruction, as do people who were highly motivated (another intrapersonal variable, measured through another psychometric instrument) at the point at which instruction commenced-.

But the evidence also indicates that students instructed by teachers judged to be highly competent scored higher than those instructed by the less competent, with competence assessed perhaps through the observational ratings of third-party experts; we might construe "competence" as an intrapersonal characteristic, but of the teacher rather than the learner and therefore an extrapersonal (or stimulus) determinant in relationship to the learner. Suppose, finally, that the evidence also indicates that students instructed by teachers who are themselves native speakers of Chinese (a characteristic similarly intrapersonal for the teacher and extrapersonal for the learner) score higher on those mastery examinations.

The univariate approach to such evidence might content itself with a *series* of disparate statements linking each variable independently to the criterion (e.g., bright people can master Chinese; highly motivated people can master Chinese; etc.). But the multivariate approach would seek to *meld* the evidence into an economically-constructed statement, perhaps to the effect that "bright, highly-motivated non-native speakers of Chinese are likely to master the Chinese language, provided they receive competent instruction from teachers who are native-speakers."

Threshold values and interactive blends

Cattell would undoubtedly wish to specify with mathematical precision the specific "weights" (derived from such statistical methodologies as multiple regression or multiple discriminant analysis) attached to each variable in the statement. Alternately, if we adopt the perspectives of the biomedical sciences, we might organize the data somewhat differently.

Our data set consists essentially of a series of measures of correlation or association. But even very high coefficients may mask important relationships. Suppose that we organize the data into categories that approximate nosologic groups (viz., those learners who have demonstrated mastery vs. those who have not). When we inspect, say, Verbal IQ scores in the two groups, we may find that no learner whose score is 130 or higher (equivalent to +2.0 standard deviation units above the mean, at the 97th percentile) is to be found in the "no mastery" group. Suppose that we also find, as we inspect correlations between other variables only for learners whose IQ scores fall at or above that threshold, that those measures are weak or do not differ significantly from zero. We are now justified in regarding that level of intelligence as a *threshold level* for language mastery in the absence of high motivation, competent instruction, or national origin of the instructor; in short, we may be able to support the proposition that very high verbal intelligence constitutes a *sufficient* condition for mastery without regard to the intervening or interactive effects of other variables.

But, when we inspect measures of correlation with the other variables for learners with scores below the threshold level, we may find *differential* associations. In the "mastery" group, we may find that, when intelligence is relatively lower, motivation and instructor competence are relatively higher, while in the "non-mastery" group, when intelligence is relatively higher, motivation and instructor competence are relatively lower. We may now be in a position to propose that, *below* a threshold level sufficient in and of itself to account for the effect, language mastery is a function of the *interactive blend* between intelligence, motivation, instructor competence, and whether the instructor is a native speaker or not. So also we may find that, in some episodes of criminal aggression, a particularly potent antecedent (e.g., recent, massive damage to the frontal lobes leading to abrupt, unprovoked, unfocused aggression) may emerge as a "sufficient" condition, while in most episodes we will uncover instead the congealing of several variables, both intrapersonal and extrapersonal.

We have thus far considered a wide array of variables that have been found individually and serially to be related to aggressive criminal violence. It remains to construct a cognitive model of the *interactive process* that links neuropathology, demography, patterns of socialization and social influence, and differentiating psychological traits as interactive precursors to each other and to criminal aggression in tinder-box circumstances.

THE CHOREOGRAPHY OF THE DARE

Nearly 40 years ago, Redl & Wineman (1957) developed the construct "the choreography of the dare" to describe interaction between parents and children in what today would be termed "dysfunctional families." The construct is eminently appropriate in describing the process dynamics of tinder-box situations.

What has come to be called the self-fulfilling prophecy (Wineburg, 1987) is quintessentially illustrated in tinder-box situations peopled by impulsive risk-seekers who misconstrue the costs and risks associated with character contests within self-selected social environments that aid, abet, or otherwise approbate and reinforce both impulsivity and risk-seeking.

At the risk of offending the literary scholars among our academic colleagues who follow Derrida and Habermaas, we confess the fixed belief that the poet has frequently led where the behavioral scientist has followed. Since we despair of more aptly depicting the self-fulfilling prophecy, or the mutuality of a taste for risk, or the choreography of the dare, we turn to *War Is Kind,* the 1897 collection of free verse by Stephen Crane, an American author perhaps (and unfortunately) remembered today only for his moralistic *Red Badge of Courage*:

> *Two youth, in apparel that glittered,*
> *Went to walk in a grim forest.*
> *One was an assassin, the other a victim.*
> *They chanced to meet.*
> *"I," said the assassin, "am an assassin."*
>
> *"And I," said the victim, "am a victim.*
> *"And, believe me, sir, I am enchanted*
> *"To die thus, in the best medieval fashion."*
>
> *Then took he the wound, gladly, and died, smiling.*

In his remarkable field study of social interaction in the Philadelphia ghetto, sociologist Elijah Anderson (1990, 177-178) provides an instructive description of "gritting," an interactive choreography that "could easily be compared to threatening animal behavior" played against a "quasi-military swagger to the beat of 'rap' songs in public places":

> When I walk the street, I put this expression on my face that tells the next person I'm not to be messed with. That "You messing with the wrong fellow. You just try it, try it." And I know when cats are behind me. I be just lookin' in the air, letting them know I'm checking them out. Then I'll put my hand in my pocket, even if I ain't got no gun. Nobody wants to get shot, that shit burns, man . . . Some guys go to singing. They try to let people know they crazy. Cause if you crazy, they'll leave you . . . They catch your drift quick.

The costume has changed, from Crane's non-specific "apparel that glittered," to Anderson's "uniform" of "radio, sneakers, gold chain, athletic suit"; the locale is no longer Crane's "grim forest," or perhaps that grim forest has been transformed into Anderson's inner-city ghetto; what has remained constant is the choreography of the dare.

"Young male syndrome" and the taste for risk

As we saw in Chapter 4, the demography of risk for both offending and for victimization in aggressive criminal violence centers in the male gender and in the late adolescent and early adulthood age ranges. Wolfgang & Ferracuti (1967) had early identified chronological age as a major attribute disposing attraction to a "subculture of violence." Congruently, Holinger (1979) identified "fatal violence" (through homicide, suicide, or accident) as the leading cause of death among victims from the age of 19-34 in the U.S. Marohn, Locke, Rosenthal & Curtiss (1982) observed a similar, very strong confluence between homicide, suicide, and accidental death among adolescents.

Such propensity toward (fatal) violence has been interpreted by Wilson & Daly (1985) as indicative of a "young male syndrome," in which "status competition, 'taste for risk,' dare-devilry and gambling" are principal features. Observing that the data from some 700 homicides in Detroit demonstrate that "victim and offender populations were almost identical, with unemployed, unmarried young men greatly over-represented," these investigators propose that the "taste for risk" is "primarily a masculine attribute and is *socially facilitated by the presence of peers in pursuit of the same goals.*"

Clarke (1985) and other commentators have opined that such a "taste for risk" likely declines with advancing age. Such an interpretation seems consistent with the findings of Loeber (1982), Ageton (1983), Holland & McGarvey (1984), Blumstein & Cohen (1987), and Hare, McPherson & Forth (1988) on the age-related decline in the emission of violent behavior; with those of Colligan, Osborne, Swenson & Offord (1988) on the age-related decline in mania and psychopathy to emanate from the Mayo Clinic restandardization of the MMPI; with those of Farley (1986) on thrill-seeking as a function of age; and with the data (Chapter 4) on the demography of aggressive criminal violence.

Character contests

As if to underscore the impact of the normative expectations held by one's peers, both Felson (1982) and Steadman (1982) confirmed that the *presence of third parties* in a conflict situation (sometimes of the opposite gender) tends to potentiate the probability of violence, with that finding corroborated by Henderson & Hewstone (1984) and further supported by the Russell & Pigat (1991) study on enjoyment and approval of violence reviewed in Chapter 4. Felson, Ribner & Siegel (1984) found the degree of potentiation particularly powerful among younger combatants, and Felson (1993) has identified "assertive self-presentation" as a component. In a joint analysis, Felson & Steadman (1983) indeed identified what they described as a "systematic pattern" in a study of conflicts that ended in fatality:

> They began with identity attacks, followed by attempts and failures to influence the antagonists. Threats were made, and finally the verbal conflict ended in physical attack . . . retaliation is a key principle in the escalation of these incidents in that aggressive actions by the victim were associated with aggressive actions by the offender and the likelihood that the victim would be killed.

Following Goffman's (1967) description of what he calls the process of "social definition," Luckenbill (1977) has termed the phenomenon described by Felson and Steadman and their colleagues a "character contest," in which both the prospective victim and the prospective offender accept (or acquiesce to) violence as a means of conflict resolution. In such circumstances, whether one emerges from the contest as one sort of crime statistic or another (or, for that matter, whether the contest ends in a charge of aggravated assault short of homicide, or indeed ends without formal criminal charges) may represent no more than the luck of the draw, abetted to be sure by physical agility.

Strong empirical validation for the suppositions which undergird the notion of the character contest is found in a study by Fishbain, Fletcher, Aldrich & Davis (1987) which contrasted subjects who had died while playing Russian roulette with others who had committed suicide, with the former distinguished by a history of drug and alcohol abuse; the investigators opined that they "were trying to treat their depression through risk-taking behavior." The proposition that behavior that involves deliberate risk to life is surely CNS-arousing (and therefore corrective for depressive states) is unexceptionable.

Conceptually, the character contest has much in common with Farley's (1986) empirically-derived description of the thrill-seeking personality and is quite congruent with the description that Feldman & Quenzer (1984, 248-252) provide of intermale aggression among members of infra-human species. It also quintessentially illustrates the legacy of the ethos of the frontier. Among literary observers, prison psychologist Robert Lindner's case study *Rebel Without a Cause* (which became a "cult classic" motion picture of the mid-1950s) hinges upon precisely such a character contest, to which both participants readily agree and which ends in lethal violence, albeit technically by accident. Similarly, novelist Aldous Huxley proffers in *The Genius and the Goddess* a description of a "game" once popular among young men in this country, in which two contestants drive automobiles at each other, head-on, at high speed; whomsoever first applies the brakes is declared to be "Chicken." Among young men in the mid-1990s, a new version of that game is played with four-wheel drive trucks with oversized tires spinning in mud flats. Similar scenes are memorialized cinematically in literally thousands of Hollywood films and television productions featuring "shoot-outs" between gunmen of the Old West or in Crane's "grim forests," or Anderson's ghetto streets, in depictions of "character contests" enacted precisely in accord with the ethos of the frontier [NOTE 1].

Risk-seeking victims and offenders

A behavioral situation in which each of two participants at least tacitly consents to violence, and perhaps in which both lubricate themselves for that violence by means of alcohol or drugs, surely sounds like "tinder-box" circumstances writ large and peopled by the "risk takers" described by Silver, Yudofsky & Hales (1987), whose propensities for violence inhere in brain dysfunction. Perceptions of violence as normal and normative are, as we have seen in Chapter 3, supported by mutual use or abuse of alcohol and drugs (Beck et al., 1993) and, as we have seen in Chapters 2 and 3, likely by a high incidence of neuropathology as well (Williams, 1969; Yeudall, 1979; Langevin, 1988; Demeter et al., 1988, 1989; Galski, 1990; Volavka, 1991). Support for the hypothesis that the person who emerges from the contest as victim has more or less agreed to participate in the choreography of the dare and/or has either sought or consented to remain within the confines of a violent subculture is found in the studies by Budd (1982), Abel (1986, 1987, 1988), and Welte & Abel (1989) on toxic levels of alcohol in the blood of homicide victims (Chapter 3), and that of Demeter et al. (1988, 1989) on dysfunctions in the metabolism of serotonin in the brains of victims and of Waller (1972) on blood alcohol levels in pedestrian victims in traffic fatalities (as we saw in Chapter 4).

There is some evidence that violence is perceived as normative by some victims as well as by offenders. Among some 97 variables assessed in a review of a wide array of studies on spouse abuse perpetrated by husbands, Hotaling & Sugarman (1986) found that "Only witnessing violence in the wife's family of origin was consistently associated with being victimized by violence." Exposure to such violence as a child and adolescent apparently produces either or both an expectation of and tolerance for such behavior in adulthood — and, to the extent to which the victimized spouse nonetheless elects to remain within an abusive relationship, she (or he) has acquiesced to spousal violence as "normative" and "normal." Similarly, in a study which compared Black women who committed homicide with their victims on a number of social characteristics, McClain (1982) concluded that the two groups "exhibit essentially similar behavior patterns that increase their probability of involvement in homicide," so that who became the victim and who the offender was indeed essentially a matter of the luck of the draw in a specific behavioral interaction. Similar findings were reported by Mann (1990): "Black female homicide offenders . . . kill those closest to them in homicides that are intraracial and intrafamilial."

More pointedly, in his remarkable study of the characteristics of inmates who aggress against other inmates in contrast to those who become the victims of aggression while incarcerated (i.e., the "violent vs. the victimized" in state prison populations), Wright (1991) found that the "most deviant personality types" (those with the most significant psychopathology, whose profiles matched those of Groups Charlie and How in the Megargee-Bohn Typology Study), "are clearly over-represented among the *victimized*." Accordingly, Wright concluded (3, 6) that, in "the exploitive environment found in today's prisons . . . a world in which the prospect and often the reality of violence are facts of everyday life . . . *victims may be aggressors who lose in contests of wills*."

Though the victim-to-be may self-select a social environment with a high tolerance for violence and may even acquiesce to violence as a mode of conflict resolution, he or she rarely foresees (much less agrees to) enacting the role of victim — one suspects, as a function of the habitual misconstruing of costs and benefits associated with risk-seeking behavior. In their definitive study of chronic delinquency in relation to drug abuse, Inciardi, Horowitz & Pottieger (1993, 104-105) provide a remarkable first-hand account of an interaction that escalates from voluntary participation (as an offender) in a relatively "victim-less" crime ("commercialized vice," known more familiarly as prostitution) to victimization in physical assault. The putative offender had voluntarily agreed to exchange sex for drugs, but instead she becomes a victim:

> I was in this graveyard [a room in an abandoned building used for selling and smoking crack] off 103rd, givin' this man a blow job for a taste of his crack. But he was so strung out, so wasted, so fucked up from doin' crack that he couldn't get it up . . . he got fuck-all kick-ass mad . . . Like it was my fault, the mother fucker . . . He keeps slappin' me, sayin' that I couldn't give good head.

Sexual assault in the context of the dare

However appropriate the choreography of the dare may be as a conceptualization for certain episodes of homicide and assault, surely it seems inapplicable to sexual assault. Indeed, to so apply the construct is tantamount to asserting that victims of sexual assault elect to place themselves at risk.

Yet we recall from National Crime Victimization Survey data reviewed in Chapter 4 that victims and offenders were known to each other in 70% of acknowledged cases of single-offender victimization (with relatives or ex-relatives the offenders in 4% and friends or acquaintances the offenders in 66%), with predatory sexual aggression perpetrated by strangers comprising the remaining 30%. In predatory sexual aggression, in which the victim may be chosen virtually at random, it is clear that the choreography of the dare does not approximate the dynamic between victim and offender. But in a literal sense that choreography may nonetheless operate between an offender and his (or her) peers who urge him/her into predatory aggression.

Some elements of the choreography of the dare may be discernible in the 70% of the cases that do not fall into the predatory category. A study conducted by Silverman, Kalick, Bowie & Edbril (1988) at the Rape Crisis Center at Boston's Beth Israel Hospital proves instructive. Subjects were 1000 consecutive Center admittees, categorized as victims of (heterosexual) "confidence rape" (i.e., those victims who had been assaulted by friends, relatives, or acquaintances, 75% of the time in places where they had willingly gone with their assailants) or as victims of "blitz rape" (i.e., those assaulted by strangers, 63% of the time in a surprise attack in their own homes). In only 25% of the cases of "confidence" rape was a weapon used by the assailant vs. 54% of the time in "blitz" rape; the victim's life was threatened 49% of the time in the "blitz" situation vs. 35% of the time in the "confidence" situation. Nonetheless, the extent of resistance among "blitz" victims (67%) did not differ significantly from that of "confidence" victims (76%) in a relatively less life-threatening situation. The "confidence" rape victim, then, apparently believed she had reason to trust the offender-to-be in consequence of a prior non-threatening relationship, since she had willingly accompanied her offender to the place destined to be the site of the assault; and fear or intimidation emerges as the modal mechanism through which the offender gains compliance. Though we court the indignation of some of our feminist colleagues, the misconstruing of costs, benefits, and risks associated with behavior on the part both of the victim and of the offender seems palpable [NOTE 2].

Several researchers have addressed factors associated with victim resistance in sexual assault. As a general observation, Walker & Browne (1985, 179) have commented that women "are socialized to adapt and submit" to the instructions and demands of men, so that, during childhood, they do not "develop adequate self-protection skills, especially if they come from homes" with a high tolerance for the degradation or subservience of women.

In counterpoint, Burnett, Templer & Barker (1985), in a study of personality characteristics of victims who had been resistant or compliant to the threat of rape, found that resistant victims were characterized by a generally "fearless" attitude and that the absence of a weapon and a previous acquaintance with their assailants contributed to resistance. Levine-MacCombie & Koss (1986) and Amick & Calhoun (1987) reported similar findings in studies of victims who had successfully resisted "acquaintance rape." And, in a study of resistance of victims in 41 attempted rapes and 95 completed rapes perpetrated by 72 offenders as inferred from official police accounts of these crimes, Quinsey & Upfold (1985, 40) found that:

> Victims were more likely to avoid being raped when they resisted, particularly when they screamed or yelled for help. There was no positive association between victim resistance and the probability of subsequent injury. Previous reports of resistance being related to victim injury [may mask the fact that] victims resist more strongly when they are being injured.

However that may be, there is scant comfort in the datum that, of the 136 victims studied by Quinsey & Upfold, nearly half sustained physical injuries in addition to sustaining the degradation of sexual assault, whether attempted or completed.

Differences between groups of victims who do and do not report an episode of rape or attempted rape, either to law enforcement officials or to other public agencies, have been analyzed in several studies. Williams (1984) interviewed 246 rape victims who had contacted Seattle Rape Relief, a feminist rape crisis center, of whom 59% had reported the assault to police. Based on information obtained through structured interviews, Williams found that the assault was *more likely* to have been reported if it shared the characteristics of a predatory or "blitz" attack, i.e., when the assailant was a stranger, when the attack involved illegal entry or a chance encounter in a public place, when force was used or threatened, and when the victim sustained injury.

As if to provide validation across both cultures and legal traditions, Shaalan, El-Akaboui & El-Kott (1983), in a study of victims of rape in Egypt, concluded that "reporting rape involved as much scandal for the victims as for the offenders, no matter how innocent the victims." In a study of victims who had sought treatment at crisis intervention centers or other social agencies in Chicago, Peretti & Cozzens (1983) asked subjects to retrospectively reconstruct reasons for reporting or not reporting the offense formally. Their characterization of victims who failed to report (84):

> These women found it difficult to accept the possibility that mere chance factors might have led them to be in the rape victim position. In essence, they seemed overly concerned with "something" they had either done, or something that they had failed to do, which might have been responsible for their being the victim of the rapist.

Again courting indignation, we observe that, in a majority of cases of "confidence" assault, that "something" contributed by the victim may have been the mis-construing of risks.

FROM NEUROGENIC IMPULSIVITY TO TINDER-BOX AGGRESSION: AN INTERACTIVE PROGRESSION

We have characterized some rather large proportion of episodes of aggressive criminal violence as occurring under what we have termed "tinder-box" circumstances. We have speculated that the essential components in such tinder-box circumstances are *two* actors, known to each other, *each of whom has a taste for risk,* and an *environment* that regards the taking of risks as normal or normative, so that the social milieu which envelopes both actors tolerates or reinforces risky behavior. We have also opined that some (perhaps quite large) proportion of episodes may have their remote origins in disordered neurology that inclines toward impulsivity, surely on the part of offenders and perhaps also on the part of victims.

Consideration of data that address an array of variables provides some flavor of the varied "blends" through which variables reinforce and potentiate each other. In particular, we have highlighted the interplay between family dysfunction, substance abuse, negative behavioral modeling in the family, and the reinforcing effect of long-distance vicarious modeling by means of entertainment and information media, reinforced by formal sanctions so lightly enforced that their stimulus value is lost, especially among the habitually impulsive who characteristically misconstrue costs, risks, and benefits associated with various courses of behavior. We have reviewed data from several investigations that suggest the interaction between an age-related "taste for risk," the self-selection of environments peopled by like-minded persons, the willingness to acquiesce to violence in a "character contest" to resolve interpersonal disputes, yielding a devastating portrayal of a set of "tinder-box" circumstances in which the question of which of two more-or-less willing participants emerges as the victim and which as the offender may be merely the luck of the draw.

It remains to propose the characteristic progression that links neuropathology, demography, patterns of socialization and social influence, and differentiating psychological traits as precursors to each other and to criminal aggression in the tinder-box circumstance in interactive, multivariate fashion, avoiding reliance on *this and this alone* formulations.

We have seen that an overwhelming preponderance of aggressive offenders in a number of studies demonstrate neuropathology, most frequently inclining toward neurogenic hyperarousability (Chapter 2). But the data on the incidence of serious head trauma leading to neurologic anomaly (also reviewed in Chapter 2) indicate some 7 million cases per year. Clearly, except in very rare cases (prototypically, sudden-onset brain injury resulting in unprovoked violence), neuropathology in isolations does not constitute a sufficient condition for criminal aggression. We have seen that a large proportion of offenders, both aggressive and non-aggressive, are frequently neurochemically influenced; but the data on widespread alcohol and drug use in the population at large (Chapter 3) argue that alcohol or drug use or abuse in isolation does not constitute a sufficient condition to account for criminal aggression. Similarly, social influences ranging from long-distance vicarious conditioning of the acceptability of violence to the non-deterrent effects of formal sanctions (Chapter 4) seem not to constitute a sufficient condition in isolation from other variables. We have found that the "verbal deficit" in intelligence and impulsivity and psychopathy as psychological traits differentiate aggressive offenders (Chapter 5), but there is no evidence that all persons who exhibit that deficit or those traits aggress criminally, so that these cannot be regarded as sufficient conditions in isolation from other contributing sources.

Except in the rarest of circumstances (e.g., sudden-onset neurologic trauma or acute neurotoxicity), *either-or* formulations do little to illuminate the dynamics of aggressive criminal violence. But *both-and* formulations reveal interactive blends sufficient to render aggressive violence comprehensible. On the opposite page, we sketch a cognitive map that models a (hypothetically) stepwise, interactive progression between neurogenic impulsivity and tinder-box aggression as a conceptual guide to a process psychology of that proportion of episodes of aggressive criminal violence that occur under tinder-box conditions.

Some episodes display a stepwise progression through each cell. But there are also leaps, lapses, and pauses, and interactive effects at various steps may prove particularly potent. Thus:

- A child may *both* enter the world with a congenital anomaly in brain or central nervous system dysfunction [Cell 1] *and* may be greeted with harsh child-rearing practices that exacerbate that condition [Cell 2], *or* a child may enter the world with perfectly normal CNS functioning and without brain anomaly but suffer injury *as a result* of harsh child-rearing practices [Cell 2], as did the majority of abused children studied by Ito and his associates (1993). Many such injuries to children as a result of harsh child-rearing practices are themselves acts of criminal aggression [Cell 12].

- Families who display such harsh child-rearing practices [Cell 2] are likely *also* to provide negative or aggressive role models [Cell 3], but even in the absence of congenital or induced neuropathology, such role models are likely to induce impulsivity and the need for serial stimulation [Cell 4], with additional reinforcement issuing from long-distance vicarious conditioning, primarily through entertainment media.

- Alternately, if there is neuropathology with hyperarousability [Cell 1], whatever its genesis, there is likely to ensue the impulsive need for serial stimulation [Cell 4], even in the absence of harsh child-rearing practices or negative role models [Cells 2, 3].

- Whatever its source, if the onset of impulsivity [Cell 4] as a pattern of behavior occurs early enough in life, learning problems in school [Cell 5] are likely to

FIGURE 6.1: FROM NEUROGENIC IMPULSIVITY TO TINDER-BOX AGGRESSION — A GENERAL MODEL FOR A STEPWISE, INTERACTIVE PROGRESSION

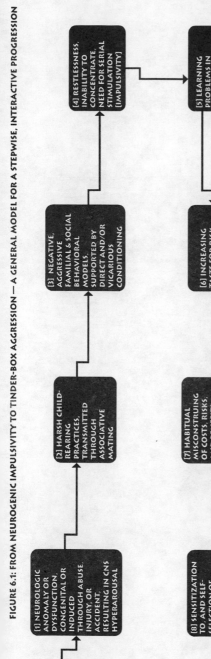
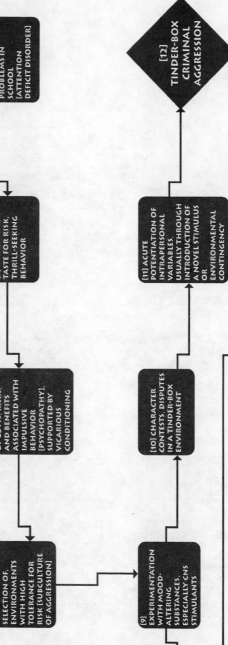

FIGURE 6.1: FROM NEUROGENIC IMPULSIVITY TO TINDER-BOX AGGRESSION — A GENERAL MODEL FOR A STEPWISE, INTERACTIVE PROGRESSION

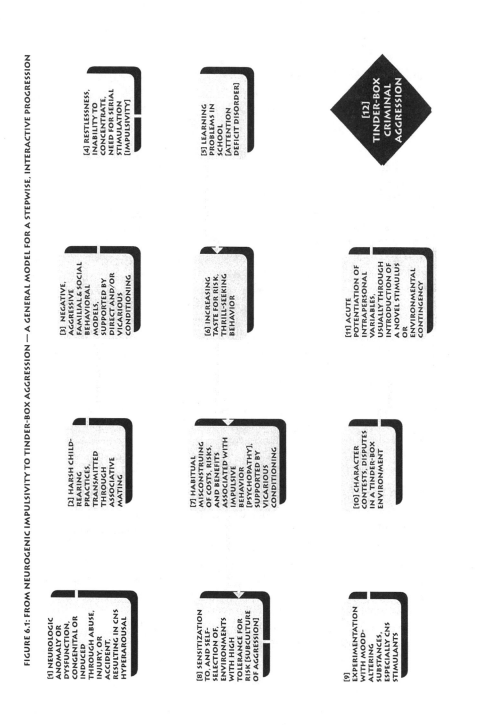

[1] NEUROLOGIC ANOMALY OR DYSFUNCTION, CONGENITAL OR INDUCED THROUGH ABUSE, INJURY, OR ACCIDENT, RESULTING IN CNS HYPERAROUSAL

[2] HARSH CHILD-REARING PRACTICES, TRANSMITTED THROUGH ASSOCIATIVE MATING

[3] NEGATIVE, AGGRESSIVE FAMILIAL & SOCIAL BEHAVIORAL MODELS, SUPPORTED BY DIRECT AND/OR VICARIOUS CONDITIONING

[4] RESTLESSNESS, INABILITY TO CONCENTRATE, NEED FOR SERIAL STIMULATION [IMPULSIVITY]

[5] LEARNING PROBLEMS IN SCHOOL [ATTENTION DEFICIT DISORDER]

[6] INCREASING TASTE FOR RISK, THRILL-SEEKING BEHAVIOR

[7] HABITUAL MISCONSTRUING OF COSTS, RISKS, AND BENEFITS ASSOCIATED WITH IMPULSIVE BEHAVIOR [PSYCHOPATHY], SUPPORTED BY VICARIOUS CONDITIONING

[8] SENSITIZATION TO, AND SELF-SELECTION OF, ENVIRONMENTS WITH HIGH TOLERANCE FOR RISK [SUBCULTURE OF AGGRESSION]

[9] EXPERIMENTATION WITH MOOD-ALTERING SUBSTANCES, ESPECIALLY CNS STIMULANTS

[10] CHARACTER CONTESTS, DISPUTES IN A TINDER-BOX ENVIRONMENT

[11] ACUTE POTENTIATION OF INTRAPERSONAL VARIABLES, USUALLY THROUGH INTRODUCTION OF A NOVEL STIMULUS OR ENVIRONMENTAL CONTINGENCY

[12] TINDER-BOX CRIMINAL AGGRESSION

follow, especially if there is also present a relative "verbal deficit" pattern in the organization of cognitive abilities, and, as McCance-Katz, Leal & Schottenfeld (1995) have demonstrated, such learning problems in interaction with such impulsivity are likely to incline the person toward sensation-seeking and risk-seeking behaviors [Cell 6].

- When a person becomes habituated to risk-seeking [Cell 6] and to serial stimulation [Cell 4], he or she is likely to develop the habit of misconstruing the costs, benefits, and risks [Cell 7] associated with impulsive behavior; and he or she will have little choice but to seek out and self-select those subcultural environments that tolerate thrill-seeking [Cell 8]. Experimentation with mood-altering substances has become a standard accoutrement of such environments [Cell 9].

- But a sudden-onset neurological injury even after childhood or adolescence [Cell 1] may issue a biological imperative to search out mood-altering substances [Cell 9] even when the pattern of development had been quite positively socialized pre-morbidly; and the perfectly neurologically-normal may be led to such substances through role models and vicarious influences [Cell 9]. Moreover, virulent substance abuse [Cell 9] may itself result in neurologic damage [Cell 1], which may then perpetuate into impulsivity [Cell 4] and psychopathy [Cell 7]

- Without question, character contests [Cell 10] arise readily in contexts that tolerate risk-seeking behavior [Cell 8], and prospective acute potentiators [Cell 11] lie everywhere. But tinder-box criminal violence [Cell 12] itself may engender neuropathology [Cell 1], or additional neuropathology. When that occurs, the cycle renews itself. Hence, neuropathology may represent *both* the starting point *and* the terminus in the interactive progression toward aggressive criminal violence.

Neurogenesis vs. social learning: An analogy

In a review of the research evidence that links alcoholism with "biological markers and precursors," the prestigious Group for the Advancement of Psychiatry (1991) observed that it has now been clearly established that, in some people, alcoholism is virtually an inherited disease and that "efforts to map the gene or genes that convey a vulnerability to alcoholism are underway." Moreover, what may be congenital, if not hereditary, dysfunctions in the neurohormonal system have also been firmly linked to alcoholism.

Suppose, for the sake of analogy, that Person X has indeed inherited the gene (or the set of genes) that yields such vulnerability to alcoholism and that he or she also suffers those neurohormonal dysfunctions that predispose to alcoholism — but that he or she has been raised in a traditionally strict Moslem culture, in which neither role models for the ingestion of beverage alcohol nor purchasable beverage alcohol are available. Would we expect that person to become addicted to alcohol? Or is it not more reasonable to suppose that the biological precursors are, at best, *necessary but not sufficient* conditions for the development of alcoholism? If that is so, Person X may remain forever *prone* to alcoholism — but, in the absence of socially conditioned role models and the availability of the substance itself, forever free of that addiction.

Analogically, that situation may not be very different from the linkage between neuropathology and tinder-box aggression. Neuropathology (or, at least, neurologic anomaly) that results in persistent hyperarousability is very likely a contributory factor in a very large proportion of cases of tinder-box criminal aggression (and, indeed, were transitory states of organic dementia consequent upon the ingestion of mood-altering drugs to be added to the grouping, perhaps in a major proportion of all such cases). But it is not our contention that neuropathology alone is prototypically a "sufficient" antecedent condition to criminal aggression of the tinder-box variety. There are exceptions in the rarest circumstances, in which acute, well-documented neurologic trauma precipitates sudden-onset aggressive behavior (Phineas Gage and Charles Whitman, whom we met in Chapter 2; Larry, whom we shall introduce later in this chapter), and thus may constitute a sole and sufficient condition even in the absence of negative neurochemical or social influences or psychological traits. Instead, neuropathology represents the substratum that is *potentiated* by interactive blends.

Nor do we hold that every citizen who not only views but applauds Clint Eastwood's celebrated "Go ahead, kid; make my day" statement is, by virtue of the force of social imitation and vicarious conditioning alone, destined to arm himself or herself with an appropriately menacing Colt Magnum to walk the San Francisco waterfront (or its analogue elsewhere) in search of societal predators worthy of execution by a tough-minded rogue cop who has appointed himself sole arbiter of the good, the true, the beautiful, *or* the just. Instead, the issue may turn on the *interaction* between significant neuropathology (perhaps indeed experienced as restlessness, but construed as fearlessness in the face of societal predators) and an attractively violent role model, presented via a popular entertainment medium, on the one hand, and the availability of a weapon, on the other. That interactive mix may indeed yield a *sufficient* condition for violence, undertaken for what the actor construes as society's betterment when the role model is positive and pro-social and when the actor construes himself or herself among the "good guys," but undertaken for quite contrary purposes when the actor construes himself or herself and his or her role model in diametric ways.

Neurogenesis, socialization, channelization

The present state of the evidence in the neurosciences inclines us strongly to the belief that a taste for risk may have its origins in brain function anomalies of one or another sort, whether structural or neurochemical, that result in a condition of persistent hyperarousability. For us, the case is attractively persuasive, but not yet compelling. The evidence is not so clear that it can as yet be posited axiomatically that such anomalies lead invariably to violent or aggressive behavior — for, while it may be the case that some very large proportion of the cases of tinder-box violence have their origin in brain dysfunction, it may *not* simultaneously be the case that nearly all instances of brain dysfunction lead to such violence.

What intervenes, of course, is the complex process of socialization; and that process incorporates such elements as the influence of role models within and outside the family, the intergenerational transmission of patterns of behaving, long distance vicarious influences, social imitation, *in vivo* exposure to environments that elicit and/or constrain behaviors of various sorts.

In the course of development, some people are socialized into quite peaceable and pro-social environments, so that whatever proclivities one may feel toward the emission of anti-social, aggressive, or violent behavior is quickly either suppressed or channelized into pathways the sociocultural envelope deems positive (Zaleski, 1984). Others are socialized into anti-social, or at least a-social environments, in which anti-social, aggressive, and violent behavior is readily modeled and easily learned by social imitation.

To judge by the enormous popularity of motion pictures in which even "good guy" heroes behave in incredibly violent ways in order to achieve purposes that are presented and widely perceived as essentially *not* anti-social, one can only conclude that the central thrust of the society at large is toward the image of the frontiersman who defines the law for himself. That image, as American cultural historians have said for a century (as we saw in Chapter 4), conveys the portrait of the invincible hero who constitutes himself the sole arbiter of the good, the true, and the just, who sets himself beyond the formal requirements of the law — and who may well, as Farley (1986) intimates, thrive on thrill-seeking for its own sake. Shorn of its romanticism, of course, that portrait reveals a set of beliefs and behaviors deeply corrosive to societal order through the rule of law.

Some interpreters will assert that diametric sociocultural milieux are sufficient in and of themselves to account for diametric differences in behavior. We assert, not quite to the contrary, that the *interaction* between a sociocultural environment of the anti-social or a-social sort and a neurogenic proclivity toward impulsivity yields a geometric progression in which one potentiates the other. Moreover, we assert that a sufficiently compelling neurogenic proclivity will propel one to *self-select* an environment that he or she construes as encouraging the discharge of impulse into behavior. Nonetheless, it is patently not the case that all, or perhaps not even the majority, of those persons who suffer neurologic dysfunction will eventually behave in violently criminal ways; and, quite clearly, *socialization* and *channelization* are key constructs in understanding why they do not.

The experience of restlessness

But, proceeding from what we have clearly labeled as a belief, there appears to us a characteristic developmental sequence flowing from neurologic dysfunction that yields in its path psychological and social consequences of substantial import.

It is reasonable to believe that the person who suffers brain function anomaly resulting in hyperarousability — especially at a sub-clinical level of severity that is *not* the subject of medical attention — experiences that anomaly merely as "restlessness," as an inability to concentrate on a particular or single topic for an appreciable length of time. As a result, he or she is propelled constantly to seek *serial* sources of stimulation and excitement.

Inevitably, the constant search for serial stimulation in order to relieve restlessness in the here-and-now rivets the person to the present, precluding consideration of the future. But he or she construes such restlessness not as something alien to how he or she construes the self, but rather as part and parcel of the self — as what our psychodynamicist colleagues would term *ego-syntonic*, rather than *ego-alien*, characteristics of the self. Indeed, the prototypical person here described may be volubly proud that he/she "can't sit still — have to be up and doing," etc., etc., with little or no awareness of how distant such a pattern of behavior is from that of most members of the relevant age cohort.

In its turn, an inability to concentrate impedes the capacity to construe long-term goals and objectives and the capacity to construe the means to achieve those goals and objectives. These very capacities are generally conceded to form the foundation for that *planfulness* that characterizes self-sufficient, responsible adults who are able to postpone gratification of momentary impulses in favor of achieving long-term goals.

Observers will say that the subject of our exemplary sequence has a short attention span. Because of that limited capacity to concentrate coupled with the propulsion toward constant craving for sources of stimulation, he or she is likely to experience learning problems at school, often formally diagnosed as "attention deficit disorder" or "attention deficit disorder with hyperactivity." Differential psychologists might want to group the composite of anomalous brain function and its sequelae under the trait-label "impulsivity," believing that, once such a trait has been named, it acquires some metaphysical reality apart from the *aggregate behaviors* for which it is a label. In its turn, that behavior which results from impulsivity rather than from planfulness is typically described as "violent," whether criminally aggressive or not.

The continual search for stimulation

Phenomenologically, the person we have described will experience "boredom" with great regularity, and, to combat boredom, will constantly and serially seek new sources of stimulation, either or both in the form of novel activities or new people with whom to engage in those activities. Indeed, three decades ago Quay (1965) saw in the need for constant stimulation the seeds of psychopathy.

By early adolescence in today's world with its surfeit of drugs and alcohol, those efforts will almost surely lead to experimentation with mood-altering substances, particularly the central nervous system stimulants. In using such substances, he or she may actually be choosing a form of self-medication for an undiagnosed neurological disorder. But, as we have seen, people who use mood-altering substances, whether central nervous system stimulants or depressants, are at risk for both closed and open head injury, the result of which will almost certainly be an exacerbation of an underlying neurological disorder. Attempts to change the behavior of the person thus described, especially through aversive means, typically fail to produce positive results. Instead, it seems to be the case that such aversive treatment may in itself be greeted as a novel form of stimulation.

Substantial empirical evidence links such early learning problems as "attention deficit disorder" to the later emission of criminal behavior; early learning problems are held, in turn, to be precursors to the development of psychopathic deviation in adolescence (Lilienfeld & Waldman, 1990; Tremblay, Pihl, Vitaro & Dobkin, 1994); impulsivity and psychopathic deviation are highly correlated, as are impulsivity, psychopathic deviation, habituation to mood-altering substances, and certain forms of neurological anomaly, especially in the morphology and biochemistry of the left hemisphere and the frontal lobes; those who score high on measures of psychopathy customarily have few friendships (and these are often quite shallow) and are typically described as "unable to profit from experience," so that even the aversive threat or experience of penal incarceration appears to affect their behavior minimally.

Perhaps because those of us who are not impulsive and/or do not experience a strong taste for risk tend to shun the company of those who are and who do, the latter soon enough encounter others like themselves, even if they have not been socialized in environments that reflect a culture of violence and/or a taste for risk.

That conjugation is certain to produce a social environment in which impulsive behavior is construed as normal or perhaps even as desirable — an environment in which the satiation of one's taste for risk through impulsive and violent behavior is a normative expectation, especially when biochemical lubricants are added and weapons are available. Just that sort of environment enveloped those who were more readily initiated into "crack"-cocaine use/abuse in the New York city neighborhoods studied by Fagan & Ko-Lin (1991). Such environments, with their high tolerance for risky behavior, present unprecedented *opportunity* to behave *without* deterrence and with the full expectation of *impunity;* they systematically reinforce the mis-construing of costs, risks, and benefits associated with deviant courses of behavior [NOTE 3].

The like-minded "playmate" who becomes a victim

Interpersonal disputes or character contests are inevitable in any social environment, and perhaps more so in the environments peopled by the neurogenic risk-seekers we have just described. Such disputes or character contests may, in fact, be kept alive by mutual agreement between the protagonists rather than reconciled, *precisely because* they provide the rationale for a fine bout of "mixing it up" with one's "playmates" — that is to say, they may be kept at a "simmering" point by relatively conscious and deliberate decision on the part of *both* disputants. Indeed, adolescent and late-adolescent street gangs rather clearly consist of like-minded playmate, often in search of their counterparts.

But those deliberately-simmering disputes and character contests add another element to the tinder-box, one in which it requires only what observers may construe as merely a "chance spark" to ignite into criminal aggression.

Since an analogy to sheer internal combustion implies only one actor rather than two or several, it seems inapplicable here. Yet only a subset of those disputes or character contests between contending actors are in fact ignited into aggressive violence — or even into such aggravated assault as comes to the attention of law enforcement authorities. Why? Given a behavioral situation in which the elements for conflagration have been aggregated into a tinder-box, what accounts for an episode of criminal aggression at *this* moment, but not at some prior moment?

The intellectual shorthand, of course, is *acute potentiation*, typically of one or more intrapersonal variables, typically by the introduction of a new and powerful stimulus determinant or environmental contingency *or* because the salience of one or more determinants or contingencies has rapidly escalated, perhaps because new observers have been added to the audience to a long-enacted "dance of the dare" — with such potentiation sufficient to interactively transform those intrapersonal variables Cattell would call "traits" into a "state" of readiness-to-act. Such an interpretation is consistent with the research of Russell & Pigat (1991) we reviewed in Chapter 4 on the effect of endorsement of violence by "others" in a passive behavioral situation on the subject's attitudes toward violent behavior and that reported by Mehrabian (1995), also reviewed in Chapter 4, that suggests that the acceptability of violent behavior covaries with social dependency needs. Though that process is in fact quite orderly, at least at the point of post-dictive reconstruing, phenomenologically it is frequently not experienced as the product of conscious deliberation or what most of us would regard as "decision."

Indeed — and here we must stress the speculative nature of our conjecture — it seems likely that the denizens of such risky environments regard each other not as "enemies," but in fact (and consistent with what the psychodynamicists would term "fixation" at a pre-adult level of psychosocial development) rather as "playmates."

Now, one surely wants to "mix it up" with one's playmates, often in very stimulating rough-and-tumble ways; that much is a "rational choice," or at least as rational a choice as the neurogenically impulsive is able to make. But one does not want to harm one's playmates in any significant, much less life-threatening, way. Indeed, if our conjectures to this point are not woefully off the mark, to resolve a long-standing dispute or character contest would be, for the risk-seeker, quite counter-productive — for a long-standing dispute, with recurrent violent exchanges between the disputants, is in itself precisely the source of stimulation risk-seekers pursue when they self-select what we have termed "risky environments." A conceptual model that invokes acute potentiation of one or another intrapersonal variable or a rapid increase in the salience of one or another stimulus determinant and/or environmental contingency is consistent with Farley's research on thrill-seeking behavior, Lindner's theme in the case study *Rebel without a Cause,* and Huxley's account of the game of "Chicken."

Hence, in the final irony, the person who, driven by disordered neurology and spurred by impulsivity and the self-selection of risky environments, has committed an act of aggressive tinder-box criminal violence will characteristically denominate his or her behavior as unintentional, as an "accident." Phenomenologically, he or she may be offering quite an accurate interpretation of how he or she has construed the situation. And, as we have seen, in such tinder-box circumstances who emerges as victim and who as offender may turn on the luck of the draw.

The phenomenology of risk

Central to our explanation of tinder-box criminal aggression is the notion that those prone to the taking of risks *self-select* those environments in which risky behavior is not unusual, but quite normative — those environments in which, in Wright's (1991) description, "the prospect and often the reality of violence are facts of everyday life." Now, how in the world does such a choice, patently irrational to you and to us, come to be construed as normative or desirable?

We have earlier argued that, at bottom, the pivot that guides the behavior of those persons who are labeled, on the basis of psychometric tests, as psychopathically deviate is essentially the *mis-construing* of the costs, benefits, and risks associated with behavior — invariably in the direction of *under*-estimating costs and risks and of *over*-estimating benefits. What requires further elaboration is the matter of how risks are construed and particularly how risks are *experienced*.

We do not know you, but we would wager a guess that you and we would not behave terribly differently from each other in some situations. At 3:00 a.m. and fully sober, we daresay both of us would be willing to risk breaking the law by running a red light in a non-residential area. The process of construing that stimulus situation would for each of us doubtless include consideration of the sanction attached to the behavior — i.e., breaking a law that speaks to a behavior that is *mala prohibita* rather than *mala in se,* with a sanction that is typically limited to a fine, but with no prospect (given the hour and some small vigilance on our part) of instant deterrence and but little probability of detection thereafter.

Neither of us is likely to construe our *physical* safety as in jeopardy. To the extent that we construe the prospect of arrest and prosecution as unlikely *and* construe our physical safety as not likely to be compromised, we are behaving rather like the "reasonable adventurer" described by Harvey (1962) or the "eternally optimistic gambler" described by Atlas & Peterson (1990) or Michael Maccobby's (1977, 1988) "corporate gamesman," who in essence is willing to place bets only when losing seems to have a markedly low probability and winning seems to have, on objective and publicly verifiable criteria, a substantially better than even probability.

Our belief is that the habitual risk-takers we have described, especially when their risk-taking habits have a neurogenic etiology, are quite *unreasonable* adventurers. Many persistent malefactors we have known over the course of the years, within and outside correctional institutions, have spoken of the exhilaration they have experienced, particularly when they have eluded detection under "close call" conditions. A large proportion of them have referred to that exhilaration as "the Frizzle," that special feeling that arises when one knows he or she has "gotten over" on another — and preferably, on someone in a position of formal authority. Certainly, few who have so described that exhilaration have troubled to trace the term etymologically, so that they are unlikely to know that in an earlier time (as an English corruption of the French *frisson*) it denoted "that which has been fried." Though the specific referent is substance abuse, the description given by medical pharmacologist Renata Bluhm of Vanderbilt (Roueche, 1991, 73) is quite apt:

> Adrenaline is turned on by more than the drug itself. [Users] know there is a risk — anything might happen — and *that risk is part of the experience.* There is an excitement in a jump into the unknown.

Were you or we to wander into the sort of environment we have denominated as part of the tinder-box circumstance — say, a dingy bar whose denizens appear at least alcohol-inebriated if not drug-intoxicated as well, with many of them brandishing weapons, and with loud arguments on the periphery — we daresay that each of us would experience a threat to our physical safety. That experience will doubtless involve the classic physiological indicators of apprehension, stress, anxiety — clammy palms, lowering of peripheral body temperature (a combination that many, quite accurately, describe as "breaking out into a cold sweat"), increased heart rate, the elements indeed of "The Frizzle" as we have described it, with help from Renata Bluhm. For most, that experience is quite unpleasant; your behavioral response and ours is likely to be *flight,* as we seek to distance ourselves from those fear-provoking stimuli and circumstances. On the other hand, and usually only long after we have fled from those noxious stimuli and achieved sufficient physical safety to permit rumination, if we are genuinely honest with ourselves we may admit that, for a moment back there, The Frizzle felt "kind of good" — but only for a moment, mind you.

Our contention is that, for the *unreasonable* adventurer, the habitual risk-seeker, the phenomenology of The Frizzle is assuredly *not* experienced as (at best) momentarily positive but quickly to be terminated, but rather as pleasurable in and of itself — and therefore to be prolonged. Perhaps anticipating the work of Farley on thrill-seeking behavior, novelist Aldous Huxley aptly described such phenomenology in his 1955 *The Genius and the Goddess:* "You want some special kind of thrill, and you deliberately work away at yourself until you get it — a green or bruise-colored lump of fear; for fear, of course, is a thrill like any other, *fear is a hideous kind of fun.*"

Moreover, for the unreasonable adventurer for whom risk-taking issues from a neurogenic etiology, it may be that the *threshold* for the phenomenology of The Frizzle (in a very real sense, and as a result of neurological anomaly that results in persistent hyperarousability) is substantially higher than for you and us; the findings of Farley & Sewell (1976) on thrill-seeking and sensation-seeking among juvenile delinquents certainly seem to argue in that direction. If that conjecture is anywhere near the mark, then we might expect *both* that the habitual risk-seeker not only does not perceive danger to physical safety in situations that would provoke apprehension followed by flight in you and us *but also* that, once he or she has penetrated the risky environment sufficiently to step over his or her own ipsative threshold for apprehensive anxiety, he or she construes the adrenaline-pumping experience of stress as pleasurable — and thus behaves in ways so as to continue or increase the sense of risk.

Unreasonable adventurers seeking "The Frizzle"

Just as one might become habituated to the normal dosages in prescription medication and thus require ever escalating dosages in order to achieve a medically therapeutic effect, so it may also be the case that the threshold for the apprehension of risk escalates for habitual risk-seekers, who will in turn require ever greater and more palpable threat to physical safety before the pleasurable experience of The Frizzle is engaged. For the alexithymic who lacks the verbal capacity to construe the costs associated with risky behavior and the sanctions which may follow such behavior, the rate of escalation may be exponential.

An attractive alternative hypothesis might argue that, among at least some unreasonable adventurers whose habitual risk-taking behavior has a neurogenic etiology, the experience of stress, tension, anxiety, or fear is *neurochemically inhibited* in very direct ways as a consequence of neurologic anomaly or dysfunction; another might argue that those responses are inhibited in consequence of *social imitation* of fearless "macho" figures, who may of course themselves be subject to neurologic anomalies.

To the extent that he or she is successful in avoiding painful physical or social consequences even as the threshold escalates, at some extreme point a third-party observer might be tempted to characterize the *successful* unreasonable adventurer as feeling immune to the negative consequences of risky behavior; and, in common with such usage in the behavioral sciences, to attribute such a feeling of immunity to *grandiosity*, understood as an internal quality or characteristic of personality. An alternate interpretation might focus on alexithymia as a barrier to perceiving or understanding prospective sanctions; for the person whose capacity to mediate verbally is impaired and whose cognitions are therefore relatively more bound by stimuli in the here-and-now, the distant threat of an intrusive sanction in the remote and vaguely defined future may hold very little stimulus value.

For us, such a feeling of immunity (or indeed of grandiosity, if one prefers) *results from* behavior that has been positively reinforced; and, even though in a kind of intellectual shorthand, we might describe that immunity or grandiosity as a driving force for ever greater escalation in future risky behavior. But to assert that the "trait" pre-exists behavior in any meaningful way (as a "potentiality" to behave that pre-exists behavior but can only be inferred as a potentiality after one has observed the behavior) is simply to mis-construe the interactive calculus that is the very focus of what Cattell calls *process* psychology.

Thus far, we have described the phenomenology of risk-seeking as largely *visceral and emotional* for unreasonable adventurers, but as essentially *cognitive* for you and us. If that conjecture is not woefully inadequate, we may have reached a nexus that connects the person who *habitually or persistently* commits crimes of aggression with little regard for the consequences of that behavior and the person who repeatedly commits crimes against property but has *successfully eluded sanction*. In the first case, sanctions will have little deterrent value, since what might be called motivation is largely visceral and emotional rather than verbally mediated; in the second case, sanctions may have major deterrent value, if motivation is largely cognitive, not visceral and emotional.

And, to understand that both the former and the latter might appropriately be denominated by the differentialist (or even the psychodynamicist) as exhibiting a personality characteristic called "grandiosity," while *simultaneously* understanding that the former and the latter have arrived at what appears to be the same point by means of very different pathways, involving very different sequences of positively and negatively reinforced behavior, is to have understood the cognitive operations that quintessentially characterize process psychology.

Tinder-box elements in multiple-offender and multiple-victim aggression

We propose the tinder-box model as explanatory in a specific set of situations involving primarily single offenders and single victims who are known to each other and who mutually share a sociocultural environment with a high taste for risk. Those situations constitute only a subset of the universe of aggressive criminal violence. But certain components in the model are likely operative in multiple-offender and in multiple-victim episodes as well.

A number of investigators, including Campbell (1991) and Ko-Lin, Kelly & Fagan (1993), have amply demonstrated that gang-perpetrated crime, including crimes of violence, pivots on a mutual taste for risk and the self-selection of risky environments, an observation further supported by the Russell & Pigat (1991) study on mutual enjoyment of violence, especially among subjects with strong "social dependency" needs. Though evidence bearing on the neurologic status of gang members even when incarcerated is not readily available, there is indication of learning problems in school and of dysfunctional family backgrounds; negative, aggressive role models and repetitive and persistent character contests constitute the very focus for social interaction among gang members and between members of one gang and another.

Empirical evidence on multiple-victim/single-offender episodes of violence is more elusive, although impressionistic and journalistic accounts (ranging from Truman Capote's *In Cold Blood* to Joseph McGinniss' *Fatal Vision* and sometimes including putatively autobiographical books by offenders on death row "dictated" to journalists) abound. In rare circumstances (i.e., that of Whitman, the Texas Tower sniper we met in Chapter 2, whose brain tumor was excised after he was killed by police), clinical data point unerringly to a neurogenic substratum for homicidal violence. In such cases as that of the "mad Chinese physicist" who killed four faculty, students, and administrators (including the distinguished psychologist Anne Cleary) and injured two others at the University of Iowa (Myers, 1991) because he had not been awarded a post-doctoral fellowship, the acutely potentiating effect of the character contest is unmistakable.

Similarly, in the case of Mark Spotz (Sampson, 1995), what started as a character contest between brothers, both intellectually limited and likely neurologically impaired, ended in the deaths not only of a "playmate" but of three motorists who happened to traveling the same highways as the offender fled. The string of killings started when Spotz argued with his brother over a gerbil recently acquired by the son of the brother's girl friend; the argument escalated into violence when the brother slashed Spotz, who retaliated with fatal gunfire. Spotz, 23, and his 17-year-old girl friend sped from the scene in western Pennsylvania; when their automobile ran out of fuel in West Virginia, they simply commandeered that of a passing motorist; when he resisted, he was killed; and the scenario repeated itself twice over.

The distinction we made in Chapter 1 between aggressive and instrumental violence blurs in this case: What had started as a tinder-box dispute between "playmates" in a mutually-familiar environment in one state, acutely potentiated by novel stimuli, had vastly overflowed into instrumental violence in another state, resulting in serial murders of victims with no connection whatever to the tinder-box of brother-to-brother interaction.

CASE VIGNETTES AND A CASE STUDY

Thus far, we have been concerned with the elements that comprise the tinder-box; we have not essayed to convey the flavor of how these elements blend with, reinforce, and potentiate each other in the behavioral repertoire of an individual actor, so that he or she comes to construe violence as desirable, acceptable, tolerable, or "normal," or perhaps normal in response to certain stimuli in certain psychosocial environments which themselves seem either to evoke, expect, or tolerate violent behavior.

While clinical case study is not a very satisfactory research methodology in the quest for new knowledge, it remains unsurpassed as a means to illustrate how the engines of behavior actually operate in real-world terms and among real-world people. Hence, the classic way to illustrate the manner in which the elements in the tinder-box intersect (or perhaps even, collide) with each other so as to eventuate in criminal aggression is by means of detailed examination of individual cases, the parameters of which have been reasonably well documented. In this section, we present brief case vignettes and a comprehensive case study, drawn from our work and that of our colleagues with aggressive offenders; although each is factual in all significant particulars, consistent with Federal guidelines and current ethical canons, we here render these as fictionalized accounts.

Larry

Acute neurologic trauma as "sufficient" condition

We first met Larry in his attorney's office, under what proved to be rather inauspicious circumstances. We had been asked by the attorney to meet with

Larry in connection with charges of atrocious assault and malicious destruction of property, to which, in consequence of a history of acute neurologic trauma resulting from industrial accident, the attorney intended to prepare a psychological defense.

The office was located on the second floor of a small professional building (which had indeed been built by the construction company of which Larry was part-owner with his father). We had arrived somewhat before the hour and were mindlessly thumbing magazines long out of date when a tall, very large, middle-aged man (whom we later learned to be Larry) and a shorter, older man (his father) entered the waiting room and greeted the secretary relatively amiably. She told the newcomers that "He'll be off the phone in a couple of minutes; why don't you take a seat?" Later, Larry insisted that he asked: "Where to?" To the best of our recollection, she responded "Oh, the window I guess," with a gesture. Whereupon, Larry picked up a chair and threw it through the second-story window, shattering glass; fortunately, when it landed it damaged only his own vehicle. In the consultation that followed, Larry told his attorney and us that the secretary had clearly told him to throw the chair through the window.

Such confabulation in response to mental discoordination is quite consistent with the acute neurologic damage Larry had sustained in an accident on a construction site some three years earlier. Serving as the site construction supervisor, Larry (wearing the customary hard hat) had been directing the operations of a crane (operated by a subcontractor) raising a sheet of plate glass for installation when the crane malfunctioned, setting the glass free; it shattered, and a fragment pierced Larry's helmet, fracturing his skull, and shearing though brain tissue.

Investigation (by the liability insurance carrier) determined that the incident occurred as a result of equipment flaw rather than operator error; since the subcontractor had rented the equipment from a service that carried huge liability insurance against just such incidents, he had been accorded substantial medical and neuropsychiatric treatment before we met him, including nearly two years in a leading neuropsychiatric hospital specializing in brain trauma rehabilitation. During the course of that treatment, hospital staff had thoroughly assembled records concerning Larry's educational and psychosocial history prior to the accident.

Larry had been an average student and an interscholastic athlete (baseball) in high school. Records from that era indicated a mild "verbal deficit" pattern, with a WISC VIQ of 99 and PIQ of 109 in 9th grade. Probably in view of that pattern, and given his father's occupation and Larry's intention to join the firm, the school counselor had advised Larry to attend a community college in pursuit of a degree in engineering technology. He followed this course while working part-time for his father and earned the degree in four years rather than the customary two.

When tested on the WAIS-R at the point of admission to the rehabilitation hospital (as part of a comprehensive neuropsychological assessment), VIQ was reported at 72 and PIQ at 87; again, the "verbal deficit" was in evidence but paled before the amount of deterioration indicated. Several attempts were made to administer the MMPI, both at admission and subsequently, but abandoned because of Larry's extraordinarily limited span of attention; in any case, post-accident scores would have proved less informative than pre-accident results.

Except for a short-lived marriage (some 30 months) to a woman who had left him for another (in Larry's father's account, because she felt neglected by Larry in favor of his work obligations), there was nothing "remarkable or contributory" (in the parlance of hospital records) in the social history. Larry's mother had died a few months before his wife left him, so he moved into his parents' home and was residing there at the time of the accident.

According to the World Health Organization's *International Classification of Diseases, 10: Classification of Mental and Behavioural Disorders* (1992, 66-67)

Organic personality disorder . . . is characterized by significant alteration of the habitual patterns of premorbid behavior. The expression of emotions, needs, and impulses is particularly affected. Cognitive functions may be defective mainly or even exclusively in the area of planning and anticipating likely personal and social consequences . . .

Among the diagnostic criteria for the disorder, ICD-10 enumerates:

In addition to an established history or other evidence of brain disease, damage, or dysfunction . . . cognitive disturbances, in the form of suspiciousness or paranoid ideation . . . Marked alteration in the rate and flow of language production, with features such as circumstantiality, over-inclusiveness, viscosity, and hypergraphia . . . altered emotional behavior, characterized by emotional lability, shallow and unwarranted cheerfulness . . . and easy change to irritability or shot-lived outbursts of anger and aggression . . . Expression of needs and impulses without consideration of consequences or social convention (the patient may engage in dissocial acts, such as stealing, inappropriate sexual advances, or voracious eating, or may exhibit disregard for personal hygiene).

Each of these behaviors was documented in abundance in the hospital records, including many physical assaults against hospital personnel (most frequently, ward orderlies or food service workers, when Larry decided not to like the meal on offer). The hospital record also contained detailed accounts of many efforts to control impulsive and assaultive behavior through medications; these efforts had uniformly failed, principally because the injury had damaged or destroyed the very receptor sites in the brain at which these neurochemicals interact or had altered the normally-occurring production of the neurotransmitters with which they interact.

Indeed, certain pharmacological preparations were observed to produce strongly paradoxical effects (e.g., even administered intravenously, the "major tranquilizers" proved excitatory). Larry had been discharged, in essence, because the professional staff at the hospital felt there was little more than could be done reconstructively. And that judgment in no way diminishes the remarkable extent to which Larry had recovered from neurologic trauma that, as recently as the mid-1960s, might have left him a hopeless invalid.

The sorry tales detailed in hospital notes were amplified by Larry's father. In the period of time since Larry had been discharged from hospital (slightly less than a year), he had *inter alia* assaulted physically a clerk at a convenience store who he accused of short-changing him (erroneously, and as a result of cognitive deficit), struck a neighbor with a snow shovel (because he believed the neighbor had piled snow on his father's property), and "propositioned" both a 16-year-old girl and a 62-year-old widow in the neighborhood.

Some of these episodes were dismissed or shrugged off because the "victims" understood his medical condition and that he was not "really" responsible for his actions; still, his erratically impulsive and hostile behavior had earned for him the appellation "Crazy Larry" among neighbors, and, in consequence of his size (6'4" and 270 pounds) he had become a figure to be feared and avoided; for his part, Larry rankled when he heard the nickname. In other cases, police had been summoned, but (in a pattern documented at least since the time of Phineas Gage) once the responding officers learned Larry's history, charges were not filed.

The instant case was different. On a weekday about six weeks before our meeting, Larry was at home alone. There appeared in the neighborhood a delivery van from Amalgamated Parcel Services; in routine fashion, the driver (the "regular" for the route, a young, thin Black man who knew Larry) made calls at several houses.

As he was preparing to leave, Larry accosted him, demanding to know why the package he had been expecting from a mail-order house famous for providing woolen shirts had not been delivered. The driver told him that the package was not aboard; Larry persisted, claiming that he personally wanted to inspect every package still on the truck. In his statement to police, the driver reported that he next said something to the effect *Don't be crazy, Larry;* I got to be on my way. Apparently, Larry failed to hear, or to appreciate, the comma, for the driver continued: "Next he punches me, shoves me out the truck; I'm lying in the street, my nose is broken, and the truck's gone." Neighbors called police.

Larry and the truck were found about 90 minutes later, in the parking lot of a nearby shopping center. By that time, Larry had opened, in what must have been a frenzied manner, about 300 packages. Each time, when he found that the package did not contain his coveted woolen shirts, he destroyed the contents, smashing glass and wooden objects with his feet, tearing clothing, underwear, draperies, etc., and causing thousands of dollars in damage. It required six officers to subdue Larry sufficiently to take him to a holding cell.

Because he knew something of Larry's history, the driver was not inclined to press charges; Amalgamated proved adamantly less forgiving. Larry's father was beside himself; although he had serially engaged the services of several home health aides, each had left abruptly, usually as a result of physical or verbal abuse by Larry. Though the insurance carrier for the equipment company was providing Larry substantial disability compensation, the father had a business to run, one that often demands very long days; though he seemed able to control his son's behavior absolutely and effortlessly, he could not afford on economic grounds alone to remain at home as Larry's watch dog.

Larry's father had offered to make restitution to Amalgamated, the public prosecutor showed no burning desire to try the case, and his attorney had even proposed to Amalgamated that "trial in the press," with headlines trumpeting its insensitive treatment of a brain-damaged citizen might tarnish its image. But these strategies availed not; and thus we had been summoned for a case conference.

In the state in which Larry lived, the relevant positive and case law requires that, if a defendant is found not to be culpable by reason of insanity, the judge has no option but to sentence the defendant to confinement in the state's forensic psychiatric hospital; the law provides, further, that "sanity hearings" are to be held periodically thereafter to determine whether the defendant can be released without threat of danger to public safety. In Larry's case, the public prosecutor seemed more than delighted not to oppose such a plea; accordingly, Larry was so sentenced.

Case notes from this confinement indicate that, after a predictably hostile period of adjustment, Larry seemed to be faring rather well. Because the earlier hospital records had reported the futility of medication, none was prescribed. Some minor alterations were undertaken on the hospital grounds about three months after Larry's admission. He expressed interest in volunteering his assistance; because there had been no impulsive outbursts, nor indeed any other contraindications, since early in his stay in hospital, his "case manager" acceded. For three weeks, Larry expertly laid brick alongside the contractor and his employees; case notes enthuse about his positive adjustments. Then, on a Thursday morning, he apparently simply walked off the hospital grounds.

That happened four years ago as of this writing. His father, now re-married, has not heard from Larry. For some months after his disappearance, disability compensation checks continued to arrive at the house. When the father informed the insurance company of Larry's absconsion, the checks stopped; the insurance company periodically asks the father whether Larry has returned, suggesting that Larry has not otherwise re-directed those checks. At this point, if he is alive, Larry is technically a fugitive from justice.

- *In the schematic representation presented earlier, we plot this case as a 1-10-12 progression. The evidence of acute onset neurologic disorder is clear and well-documented, resulting in cognitive and behavioral consequences (impaired cognitive capacity, paranoid ideation, confabulation) that render a casual interaction and/or remark into a character contest out of proportion to*

Figure 6.2: Larry's progression from neurologic injury to violence

the actual provocative stimuli. There is little evidence of negative behavioral or social influence or of CNS-active substance abuse either before or after neurologic injury. A graphic representation of Larry's case appears below.

Big Al and Tiny Tony

Character contest with grievous bodily harm

Tillton lies some 65 miles west of New York City and 35 miles north of Philadelphia and serves as the seat of an eastern Pennsylvania county whose landscape is frequently compared to the rolling English countryside. Except for the commuter railroad station that links the town to Philadelphia, the visitor would find great similarity between Tillton and a small midwestern city; there is virtually no resemblance to either New York or Philadelphia. Tillton's 1990 population was just under 9000, and that of the county it serves as seat a sparsely-populated half-million. A century ago, Tillton was a thriving, if small, industrial center, specializing in agricultural implements. Today, some of the abandoned factories have been reclaimed by young urban professionals who do not mind long commutes when they can be exchanged for gentrified loft-like living spaces in a country town. In calendar year 1993, there were no homicides in Tillton, although two rapes, 29 assaults, and nearly 190 property crimes were reported. The minority population aggregates to 7%, well below the comparable proportion for the state.

Big Al McCarthy was born in Tillton in 1970, the second son and third child of a family whose roots extend to the early 19th century. Al's father is a licensed plumber with his own practice, which has proved quite profitable in recent years as a result of gentrification. Mother has never worked outside the home, but she has consistently maintained a high level of activity on behalf of the church to which the family belongs.

Al's older brother, now an agronomist employed by state government, and his sister, a teacher in a community some 30 miles distant, early distinguished themselves in the religious school which all three attended; Al did not so distinguish himself. His father recalls with some disappointment learning, when Al was a sophomore in high school, that his youngest son likely would not be able to master the body of knowledge required to enter a licensed trade like plumbing. Nor did Al's stature, responsible for his nickname, provide consolation, for a certain awkwardness and incoordination precluded his selection for interscholastic athletic teams. Still, Big Al was known as an easy-going chap, never a problem in school, and certainly never involved in law-breaking behavior.

The McCarthys lived in half of what, in local parlance, is called a "duplex" house. Into the other half, as renters, moved the Martinez family when Al was aged 10. Rafael, scion of the clan, had come to the United States as a migrant agricultural worker some seven years earlier from his native Guadalajara in Mexico, worked diligently, saved his money, dropped out of the migrant stream when a position became available in the small pottery in Tillton that produces decorative tiles similar to those manufactured in the plant in his home town where he worked as a young man, gained permanent resident status, and sent for his family. Tony, youngest in the family, was called Niño ("the Little One"), but the appellation changed when he entered the same religious school Big Al attended.

Though Tiny Tony is two years older than Big Al, because his native language was Spanish and his grasp of English poor, he was placed in the same grade. That circumstance and the proximity of residence sparked a continuing, close relationship between the boys, despite the striking difference in their stature and physique, with Al extra-tall and lanky and Tony short and square; they were not infrequently referred to as "Mutt and Jeff." The friendship endured through the high school years, which were academically undistinguished for both and uneventful in other ways. Their relationship could be characterized as a typical "rough-house" friendship between adolescent males, with considerable good-natured jostling and an occasional, equally good-natured according to observers, bout of ethnically-tinged name-calling.

At high school graduation, both Al and Tony obtained employment in the pottery, where Rafael had risen steadily to a supervisory position. Al became a driver who shuttled shipping cartons to freight depots, while Tony worked as a packer. Each continued to live at home. About two years later, Al and Tony jointly decided that each should purchase a truck, considered within the context of their phenomenological world something of a "macho" accouterment. Shortly after, Tony began to don a roughly Southwestern costume (tailored shirt, custom jeans, boots, string tie, elaborately tooled belt, Stetson) as his "dress-up" clothing, and, to his parents' surprise, Al followed Tony's lead. The two young men also began to frequent Carl's County Carousel, a tavern with a "country and western" flavor and decor that featured "line dancing" to live music on Friday and Saturday nights. Neither set of parents objected to alcohol consumption, and besides the boys were well past adulthood; but a pattern that would qualify under the rubric of "episodic dyscontrol" of alcohol consumption was soon enough in evidence. Nonetheless, no one seemed particularly worried, since the episodes were strictly limited to the first two nights of each weekend.

Those were the circumstances that prevailed on a Friday night in November 1992, when Al and Tony arrived at Carl's Carousel, each in his own truck. Eyewitnesses later recalled nothing unusual in the behavior of the boys toward each other or toward other patrons. Each danced a few times with girls they had known casually as fellow patrons. According to witnesses, there was the usual, fairly deliberate maneuvering toward each other on the dance floor, leading to collisions, followed by name-calling; but that was unusual neither for Big Al, Tiny Tony, or other patrons; it was instead part of the fun at Carl's Carousel. Then Adrianna and Luz entered Carl's establishment for the first time.

Witnesses later remembered that the newcomers were relatively quickly noticed and asked to dance. Those near Al and Tony remember that Tony addressed the girls in Spanish, to which Al apparently took exception. One witness believes that Al said of one of the girls something like "She's mine," to which Tony replied to the effect "You're not man enough for that *bella muchacha,* Gringo," followed by the typical good-natured pushing and shoving, to the considerable delight of all, apparently including Adrianna and Luz.

In her statement to police, Adrianna described the next set of events as having occurred "in a flash. Before you know it, they both got beer bottles in their hands, lunging at each other like fools, and the others, they're just egging them on. Then somebody's bottle gets broken, and there's more lunging, and then Tony, he's bleeding from his eyes."

In the aftermath of the confrontation, Tiny Tony lost the use of his left eye. Big Al pled guilty to a charge of aggravated assault with grievous bodily harm (rather contrary to the advice of his attorney, who claimed that, because Tony had also been "armed," a better plea-bargain leading to a non-custodial sentence seemed eminently possible). Nonetheless, Al was sentenced to 3-5 years in prison; he was released after serving eleven months. He did not return to work at the pottery; instead, he serves as a plumber's helper and general laborer for his father.

The case made headlines only when, at the time of sentencing, Tony's mother addressed the court in halting English, asserting that the sentence would have been longer if the victim had emerged as the offender, because, she said, "a Gringo eye is worth more than a Mexican eye." Tony continues to work at the pottery and occasionally visits Carl's Carousel, where he has become something of a folk legend, enhanced by a rather sinister visage highlighted by a black eye-patch; the family has moved to a small village outside Tillton. A civil case filed by Tony against Al for monetary damages issuing from the loss of the eye is pending.

- *This case quintessentially illustrates the character contest. There is only moderate evidence of underlying neuropathology, inferable from school records and from Al's periodic motor incoordination; but its extent in either actor very likely does not exceed the "no observable effect" level. There is no evidence of overtly negative behavioral models in the home or family but considerable evidence of a long-simmering, long-unresolved character con-*

Figure 6.3: Tony: A small taste for risk, a mildly deviant subcultures, and a long-simmering character contest meet acute potentiation

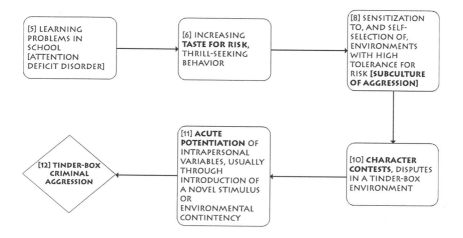

test. And the influence both of a novel stimulus determinant and the presence of third parties in the choreography of the dare is clear and paramount. If we turn to our schematic, we might characterize this case as following a 5-6-8-10-11-12 progression, as represented here.

Mark

Epilepsy, Love Boat, and death

New Caledonia is a city of some 40,000 about 50 miles from Manhattan, a county seat, and home to a public university with an enrollment of about 30,000. Surrounded by suburbs and "exurbs" in a New York corridor that is itself among the two dozen largest standard metropolitan statistical area in the country, some 70% of its "permanent" (non-student) population is either Black or Hispanic, with a high rate of crime, delinquency, and unemployment. In contrast to the relative tranquillity of Tillton, there were five murders (121% higher than its state's average), 16 rapes (127% higher than the state average), 283 assaults (146% higher), and 3056 property crimes (73% higher) during 1993 to keep its 135 (still mostly white) police officers busy. Economically, it was once an important center for the manufacture of men's clothing, and it continues as the home base for a major manufacturer of pharmaceuticals and surgical supplies.

Mark Jenkins was born in New Caledonia in 1961, the oldest child and only son of a father who worked as a mail carrier and a mother who worked as a housekeeper in a dormitory complex at the university; the family, to which a daughter was added when Mark was 4, lived in a neighborhood comprised largely of Black families stably employed in blue-collar occupations. At the age of 10, while (at his own insistence) helping his father clean the rain gutters, Mark fell from a ladder at a height of about a story and a half, suffering concussion that perpetuated as epilepsy, with seizures largely *petit mal* in character, but sometimes involving loss of consciousness and hallucinosis and periodically escalating to the level of *grand mal*, largely dependent on how faithful Mark remained to the prescribed use of anticonvulsant medication. It is relevant that Mark's injury occurred in the relatively early days of the massive knowledge explosion in the neurosciences and before the emergence of a panoply of clinical methods for neurotherapy and cognitive rehabilitation.

Whether as a result of brain trauma or otherwise, Mark performed poorly in school. By the age of 12, he was skipping class regularly and, despite strict instructions from his physician and his parents, he began to drink alcohol and smoke marijuana with other members of his "street corner set." He was arrested on several occasions as a juvenile, along with other members of the "set," primarily for shoplifting or disorderly conduct but on two occasions for burglary; on each occasion, he was placed on probation. Shortly after his 17th birthday, Mark dropped out of school, having progressed only to the 10th grade. Even in the relatively difficult economic times of the late-1970s, he obtained employment in a small plastics factory. But his work record over the next 8 years or so proved highly sporadic, with some voluntary terminations (when Mark simply failed to show up for work), dismissals for lateness of absence, and other dismissals because he suffered mild seizures at work, in situations in which his condition made it unsafe for him to operate machinery. During this period, largely at his parents' urging issuing from their own exasperation with patterns of behavior of which they strongly disapproved, he moved out of the family home, cohabiting for relatively short periods with live-in girl friends; not infrequently, they supported him, most often through welfare payments. For her part, Mark's sister remained at home, graduated from high school, attended a semester in the county college, and became pregnant. She bore a son and later a daughter.

In early 1987, on an evening during which he had been drinking heavily, Mark was injured physically in a barroom brawl, suffering concussion. Mark was no stranger to such brawls, in which, like the subjects in Group How in the Megargee-Bohn Typology Study, he emerged more typically as victim than as offender. But that episode seemed to prove something of a turning point in his life. Upon release from the hospital, he joined Alcoholics Anonymous and resolved to pursue his pharmacotherapy religiously. With the aid of his AA sponsor and despite what can only be regarded as an atrocious employment record, he obtained work in a small factory that manufactured guitar picks. For a time, he participated in the activities of the Nation of Islam; although he eventually withdrew, the Nation's strong prohibition against alcohol (and drugs) reinforced the central messages from AA, which he continued to sporadically attend. Mark supplemented his meager income through petty theft, often from inebriated geriatrics; there were three arrests but no prosecutions.

During this period, he moved in with Sadie, a woman with whom he had earlier shared a sexual relationship, and her two children, neither of whom had been fathered by Mark. The relationship and living circumstances seemed relatively satisfactory until Fall 1990. Because he had no access to health insurance, Mark had foregone his anticonvulsant medication, but the periodic seizures he suffered were minor, often only minutes in length, and neither overly intrusive nor obtrusive. In late October, however, he suffered a seizure at work that became visible to all; others ensued in early November. At mid-month, there was a seizure of sufficient severity that his employers had him transported to hospital via ambulance. When discharged, he was given a supply of anticonvulsant medication sufficient for several weeks and warned direly to strictly conform to the pharmacotherapeutic regimen. But when he returned to work several days later, his employers told him that they could not longer trust him to operate the plastic press; they offered him an alternate position in the packing department, at a lower hourly wage.

That brings us to a cold, rainy Friday in November, indeed the day before Mark's birthday. Because he had lost several days' wages during the past weeks as a result of the now-recurrent seizures and because he had been "downgraded" to a lower-paying position, Mark gave Sadie less than his agreed-upon "half" of the household's expenses. Exasperated, Sadie ordered Mark from the premises, there and then, further implying that he had imperiled their life together by failing to control his seizure disorder. Mark apparently pleaded with her to reconsider; demonstrating his intent to follow the program of anticonvulsant medication, he downed a pill on the spot. But whatever amount of rational suasion Mark was able to muster moved her not in the least. He packed his meager belongings into a duffel bag. Because the telephone had been disconnected for non-payment, Mark was unable to contact his parents from the apartment. Instead, he made for the nearest public phone, located in Nettie's Bar.

Nettie's Bar is an institution of some renown in New Caledonia, widely known as a marketplace where anything (from barbiturates to amphetamines to crack to LSD) and everyone (man, woman, child) is available for purchase. Though it had once been a haunt of Mark's, he had rarely entered the establishment since "straightening himself out" after the injuries of two years earlier. From Nettie's, Mark contacted his father, who grudgingly and reluctantly agreed to come to fetch him to the family home.

While waiting, Mark decided to order a Rye whiskey, even though he had not been near alcohol for years; it was, after all, the day before his birthday, the job was going down the tube, and his "woman" had thrown him out. Shortly after, Slim entered Nettie's. Slim had been a friend during the old street corner days, but he now owned a small fish market nearby, which he had "inherited" from his aunt, and, as he liked to put it, he "moved with the carriage trade." During his aunt's day, the back room was used primarily for gambling and for the sale of "moonshine" liquor, and the customers were invariably older and even elderly Blacks. After the establishment became Slim's Fishery, it was rumored that whatever (but not whoever) was not on offer at Nettie's could be found in Slim's back room.

Given the proximity to the university and its throngs of students, however, Slim had carved out a new "market corner," specializing in "designer drugs" fabricated from readily-available (and legally-obtainable) chemicals that nonetheless mimic the effects of controlled dangerous substances and frankly aimed at students. At the time in question, the most recent addition to Slim's "product line" had been "Love Boat," a "cigarette" fabricated with formaldehyde-soaked smoking tobacco that virulently mimics the effects of cocaine. Once ingested by inhalation, the substance follows the route of aldehyde metabolism, emerging as aldehyde dehydrogenase or aldehyde reductase, enzymes which are implicated in the catabolism of norepinephrine and monoamine oxidase. The phenomenological experience of the user will mimic that of the ingestion of cocaine, crack, amphetamine, or another psychotomimetic which interferes with monoamine oxidase.

University health authorities called upon to treat students after visits to Slim's back room had frequently complained to New Caledonia police, but whatever investigations had ensued led neither to arrest nor to conviction. It was widely rumored that Slim frequently provided police with information about the movement of "hard" drugs into New Caledonia and that such information had led to many seizures by police. There is, of course, no way of verifying that rumor, but such cooperation clearly seems to have been in Slim's interest, since it represented a way of constraining the competition.

As investigators later reconstructed the interaction, Slim observed Mark's hang-dog expression, asked its cause, heard Mark's tale of woe, then, handing Mark his own "reefer," said something like "Take a hit of this; it'll make you feel better." Since Mark had smoked marijuana with Slim many and many a time in the street corner days, it is likely that he construed what he was being offered as that substance; as later events demonstrated, it was instead "Love Boat." Shortly after, Mark's father arrived, and the two left for the family home; it was now nearly midnight.

Once at home, the father retired, instructing Mark to sleep on the couch; the son replied that he wasn't tired yet, instead felt rather invigorated, and would stay up watching television for a while. At 12:45 or so, the father was awakened by shouts from the living room; he recalls hearing Mark, clad in his underwear, bellowing at the television set, using terms like "the Great Satan." Entering the room, the father observed his son in what can most economically be described as an intensely manic state. When the father remonstrated, in the father's account, his son began to bellow at him, calling him "the Great Satan" and making what the father construed as menacing gestures.

Mark's father is a cautious man who has lived in inner-city circumstances for decades. During the early 1980s, following an epidemic of such incidents nationwide, there had been many "push-in" robberies and assaults in the neighborhood. Invariably, the victim had been an older retiree and the offenses had been timed to coincide with the delivery of pension and/or Social Security checks. Since both he and his wife were now retired, for the protection of his family and property he had taken to keeping near the front door a baseball bat that had been hollowed out and filled with lead.

Bellowing further about "the Great Satan," Mark lunged at his father, fists clenched, head first; the father sidestepped toward the door, where he encountered the bat. The shouting awakened his wife, his daughter, and his granddaughter from their sleep in other parts of the house; Mark seemed impervious to his father's exhortations to calm down and quiet down and seemed ready to rush at his father again; the baseball bat was close to hand. The father delivered a healthy blow with the bat to his son's head in the vicinity of the left ear.

It is probable that Mark construed that blow (to the extent that he was able to impart meaning to the data of his experience at all at that point) as palpable evidence that his father had become indeed "the Great Satan" or one of his demonic minions. His response was to make for the kitchen (the adjacent room), where he fumbled for the largest kitchen knife he could find, cutting his left hand badly in the process. By this time, with the exception of the 6-year-old grandson who slept in an attic bedroom, the household was fully roused. Holding the bat at the ready, the father ordered his wife, daughter, and granddaughter to leave the house, instructing them to call the police, a task accomplished with alacrity next door; then he also exited the house.

On the same evening, the New Caledonia police had conducted a major round-up of "hard drug" dealers in a public park near the campus, along with their customers, most of whom were university students; there are some in New Caledonia who believe that Slim had alerted police of the movement into the city of a quantity of high-quality cocaine intended for the university market. In the manner of those law enforcement officials who derive the prescriptions for their own behavior not from commonly-accepted police practices but from tabloid television, the nine officers who had conducted the raid had garbed themselves in the costume of "special weapons and tactics" teams, armed themselves with semi-automatic weapons, and had even daubed on facial camouflage in the manner of jungle guerrillas. They had just rolled into headquarters when five of them were dispatched to quell the disturbance Mark had engendered. Mark had, of course, long been known to New Caledonia police, first as a juvenile and later as an adult offender, so that a complaint to the effect that he was "armed and dangerous" came as no surprise. No one at headquarters recalled that his offenses had consistently been property rather than violent crimes, but they recalled him by name.

Of the several police officers and Federal agents with whom we have discussed the phenomenology of participating in drug raids, whether on the fairly large scale in New Caledonia that night or in smaller assaults on "crack houses," a preponderance have used the term "feeling pumped up" to describe their own experiences. The descriptions rather strongly resemble Renata Bluhm's description of the adrenaline-releasing effects of "a jump into the unknown." It is a reasonable surmise that, having just returned from a raid that netted a total of 17 arrestees (five dealers, 12 student customers) and still clad in SWAT gear, some of the officers dispatched to Mark's parents' home still felt "pumped up."

When they arrived at the scene, the neighborhood was alive with people whose sleep had been disturbed — as had that of Mark's nephew, who had joined his uncle. What the officers beheld on the front porch of the house was a young Black man wielding a knife in his right hand; his left hand rested on his nephew's left shoulder. Blood was clearly visible on Mark's undershirt and also on his nephew's pajama top.

With exquisite precision, seven police bullets cut a neat diagonal swath from Mark's left shoulder to his right hip. The ambulance that had accompanied the officers moved Mark to hospital. Both transfusion and surgery were required; in order to match blood type, two vials were extracted from Mark's body. They remained in hospital. Since massive damage had been done to arteries and lungs, surgery proved ineffective; Mark died three days later.

In New Caledonia, there is an active chapter of the Black People's Unity Coalition, an organization whose political viewpoints reflect those of the Black Panthers of the mid-1960s. By the time of Mark's death, it had been learned that only his blood, and no one else's, had been shed. The "spin" given to events by BPUC leaders was that five white police officers with itchy trigger fingers had killed a young Black man whose only crime had been that he had cut himself with a knife in his mother's kitchen; and, moreover, this episode constituted merely the latest example of police brutality in an organized effort at genocide against the Black population nationwide; etc. The official response from police was that clearly inebriated Mark had equally clearly taken his nephew hostage and stood at the point of murdering the child. Journalists had a field day.

A confrontation of that sort between an energized minority population and a predominantly white police force is dangerous in any city, but perhaps more so in a city with a university whose students are about 80% white. The public prosecutor decided to proceed with charges against the officer who had shot Mark and the officer in charge of the detail.

During evidence presented before the grand jury, a psychopharmacologist from the university provided expert witness testimony about Mark's neuro-chemical condition preceding the shooting, especially in relation to his long-di-agnosed epilepsy. While anticonvulsants raise the threshold for seizure, alcohol lowers that threshold; Mark had ingested alcohol voluntarily, nor was he a stranger to the effects of that substance, or to the biochemical "yo-yo" effect that follows ingestion of both alcohol and anticonvulsants. In the blood samples which had remained in hospital, there was evidence of the medication (consistent with Sadie's statement) and of alcohol, but not at toxic levels (consistent with eyewitness statements that Mark had ingested but one shot of whiskey at Nettie's).

But there was also found a concentration of aldehyde dehyrogenase, an enzyme which interferes with the metabolism of norepinephrine and monoamine oxidase and produces an effect that mimics a massive dose of cocaine; and that is consistent with the statements of other patrons at Nettie's that the "reefer" given to Mark by Slim on the fatal night in fact contained the substance constructed with formaldehyde called "Love Boat," at least in the New Caledonia formulary. Slim declined to make any statement about its contents; instead, urgent family business called him to Florida.

The psychopharmacologist also testified that, in her opinion, it was not probable but virtually certain that Mark was already deeply in a state of hallucinatory delirium before his father delivered the blow to the left temporal lobe, a blow that almost certainly exacerbated the hallucinatory delirium and that was perhaps sufficient in itself to elicit disorientation and mental and emotional discoordination. She might have added that, with the combination of medication, alcohol, and formaldehyde in addition to the underlying epilepsy, there was little doubt that Mark's brain was virtually in the condition of neurochemical barrage (Lezak, 1995, 314). Though the prosecutor thanked her for her testimony, it is rumored that he wondered aloud how officers responding to a crisis could possibly have intuited all that; since the proceedings of grand juries are not made public, it is not possible to verify the rumor. In all, the grand jury deliberated for some 24 minutes before declining to indict the officers, who quickly returned to duty.

Slim now tells people who ask about the matter (most do not) that it's a shame that Mark's gone because "his Daddy done him in." For his part, the father appears to hold the view that he acted as any normal person would when faced with a raving, obviously intoxicated son. He is a cautious man; he was at some pains throughout the set of events here recounted to cast no blame in the direction of police, rather deliberately distancing himself from BPUC spokespersons.

In the aftermath of the event, the New Caledonia police undertook "community relations" training with renewed vigor and launched an "affirmative action" program to recruit minority officers. Leaders of the BPUC continue to call press conferences about episodes of police brutality. Nettie's Bar remains the Mecca it has long been both for the community and for a portion of the student body who "cop and scram," and Slim continues to operate the Fishery. Mark's family has remained in its house, and his father still keeps the baseball bat near the front door.

There has been a great deal of fairly glib discussion professionally and journalistically about "victim-less" crime. Mark became a crime-less victim, at least so far as the official record is concerned.

- *In this case, the 1-9-10-1 "vicious circle" loop in our schematic predominates. There is pre-existing neuropathology, induced through head trauma at the age of 10, which inclines to experimentation with mood-altering substances (perhaps even in an effort to self-medicate), which leads to confrontations with others in barroom brawls, which leads to further head trauma. There is also substantial evidence of negative social, though not familial, role models (3) and of learning problems (5), habituation to a subculture of deviance (8), both in continued association with the "street corner set" and in familiarity with Nettie's, for an increasing taste for risk (6) in his property crimes as a juvenile and adult, and some evidence of impairment in the capacity to accurately assess costs, risks, and benefits associated with behavior, in particular failure to adhere to prescribed medication (7). Perhaps most importantly, ingestion of biochemical substances with antagonistic neurologic effects constitutes acute potentiation (11) of intrapersonal variables, even though Mark apparently did not understand that the "reefer" contained not a CNS depressant but a volatile CNS stimulant. This rather complex pattern is graphically represented on the next page.*

Figure 6.4: Mark: From chronic neurologic disorder to crime-less victim in a complex interactive pathway

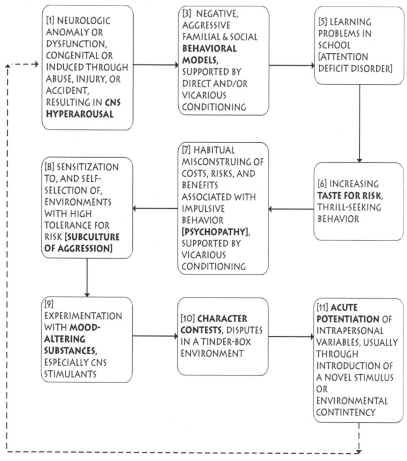

Squire

If we inspect any of the cells in our schematic, at one point or another Squire is to be found; his history thus unfolds in a fully interactive pathway. Squire was "state-raised" and no stranger to the insides of prisons. His story involves victimization in incestuous homosexual child abuse, anti-social explosiveness in adolescence, neurologic dysfunction, and the retributive killing of one prison inmate by another. Ultimately, it may not be an unusual tale.

The path to sexual victimization

Squire was born to a non-commissioned officer in the U.S. Army and his wife (whom we shall call Kay) during that brief lull between the end of World War II and the beginning of the Korean conflict (we never got around to calling it a war) in 1951. Because his father's unit was dispatched to Korea early in that first of America's Asian adventures, Kay moved herself and her son back to her family's farm in a northeastern state to await the return of her husband.

But neither fate nor the military forces of North Korea, widely regarded as a puppet state of the then-virulently Maoist People's Republic of China, would have it so. The husband-father was killed in action in the early days of the armed conflict, when his son was barely a year old. In accordance with U.S. military custom, the news of the death was borne in person by another non-commissioned officer, whom we shall call Art.

So far as we know or have been able to determine, Kay and Art had not known each other until that morbid occasion. Thereafter, however, they began to "keep company" (as one termed it in the 1950s, if not thereafter), and a marriage ensued in due course. The happy bridegroom left the Army after his enlistment terminated, ending some 12 years of service, and repaired to Kay's family's farm; in view of a service-connected injury, Art was entitled to a small monthly pension as a disabled veteran. In the succeeding years, two children were born of the new union.

After a time, as death claimed his in-laws, Art and his bride found themselves the sole owners of the farm property, which by now had become relatively valuable as the cities and the suburbs of the northeast began to expand under the pressure of the "baby boom" of that era.

Because land prices had begun to escalate, Art found that the proceeds from the sale of parcels of property, when combined with his small disability pension, made it unnecessary for him either to hold a job outside the farm or even to work the farm assiduously. Instead, he had both the leisure and the income to indulge a taste for beverage alcohol. He had certainly stumbled upon someone's notion of an approximation to the lifestyle of the country gentleman.

Revelation of victimization — and its aftermath

There the story might have ended (and reasonably idyllically at that) had it not been the case that, at the break of the decade, the child welfare agency in the state in which the family lived launched an early and vigorous campaign to promote awareness of child sexual abuse. Then as now, such campaigns often began with "awareness" sessions in the public schools conducted by social workers from the state's official child welfare agency, who urge their hearers not only to sensitize themselves to unwarranted advances from adults or from older children but to report such episodes and their sequelae to their teachers or other adults in positions of formal authority.

Thus it was that Squire revealed that, for some three years past, his stepfather had treated him as a love object. The response of the school, child welfare, and law enforcement authorities was electric. In short order, Squire was removed from the home to be placed under the guardianship of the child welfare agency, while Art was indicted.

Art was represented by a skillful attorney, who advised him immediately upon release on bail to enter into sustained psychotherapy. He also advised Art to plead guilty, thus obviating a jury trial and reducing the single court proceeding to the imposition of sentence. During that session, the attorney was able to bring forward for the perusal of the sentencing judge Art's relatively distinguished service record and the reports of the treating psychotherapist, with the outcome that Art was given a 10-year suspended sentence and placed on probation, with the strict condition that he continue outpatient psychotherapy. These events convey some flavor, in real life terms, of the origins of the data on the relative infrequency of intrusive sanction for aggressive crime recounted in Chapter 4. There is no evidence, by the way, that Art ever complied with that condition of probation, or that anybody cared very much whether he did or did not.

The sentence satisfied almost everybody — except the child welfare agency. There was then, as there is now, in the state in question an ironclad regulation that an offender who has been convicted of child abuse is not to be permitted to share a domicile with his or her victim. Clearly, the agency told Kay, Art would have to leave the family home. Indeed, since the laws governing divorce in that state, then as now, listed conviction of a spouse for a sexual offense as a ground for the immediate dissolution of the marital union, it would not have been untoward to expect Kay to divorce Art.

Removal from the family: What is reinforced?

But Kay was not so minded. Instead, she surrendered custody of her son to the child welfare agency. Because his biological father was deceased and because Art had never formally adopted him, only Kay enjoyed parietal rights over the child. Thus, Squire was removed from the temporary shelter into which he had been placed and put instead into the first of a series of foster homes.

Now we have a pretty picture: Society, through one of its recognized agents (the child welfare agency), operating in conjunction with another of its agents (the schools), urges one of its small citizens to reveal wrongdoing. He does; and for his trouble he is, to borrow the Bard's phrase, untimely ripped from the bosom of his family. He was deposited, as it developed, into totally unfamiliar school and social environments in an inner-city neighborhood. Because Art had been given a 10-year sentence, and because Squire was at that point already 11 years old, the decision to seek foster-care placement meant, in essence, that he would never live with his family again — at least not before he attained adulthood. What a marvelous set of messages concerning our values, our system of justice, and the rights and obligations of our citizens was thereby conveyed.

It was, of course, many decades after these events that we were able to interview Squire — who, incidentally, acquired his nickname in that first inner-city foster home. What he remembers and what he is willing to reveal about what he remembers may be quite different. But, in any event, it certainly seemed to us that, even at a remove of more than a quarter century, there was more than a tinge of regret as he recounted the decision to reveal Art's wrong-doing.

That regret, which the accumulated research evidence indicates is by no means uncommon among victims of incestuous child abuse (Pallone, 1990-b, 46-49), appears to pivot largely on lack of awareness of the likely consequences: On one day, life is normal, even comfortable, with the abused child (perhaps only at the margin of awareness) even enjoying the "special" relationship he or she shares with a parent or sibling; on what appears to be only the next day, life is a shambles, the non-abusing parent is tearful and even accusatory, and the world appears to have turned upside down.

In such circumstances, especially when siblings also lay the burden for disruption in their lives upon the victim in one variation of the "blame the victim" scenario that has become a popular international pastime (Ibid., 41-44), there is little mystery in the retrospective assessment by victims that, if they had it to do over again, they would continue to endure the abuse (and, perhaps, also enjoy the benefits of that "special relationship" with an abusing parent or sibling) rather than undergo the tumult that ensues upon its revelation.

Hostility and impulsivity in the behavioral repertoire

The records we have been able to obtain from that era reveal not regret, but rather anger in great abundance. Further, the anger was omni-directional, emitted in explosive and disruptive behavior both in school and in the foster home; the behavior in school was quite in contrast to that observed by his former teachers. Within short order, these first foster parents gave up the ghost and, at their request, the child welfare agency transferred Squire to another placement.

This pattern was to repeat itself over the course of the next several years, with greater and greater vehemence exhibited in the pattern of explosive and disruptive behavior. That behavior became most virulent whenever an adult male — whether teacher, police officer, or Boy Scout Troop Leader — attempted to assert his quite legitimate authority over Squire. We need not long detain ourselves with discussions of stimulus generalization and discrimination to underscore the source of such razor-edge hostility.

There finally came a day in 1967 when Squire came before the same juvenile judge before whom he had appeared many times in the past. Squire was at that point 17 years old, nominally still enrolled in high school, and generally considered uncontrollable by the child welfare agency. Despite an escalating record of juvenile acts, he had not served time in a reformatory — very probably because sentencing judges regarded his background as explanatory if not exculpatory of whatever had been his instant delinquent behavior. On this occasion, however, the judge gave Squire a choice of the sort popular in an era in which the nation was at war (Vietnam), universal military conscription was the order of the day, and the possession of a high school diploma was not yet a prerequisite to enlistment. The choice: Tomorrow, you will *either* be in the uniform of one of the armed services, *or* I will sentence you to a maximum term in a juvenile reformatory.

Acute neurological toxicity potentiates criminal behavior

It was to the Navy that Squire presented himself and, after a series of tests of cognitive ability and vocational aptitude, the Navy accepted his enlistment. Photographs taken then for identification purposes show Squire much as he looks today: tall (6'4"), thin virtually to the point of emaciation, a narrowing of the eyes that would be interpreted by most people as an unspoken challenge, a positioning of jaw and lips that most would interpret as a smirk rather than a smile.

Not incidentally, it was apparently at this point that Squire first *heard* an adult who told him that he was more intelligent than average; doubtless, that message had been conveyed repeatedly by school officials but ignored. Now, however, intellectual standing had real meaning, for it qualified Squire to undergo training in a specialized Navy school.

We have not been able to obtain access to Squire's scores to that series of examinations given at the time of enlistment. However, we administered the Hartford-Shipley Institute for Living Scale (Suinn, 1960; Wiens & Banaka, 1960; Zachary, 1990), a measure of intelligence developed at the Hartford Retreat (the oldest psychiatric hospital in the United States) and derived from the original Wechsler-Bellevue Scales. On this instrument, Squire's intelligence quotient was estimated to be 114, a figure that would place him on the border between the groups labeled "bright normal" and "superior" among adults. We have no particular reason to believe that Squire has become either more or less intellectually able in the years intervening between examination by the Navy and our administration of the Hartford-Shipley. Squire declined to "sit through" the roughly 90-120 minutes it would have required to administer the Wechsler Adult Intelligence Scale, but our clinical supposition is that he most assuredly would have displayed a high Performance than Verbal Score; in many other ways, there were indications of "verbal deficit" in relation to relatively high general intelligence.

From among the choices the Navy presented to him, he elected training as a ship-to-shore radio operator. Service records indicate a relatively large number of relatively minor disciplinary infractions, primarily involving insubordination to military superiors, during training; but Squire graduated, only a few weeks late, and was assigned to an aircraft carrier shortly to embark for Southeast Asia.

For the next three years, punctuated by appropriate "rest and relaxation" rotations, Squire served aboard that carrier, whose principal mission was the fueling and refueling of Navy and Marine planes and helicopters with Dioxin, an herbicide better known as Agent Orange which has since become notorious for its acute neurological and physiologic toxicity (Roberts, 1991). Like everyone else aboard the carrier, Squire ingested Agent Orange through respiration and through dermal contact on a daily basis. According to neuropsychologist David Hartman (1988, 238) of the University of Illinois Medical Center:

> Over 100 million pounds of this potent herbicide were applied by the United States as a defoliant in Viet Nam. Agent Orange has been linked to a variety of toxic effects, including cloracne, porphyria cutanea tarda, liver disorders and immune system abnormalities . . . Veterans who had been exposed reported significantly more subjective psychological difficulties both on the MMPI and self-report inventories. Problems reported included depression, anxiety, rage attacks, and irritability.

Squire's account of his time aboard ship suggests a great frequency of hostile encounters with military superiors, including physical confrontations, brawls, fist fights; such a pattern is surely in conformance with the record of his earlier behavior during adolescence — and it is simultaneously consistent with potentiation of that earlier pattern as a consequence of acute Dioxin toxicity. Nonetheless, few formal disciplinary actions are recorded in Squire's military records during this period. It may, of course, be the case that Squire's memory has romanticized the past, that he was really mild as a lamb aboard ship; or it may be that, since acute Dioxin toxicity was surely prevalent among the crew, the military had no choice but to overlook episodes of hostile insubordination it might in other times and at other places have prosecuted.

Opting for a criminal lifestyle

Among the several friends Squire made while aboard the carrier was a young, devil-may-care pilot whom we shall call Mike, who apparently became a hero to disaffected enlisted men because of his own negative attitudes toward authority. Those attitudes, however, were offset by what were in Squire's account spectacular successes in fearless combat missions. Such fearlessness, according to Squire (and here his account finds some corroboration in published accounts of the war in Vietnam), was in part attributable to central nervous system stimulants ingested by combatants precisely to enhance their fighting capacity.

We have been able to confirm little about this officer and virtually nothing about his history prior to entering the Navy; but we are nonetheless struck by certain similarities between Squire's description and the portrait of the neurogenic risk-taker drawn by Silver, Yudofsky & Hales (1987), right down to the biochemical lubrication of the disposition to take risks. Here, surely, we have mutual reinforcement in risk-taking behaviors on the part of the pilot, who alternately risks his life in combat and risks his career through little-disguised contempt for his superiors. Nor is there any serious question as to why Squire found Mike an attractive behavioral model.

Mike's tour, and his enlistment, ended about three months before Squire's. The two had already planned to return to the West Coast city which had been Mike's home and there to pursue auto theft as a career. Mike had engaged in such activity on a part-time basis while in high school and college and, after training and experience as a Navy pilot, had perfected a variety of skills required to coax an engine into life in the absence of an ignition key; Mike also averred that he still had many contacts with operators of "chop shops" and dealers in stolen autos and auto parts. Squire had little such experience, but he had amply demonstrated his mechanical aptitude while on tour; moreover, he had become highly skilled in electronic communication devices, and these figured prominently into Mike's planning.

The two partners planned to devote the proceeds from these activities to the pursuit of a luxuriant lifestyle, itself lubricated with plentiful supplies of central nervous system stimulants. That such plans were made while the two were actively Dioxin-toxic is surely congruent with Stoudemire's (1987) description of the "pseudopsychopathic" variety of organic personality disorder. That they were made aboard a military ship in the territorial waters of a foreign nation by American servicemen who had been rendered neurologically toxic as a direct result of their pursuit of their nation's objectives simply boggles the mind.

In the event, the reality proved more satisfying than the planning. Mike and Squire found, within six months or so, that they needed three additional members in their firm; these they recruited from among their former shipmates. In Squire's account, which may romanticize the past, the group was able to acquire up to eight to ten automobiles per day, typically ordered to specification (a maroon Audi, a gold Mark IV, and the like). In the main, the vehicles were "ordered" by "chop shop" operators — who planned to cannibalize them for parts, rather than to re-sell the entire unit.

However exaggerated the figure may be, what is certain is that, after three and a half years of successful operation and on an occasion on which Squire's electronic communication network had failed them, Squire, Mike, and their confreres were arrested and charged with 60 counts of auto theft.

Mike was nothing if not meticulous; thus, he had kept extra-ordinarily accurate records of all his business transactions. Since these were highly congruent with the records of the organizations to which the group had sold the stolen vehicles, there seemed little point in denial. Accordingly, Squire pled guilty, and, in a plea-bargain predicated to some large extent on the fact that he had no prior criminal convictions in any state as an adult, he was given a relatively light sentence, of three to five years.

In light of the legislative and administrative regulations governing parole in the state in which he was sentenced, we might have expected Squire to serve only a year, or roughly 33% of the minimum sentence that had been handed down. But that outcome would have required some degree of cooperation of his part, or at least a willingness to hold his impulsive hostility in check; instead, disciplinary infractions and altercations while in prison extended his stay by something over a year beyond his first parole eligibility, with the result that he actually served some 26 months of this sentence.

An attempt to diversify leads to Federal prison

Upon parole, Squire lost little time in absconding from the jurisdiction of that state and its parole officers. Gathering what valuables he could and exchanging them for drugs and cash, he set off cross-country in a rather vague plan to return to the northeast.

Since he had by now perfected the skills of auto theft, it seemed a simple enough matter to steal a car in one city, drive it some 150 to 200 miles or so, abandon it, steal another, repeat the process — the while, selling whatever of value had been left it the vehicle by its owner (camera, portable radio, briefcase, etc.) for cash as he traveled.

Thus it came to pass that, on a Saturday afternoon during May, Squire found himself in a public park in a small city in a southern state. He was, in point of fact, scouting a likely prospect for transportation — when, miracle of miracles, there came into view an unattended armored truck. Never in his wildest dreams had Squire even conceived such a possibility.

Years later, he recounts jumbled thoughts about Southerners and hick towns and the like when he contemplates stumbling upon that armored truck. Squire recollects that he had the vehicle hot-wired and moving within 90 seconds. Later events demonstrated that the driver and guard were no more than 200 feet away, in a coffee shop, and that one caught a glimpse of Squire sufficient to provide a reasonable description.

Since an armored truck is relatively more identifiable even than a maroon Audi, Squire determined to abandon the vehicle at the earliest opportunity; therefore, he bore south, crossed the boundary between one state and another, and headed directly into the Gulf of Mexico, along the way stuffing his duffel bag with bundles of dollars. In his account, within 45 minutes of first spotting the truck, the vehicle was submerged in the Gulf along with about $500,000 in cash, while he, his duffel bag, and another 200,000 U.S. dollars were hitch-hiking eastward.

Crime specialization rather than graduation from one sort of offense to another is likely characteristic of the offender who successfully eludes apprehension. Squire had specialized in auto theft and had been successful for a reasonably long period. He probably should have left armored trucks alone, for he had no notion of the operations of the banking industry, of serial number registration, and the like; nor had he considered that, because of various contingencies like propinquity to the border between one state and another, the armored truck that presented itself as a powerful stimulus determinant might itself be engaged in interstate transportation of bank funds — and that, therefore, its theft might represent a Federal offense, no less than transporting across state lines a stolen vehicle of any sort.

Only 23 days elapsed between the theft and Squire's apprehension by Federal officials. When arrested, he had with him nearly $185,000 of the $200,000 he had taken. The balance had been used to purchase an automobile and clothes and for incidental expenses; every dollar he had spent had become a signpost pointing to his whereabouts. Once again, Squire entered a guilty plea; but, because he now had a prior adult conviction, his sentence was not so lenient. It was to be served in a Federal penitentiary.

Re-traumatization potentiates disposition toward violence

It is beyond the scope of this volume to delve in detail into the ethos of prison life. Instead, the reader is referred to the comprehensive work of Toch & Adams (1989) and of Wright (1991). For our purposes, it will suffice to observe that virtually each prison has its rites of initiation.

And, in common with many other institutions and despite the best efforts of prison staff, the Ritual of 'Hood was in full flower when Squire arrived at the penitentiary to which he was assigned. The Ritual of 'Hood is a ceremony in which a new inmate is "robbed of his manhood" through anal rape. In some institutions, as in that in which Squire was incarcerated, those longer-term inmates who have established themselves in leadership positions may cast lots to determine which new inmate constitutes whose legitimate prey.

Thus it was that Samb drew Squire. As the court papers later verified, Samb (apparently, short for "Sambo") was a mid-40s, often-convicted dealer in drugs, weapons, and other contra-band. Among those of Squire's fellow inmates we were able to interview, there was general agreement that Samb had established himself within the institution in part because he was able to trade favors and merchandise on the inside for favors and merchandise on the outside, since he maintained active contact with his compatriots still at liberty.

Because of what follows, it is important to observe that, while Samb appeared phenotypically to be an American black, his accent immediately marked him as other than a native American. A native of a Francophone Caribbean island republic, Samb was certainly heterosexual by choice; but, like many in the Caribbean culture, he did not regard sexual relations between men in situations in which women were not available as constituting homosexuality. There was even some indication among some inmates that we interviewed that Samb indeed had interest in the Ritual of the 'Hood only to the extent that his participation was required in order to maintain his position of authority within the prison's inmate community.

Some three months after he had entered the institution, Squire became the object of the Ritual of the 'Hood. The locale was a common shower room on the inmate wing where he, but not Samb, resided. Samb was to be assisted by two other inmates over whom he exerted virtually dictatorial influence. These two held Squire, spread-eagle style, facing a wall while Samb prepared himself for penetration.

It happened, however, that a disturbance elsewhere on the wing brought a contingent of guards to the entrance. The attempt was quickly abandoned — and never repeated. Squire had neither cried out in terror during the attempt, nor did he report it to prison authorities — though, if he had, Samb would doubtless have responded with an ironclad alibi.

Nonetheless, word quickly spread of an attempt that had been foiled and of the fearlessness with which it had been greeted by its intended victim. Other inmates regarded Squire's apparently Stoic attitude toward the incident as the mark of one who fully understood and accepted the rite of initiation for what it was.

Word of this episode, combined with a distorted version of his background, stimulated in the inmate community a portrait of Squire as a genuine tough guy; when commingled with tales about his military experiences in Vietnam, Squire was regarded as an ace jungle fighter who had personally accounted for the demise of thousands of the enemy.

For his part, Squire returned to his work in the prison's electronics workshop and kept his counsel for the next six months. When we question him about his immediate response to this incident or ask him about his feelings during the attack itself, Squire will only tell us: *"I knew what I had to do."* It seems to us self-evident that Squire had re-lived during the attack the trauma he had experienced years earlier with Art. But even that self-evidence may lie only in our interpretation. What the record shows is that, six months after the attack just described, Samb was found dead in his cell in a very different wing of the prison. He had been strangled with a set of fine, very strong, razor-sharp wires which had sliced skin, flesh, and muscle. On the dead man's chest had been placed a sign that read *Good-bye, Gook*; it was signed *Squire*.

Construing lethal violence as an acceptable behavior

Even some years after our first acquaintance with Squire, we cannot be sure of whether he is being candid with us when he insists that the thought *I knew what I have to do* came to him whole and entire during the attempted rape. Squire affirms, and later events surely confirm, that the thought — even upon first thinking — conveyed that *I must kill Samb*, so that the behavioral goal was simultaneously construed and adopted, even though it was some time later that Squire construed the means by which to achieve that goal in specific steps.

How it came to be that Squire came to construe the killing of Samb as a desirable behavior is perfectly *post*-dictable. We have already observed that Squire's hostility, impulsivity, and explosiveness in late childhood and adolescence emerged in the aftermath of his removal from the family home following revelation of homosexual child abuse. Our psychoanalytic colleagues will comment that the principal dynamic at play was surely displacement of anger and aggression from Art (an inaccessible target) primarily to adult males in positions of authority, who were relatively more accessible as targets.

But it is also worth observing that the very act of removal weakened whatever inclination Squire may have had to embrace pro-social beliefs and values; and that, despite his many appearances in juvenile court, no strongly intrusive sanctions had been imposed on Squire. We should not be surprised to find, then, that the prospect or threat of punishment had little deterrent effect on his behavior, then or later; as we noted in our discussion of the apparent lack of deterrent effect associated with judicially-imposed sanctions, a lenient sanction has little effect on behavior. Moreover, intrusive sanction had merely been threatened but not imposed on Art, so that the expectation of impunity had been elicited early and was subsequently reinforced by Squire's own experiences in juvenile court. Finally, his single adult conviction for auto theft had resulted in a relatively lenient sentence. If one of the characteristics of the psychopathic personality is an absence of fear of punishment, Squire's case surely illustrates the social learning processes that result in such a condition.

But Art was by no means Squire's only behavioral model for the acceptability of violent behavior. He was succeeded, first, by a wide array of foster-siblings in the succession of homes in which Squire was placed and, second, by the heroic figure of Mike.

We have suggested something of the hero worship in which Squire held Mike and of Mike's reputation as an obstreperous but fearless combat pilot. Our psychoanalytic colleagues may see in this hero worship something like a latent homosexual attachment, as to an older brother — and perhaps reminiscent of an attachment to Art, through the process they would label as "identification with the aggressor." We would not be disposed to quarrel overlong, but we would point out that, if there was homosexual content to the attachment, it remained quite latent.

A legacy from Art and from "America's racist war"

According to Squire, Mike flew a minimum of two combat missions daily in a fighter-bomber; each of those missions presumably resulted in death for the enemy. In light of Squire's message on Samb's body, it is worth observing that, in Vietnam, the enemy was indeed a citizen of a former French colony that has been Francophone for most of its existence — and that the enemy was routinely referred to as "Gook."

It is also worth observing that, so far as we know, criminal violence had played little part in Mike's life before the war or since. Many journalistic accounts of the Vietnam war, however, have detailed the extent to which American military leadership fostered the view of the north Vietnamese as an inferior people, expressed in the slogan: "The only good Gook is a dead Gook." There was, in that process, a peculiar twist to familiar themes of racism; for, in this case, it was not racial difference but nationality purely and simply on which the judgment of superiority vs. inferiority was to pivot — that is, since a message that merely portrayed whites as superior to non-whites might have yielded disturbances between the races within the American military, it was necessary to transmit a message that combined Americans of different races into a phenomenological *us* perceived as superior to *them*. That certainly is racism in a new key. That depiction represented an addition to the traditional military effort to personalize or, as White (1995) has it, to "demonize," the enemy by invariably referring to the enemy as *he,* never as *them.*

Both before and after the sitting President told the citizenry that the Gulf War against Iraq had freed us of our "Vietnam complex," many commentators have referred to the misadventure in Vietnam as America's most racist war, surpassed perhaps only by the organized and successful effort to drive Native Americans from the plains and the southwest during the 19th century. In the standard formulation, Vietnam constituted a war in which white people conscripted Black people to kill yellow people, while providing all manner of deferments from the draft for young white men. Perhaps no single episode encapsulates the volatile American attitude toward Vietnam and its people than the My Lai massacre.

In 1968 in the remote village of My Lai in South Vietnam, William Calley, a (white) junior officer in the U.S. Army, directed and participated in the wholesale massacre of non-combatant women and children. Following a substantial public outcry engendered by press coverage during television's first "live" war, Calley was later court-martialed and convicted — an outcome that considerably troubled many then serving in the military as well as some large segment of U.S. citizens who failed to discriminate between what is the "legitimate" killing of an armed enemy and what is an unjustified atrocity perpetrated on a non-combatant. In a remarkable analysis before the war ended entitled "It Never Happened — and Besides, They Deserved It," Edward Opton (1971, 52-56), a research psychologist at the Wright Institute in Berkeley, reconstructed the psychological forces that had led to the construing of mass lethal violence as normative and/or to be applauded:

> The My Lai massacre was only a minor step beyond the standard, official, routine United States policy in Viet Nam. This official policy is to obliterate not just whole villages but whole districts and virtually whole provinces . . . These small-scale war crimes have become so common that our reporters seldom report them; they are no longer news. They have become routine to many of our soldiers [who] have developed the classical psychological methods of justifying what they see happening. They come to think of the Vietnamese not as humans like themselves or even, as the Army indictment for the My Lai massacre put it, as "Oriental human beings," but as something less than human. It is only a small further step to the conclusion that "the only good dink is a dead dink" . . . The furor over the My Lai massacre must have seemed grimly illogical to the troops in the field . . The best way to kill civilians is with bombs, rockets, artillery shells, and napalm. Those who kill women and children in these ways are called heroes. How is it that to kill women and children at less than 500 paces is an atrocity, but at more than 500 paces an act of heroism?

Racism of the traditional sort was apparently a problem neither for Mike nor for Squire; two of the three former ship-mates they invited to become members of their auto theft "firm" were black Americans themselves. Whether these two new recruits shared Squire's notions about Gooks is not known. Our psychoanalytic colleagues may be interested to know that Art's military decorations emanated from the campaign in the Pacific during World War II, so that the enemy were the Japanese. To the extent that Squire admits to a negative view of Asians which pre-existed his entrance into the Navy, there may be an element that our colleagues will surely term "identification with the aggressor" that rendered Squire rather fertile ground for racism in a new key.

Elements in the interactive blend

So: Let us start with that remote anti-Asian seedbed. Blend in the effects of an active anti-Gook campaign undertaken by the American military as personally filtered through Squire's relationship with Mike. Flavor with long-standing hostility and impulsivity. Stir in a disregard of consequence, born of an expectation of impunity itself resting on the observation that intrusive sanctions are rarely applied — whether to Squire or to Art.

Add, finally and just before the cauldron overflows, what may be the ultimate stimulus determinant that is most likely to elicit an extreme response — an attempt by a Francophone Gook to do to Squire by force what Art had done so often in the past by cajolery. That Squire then construes lethal violence as an acceptable, desirable behavior is not surprising; nor is it surprising that, for him, the thought seems to spring whole and entire — surely, it had been germinating long enough.

But the conviction that Samb must die is quite different from planning *how* he is to die. While Squire is willing enough to discuss with us how he fashioned the garrote he used from parts readily available to him in the prison's electronic workshop (where he repaired a variety of radio and video transmitting devices), he has been no more forthcoming with us about how he traveled from his cell to Samb's in another wing (and back) than he was during the subsequent investigation or at court.

Almost certainly, the subornation of prison staff was involved; and we certainly admire Squire's unwillingness to involve others in criminal charges. Further, in consequence of extensive prison "grapevines," it is difficult for us to believe that other inmates did not know of Squire's plans; but we are unlikely ever to have the answers to these questions. They are important to us only to the extent that they would establish (or disconfirm) that a large segment of the prison community had in fact acquiesced to violence — that is to say, agreed to a "character contest" — as an acceptable way of resolving the long-standing grievance Squire held toward Samb.

Proud confession, resulting sentence

Because Squire had in essence confessed to the slaying of Samb in the message he placed on the latter's chest, there was little question of entering any plea but "guilty." During the sentencing process, Squire's attorney (from the Office of the Federal Public Defender) adduced evidence of the widespread knowledge within the prison that Samb had attempted to perpetrate the Ritual of the 'Hood on Squire and of Squire's service during the Vietnam war, with a small mention of Dioxin exposure. The sentence was 18 years, on a charge reduced to manslaughter, to be served subsequently to Squire's then-current sentence for theft of the armored truck.

In our interview years after these events, we asked the attorney why she did not present as an argument the details of Squire's background, his removal from the home, and the like; by then, professional knowledge of the "new" psychiatric disease called "post-traumatic stress disorder" had burgeoned, and it was widely believed to be the case that the re-living of one component of a trauma was likely to re-instill whatever feelings the patient had experienced during the original trauma. Thus, if Squire had experienced rage as a child victimized by Art, it is likely that he experienced rage during the attempt by Samb; the strength of the rage had likely increased exponentially.

Perhaps well and true, replied the attorney, but still *explanatory* and not *exculpatory;* after all, six months had elapsed between the attempt on Squire and Samb's killing, and that is a very long time for rage to continue unabated.

Moreover, she said, in a prison population the fact of child abuse, however brutal and demeaning, is not in the least unusual — a clinical observation later confirmed empirically by Wright (1991).

Squire's MMPI profile and the post-diction of violence

During the course of our many contacts with Squire, we became interested in pursuing a clinical "hunch" of our own. Between the time of Samb's murder and our work with Squire, the Megargee-Bohn Typology Study had been published and cross-validated, as detailed in Chapter 5. Though the typology was not yet in use in the facility in which Squire was confined, we wanted to know to which of the Megargee-Bohn offender groups Squire might be assigned on an actuarial basis alone — and whether that assignment comported with his actual offense record. Accordingly, Squire agreed to complete the MMPI. Both our clinical sorting and computerized actuarial sorting, by means of the technologically sophisticated program called the Weathers Report (discussed in Chapter 5), indicated that the best "fit" occurs between Squire's profile and that of Group Charlie in the Megargee-Bohn Typology. Both sets of scores are reported graphically on the next page.

A narrative "interpretation" accompanies the Weathers Report exercise in determining best fit between profiles. The narrative merely reports statements that have been found to be empirically associated with membership in the group of best fit; it is clear that the narration deals with what *has been*, and thus quite obviously *post*-dicts rather than *pre*dicts — and does so entirely on an actuarial basis. For Squire, the actuarially-based narrative generated by computer reads, in part:

> The client is a member of Group Charley with a fit of high accuracy . . . This is a bitter, hostile, antisocial person who is sensitive to perceived insults and lashes out readily. Acting-out and aggressive behavior is common. This individual has some proclivity for crimes against persons, fraud, and possession of contraband other than drugs. This person is likely to have come from a stressful, deviant, inadequate family of origin. Discipline is likely to have been inadequate, possibly because of lack of contact with the father, and as a result, [persons in this group] tend to be estranged from their family. A paranoid, suspicious resentment haunts life . . . There is an antagonistic, aggressive style that tends to alienate others. There tends to be an extensive criminal history . . . There is usually substantial authority conflict [and] significant emotional difficulties as well as social constriction, poor sociability, [which may] result in difficulty adapting to incarceration.
>
> This is a hostile loner who is socially withdrawn and aggressive. There is considerable inner turmoil with high levels of state and trait anxiety, poor adjustment, deviant value system . . . Other people are seen as potential threats, instead of as avenues for emotional support. Relationships with others tend to be acrimonious and exploitive . . . This individual has not been able to either internalize or live by ordinary cultural values . . . Institutional infractions tend to involve violence. [Prisoners in this group] respond to hostility when provoked, but do not actively seek out trouble . . . Institutional treatment is unlikely to have any significant impact on this individual.

In Chapter 5, we confessed our commitment to actuarial rather than purely clinical methods of assessment, denominating that commitment not merely a matter of personal preference but instead a conviction that flows from rigorous consideration of the relevant evidence (Dawes, Faust & Meehl, 1989). Even so, the congruence between the actuarially-generated description here quoted and the factual record of Squire's psychosocial and offense history is truly remarkable.

Postscript: Expectation of impunity yields another victim of incest

The reader may wonder how it came to pass that we became familiar with Squire and his story. In truth, the route was circuitous, for we began with Karen.

In 1963, Squire had been out of the family home for some time; he was a teen-ager and already well on his way to perfecting hostile, impulsive, aggressive behavior as a leading feature of his behavioral repertoire. Art and Kay were still reasonably young; they decided to have another child, whom they named Karen.

In 1977, Squire had been in and out of the Navy, in and out of the West Coast prison, and convicted of manslaughter in a Federal prison; Karen was 14. It was in that year that the state's child welfare agency initiated a new campaign on child

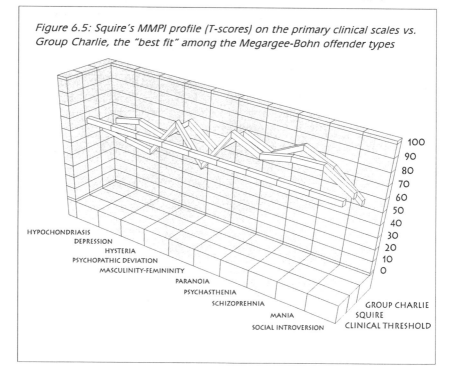

Figure 6.5: Squire's MMPI profile (T-scores) on the primary clinical scales vs. Group Charlie, the "best fit" among the Megargee-Bohn offender types

sexual abuse. History had repeated itself. Workers for the agency called upon us to evaluate Karen. It was in delving into her father's criminal history that we learned that she had a half-brother who had been similarly victimized; Karen knew nothing of Squire — not even of his existence; Kay had long since lost contact with him, so she knew nothing of his current incarceration for manslaughter.

Art pled guilty and was convicted, as he had anticipated — but, on this occasion, because of the prior conviction, he was sentenced to an indeterminate 15-year sentence, to be served in his state's special prison for repetitive sex offenders. Art believed the sentence harsh and engaged repeated appeals, all of which were denied; his belief was certainly justified on the basis of his earlier experience, which had led him to expect impunity.

With Art's departure for prison, Kay became more and more morose. She intensified those feelings with alcohol. Shortly, she began openly to blame Karen for the loss of Art. For her part, Karen entered a psychiatric hospital some months after Art's incarceration and Kay's embrace of alcohol; there have been seven subsequent admissions.

Neither Art, nor Kay, nor the sentencing judge, nor the probation officer who prepared the recommendation concerning disposition, nor the social worker for the child welfare agency to whom Karen reported her victimization, seem in the least concerned or even curious about Squire — and even less, about a "Gook" who was murdered in his prison cell.

NEUROPATHOLOGY, CULPABILITY, AND CORRECTIONAL REHABILITATION

Though the evidence of a statistical association (technically, no more than a correlative association) between brain morphological and/or neurochemical anomalies and violent criminal behavior is relatively strong, the state of the evidence does not yet permit determination of precedent and antecedent (much less, of "cause and effect") relationships. But the scientific picture on the neurogenesis — as distinct from the biogenesis, at least in the sense of inherited constitutional predispositions, as Herrnstein (1990) appears to understand the term — of violence is currently richly persuasive, though not yet definitive. Given what is currently either known or hypothesized about brain and neurochemical anomalies thought to "control" impulsivity and aggression, and in light of evidence about the incidence of anomalies in brain and neurochemical functioning among violent offenders, it may well be the case that research in the neruosciences will, in the relatively short term, demonstrate conclusively that criminally aggressive behavior is "triggered" by very primitive neurophysiological or neurochemical processes over which the individual can be expected to exert little *volitional* control.

Neuropathology and the M'Naghten Standard

Some rather silly academic debates about antecedent and consequent conditions might then be expected — concerning whether, for example, such personality traits as are measurable through psychometric or clinical instruments result from disordered neuropsychological processes or whether such traits (presumably acquired as the remnants of disordered developmental or learning processes) dictate disordered neuropsychological processes. But the more salient debates will concern the implications of revolutionized understandings of the genesis of violent behavior that is formally criminal for societal and legislative notions of culpability, as Wilson & Herrnstein (1985, 504-505) have somewhat satirically foreseen:

> If society should not punish acts that science has shown to have been caused by antecedent conditions, then every advance in knowledge about why people behave as they do may shrink the scope of criminal law. If, for example, it is shown that [violent] offenders suffer from abnormal hormones combined with certain atypical relations with their parents, then, by the existing standards of responsibility, why should their attorneys not demand acquittal on grounds of bad hormones combined with a particular family history?

Quite clearly, advances in knowledge about the neurogenesis of violence will inevitably "shrink the scope of criminal law" — indeed, as effectively as the scope of the law underwent "shrinkage" a century and a half ago when then-current scientific knowledge led to the initial formulation of the M'Naghten Standard in 1843, when the hapless Daniel M'Naghten, a disappointed seeker of a political appointment in a government bureau, claimed to have received a message from God instructing him to kill the Prime Minister. M'Naghten's shot went wide of its mark but struck and killed the Prime Minister's secretary. That event occurred nearly 45 years after Hadfield (whom we met in Chapter 2) had been found non-culpable of his attempt to assassinate George III in consequence of hard evidence of neuropathology, not a psychotic belief in personal communication with the divine, or at least not a psychotic belief in communication with the Almighty that is posited as *independent of* the imperatives of neuropathology.

In the late 20th century, we can barely comprehend the *zeitgeist* that must have prevailed at the time of M'Naghten's trial to yield the situation in which M'Naghten rather than Hadfield should have become precedental as the basis for exculpation throughout the English-speaking nations of the world.

If one is given to analogical rumination, one might conclude that Hadfield is to M'Naghten as (approximately) science is to mythology. Alternately, that M'Naghten and not Hadfield became precedental is perhaps no more surprising than that Freud forsook a promising career in neurology to invent the murky, mystic, mythical world of id, ego, superego. And, if we speculate even further, we might wonder whether — had the powerful investigative techniques of the neurosciences of the last half of the twentieth century been available in 19th century Vienna — Freud might never have experienced an intellectually compelling need for such invention.

Directionality and culpability

Directionality (or determination of "cause" vs. "effect") may not be pertinent in fixing culpability for a particular offense, unless it be the case that the putatively "triggering" brain or neurochemical anomaly can be demonstrated to have arisen *consequent* to that offense.

Consider a situation, for example, in which earlier, documented episodes of criminal violence have *resulted* in neuropsychological anomalies of such character that violent aggressivity is virtually beyond the volitional control of the individual, and in which there is also documented evidence that the individual in question was free of such anomalies prior to those earlier episodes. In an *instant* case of criminal violence subsequent to the onset of such anomalies, what degree of culpability should attach to that individual? In that situation, whether the earlier episodes of violent behavior that "caused" those anomalies themselves constituted "willful misconduct" may be quite irrelevant.

Though a formal diagnosis of "organic psychosis" as the perpetuation of brain injury (as in Larry's case) or of morphologic or neurochemical disorder would seem to fit within legislatively established criteria for nonculpability, most current formulations of the criteria for culpability and exculpation as reflected in the M'Naghten Standard and its variants are not readily applicable to cases in which criminal behavior is triggered by brain or neurochemical dysfunction.

We may ultimately come to regret that M'Naghten, and not Hadfield, provided the overarching guidelines. In particular, in the light of evidence that links, even correlatively, psychopathy with neurophysiological and neurochemical dysfunction, the endorsement by the American Psychiatric Association (1984, 17) of the American Law Institute's exclusion of psychopathic deviation as an acceptable basis for a plea of nonculpability — viz., that "the terms 'mental disease or defect' do not include an abnormality manifested only by repeated antisocial conduct" — may need substantial discerning reconsideration.

Correctional rehabilitation and management of neurogenic violence

However engaging at the conceptual level, the question of directionality is significant primarily to a theory of criminogenesis. At the practical level of correctional management, the mere fact that propensities for violent behavior co-exist with brain dysfunctions is the salient issue, whatever the direction of the relationship. If reconsideration of culpability in the light of the accumulating evidence on the neurogenesis of violence maintains the current narrow grounds for exculpation, responsibility for the management of neurogenically violent offenders will remain within the province of correctional institutions. If such reconsideration results in a broadening of the grounds for exculpation, responsibility for the management of offenders whose criminal violence has been triggered neurogenically is likely to be transferred from the province of correctional institutions to that of the mental hospitals. Hence, whatever the result of the inevitable conceptual debates as the evidence for the neurogenesis of criminal violence accumulates, at the practical level the matter of methods of control remains at issue.

Bound as they are to traditional modes of (largely verbally mediated) psychotherapy, neither set of institutions seems presently well prepared to accommodate the major paradigm shift that has yielded "new methods for diagnosing psychiatric disorders, clarifying their pathophysiology, and developing more specific and effective therapies," of which Coyle (1988) has spoken. If neurogenic criminally violent behavior is to be effectively managed, it seems clear that responsive methods of management must address such behavior at its molar roots, utilizing precisely those "specific and effective" methods that have emerged from the explosion in neuroscientific knowledge.

Neurosurgery in neurogenic aggression

As an illustration, consider a case of "quite savage acts of aggression" managed neither in a correctional facility nor a psychiatric hospital but rather at the Kemsley Unit of St. Andrew's Hospital, Northampton, England, a medical installation for the rehabilitation of head trauma. The methods employed correspond neither to those standard in correctional facilities (i.e., externally applied behavior control) nor to those standard in mental hospitals (i.e., psychotropic medication combined with supportive psychotherapy). Instead, following the failure of a regimen consisting of pharmacotherapy and behavior therapy, effective management required application of advanced neurosurgery, as described by Wood (1987, 72):

> [An] aggressive behavior pattern . . . occurred in a 19-year-old patient who had sustained a severe head injury 28 months earlier. He had no serious physical sequelae. From admission, the patient was known to have an abnormal EEG, suggesting that an electrical anomaly was responsible for his unprovoked, volatile outbursts which included quite savage acts of aggression.
>
> This [condition] was treated from admission by a combination of carbamazepine [a medication intended for the relief of epileptic seizures, usually marketed under the trade name Tegretol] and behaviour management. There was, however, only a temporary reduction in aggressive behaviour and, instead of continuing to improve, his behaviour deteriorated.
>
> It was then noticed that the patient had intermittent nasal discharge of cerebro-spinal fluid (CSF). Neurological investigations showed that this intermittent CSF discharge was due to increases in intra-cranial pressure, forcing CSF through a tear in the dura [the fibrous membrane covering the brain and spinal cord]. The build-up of

pressure within the skull probably precipitated an electrical discharge in the limbic system, profoundly affecting behaviour. The patient was transferred back to a neuro-surgical unit long enough for a ventriculo-peritoneal shunt to be inserted. The frequency of aggression before and after the shunt operation to reduce intra- cranial pressure [was] very different . . . confirming that neurological, not psychological, factors were responsible for the aggressive behavior.

Because the surgery performed in this case remediated a medically-verified neurological impairment (itself the result of accidental injury), the regimen followed differs fundamentally from the "serious and indiscriminate destruction of brain tissue [that] would render almost any offender so incapacitated as to be unable to think or act with sufficient efficiency to engage in . . . criminal behavior" vilified by Halleck (1987, 175) as ethically unacceptable in the treatment of offenders.

Cognitive rehabilitation and impulse control

Though less dramatically, a variety of techniques for cognitive rehabilitation, often based on computerization and programmed learning, have been developed by neuropsychologists in treatment facilities for patients with head injury (or, less often, those who are suffering the effects of prolonged biochemical insult to the brain through the use of alcohol or virulently psychotomimetic substances) in medical installations devoted to brain injury rehabilitation (Franzen & Sullivan, 1987; Yohman, Schaeffer & Parsons, 1988). Not to be confused with cognitive-behavior therapy, cognitive rehabilitation techniques constitute a set of sophisti-cated methods for "teaching" patients to compensate for cognitive functions which have been impaired as a consequence of injury to brain tissue "using the learning theory concepts of componential learning, approximation, and rein-forcement for success" (Franzen & Sullivan, 1987, 443).

Cognitive rehabilitation regimens have been successful in addressing deficits in memory and problem-solving capacity but are also employable to retrain (or train) patients with impairments in impulse control, by "teaching" patients to increase their attention span, inhibit urges to behave, foresee consequences, and consider alternatives. In the aggregate, these techniques derive from a knowledge base in clinical neuropsychology rooted in the psychology of learning rather from the armamentarium of clinical psychotherapy (Miller, 1991; Weinstein, 1994).

The following case, treated at the Robert Wood Johnson Lifestyle Institute in New Jersey, an installation specializing in rehabilitation medicine, illustrates the application of these techniques to problems in impulse control (Cicerone & Wood, 1987, 111-112):

The client is a 20 year old right-handed man who had sustained a closed head injury in a motor vehicle accident four years earlier. Computed tomography performed shortly after his hospital admission showed multiple contusions, right cerebral edema with right to left midline shift, and a right frontal intracerebral hematoma . . . There was continued improvement over the next three months . . . More recently, the family became concerned over his marked impulsivity and interpersonal difficulties. He frequently interrupted conversations with other family members and friends, his own speech became expansive and circumstantial, and it often appeared as if "he doesn't think before he does something." Initial neuropsychological evaluation was conducted four years after his injury . . . Neuropsychological evaluations were most notable for marked impaired of planning ability and difficulty evaluating results of his own actions [and] disturbances of "higher executive functions" (e.g., initiation, planning, and self-regulation) . . required him to verbalize a plan before and during execution of the training task and then to gradually fade overt verbalization.

The training task was a modified version of the "Tower of London," which requires the subject to move three different color beads onto three different sized pegs from a specified starting position in a restricted number of moves . . . The self-instructional training was conducted in three stages. Throughout the course of training, the client received general instructions about various aspect of planning and problem solving, e.g., problem formulation, goal definition, subgoal identification, consideration of alternatives, and self-evaluation of results . . treatment effects to everyday behavior . . . there was an implicit demand for self-monitoring built into the training procedure. Replication of real-life examples during treatment allowed the client to compare his behavior in those situations with the solution he arrived at using the treatment strategy. He could also evaluate any discrepancy between his actual and planned solutions.

A variety of psychometric measures demonstrated not only significant im-provement in the *in vitro* tasks at hand but generalization of effect to a wide array of "real life" situations, with a "systematic reduction and eventual cessation in target behaviors" during the course of training and during a follow-up period.

Non-therapeutic use of mood-altering substances

On the basis of their own research and that of others on the neurochemistry of criminal violence, Virkkunen, Nuutila, Goodwin & Linnoila (1987, 245-246) hold that even the present state of knowledge yields important implications for the pharmacological management of violent offenders:

[Deficiencies in a metabolite of monoamine oxidase are] associated with aggression dyscontrol by being conducive of a heightened aggressive drive . . . more specifically with a deficiency of impulse control and because of this with dyscontrol of intraper-sonal and interpersonal aggression . . . Aggressivity and impulse control problems are very closely related, especially in violent offenders . . . In controlled clinical studies, both tryptophan and lithium carbonate have been found to be effective in reducing violent acts by habitually impulsive and violent offenders, and by adolescents with undersocialized aggressive conduct disorders characterized by severe aggressiveness and explosive impulsivity . . . Thus, it seems that lithium carbonate may rather specifically ameliorate impulse control problems.

The implications might seem to flow in the direction of the administration of psychotropic medication in those settings charged with the management of neurogenically violent offenders. But the right of patients (even involuntarily committed patients) to refuse medication for the treatment of mental illness, deriving from "the basic assumption in our society that all persons have the right to control intrusions on their bodies" (Appelbaum, 1988, 413), has now been firmly established (Brooks, 1986; Rodenhauser, 1984). In *Large v. Superior Court* (714 P.2D 399, Arizona, 1986) and *People v. Delgado* (A042371, First Appellate District, California, 1989), state courts had specifically extended that right to prisoners as well. Moreover, it is a reasonable speculation that some portion of neurogenically violent offenders would regard their disorders as ego-syntonic and thus perceive themselves as scarcely in need of pharmacotherapeutic treatment for a condition they do not perceive as an abnormality.

However, in a 1990 decision (*Washington v. Harper*, 88-599), the scope of which is really quite limited but would seem to include neurogenically violent offenders, the U.S. Supreme Court opened a "window" on the matter of involuntary administration of psychotropic medication to prisoners. The specific case concerned the acceptability under the Constitution of the procedures used in the State of Washington to determine whether psychoactive medication should be administered to an inmate against his or her will. Those procedures require the decision of a review board composed of a prison psychiatrist, a prison psychologist, and a correctional administrator to over-rule the inmate's declination; the inmate has the right to be represented by an "advisor," but not by an attorney [NOTE 4].

The key phrases in the Supreme Court's decision hold that the state is Constitutionally permitted (with emphases added) "to treat a prison inmate who has a serious mental illness with antipsychotic drugs against his will, *if the inmate is dangerous to himself or others.*" Since the Court has applied the "clear and imminent danger" test [NOTE 5], the scope of the decision appears limited to those situations in which an inmate presents an imminent threat of violence *within* the correctional setting.

That is a situation at some considerable conceptual and operational distance from the involuntary administration of medication to treat a disorder *on account of which* an inmate has become an inmate but which cannot reasonably be linked to the prospect of suicide or assault while in custody — as, for example, in the administration of hormone-suppressing pharmacologic agents to focused pedophiles confined judicially for treatment, but in an institution for adults, a class of victim toward whom such offenders have shown no prior violent disposition.

Even though the scope of *Washington v. Harper* would seem to preclude such aggressive pharmacotherapy as, for example, chemical castration by means of hormone-suppressing pharmacological agents in the rehabilitative treatment of sex offenders (Pallone, 1990-b, 85-86), the window has been opened for future litigation — perhaps, indeed, brought by sex offenders as plaintiffs who would prefer chemical castration (followed by release) to continued confinement for treatment that is nonpharmacotherapeutic.

There is every reason to believe, however, that neurogenically violent offenders in custody (and, more particularly, those for whom there is corroborative evidence, as from the MMPI, that mania and impulsivity are characteristic patterns of behavior) may fall within even the narrow scope of the *Harper* window.

Paradigm shift: New knowledge, new skills

The body of knowledge and skill marshaled either in the control of neurogenic violence by means of advanced neurosurgery or in the control of impulsivity through cognitive rehabilitation regimens are not commonly available in correctional facilities; nor, for that matter, is it likely that that knowledge and those skills will become commonly available in most public mental hospitals until the paradigm shift courses its predictably slow way through the mental health system. Whatever the mechanism and whatever the setting, the general direction is clear — viz., that techniques for the management of neurogenic propensities to violence should pivot on strategies for control that marshal the "nearly logarithmic" advances in neuropsychiatry, neurochemistry, and even neurosurgery of which Coyle (1988) has written. And, against the offender's right not to have his/her body intruded upon against his/her will, whether by involuntary psychotropic medication or by surgical implants into brain tissue, must be balanced, as Monahan (1981) suggested, "his next victim's right not to become his next victim."

AGGRESSIVE VIOLENCE AND RATIONAL CHOICE

In this chapter, we have offered a process psychology paradigm for aggressive criminal violence, incorporating its bio-psycho-social engines, along with portrayals of several interactive "blends" in which neuropsychological, personality, social learning, and stimulus determinants interact in such a way that an individual behaver construes violence as an acceptable, tolerable, or "normal" way to behave and the prospect for aggressive violence thus enters that individual's behavioral repertoire. In particular, we have stressed the interplay between neuropathology, family dysfunction, substance abuse, negative behavioral modeling in the family and community, and the reinforcing effect of long-distance vicarious modeling by means of entertainment media. We have proposed that interaction between an age-related "taste for risk," the self-selection of environments peopled by like-minded persons, the willingness to agree to violence in "character contests" to resolve interpersonal disputes yields a devastating portrayal of a set of "tinder-box" circumstances in which the question of which of two relatively willing participants emerges as the victim and which as the offender may turn on the luck of the draw.

In this chapter as in others, with the single exception of rapid-onset organic psychosis resulting for major brain damage, we have portrayed an orderly and by no means irrational or incomprehensible progression from neurogenic hyper-arousability toward aggressive criminal violence. From the perspective of the aggressor (even the organically-psychotic aggressor), his or her "choices" — whether to respond to the impulse to behave, whether to select those environ-ments in which impulsive behavior is tolerated, whether to participate in or avoid a character contest — represent "rational" decisions, experienced pheno-menologically as ego-syntonic, not as ego-alien. Indeed, the definition of self may inhere precisely in impulsivity, psychopathy, the taste for risk, and comfort in an environment in which one feels he or she "fits."

Yet there lingers a hint of dissonance after such an analysis; perhaps many of us would prefer an older tradition in the psychological analysis of criminal aggression that attributes "badness" to "madness." There is something troubling about the disjunction, something residually disturbing about the proposition that the cruel and deliberate aggression of one human being against another is *not* the product of what we can recognize as pathological psychological processes but instead the product of a predictable progression that leads to what the actor at least perceives as "rational choice."

Have we, perhaps, become so inured to "forgiving," to simply writing off, to exculpating in a very real sense, those acts of cruelty which are patently the product of disordered minds that some of us would much prefer it to be the case that all such acts of aggressive criminal violence be attributed to incapacitating mental disorder? And is that a way of saying that, among those of us who have been reasonably well socialized in concert with prevailing social norms and values, psychological deviance is more understandable — and, to that extent, more "acceptable" — than acts of aggressive violence that reflect that the aggressors themselves perceive as *rational choices*? Axiomatically, if not really by definition, the actions of a madman are unpredictable. Not so those of an actor following an orderly progression dictated by a dynamic calculus between intrapsychic and extra-psychic variables which begins with neurogenic hyper-arousability. Yet each step in that progression is discoverable and, once discov-ered, susceptible to control.

THE CHAPLAIN'S DILEMMA

In the small pantheon of intellectual giants in scientific psychology in the 20th century, alongside Cattell stands the late Burrhus Frederic (B.F.) Skinner. Nearly half a century ago, before the revolution in the neurosciences, at the very dawn of the emergence of neuropsychopharmacology, and before he could have antici-pated the laser beam, much less its prospective uses in neurosurgery, Skinner (1948) outlined his vision for Walden II, a "new world order" based on the principles of operant conditioning, in which each gives according to his or her ability and receives according to his or her need — and in which interpersonal aggression is unknown. In perhaps a prophetic scene in the novel, Skinner casts his protagonist (tellingly, a drop-out or flunk-out from a doctoral program in psychology) in conversation with a former professor of his, a philosopher named (with high ironic symbolism) Augustine Castle. The protagonist asks: "What would you do if I told you that we have a science of behavior that is capable of producing a well-ordered world, free from want, or hunger, or aggression?" Castle's response: "I think I would dump your 'science of behavior' into the ocean."

After Hans Eysenck published the first edition of *Crime and Personality* in 1964, objections were lodged from many quarters about the methods of "rehabilitation" he proposed for aggressive offenders, pivoting largely on aversive behavior therapy and pharmacological control of behavior; the neurosciences had not yet undergone that knowledge explosion that unleashes the prospect of neurosurgery, intravenous neruopharmacology, and even lithiumizing the water supply. Among Eysenck's critics, none was more eloquent than novelist Anthony Burgess, whose *A Clockwork Orange* tells the story of Alex, a delinquent 15-year-old who, within the space of a thrill-seeking few days abetted to be sure by central nervous system stimulants, beats an old man senseless, leads the gang rape of a suburban housewife and two 11-year-old girls, and murders an old woman. Imprisoned, Alex is subjected to correctional rehabilitation methods that render him *incapable* of aggressive criminal behavior. But the result much troubles the prison chaplain: "What does God want? Does God want *goodness* or the *choice of goodness*? Is the man who *chooses the bad* perhaps in some way better than the man who *has the good imposed upon him*?" Skinner and Burgess wrote their novels before the vehicles through which to "impose the good" came to encompass adding lithium to drinking water, correcting naturally-occurring dysfunctions in brain biochemistry or those induced through injury by means of pharmacology, or adapting laser beams to psychosurgery. Even so, there seems little doubt about how Professor Castle would respond to the chaplain's question.

By the time he published the second edition, Eysenck (1977, 182) felt compelled to answer those critics who had decried the loss of personal freedom on the part of the offenders so treated:

> I have had many requests from prisoners (who had nothing whatever to gain by making such requests) for radical treatment of what they recognized as impulses driving them in directions in which they did not want to go. There is a war going on within the prisoner, and his better self is asking for help. *That is the ethical basis of the methods here suggested.*

Daniel Koshland, distinguished editor of the journal of the American Association for the Advancement of Science, may or may not know Skinner's Professor Castle or Burgess' prison chaplain. But he knows the brain and its relationship to criminal violence (1992):

There is no simple dividing line between sane crime and insane crime . . . The brain is an organ, and like other organs — the heart, the lungs, the liver — has an internal biochemistry that can break down. Because of the special role of the brain, there are those who want to believe that it can only be affected by the environment; they refuse to face the fact that the brain, like other organs, while functioning effectively in most areas, may have one part go awry and cause major malfunction. If we treat the brain as another organ, then the fact that an elephant or a human goes berserk is as easy to comprehend and as difficult to unravel as cystic fibrosis, tuberculosis, or AIDS. Sometimes the damage to the organ will be hereditary and sometimes environmental, but it is not mysterious that a large fraction of the organ can behave perfectly correctly while a small section has totally abnormal qualities.

According to *Scientific American* writer Wayt Gibbs (1995, 101), leading neuropsychiatrist Stuart Yudofsky, whose work we have encountered many times in this volume, now holds that, within the near term, "we're going to be able to diagnose many people who are *biologically brain-prone to violence*," creating conditions that yield "the opportunity to prevent tragedies" by screening "people at high risk" for aggressive criminal offending. Quite without reference to the paradigm lag that typically impedes communication between behavioral science disciplines, Gibbs also recounts the responses of some criminologists and sociologists to Yudofsky's statement, which range from skepticism that the state of the neurosciences is nearly so advanced to derision predicated on a far greater (and perhaps commendable) humanitarian concern for the false positive than for the false negative that would do Professor Castle and Burgess' chaplain proud.

In the late 18th century, the Quakers of Pennsylvania replaced the prison (a place where malefactors were confined so that they could be incapacitated and punished) by inventing the "penitentiary" as a place where malefactors were to be confined so that they could perform penance and thus expiate wrong-doing. That invention is eminently consistent with the belief in communication with the Almighty on which the M'Naghten standard pivots and is clearly comprehensible to Professor Castle and to Burgess' chaplain. Hadfield leads elsewhere.

NOTES

1. Indeed, a film such as *High Noon* remains memorable 40 years after its release precisely because it depicts the process through which one member of the dyad in a character contest of long standing refuses to further engage in a recurrently choreographed dare because he has now encumbered himself with the adult social responsibility of marriage; nor is it accidental that the new wife is a mail-order bride from a relatively more lawfully ordered city of the East. It is not difficult to see in such a process a graduation from the mores of a violent subculture to embrace those of the larger, less violent society — or perhaps both the very "burn out" in violent behavior empirically identified by Hare, McPherson & Forth (1988) and one of the developmental pivots therefor.

2. We understand that this sentiment comes perilously close to "blaming the victim," an activity which we have elsewhere (Pallone, 1990), with particular focus on sexual

assault, decried as an "international pastime." A substantial body of research evidence of international dimensions has demonstrated a generalized tendency for *women* cast in the role of third-party observers to display greater sympathy for, and to attribute less blame toward, the female victim, and conversely for men to display less sympathy and to attribute more blame toward the victim. In the typical experimental situation, observers are provided a variety of descriptions of sexual assaults, along with background information about victims and offenders, their past relationships, etc., sometimes with photographs; each variable is "experimentally manipulated" to increase or decrease the salience of certain characteristics. Respondents are then asked to judge to what extent blame should fall to the victim and/or to the offender.

The "blame the victim" effect (Berrenberg, Rosnik & Kravcisin, 1991), with male-female gender differences between respondents, obtains whether the respondents cast in the role of third-party observers are college and university undergraduates in the United States (Best & Demmin, 1982; Deitz, Littman & Bentley, 1984; Hall, Howard & Boezio, 1986; Karuza & Carey, 1984; Kraulewitz, 1982; Larmand & Pepitone, 1982; Mosher & Anderson, 1986; Pugh, 1983; Thornton & Ryckman, 1983; Thornton, Ryckman & Robbins, 1982; Wyer, Bodenhausen & Gorman, 1985); or undergraduates in Canada (Yarmey, 1985) or Germany (Smith, Tritt & Zollmann, 1982) or India (Kanekar, Pinto & Mazudmar, 1985; Kanekar & Vaz, 1983) or Sicily (DiMaria & DiNuovo, 1986); or non-student citizens of Britain (Howells et al., 1984; Sealy & Wain, 1980) or Canada (Yarmey, 1985); or, more disturbingly, nursing (Alexander, 1980; Damrosch, 1985) or medical students in the United States (Gilmartin, 1983), who might be expected to serve at some future point on the staff of crisis intervention centers; and even among spouses whose partners have been victimized (Earl, 1985). This effect is especially strong when the experimental depictions suggest that the victim failed to take appropriate precautions (Pallak & Davies, 1982) or had herself consumed alcohol prior to, or during, the interaction that led to the rape attempt (Richardson & Campbell, 1982). In an astounding and particularly troubling finding, Deitz, Littman & Bentley (1984) reported that "subjects responded least favorably to an unattractive rape victim, particularly when she resisted the rape by fighting with her attacker." Apparently, not even behavioral science researchers are immune from the tendency to blame the victim. Thus, Myers, Templer & Brown (1984) concluded that "rape vulnerability" was a product of psychosocial incompetence on the part of the victim. Even more disturbingly, in an analysis of the decisions of British appellate courts in cases in which the penalty for incest was at issue, Mitra (1987) found that "where the daughter was not a virgin, the court all but held her responsible." The underlying sexism is so rampant that it requires no interpretation. As one might expect, of course, the same effect is observed among rapists themselves (McDonald & Paitich, 1982-83; Scully & Marolla, 1984, 1985), so that it might be concluded, as Burt (1983) has suggested, that offenders and the general public equally enjoy "blame the victim" as a pastime. One might be tempted to grimace sadly, shake one's head in disbelief, or do whatever one does when confronted with an unpleasant reality and try to suppress the evidence — were it not the fact that the respondents in these studies are, however remotely or proximately, prospective jurors in sexual assault cases.

Indeed, there is some evidence that the "blame the victim" effect operates in the same way among members of criminal court juries as among "grab group" respondents presumably representative of the larger society. In their study of empathy toward both victim and offender among a sample of nearly 600 undergraduates and another of 170 jurors, Deitz, Blackwell, Daley & Bentley (1982) found parallel patterns and further reported that lack of empathy for the victim indeed influenced "jurors' ratings of defendant guilt and their recommended sentences for the defendant and their attributions of responsibility for the crime." Deitz and his colleagues interpreted their results in relation to "the low conviction rate for sexual assault cases and the importance of juror selection as a vehicle for increasing the number of just convictions." Relatively congruent results were reported by LaFree, Reskin & Visher (1985) in a study of the responses of 360 jurors who had served in rape trials to information about a victim's extramarital sexual behavior and its impact on their judgments of her assailant's guilt.

Some suggestion as to the fundamental dynamics around which the game of "blame the victim" pivots might be found in a study of Malamuth, Heim & Feshbach (1980) on the sexual responsiveness of college students to rape depictions of varying character. In sequential experiments, the investigators first determined that their subjects became more sexually aroused by depictions of consensual sex than by depictions of sexual assault. In the second experiment, the victim in criminal sexual violence was portrayed as experiencing an involuntary orgasm during the assault, with the result that this portrayal "disinhibited subjects' sexual responsiveness and resulted in levels of arousal comparable to those elicited by depictions of mutually consenting sex." Moreover, "female subjects were most aroused when the rape victim was portrayed as experiencing an orgasm and no pain" but "males were most aroused when the victim experienced [both] an orgasm and pain." Malamuth and his associates interpreted their results in relation to a belief common among rapists "that their victims derive pleasure from being assaulted." To judge by the universality of responses to the "blame the victim" situation, that belief is by no means limited to those who perpetrate crimes of sexual violence.

3. Some of our colleagues see in our views on the aggregation of neurogenically impulsive persons into mutually self-selected environments with a high tolerance for risky behavior a variation of the classic "differential association" hypothesis of premier criminologist Edwind Sutherland (1947; Sutherland & Cressey, 1978; Gaylord & Galliher, 1988). Although a cross-sectional, external perspective would seem to suggest significant similarities, it remains the case that, in Sutherland's view, the variables which elicit association between "like-minded" persons are essentially sociodemographic, while, in our view, those variables are essentially neuropsychological. Nor will it prove surprising that we see something more than a temporal link between neuropsychological dysfunction and sociodemographic variables.

4. It is a matter of some interest that the American Psychiatric Association filed an amicus brief favoring the position of the state, while the American Psychological Association filed its amicus brief on the side of the inmate. The position of the American Psychological Association is particularly curious at a time when a vocal segment of its membership had raised a clamor demanding that psychologists be granted the right to prescribe psychoactive medication in their own clinical practices. For their part, psychiatrists have stoutly resisted that clamor — and, one says thankfully, with very good reason, for the pace of change produced by the major paradigm shift of which Coyle (1988) has written has been so rapid that even many psychiatrists have found themselves outdated in their knowledge of neuropsychopharmacology, as Rubinson, Asnis & Friedman of the Albert Einstein College of Medicine (1988) suggested in their study of "significant errors" in the diagnosis of depression and the consequent decision not to use somatic treatment.

5. The "clear and imminent danger" principle has been articulated most clearly in court decisions concerning the duty of mental health professionals to warn persons whom they have reason to believe are in danger of becoming victims of violence, even when such a belief arises during the course of psychotherapeutic transactions whose confidentiality is otherwise protected by law. The key decisions arose in the *Tarasoff* case. In *Tarasoff v. Regents*, the Supreme Court of California affirmed in 1976 that the psychologist who had treated an emotionally disturbed student at the University of California (who admitted during treatment an intention to slay his former girl friend) had a duty to warn the prospective victim and that this duty extended to the psychiatrist who had supervised the treating psychologist and to the Regents of the University, in whose name both were acting; in a 1980 decision in *Thompson v. County of Alameda,* the same Court articulated "the requirement that there be a readily identifiable victim before a duty to warn can be imposed" (Simon, 1987, 309). Litwack & Schlesinger (1987) have reviewed a number of court decisions that have placed upon mental health professionals at a minimum the duty to warn those they have reason to believe are in "imminent danger" of victimization on the basis of information revealed by patients. Such a duty requires that the clinician make a "prediction" of violence, albeit with the overt purpose of defeating that prediction (Hall, 1984).

Renowned legal scholar George Dix (1983) has underscored the capital distinction between an assessment of clear and imminent danger to a particular prospective victim, as explicated in the *Tarasoff* decision, and a more generalized opinion about the prospect that a particular person, at some future time and under some unspecified set of conditions, might perpetrate a violent crime. As Dix puts it (256): "there is little reliable evidence verifying claims made by some members of the [mental health] profession of predictive skill. Such research as is available concerns mostly long term predictions concerning the conduct of persons without traditional mental illness; this research suggests minimal predictive skill . . . Psychiatrists' predictive ability is substantially greater when it is called into play concerning the short-term risk posed by persons whose assaultive tendencies are related to symptoms of identifiable serious mental illness. But claims of predictive skill even in these situations might be acknowledged to rest only upon intuition." It is presumably the matter of short-term risk (Tardiff, 1989; Waite, 1995) that guided the Court's thinking in *Washington v. Harper.* But the "clear danger" issue had been broadened by the Court in another landmark case that dealt with the prediction of violence not in the immediate future or against a specific prospective victim. Instead, in *Barefoot v. Estelle*, 1983, a case which challenged capital punishment, the U.S. Supreme Court upheld the Constitutional permissibility of the prosecution's use of expert psychiatric testimony that plaintiff (who had slain a police officer, apparently with premeditation and careful delibera-tion) would continue to behave in homicidally violent ways unless he was executed, despite a dissenting *amicus* brief submitted by the American Psychiatric Association, recounting an earlier Task Force Report (1974) on the assessment of violence, which had warned: "The state of the art regarding predictions of violence is very unsatisfac-tory. The ability of psychiatrists or any other professionals to reliably predict future violence is unproved." Incredibly, the Court also held that such expert testimony "need not be based on personal examination of the defendant and may be given in response to hypothetical questions" (Amnesty International, 1987, 217-218).

REFERENCES

Abel, Ernest L. 1986. Guns and blood alcohol levels among homicide victims. *Drug & Alcohol Dependence*, 18, 253-257.

Abel, Ernest L. 1987. Drugs and homicide in Erie County, New York. *International Journal on Addictions*, 22, 195-200.

Abel, Ernest L. 1988. Guns and blood alcohol levels among homicide victims. *Drug & Alcohol Dependence*, 18, 253-257.

Adler, Freda. 1983. *Nations Not Obsessed With Crime*. Littleton, CO: Rothman.

Adler, Freda. 1986. Jails as a repository for former mental patients. *International Journal of Offender Therapy & Comparative Criminology*, 30, 225-236.

Adinoff, Bryon, H. Katherine O'Neill & James C. Ballenger. 1995. Alcohol withdrawal and limbic kindling. *American Journal on the Addictions*, 4, 5-17.

Ageton, Suzanne S. 1983. The dynamics of female delinquency, 1976-1980. *Criminology*, 21, 555-584.

Akesson, Hans O., & Jan Wahlstrom. 1977. Length of the Y-chromosomes in men examined by forensic psychiatrists. *Human Genetics*, 39, 1, 1-5.

Alcohol, Drug & Mental Health Administration. 1980. Symposium on homicidal violence among Black males. *Public Health Reports*, 96, 6, 549-561.

Alexander, Cheryl S. 1980. The responsible victim: Nurses' perceptions of victims of rape. *Journal of Health & Social Behavior*, 21, 22-33.

Alexander, E. Carelene, Heidi N. Wolfson, David J. Scrams & Beth Menees Rienzi. 1995. Provocation, hostility, aggression, and victimization: firefighters and incarcerated felons. *Journal of Offender Rehabilitation*, 22 (1/2), 47-58.

Alexander, Franz, & Frederick Staub. 1956. *The Criminal, the Judge, and the Public*. Glencoe, IL: Free Press. Originally published in Berlin, 1931 (German).

Allen, H.E., & C.C. Simonsen. 1975. *Corrections in America*. New York: Benziger, Bruce.

American Bar Association. 1989. *ABA Criminal Justice Mental Health Standards*. Washington, DC: The Association.

American Psychiatric Association. 1954. *Diagnostic and Statistical Manual of Mental Disorders*. Washington, DC: The Association.

American Psychiatric Association. 1968. *Diagnostic and Statistical Manual of Mental Disorders, Second edition*. Washington, DC: The Association.

American Psychiatric Association. 1974. *Clinical Aspects of the Violent Individual*. Washington, DC: The Association.

American Psychiatric Association. 1980. *Diagnostic and Statistical Manual of Mental Disorders, Third edition*. Washington, DC: The Association.

American Psychiatric Association. 1984. *Issues in Forensic Psychiatry*. Washington, DC: American Psychiatric Press.

American Psychiatric Association. 1987. *Diagnostic and Statistical Manual of Mental and Emotional Disorders, Third edition, Revised*. Washington, DC: The Association.

American Psychiatric Association. 1994. *Diagnostic and Statistical Manual of Mental and Emotional Disorders, Fourth edition*. Washington, DC: The Association.

American Psychological Association. 1978. Report of the task force on the role of psychology in the criminal justice system. *American Psychologist*, 33, 633-638.

Ames, Donna, Jeffrey L. Cummings, William C. Wirshing, Bruce Quinn & Michael Mahler. 1994. Repetitive and compulsive behavior in frontal lobe degenerations. *Journal of Neuropsychiatry & Clinical Neurosciences*, 6, 110-113.

Amick, Angelynne E., & Karen S. Calhoun. 1987. Resistance to sexual aggression: Personality, attitudinal, and situational factors. *Archives of Sexual Behavior,* 16, 153-164.

Amnesty International. 1987. *United States of America: The Death Penalty.* London: Amnesty International.

Anastasi, Anne. 1988. *Psychological Testing,* 6th ed. New York: Macmillan.

Anderson, Craig A., & Donna C. Anderson. 1984. Ambient temperature and violent crime: Tests of the linear and curvilinear hypotheses. *Journal of Personality & Social Psychology,* 46, 91-97.

Anderson, Elijah. 1990. *Streetwise: Race, Class, and Change in an Urban Community.* Chicago: University of Chicago Press.

Anderson, Wayne P., & William R. Holcomb. 1983. Accused murderers: Five MMPI personality types. *Journal of Clinical Psychology,* 39, 761-768.

Andreasen, Nancy C., Daniel S. O'Leary & Stephan Arndt. 1993. Neuroimaging and clinical neuroscience: Basic issues and principles. In John M. Oldham, Michelle B. Riba & Allan Tasman (eds.), *American Psychiatric Press Review of Psychiatry, Volume 12.* Washington, DC: American Psychiatric Press.

Andreasen, Nancy C., Michael Flaum, Victor Swayze II, Daniel S. O'Leary, Randall Alliger, Gregg Cohen, James Ehrhardt & William T.C. Yuh. 1993. Intelligence and brain structure in normal individuals. *American Journal of Psychiatry,* 150, 130-134.

Andreasen, Nancy C., Gregg Cohen, Greg Harris, Ted Cizadlo, Jussi Parkkinen, Karim Rezai & Victor W. Swayze. 1992. Image processing for the study of brain structure and function: problems and programs. *Journal of Neuropsychiatry & Clinical Neurosciences,* 4, 125-133.

Angier, Natalie. 1995. Does testosterone equal aggression? Maybe not. *New York Times,* 20 June, A-1.

Appelbaum, Paul S. 1987. *Allen v. Illinois*: The Fifth Amendment and the sexually dangerous person. *Hospital & Community Psychiatry,* 38, 25-26.

Appelbaum, Paul S. 1988. The right to refuse treatment with antipsychotic medication. *American Journal of Psychiatry,* 145, 413-419.

Appelbaum, Paul S., & Steven K. Hoge. 1986. Empirical research on the effects of legal policy on the right to refuse treatment. In *The Right to Refuse Antipsychotic Medication.* Washington, DC: Commission on the Mentally Disabled, American Bar Association. Pp. 87-96.

Arboleda-Florez, Julio. 1981. Post-homicide psychotic reaction. *International Journal of Offender Therapy & Comparative Criminology,* 25, 47-52.

Archer, Dane, Rosemary Gartner & Marc Beittel. 1983. Homicide and the death penalty: A cross-national test of a deterrence hypothesis. *Journal of Criminal Law & Criminology,* 74. 991-1013.

Archer, John. 1994. Testosterone and aggression. In Marc Hillbrand & Nathaniel J. Pallone (eds.), *The Psychobiology of Aggression.* New York: Haworth. Pp. 3-26.

Archer, Robert P. 1995. The many faces of psychopathy. *Contemporary Psychology,* 40, 518-520.

Arizona appeals court says state hospital psychiatrist owed duty to protect victim from violent acts of his patient. 1991. *Register Report: Newsletter for Psychologist Health Service Providers,* 17 (1), 19.

Arnold, Larry, Russell Fleming & Valerie Bell. 1979. The man who became angry once: A study of overcontrolled hostility. *Canadian Journal of Psychiatry,* 24, 762-766.

Arnold, L.S., V.L. Quinsey & I. Velner. 1977. Overcontrolled hostility among men found not guilty by reason of insanity. *Canadian Journal of Behavioral Science,* 9, 333-340.

Aronowitz, Bonnie, Michael Leibowitz, Eric Hollander, Enrizo Fazzini, Cecile Durlach-Misteli, Maxim Frenkel, Serge Mosovich, Robin Garfinkel, Jihad Saoud, Donato Del Bene, Lee Cohen, Andrei Jaeger & A. Lawrence Rubin. 1994. Neuropsychiatric and neuropsychological findings in conduct disorder and attention-deficit hyperactivity disorder. *Journal of Neuropsychiatry & Clinical Neurosciences,* 6, 245-249.

Astin, Alexander W., William S. Korn & Ellyne R. Riggs, 1993. *The American Freshman: National Norms for Fall 1993.* Los Angeles: Higher Education Research Institute, University of California at Los Angeles.

Atlas, Gordon D., & Christopher Peterson. 1990. Explanatory style and gambling: How pessimists respond to losing wagers. *Behaviour Research & Therapy*, 28, 523-529.

Ayoub, Catherine, & Marion Jacewitz. 1982. Families at risk for poor parenting: A model for service delivery, assessment, and intervention. *Child Abuse & Neglect*, 6, 351-358.

Bailey, William C. 1975. Murder and capital punishment: Some further evidence. *American Journal of Orthopsychiatry*, 45, 669-688.

Bailey, William C. 1976-*a*. Some further evidence on homicide and a regional culture of violence. *Omega: Journal of Death & Dying*, 7, 145-170.

Bailey, William C. 1976-*b*. Use of the death penalty v. outrage at murder: Some additional evidence and considerations. *Crime & Delinquency*, 22, 31-39.

Bailey, William C. 1980. Deterrent effect of the death penalty: An extended time series analysis. *Omega: Journal of Death & Dying*, 10, 234-259.

Bailey, William C. 1983. The deterrent effect of capital punishment during the 1950s. *Suicide & Life-Threatening Behavior*, 13, 95-107.

Bailey, William C. 1985. Disaggregation in deterrence and death penalty research: The case of murder in Chicago. *Journal of Criminal Law & Criminology*, 74, 827-859.

Bailey, William C. 1990. Murder, capital punishment, and television: Execution publicity and homicide rates. *American Sociological Review*, 55, 628-633.

Bailey, William C., & Ruth D. Peterson. 1989. Murder and capital punishment: A monthly time-series analysis of execution publicity. *American Sociological Review*, 54, 722-743.

Baldwin, James. 1963. *The Fire Next Time*. London: Michael Joseph.

Baldwin, J.A., & J.E. Oliver. 1975. Epidemiology and family characteristics of severely-abused children. *British Journal of Preventive & Social Medicine*, 29, 205-221.

Ball, John C., & David N. Nurco. 1984. Criminality during the life course of heroin addiction. *National Institute on Drug Abuse, Research Monograph Series*, 49. Pp. 305-312.

Ball, John C., Lawrence Rosen, John A. Flueck & David N. Nurco. 1982. Lifetime criminality of heroin addicts in the United States. *Journal of Drug Issues*, 12, 225-239.

Ball, John D., Robert P. Archer, Frederick A. Struve & John A. Hunter. 1987. MMPI correlates of a controversial EEG pattern among adolescent psychiatric patients. *Journal of Clinical Psychology*, 43, 708-714.

Bandura, Albert. 1962. Social learning through imitation. In Marshall R. Jones (ed.), *Nebraska Symposium on Motivation*. Lincoln: University of Nebraska Press. Pp. 211-274.

Bandura, Albert. 1965. Influence of models' reinforcement contingencies on the acquisition of imitative responses. *Journal of Personality & Social Psychology*, 1, 589-595.

Bandura, Albert. 1969. *Principles of Behavior Modification*. New York: Holt Rinehart Winston.

Bandura, Albert. 1973. *Aggression: A Social Learning Analysis*. Englewood Cliffs, NJ: Prentice Hall.

Bandura, Albert. 1977. Self-efficacy: Toward a unifying theory of behavioral change. *Psychological Review*, 84, 191-215.

Bandura, Albert. 1978. The self-system in reciprocal determinism. *American Psychologist*, 33, 344-358.

Bandura, Albert. 1979. Mechanisms of aggression from the social learning perspective. In Hans Toch (ed.), *Psychology of Crime and Criminal Justice*. New York: Holt Rinehart Winston.

Bandura, Albert. 1985. Catecholamine secretion as a function of perceived coping self-efficacy. *Journal of Consulting & Clinical Psychology*, 53, 406-414.

Bandura, Albert. 1986-*a*. Fearful expectations and avoidant actions as coeffects of perceived self inefficacy. *American Psychologist*, 41, 1389-1391.

Bandura, Albert. 1986-*b*. From thought to action: Mechanisms of personal agency. *New Zealand Journal of Psychology*, 15, 1-17.

Bandura, Albert. 1986-*c*. *Social Foundations of Thought and Action: A Social Cognitive Theory*. Englewood Cliffs, NJ: Prentice-Hall.

Bandura, Albert. 1986-*d*. The explanatory and predictive scope of self-efficacy theory. *Journal of Social & Clinical Psychology*, 4, 359-373.

Bandura, Albert. 1989-*a*. Human agency in social cognitive theory. *American Psychologist*, 44, 1175-1184.

Bandura, Albert. 1989-*b*. Regulation of cognitive processes through perceived self-efficacy. *Developmental Psychology*, 625, 729-735.

Bandura, Albert, & Carol J. Kupers. 1964. Transmission of patterns of self-reinforcement through modeling. *Journal of Abnormal & Social Psychology*, 69, 1-9.

Bandura, Albert, & Frederick J. McDonald, 1963. Influence of social reinforcement and the behavior of models in shaping children's moral judgments. *Journal of Abnormal & Social Psychology*, 67, 274-281.

Bandura, Albert, & Theodore L. Rosenthal. 1966. Vicarious classical conditioning as a function of arousal level. *Journal of Personality & Social Psychology*, 3, 54-62.

Bandura, Albert, & Richard H. Walters. 1963. *Social Learning and Personality Development*. New York: Holt Rinehart Winston.

Bandura, Albert, Joan E. Grusec & Frances L. Menlove. 1967-a. Some social determinants of self-monitoring reinforcement systems. *Journal of Personality & Social Psychology*, 5, 449-455.

Bandura, Albert, Joan E. Grusec & Frances L. Menlove. 1967-b. Vicarious extinction of avoidance behavior. *Journal of Personality & Social Psychology*, 5, 16-23.

Bandura, Albert, Joan E. Grusec & Frances L. Menlove. 1967-c. Some social determinants of self-monitoring reinforcement systems. *Journal of Personality and Psychology*, 5, 449-455.

Bandura, Albert, Dorothea Ross & Sheila A. Ross. 1963. Vicarious reinforcement and imitative learning. *Journal of Abnormal & Social Psychology*, 67, 601-607.

Bannister, Donald, & Fay Fransella. 1971. *Inquiring Man: The Theory of Personal Constructs*. Harmondsworth, UK: Penguin.

Bannister, Donald, & J.M.M. Mair. 1968. *The Evaluation of Personal Constructs*. London: Academic.

Barabasz, Arreed, & Marianne Barabasz. 1995. Attention deficit hyperactivity disorder: Neurological basis and treatment alternatives. *Journal of Neurotherapy*, 1, 1-11.

Barack, Leonard I., & Cathy S. Widom. 1978. Eysenck's theory of criminality applied to women awaiting trial. *British Journal of Psychiatry*, 133, 452-456.

Baringa, Marcia. 1996. Social status sculpts activity of crayfish neurons. *Science*, 271, 290-291.

Barnett, Arnold. 1978. Crime and capital punishment: Some recent studies. *Journal of Criminal Justice*, 6, 291-303.

Baroff, George S. 1990. Establishing mental retardation in capital defendants, *American Journal of Forensic Psychology*, 8, 35-45.

Barsky, Arthur J., Carol Wool, Marcia C. Barnett & Paul D. Cleary. 1994, Histories of childhood trauma in adult hypochondriacal patients. *American Journal of Psychiatry*, 151, 397-401.

Bartol, Curt R. 1983. *Psychology and American Law*. Belmont, CA: Wadsworth.

Bartol, Curt R. 1991. *Criminal Behavior: A Psychosocial Approach*. Englewood Cliffs, NJ: Prentice-Hall.

Bartol, Curt R. 1992. Predictive validation of the MMPI for small-town police officers. *Professional Psychology*, 22, 127-132.

Bastian, Lisa. 1995. National Crime Victimization Survey: Criminal victimization 1993. *Bureau of Justice Statistics Bulletin*, NCJ-151658, 1-8.

Bates, Marsha E., Helene Raskin White & Erich Labouvie. 1994. Changes in sensation-seeking needs and drug use. In P. Venturelli (ed.), *Drug Use in America: Social, Cultural, and Political Perspectives*. Boston: Jones & Bartlett. Pp. 67-75.

Bateson, Gregory. 1972. *Steps to an Ecology of Mind*. New York: Ballantine.

Bateson, Gregory. 1978. The birth of a matrix, or double bind and epistemology. In Milton M. Berger (ed.), *Beyond the Double Bind: Communication and Family Systems, Theories, and Techniques with Schizophrenics*. New York: Brunner/Mazel.

Bateson, Gregory, Don D. Jackson, Jay Healey & John Weakland. 1956. Toward a theory of schizophrenia. *Behavioral Science*, 1, 251-264.

Baum, Maureen S., Ray E. Hosford & C. Scott Moss. 1984. Predicting violent behavior within a medium security correctional setting. *International Journal of Eclectic Psychotherapy*, 3, 18-24.

Bear, David. 1987. "Psychotic Trigger Reaction:" Neuro-psychiatric and neuro-biological (limbic?) aspects of homicide, reflecting on normal action. *Integrative Psychiatry*, 5, 125-127

Beck, Allen, Darrell Gilliard, Lqwrence Greenfeld, Caroline Harlow, Thomas Hester, Louis Jankowski, Tracy Snell, James Stephan & Danielle Morton. 1993. *Survey of State Prison Inmates.* Washington, DC: Bureau of Justice Statistics, U.S. Department of Justice.

Bell, Carl C. 1986. Coma and the etiology of violence. *Journal of the National Medical Association,* 78, 1167-1176.

Bell, Carl C. 1990. Neuropsychiatry and gun safety. *Journal of Neuropsychiatry & Clinical Neurosciences*, 2, 145-148.

Bellak, Leopold. 1979. *Psychiatric Aspects of Minimal Brain Dysfunction in Adults.* New York: Grune & Stratton.

Bellak, Leopold. 1992. Comorbidity of attenion deficit hyperactivity disorder and other disorders. *Ameican Journal of Psychiatry,* 149, 147-148.

Benedek, Elissa, & Dewey Cornell (eds.). 1989. *Juvenile Homicide.* Washington, D.C.: American Psychiatric Press.

Benedek, Elissa, Dewey Cornell & Lois Staresina. 1989. Treatment of the homicidal adolescent. In Elissa Benedek & Dewey Cornell (eds.), *Juvenile Homicide.* Washington, DC: American Psychiatric Press. Pp. 219-247.

Benezech, Michel M. 1984. Homicide by psychotics in France: A five-year study. *Journal of Clinical Psychiatry,* 45, 85-85.

Benezech, Michel M. Bourgeois, D. Boukhabza & Jerome Yesavage. 1981. Cannibalism and vampirism in paranoid schizophrenia. *Journal of Clinical Psychiatry,* 42, 290.

Benezech, Michel, Jacques de Witte, Jean J. Etcheparre & Marc Bourgeois. 1989. A lycanthropic murderer. *American Journal of Psychiatry* 146, 942.

Benkelfat, Chawki, Mark A. Ellenbogen, Peggy Dean, Roberta M. Palmour & Simon N. Young. 1994. Mood-lowering effect of tryptophan depletion: Enhanced susceptibility in young men at genetic risk for major affective disorders. *Archives of General Psychiatry,* 51, 687-697.

Bennett, Trevor, & Richard Wright. 1984. The relationship between alcohol use and burglary. *British Journal of Addiction,* 79, 431-437.

Ben-Porath, Yossef S., Denise D. Shondrick & Kathleen P. Stafford. 1995. MMPI-2 and race in a forensic diagnostic sample. *Criminal Justice & Behavior,* 22, 19-32.

Berelson, Bernard, & Patrician J. Salter. 1946. Majority and minority American: An analysis of magazine fiction. *Public Opinion Quarterly,* 10, 168=190.

Berelson, Bernard, & Gary A. Steiner. 1964. *Human Behavior: An Inventory of Scientific Findings.* New York: Harcourt, Brace & World.

Berg, Richard, Michael Franzen & Danny Wedding. 1987. *Screening for Brain Impairment.* New York: Springer.

Berkow, Robert J., & Andrew J. Fletcher. 1987. *The Merck Manual of Diagnosis and Therapy,* 15th ed. Rahway, NJ: Merck, Sharp & Dohme Research Laboratories.

Berkow, Robert J., & Andrew J. Fletcher. 1992. *The Merck Manual of Diagnosis and Therapy,* 16th ed. Rahway, NJ: Merck, Sharp & Dohme Research Laboratories.

Bernstein, Ira. H., & Calvin P. Garbin. 1985. A simple set of salient weights for the major dimensions of the MMPI scale variation. *Educational & Psychological Measurement,* 45, 4, 771-781.

Bernstein, Ira H., Gary Teng, Bruce D. Granneman & Calvin P. Garbin, 1987. Invariance in the MMPI's component structure. *Journal of Personality Assessment,* 51, 4, 522-531.

Berrenberg, Joy L., Danield Rosnik & Nicki J. Kravcisin. 1991. Blaming the victim: When disease-prevention programs misfire. *Current Psychology,* 9, 415-420.

Best, John B., & Herbert S. Demmin. 1982. Victim's provocativeness and victim's attractiveness as determinants of blame in rape. *Psychological Reports,* 51, 255-258.

Black, Donald W., William R. Yates & Nancy C. Andreasen. 1988. Schizophrenia, schizophreniform disorder, and delusional (paranoid) disorders. In John A. Talbott, Robert E. Hales & Stuart C. Yudofsky (eds.), *American Psychiatric Press Textbook of Psychiatry.* Washington, DC: American Psychiatric Press. Pp. 357-402.

Blackburn, Ronald. 1975-a. Aggression and the EEG: A quantitative analysis. *Journal of Abnormal Psychology,* 84, 359-365.

Blackburn, Ronald. 1975-b. An empirical classification of psychopathic personality. *British Journal of Psychiatry,* 127, 456-460.

Blackburn, Ronald. 1979. Cortical and autonomic arousal in primary and secondary psychopaths. *Psychophysiology,* 16, 143-150.

Blackburn, Ronald. 1993. *The Psychology of Criminal Conduct: Theory, Research, and Practice.* Chicherster, UK: Wiley.

Blackburn, Ronald, & Clive Maybury. 1985. Identifying the psychopath: The relation of Cleckey's criteria to the interpersonal domain. *Personality & Individual Differences,* 6, 375-386.

Blackman, Nathan, John T. Lum & Robert J. VanderPearl. 1974. Disturbed communications: A contributing factor in sudden murder. *Mental Health & Society,* 11, 345-355.

Blackson, Timothy C., Ralph E. Tarter, Christopher S. Martin & Howard B. Moss. 1994. Temperament mediates the effects of family history of substance abuse on externalizing and internalizing child behavior. *American Journal on Addictions,* 3, 58-66.

Blanchard, Jack J., & John M. Neale. 1994. The neuropsychological signature of schizophrenia: Generalized or differential deficit? *American Journal of Psychiatry,* 151, 40-48.

Bluestone, Harvey, & Sheldon Travin. 1984. Murder: The ultimate conflict. *American Journal of Psychoanalysis,* 44, 147-167.

Blum, Richard H. 1981. Violence, alcohol, and setting: An unexplored nexus. In James J. Collins, Jr. (ed.), *Drinking and Crime.* New York: Guilford. Pp. 110-142.

Blumenthal, Deborah. 1991. How to keep guns safely. *New York Times,* 30 March, 36.

Blumstein, Alfred, & Jacqueline Cohen. 1987. Characterizing criminal careers. *Science,* 237, 985-991.

Blumstein, Alfred, & S. Moitra. 1980. Identification of "career criminals" from "chronic offenders" in a cohort. *Law & Policy Quarterly,* 2, 321-334.

Bockar, Joyce A. 1976. *Primer for the Nonmedical Psychotherapist on Psychoactive Medication.* New York: Spectrum.

Bonkalo, A. Electroencephalograpy in criminology. *Canadian Psychiatric Association Journal,* 12, 281-286.

Boulton, Alan A., Bruce A. Davis, Peter H. Yu, Stephen Wormith, & Donald Addington. 1983. Trace acid levels in the plasma and MAO activity in the platelets of violent offenders. *Psychiatry Research,* 8, 19-23.

Bourget, Dominique, & John M. Bradford. 1990. Homicidal parents. *Canadian Journal of Psychiatry,* 35, 233-238.

Boverie, Patricia E., Dennis J. Scheuffele & Elizabeth J. Raymond. 1995. Multimethodological approach to examining risk-taking. *Current Psychology,* 13, 289-302.

Bowers, William J. 1983. *Executions in America, 1864-1982: A Study of Death as Punishment.* Boston: Northeastern University Press.

Bowers, William J., Glenn L. Pierce & John F. McDevitt. 1983. *Legal Homicide: Death as Punishment in America, 1864-1982.* Boston: Northeastern University Press.

Bracha, H. Stefan, Richard L. Livingston, Jeffrey Clothier, Beverly B. Linington & Craig N. Karson. 1993. Correlation of severity of psychiatric patients' delusions with right hemispatial inattention (left-turning behavior). *American Journal of Psychiatry,* 150, 330-332.

Bracha, H. Stefan, E. Fuller Torrey, Irving I. Gottesman, Llewellyn B. Bigelow & Christopher Cunniff. 1992. Second-trimester markers of fetal size in schizophrenia: a study of monozygotic twins. *American Journal of Psychiatry,* 149, 1356-1361.

Bradford, John M., & D. McLean. 1984. Sexual offenders, violence, and testosterone: A clinical study. *Canadian Journal of Psychiatry,* 29, 335-343.

Branch, Curtis, Jeanne Brooks-Gunn, John M. Broughton, Morton Deutsch, Herbet P. Ginsburg, Maxine Greene, Howard E. Gruber, Deanna Kuhn & A. Harry Passow. 1995. Statement on race differences in intelligence occasioned by *The Bell Curve. Peace & Conflict,* 1, 99-100.

Brenner, M. Harvey, & Robert T. Swank. 1986. Homicide & economic change: Recent analyses of the Joint Economic Committee Report of 1984. *Journal of Quantitative Criminology,* 2, 81-103.

Briere, John, Neil Malamuth & James V. Check. 1985. Sexuality & rape-supportive beliefs. *International Journal of Women's Studies,* 8, 398-403.

Brinson, Jesse A. 1994. The incarceration of Black males: Unsettled questions. *Journal of Offender Rehabilitation,* 20 (3/4), 85-96.

Brody, Baruch. 1980. *Mental Illness: Law and Public Policy.* Boston: D. Reidel.

Brody, Erness Bright, & Nathan Brody. 1976. *Intelligence: Nature, Determinants, and Consequences.* New York: Academic.

Brooks, Alexander D. 1986. The effect of law on the administration of antipsychotic medications. In Laurence Tancredi (ed.), *Ethical Issues in Epidemiologic Research.* New Brunswick, NJ: Rutgers University Press. Pp. 183-200.

Brown, Phil, & Christopher J. Smith. 1988. Mental patients' rights: An empirical study of variation across the United States. *International Journal of Law & Psychiatry,* 11, 157-165.

Brown, Rosemary, Nigel Colter, Nicholas Corsellis, Timothy J. Crow, Christopher D. Frith, Roger Jagoe, Eve C. Johnstone & Laura Marsh. 1986. Postmortem evidence of structural brain changes in schizophrenia: Differences in brain weight, temporal horn area, and parahippocampal gyrus compared with affective disorder. *Archives of General Psychiatry,* 43, 36-42.

Brown, Serena-Lynn, Alexander Botsis & Herman M. Van Praag. 1994. Serotonin and aggression. In Marc Hillbrand & Nathaniel J. Pallone (eds.), *The Psychobiology of Aggression.* New York: Haworth. Pp. 27-40.

Brown, Stephen J., Jesse R. Fann & Igor Grant. 1994. Postconcussional disorder: Time to acknowledge a common source of neurobehavioral morbidity. *Journal of Neuropsychiatry & Clinical Neurosciences,* 6, 15-22.

Bryant, Ernest T., Monte L. Scott, Christopher D. Tori & Charles J. Golden. 1984. Neuropsychological deficits, learning disability, and violent behavior. *Journal of Consulting & Clinical Psychology,* 52, 323-324.

Budd, Robert D. 1982. The incidence of alcohol use in Los Angeles county homicide victims. *American Journal of Drug & Alcohol Abuse,* 9, 105-111.

Buikhuisen, Wouter. 1982. Aggressive behavior and cognitive disorders. *International Journal of Law & Psychiatry,* 5, 205-217.

Buikhuisen, Wouter, & B.W.G.P. Mejs. 1983. Psychosocial approach to recidivism. In Katherin T. van Dusen & Sarnoff A. Mednick (eds.), *Prospective Studies of Crime and Delinquency.* Boston: Kluwer-Nijhoff. Pp. 99-115.

Buikhuisen, Wouter, & Sarnoff A. Mednick. 1988. *Explaining Criminal Behaviour: Interdisciplinary Approaches.* Leyden: Brill.

Bukowski, Nilzete T., & Roselane Gehrke. 1979. O Rorschach em homicidas. *Psico,* 16, 5-27.

Bureau of the Census, U.S. Department of Commerce. 1988. *Profile of State Prison Inmates.* Washington, DC: Bureau of Justice Statistics, U.S. Department of Justice. Report NCJ-109926.

Bureau of the Census, U.S. Department of Commerce. 1989. *Statistical Abstract of the United States.* Washington, DC: U.S. Government Printing Office.

Bureau of Justice Statistics, U.S. Department of Justice. 1980. *Profile of Jail Inmates: National Prisoner Statistics Report* SD NPS J-6, NCJ-65412. Washington, DC: The Bureau.

Bureau of Justice Statistics, U.S. Deparment of Justice. 1983. *Report to the Nation on Crime and Justice: The Data.* Washington, DC: The Bureau. NCJ-87068.

Bureau of Justice Statistics. 1988. *Criminal Victimization in the United States: Trends.* Washington, DC: U.S. Department of Justice.

Bureau of Justice Statistics. 1994. *Criminal Victimization in the United States.* Washington, DC: U.S. Department of Justice.

Bureau of Justice Statistics. 1990. *Population Density in Local Jails.* Washington, DC: U.S. Department of Justice.

Bureau of Justice Statistics. 1991. *Prisoners in 1990.* Washington, DC: U.S. Department of Justice.

Burgess, Ann W., Carol R. Hartman & Arlene McCormack. 1987. Abused to abuser: Antecedents of socially deviant behaviors. *American Journal of Psychiatry,* 144, 1431-1436.

Burgess, Ann W., Carol R. Hartman, Robert K Ressler, John E. Douglas, et al. 1986. Sexual homicide: A motivational model. *Journal of Interpersonal Violence,* 1, 251-272

Burke, Jack D., & Darrel A. Regier. 1988. Epidemiology of mental disorders. In John A. Talbott, Robert E. Hales & Stuart C. Yudofsky (eds.), *American Psychiatric Press Textbook of Psychiatry*. Washington, DC: American Psychiatric Press. Pp. 67-90.

Burnett, Robbie C., Donald I. Templer, & Patrick C. Barker. 1985. Personality variables and circumstances of sexual assault predictive of a woman's resistance. *Archives of Sexual Behavior,* 14, 183-188.

Bursten, Ben. 1985. Detecting child abuse by studying the parents. *Bulletin of the American Academy of Psychiatry & the Law,* 13, 273-281.

Burt, Martha R. 1983. Justifying personal violence: A comparison of rapists and the general public. Victimology, 8, 131-150.

Busch, Katie A., & James L. Cavanaugh. 1986. The study of multiple murder: Preliminary examination of the interface between epistemology and methodology. *Journal of Interpersonal Violence,* 1, 5-23.

Busch, Kenneth G., Robert Zagar, John R. Hughes & Jack Arbit. 1990. Adolescents who kill. *Journal of Clinical Psychology,* 46, 472-485.

Bush, John M. 1983. Criminality and psychopathology: Treatment for the guilty. *Federal Probation,* 47, 44-49.

Butcher, James N., Laura S. Keller & Steven F. Bacon. 1985. Current developments and future directions in computerized personality assessment. *Journal of Consulting & Clinical Psychology,* 1985, 53, 803-815.

Campbell, Anne. 1991. *The Girls in the Gang,* 2nd ed. Cambridge, MA: Blackwell.

Campbell, David E., & John L. Beets. 1978. Lunacy and the moon. *Psychological Bulletin,* 85, 1123-1129.

Campion, John F., James M. Cravens & Fred Covan. 1988. A study of filicidal men. *American Journal of Psychiatry,* 145, 1141-1144.

Cannon, Tyrone D., Sarnoff A. Mednick, Josef Parnas, Fini Schulsinger, Johannes Praestholm & Aage Vestergaard. 1994. Developmental brain abnormalities in the offspring of schizophrenic mothers: II. Structural brain characteristics of schizophrenia and schizotypal personality disorder. *Archives of General Psychiatry,* 51, 12, 955-962.

Caplan, Nathan S. 1965. The role of intellectual functioning in delinquency. In Herbert C. Quay (ed.), *Research and Theory in Juvenile Delinquency.* Princeton: Van Nostrand.

Carbonell, Joyce L. 1983. Inmate classification: A cross-tabulation of two methods. *Criminal Justice & Behavior,* 10, 285-292.

Carbonell, Joyce L., Karen M. Moorhead & Edwin I. Megargee. 1984. Predicting prison adjustment with structured personality inventories. *Journal of Consulting & Clinical Psychology,* 52, 280-294.

Cases, Olivier, Isabelle Seif, Joseph Grimsby, Patricia Gaspar, Kevin Chen, Sandrine Pournin, Ulrike Müller, Michel Aguet, Charles Babinet, Jean Chen Shih & Edward DeMaeyer, 1995. Aggressive behavior and altered amounts of brain serotonin and norepinephrine in mice lacking MAOA. *Science,* 268, 1763-1766.

Caspi, Avshalom, Terrie E. Moffitt, Phil A. Silva & Robert F. Kreuger. 1994. Are some people crime-prone? Replications of the personality-crime relationship across contries, races, and methods. *Criminology,* 32, 163-195.

Catalano, Ralph, David Dooley, Raymond W. Novaco, Georjeanna Wilson & Richard Hough. 1993. Using ECA survey data to examine the effect of job layoffs on violent behavior. *Hospital & Community Psychiatry,* 44, 361-368.

Cattell, Raymond B. 1963. Formulating the environmental situation and its perception in behavior theory. In S.B. Sells (ed.), *Stimulus Determinants of Behavior.* New York: Ronald. Pp. 46-75.

Cattell, Raymond B. 1971. *Abilities: Their Structure, Growth, and Action.* Boston: Houghton Mifflin.

Cattell, Raymond B. 1980. *Personality and Learning Theory: The Structure of Personality in Its Environment.* New York: Springer.

Cattell, Raymond B. 1985. *Psychotherapy by Structured Learning Theory.* New York: Springer.

Cattell, Raymond B., & Dennis Child. 1975. *Motivation and Dynamic Structure*. New York: Holt Rinehart Winston.

Cavallin, Hector C. 1966. Incestuous fathers: A clinical report. *American Journal of Psychiatry,* 122, 1132-1138.

Cavanaugh, James L., & Oriest E. Wasyliw. 1985. Treating the not guilty by reason of insanity outpatient: A two year study. *Bulletin of the American Academy of Psychiatry & the Law,* 13, 407-415.

Chakraborty, Ranajit, & Kenneth K. Kidd. 1991. The utility of DNA typing in forensic work. *Science,* 254, 1735-1739.

Christiansen, James L., & John M. Grzybowski. 1993. *Biology of Aging*. Boston: Mosby.

Christoffel, Katherine K., & Kiang Liu. 1983. Homicide death rates in childhood in 23 developed countries: U.S. rates atypically high. *Child Abuse & Neglect,* 7, 339-345.

Church, R.M. 1959. Emotional reactions of rats to the pain of others. *Journal of Comparative & Physiological Psychology,* 52, 132-134.

Cicerone, Keith D., & Jeanne C. Wood. 1987. Planning disorder after closed head injury: A case study. *Archives of Physical Medicine & Rehabilitation,* 68, 111-115.

Clarke, Ronald V. 1980. Situational crime prevention. *British Journal of Criminology,* 20, 136-147.

Clarke, Ronald V. 1984. Opportunity-based crime rates: The difficulties of further refinement. *British Journal of Criminology,* 75, 77-85.

Clarke, Ronald V. 1985. Delinquency, environment, and intervention. *Child Psychology & Psychiatry,* 26, 505-523.

Clarke, Ronald V. 1987. Practicalities of prevent car theft: A criminological analysis. In *Car Theft*. Sydney: National Roads & Motorists Association.

Clarke, Ronald V., & David B. Cornish. 1985. Modeling offenders' decisions: A framework for research and policy. *Crime & Justice,* 6, 147-185.

Clarke, Ronald V., & Marcus Felson. Criminology, routine activity, and rational choice. In Ronald V. Clarke & Marcus Felson (eds.), *Routine Activity and Rational Choice: Advances in Criminological Theory*. New Brunswick, NJ: Transaction Publishers. Pp. 1-14.

Clarke, Ronald V., & David Lester. 1989. *Suicide: Closing the Exits*. New York: Springer-Verlag.

Clarke, Ronald V., & David L. Weisburd. 1990. On the distribution of deviance. In Don M. Gottfredson & Ronald V. Clarke (eds.), *Policy and Theory in Criminal Justice*. Avebury, UK: Gower. Pp. 10-27.

Clarkin, John F., & Stephen W. Hurt. 1988. Psychological assessment: Tests and rating scales. In John A. Talbott, Robert E. Hales & Stuart C. Yudofsky (eds.), *American Psychiatric Press Textbook of Psychiatry*. Washington, DC: American Psychiatric Press. Pp. 225-246.

Cleare, Anthony J., & Alyson J. Bond. 1994. Effects of alterations in plasma tryptophan levels on aggressive feelings. *Archives of General Psychiatry,* 51, 12, 1004-1005.

Cleckley, Harvey. 1941. *The Mask of Sanity*. St. Louis: Mosby.

Cloninger, C. Robert, Theodore Reich & Samuel B. Guze. 1975. The multifactorial model of disease transmission: Sex differences in the familial transmission of sociopathy (antisocial personality). *British Journal of Psychiatry,* 127, 11-22.

Close, H.G., A.S.R. Goonetilleke, P.A. Jacobs & W.H. Price. 1968. The incidence of sex chromosomal anomalies in mentally subnormal males. *Cytogenetics,* 7, 277-295.

Coccarro, Emil F., Larry J. Siever, Howard M. Klar & Gail Mauer. 1989. Serotonergic studies in patients with affective and personality disorders: Correlates with suicidal and impulsive aggressive behavior. *Archives of General Psychiatry,* 46, 587-599.

Cochran, John K., Mitchell B. Chamlin & Mark Seth. 1994. Deterrence or brutalization? An impact assessment of Oklahoma's return to capital punishment. *Criminology,* 32, 107-134.

Cocozza, Joseph J., & Henry J. Steadman. 1974. Some refinements in the measurement and prediction of dangerous behavior. *American Journal of Psychiatry,* 131, 1012-1014.

Cohen, Bruce M., Ferdinando Buonanno, Paul E. Keck, Seth P. Finkelstein & Francine M. Benes. 1988. Comparison of MRI and CT scans in a group of psychiatric patients. *American Journal of Psychiatry,* 145, 1084-1088.

Cohen, Jacob. 1994. The earth is round (p < ,05). *American Psychologist,* 49, 997-1003.

Cohen, Stanley. 1988. *Against Criminology.* New Brunswick, NJ: Transaction Publishers.

Cohn, Ellen, G. 1990. Weather and violent crime: A reply to Perry and Simpson. *Environment & Behavior,* 22, 280-294.

Cole, K.D., G. Fisher & S.S. Cole. 1968. Women who kill: A sociopsychological study. *Archives of General Psychiatry,* 19, 1-8.

Colligan, Robert C., David Osborne, Wendell M. Swenson & Kenneth P. Offord. 1989. *The MMPI: A Contemporary Normative Study,* 2nd ed. Odessa, FL: Psychological Assessment Resources.

Collins, James J., Jr. 1981. Alcohol careers and criminal careers. In James J. Collins, Jr. (ed.), *Drinking and Crime.* New York: Guilford. Pp. 152-206.

Combs-Orme, Terri. 1983. Violent deaths among alcoholics: A descriptive study. *Journal of Studies on Alcohol,* 44, 938-949.

Comstock, George, A. 1986. Sexual effects of movie & TV violence. *Medical Aspects of Human Sexuality,* 20, 96-101.

Conacher, G. Neil. 1988. Pharmacotherapy of the aggressive adult patient. *International Journal of Law & Psychiatry,* 11, 205-212.

Conacher, G. Neil, & D.G. Workman. 1989. Violent crime possibly associated with anabolic steroid use. *American Journal of Psychiatry,* 146, 679.

Cook, Philip. 1982. The role of firearms in violent crime. In Marvin E. Wolfgand & Neil A. Weiner (eds.), *Criminal Violence.* Beverly Hills, CA: Sage.

Cornell, Dewey. 1989. Causes of juvenile homicide: A review of the literature. In Elissa Benedek & Dewey Cornell (eds.), *Juvenile Homicide.* Washington, DC: American Psychiatric Press. Pp. 1-36.

Cornell, Dewey G., Elissa P. Benedek & David M. Benedek. 1987-a. Characteristics of adolescents charged with homicide: Review of 72 cases. *Behavioral Sciences & the Law,* 5, 11-23.

Cornell, Dewey G., Elissa P. Benedek & David M. Benedek. 1987-b. Juvenile homicide: Prior adjustment and a proposed typology. *American Journal of Orthopsychiatry,* 57, 383-393.

Cornell, Dewey G., Elissa P. Benedek & David M. Benedek. 1989. A typology of juvenile homicide offenders. In Elissa Benedek & Dewey Cornell (eds.), *Juvenile Homicide.* Washington, DC: American Psychiatric Press. Pp. 59-84.

Cornell, Dewey G., Carolee Miller & Elissa P. Benedek. 1987. MMPI Profiles of adolescents charged with homicide. *Behavioral Sciences & the Law,* 6, 401-407.

Cornell, Dewey G., Lois Staresina & Elissa P. Benedek. 1989. Legal outcome of juveniles charged with homicide. In Elissa Benedek & Dewey Cornell (eds.), *Juvenile Homicide.* Washington, DC: American Psychiatric Press. Pp. 163-182.

Cornish, Derek. 1993. Theories of action in criminology: Learning theory and rational choice approaches. In Ronald V. Clarke & Marcus Felson (eds.), *Routine Activity and Rational Choice: Advances in Criminological Theory.* New Brunswick, NJ: Transaction Publishers. Pp. 351-382.

Cosgrove, Judith, & Terry G. Newell. 1991. Recovery of neuropsychological functions during reduction to use of phencyclidine. *Journal of Clinical Psychology,* 47, 159-169.

Coyle, Joseph T. 1988. Neuroscience and psychiatry. In John A. Talbott, Robert E. Hales & Stuart C. Yudofsky (eds.), *American Psychiatric Press Textbook of Psychiatry.* Washington, DC: American Psychiatric Press. Pp. 3-32.

Crittenden, Patricia M., & Susan E. Craig. 1990. Developmental trends in the nature of child homicide. *Journal of Interpersonal Violence,* 1990, 5, 202-216.

Cromwell, Paul F., Jr., George C. Killinger, Hazel B. Kerper & Charles Walker. 1985. *Probation and Parole in the Criminal Justice System.* St. Paul, MN: West.

Cronbach, Lee J. 1971. Test validation. In Robert L. Thorndike (ed.), *Educational Measurement.* Washington, DC: American Council on Education. Pp. 443-507.

Cronbach, Lee J., & Goldine C. Gleser. 1965. *Psychological Tests and Personnel Decisions.* Urbana: University of Illinois Press.

Croughan, Jack L. 1985. The contribution of family studies to understanding drug abuse. In Lee N. Robins (ed.), *Studying Drug Abuse.* New Brunswick, NJ: Rutgers University Press. Pp. 93-116.

Cullum, C. Munro, & Erin D. Bigler. 1988. Short form MMPI findings in patients with predominantly lateralized cerebral dysfunction: Neuropsychological and computerized axial tomography-derived parameters. *Journal of Nervous & Mental Disease,* 176, 332-342.

Curtiss, Glenn, Mary D. Feczko & Richard C. Marohn. 1979. Rorscach differences in normal and delinquent white male adolescents: A discriminant function analysis. *Journal of Youth & Adolescence,* 8, 379-392.

Dabbs, James M., Robert L. Frady, Timothy S. Carr & Norma F. Besch. 1987. Saliva testosterone and criminal violence in young adult prison inmates. *Psychosomatic Medicine,* 49, 174-182.

Dabbs, James M., Timothy S. Carr, Robert L. Frady & Jasmin K. Riad. 1995. Testosterone, crime, and misbehavior among 692 male prison inmates. *Personality & Individual Differences,* 18, 5, 627-633.

Dahlstrom, W. Grant, James H. Panton, Kenneth P. Bain & Leona E. Dahlstrom. 1986. Utility of the Megargee & Bohn MMPI typological assessments: Study with a sample of death row inmates. *Criminal Justice & Behavior,* 13, 5-17.

Dallas, Dan. 1978. Savagery, show and tell. *American Psychologist,* 33, 388-390.

Daly, Martin, & Margo Wilson. 1989. Homicide and cultural evolution. *Ethology & Sociobiology,* 10, 99-110.

Damasio, Hanna, Thomas Grabowski, Randall Frank, Albert M. Galaburda & Antonio R. Damasio. 1994. The return of Phineas Gage: Clues about the brain from the skull of a famous patient. *Science,* 264, 1101-1105.

Damorsch, Shirley P. 1985. How perceived carelessness and time of attack affect nursing students' attributions about rape victims. *Psychological Reports,* 56, 531-536.

Daniel, Anasseril E., & Philip W. Harris. 1982. Female homicide offenders referred for pre-trial psychiatric examination: A descriptive study. *Bulletin of the American Academy of Psychiatry & the Law,* 10, 261-269.

Daniel, Anasseril E., Philip W. Harris & Sayed A. Husain. 1981. Differences between midlife female offenders and those younger than 40. *American Journal of Psychiatry,* 138, 1225-1228.

Danicl, Chris. 1992. Anger control bibliotherapy with a convicted murderer under life sentence: A clinical report. *Journal of Offender Rehabilitation,* 18, 301-310.

Daniel, David G., Jeffrey R. Zigun & Daniel R. Weinberger. 1992. Brain imagining in neuropsychiatry. In Stuart C. Yudofsky & Robert E. Hales (eds.), *American Psychiatric Press Textbook of Neuropsychiatry,* 2nd ed. Washington, DC: American Psychiatric Press.

Danto, Bruce. 1971. Firearms and their role in homicide and suicide. *Life-Threatening Behavior,* 1, 10-17.

Danto, Bruce. 1985. *Identification and Control of Dangerous and Mentally Disordered Offenders.* Laguna Hills, CA: Eagle.

Daradkeh, Tewfik K. 1990. The possible reasons behind a high intentional homicide rate in Jordan. *Dirasat,* 1988, 15, 59-69.

Davidovich, Jessica R. 1990. Men who abuse their spouses: Social and psychological supports. *Journal of Offender Rehabilitation,* 15, 28-30.

Davis, Bruce A., Peter H. Yu, Alan A. Boulton, J. Stephen Wormith & Donald Addington. 1983. Correlative relationships between biochemical activity and aggressive behavior. *Progress in Neuro-psychopharmacology & Biological Psychiatry,* 7, 529-535.

Davis, Gary, & Richard G. Hoffman. 1991. MMPI and CPA scores of child molesters before and after incarceration-for-treatment. *Journal of Offender Rehabilitation,* 17 (1/2), 77-86.

Davis, Glen E., & Harold Leitenberg. 1987. Adolescent sex offenders. *Psychological Bulletin,* 101, 417-427.

Davis, Hilton. 1974. What does the P scale measure? *British Journal of Psychiatry,* 125, 161-167.

Davis, Kenneth L., Rene S. Kahn, Grant Ko & Michael Davidson. 1991. Dopamine in schizophrenia: A review and reconceptualization. *American Journal of Psychiatry,* 148, 1474-1486.

Davis, Richard. 1993. Biological tests of intelligence as culture fair. *American Psychologist,* 48, 695-696.

Dawes, Robyn M. 1993. Prediction of the future versus an understanding of the past: A basic asymmetry. *American Journal of Psychology*, 106, 1-24.

Dawes, Robyn M., David Faust & Paul E. Meehl. 1989. Clinical versus actuarial judgment. *Science*, 243, 1668-1674.

Dawson, E.B, T.D. Moore & W.J. McGanity. 1972. Relationship of lithium metabolism to mental hospital admission and homicide. *Diseases of the Nervous System*, 33, 546-556.

Day, Lincoln H. 1984. Death from non-war violence: An international comparison. *Social Science & Medicine*, 19, 917-927.

deCastro, Ferreira Elsa, F. Pimenta & I. Martins. 1989. The truth about suicide in Portugal. *Acta Psychiatrica Scandinavica*, 80, 334-339.

Decker, Scott H., & Carol W. Kohlfeld. 1984. A deterrence study of the death penalty in Illinois, 1933-1980. *Journal of Criminal Justice*, 12, 367-377.

DeFrances, Carol J., & Steven K. Smith. 1994. Crime and neighborhoods. *Crime Data Briefs*, June. Washington, DC: Office of Justice Programs, U.S. Department of Justice.

Deitz, Sheila R., Karen T. Blackwell, Paul C. Daley & Brenda J. Bentley. 1982. Measurement of empathy toward rape victims and rapists. *Journal of Personality & Social Psychology*, 43, 372-384.

Deitz, Sheila R., Madeleine Littman & Brenda J. Bentley. 1984. Attribution of responsibility for rape: The influence of observer empathy, victim resistance, and victim attractiveness. *Sex Roles*, 10, 261-280.

Dell, Suzanne. 1983. The detention of diminished responsibility homicide offenders. *British Journal of Criminology*, 23, 50-60.

Dell, Suzanne, & Alan Smith. 1983. Changes in the sentencing of diminished responsibility homicides. *British Journal of Psychiatry*, 142, 20-34.

Dembo, Richard, Max Dertke, Lawrence LaVoie, Scott Borders et al. 1987. Physical abuse, sexual victimization & illicit drug use: a structural analysis among high risk adolescents. *Journal of Adolescence*, 10, 13-34.

Dembo, Richard, Mark Washburn, Eric D. Wish, James Schneider, Alan Getreu, Estellita Berry, Linda Williams & William R. Blount. 1987. Further examination of the association between marijuana use and crime among youths entering a juvenile detention center. *Journal of Psychoactive Drugs*, 19, 361-373.

Demeter, Erzsebet, Kornelia Tekes, Kalman Jaorossy, Miklos Palkovitz et al. 1988. Does -sup-3H-imipramine binding asymmetry indicate psychiatric illness? *Acta Psychiatrica Scandinavica*, 77, 746-747.

Demeter, Erzsebet, Kornelia Tekes, Kalman Jaorossy, Miklos Palkovitz et al. 1989. The asymmetry of -sup-3H imipramine binding may predict psychiatric illness. *Life Sciences*, 44, 1403-1410.

Denkowski, George C., & Kathryn M. Denkowski. 1985. The mentally retarded offender in the state prison system: Identification, prevalence, adjustment, and rehabilitation. *Criminal Justice & Behavior*, 12, 55-70.

Denno, Deborah W. 1990. *Biology and Violence: From Birth to Adulthood*. Cambridge, UK: Cambridge University Press.

Deuser, William E., Kristina M. DeNeve, Kathryn B. Anderson & Mark D. Wood. 1991. Temperature and aggression: Symmetries and asymmetries. American Psychological Society, Washington, 15 June.

DeWolfe, A.S., & J.J. Ryan. 1984. PIQ > VIQ index in a forensic sample: A reconsideration, *Journal of Clinical Psychology*, 40, 291-294.

DeYoub, Paul L. 1984. Hypnotic stimulation of antisocial behavior: A case report. *International Journal of Clinical & Experimental Hypnosis*, 32, 301-306.

DiLalla, Lisabeth Fisher, & Irving I. Gottesman. 1991. Biological and genetic contributors to violence: Widom's untold tale. *Psychological Bulletin*, 109, 125-129.

DiMaria, Franco, & Santo DiNuovo. 1986. Judgments of aggression by Sicilian observers. *Journal of Social Psychology*, 126, 187-196.

Dix, George E. 1983. A legal perspective on dangerousness: Current status. *Psychiatric Annals*, 13, 243-256.

Doerner, William G. 1975. A regional analysis of homicide rates in the United States. *Criminology,* 13, 90-101.

Dollard, John. 1937. *Caste and Class in a Southern Town.* New Haven: Yale University Press.

Donnerstein, Edward I., & Daniel G. Linz. 1986. Mass media sexual violence and male viewers: Current theory and research. *American Behavioral Scientist,* 29, 601-618.

Donnerstein, Edward, & Steven Penrod. 1984. The effects of multiple exposures to filmed violence against women. *Journal of Communication,* 34, 130-147.

D'Orban, P.T. 1990. Female homicide. *Irish Journal of Psychological Medicine,* 7, 64-70.

D'Orban, P.T., & Art O'Conner. 1989. Women who kill their parents. *British Journal of Psychiatry,* 154, 27-33.

D'Souza, Dinesh. 1995. *The End of Racism.* New York: Free Press.

Douglass, John E., Robert K. Ressler, Ann W. Burgess & Carol R. Hartman. 1986. Criminal profiling from crime scene analysis. *Behavioral Science & the Law,* 4, 401-421.

Dubovsky, Steve L. 1987. Severe nortriptyline intoxication due to change from a generic to a trade preparation. *Journal of Nervous & Mental Disease,* 175, 115-117.

Duckitt, John. 1993. Prejudice and behavior: A review. *Current Psychology,* 11, 291-307.

Duffy, Frank H., G.B. McAnulty & M.S. Albert. 1993. The pattern of age-related differences in electrophysiological activity of healthy males and females. *Neurobiology of Aging,* 14, 73-84.

Duffy, James D., & John J. Campbell. 1994. The regional prefrontal syndromes: A theoretical and clinical overview. *Journal of Neuropsychiatry & Clinical Neurosciences,* 6, 379-387.

Dull, Thomas R., & David J. Giacopassi. 1988. Dry, damp, and wet: Correlates and presumed consequences of local alcohol ordinances. *American Journal of Drug & Alcohol Abuse,* 14, 499-514.

DuToit, L., & J. Duckitt. 1990 Psychological characteristics of over- and under-controlled violent offenders. *Journal of Psychology, 124 125-141.*

Earl, William L. 1985. Rape as a variable in marital therapy: Context and treatment. *Family Therapy,* 12, 259-272.

Edel, Wilbur. 1995. *Gun Control: Threat to Liberty or Defense against Anarchy?* Westport, CT: Praeger.

Edinger, Jack D. 1979. Cross-validation of the Megargee MMPI typology for prisoners. *Journal of Consulting & Clinical Psychology,* 47, 234-242.

Edinger, Jack D., David L. Reuterfors & S. Susan Logue, 1982. Cross-validation of the Megargee MMPI typology: A study of specialized inmate populations. *Criminal Justice & Behavior,* 9, 184-203.

Ehrlich, Isaac. 1975-*a*. The deterrent effect of capital punishment: A question of life and death. *American Economic Review,* 65, 397-417.

Ehrlich, Isaac. 1975-*b*. Deterrence: Evidence and interference. *Yale Law Journal,* 85, 209-227.

Elion Victor H., & Edwin I. Megargee, 1975. Validity of the MMPI Pd scale among black males. *Journal of Consulting & Clinical Psychology,* 43, 166-172.

Ellis, Robert H., & Joel S. Milner. 1981. Child abuse and locus of control. *Psychological Reports,* 48, 507-510.

Engel, Jerome. 1989. *Seizures and Epilepsy: Contemporary Neurology.* Philadelphia: Davis.

Erikson, Kai. 1966. *Wayward Puritans: A Study in the Sociology of Deviance.* New York: Wiley.

Erlanger, Howard S. 1974-*a*. The empirical status of the subculture of violence thesis. *Social Problems,* 22, 280-292.

Erlanger, Howard S. 1974-*b*. Social class and corporal punishment in childrearing: A reassessment. *American Sociological Review,* 39, 68-65.

Exner, John E. 1993. *The Rorschach: A Comprehensive System,* 3d ed. New York: Wiley.

Eysenck, Hans J. 1964. *Crime and Personality.* London: Routledge & Kegan Paul.

Eysenck, Hans J. 1967. *Biological Basis of Personality.* Springfield, IL. Charles C. Thomas.

Eysenck, Hans J. 1977-a. *Crime and Personality,* 2nd ed. London: Routledge & Kegan Paul.

Eysenck, Hans J. 1977-b. Personality and factor analysis: A reply to Guilford. *Psychological Bulletin,* 84, 405-411.

Eysenck, Hans J. 1995. The biological bases of crime. *Contemporary Psychology*, 40, 3, 210-211.

Eysenck, Hans J., & Sybil B. Eysenck. 1974. An improved short questionnaire for the measurement of extraversion and neuroticism. *Life Sciences*, 3, 1103-1109.

Eysenck, Hans J., & Gisli H. Gudjunsson. 1989. *The Causes & Cures of Criminality*. New York: Plenum Press.

Eysenck, Sybil B., & Hans J. Eysenck. 1977-a. Personality differences between prisoners and controls. *Psychological Reports*, 40, 1023-1028.

Eysenck, Sybil B., & Hans J. Eysenck. 1977-b. The place of impulsiveness in a dimensional system of personality description. *British Journal of Social & Clinical Psychology*, 16, 57-68.

Eysenck, S.B.G., J. Rust & Hans J. Eysenck. 1977. Personality and the classification of adult offenders. University of London, London. *British Journal of Criminology*, 17, 169-179.

Fagan, Jeffrey. 1989. The social organization of drug use and drug dealing among urban gangs. *Criminology*, 27, 633-639.

Fagan, Jeffrey. 1992. Drug selling and licit income in distressed neighborhoods: The economic lives of street-level drug users and dealers. In Adelle V. Harrell & George E. Peterson (eds.), *Drugs, Crime, and Social Isolation: Barrierts to Urban Opportunity*. Washington, DC: Urban Institute Press.

Fagan, Jeffrey, & Chin Ko-Lin. 1991. Social processes of initiation into crack. *Journal of Drug Issues*, 21, 313-343.

Fanon, Frantz. 1965. *The Wretched of the Earth*. Translated by Constance Farrington. New York: Grove.

Farley, Frank. 1986. The big T in personality. *Psychology Today*, May, 44-52.

Farley, Frank, & Trevor Sewell. 1976. Test of an arousal theory of delinquency. *Criminal Justice & Behavior*, 3, 315-320.

Farrington, David P., Leonard Berkowitz & Donald J. West. 1982. Differences between individual and group fights. *British Journal of Social Psychology*, 21, 323-333.

Fattah, Ezzat A. 1991. *Understanding Criminal Victimization: An Introduction to Theoretical Victimology*. Toronto: Prentice-Hall.

Fattah, Ezzat A. 1993. The rational choice/opportunity perspectives as a vehicle for integrating criminological and victimological theories. In Ronald V. Clarke & Marcus Felson (eds.), *Routine Activity and Rational Choice: Advances in Criminological Theory*. New Brunswick, NJ: Transaction Publishers. Pp. 225-258.

Fausto-Sterling, Anne. 1993. Sex, race, brains, and calipers. *Discover*, October, 32-37.

Fedoroff, J. Paul, Sergio E. Starkstein, Alfred W. Forrester, Fred H. Geisler, Ricardo E. Jorge, Stephan V. Arndt & Robert G. Robinson. 1992. Depression in patients with acute traumatic brain injury. *American Journal of Psychiatry*, 149, 918-923.

Fedoroff, J. Paul, & Shari Pinkus. 1996. A test of the abuse-to-abuser hypothesis of the genesis of pedophilia. In Eli Coleman, S. Margretta Dwyer & Nathaniel J. Pallone (eds.), *Sex Offender Treatment: Biological Dysfunction, Intrapsychic Conflict, Interpersonal Violence*. New York: Haworth.

Fein, Robert A. 1985. How the insanity acquittal retards treatment. *Law & Human Behavior*, 8, 283-292.

Feldman, Esther, Bonnie Levin, Herbert Lubs, Mark Rabin, Marie Louise Lubs, Bonnie Jallad & Alex Kusch. 1993. Adult familial dyslexia: A retrospective developmental and psychosocial profile. *Journal of Neuropsychiatry & Clinical Neurosciences*, 5, 195-199.

Feldman, Marilyn, Katherine Mallouh & Dorothy Otnow Lewis. 1986. Filicidal abuse in the histories of 15 condemned murderers. *Bulletin of the American Academy of Psychiatry & the Law*, 1986, 14, 345-352.

Feldman, Robert S., & Linda F. Quenzer. 1984. *Fundamentals of Neuro-psychopharmacology*. Sunderland, MA: Sinauer.

Felson, Richard B. 1982. Impression management and the escalation of aggression and violence. *Social Psychology Quarterly*, 45, 245-254.

Felson, Richard B. 1993. Predatory and dispute-related violence: A social interactionist approach. In Ronald V. Clarke & Marcus Felson (eds.), *Routine Activity and Rational Choice: Advanced in Criminological Theory.* New Brunswick, NJ: Transaction Publishers. Pp. 103-126.

Felson, Richard B., & Henry J. Steadman. 1983. Situational factors in disputes leading to criminal violence. *Criminology,* 21, 59-74.

Felson, Richard B., & Henry J. Steadman. 1984. Self-reports of violence. *Criminology,* 22, 321-342.

Felson, Richard B., Stephen A. Ribner & Meryl S. Siegel. 1984. Age and the effect of third parties during criminal violence. *Sociology & Social Research,* 68, 452-462.

Ferster, David, & Nelson Spruston. 1995. Cracking the neuronal code. *Science,* 270, 756-758.

Fiddes, Dorothy D. Scotland in the seventies: Adolescents in care and custody — A survey of adolescent murder in Scotland. *Journal of Adolescence,* 4, 47-65.

Finkelhor, David, & Jennifer Dzuiba-Leatherman. 1994. Victimization of children. *American Psychologist,* 49, 173-183.

Finlay, Barbara L., & Richard B. Darlington. 1995. Linked regularities in the development and evolution of mammalian brains. *Science,* 268, 1579-1584.

Finlay, William. 1991. Revelations reassessed — A history of the Hawthorne experiments. *Science,* 254, 1820-1821.

Finley, Wayne H., Clarence E. McDanal, Sara C. Finley & Clarence J. Rosecrans. 1973. Prison survey for the XYY karyotype in tall inmates. *Behavior Genetics,* 1, 97-100.

Fishbain, David A. 1986. Suicide pacts and homicide. *American Journal of Psychiatry,* 143, 1319-1320.

Fishbain, David A., James R. Fletcher, Timothy E. Aldrich & Joseph H. Davis. 1987. Relationship between Russian roulette deaths and risk-taking behavior: A controlled study. *American Journal of Psychiatry,* 144, 563-567

Fishbein, Diana H. 1992. The psychobiology of female aggression. *Criminal Justice & Behavior,* 19, 99-126.

Fishbein, Diana H., & Susan E. Pease. 1994. Diet, nutrition, and aggression. In Marc Hillbrand & Nathaniel J. Pallone (eds.), *The Psychobiology of Aggression.* New York: Haworth. Pp. 117-144.

Fisher, G. 1970. Discriminating violence emanating from over-controlled versus under-controlled aggressivity. *British Journal of Social & Clinical Psychology,* 9, 54-59..

Flanagan, Timothy J., & Katherine M. Jamieson. 1988. *Sourcebook of Criminal Justice Statistics.* Washington, DC: Bureau of Justice Statistics, U.S. Department of Justice.

Flanagan, Timothy J., & Maureen McLeod. 1983. *Sourcebook of Criminal Justice Statistics.* Washington, DC: Bureau of Justice Statistics, U.S. Department of Justice.

Fletcher, Jack M., Linda Ewing-Cobbs, Michael E. Miner, Harvey S. Levin & Lauren Eisenberg. 1990. Behavioral changes after closed head injury in children. *Journal of Consulting & Clinical Psychology,* 1990, 58, 93-98.

Flor-Henry, P., R.A. Lang, Z.J. Koles & R.R. Frenzel. 1991. Quantitative EEG studies of pedophilia. *International Journal of Psychophysiology,* 10, 253-258.

Fogel, Barry S. 1994. The significance of frontal system disorders for medical practice and health policy. *Journal of Neuropsychiatry & Clinical Neurosciences,* 6, 343-347.

Fogel, C.A., S.A. Mednick & N. Michelsen. 1985. Hyperactive behavior and minor physical anomalies. *Acta Psychiatrica Scandinavica,* 72, 551-556.

Fornazzari, Luis, Karl Farcnik, Isaac Smith, Gerald A. Heasman & Mas Ichise. 1992. Violent visual hallucinations and aggression in frontal lobe dysfunction: Clinical manifestations of deep orbitofrontal foci. *Journal of Neuropsychiatry & Clinical Neurosciences,* 4, 42-44.

Forrest, David V. 1987. Psychosocial treatment in neuropsychiatry. In In Robert E. Hales & Stuart C. Yudofsky (eds.), *American Psychiatric Press Textbook of Neuropsychiatry.* Washington, DC: American Psychiatric Press. Pp. 387-410.

Forst, Brian. 1983. Capital punishment and deterrence: Conflicting evidence? *Journal of Criminal Law & Criminology,* 74, 927-942.

Forst, Brian. 1995. Prosecution and sentencing. In James Q. Wilson (ed.), *Crime and Public Policy.* New Brunswick, NJ: Transaction Publishers. Pp. 165-182.

Foucault, Michel. 1978. *Discipline and Punish: The Birth of The Prison.* New York: Pantheon.

Fowler, Raymond D. 1976. Sweeping reforms ordered in Alabama prisons. *American Psychological Association Monitor,* 7(April), 1, 15.

Fowler, Raymond D. 1985. Landmarks in computer-assisted psychological assessment. *Journal of Consulting & Clinical Psychology,* 1985, 53, 748-759.

Fowler, Raymond D. 1988. Assessment for decision in a correctional setting. In Donald R. Peterson & Daniel B. Fishman (eds.), *Assessment for Decision.* New Brunswick, NJ: Rutgers University Press. Pp. 214-239.

Fowles, George P. 1988. Neuropsychologically impaired offenders: Considerations for assessment and treatment. *Psychiatric Annals,* 18, 692-697.

Frances, Richard J., & John E. Franklin. 1987. Alcohol-induced organic mental disorders. In Robert E. Hales & Stuart C. Yudofsky (eds.), *American Psychiatric Press Textbook of Neuropsychiatry.* Washington, DC: American Psychiatric Press. Pp. 141-156.

Frances, Richard J., & John E. Franklin. 1988. Alcohol and other psychoactive substance abuse disorders. In John A. Talbott, Robert E. Hales & Stuart C. Yudofsky (eds.), *American Psychiatric Press Textbook of Psychiatry.* Washington, DC: American Psychiatric Press. Pp. 313-356.

Francione, Gary L. 1995. *Animals, Property, and the Law.* Philadelphia: Temple University Press.

Franke, Richard H., Edward W. Thomas & Allen J. Queenen. 1977. Suicide and homicide: Common sources and consistent relationships. *Social Psychiatry,* 12, 149-156.

Franklin, Ronald D., David B. Allison & Thomas Smith. 1992. Alcohol, substance abuse, and violence among North Carolina prison admissions, 1988. *Journal of Offender Rehabilitation,* 17 (3/4), 101-112.

Fransella, F., & D. Bannister. 1977. *A Manual for Repertory Grid Technique.* London: Academic Press.

Franzen, Michael D., & Mark R. Lovell. 1987. Neuropsychological assessment. In Robert E. Hales & Stuart C. Yudofsky (eds.), *American Psychiatric Press Textbook of Neuropsychiatry.* Washington, DC: American Psychiatric Press. Pp. 41-54.

Franzen, Michael D., & Carl Rollyn Sullivan. 1987. Cognitive rehabilitation of patients with neuropsychiatric disabilities. In Robert E. Hales & Stuart C. Yudofsky (eds.), *American Psychiatric Press Textbook of Neuropsychiatry.* Washington, DC: American Psychiatric Press. Pp. 439-450.

Frantzen, Allen J. 1983. *The literature of penance in Anglo-Saxon England.* New Brunswic, NJ: Rutgers University Press.

Freud, Anna. 1946. *The Ego and the Mechanisms of Defense.* New York: International Universities Press.

Frishtik, Mordechai. 1988. The probation officer's recommendations in his "investigation report." *Journal of Offender Rehabilitation,* 13, 101-132.

Fry, Lincoln J. 1985. Drug abuse and crime in a Swedish birth cohort. *British Journal of Criminology,* 25, 46-59.

Furlong, Michael J., & Donald A. Leton. 1977. The validity of MMPI scales to identify potential child abusers. *Journal of Clinical Child Psychology,* 6, 55-57.

Gabel, Stewart, & Richard Shindledecker, 1993. Parental substance abuse and its relationship to severe aggression and antisocial behavior in youth. *American Journal on Addictions,* 2, 1, 48-59.

Gabel, Stewart, John Stadler, Janet Bjorn, Richard Shindledecker & Charles J. Bowen. 1995. Homovanillic acid and monoamine oxidase in sons of substance-abusing fathers: Relationship to conduct disorders. *Journal of Studies on Alcohol,* 56, 135-139.

Gabrielli, William F., Jr., Sarnoff A. Mednick & Jan Volavka. 1982. Electroencephalograms in children of alcoholic fathers. *Psychophysiology,* 19, 404-407.

Galiher, John F., Gregory Ray & Brent Cook. 1992. Abolition and reinstatement of capital punishment during the Progressive Era and early 20th century. *Journal of Criminal Law & Criminology,* 83, 538-576.

Galski, Thomas, Kirtley E. Thornton & David Shumsky. 1990. Brain dysfunction in sex offenders. *Journal of Offender Rehabilitation,* 16, 65-80.

Gandelman, Ronald. 1980. Gonadal hormones and the induction of intraspecific fighting in mice. *Neuroscience & Biobehavioral Reviews*, 4, 133-140.

Garofalo, James, & Maureen McLeod. 1990. Improving the use and effectiveness of Neighborhood Watch programs. In Larry J. Siegel (ed.), *American Justice: Research of the National Institute of Justice*. St. Paul, MN: West. Pp. 62-66.

Garza-Tevino, Enrique S. 1994. Neurobiological factors in aggressive behavior. *Hospital & Community Psychiatry*, 45, 7, 690-699.

Gastil, Raymond D. 1971. Homicide and a regional culture of violence. *American Sociological Review*, 36, 412-427.

Gaylord, Mark S., & John F. Galliher. 1988. *The Criminology of Edwin Sutherland*. New Brunswick, NJ: Transaction Publishers.

Gearing, Milton L. 1979. The MMPI as a primary differentiator and predictor of behavior in prison: A methodological critique and review of the recent literature. *Psychological Bulletin*, 86, 929-963.

Geen, Russell G., & Leonard Berkowitz. 1969. Some conditions facilitating the occurrence of aggression after the observation of violence. In Leonard Berkowitz (ed.), *Roots of Aggression*. New York: Atherton.

Geiger, Sara G. 1960. Organic factors in delinquency. *Journal of Social Therapy*, 6 (4). 1-16.

Gelberg, Lillian, Lawrence S. Linne & Barbara D. Leake. 1988. Mental health, alcohol and drug use, and criminal history among homeless adults. *American Journal of Psychiatry*, 145, 191-196.

Gelles, Richard J., & Ellen F. Hargreaves, 1990. Maternal employment and violence toward children. In Murray A. Straus & Richard J. Gelles (eds.), *Physical Violence in American Families: Risk Factors and Adaptions to Violence in 8145 Families*. New Brunswick, NJ: Transaction Publishers. Pp. 279-289.

Genet, Jean. 1960. *The Blacks: A Clown Show*. Trans. Bernard Frechtman. New York: Grove.

George, Jennifer M. 1991. State or trait: Effects of positive mood on prosocial behaviors at work. *Journal of Applied Psychology*, 76, 299-307.

Gerbner, George. 1993. "Miracles" of communication technology: Powerful audiences, diverse choices, and other fairy tales. In J. Wasko (ed.), *Illuminating the Blind Spots*. New York: Ablex.

Gerbner, George. 1995. Television violence: The power and the peril. In Gail Dines & Jean M. Humez (eds.), *Gender, Race, and Class in Media*. Thousand Oaks, CA: Sage. 5467-5557.

Gerbner, George, & Nancy Signorelli. 1990. *Violence Profile 1967 through 1988-89: Enduring Patterns*. Philadelphia: Annenberg School of Communications, University of Pennsylvania.

Gessner, Theodore L., Jennifer A. O'Connor, Timothy C. Clifton, Mary Shane Connelly & Michael D. Mumford. The development of moral beliefs: A retrospective study. *Current Psychology*, 12, 236-259.

Gibbs, John J., & Peggy L. Shelly. 1982. Life in the fast lane: A retrospective view by commercial thieves. *Journal of Research in Crime & Delinquency*, 19, 299-330.

Gibbs, W. Wayt. 1995. Trends in behavioral science: Seeking the criminal element — Scientiests are homing in on social and biological risk factors that they believe predispose individuals to criminal behavior. *Scientific American*, 272, 100-107.

Giedd, Jay N., F. Xavier Castellanos, B.J. Casey, Patricia Kozuch, A. Catherine King, Susan D. Hamburger & Judith L. Rapoport. 1994. Quantitative morphology of the corpus callosum in attention deficit hyperactivity disorder. *American Journal of Psychiatry*, 151, 665-669.

Gilandas, Alex, Stephen Touyz, Pierre J.V. Beumont & H.P. Greenberg. 1984. *Handbook of Neuropsychological Assessment*. Sydney: Grune & Stratton.

Gillies, Hunter. 1976. Homicide in the west of Scotland. *British Journal of Psychiatry*, 128, 105-127.

Gilmartin, Zena Pat. 1983. Attribution theory and rape victim responsibility. *Deviant Behavior*, 4, 357-374.

Glaser, Daniel. 1976. Achieving better questions: A half century's progress in correctional research. *Federal Probation*, 4, 3-9.

Glaser, Daniel. 1979. Capital punishment: Deterrent or stimulus to murder? Our unexamined deaths and penalties. *University of Toledo Law Review*, 10, 317-333.

Glueck, Sheldon, & Eleanor Glueck. 1956. *Physique and Delinquency*. New York, Harper.

Godkin, Edwin Lawrence. 1898. *Problems of Modern Democracy: Political and Economic Essays,* 3rd ed. New York: Harcourt.

Goeppinger, H. 1975. Homicide and criminal career: A first provisional report of the investigations of murderers at Tubingen. *Rassegna di Criminologia,* 6, 39-45.

Goetting, Ann. 1988-a. Patterns of homicide among women. *Journal of Interpersonal Violence,* 3, 3-19.

Goetting, Ann. 1988-b. When females kill one another: The exceptional case. *Criminal Justice & Behavior,* 15, 179-189.

Goetting, Ann. 1988-c. When parents kill their young children. *Journal of Family Violence,* 3, 339-346.

Goetting, Ann. 1989-a. Men who kill their mates: A profile. *Journal of Family Violence,* 4, 285-296.

Goetting, Ann. 1989-b. Patterns of homicide among children. *Criminal Justice & Behavior,* 16, 63-80.

Goetting, Ann. 1989-c. Patterns of marital homicide: A comparison of husbands and wives. *Journal of Comparative Family Studies,* 20, 341-354.

Goffman, Erving. 1963. *Stigma: Notes on the Management of a Spoiled Identity.* Englewood Cliffs, NJ: Prentice-Hall.

Goffman, Erving. 1967. *Interaction Ritual: Essays on Face-to-Face Behavior.* Garden City, NY: Anchor.

Golann, Stuart, & William J. Fremouw (eds.). 1976. *The Right to Treatment for Mental Patients.* New York: Irvington.

Goleman, Daniel. 1985. Violence against women in films. *Victimology,* 8, 21-22.

Gomme, Ian M. 1985. Predictors of status and criminal offences among male and female adolescents in an Ontario community. *Canadian Journal of Criminology,* 27, 147-159.

Gordon, Alistair M. 1983. Drugs and delinquency: A ten-year follow-up of drug clinic patients. *British Journal of Psychiatry,* 142, 169-173.

Gordon, Robert A. 1986. Scientific justification and the race-IQ-delinquency model. In Timothy F. Hartnagel & Robert A. Silverman (eds.), *Critique and Explanation.* New Brunswick, NJ: Transaction Publishers. Pp. 91-131.

Gorenstein, Ethan E. 1982. Frontal lobe functions in psychopaths. *Journal of Abnormal Psychology,* 91, 368-379.

Gorenstein, Ethan E., & Joseph P. Newman. 1980. Disinhibitory psychopathology: A new perspective and model for research. *Psychological Review,* 87, 301-315.

Gossop, Michael R., & Sybil B. Eysenck. 1983. A comparison of the personality of drug addicts in treatment with that of a prison population. *Personality & Individual Differences,* 4, 207-209.

Gottfredson, Linda S. 1994. The science and politics of race-norming. *American Psychologist,* 49, 955-963.

Gottfredson, Linda S. 1995. The egalitarian fiction. In Nathaniel J. Pallone & James J. Hennessy (eds.), *Fraud and Faillible Judgment: Varieties of Deception in the Social and Behavioral Sciences.* New Brunswick, NJ: Transaction Publishers. Pp. 95-106.

Gottfredson, Michael R. & Travis Hirschi. 1994. Aggression. In Travis Hirschi & Michael R. Gottfredson (eds.), *The Generality of Deviance.* New Brunswick, NJ: Transaction Publishers. Pp. 23-45.

Gottlieb, Peter, G. Gabrielsen & Peter Kramp. 1988. Increasing rates of homicide in Copenhagen from 1959 to 1983. *Acta Psychiatrica Scandinavica,* 77, 301-308.

Grace, W.C., & M.E. Sweeney. 1986. Comparison of the P>V sign on the WISC-R and WAIS-R in delinquent males. *Journal of Clinical Psychology,* 42, 173-176.

Graham, John R. 1987. *The MMPI: A Practical Guide,* 2nd ed. New York: Oxford University Press.

Graham, John W., Gary Marks & William B. Hansen. 1991. Social influence processes affecting adolescent substance use. *Journal of Applied Psychology,* 76, 291-298.

Graham, Mary G. 1990. Controlling drug abuse and crime: A research update. In Larry J. Siegel (ed.), *American Justice: Research of the National Institute of Justice.* St. Paul, MN: West. Pp. 101-113.

Grant, Brian L., & Cooons, David J. 1983. Guilty verdict in a murder committed by a veteran with post-traumatic stress disorder. *Bulletin of the American Academy of Psychiatry & the Law,* 11, 355-358.

Greenberg, Stephanie W. 1981. Alcohol and crime: A methodological critique of the literature. In James J. Collins, Jr. (ed.), *Drinking and Crime.* New York: Guilford. Pp. 70-109.

Greene, Roger L. 1987. Ethnicity and MMPI performance: A review. *Journal of Consulting & Clinical Psychology,* 55, 497-512.

Greene, Roger L. 1988. The relative efficacy of F-K and the obvious and subtle scales to detect overreporting of psychopathology on the MMPI. *Journal of Clinical Psychology,* 44, 152-159.

Greene, Roger L. 1990. Stability of MMPI scale scores within four codetypes across forty years. *Journal of Personality Assessment,* 55, 1-6.

Greenfield, Susan A. 1995. *Journey to the Centers of the Mind: Toward a Science of Consciousness.* New York: W.H. Freeman.

Greenwood, Peter W. 1995. Controlling the crime rate through imprisonment. In James Q. Wilson (ed.), *Crime and Public Policy.* New Brunswick, NJ: Transaction Publishers. Pp. 251-270.

Grier, William, & Price Cobbs. 1968. *Black Rage.* New York: Basic.

Griswold, David B. 1984. Crime prevention and commercial burglary: A time series analysis. *Journal of Criminal Justice,* 12, 493-501.

Gross, Lawrence S. 1987. Neuropsychiatric aspects of vitamin deficiency states. In Robert E. Hales & Stuart C. Yudofsky (eds.), *American Psychiatric Press Textbook of Neuropsychiatry.* Washington, DC: American Psychiatric Press. Pp. 287-306.

Group for the Advancement of Psychiatry, Committee on Alcoholism and the Addictions. 1991. Substance abuse disorders: A psychiatric priority. *American Journal of Psychiatry,* 148, 1291-1300.

Gruber, Howard E. 1995. Curving the bell. *Peace & Conflict,* 1, 97-98.

Gudjonsson, G. H., H. Petursson, H. Sigurdardottir & S. Skulason. 1991. Overcontrolled hostility among prisoners and its relationship with denial and personality scores. *Personality & Individual Differences,* 12 1, 17-20.

Guilford, Joy Paul. 1967. *The Nature of Human Intelligence.* New York: McGraw-Hill.

Gualtieri, Thomas, Mark Chandler, Tena B. Coons & Lloyd T. Brown. 1989. Amantadine: A new clinical profile for traumatic brain injury. *Clinical Neuropharmacology,* 12, 258-270.

Gunn, John C. 1978-a. Epileptic homicide: A case report. *British Journal of Psychiatry,* 132, 510-513.

Gunn, John C. 1978-b. *Psychiatric Aspects of Imprisonment.* New York: Academic.

Gunn, John. 1982. An English psychiatrist looks at dangerousness. *Bulletin of the American Academy of Psychiatry & the Law,* 10, 143-153.

Gur, Raquel E., Susan M. Resnick, Ruben C. Gur, Abass Alavi, Stanley Caroff, Michael Kushner & Martin Reivich. 1987. Regional brain function in schizophrenia: Repeated evaluation with positron emission tomography. *Archives of General Psychiatry,* 44, 126-129.

Gur, Ruben C., Lyn Harper Mozley, P. David Mozley, Susan M. Resnick, Joel S. Karp, Abass Alavi, Steven E. Arnold & Raquel E. Gur. 1995. Sex differences in regional cerebral glucose metabolism during a resting state. *Science,* 267, 528-536.

Gustafson, Roland. 1994. Alcohol and aggression. In Marc Hillbrand & Nathaniel J. Pallone (eds.), *The Psychobiology of Aggression.* New York: Haworth. Pp. 41-80.

Hall, Calvin S., & Gardner Lindzey. 1970. *Theories of Personality,* 2nd ed. New York: Wiley.

Hall, Eleanor R., Judith A. Howard & Sherrie L. Boezio. 1986. Tolerance of rape: A sexist or antisocial attitude? *Psychology of Women Quarterly,* 10, 101-117.

Hall, Gordon C. 1988. Criminal behavior as a function of clinical and actuarial variables in a sexual offender population. *Journal of Consulting & Clinical Psychology,* 56, 773-775.

Hall, Harold V. 1984. Predicting dangerousness for the courts. *American Journal of Forensic Psychology,* 2, 5-25.

Hall, Harold V., & Douglas McNinch. 1988. Linking crime-specific behavior to neuropsychological impairment. *International Journal of Clinical Neuropsychology,* 10, 113-122.

Hall, Robert W. 1989. A study of mass murder: Evidence of underlying cadmium and lead poisoning and brain involved immunoreactivity. *International Journal of Biosocial & Medical Research,* 11, 144-152.

Halleck, Seymour L. 1987. *The Mentally Disordered Offender.* Washington, DC: American Psychiatric Press.

Halperin, Jeffrey M., Vanshdeep Sharma, Larry J. Siever, Susan T. Schwartz, Kristin Matier, Gibsi Wornell, & Jeffrey H. Newcorn. 1994. Serotonergic function in aggressive and nonaggressive boys with attention deficit hyperactivity disorder. *American Journal of Psychiatry,* 151, 243-248.

Hamburg, David A., & Michelle B. Trudeau (eds.). 1981. *Bio-Behavioral Aspects of Aggression.* New York: Liss.

Hammersley, Richard, & Valerie Morrison. 1987. Effects of polydrug use on the criminal activities of heroin users. *British Journal of Addiction,* 82, 899-906

Hammersley, Richard, & Valerie Morrison. 1988. Crime amongst heroin, alcohol, and cannabis users. *Medicine & Law,* 7, 185-193.

Hammond, W. Rodney, & Betty Yung. 1993. Psychology's role in the public health response to assaultive violence among young African-American men. *American Psychologist,* 48, 142-154.

Hansmann, Henry B., & John M. Quigley. 1982. Population heterogeneity and the sociogenesis of homicide. *Social Forces,* 61, 206-224.

Harding, Richard W. 1993. Gun use in crime, rational choice, and social learning theory. In Ronald V. Clarke & Marcus Felson (eds.), *Routine Activity and Rational Choice: Advances in Criminological Theory.* New Brunswick, NJ: Transaction Publishers. Pp. 85-102.

Hare, Robert D. 1970. *Psychopathy: Theory and Research.* New York: Wiley.

Hare, Robert D. 1979. Psychopathy and laterality of cerebral function. *Journal of Abnormal Psychology,* 88, 605-610.

Hare, Robert D. 1982. Psychopathy and physiological activity during anticipation of an aversive stimulus in a distraction paradigm. *Psychophysiology,* 19, 266-271.

Hare, Robert D. 1984. Performance of psychopaths on cognitive tasks related to frontal lobe function. *Journal of Abnormal Psychology,* 93, 133-140.

Hare, Robert D. 1985. Comparison of procedures for assessment of psychopathy. *Journal of Consulting & Clinical Psychology,* 53, 7-16.

Hare, Robert D. 1991. *The Hare Psychopathy Checklist — Revised (PCL-R).* North Tonawanda, NY: Multi-Health Systems.

Hare, Robert D. 1993. *Without Conscience: The Disturbing World of the Psychopaths among Us.* New York: Pocket.

Hare, Robert D., & Leslie M. McPherson. 1984. Psychopathy and perceptual asymmetry during verbal dichotic listening. *Journal of Abnormal Psychology,* 93, 141-149.

Hare, Robert D., & Leslie M. McPherson. 1985. Violent and aggressive behavior by criminal psychopaths. *International Journal of Law & Psychiatry,* 7, 35-50.

Hare, Robert D., Leslie M. McPherson & Adelle E. Forth. 1988. Male psychopaths and their criminal careers. *Journal of Consulting & Clinical Psychology,* 56, 710-714.

Hare, Robert D., Timothy Harpur, A. Ralph Hakstian & Adelle E. Forth. 1990. The revised psychopathy checklist: Reliability and factor structure. *Journal of Personality Assessment,* 2, 338-341.

Harlow, John M. 1868. Recoverty from the passage of an iron bar through the head. *Publications of the Massachusetts Medical Society,* 2, 327-329.

Harring, Sidney L. 1983. *Policing a Class Society: The Experience of American Cities, 1865-1915.* New Brunswick, NJ: Rutgers University Press.

Harris, Jay E., & Anneliese A. Pontius. 1975. Dismemberment murder: In search of the object. *Journal of Psychiatry & Law,* 3, 7-23.

Harrison, M.J.G., & T.G. Tennent. 1972. Neurological anomalies in XYY males. *British Journal of Psychiatry,* 120, 557, 447-448.

Harry, Bruce. 1983. Movies and behavior among hospitalized mentally disordered offenders. *Bulletin of the American Academy of Psychiatry & the Law,* 4, 359-364.

Hart, Cedric J. 1987. The relevance of a test of speech comprehension deficit to persistent aggressiveness. *Personality & Individual Differences*, 8, 371-384.

Hartman, David E. 1988. *Neuropsychological Toxicity*. New York: Pergamon.

Harvey, O.J. 1962. Personality factors in resolution of conceptual incongruities. *Sociometry*, 25, 336-352.

Haskell, Martin R., & Lewis Yablonsky. 1974. *Crime and Delinquency*. Chicago: Rand McNally.

Hassan, A.M., & P.S. Ward. 1991. On the primacy of the brain. *Current Psychology*, 10, 103-111.

Hathaway, Starke R., & Paul E. Meehl. 1956. Psychiatric implications of code types. In George S. Welsh & W. Grant Dahlstrom (eds.), *Basic Readings on the MMPI in Psychology and Medicine*. Minneapolis: University of Minnesota Press. Pp. 136-144.

Hawkins, Darnell F. 1989. Intentional injury: Are there no solutions? *Law, Medicine & Health Care*, 17, 32-41.

Hayman, L. Anne, & Vincent C. Hinch. 1992. *Clinical Brain Imaging*. St. Louis: Mosby.

Hays, J. Ray, Kenneth S. Solway & Donna Schreiner. 1978. Intellectual characteristics of juvenile murderers versus status offenders. *Psychological Reports*, 43, 80-82.

Heath, Linda, Candace Kruttschnitt & David Ward. 1986. Television and violent criminal behavior: Beyond the bobo doll. *Violence & Victims*, 1, 177-190.

Heather, Nick. 1976. Specificity of schizophrenic thought disorder: A replication and extension of previous findings. *British Journal of Social & Clinical Psychology*, 15, 131-137.

Heather, Nick. 1977. Personal illness in "lifers" and the effects of long-term indeterminate sentences. *British Journal of Criminology*, 17, 378-386.

Heberling, Jon L. 1973. Judicial review of the guilty plea. *Lincoln Law Review*, 7, 137-150.

Heilbrun, Alfred B. 1978. Psychopathy and violent crime. *Journal of Consulting & Clinical Psychology*, 47, 509-516.

Heilbrun, Alfred B. 1982. Cognitive models of criminal violence based upon intelligence and psychopathy levels. *Journal of Consulting & Clinical Psychology*, 50, 546-557.

Heilbrun, Alfred B. 1990. Differentiation of death-row murderers and life-sentence murderers by antisociality and intelligence measures. *Journal of Personality Assessment*, 54, 617-627.

Heilbrun, Alfred B., & Mark R. Heilbrun. 1985. Psychopathy and dangerousness: Comparison, integration, and extension of two psychopathic typologies. *British Journal of Clinical Psychology*, 24, 181-195.

Heinrichs, Douglas W., & Robert W. Buchanan. 1988. Significance and meaning of neurological signs in schizophrenia. *American Journal of Psychiatry*, 145, 11-18.

Heinsohn, Robert, & Craig Packer. 1995. Complex cooperative strategies in group-territorial African lions. *Science*, 269, 1260-1262.

Heller, Melvin S., William H. Taylor, Saundra M. Ehrlich & David Lester. 1984. The association between psychosis and violent crime: A study of offenders evaluated at a court psychiatric clinic. *Journal of General Psychology*, 110, 263-266.

Henderson, Monika. 1983. An empirical classification of non-violent offenders using the MMPI. *Personality & Individual Difference*, 4, 671-677.

Henderson, Monika, & Miles Hewstone. 1984. Prison inmates' explanations for interpersonal violence: Accounts and attributions. *Journal of Consulting & Clinical Psychology*, 52, 789-794.

Hennessy, James J., & Laurie Kepecs-Schlussel. 1992. Psychometric scaling techniques applied to rates of crimes and victimization, I: Major population centers. *Journal of Offender Rehabilitation*, 18, 5-78.

Hennigan, Karen M. 1982. Impact of the introduction of television on crime in the United States: Empirical findings and theoretical implications. *Journal of Personality & Social Psychology*, 42, 461-477.

Herrnstein, Richard. 1990. Biology and crime. In Larry J. Siegel (ed.), *American Justice: Research of the National Institute of Justice*. St. Paul, MN: West. Pp. 11-14.

Herrnstein, Richard J., & Charles Murray. 1994. *The Bell Curve: Intelligence and Class Structure in American Life*. New York: Free Press.

Hillbrand, Marc, Diane Langlan, Christine W. Nelson, Janelle E. Clark & Simone M. Dion. 1994. Cerebral lateralization and aggression. In Marc Hillbrand & Nathaniel J. Pallone (eds.), *The Psychobiology of Aggression.* New York: Haworth. Pp. 81-90.

Hindler, C.G. 1989. Epilepsy and violence. *British Journal of Psychiatry,* 155, 246-249.

Hinds, Lennox S. 1978. *Illusions of Justice.* Iowa City: School of Social Work, University of Iowa.

Hinsie, Leland E., & Robert Jean Campbell. 1970. *Psychiatric Dictionary,* 4th ed. New York: Oxford University Press.

Hirsch, Charles S., Norman B. Rushforth, Amasa B. Ford & Lester Adelson. 1973. Homicide and suicide in a metropolitan county: Long-term trends. *Journal of the American Medical Association,* 223, 900-905.

Hirschi, Travis. 1995. Crime and the family. in James Q. Wilson (ed.), *Crime and Public Policy.* New Brunswick, NJ: Transaction Publishers. Pp. 53-68.

Hirschi, Travis, & Michael J. Hindelang. 1977. Intelligence and delinquency: A revisionist review. *American Sociological Review,* 42, 571-587.

Hirschi, Travis, & Michael R. Gottfredson. 1994. The generality of deviance. In Travis Hirschi & Michael R. Gottfredson (eds.), *The Generality of Deviance.* New Brunswick, NJ: Transaction Publishers. Pp. 1-22.

Hoffman, Michelle. 1991. NMDA receptor cloned — twice. *Science,* 254, 801-89\02.

Hofmann, Frederick G., & Adele D. Hofmann. 1975. *A Handbook on Drug and Alcohol Abuse: The Biomedical Aspects.* New York: Oxford University Press.

Holcomb, William R., & Nicholas Adams. 1982. Racial influences on intelligence and personality measures of people who commit murder. *Journal of Clinical Psychology,* 38, 793-796.

Holcomb, William R., & Nicholas A. Adams. 1985. Personality mechanisms of alcohol-related violence. *Journal of Clinical Psychology,* 41, 714-722.

Holcomb, William R., Nicholas A. Adams & Howard M. Ponder. 1984. Are separate black and white MMPI norms needed? An IQ-controlled comparison of accused murderers. *Journal of Clinical Psychology,* 40, 189-193.

Holcomb, William R., Nicholas A. Adams & Howard M. Ponder. 1985. The development and cross-validation of an MMPI typology of murderers. *Journal of Personality Assessment,* 49, 240-244.

Holcomb, William R., Nicholas A. Adams, Howard M. Ponder & Wayne P. Anderson. 1984. Cognitive and behavioral predictors of MMPI scores in pretrial psychological evaluations of murderers. *Journal of Clinical Psychology,* 40, (2) 592-597.

Holinger, Paul C. 1979. Violent deaths among the young: Recent trends in suicide, homicide, and accidents. *American Journal of Psychiatry,* 136, 1144-1147.

Holinger, Paul C. 1980. Violent deaths as a leading cause of mortality: An epidemiologic study of suicide, homicide, and accidents. *American Journal of Psychiatry,* 137, 472-476.

Holinger, Paul C., & Elaine H. Klemen. 1982. Violent deaths in the United States, 1900-1975: Relationships between suicide, homicide, and accidental deaths. *Social Science & Medicine,* 16, 1928-1938.

Holinger, Paul C., Daniel Offer & Eric Ostrov. 1987. Suicide and homicide in the United States: An epidemiologic study of violent death, population changes, and the potential for prediction. *American Journal of Psychiatry,* 144, 215-219.

Holland, James G., & B.F. Skinner. 1961. *The Analysis of Behavior.* New York: McGraw-Hill.

Holland, Terrill R., & Bill McGarvey. 1985. Crime specialization, seriousness progression, and Markov chains. *Journal of Consulting & Clinical Psychology,* 52, 837-840.

Holland, Terrill R., Gerald B. Beckett & Norman Holt. 1982. Prediction of violent versus nonviolent recidivism from prior violent and nonviolent criminality. *Journal of Abnormal Psychology,* 91, 178-182.

Holland, Terrill R., Gerald E. Beckett & Mario Levi. 1981. Intelligence, personality, and criminal violence: A multivariate analysis. *Journal of Consulting & Clinical Psychology,* 49, 106-111.

Holland, Terrill R., Norman Holt & Gerald E. Beckett. 1982. Prediction of violent versus nonviolent recidivism from prior violent and nonviolent criminality. *Journal of Abnormal Psychology,* 91, 178-182.

Holland, Terrill R., Mario Levi & Gerald E. Beckett. 1983. Associations between violent and non-violent criminality: A canonical contingency-table analysis. *Multivariate Behavioral Research*, 16, 237-241.

Holland,Terrill R., Norman Holt, Mario Levi & Gerald E. Beckett. 1983. Comparison and combination of clinical and statistical predictions of recidivism among adult offenders. Journal of Applied Psychology, 68, (2) 203-211.

Hollin, Clive R. 1990. *Cognitive-Behavioral Interventions with Young Offenders*. New York: Pergamon.

Holmes, Ronald M., & James E. deBurger. 1985. Profiles in terror: The serial murderer. *Federal Probation*, 49, 29-34.

Hoppe, C.M., & R.D. Singer. 1976. Overcontrolled hostility, empathy, and egocentric balance in violent and nonviolent psychiatric offenders. *Psychological Reports*, 39, 1303-1308.

Horowitz, Irving Louis. 1995. The Rushton file: Racial comparisons and media passions. *Transaction/Society*, 32, 7-17.

Hosch, Harmon M., & D. Steven Cooper. 1982. Victimization as a determinant of eyewitness accuracy. *Journal of Applied Psychology*, 67, 649-652.

Hotaling, Gerald T., & David B. Sugarman. 1986. An analysis of risk markers in husband to wife violence: The current state of knowledge. *Violence & Victims*, 1, 101-124.

Howard, Richard C. 1984. The clinical EEG and personality in mentally abnormal offenders. *Psychological Medicine*, 14, 569-580.

Howard, Richard C., Roger Bailey & Alison Newman. 1984. A preliminary study of Hare's "Research Scale for the Assessment of Psychopathy" in mentally-abnormal offenders. *Personality & Individual Differences*, 5, 389-396.

Howells, Kevin, et al. 1984. Perceptions of rape in a British sample: Effects of relationship, victim status, sex, and attitudes to women. *British Journal of Social Psychology*, 21, 35-40.

Howieson, Diane B., & Muriel Lezak. 1992. The neuropsychological examination. In Robert E. Hales & Stuart C. Yudofsky (eds.), *American Psychiatric Press Textbook of Neuropsychiatry*, 2nd ed. Washington, DC: American Psychiatric Press. Pp. 127-150.

Hubble, L.M., & M. Groff. 1980. WISC-R profiles of adjudicated delinquents later incarcerated or released on probation. *Psychological Reports*, 47. 482-483.

Hucker, S., R. Langevin, G. Wortzman & J. Bain. 1986. Neuropsychological impairment in pedophiles. *Canadian Journal of Behavioural Science*, 18, 440-448.

Huff-Corzine, Lin, Jay Corzine & David C. Moore. 1986. Southern exposure: Deciphering the south's influence on homicide rates. *Social Forces*, 64, 906-924.

Hull, Debra B., & Jacqueline Burke. 1991. The religious right, attitudes toward women, and tolerance for sexual abuse. *Journal of Offender Rehabilitation*, 17, 1-12.

Humphrey, John A., & Harriet J. Kupferer. 1977. Pockets of violence: An exploration of homicide and suicide. *Diseases of the Nervous System*, 38, 833-837.

Humphrey, John A., & Stuart Palmer. 1987. Stressful life events and criminal homicide. *Omega: Journal of Death & Dying*, 17, 299-308.

Hunt, Dana E., Douglas S. Lipton & Barry Spunt. 1984. Patterns of criminal activity among methadone clients and current narcotics users not in treatment. *Journal of Drug Issues*, 14, 687-702.

Husain, Arshad, Daniel E. Anasseril & Phillip W. Harris. 1983. A study of young age and mid-life homicidal women admitted to a psychiatric hospital for pretrial evaluation. *Canadian Journal of Psychiatry*, 28, 109-113.

Hutton, H.E., M. H. Miner, J.R. Blades & V.C. Langfeldt. 1992. Ethnic differences on the MMPI overcontrolled-hostility scale. *Journal of Personality Assessment*, 58, 260-268.

Huxley, Aldous. 1953. *The Devils of Loudon*. New York: Harper.

Huxley, Aldous. 1955. *The Genius and the Goddess*. London: Chatto & Windus.

Hyman, Steven E., & Eric J. Nestler. 1993. *The Molecular Foundations of Psychiatry*. Washington, DC: American Psychiatric Press.

Inciardi, James A. 1982. The production and detection of fraud in street studies of crime and drugs. *Journal of Drug Issues,* 12, 285-291.

Inciardi, James A., Anne E. Pottieger & Charles E. Faupel. 1982. Black women, heroin, and crime: Some empirical notes. *Journal of Drug Issues,* 12, 241-250.

Inciardi, James A., Ruth Horowitz & Anne E. Pottieger. 1993. *Street Kids, Street Drugs, Street Crime: An Examination of Drug Use and Serious Delinquency in Miami.* Belmont, CA: Wadsworth.

Infomerica. 1995. *Crime USA.* Orinda, CA: Informerica.

International Criminal Police Organization. 1991. *International Crime Statistics.* Lyons, FR: ICPO-Interpol General Secretariat.

Ito, Yutaka, Martin H. Teicher, Carol A. Glod, David Harper, Eleanor Magnus & Harris A. Gelbard. 1993. Increased prevalence of electrophysiological abnormalities in children with psychological, physical, and sexual abuse. *Journal of Neuropsychiatry & Clinical Neurosciences,* 5, 401-408

Jackson, Douglas N., L. Hournay & N.J. Vidmar. 1972. A four-dimensional interpretation of risk-taking. *Journal of Personality,* 40, 483-501.

Janeskela, Galan M., & Martin G. Miller. 1985. An exploratory study of delinquency, criminal offenses, and juvenile status offenders via the cross-validation design. *Adolescence,* 20, 161-170.

Jarvinen, Liisa. 1977. Personality characteristics of violent offenders and suicidal individuals. *Annals of the Finnish Academy of Sciences,* 19-30.

Jason, Janine. 1984. Centers for Disease Control and the epidemiology of violence. *Child Abuse & Neglect,* 8, 279-283.

Javitt, Daniel C., & Stephen R. Zubin. 1991. Recent advances in the phencyclidine model of schizophrenia. *American Journal of Psychiatry,* 148, 1301-1308.

Jensen, Arthur R. 1965. Maudsley Personality Inventory. In Oscar K. Buros (ed.), *The Sixth Mental Measurement Yearbook.* Highland Park, NJ: Gryphon. Pp. 288-291.

Jensen, Arthur R. 1980. *Bias in Mental Testing.* New York: Free Press.

Johnson, Dennis L., James G. Simmons & B. Carl Gordon. 1983. Temporal consistency of the Meyer-Megargee inmate typology. *Criminal Justice & Behavior,* 10, 263-268.

Johnston, Lloyd D., Patrick M. O'Malley & Jerald G. Bachman, 1987. Psychotherapeutic, licit, and illicit use of drugs among adolescents: An epidemiological perspective. *Journal of Adolescent Health Care.* 8, 36-51.

Jones, Taz, William B. Beidelman & Raymond O. Fowler. 1981. Differentiating violent and non-violent prison inmates by use of selected MMPI scales. *Journal of Clinical Psychology,* 37, 673-678.

Joseph, J.A., & G.S. Roth. 1983. Mechanisms. In D. Samuel, S. Algeri, H. Gersho, V.E. Grimm & G. Toffano (eds.), *Aging of the Brain.* New York: Raven.

Joseph, J.A., R. Villalobos-Molina, K. Yamagami & G.S. Roth. 1995. Age-specific alterations in muscarinic stimulation of K+-evoked dopamine release from striatal slices by cholesterol and S-adenosyl-L-metionine. *Brain Research,* 673, 185-193.

Joseph, Rhawn. 1990. *Neuropsychology, Neuropsychiatry, and Behavioral Neurology.* New York: Plenum.

Junger, Marianne. 1994. Accidents. In Travis Hirschi & Michael R. Gottfredson (eds.), *The Generality of Deviance.* New Brunswick, NJ: Transaction Publishers. Pp. 81-112.

Jutai, Jeffrey W., Robert D. Hare & John F. Connolly. 1987. Psychopathy and event-related brain potentials (ERPs) associated with attention to speech stimuli. *Personality & Individual Differences,* 8, 175-184.

Kahn, Marvin W. 1959. A comparison of personality, intelligence, and social history of two criminal types. *Journal of Social Psychology,* 49, 33-40.

Kahn, Marvin W. 1971. Murderers who plead insanity: A descriptive factor-analytic study of personality, social, and history variables. *Genetic Psychology Monographs,* 84, 275-360.

Kahn, Marvin W., & W.E. Kirk. 1968. The concepts of aggression: A review and reformation. *Psychological Record,* 18, 559-573.

Kahn, Marvin W., & Lawrence Raifman. 1981. Hospitalization versus imprisonment and the insanity plea. *Criminal Justice & Behavior,* 8, 483-490.

Kalichman, Seth C. 1988. MMPI profiles of women and men convicted of domestic homicide. *Journal of Clinical Psychology,* 44, 847-853.

Kalmuss, Debra S., & Murray A. Straus. 1990. Wife's marital dependency and wife abuse. In Murray A. Straus & Richard J. Gelles (eds.), *Physical Violence in American Families: Risk Factors and Adaptions to Violence in 8145 Families.* New Brunswick, NJ: Transaction Publishers. Pp. 360-382.

Kandel, E.R., J.H. Schwartz & T.M. Jessell (eds.) 1991. *Principles of Neural Science,* 3rd edition. New York: Elsevier.

Kandel, Elizabeth, Sarnoff A. Mednick, Lisa Kirkegard-Sorensen, Barry Hutchings et al. 1988. I.Q. as a protective factor for subjects at high risk for antisocial behavior. *Journal of Consulting & Clinical Psychology,* 56, 224-226.

Kanekar, Suresh, & Laura Vaz. 1983. Determinants of perceived likelihood of rape and victim's fault. *Journal of Social Psychology,* 120, 147-148.

Kanekar, Suresh, Nirmala J. Pinto & Deepa Mazumdar. 1985. Causal and moral responsibility of victims of rape and robbery. *Journal of Applied Social Psychology,* 15, 622-637.

Kaplan, Edith. 1990. The process approach to neuropsychological assessment of psychiatric patients. *Journal of Neuropsychiatry & Clinical Neurosciences,* 2, 72-87.

Kaplun, David, & Robert Reich, 1976. The murdered child and his killers. *American Journal of Psychiatry,* 133, 809-813.

Karmen, Andrew. 1990. *Crime Victims,* 2nd ed. Belmont, CA: Wadsworth.

Karuza, Jurgis, & Thomas O. Carey. 1984. Relative preference and adaptiveness of behavioral blame for observers of rape victims. *Journal of Personality,* 52, 249-260.

Kaufman, Alan S., & Nadeen L. Kaufman 1993. *Manual for the Kaufman Brief Intelligence Test.* Circle Pines, MN: American Guidance Service.

Kaufman, Alan S., & Nadeen L. Kaufman 1994. *K-SNAP; Kaufman Short Neuropsychological Assessment Procedure: Manual.* Circle Pines, MN: American Guidance Service.

Kaufman, Joan, & Edward Zigler. 1987. Do abused children become abusive parents? *American Journal of Orthopsychiatry,* 57, 186-192.

Kelley, Katherine A. 1985. Nine social indicia as functions of population size or density. *Bulletin of the Psychonomic Society,* 23, 24-26.

Kelly, George A. 1955. *The Psychology of Personal Constructs.* New York: Norton.

Kelly, George A. 1963. *A Theory of Personality: The Psychology of Personal Constructs.* New York: Norton.

Kelly, George A. 1967. A psychology of the optimal man. In Brendan H. Maher (ed.), *The Goals of Psychotherapy.* New York: Appleton-Century-Crofts.

Kelly, George A. 1969. *Clinical Psychology and Personality: The Selected Papers of George Kelly.* Edited by Brendan Maher. New York: Wiley.

Kelly, George A. 1970. Behavior is an experiment. In D. Bannister (ed.), *Perspectives in Personal Construct Theory.* London: Academic. Pp. 255-269.

Kelly, George A. 1980. A psychology of the optimal man. In Alvin W. Landfield & Larry M. Leitner (eds.), *Personal Construct Psychology.* New York: Wiley. Pp. 33-34.

Keltikangas-Jarvinen, Liisa. 1978. Personality of violent offenders and suicidal individuals. *Psychiatrica Fennica,* 14, 57-63.

Keltikangas-Jarvinen, Liisa. 1980. Rorschach and TAT protocols of violent identical twins: A case report. *Psychiatria Fennica,* 16, 77-80.

Keltikangas-Jarvinen, Liisa. 1982. Alexithymia in violent offenders. *Journal of Personality Assessment,* 46, 462-467.

Kennedy, Thomas D. 1986. Trends in inmate classification: A status report of two computerized psychometric approaches. *Criminal Justice & Behavior,* 13, 165-184.

Kepecs-Schlussel, Laurie, & James J. Hennessy. 1995. Psychodemographic characteristics of homicide and larceny offenders imprisoned in the State of New York. Paper presented at the annual meeting of the American Psychological Association, New York, August.

Kessler, Ronald C., Geraldine Downey, J. Ronald Milavsky & Horst Stipp. 1988. Clustering of teenage suicides after television news stories about suicides; A reconsideration. *American Journal of Psychiatry,* 145, 1379-1383.

Kinard, E. Milling. 1982. Child abuse and depression: Cause or consequence? *Child Welfare,* 61, 403-413.

King, D.P. 1973. Firearms and crime. *Criminologist,* 8, 50-58.

King, David R. 1978. The brutalization effect: Execution publicity and the incidence of homicide in South Carolina. *Social Forces,* 57, 683-687.

Kitahara, Michio. 1986. Dietary tryptophan ratio and homicide in western and southern Europe. *Journal of Orthomolecular Medicine,* 1, 13-16.

Klaus, Patsy A., Michael R. Rand & Bruce M. Taylor. 1983. The victim. *Report to the Nation on Crime and Justice: The Data.* Washington, DC: Bureau of Justice Statistics, U.S. Department of Justice. NCJ-87068.

Klein, David, Maurice S. Reizen, George H. van Amburg & Scott A. Walker. 1977. Some social characteristics of young gunshot fatalities. *Accident Analysis & Prevention,* 9, 177-182.

Klein, Lawrence, Brian Forst & Victor Filatov. 1978. The deterrent effect of capital punishment: An assessment of the estimates. In Alfred Blumstein (ed.), *Deterrence and Incapacitation: Estimating the Effects of Criminal Sanctions on Crime Rates.* Washington, DC: National Academy of Sciences. Pp. 336-360.

Klinge, Valerie, & John Dorsey. 1993. Correlates of the Woodcock-Johnson reading comprehension and Kaufman Brief Intelligence Test in a forensic psychiatric population. *Journal of Clinical Psychology,* 49, 593-598.

Knutson, John F. 1995. Psychological characteristics of maltreated children: Putative risk factors and consequences. *Annual Review of Psychology,* 46, 401-431.

Kolb, Douglas, & E.K. Eric Gunderson. 1985. Research on alcohol abuse and rehabilitation in the U.S. Navy. In Marc A. Schuckit (ed.), *Alcohol Patterns and Problems.* New Brunswick, NJ: Rutgers University Press. Pp. 157-178.

Kokkevi, Anna, & Helen Agathonos. 1988. Intelligence and personality profile of battering parents in Greece: A comparative study. *Child Abuse & Neglect,* 11, 93-99.

Ko-Lin, Chin, Robert J. Kelly & Jeffrey A. Fagan. 1993. Methodological issues in studying Chinese gang extortion. *Gang Journal,* 2, 25-36.

Koshland, Daniel. 1992. Elephants, monstrosities, and the law. *Science,* 255, 777.

Kosslyn, Stephen M. 1994. *Image and Brain.* Cambridge, MA: MIT Press.

Krakowski, Menahem I., Antonio Convit, Judith Jaeger & Shang Lin. 1989. Neurological impairment in violent schizophrenic inpatients. *American Journal of Psychiatry,* 146, 849-853.

Kramer, Morton. 1977. *Psychiatric Services and the Changing Institutional Scene, 1970-1985.* Washington, DC: U.S. Government Printing Office.

Kraulewitz, Judith E. 1982. Reactions to rape victims: Effects of rape circumstances, victim's emotional response, and sex of helper. *Journal of Counseling Psychology,* 29, 645-654.

Kruesi, Markus J., Judith L. Rapoport, E. Mark Cummings & Carol J. Berg. 1987. Effects of sugar and aspartame on aggression and activity in children. *American Journal of Psychiatry,* 144 1487-1490.

Kudryavtsev, V.N. 1974. The structure of criminality and social change. *United Nations Social Defence Research Institute,* 8, 23-39.

Kurlychek, Robert T., & L. Jordan. 1980. MMPI profiles and code types of responsible and non-responsible criminal defendants. *Journal of Clinical Psychology,* 36, 2, 1980, 590-593.

Kunce, Joseph T., Joseph J. Ryan & C. Cleary Eckelman. 1976. Violent behavior and differential WAIS characteristics. *Journal of Consulting & Clinical Psychology,* 44, 42-45.

Kundu, Ramanath, & Gita Bhaumik. 1982. Some affective personality qualities of murderers: A research note. *Personality Study & Group Behavior,* 2, 36-43.

Laborit, Henri-Marie. 1977. *Decoding the Human Message.* Trans. Stephen Bodington & Alison Wilson. New York: St. Martin's.

LaFree, Gary D., Barbara F. Reskin & Christy A. Visher. 1985. Jurors' responses to victims' behavior and legal issues in sexual assault trials. *Social Problems,* 32, 389-407.

Lalli, M., & S.H. Turner. 1968. Suicide and homicide: A comparative analysis by race and occupational levels. *Journal of Criminal Law, Criminology, Police Science,* 59, 191-200.

Lalumiere, Martin L., & Vernon L. Quinsey. 1994. The discrimination of rapists from non-sex offenders using phallometric measures: A meta-analysis. *Criminal Justice & Behavior,* 21, 150-175.

Lamb, H. Richard. 1988. Community psychiatry and prevention. In John A. Talbott, Robert E. Hales & Stuart C. Yudofsky (eds.), *American Psychiatric Press Textbook of Psychiatry.* Washington, DC: American Psychiatric Press. Pp. 1141-1160.

Lamb, H. Richard, & Robert W. Grant. 1982. The mentally ill in an urban county jail. *Archives of General Psychiatry,* 39, 17-22.

Lancaster, Neville P. 1978. Necrophilia, murder, and high intelligence: A case report. *British Journal of Psychiatry,* 132, 605-608.

Landau, Simha F. 1988. Violent crime and its relation to subjective social stress indicators: The case of Israel. *Aggressive Behavior,* 14, 337-362.

Lande, Raymond G. 1993. The video-violence debate. *Hospital & Community Psychiatry,* 44, 4, 347-351.

Lane, J., & J.S. Kling. 1979. Construct validation of the overcontrolled hostility scales of the MMPI. *Journal of Consulting & Clinical Psychology,* 47, 781-782.

Lang, Reuben A., & Ron Langevin. 1991. Parent-child relations in offenders who commit violent sexual crimes against children. *Behavioral Sciences & the Law,* 3, 403-419.

Lang, Reuben A., Roger Holden, Ron Langevin, George M. Pugh et al. 1987. Personality and criminality in violent offenders. *Journal of Interpersonal Violence,* 2, 179-195.

Langevin, Ron. 1982. Diagnosis of killers seen for psychiatric assessment: A controlled study. *Acta Psychiatrica Scandinavica,* 66, 216-228.

Langevin, Ron, Dennis Marentette & Bruno Rosati. 1995. Why therapy fails with some sex offenders: Learning difficulties examined empirically. *Journal of Offender Rehabilitation,* 23 (3/4), 145-157.

Langevin, Ron, Mark Ben-Aron, George Wortzman & Robert Dickey. 1987. Brain damage, diagnosis, and substance abuse among violent offenders. *Behavioral Sciences & the Law,* 5, 77-94.

Langevin, R., D. Paitich, B. Orchard, L. Handy & A. Russon. 1982-a. Diagnosis of killers seen for psychiatric assessment. *Acta Psychiatrica Scandinavica,* 66, 216-228.

Langevin, R., D. Paitich, B. Orchard, L. Handy & A. Russon. 1982-b. The role of alcohol, drugs, suicide attempts and situational strains in homicide committed by offenders seen for psychiatric assessment. *Acta Psychiatrica Scandinavica,* 66, 229-242.

Langevin, R., P. Wright & L. Handy. 1989. Characteristics of sex offenders who were sexually victimized as children. *Annals of Sex Research,* 2, 227-253.

Langevin, R., G. Wortzman, R. Dickey, P. Wright & L. Handy. 1988. Neuropsychological impairment in incest offendrs. *Annals of Sex Research,* 1, 401-415.

Larrance, Deborah T., & Craig T. Twentyman. 1983. Maternal attributions and child abuse. *Journal of Abnormal Psychology,* 92, 449-457.

Larmand, K. & Albert Pepitone. 1982. Judgments of rape: A study of victim-rapist relationship and victim sexual history. *Personality & Social Psychology Bulletin,* 8, 134-139.

Laufer, William S., Dana K. Skogg & James M. Day. 1982. Personality and criminality: A review of the California Psychological Inventory. *Journal of Clinical Psychology,* 38, 562-573.

Laybourn, Ann. 1986. Traditional strict working class parenting: An undervalued system. *British Journal of Social Work,* 16, 625-644.

Leibman, Faith H. 1989. Serial murderers: Four case histories. *Federal Probation,* 53, 41-45.

Lemaku, Paul V. 1961. Notes on the development of mental hygiene in the Johns Hopkins School of Hygiene and Public Health. *Bulletin of the History of Medicine,* 35, 169-174.

Lesco Philip A. 1989. Murder-suicide in Alzheimer's disease. *Journal of the American Geriatrics Society,* 37, 167-168.

Lester, David. 1973. Variation in homicide rate with latitude and longitude in the United States. *Perceptual & Motor Skills,* 36, 532.

Lester, David. 1977. The relationship between suicide and homicide. *Corrective & Social Psychiatry & Journal of Behavior Technology, Methods & Therapy*, 23, 83-84.

Lester, David. 1980. Variation in suicide and homicide by latitude and longitude. *Perceptual & Motor Skills*, 51, 1346.

Lester, David. 1981. Freedom of the press and personal violence: A cross-national study of suicide and homicide. *Journal of Social Psychology*, 114, 267-269.

Lester, David. 1986-*a*. Interaction of divorce, suicide, and homicide. *Journal of Divorce*, 9, 103-109.

Lester, David. 1986-*b*. The distribution of sex and age among victims of homicide: A cross-national study. *International Journal of Social Psychiatry*, 32, 47-50.

Lester, David. 1987-*a*. National distribution of blood groups, personal violence (suicide and homicide), and national character. *Personality & Individual Differences*, 8, 575-576.

Lester, David. 1987-*b*. Religion, suicide, and homicide. *Social Psychiatry*, 22, 99-101.

Lester, David. 1987-*c*. Religiosity and personal violence: A regional analysis of suicide and homicide rates. *Journal of Social Psychology*, 127, 685-686.

Lester, David. 1987-*d*. Substitution of method in suicide and homicide: A regional analysis. *Psychological Reports*, 60, 278.

Lester, David. 1988-*a*. A regional analysis of suicide and homicide rates in the USA: Search For broad cultural patterns. *Social Psychiatry & Psychiatric Epidemiology*, 23, 202-205.

Lester David. 1988-*b*. Economic factors and suicide. *Journal of Social Psychology*, 128, 245-248.

Lester, David. 1988-*c*. Gun control, gun ownership, and suicide prevention. *Suicide & Life-Threatening Behavior*, 18, 176-180.

Lester, David. 1989. The deterrent effect of executions on homicide. *Psychological Reports*, 64, (1) 306.

Lester, David, & Mary E. Murrell. 1982. The preventive effect of strict gun control laws on suicide and homicide. *Suicide & Life-Threatening Behavior*, 12, 131-140.

Levenson, Michael R. 1990. Risk taking and personality. *Journal of Personality & Social Psychology*, 58, 1073-1080.

Levi, J., S. Oppenheim & D. Wechsler. Clinical use of the mental deterioration index of the Wechsler-Bellevue scale. *Journal of Abnormal & Social Psychology*, 40, 405-407.

Levin, Jerome D. 1987. *Treatment of Alcoholism and Other Addictions*. Northvale, NJ: Jason Aronson.

Levine-MacCombie, Joyce, & Mary P. Koss. 1986. Acquaintance rape: Effective avoidance strategies. *Psychology of Women Quarterly*, 10, 311-319.

Lewandowski, Lawrence J., & Barbara Forsstrom-Cohen. 1986. Neurological bases of youth violence. In Steven J. Apter & Arnold P. Goldstein (eds.), *Youth Violence*. Elmsford, NY: Pergamon.

Lewin, Kurt. 1951. *Field Theory in the Social Sciences*. New York: Wiley.

Lewis, Collins E., C. Robert Cloninger & John Pais. 1983. Alcoholism, antisocial personality, and drug use in a criminal population. *Alcohol and Alcoholism*, 18, 53-60.

Lewis, Dorothy Otnow. 1990. Neuropsychiatric and experiential correlates of violent juvenile delinquency. *Neuropsychology Review*, 1, 125-136.

Lewis, Dorothy O., Richard Lovely, Catherine Yeager & George Ferguson. 1988. Intrinsic and environmental characteristics of juvenile murderers. *Journal of the American Academy of Child & Adolescent Psychiatry*, 27, 582-587.

Lewis, Dorothy O., Shelley S. Shanok, Madeline Grant & Eva Ritvo. 1983. Homicidally aggressive young children: Neuropsychiatric and experiential correlates. *American Journal of Psychiatry*, 140, 148-153.

Lewis, Dorothy O., Catherine A. Yeager, Richard Lovely, Abby Stein & Celeste S. Cobham-Portorreal. 1994. A clinical follow-up of delinquent males: Ignored vulnerabilities, unmet needs, and the perpetuation of violence. *Journal of the American Academy of Child & Adolescent Psychiatry*, 33, 518-528.

Lewontin, Richard C., & Daniel L. Hartl. 1991. Population genetics in forensic DNA typing. *Science*, 254, 1745-1750.

Lezak, Muriel Deutsch. 1995. *Neuropsychological Assessment,* 3rd ed. New York: Oxford University Press.

Lidberg, Lars. 1985. Platelet monoamine oxidase activity and psychopathy. *Psychiatry Research,* 16, 339-343.

Lieber, Arnold L. 1978. Human aggression and the lunar synodic cycle. *Journal of Clinical Psychiatry,* 39, 385-392.

Lieber, Arnold L., & Carolyn R. Sherin. 19 1972. Homicides and the lunar cycle: Toward a theory of lunar influence on human emotional disturbance. *American Journal of Psychiatry,* 129, 69-74.

Liederman, Jacqueline. 1988. Misconceptions and new conceptions abut early brain damage, functional asymmetry, and behavioral outcome. In Dennis L. Molfese & Sidney J. Segalowitz (eds.), *Brain Lateralization in Children.* New York: Guilford. Pp. 375-400.

Lilienfeld, Scott O., & Irwin D. Waldman. 1990. The relationship between childhood attention-deficit hyperactivity disorder and adult antisocial behavior re-examined: The problem of heterogeneity. *Clinical Psychology Review,* 10, 699-725.

Lindgren, Scott D., Dennis C. Harper, Lynn C. Richman & James A. Stebbens. 1986. Mental imbalance and the prediction of recurrent delinquent behavior. *Journal of Clinical Psychology,* 42, 821-825.

Lindner, Robert M. 1949. *Handbook of Correctional Psychology.* New York: Philosophical Library.

Lindner, Robert M. 1961. *The Fifty-Minute Hour.* New York: Bantam.

Lindquist, Charles A., Terry D. Smusz & William Doerner. 1985. Causes of conformity: An application of control theory to adult misdemeanant probationers. *International Journal of Offender Therapy & Comparative Criminology,* 29, 1-14.

Lindqvist, Per. 1986. Criminal homicide in northern Sweden, 1970-1981. Alcohol intoxication, alcohol abuse, and mental disease. *International Journal of Law & Psychiatry,* 8, 19-37.

Linz, Daniel G., Edward Donnerstein & Steven Penrod. 1984. The effects of multiple exposures to filmed violence against women. *Journal of Communication,* 34, 130-147.

Linz, Thomas D., Stephen R. Hooper, George W. Hynd, Walter Isaac & Lu Juan Gibson. 1990. Frontal lobe functioning in conduct disordered juveniles: Preliminary findings. *Archives of Clinical Neuropsychology,* 5, 411-416.

Litwack, Thomas R., & Louis B. Schlesinger. 1987. Assessing and predicting violence: Research, law, and applications. In Irving B. Weiner & Allen K. Hess (eds.), *Handbook of Forensic Psychology.* New York: Wiley. Pp. 205-257.

Livesley, W. John, Kerry L. Jang, Douglas N. Jackson & Philip A. Vernon. 1993. Genetic and environmental contributions to dimensions of personality disorder. *American Journal of Psychiatry,* 150, 1826-1831.

Loeber, Rolf. 1982. The stability of antisocial and delinquent child behavior: A review. *Child Development,* 53, 1431-1446.

Loeber, Rolf. 1990. Families and crime. In Larry J. Siegel (ed.), *American Justice: Research of the National Institute of Justice.* St. Paul, MN: West. Pp. 15-18.

Loeber, Rolf, & Karen B. Schmaling. 1985. The utility of differentiating between mixed and pure forms of antisocial child behavior. *Journal of Abnormal Child Psychology,* 13, 315-334.

Loeber, Rolf, Wendy Weissman & John B. Reid. 1983. Family interactions of assaultive adolescents, stealers, and nondelinquents. *Journal of Abnormal Child Psychology,* 11, 1-14.

Loevinger, Jane. 1976. *Ego Development: Conceptions and Theories.* San Francisco: Jossey-Bass.

Loftin, Colin, & Robert H. Hill. 1974. Regional subculture and homicide: An examination of the Gastil-Hackney thesis. *American Sociological Review,* 39, 714-724.

Loftin, Colin, & David McDowall. 1984. The deterrent effects of the Florida felony firearm law. *Journal of Criminal Law & Criminology,* 75, 250-259.

Loftin, Colin, Milton Heumann & David McDowall. 1983. Mandatory sentencing and firearms violence: Evaluating an alternative to gun control. *Law & Society Review,* 17, 287-318.

Louscher, P. Kent, Ray E. Hosford & C. Scott Moss. 1983. Predicting dangerous behavior in a penitentiary using the Megargee typology. *Criminal Justice & Behavior,* 10, 269-284.

Loew, Franklin M. 1981, Statement on behalf of the Institute of Laboratory Animal Resources, National Research Council. In *The Use of Animals in Medical Research & Testing.* Washington, DC: U.S. Government Printing Office. Pp. 151-172.

Lore, Richard K., & Lori A. Schultz. 1993. Control of human aggression: A comparative perspective. *American Psychologist,* 48, 16-25.

Lowenstein L.F. 1988. Licence to kill: Is there a case for the death penalty? *Journal of Rehabilitation,* 252, 32-36.

Lowenstein, L.F. 1989. Homicide: A review of recent research (1975-1985). *Criminologist,* 13, 74-89.

Luckenbill, David F. 1977. Criminal homicide as a situated transaction. *Social Problems,* 25, 175-186.

Luxenbrg, Jay S., Susan E. Swedo, Martine F. Flament, Robert P. Friedland, Judith Rapoport & Stanley L. Rapoport. 1988. Neuroanatomical abnormalities in obsessive compulsive disorder detected with quantitative X-ray computed tomography. *American Journal of Psychiatry,* 145, 1089-1093.

Lykken, David T. 1987. Psychopathic personality. In Raymond J. Corsini (ed.), *Concise Encylopedia of Psychology.* New York: Wiley. Pp. 926-927.

MacCrimmon, K.R., & D.A. Wehrung. 1985. A portfolio of risk measures. *Theory & Decision,* 19, 1-29.

Maccoby, Michael. 1976. *The Gamesman: The New Corporate Leader.* New York: Simon & Schuster.

Maccoby, Michael. 1988. *Why Work: Leading the New Generation.* New York: Simon & Schuster.

Maguire, Kathleen, & Timothy J. Flanagan. 1991. *Sourcebook of Criminal Justice Statistics.* Washington, DC: Bureau of Justice Statistics, U.S. Department of Justice.

Maguire, Kathleen, & Ann L. Pastore. 1994. *Sourcebook of Criminal Justice Statistics.* Washington, DC: Bureau of Justice Statistics, U.S. Department of Justice.

Maher, Brendan H. 1969. *Clinical Psychology and Personality: The Selected Writings of George Kelly.* New York: Wiley.

Mahoney, Michael J. 1976. *Scientist as Subject: The Psychological Imperative.* Cambridge, MA: Ballinger.

Main, Mary, & Ruth Goldwyn. 1984. Predicting rejection of her infant from mother's representation of her own experience: Implications for the abused-abusing intergenerational cycle. *Child Abuse & Neglect,* 8, 203-217.

Maisto, Stephen A. 1995. The ABCs of researching AA. *Contemporary Psychology,* 40, 137-138.

Malamuth, Neil M. 1983. Factors associated with rape as predictions of laboratory aggression against women. *Journal of Personality & Social Psychology,* 50, 953-962.

Malamuth, Neil M. 1986. Predictors of naturalistic sexual aggression. *Journal of Personality & Social Psychology,* 50, 953-962.

Malamuth, Neil M. 1988. Predicting laboratory aggression against female and male targets: Implications for sexual aggression. *Journal of Research in Personality,* 22, 474-495.

Malamuth, Neil M., & John Briere. 1986. Sexual violence in the media: Indirect effects on aggression against women. *Journal of Social Issues,* 42, 75-92.

Malamuth, Neil M., & Paul Centi. 1986. Repeated exposure to violent and non-violent pornography: Likelihood or raping ratings and laboratory aggression against women. *Aggressive Behavior,* 12, 129-137.

Malamuth, Neil M., & James V. Check. 1985. The effects of aggressive pornography on beliefs in rape myths: Individual differences. *Journal of Research in Personality,* 19, 299-320.

Malamuth, Neil M., Maggie Heim & Seymour Feshbach. 1980. Sexual responsiveness of college students to rape depictions. *Journal of Personality & Social Psychology,* 38, 399-408.

Malloy, Paul F., & Emily D. Richardson. 1994. The frontal lobes and content-specific delusions. *Journal of Neuropsychiatry & Clinical Neurosciences,* 6, 455-466.

Mallory, C.H., & C.E. Walker. 1972. MMPI O-H scale responses of assaultive and nonassaultive prisoners and associated life history variables. *Educational & Psychological Measurement*, 32, 1125-1128.

Malmquist, Carl P. 1990. Depression in homicidal adolescents. *Bulletin of the American Academy of Psychiatry & the Law*, 18, 23-26.

Malmquist, Carl P., & Paul E. Meehl. 1978. Barabbas: A study in guilt-ridden homicide. *International Review of Psychoanalysis*, 5, 149-174.

Manderscheid, Ronald W., Michael J. Witkin, Marilyn J. Rosenstein, Laura J. Milazzo-Sayre, Helen E. Bethel & Robin L. MacAskill. 1985. Specialty mental health services: System and patient characteristics. In Carl A. Taube & Sally A. Barrett (eds.), *Mental Health, United States 1985*. Rockville, MD: Division of Biometry & Epidemiology, National Institute of Mental Health, U.S. Department of Health & Human Services. Pp. 7-69.

Mann, Charles. 1995. Regulating cyberspace, *Science*, 268, 628-629.

Mann, Coramae R. 1990. Black female homicide in the United States. *Journal of Interpersonal Violence*, 5, 176-201.

Mann, Jim, Walter Stenning & Christopher Borman. 1992. The utility of the MMPI-2 with pedophiles. In Eli Coleman, S. Margretta Dwyer & Nathaniel J. Pallone (eds.), *Sex Offender Treatment: Psychological and Medical Approaches*. New York: Haworth. Pp. 59-74.

Marohn, Richard C., Ellen M. Locke, Ronald Rosenthal & Glenn Curtiss. 1982. Juvenile delinquents and violent death. *Adolescent Psychiatry*, 10, 147-170.

Marolla, Joseph A., & Diana Scully. 1986. Attitudes toward women, violence, and rape: A comparison of convicted rapists and other felons. *Deviant Behavior*, 7, 337-355.

Marongiu, Pietro, & Ronald V. Clarke. 1993. Ransom kidnapping in Sardinia, subculture theory, and rational choice. In Ronald V. Clarke & Marcus Felson (eds.), *Routine Activity and Rational Choice: Advances in Criminological Theory*. New Brunswick, NJ: Transaction Publishers. Pp. 179-200.

Martell, Daniel A. 1991. Homeless mentally disordered offenders and violent crimes. *Law & Human Behavior*, 15, 333-347.

Martin, Martha B., Cynthia M. Owen & John M. Morisha. 1987. An overview of neurotransmitter and neuroreceptors. In Robert E. Hales & Stuart C. Yudofsky (eds.), *American Psychiatric Press Textbook of Neuropsychiatry*. Washington, DC: American Psychiatric Press. Pp. 55-87.

Martin, Ronald L., C. Robert Cloninger & Samuel B. Guze. 1982. The natural history of somatization and substance abuse in women criminals: A six year follow-up. *Comprehensive Psychiatry*, 23, 528-537.

Martinius, Joest. 1983. Homicide of an aggressive adolescent boy with right temporal lesion. *Neuroscience & BioBehavioral Reviews*, 7, 419-422.

Master, Franklin D. 1984. Punishment of the mentally ill offender: The state of Nevada v. Patrick Henry Lizotte. *American Journal of Forensic Psychiatry*, 5, 17-27.

Matarazzo, Joseph D. 1972. *Wechsler's Measurement and Appraisal of Adult Intelligence, 5th Edition*. Baltimore: Williams & Wilkins.

Mathew, Roy J., William H. Wilson, Dan G. Blazer & Linda K. George. 1993. Psychiatric disorders in adult children of alcoholics: Data from the Epidemiologic Catchment Area project. *American Journal of Psychiatry*, 150, 793-800.

Maunsell, John H.R. 1995. The brain's visual world: Representation of visual targets in cerebral cortex. *Science*, 270, 764-769.

Mawson, A.R., & Keith W. Jacobs. 1978. Corn consumption, tryptophan, and cross-national homicide rates. *Journal of Orthomolecular Psychiatry*, 7, 227-230.

Mayhew, Pat, & David Elliott. 1990. Self-reported offending, victimization, and the British crime survey. *Violence & Victims*, 5, 82-96.

McAfee, James K., & Michele Gural. 1988. Individuals with mental retardation and the criminal justice system. *Mental Retardation*, 26, 5-12.

McCance-Katz, Elinore F., & Lawrence H. Price. 1992. Depression associated with Vitamin A intoxication. *Psychosomatics*, 33, 57.

McCance-Katz, Elinore F., Jorge Leal & Richard S. Schottenfeld. 1995. Attention deficit hyperactivity disorder and cocaine abuse. *American Journal on the Addictions,* 4, 88-91.

McClain, Paula D. 1982. Black female homicide offenders and victims: Are they from the same population? *Death Education,* 6, 265-278.

McCrady, Barbara S., & William R. Miller (eds.), *Research on Alcoholics Anonymous: Opportunities and Alternatives.* Piscataway, NJ: Publications Division, Center of Alcohol Studies, Rutgers University.

McCreary, Charles P. 1976. Trait and type differences among male and female assaultive and non-assaultive offenders. *Journal of Personality Assessment,* 40, 617-621.

McDonald, Angus, & Daniel Paitich. 1981. A study of homicide: The validity of predictive test factors. *Canadian Journal of Psychiatry,* 26, 549-554.

McDonald, Angus & Daniel Paitich. 1982-83. Psychological profile of the rapist. *American Journal of Forensic Psychiatry,* 3, 159-172.

McDowall, David. 1986. Poverty and homicide in Detroit, 1926-1978. *Violence & Victims,* 1, 23-34.

McEwan, Alexander W. 1983. Eysenck's theory of criminality and the personality types and offenses of young delinquents. *Personality & Individual Differences,* 4, 201-204.

McFarland, Sam G. 1983. Is capital punishment a short-term deterrent to homicide? A study of the effects of four recent American executions. *Journal of Criminal Law & Criminology,* 74, 1014-1032.

McGahey, Richard. 1990. Jobs and crime. In Larry J. Siegel (ed.), *American Justice: Research of the National Institute of Justice.* St. Paul, MN: West. Pp. 24-27.

McGarrell, Edmund F., & Timothy J. Flanagan. 1985. *Sourcebook of Criminal Justice Statistics.* Washington, DC: Bureau of Justice Statistics, U.S. Department of Justice.

McGehee, Daniel S., Mark J.S. Heath, Shari Gelber, Piroska Devay & Lorna W. Role. 1995. Nicotine enhancement of fact excitatory synaptic transmission in CNS by presynaptic receptors. *Science,* 269, 1692-1696.

McGlothlin, William H. 1985. Distinguishing effects from concomitants of drug use: The case of crime. In Lee N. Robins (ed.), *Studying Drug Abuse: Series in Psychosocial Epidemiology, VI.* New Brunswick, NJ: Rutgers University Press. Pp. 153-172.

McGovern, Francis J., & Jeffrey S. Nevid. 1986. Evaluation apprehension on psychological inventories in a prison-based setting. *Journal of Consulting & Clinical Psychology,* 54, 576-578.

McGurk, Barry J. 1978. Personality types among homicides. *British Journal of Criminality,* 18, 146-161.

McGurk, Barry J. 1981. Validity and utility of a typology of homicides based on Megargee's theory of control. *Personality & Individual Differences,* 2, 129-136.

McGurk, Barry J., & Neil Bolton. 1981. A comparison of the Eysenck Personality Questionnaire and the Psychological Screening Inventory in a delinquent sample and a comparison group. *Journal of Clinical Psychology,* 37, 874-879.

McGurk, Barry J., & Cynthia McDougall. 1981. A new approach to Eysenck's theory of criminality. *Personality & Individual Differences,* 2, 338-340.

McKinley, J. Charnley, & Starke R. Hathaway. 1956. Scales 3 (Hysteria), 9 (Hypomania), and 4(Psychopathic deviate). In George S. Welsh & W. Grant Dahlstrom (eds.), *Basic Readings on the MMPI in Psychology and Medicine.* Minneapolis: University of Minnesota Press. Pp. 87-103.

McKinley, J. Charnley, Starke R. Hathaway & Paul E. Meehl. 1956. The K scale. In George S. Welsh & W. Grant Dahlstrom (eds.), *Basic Readings on the MMPI in Psychology and Medicine.* Minneapolis: University of Minnesota Press. Pp. 112-123.

Mechanic, David. 1980. *Mental Health and Social Policy,* 2d ed. Englewood Cliffs, NJ: Prentice-Hall.

Mednick, Sarnoff A. & Karl O. Christiansen. 1977. *Biosocial Bases of Criminal Behavior.* New York: Gardner.

Mednick, Sarnoff A., & Jan Volavka. 1980. Biology and crime. In Norval Morris & Michael Tonry (eds.), *Crime and Justice: An Annual Review of Research.* Chicago: University of Chicago Press.

Mednick, Sarnoff A., William F. Gabrielli & Barry Hutchings. 1984. Genetic influences in criminal convictions: evidence from an adoption cohort. *Science,* 224, 891-894.

Mednick, S.A., T.D. Cannon, G.E. Barr & M. Lyon (eds.). 1991. *Fetal Neural Development and Adult Schizophrenia.* New York: Cambridge University Press.

Meehl, Paul E. 1954. *Clinical versus Statistical Prediction: A Theoretical Analysis and a Review of the Evidence.* Minneapolis: University of Minnesota Press.

Meehl, Paul E. 1995. Bootstraps taxonometrics: Sovling the classification problem in psychopathology. *American Psychologist,* 50, 266-275.

Megargee, Edwin I. 1966. Undercontrolled and overcontrolled personality types in extreme antisocial aggression. *Psychological Monographs,* 80, 3 (Number 611).

Megargee, Edwin I. 1970. The prediction of violence with psychological tests. In Charles S. Spielberger (ed.), *Current Topics in Clinical and Community Psychiatry.* New York: Academic Press.

Megargee, Edwin I. 1976. The prediction of dangerous behavior. *Criminal Justice & Behavior,* 3, 3-22.

Megargee, Edwin I. 1977. New classification system for criminal offenders. *Criminal Justice & Behavior,* 4, 1-116.

Megargee, Edwin I. 1982. Psychological correlates and determinants of criminal violence. In Marvin E. Wolfgang & Neil A. Weiner (eds.), *Criminal Violence.* Beverly Hills, CA: Sage.

Megargee, Edwin I. 1984. A new classification system for criminal offenders: VI differences among the types on the Adjective Checklist. *Criminal Justice & Behavior,* 11, 349-376.

Megargee, Edwin I. 1986. A psychometric study of incarcerated presidential threateners. *Criminal Justice & Behavior,* 13, 243-260.

Megargee, Edwin I., & Martin J. Bohn. 1977. Empirically-determined characteristics of the ten types. *Criminal Justice & Behavior,* 4, 149-210.

Megargee, Edwin I., & Martin J. Bohn. 1979. *Classifying Criminal Offenders: A New System Based on the MMPI.* Beverly Hills, CA: Sage.

Megargee, Edwin I., & Joyce L. Carbonell. 1985. Predicting prison adjustment with MMPI correctional scales. *Journal of Consulting & Clinical Psychology,* 53, 874-883.

Megargee, Edwin I., & Patrick E. Cook. 1975. Negative response bias and the MMPI overcontrolled hostility scale. *Journal of Consulting & Clinical Psychology,* 43, 725-729.

Megargee, Edwin I., J.C. Cook & H.T. Mendelsohn. 1967. The development and validation of an MMPI scale of assaultiveness in overcontrolled individuals. *Journal of Abnormal Psychology,* 72, 519-528.

Meharry Medical College. 1991. *Psychiatrist Carl Bell.* Nashville, TN: The College.

Mehlman, P.T., J.D. Higley, I. Faucher, A.A. Lilly, D.M. Taub, J. Vickers, S.J. Suomi & M. Linnoila. Low CSF 5-HIAA concentrations and severe aggression and impaired impulse control in nonhuman primates. *American Journal of Psychiatry,* 151, 1485-1491.

Mehrabian, Albert. 1995. Theory and evidnece bearing on a scale of trait arousability. *Current Psychology,* 14, 3-28.

Meloy, J. Reid. 1988. *The Psychopathic Mind: Origins, Dynamics, Treatment.* Northvale, NJ: Jason Aronson.

Menninger, W. Walter. 1984. Guns and violence: An American phenomenon. *American Journal of Social Psychiatry,* 4, 37-40.

Merbitz, Charles, Santosh Jain, Gleeann L. Good & Ada Jain. 1995. Reported head injury and disciplinary rule infractions in prison. *Journal of Offender Rehabilitation,* 22 (3/4), 11-20.

Messer, Stephen C., Tracy L. Morris & Alan M. Gross. 1990. Hypoglycemia and psychopathology: A methodological review. *Clinical Psychology Review,* 10, 631-648.

Messick, Samuel. 1900. Test validity and the ethics of assessment. *American Psychologist,* 25, 1012-1027.

Messner, Steven F. 1982. Poverty, inequality, and the urban homicide rate: Some unexpected findings. *Criminology,* 20, 103-114.

Messner, Steven F. 1983. Regional and racial effect on the urban homicide rate: The subculture of violence revisited. *American Journal of Sociology,* 88, 997-1007.

Messner, Steven F. 1985. Regional differences in the economic correlates of urban homicide rate: Some evidence on the importance of cultural context. *Criminology,* 21, 477-488.

Messner, Steven F. 1986. Television violence and violent crime: An aggregate analysis. *Social Problems,* 33, 218-235.

Michael, Richard P., & Doris Zumpe. 1983-a. Annual rhythms in human violence and sexual aggression in the United States and the role of temperature. *Social Biology,* 30, 263-278.

Michael, Richard P., & Doris Zumpe. 1983-b. Sexual violence in the United States and the role of season. *American Journal of Psychiatry,* 140, 883-886.

Milavsky, J. Ronald. 1990. TV and violence. In Larry J. Siegel (ed.), *American Justice: Research of the National Institute of Justice.* St. Paul, MN: West. Pp. 11-14.

Milburn, Thomas W. 1963. Design for the study of deterrence. In S.B. Sells (ed.), *Stimulus Determinants of Behavior.* New York: Ronald. Pp. 224-235.

Milgram, Stanley. 1963. Behavioral study of obedience. *Journal of Abnormal & Social Psychology,* 67, 371-378.

Milgram, Stanley. 1965. Some conditions of obedience and disobedience to authority. *Human Relations,* 18, 57-85.

Milgram, Stanley. 1974. *Obedience to Authority: An Experimental View.* New York: Harper & Row.

Miller, Lawrence. 1988. Neuropsychological perspectives on delinquency. *Behavioral Sciences & the Law,* 6, 409-428.

Miller, Lawrence. 1991. Psychotherapy of the brain-injured patient: Principles and practices. *Cognitive Rehabilitation,* 9, 24-30.

Miller, Lawrence. 1994. Traumatic brain injury and aggression. In Marc Hillbrand & Nathaniel J. Pallone (eds.), *The Psychobiology of Aggression.* New York: Haworth. Pp. 91-104.

Miller, Neal E., & John Dollard. 1950. *Social Learning and Imitation.* New Haven: Yale University Press.

Miller, S.J., Simon Dinitz & J. P. Conrad. 1982. *Careers of the Violent.* Lexington, MA: Heath.

Millon, Theodore. 1990. *Toward a New Personology: An Evolutionary Model.* New York: Wiley.

Mills, Shari, & Adrian Raine. 1994. Neuroimaging and aggression. In Marc Hillbrand & Nathaniel J. Pallone (eds.), *The Psychobiology of Aggression.* New York: Haworth. Pp. 145-158.

Mindus, Per, Steven A. Rasmussen & Christer Lindquist.1994. Neurosurgical treatment for refractory obsessive-compulsive disorder: Implications for understanding frontal lobe function. *Journal of Neuropsychiatry & Clinical Neurosciences,* 6, 467-477.

Mischel, Walter. 1973. Toward a cognitive social learning reconceptualization of personality. *Psychological Review,* 80, 252-253.

Mischel, Walter. 1979. On the interface of cognition and personality: Beyond the person-situation debate. *American Psychologist,* 34, 740-754.

Mitra, Charlotte L. 1987. Judicial discourse in father-daughter incest appeal cases. *International Journal of the Sociology of the Law,* 15, 121-148.

Moffitt, Terrie E. 1988. Neuropsychology and self-reported early delinquency in an unselected birth cohort. In Terrie E. Moffitt & Sarnoff A. Mednick (eds.). 1988. *Biological Contributions to Crime Causation.* Amsterdam: Martinus Nijhof.

Moffitt, Terrie E. 1993. Adolescence-limited and life-course-persistent antisocial behavior: A developmental taxonomy. *Psychological Bulletin,* 100, 674-701.

Moffitt, Terrie E. 1994. *Juvenile Delinquency: Seed of A Career in Violent Crime, Just Sowing Wild Oats — or Both?* Washington, DC: Federation of Behavioral, Psychological & Cognitive Sciences.

Moffitt, Terrie E., & Sarnoff A. Mednick (eds.). 1988. *Biological Contributions to Crime Causation.* Amsterdam: Martinus Nijhof.

Moffitt, Terrie E., Sarnoff A. Mednick & William F. Gabrieli, Jr. 1989. Predicting careers of criminal violence: Descriptive data and predispositional factors. In David A. Brizer & Martha L. Crowner (eds.), *Current Approaches to the Prediction of Violence.* Washington, DC: American Psychiatric Press. Pp. 13-34.

Monahan, John. 1976. The prediction of violence. In John Monahan (ed.), *Community Mental Health and the Criminal Justice System.* New York: Pergamon. Pp. 13-34.

Monahan, John. 1981. *The Clinical Prediction of Violent Behavior.* Washington, DC: U.S. Department of Health & Human Services.

Monahan, John, & Henry J. Steadman. 1982. Crime and mental disorder: An epidemiological approach. In Michael Tonry & Norval Morris (eds.), *Crime and Justice,* IV. Chicago: University of Chicago Press.

Montgomery, Lori. 1995. Experts downplay gene-crime link: If there is such a thing, conferees said, it alone would not control crime. *Philadelphia Inquirer,* 25 September, A3.

Moore, Mark H. 1995. Controlling criminogenic commodities: Drugs, guns, and alcohol. in James Q. Wilson (ed.), *Crime and Public Policy.* New Brunswick, NJ: Transaction Publishers. Pp. 125-144.

Morand, Claud, Simon M. Young & Frank R. Ervin. 1983. Clinical response of aggressive schizophrenics to oral tryptophan. *Biological Psychiatry,* 18, 575-578.

Morris, Desmond. 1969. *The Naked Ape.* New York: Dell.

Mosher, Donald L. & Ronald D. Anderson. 1986. Macho personality, sexual aggression, and reactions to guided imagery of realistic rape. *Journal of Research in Personality,* 20, 77-94.

Moss, C. Scott, Mark E. Johnson & Ray E. Hosford. 1984. An assessment of the Megargee typology in lifelong criminal violence. *Criminal Justice & Behavior,* 11, 225-234.

Moss, Howard B., & Ralph E. Tarter. 1993. Substance abuse, aggression, and violence. *American Jounral on Addictions,* 2, 2, 149-160.

Moss, Howard B., George L. Panzak & Ralph E. Tarter. 1992. Personality, mood, and psychiatric symptoms among anabolic steroid users. *American Journal on Addictions,* 1, 4, 315-324..

Motiuk, Laurence L., James Bonta & Don A. Andrews. 1986. Classification in halfway houses: The relative and incremental predictive criterion validities of the Megargee MMPI and LSI systems. *Criminal Justice & Behavior,* 13, 33-46.

Mouridsen, Svend E., & Kai Tolstrup. 1988. Children who kill: A case study of matricide. *Journal of Child Psychology & Psychiatry & Allied Disciplines,* 29, 511-515.

Moyer, K.E. 1968. Kinds of aggression and their physiological basis. *Community & Behavioral Biology,* 2, 65-87.

Mrad, David F., Robert I. Kabacoff & Paul Duckro. 1983. Validation of the Megargee typology in a halfway house setting. *Criminal Justice & Behavior,* 10, 252-262.

Mullen, P.E. 1984. Mental disorder and dangerousness. *Australian & New Zealand Journal of Psychiatry,* 18, 8-17.

Mulvey, Edward P. 1994. Assessing the evidence of a link between mental illness and violence. *Hospital & Community Psychiatry,* 45, 13-19.

Murray, A.M., & J.L. Waddington. 1991. Age-related changes in the regulation of behavior by D-1:D-2 dopamine receptor interactions. *Neurobiology of Aging,* 12, 431-435.

Musick, David. 1995. *An Introduction to the Sociology of Juvenile Delinquncy.* Albany: State University of New York Press.

Myers, Mary B., Donald I. Templer & Ric Brown. 1984. Coping ability in women who become victims of rape. *Journal of Consulting & Clinical Psychology,* 52, 73-78.

Myers, Steven Lee. 1991. Student opens fire at U. of Iowa, killing 4 before shooting himself. *New York Times,* November 2, A-8.

Myers, Wade C., & Anthony Caterine. 1990. Tarasoff and threats of patricide by a 9-year-old boy. *American Journal of Psychiatry,* 147, 535-536.

Myers, Wade C., & John P. Kemph. 1990. DSM-III—R classification of murderous youth: Help or hindrance? *Journal of Clinical Psychiatry,* 51, 239-242.

Nathan, Peter E., & Anne-Helene Skinstad. 1987. Outcomes of treatment for alcohol problems: Current methods, problems, and results. *Journal of Consulting & Clinical Psychology,* 55, 332-340.

National Center for State Courts, U.S. Department of Justice. 1979. *State Court Caseload Statistics.* Washington, DC: National Criminal Justice Statistics and Information Service.

National Institute on Drug Abuse, Substance Abuse & Mental Health Administration, U.S. Department of Health & Human Services. 1994. *Preliminary Estimates from the 1993 National Household Survey on Drug Abuse.* Rockville, MD: Department of Health & Human Services.

Needleman, Harvey. 1983. Lead at low dose and the behavior of children. *Neurotoxicology* 4, 121-133.

Needleman Harvey L. 1989. The persistent threat of lead: A singular opportunity. *American Journal of Public Health,* 79, 643-645.

Nemeroff, Charles B., Michael J. Owens, Garth Bissette, Anne C. Andorn & Michael Stanley. 1988. Reduced corticotropin releasing factor binding sites in the frontal cortex of suicide victims. 1988. *Archives of General Psychiatry,* 45, 577-579.

Nelson, Matt. 1996. Minneapolis sets grim milestones: '95 murder rate makes it one of deadliest cities. *Newsday,* 28 January, A-21.

Nelson, Randy J., Gregory E. Demas, Paul L. Huang, Mark C. Fishman, Valina L. Dawson, Ted M. Dawson & Solomon H. Snyder. 1995. Behavioural abnormalities in male mice lacking neuronal nitric oxide synthase. *Nature,* 378, 383-386.

Newcomb, Michael D., & P.M. Bentler. 1988. Impact of adolescent drug use and social support on problems of young adults: A longitudinal study. *Journal of Abnormal Psychology,* 97, 64-75.

Neylan, Thomas C., Charles F. Reynolds III & David J. Kupfer. 1992. Electrodiagnostic techniques in neuropsychiatry. In Stuart C. Yudofsky & Robert E. Hales (eds.), *American Psychiatric Press Textbook of Neuropsychiatry,* 2nd ed. Washington, DC: American Psychiatric Press.

Niemeyer, Robert A. 1985. *The Development of Personal Construct Theory.* Lincoln, NE: University of Nebraska Press.

Niemeyer, Robert A. 1988. Integrative directions in personal construct therapy. *International Journal of Personal Construct Psychology,* 1, 283-297.

Niemeyer. Robert A. 1990. George A. Kelly: In memoriam. *History of Psychology Newsletter,* 22, 3-14.

Niemeyer, Robert A., & Gregory J. Niemeyer. 1987. *Personal Construct Therapy Casebook.* New York: Springer.

Nowinski, George. 1993. Questioning the answers: Reseach and the AA traditions. In Barbara S. McCrady & William R. Miller (eds.), *Research on Alcoholics Anonymous: Opportunities and Alternatives.* Piscataway, NJ: Publications Division, Center of Alcohol Studies, Rutgers University. Pp. 46-70.

Nurco, David N., John C. Ball, John W. Shaffer & Thomas E. Hanlon. 1985. The criminality of narcotic addicts. *Journal of Nervous & Mental Disease,* 173, 94-102.

Nurco, David N., John W. Shaffer, John C. Ball & Timothy W. Kinlock. 1984. Trends in the commission of crime among narcotic addicts over successive periods of addiction and nonaddiction. *American Journal of Drug & Alcohol Abuse,* 10, 481-489.

O'Brien, Robert M. 1987. The interracial nature of violent crimes: A re-examination. *American Journal of Sociology,* 92, 817-835.

O'Carroll, Patrick W. 1990. Homicides among Black males 15-24 years of age, 1970-84. *Public Health Surveillance of 1990: Injury Control Objectives of the Nation,* 37, 53-60.

O'Carroll, Patrick W., & James A. Mercy. 1989. Regional variation in homicide rates: Why is the West so violent? *Violence & Victims,* 4, 17-25.

O'Connor, Michael E. 1984. The perception of crime and criminality: The violent criminal and swindler as social types. *Deviant Behavior,* 5, 255-274.

O'Malley, Stephanie S., Adam J. Jaffe, Grace Chang, Richard S. Schottenfeld, Roger E. Meyer & Bruce Rounsaville. 1992. Naltrexone and coping skills therapy for alcohol dependence. *Archives of General Psychiatry,* 49, 881-887.

Oetting, E.R., & Fred Beauvais. 1990. Adolescent drug use: Findings of national and local surveys. *Journal of Consulting & Clinical Psychology,* 58, 385-394.

O'Leary, K. Daniel, & G. Terence Wilson. 1975. *Behavior Therapy: Application and Outcome.* Englewood Cliffs, NJ: Prentice-Hall.

Olfson, Mark. 1987. Weir Mitchell and lithium bromide. *American Journal of Psychiatry,* 144, 1101-1102.

Oliver, J.E. 1993. Intergenerational transmission of child abuse: Rates, research, and clinical implications. *American Journal of Psychiatry,* 150, 1315-1324.

Ollendick, T.H. 1979. Discrepancies between verbal and performance IQs and subtest scatter on the WISC-R for juvenile delinquents. *Psychological Reports*, 45, 563-568.

Opton, Edward W. 1971. It never happened — and besides they deserved it. In Nevitt Sanford & Craig Comstock (eds.), *Sanctions for Evil*. San Francisco: Jossey-Bass. Pp. 49-70.

Owens, David J., & Murray A. Straus. 1975. The social structure of violence and approval of violence as an adult. *Aggressive Behavior*, 1, 193-211.

Pallak, Suzanne R. & Jacqueline M. Davies. 1982. Finding fault versus attributing responsibility: Using facts differently. *Personality & Social Psychology Bulletin*, 8, 454-459.

Palley, Howard A., & Dana A. Robinson. 1988. Black on Black crime. *Transaction/Society*, 25, 59-62.

Pallone, Nathaniel J. 1986. *On the Social Utility of Psychopathology: A Deviant Majority and Its Keepers?* New Brunswick, NJ: Transaction Publishers.

Pallone, Nathaniel J. 1988. Advocacy scholarship on the death penalty in the USA. *Transaction/Society*, 26, 177-180.

Pallone, Nathaniel J. 1989. Controlled dangerous substances and felony crime: Data from recent studies in the US. In Raagnar Waahlberg (ed.), *Prevention and Control: Realities and Aspirations*, Volume III. Oslo: National Directorate for the Prevention of Alcohol & Drug Problems. Pp. 498-507.

Pallone, Nathaniel J. 1990-a. Drug use and felony crime: Biochemical credibility and unsettled questions. *Journal of Offender Rehabilitation*, 15, 85-109.

Pallone, Nathaniel J. 1990-b. *Rehabilitating Criminal Sexual Psychopaths: Legislative Mandates, Clinical Quandaries*. New Brunswick, NJ: Transaction Publishers.

Pallone, Nathaniel J. 1991. *Mental Disorder among Prisoners*. New Brunswick, NJ: Transaction Publishers.

Pallone, Nathaniel J. 1992. The MMPI in police officer selection: Legal constraints, case law, empirical data. *Journal of Offender Rehabilitation*, 17 (3/4), 199-216.

Pallone, Nathaniel J. 1996. Sadistic criminal aggression: Perspectives from psychology, criminology, neuroscience. In Louis B. Schlesinger (ed.), *Explorations in Criminal Psychopathology: Clinical Syndromes with Forensic Applications*. Springfield, IL: Charles C. Thomas.

Pallone, Nathaniel J., & James J. Hennessy. 1977. Some correlates of recidivism among misdemeanants and minor felons. *Journal of Social Psychology*, 101, 321-322. .

Pallone, Nathaniel J., & James J. Hennessy. 1992. *Criminal Behavior: A Process Psychology Analysis*. New Brunswick, NJ: Transaction Publishers.

Pallone, Nathaniel J., & James J. Hennessy. 1993. Tinderbox criminal violence: Neurogenic impulsivity, risk-taking, and the phenomenology of rational choice. In Ronald V. Clarke & Marcus Felson (eds.), *Routine Activity and Rational Choice: Advances in Criminological Theory*. New Brunswick, NJ: Transaction Publishers. Pp. 127-158.

Pallone, Nathaniel J., & James J. Hennessy. 1994-95. Luther's call and nitrogen narcosis. *Current Psychology*, 13, 371-373.

Pallone, Nathaniel J., & Daniel S. LaRosa. 1979. Mental health specialists and services in correctional facilities: Who does what? *Journal of Offender Rehabilitation*, 4, 33-41.

Pallone, Nathaniel J., & Richard J. Tirman. 1978. Correlates of substance abuse remission in alcoholism rehabilitation: Effective treatment or symptom abandonment? *Journal of Offender Rehabilitation*, 3, 7-18.

Pallone, Nathaniel J., & Eric Workowski. 1994. Overview: Crime, children, and adolescents. In Nathaiel J. Pallone (ed.), *Young Victims, Young Offenders*. New York: Haworth. Pp. 1-9.

Pallone, Nathaniel J., James J. Hennessy & Daniel S. LaRosa. 1980. Professional psychology in state correctional institutions: Present status and alternate futures. *Professional Psychology*, 11, 755-763.

Palmer, Stuart. 1981. Sex differences in criminal homicide and suicide in England & Wales and in the United States. *Omega*, 11, 255-270.

Panton, James H. 1976. Personality characteristics of death-row prison inmates. *Journal of Clinical Psychology*, 32, 306-309.

Panton, James H. 1977. Personality characteristics of drug pushers incarcerated within a state prison population. *Quarterly Journal of Corrections,* 1, 11-13.

Panton, James H. 1978. Personality differences between rapists of adults, rapists of children, and non-violent sexual molesters of female children. *Research Communications in Psychology, Psychiatry & Behavior,* 3, 385-393.

Panton, James H. 1979. MMPI profile configurations associated with incestuous and non-incestuous child molesting. *Psychological Reports,* 45, 335-338.

Paretsky, Sara. 1991. Soft spot for serial murder: Why do women buy violence against women? *New York Times,* 28 April, E-17.

Parisi, Nicolette, Michael R. Gottfredson, Michael J. Hindelang & Timothy J. Flanagan. 1979. *Sourcebook of Criminal Justice Statistics.* Washington, DC: Bureau of Justice Statistics, U.S. Department of Justice.

Parkchester Journal. 1991. Risk lures teen-agers to "surf" on the subways. *New York Times,* 28 November, B-8.

Parker, Kevin C., R. Karl Hanson & John Hunsley. 1988. MMPI, Rorschach, and WAIS: A meta-analytic comparison of reliability, stability, and validity. *Psychological Bulletin,* 103, 367-373.

Parrington, Vernon Louis. 1930. *Main Currents in American Thought.* New York: Harcourt Brace.

Parwatikar, S.D., William R. Holcomb & Karl A. Menninger. 1985. The detection of malingered amnesia in accused murderers. *Bulletin of the Academy of Psychiatry & the Law,* 13, (1) 97-103.

Pasamanick, Benjamin. 1962. A survey of mental disease in an urban population. *American Journal of Psychiatry,* 119, 299-305.

Passell, Peter, & John B. Taylor. 1977. The deterrent effect of capital punishment: Another view. *American Economic Review,* 67, 445-458.

Pearl D., L. Bouthilet & J. Lazar. 1982. *Television and Behavior: Ten Years of Scientific Progress and Implications for the Eighties,* U.S. Department of Health, Education & Welfare Publication ADM 82-1195. Washington, DC: U.S. Government Printing Office.

Pearson, Frank S., & Jackson Toby. 1991. Fear of school-related predatory crime. *Sociology & Social Research,* 75, 117-125.

Pennsylvania appeals court says patient's psychologist and counselor not liable for failing to warn victim strangled by patient. 1991. *Register Report: Newsletter for Psychologist Health Service Providers,* 17(1), 19.

Penrose, Lionel S. 1939. Mental disease and crime: Outline of a comparative study of European statistics. *Medical Psychology,* 19, 1-15.

Percy, Walker. 1987. *The Thanatos Syndrome.* New York: Farrar, Straus, Giroux.

Perdue, William C., & David Lester. 1974. Racial differences in the personality of murderers. *Perceptual & Motor Skills,* 38, 726.

Peretti, Peter O., & Nancy Cozzens. 1983. Characteristics of female rapees not reporting and reporting the first incidence of rape. *Corrective & Social Psychiatry & Journal of Behavior Technology, Methods & Therapy,* 29, 82-87.

Pernanen, Kai. 1981. Theoretical aspects of the relationship between alcohol use and crime. In James J. Collins, Jr. (ed.), *Drinking and Crime.* New York: Guilford. Pp. 1-69.

Perry, Josephus D., & Miles E. Simpson. 1987. Violent crimes in a city: Environmental determinants. *Environment & Behavior,* 19, 77-90.

Perry, Samuel. 1987. Substance-induced organic mental disorders. In Robert E. Hales & Stuart C. Yudofsky (eds.), *American Psychiatric Press Textbook of Neuropsychiatry.* Washington, DC: American Psychiatric Press. Pp. 157-176.

Petee, Thomas A., & Anthony Walsh, 1987 Violent delinquency, race, and the Wechsler performance-verbal discrepancy. *Journal of Social Psychology,* 127, 3, 353-354.

Petersen, K.G. Ingemar, M. Matousek, Sarnoff A. Mednick, J. Volavka & V. Pollock. 1982. EEG antecedents of thievery. *Acta Psychiatrica Scandinavica,* 65, 331-338.

Petersilia, Joan. 1980. Criminal career research: A review of recent evidence. In Norval Morris & Michael Tonry (eds.), *Crime and Justice, II.* Chicago: University of Chicago Press. Pp. 321-379.

Petti, Theodore A., & Leonard Davidman. 1981. Homicidal school-age children: Cognitive style and demographic features. *Child Psychiatry & Human Development*, 12, 82-89.

Peyser, Marc, Andrew Murr & Rob French. 1995. Danger online: Teens vanish into cyberspace — Were they lured away by computer pals? *Newsweek*, 19 June, 42.

Petursson, Hannes, & Gisli H. Gundjonsson. 1981. Psychiatric aspects of homicide. *Acta Psychiatrica Scandinavica*, 64, 363-371.

Phillips, David P. 1983. The impact of mass media violence in U.S. homicides. *American Sociological Review*, 48, (4) 560-568.

Phillips, David P., & John E. Hensley. 1984. When violence is rewarded or punished: The impact of mass media stories on homicide. *Journal of Communication*, 34, 101-116.

Pichot, Pierre. 1978. Psychopathic behaviour: A historical overview. In Robert D. Hare & Daisy Schalling (eds.), *Psychopathic Behaviour: Approaches to Research*. New York: John Wiley. Pp. 56-70.

Pierce, Michael R. 1979. MMPI profiles of inmates imprisoned for drug-related crimes. *Journal of Forensic Psychology*, 7, 17-21.

Pierce, Lois H., & Robert L. Pierce. 1987. Incestuous victimization by juvenile sex offenders. *Journal of Family Violence*, 2, 351-364.

Pokorny, Alex D., & Joseph Jachimczyk. 1974. The questionable relationship between homicides and the lunar cycle. *American Journal of Psychiatry*, 131, 827-829.

Polman, Dick. 1995. Reeling underneath Hollywood's thumb: Worldwide, lust for U.S. Films is fierce — Some fret about "cultural totalitarianism." *Philadelphia Inquirer*, 26 March, A-1, A-18.

Polich, J. Michael, & Charles T. Kaelber. 1985. Sample survey and the epidemiology of alcoholism. In Marc A. Schuckit (ed.), *Alcohol Patterns and Problems*. New Brunswick, NJ: Rutgers University Press. Pp. 43-77.

Pollock, V.E., John Briere, Lon Schneider & Joachim Knop. 1990. Childhood antecedents of antisocial behavior: Parental alcoholism and physical abusiveness. *American Journal of Psychiatry*, 147, 1290-1293.

Pontius, Anneliese A. 1987. "Psychotic Trigger Reaction" — Neuropsychiatric and neurobiological (limbic?) aspects of homicide, reflecting on normal action. *Integrative Psychiatry*, 5, 116-124.

Pontius, Anneliese A. 1989. Subtypes of limbic system dysfunction evoking homicide in limbic Psychotic Trigger Reaction and temporal lobe epilepsy — Evolutionary constraints. *Psychological Reports*, 65, 659-671.

Pope, Harrison G., & David L. Katz. 1990. Homicide and near-homicide by anabolic steroid users. *Journal of Clinical Psychiatry*, 51, 28-31.

Poussaint, Alvin F. 1983. Black-on-black homicide: A psychological-political perspective. *Victimology*, 8, 161-169.

Prentky, Robert A. 1985. The neurochemistry and neuroendocrinology of sexual aggression. In David Farrington & John Gunn (eds.), *Aggression and Dangerousness*. New York: Wiley. Pp. 7-56.

Prendergast, William E. 1991. *Treating Sex Offenders in Correctional Instiutions and Outpatient Clinics: A Guide to Clinical Practice*. New York: Haworth.

Prendergast, William E. 1993. *The Merry-Go-Round of Sexual Abuse: Identifying and Treating Survivors*. New York: Haworth.

President's Commission on Law Enforcement and Administration of Justice. 1967. *Task Force Report: Science and Technology*. Washington, DC: U.S. Government Printing Office.

Pritchard, David. 1986. Homicide and bargained justice: The agenda setting effect of crime news on prosecutors. *Public Opinion Quarterly*, 50, 143-159.

Pruitt, Charles R., & James Q. Wilson. 1983. A longitudinal study of the effect of race on sentencing. *Law & Society Review*, 17, 613-635.

Pugh, M.D. 1983. Contributory fault and rape convictions: Loglinear models for blaming the victim. *Social Psychology Quarterly*, 46, 233-242.

Putnins, Aldis L. 1982. The Eysenck Personality Questionnaires & delinquency prediction. *Personality & Individual Differences*, 3, 339-340.

Quay, Herbert C. 1965. Psychopathic personality as pathological stimulation seeking. *American Journal of Psychiatry,* 122, 180-183.

Quay, Herbert C. 1987. *Handbook of Juvenile Delinquency.* New York: Wiley.

Quinsey, Vernon L., & Douglas Upfold. 1985. Rape completion and victim injury as a function of female resistance strategy. *Canadian Journal of Behavioural Science,* 17, 40-50.

Quinsey, Vernon L., Terry C. Chaplin, & Douglas Upfold. 1984. Sexual arousal to non-sexual violence and sadomasochistic themes among rapists and non-sex offenders. *Journal of Consulting & Clinical Psychology,* 52, 651-657

Quinsey, V.L., A. Maguire, & G.W. Varney. 1983. Assertion and overcontrolled hostility among mentally disordered murderers. *Journal of Consulting & Clinical Psychology,* 51, 550-556..

Rachlin, Stephen, Abraham L. Halpern & Stanley L. Portnow. 1984. The volitional rule, personality disorders and the insanity defense. *Psychiatric Annals,* 14, 139-141, 145-147.

Rada, Richard T., & Robert Kellner. 1976. Thiothixene in the treatment of geriatric patients with chronic organic brain syndrome. *Journal of the American Geriatrics Society,* 24, 105-107.

Rada, Richard, D.R. Laws, Robert Kellner, Laxmi Stivasta & Glenn Peake. 1983. Plasma androgens in violent and non-violent sex offenders. *Bulletin of the American Academy of Psychiatry & the Law,* 11, 149-158.

Rafuls, William A., Irl Extein, Mark S. Gold & Frederick C. Goggins. 1987. Neuropsychiatric aspects of endocrine disorders. In Robert E. Hales & Stuart C. Yudofsky (eds.), *American Psychiatric Press Textbook of Psychiatry.* Washington, DC: American Psychiatric Press. Pp. 307-325.

Raine, Adrian, 1993-a. Features of borderline personality and violence. *Journal of Clinical Psychology,* 49, 277-280.

Raine, Adrian. 1993-b. *The Psychopathology of Crime: Criminal Behavior as a Clinical Disorder.* San Diego: Academic.

Raine, Adrian, & Peter H. Venables. 1988. Enhanced P3 evoked potentials and longer P3 recovery times in psychopaths. *Psychophysiology,* 25, 30-38.

Raine, Adrian, Mary O'Brien, Norine Smiley & Angela Scerbo. 1990. Reduced lateralization in verbal dichotic listening in adolescent psychopaths. *Journal of Abnormal Psychology,* 99, 272-277.

Ram, P. Kodanda. 1987. A comparative study of murderers and recidivists using Eysenck's personality inventory. *Indian Journal of Clinical Psychology,* 14, 100-101.

Rattner, Arye. 1990. Social indicators and crime rate forecasting. *Social Indicators Research,* 22, 83-95.

Rausch, K., & J.F. Knutson. 1991. The self-report of personal punitive childhood experiences and those of siblings. *Child Abuse & Neglect,* 15, 29-36.

Redl, Fritz, & David Wineman. 1957. *The Aggressive Child.* New York: Free Press.

Reiss, Albert J., Jr., & Jeffrey A. Roth (eds.). 1993. *Understanding and Preventing Violence.* Washington, DC: National Academy Press.

Richardson, Deborah, & Jennifer L. Campbell. 1982. Alcohol and rape: The effect of alcohol on attributions of blame for rape. *Personality & Social Psychology Bulletin,* 8, 468-476.

Richardson, Philip, Mark J. Morein & John G. Phin. 1978. *Criminal Justice Drug Abuse Surveillance System.* Arlington, VA: Creative SocioMedics.

Rieber, Robert W. 1990. In search of the impertinent question: An overview of Bateson's theory of cummunication. In Robert W. Rieber (ed.), *The Individual, Communication, and Society.* New York: Cambridge University Press.

Roberts, Leslie. 1991. More pieces in the dioxin puzzle. *Science,* 254, 277.

Robins, Lee N. 1985. Epidemiology: Reflections on testing the validity of psychiatric interviews. *Archives of General Psychiatry,* 42, 918-924.

Rodenhauser, Paul. 1984. Treatment refusal in a forensic hospital: Ill use of the lasting right. *Bulletin of the American Academy of Psychiatry & the Law,* 12, 59-63.

Rogers, Joseph, & F.E. Bloom. 1985. Neurotransmitter metabolism and function in the aging central nervous system. In C.E. Finch & E.L. Schneider (eds.), *Handbook of the Biology of Aging, 2d ed.* New York: Van Nostrand Reinhold.

Rogers, Richard. 1986. *Conducting Insanity Evaluations*. New York: Van Nostrand Reinhold.

Rohrbeck, Cynthia A., & Craig T. Twentyman. 1986. Multimodal assessment of impulsiveness in abusing, neglecting, and nonmaltreating mothers and their preschool children. *Journal of Consulting & Clinical Psychology*, 54, 231-236.

Roizen, Judy. 1981. Alcohol and criminal behavior among blacks: The case for research on special populations. In James J. Collins, Jr. (ed.), *Drinking and Crime*. New York: Guilford. Pp. 207-252.

Rose, D., & E.J. Bitter. 1982. The Palo Alto destructive content scale as a predictor of physical assaultiveness in men. *Journal of Personality Assessment*, 44, 228-233.

Rosen, Lee A., Sharon R. Booth, Mary E. Bender, Melanie L. McGrath, Sue Sorrell & Ronald S. Drabman. 1988. Effects of sugar (sucrose) on children's behavior. *Journal of Consulting & Clinical Psychology*, 56, 583-589.

Rosenthal, Barry J., & Kareem Nakkash. 1982. Drug addiction and criminality: A model for predicting the incidence of crime among a treatment population. *Journal of Drug Issues*, 12, 293-303.

Rosenthal, Robert, & Richard Rosnow. 1995. Some things you learn aren't so: Cohen's paradox, Asch's paradigm, the interpretation of interaction.*Psychological Science*, 6, 3-9.

Rosse, Richard B., & John M. Morisha. 1988. Laboratory and other diagnostic tests in psychiatry. In John A. Talbott, Robert E. Hales & Stuart C. Yudofsky (eds.), *American Psychiatric Press Textbook of Psychiatry*. Washington, DC: American Psychiatric Press. Pp. 247-277.

Rosse, Richard B., Cynthia M. Owen & John M. Morisha. 1987. Brain imaging and laboratory testing in neuropsychiatry. In Robert E. Hales & Stuart C. Yudofsky (eds.), *American Psychiatric Press Textbook of Neuropsychiatry*. Washington, DC: American Psychiatric Press. Pp. 17-40.

Roth, Jeffrey A. 1994. Firearms and violence. *National Institute of Justice Research Brief*, February. Washington, DC: Office of Justice Programs, U.S. Department of Justice.

Roueche, Berton. 1991. Annals of medicine: A good, safe tan. *New Yorker*, 11 March, 69-74.

Rouke, Byron P., & John L. Fisk. 1988. Subtypes of learning-disabled children: Implications for a neurodevelopmental model of differential hemispheric processing. In Dennis J. Molfese & Sidney J. Segalowitz (eds.), *Brain Lateralization in Children*. New York: Guilford. Pp. 547-565.

Royal College of Psychiatrists. 1987. *Drug Scenes: A Report on Drugs and Drug Dependence*. London: The College.

Rubin, Bernard. 1972. Prediction of dangerousness in mentally ill criminals. *Archives of General Psychiatry*, 25, 397-407.

Rubinson, Eileen, Gregory M. Asnis & Jill H. Friedman. 1988. Knowledge of the diagnostic criteria for major depression: A survey of mental health professionals. *Journal of Nervous & Mental Disease*, 176, 480-484.

Ruff, Carol F., Joyce L. Ayers & Donald I. Templer. 1977. The Watson and the Hovey MMPI scales: Do they measure organicity or functional psychopathology? *Journal of Clinical Psychology*, 33, 732-734.

Rushton, J. Phillipe. 1995-*a*. *Race, Evolution, and Behavior: A Life History Perspective*. New Brunswick, NJ: Tranasction Publishers.

Rushton, J. Phillipe. 1995-*b*. Race and crime: An international dilemma. *Transaction/Society*, 32, 37-41.

Russell, Gordon W., & Lianna Pigat. 1991. Effects of modeled censure/support of media violence and need for approval on aggression. *Current Psychology*, 10, 121-128.

Rutter, Michael. 1996. *Genetics of Criminal and Antisocial Behaviour*. Chichester, UK: Wiley.

Sabaté, Olivier, Dominique Campion, Thierry d'Amato, Marie Pascale Martres, Pierre Sokoloff, Bruno Giros, Marion Leboyer,, Maurice Jay, Françoise Guedj, Florence Thibaut, Sonia Dollfus, Philippe Preterre, Michel Petit, Marie-Claude Babron, Gilles Waksman, Jacques Mallet & Jean Charles Schwartz. 1994. Failure to find evidence for linkage or association between the dopamine D3 receptor gene and schizophrenia. *American Journal of Psychiatry*, 151, 107-111.

Saklofske, D.H., D.W. McKerracher & Sybil B.G. Eysenck. 1978. Eysenck's theory of criminality: A scale of criminal propensity as a measure of antisocial behavior. *Psychological Reports*, 43, 683-686.

Salloway, Stephen P. 1994. Diagnosis and treatment of patients with frontal lobe syndromes. *Journal of Neuropsychiatry & Clinical Neurosciences,* 6, 388-398.

Sampson, Pamela. 1995. Two arrested in a string of four killings: It started with a fight between two brothers, police said — It ended with four dead across central Pennsylvania. *Philadelphia Inquirer,* 4 February, B-1, B-4.

Sampson, Robert J. 1983. Structural density and criminal victimization. *Criminology,* 21, 276-293.

Satz, Paul, Henry J. Soper & Donna L. Orsini. 1988. Human hand preference: Three nondextral subtypes. In Dennis J. Molfese & Sidney J. Segalowitz (eds.), *Brain Lateralization in Children.* New York: Guilford. Pp. 281-287.

Sayle, Murrary. 1995. Letter from Hiroshima: Did the bomb end the war? *New Yorker,* 31 July, 40-64.

Schatzberg, Alan F., & Jonathan O. Cole. 1986. *Manual of Clinical Psychopharmacology.* Washington, DC: American Psychiatric Press.

Schlaug, Gottfried, Lutz Jäncke, Yanxiong Huang & Helmuth Steinmetz. 1995. In vivo evidence of structural brain asymmetry in musicians. *Science,* 267, 699-700.

Schlesinger, Steven R. 1995. Criminal procedure in the courtroom in James Q. Wilson (ed.), *Crime and Public Policy.* New Brunswick, NJ: Transaction Publishers. Pp. 183-206.

Schmideberg, Melitta. 1968. Re-examining the concepts of "rehabilitation" and "punishment." *International Journal of Offender Therapy,* 12, 25-28

Schneider, A.L., P.R. Schneider & S.G. Bazemore. 1981. In-program reoffense rates for juveniles in restitution projects. In *Oversight Hearing on Juvenile Restitution Programs,* NIJ Document 82247. Rockville, MD: National Institute for Juvenile Justice & Delinquency Prevention, U.S. Department of Justice. Pp. 286-368.

Schoenthaler, Stephen J. 1982. The effect of sugar on the treatment and control of antisocial behavior: A double-blind study of an incarcerated juvenile population. *International Journal of Biosocial Research,* 3, 1-9.

Schoenthaler, Stephen J. 1983-a. Diet and crime: An empirical examination of the value of nutrition in the control and treatment of incarcerated juvenile offenders. *International Journal of Biosocial Research,* 4, 23-59.

Schoenthaler, Stephen J. 1983-b. The Los Angeles probation department diet-behavior program: An empirical analysis of six institutional settings. *International Journal of Biosocial Research,* 5, 88-98.

Schoenthaler, Stephen J. 1983-c. The northern California diet-behavior program: An empirical examination of 3000 incarcerated juveniles in Stanislaus County juvenile hall. *International Journal of Biosocial Research,* 5, 99-106.

Schoenthaler, Stephen J. 1983-d. Types of offenses which can be reduced in an institutional setting using nutritional intervention. *International Journal of Biosocial Research,* 4, 74-84.

Schofield, William. 1986. *Psychotherapy: The Purchase of Friendship,* 2nd ed. New Brunswick, NJ: Transaction Publishers.

Schogol, Marc. 1995. Splat, you're dead — War is swell when it's paintball in the Poconos. *Philadelphia Inquirer,* 3 September, T-1, T-7.

Schrauzer, G.N., & K.P. Shrestha. 1990. Lithium in drinking water and the incidences of crimes, suicides, and arrests related to drug addictions. *Biological Trace Element Research,* 25, 105-114.

Schuckit, Marc A. 1994. Low level of response to alcohol as a predictor of future alcoholism. *American Journal of Psychiatry,* 151:184189

Schwitzgebel, Robert L., & R. Kirkland Schwitzgebel. 1980. *Law and Psychological Practice.* New York: John Wiley.

Scott, P.D. 1978. Non-accidental injury in children: Memorandum of evidence to the Parliamentary Select Committee on Violence in the Family. *British Journal of Psychiatry,* 131, 366-380.

Scull, Andrew. 1984. *Decarceration: Community Treatment and the Deviant, A Radical View.* New Brunswick, NJ: Rutgers University Press.

Scully, Diana, & Joseph Marolla. 1984. Convicted rapists' vocabulary of motive: Excuses and justification. *Social Problems,* 31, 530-544.

Scully, Diana, & Joseph Marolla. 1985. "Riding the bull at Gilley's": Convicted rapists describe the rewards of rape. *Social Problems,* 31, 530-544.

Sealy, A.P., & C.M. Wain. 1980. Person perception and juror's decisions. *British Journal of Social & Clinical Psychology*, 19, 7-16.

Sellin, Thorstin. 1959. *The Death Penalty.* Philadelphia: American Law Institute.

Sells, Saul B. 1963. Dimensions of stimulus situations which account for behavior variance. In S.B. Sells (ed.), *Stimulus Determinants of Behavior.* New York: Ronald. Pp. 3-15.

Seplow, Stephen. 1994. The more they watch, the more they fear. *Philadelphia Inquirer,* 2 December, A-1, A-21.

Seymour, Richard, & David E. Smith. 1987. *The Physician's Guide to Psychoactive Drugs.* Binghamton: Haworth.

Shaalan, Mohammed, Ahmed S. El-Akaboui, & Sayed El-Kott. 1983. Rape victims in Egypt. *Victimology,* 8, 277-290.

Shaffer, David, Madelyn Gould & Roger C. Hicks. 1994. Worsening suicide rate in Black teenagers. *American Journal of Psychiatry,* 151, 1810-1812.

Sheldon, William H. 1942. *The Varieties of Temperament: A Psychology of Constitutional Differences.* New York: Harper & Brothers.

Sheldon, William H. 1949. *Varieties of Delinquent Youth: An Introduction to Constitutional Psychiatry.* New York: Harper & Brothers.

Sheppard, Anne. 1994. Childrens' understanding of television progammes: Three exploratory studies. *Current Psychology,* 13, 124-137.

Sherman, Lawrence W. 1993. Defiance, deterrence, and irrelevance: A theory of the criminal sanction. *Journal of Research in Crime & Delinquency,* 30, 445-473.

Sherry, Michael S. 1995. A war technology: America's pursuit of precision bombing. *Science,* 269, 1599-1600.

Shockley, William. 1971. Models, mathematics, and the moral obligation to diagnose the origin of Negro IQ deficits. *Review of Educational Research,* 41, 369-377.

Shoham, Shlomo G., Giora Rahav, Rachel Markowski, Frances Chard et al. 1987. Family parameters of violent prisoners. *Journal of Social Psychology,* 127, 83-91.

Shrout, Patrick E., Michael Lyons, Bruce P. Dohrenwend, Andrew E. Skodol, Murray Solomon & Frederick Kass. 1988. Changing time frames on symptom inventories: Effects on the Psychiatric Epidemiology Research Interview. *Journal of Consulting & Clinical Psychology,* 56, 267-272.

Siever, Larry J., & Kenneth L. Davis. 1991. A psychobiological perspective on the personality disorders. *American Journal of Psychiatry,* 148, 1647-1658.

Siever, Larry J., Bonnie J. Steinberg, Robert L. Trestman & Joanne Intrator. 1994. Personality disorders. *Review of Psychiatry, Volume 13.* Wahington, DC: American Psychiatric Press.

Sila, Ante. 1977. Psychopathologic traits of perpetrators of felonious homicides. *Socijalna Psichijatrija,* 5, 3-81.

Silver, Jonathan M., Stuart C. Yudofsky & Robert E. Hales. 1987. Neuropsychiatric aspects of traumatic brain injury. In Robert E. Hales & Stuart C. Yudofsky (eds.), *American Psychiatric Press Textbook of Neuropsychiatry.* Washington, DC: American Psychiatric Press. Pp. 179-190.

Silverman, Robert A., & Leslie W. Kennedy. 1988. Women who kill their children. *Violence & Victims,* 3, 113-127.

Silverman, Daniel C., S. Michael Kalick, Sally I. Bowie, & Susan D. Edbril. 1988. Blitz rape and confidence rape: A typology applied to 1,000 consecutive cases. *American Journal of Psychiatry,* 145, 1438-1441.

Simon, Robert I. 1987. *Clinical Psychiatry and the Law.* Washington, DC: American Psychiatric Press.

Singer, Wolf. 1995. Development and plasticity of cortical processing architectures. *Science,* 270, 758-764.

Singh, Arvinder. 1980. Study of personality of murderers and the psychosocial factors related to murder. *Indian Journal of Criminology,* 8, 15-20.

Sivak, Michael. 1983. Society's aggression level as a predictor of traffic fatality rate. *Journal of Safety Research*, 14, 93-99.

Skinner, B.F. 1938. *The Behavior of Organisms: An Experimental Analysis.* New York: Appleton-Century-Crofts.

Skinner, B.F. 1957. *Verbal Behavior.* New York: Appleton-Century-Crofts.

Skinner, B.F. 1961. *Cumulative Record.* New York: Appleton-Century-Crofts.

Skinner, B.F. 1974. *About Behaviorism.* New York: Appleton-Century-Crofts.

Skinner, B.F. 1948. *Walden Two.* New York: Macmillan.

Skog, Ole-Jørgen, & Ragnar Waahlberg (eds.). 1989. *Alcohol and Drugs: The Norwegian Experience.* Oslo: National Directorate for the Prevention of Alcohol and Drug Problems.

Sloan, John H., Arthur L. Kellermann, Donald T. Reay, James A. Ferris et al. 1989. Handgun regulations, crime, assaults, and homicide: A tale of two cities. *New England Journal of Medicine,* 319, 1256-1262.

Slovic, P. 1987. Perception of risk. *Science,* 236, 280-285.

Smeaton, George, & Donn Byrne. 1987. The effects of R-rated violence & erotica, individual differences, & victim characteristics on acquaintance rape proclivity. *Journal of Research in Personality,* 21, 171-184.

Smith, Brian. 1988. Personality: Multivariate systems theory. In James Nesseleroade & Raymond B. Cattell (eds.), *Handbook of Multivariate Experimental Psychology,* 2d ed. New York: Plenum. Pp. 687-736.

Smith, Lynda B., David E. Silber & Stephen A. Karp. 1988. Validity of the Megargee-Bohn MMPI typology with women incarcerated in a state prison. *Psychological Reports,* 62, 107-113.

Smith, M. Brewster. 1991. Genocide and moral disobedience: Evil and resistance to evil in psychological perspective. *Contemporary Psychology,* 36, 384-386.

Smith, Robert J., Karen Tritt & Andreas Zollman. 1982. Sex differences in the social perception of rape victims in West Germany and the United States. *Journal of Social Psychology,* 117, 143-144.

Snyder, Solomon H. 1988. Psychotogenic drugs as models for schizophrenia: Comments on the current status of the dopamine hypothesis of schizophrenia. *Neuro-psycho-pharmacology,* 1, 197-199.

Solloway, Stephen P. 1994. Diagnosis and treatment of patients with frontal lobe syndromes. *Journal of Neuropsychiatry & Clinical Neurosciences,* 6, 388-398.

Sommers, Evelyn K., & James V. Check. 1987. An empirical investigation of the role of pornography in the verbal and physical abuse of women. *Violence & Victims,* 2, 189-209.

Sorrells, James M. 1977. Kids who kill. *Crime & Delinquency,* 23, 312-320.

Sorensen, David W.M. 1994. Motor vehicle accidents. In Travis Hirschi & Michael R. Gottfredson (eds.), *The Generality of Deviance.* New Brunswick, NJ: Transaction Publishers. Pp. 113-130.

Spearman, Charles. 1927. *The Abilities of Man.* New York: Macmillan.

Spellacy, Frank J. 1978. Neuropsychological discrimination between violent and nonviolent men. *Journal of Clinical Psychology,* 34, 49-52.

Srivastava, Shri O. 1976. A social psychological study of the condemned prisoners in Uttar Pradesh. *Social Defence,* 11, 38-49.

Srole, Leo, Thomas S. Langer, Stanley T. Michael, Marvin K. Opler & Thomas A.C. Bennie. 1962. *Mental Health in the Metropolis.* New York: McGraw-Hill.

Srole, Leo, & Anita Kassen Fischer. 1986. The Midtown Manhattan longitudinal study: Aging, generations, and genders. In Myrna M. Weissman, Jerome K. Myers & Catherine E. Ross (eds.), *Community Surveys of Psychiatric Disorders.* New Brunswick, NJ: Rutgers University Press. Pp. 77-108.

Stack, Steven. 1989. The effect of publicized mass murders and murder-suicides on lethal violence, 1968-1980: A research note. *Social Psychiatry & Psychiatric Epidemiology,* 24, 202-208.

Staub, Ervin. 1989. *The Roots of Evil: The Origins of Genocide and Other Group Violence.* Cambridge, UK: Cambridge University Press.

Steadman, Henry J. 1982. A situational approach to violence. *International Journal of Law & Psychiatry,* 5, 171-186.

Steadman, Henry J., Marilyn J. Rosenstein, Robin L. MacAskill & Ronald W. Manderscheid. 1988. A profile of mentally disordered offenders admitted to inpatient psychiatric services in the United States. *Law & Human Behavior,* 12, 91-99.

Stein, Dan J., Eric Hollander & Michael R. Leibowitz. 1993. Neurobiology of impulsivity and the impulse control disorders. *Journal of Neuropsychiatry & Clinical Neurosciences,* 5, 9-17.

Steinmetz, Suzanne K. 1980. Women and violence: Victims and perpetrators. *Journal of Psychotherapy,* 34, 334-350.

Stephen, James, & Peter Brien. 1994. Capital punishment 1993. *Bureau of Justice Statistics Bulletin,* December. Washington, DC: Office of Justice Programs, U.S. Department of Justice.

Stern, Daniel, & Nathaniel J. Pallone. 1971. Effects of brief exposure to photographic vs. prose reporting of racial aggression or harmony upon certain racial attitudes. *Journal of Social Psychology,* 85, 93-101.

Stevens, Gail Flint. 1993. Applying the diagnosis antisocial personality to imprisoned offenders: Looking for hay in a haystack. *Journal of Offender Rehabilitation,* 19 (1/2), 1-26.

Stevens, Gail Flint. 1994. Prison clinicians' perceptions of antisocial personality disorder as a formal diagnosis. *Journal of Offender Rehabilitation,* 20 (3/4), 1560-186.

Stevens, Leonard A. 1971. *Explorers of the Brain.* New York: Knopf.

Stevenson, James M., & John H. King. 1987. Neuropsychiatric aspects of epilepsy and epileptic seizures. In Robert E. Hales & Stuart C. Yudofsky (eds.), *The American Psychiatric Press Textbook of Neuropsychiatry.,* Washington, DC; American Psychiatric Press. Pp. 209-224.

Stewart, C.H.M., & D.R. Helmsley. 1979. Risk perception and likelihood of action in criminal offenders. *British Journal of Criminology,* 19, 105-119.

Stewart, C.H., & D.R. Helmsley. 1984. Personality factors in the taking of criminal risks. *Personality & Individual Differences,* 5, 119-122.

Stone, Evelyn M. 1988. *American Psychiatric Glossary.* Washington, DC: American Psychiatric Press.

Storm, Jonathan. 1994. From academia, a cry for less violence on TV. *Philadelphia Inquirer,* December 28, A-1, A-10.

Stoudemire, G. Alan. 1987. Selected organic mental disorders. In Robert E. Hales & Stuart C. Yudofsky (eds.), *American Psychiatric Press Textbook of Neuropsychiatry.* Washington, DC: American Psychiatric Press. Pp. 125-140.

Straus, Murray A. 1979-*a.* Family patterns and child abuse in a nationally representative American sample. *Child Abuse & Neglect,* 3, 213-225.

Straus, Murray A. 1979-*b.* Measuring intrafamily conflict and violence: The Conflict Tactics (CS) scales. *Journal of Marriage & the Family,* 41, 75-88.

Straus, Murray A. 1980-*a. Behind Closed Doors: Violence in the American Family.* Garden City, NY: Anchor-Doubleday.

Straus, Murray Arnold. 1980-*a.* Stress and physical child abuse. *Child Abuse & Neglect,* 4, 75-88.

Straus, Murray Arnold, & Richard J. Gelles. 1990. *Physical Violence in American Families: Risk Factors and Adaptations.* New Brunswick, NJ: Transaction Publishers.

Strauss, Abbey. 1989. Homicidal psychosis during the combined use of cocaine and an over-the-counter preparation. *Journal of Clinical Psychiatry,* 50, 147.

Suinn, Richard M. 1960. The Shipley-Hartford Retreat Scale as a screening test of intelligence. *Journal of Clinical Psychology,* 16, 419.

Surette, Ray. 1990. *The Media and Criminal Justice Policy: Recent Research and Social Effects.* Springfield, IL: Charles C. Thomas.

Surgeon General's Scientific Advisory Committee on Television and Social Behavior. 1972. *Television and Growing Up: The Impact of Televised Violence.* Washington, DC, US Public Health Service.

Sutherland, Edwin H. 1947. *Principles of Criminology,* 4th ed. Philadelphia: Lippincott.

Sutherland, Edwin H., & Donald R. Cressey. 1978. *Criminology,* 10th ed. Philadelphia: Lippincott.

Sutker, Patricia B., Albert N. Allain & Scott Geyer. 1978. Female criminal violence and differential MMPI characteristics. *Journal of Consulting & Clinical Psychology,* 46, 1141-1143.

Swift, Robert M., William Whelihan, Oleg Kuznetsov, Gregg Buongiornio & Hayden Hsuing. 1994. Naltrexone-induced alterations in human ethanol intoxication. *American Journal of Psychiatry,* 151, 1463-1467.

Szasz, Thomas. 1987. *Insanity: The Idea and Its Consequences.* New York: John Wiley.

Szasz, Thomas. 1993. *A Lexicon of Lunacy: Metaphoric Malady, Moral Responsibility, and Psychiatry.* New Brunswick, NJ: Transaction Publishers.

Szasz, Thomas. 1994. Mental illness is still a myth. *Transaction/Society,* 31 (4), 34-39.

Tardiff, Kenneth J. 1988. Violence. In John A. Talbott, Robert E. Hales & Stuart C. Yudofsky (eds.), *American Psychiatric Press Textbook of Psychiatry.* Washington, DC: American Psychiatric Press. Pp. 1037-1058.

Tardiff, Kenneth J. 1989. A model for the short-term prediction of violence potential. In David A. Brizer & Martha L. Crowner (eds.), *Current Approaches to the Prediction of Violence.* Washington, DC: American Psychiatric Press. Pp. 1-12.

Tarter, Ralph E. 1988. Are there inherited behavioral traits that predispose to substance abuse? *Journal of Consulting & Clinical Psychology,* 56, 189-196.

Tarter, Ralph E., Andrea M. Hegedus & Arthur T. Alterman. 1983. Cognitive capacities of juvenile, violent, nonviolent, and sexual offenders. *Journal of Nervous & Mental Disease,* 171, 564-567.

Tarter, Ralph E., Andrea M. Hegedus, Nancy E. Winsten & Arthur T. Alterman. 1984. Neuropsychological, personality, and familial characteristics of physically abused delinquents. *Journal of the American Academy of Child Psychiatry,* 23, 668-674.

Tarter, Ralph E., Timothy Blackson, Christopher Martin, Rolf Loeber & Howard B. Moss. 1993. Characteristics and correlates of child discipline practices in substance abuse and normal families. *American Journal on Addictions,* 2, 1, 18-25.

Taubes, Gary. 1995. Epidemiology facies its limits. *Science,* 269. 164-169.

Tauchen, Helen, Ann Dryden Witte & Harriet Griesinger. 1994. Criminal deterrence: Revisiting the issue with a birth cohort. *Review of Economics & Statistics,* 76, 399-412.

Taylor, Lathrop, & W.H. Griffith. 1993. Age-related decline in cholinergic synaptic transmission in the hippocampus. *Neurobiology of Aging,* 14, 509-515.

Taylor, Michael Alan, Frederick S. Sierles, & Richard Abrams. 1987. The neuropsychiatric evaluation. In Robert E. Hales & Stuart C. Yudofsky (eds.), *American Psychiatric Press Textbook of Neuropsychiatry.* Washington, DC: American Psychiatric Press. Pp. 3-16.

Taylor, Pamela J. 1986. Psychiatric disorder in London's life-sentenced offenders. *British Journal of Criminology,* 26, 63-78.

Teicher, Martin H., Carol A. Glod, Janet Surrey & Chester Swett. 1993. Early childhood abuse and limbic system ratings in adult psychiatric outpatients. *Journal of Neuropsychiatry & Clinical Neurosciences,* 5, 301-306.

Teplin, Linda A. 1983. The criminalization of the mentally ill: Speculation in search of data. *Psychological Bulletin,* 94, 54-67.

Thibaut, John W., & Harold H. Kelly. 1978. *Interpersonal Relations: A Theory of Interdependence.* New York: Harper.

Thionen, Jari, Jyrki Kuikka, Kim Bergstrom, Panu Harola, Jari Karhu, Olli-Pekka Rynánen & Jaana Fohr. 1995. Altered stiatal dopamine re-uptake site densities in habitually violent and non-violent alcoholics. *Nature/Medicine,* 1, 654-657.

Thornton, Billy & Richard M. Ryckman. 1983. The influence of a rape victim's attractiveness on observers' attributions of responsibility. *Human Relations,* 36, 549-561.

Thornton, Billy, Richard M. Ryckman & Michael A. Robbins. 1982. The relationship of observer characteristics to beliefs in the causal responsibility of victims of sexual assault. *Human Relations,* 35, 321-331.

Thornton, Kirtley E. 1995. The anatomy of the lie: An exploratory investigation via the quantitiative EEG (Q-EEG). *Journal of Offender Rehabilitation,* 22 (3/4), 179-210.

Thrasher, Frederic, M. 1936: *The Gang: A Study of 1313 Gangs in Chicago,* 2nd ed. Chicago: University of Chicago Press.

Tiihonen, Jari, Jyrki Kuikka, Panu Hakola, Jarmo Paanila, Juha Airaksinen, Markku Eronen & Tero Hallikainen. 1994. Acute ethanol-induced changes in cerebral blood flow. *American Journal of Psychiatry,* 151, 1505-1508.

Tiihonen, Jari, Jyrki Kuikka, Kim Bergström, Panu Hakola, Jari Kahru, Olli-Pekka Ryynänen & Jaana Fohr. 1995. Altered striatal dopamine re-uptake site densities in habitually violent and non-violent alcoholics. *Nature Medicine,* 1, 654-657.

Toborg, Mary A., & John P. Bellassai. 1987. *Assessment of Pretrial Urine Testing in the District of Columbia, I: Background and Description of the Urine Testing Program; IV: Analysis of Drug Use Among Arrestees*. Washington, DC: Toborg Associates.

Toby, Jackson. 1986. The victims of school violence. In Timothy F. Hartnagel & Robert A. Silverman (eds.), *Critique and Explanation*. New Brunswick, NJ: Transaction Publishers. Pp. 171-184.

Toby, Jackson. 1995. Crime in the schools. in James Q. Wilson (ed.), *Crime and Public Policy*. New Brunswick, NJ: Transaction Publishers. Pp. 69-88.

Toch, Hans. 1975. *Men in Crisis: Human Breakdowns in Prison*. Chicago: Aldine.

Toch, Hans (ed.) 1979. *Psychology of Crime and Criminal Justice*. New York: Holt Rinehart Winston.

Toch, Hans, & Kenneth Adams. 1988. *Coping: Maladaptation in Prisons*. New Brunswick, NJ: Transaction Publishers.

Toch, Hans, Kenneth Adams & Ronald Greene. 1987. Ethnicity, disruptiveness, and emotional disorder among prison inmates. *Criminal Justice & Behavior*, 14, 93-109.

Torrey, E. Fuller. 1988. *Nowhere to Go: The Tragic Odyssey of the Homeless Mentally Ill*. New York: Harper & Row.

Tong, Gang, Dawn Shepherd & Craig E. Jahr. 1995. Synaptic desensitization of NMDA receptors by calcineurin. *Science*, 267, 5203, 1510-1512.

Torrey, E. Fuller. 1994. Violent behavior by individuals with serious mental illness. *Hospital & Community Psychiatry*, 45, 257-268.

Tonkonogy, Joseph M., & Jeffrey L. Geller. 1992. Hypothalamic lesions and intermittent explosive disorder. *Journal of Neuropsychiatry & Clinical Neurosciences*, 4, 45-50.

Torstensson, Marie. 1987. *Drug Abusers in a Metropolitan Cohort*. Stockholm: Department of Sociology, University of Stockholm.

Tremblay, Richard E., Robert O. Phil, Frank Vitaro & Patricia L. Dobkin. 1994. Predicting early onset of male antisocial behavior from preschool behavior. *Archives of General Psychiatry*, 51, 732-739.

Tuchfeld, Barry S., Richard R. Clayton & John A. Logan. 1982. Alcohol, drug use, and delinquent criminal behavior among male adolescents and young adults. *Journal of Drug Issues*, 12, 185-198.

Turner, Frederick Jackson. 1893. The significance of the frontier in American history. *Annual Report of the American Historical Association*. Chicago: The Association. Pp. 199-227.

Ungerleider, Leslie G. 1995. Functional brain imaging studies of cortical mechanisms for memory. *Science*, 270, 769-775.

U.S. Public Health Service. 1989. *International Classification of Diseases, 9th Revision, Clinical Modification: Third Edition*. Washington, DC: U.S. Department of Health & Human Services. Publication No.(PHS) 89-1260.

U.S. Public Health Service. 1992.. *Vital Statistics of the United States — Vital and Health Statistics: Mortality Data*. Washington, DC: National Center for Health Statistics.

Valciukas, Jose A. 1991. *Foundations of Environmental and Occupational Neurotoxicology*. New York: Van Nostrand Reinhold

Valciukas, Jose A. 1995. *Forensic Neuropsychology: Conceptual Foundations and Clinical Practice*. New York: Haworth.

Valzelli, Luigi. 1981. *Psychobiology of Aggression and Violence*. New York: Raven.

van Wormer, Katherine. 1995. Execution-inspired murder: A form of suicide? *Journal of Offender Rehabilitation*, 23 (3/4), 181-197.

van Praag, Herman M. 1988. Biological psychiatry audited. *Journal of Nervous & Mental Disease*, 176, 195-199.

Veneziano, Carol A. 1986. Prison inmates and consent to treatment: Problems and issues. *Law & Psychology Review*, 10, 129-146.

Veneziano, Carol A., & Louis Veneziano. 1986. Classification of adolescent offenders with the MMPI: An extension and cross-validation of the Megargee typology. *International Journal of Offender Therapy & Comparative Criminology*, 30, 11-23.

Vigderhous, Gideon. 1975. Suicide and homicide as causes of death and their relationship to life expectancy: A cross-national comparison. *Social Biology,* 22, 338-343.

Villanueva, Michael R., Deborah D. Roman & Michael R. Tuley. 1988. Determining forensic rehabilitation potential with the MMPI: Practical implications for residential treatment populations. *American Journal of Forensic Psychology,* 6, 27-35.

Violence Epidemiology Branch, U.S. Department of Health & Human Services. 1984. *Homicide Surveillance.* Washington, DC: U.S. Government Printing Office.

Virkkunen, Matti. 1974. Suicide linked to homicide. *Psychiatric Quarterly,* 48, 276-282.

Virkkunen, Matti. 1979. Alcoholism and antisocial personality. *Acta Psychiatrica Scandinavica,* 59, 493-501.

Virkkunen, Matti. 1982-*a.* Evidence for abnormal glucose tolerance test among violent offenders. *Neuropsychobiology,* 8, 30-34.

Virkkunen, Matti. 1982-*b.* Reactive hypoglycemic tendency among habitually violent offenders: A further study by means of the glucose tolerance test. *Neuropsychobiology,* 8, 35-40.

Virkkunen, Matti. 1983-*a.* Insulin secretion during the glucose tolerance test in antisocial personality. *British Journal of Psychiatry,* 142, 598-604.

Virkkunen, Matti. 1983-*b.* Serum cholesterol levels in homicidal offenders: A low cholesterol level is connected with a habitually violent tendency under the influence of alcohol. *Neuropsychobiology,* 10, 65-69.

Virkkunen, Matti. 1984. Reactive hypoglycemic tendency among arsonists. *Acta Psychiatrica Scandinavica,* 69, 445-452.

Virkkunen, Matti. 1985. Urinary free cortisol secretion in habitually violent offenders. *Acta Psychiatrica Scandinavica,* 72, 40-44.

Virkkunen, Matti. 1986. Insulin secretion during the glucose tolerance test among habitually violent and impulsive offenders. *Aggressive Behavior,* 12, 303-310.

Virkkunen, Matti, & M.O. Huttunen. 1982. Evidence for abnormal glucose tolerance test among violent offenders. *Neuropsychobiology,* 8, 30-34.

Virkkunen, Matti, & Eila Kallilo. 1987. Low blood glucose nadir in the glucose tolerance test and homicidal spouse abuse. *Aggressive Behavior,* 13, 59-66.

Virkkunen, Matti, & Markku Linnoila. 1993. Brain serotonin, type II alcoholism, and impulsive violence. *Journal of Studies on Alcohol,* 54, 163-169.

Virkkunen, Matti, & S. Narvanen. 1987. Plasma insulin, tryptophan, and serotonin levels during the glucose tolerance test among habitually violent and impulsive offenders. *Neuropsychobiology,* 17, 19-23.

Virkkunen, Matti, Arto Nuutila & Simo Huusko. 1976. Effect of brain injury on social adaptability: Longitudinal study on frequency of criminality. *Acta Psychiatrica Scandinavica,* 53, 168-172.

Virkkunen, Matti, David F. Horrobin, Douglas K. Jenkins & Mehar S. Manku. 1987. Plasma phospholipid essentially fatty acids and prostaglandins in alcoholic, habitually violent, and impulsive offenders. *Biological Psychiatry,* 22, 1087-1096.

Virkkunen, Matti, Judith de Jong, John J. Bartko & Frederick K. Goodwin. 1989. Relationship of psychobiological variables to recidivism in violent offenders and impulsive fire setters: A follow-up study. *Archives of General Psychiatry,* 46, 600-603.

Virkkunen, Matti, Arto Nuutila, Frederick K. Goodwin, & Markku Linnoila. 1987. Cerebrospinal fluid monamine metabolite levels in male arsonists. *Archives of General Psychiatry,* 44, 241-247.

Virkkunen, Matti, Robert Rawlings, Riitta Tokola, Russell E. Poland, Alessandro Guidotti, Charles Nemeroff, Garth Bissette, Konstantine Kalogeras, Sirkka-Liisa Karononen & Markku Linnoila. 1994. CSF biochemistries, glucose metabolism, and diurnal activity rhythms in alcoholic, violent offenders, fire setters, and healthy volunteers. *Archives of General Psychiatry,* 51, 3-20.

Virkkunen, Matti, Eila Kallio, Robert Rawlings, Riita Tokola, Russell E. Poland, Alessandro Guidotti, Charles Nemeroff, Garth Bissette, Konstantine Kalogeras, Sirkka-Liisa Karonen & Markku Linnoila. 1994. Personality profiles and state aggressiveness in Finnish alcoholic, violent offenders, fire setters, and healthy volunteers. *Archives of General Psychiatry,* 51, 23-45.

Volavka, Jan. 1991. Aggression, electroencephalography, and evoked potentials: A critical review. *Neuropsychiatry, Neuropsychology & Behavioral Neurology,* 3, 249-259.

Volkow, Nora D., & Laurence R. Tancredi. 1991. Biological correlates of mental activity studied with PET [positron emisssion tomography]. *American Journal of Psychiatry,* 148, 439-443.

Volpicelli, Joseph R., Arthur I. Alterman, Motoi Hayashida & Charles P. O'Brien. 1992. Naltrexone in the treatment of alcohol dependence. *Archives of General Psychiatry,* 49, 876-880.

von Hirsch, Andrew. 1985. *Past or Future Crimes: Deservedness and Dangerousness in the Sentencing of Criminals.* New Brunswick, NJ: Rutgers University Press.

von Hirsch, Andrew. 1988. *Federal Sentencing Guidelines: The United States and Canadian Schemes Compared.* New York: Center for Research in Crime & Justice, School of Law, New York University.

Wahl, Otto F., & J. Yonatan Lefkowits. 1989. Impact of a television film on attitudes toward mental illness. *American Journal of Community Psychology,* 17, 521-528.

Waite, Bradley M. 1995. Sampling the experience of chronically aggressive psychiatric inpatients. In Marc Hillbrand & Nathaniel J. Pallone (eds.), *The Psychobiology of Aggression.* New York: Haworth. Pp. 173-186.

Wakshlag, Jacob, Virginia Vial & Ronald Tamborini. 1983. Selecting crime drama and apprehension about crime. *Human Communication Research,* 10, 227-242.

Waller, Julian. 1972. Factors associated with alcohol and responsibility for fatal highway crashes. *Quarterly Journal of Studies on Alcohol.* 33, 160-170.

Walker, Lenore E., & Angela Browne 1985. Gender and victimization by intimates. *Journal of Personality*, 53, 175-195.

Walker, Nigel. 1968. *Crime and Insanity in England: The Historical Perspective.* Edinburgh: Edinburgh University Press.

Walsh, James, John Beyer & Joanna Petee. 1987. Love deprivation, Wechsler performance>verbal discrepancy, and juvenile delinquency. *Journal of Psychology*, 121, 177-184

Walters, Glenn D. 1986-a. Correlates of the Megargee criminal classification system: A military correctional setting. *Criminal Justice & Behavior,* 13, 19-32.

Walters, Glenn D. 1986-b. Screening for psychopathology in groups and black and white prison inmates by means of the MMPI. *Journal of Personality Assessment,* 50, 257-264.

Walters, Glenn D. 1992. *Foundations of Criminal Science, Volumes 1 & 2.* New York: Praeger.

Walters, Glenn D., Thomas W. White & Roger L. Greene. 1988. Use of the MMPI to identify malingering and exaggeration of psychiatric symptomatology in male prison inmates. *Journal of Consulting & Clinical Psychology,* 56, 111-117.

Wass, Hannelore, Jane L. Raup, Karen Cerullo, Linda G. Martel *et al.* 1988-89. Adolescents' Interest in and views of destructive themes in rock music. *Omega: Journal of Death & Dying,* 19, 177-186.

Wauchope, Barbara A., & Murray A. Straus. 1990. Physical punishment and physical abuse of American children: Incidence rates by age, gender, and occupational class. In Murray A. Straus & Richard J. Gelles (eds.), *Physical Violence in American Families: Risk Factors and Adaptions to Violence in 8145 Families.* New Brunswick, NJ: Transaction Publishers. Pp. 133-148.

Webster, Rhonda L., Jay Goldstein & Alexander Segall. 1985. A test of the explanatory value of alternative models of child abuse. *Journal of Comparative Family Studies,* 16, 295-317.

Wechsler, David. 1939. *The Measurement of Adult Intelligence.* Baltimore: Williams & Wilkins.

Wechsler, David. 1941. *The Measurement of Adult Intelligence,* 2nd ed. Baltimore: Williams & Wilkins.

Wechsler, David. 1944. *The Measurement of Adult Intelligence,* 3rd ed. Baltimore: Williams & Wilkins.

Weshsler, David. 1955. *The Range of Human Capacities,* 2nd ed. Baltimore: Williams & Wilkins.

Wechsler, David. 1958. *The Measurement and Appraisal of Adult Intelligence,* 4th ed. Baltimore: Williams & Wilkins.

Wechsler, David. 1971. Intelligence: Definition, theory, and the IQ. In Robert Cancro (ed.), *Intelligence: Genetic and Envivonmental Influences.* New York: Grune & Stratton. Pp. 50-55.

Weider, A., J. Levi & F. Risch. 1943. Performances of problem children on the Wechsler-Bellevue intelligence scales and the revised Stanford-Binet. *Psychiatric Quarterly,* 17, 695-701.

Weinstein, Cheryl S. 1994. Cognitive remediation strategies. *Journal of Psychotherapy Practice & Research*, 3, 44-57.

Weissman, Myrna M., Jerome K. Myers & Pamela S. Harding. 1978. Psychiatric disorders in a U.S. Urban community. *American Journal of Psychiatry*, 135, 459-462.

Weissman, Myrna M., Jerome K. Myers & Catherine E. Ross. 1986. Community studies in psychiatric epidemiology. In Myrna M. Weissman, Jerome K. Myers & Catherine E. Ross (eds.), *Community Surveys of Psychiatric Disorders*. New Brunswick, NJ: Rutgers University Press. Pp. 1-9.

Welte, John W., & Ernest L. Abel. 1989. Homicide: Drinking by the victim. *Journal of Studies on Alcohol*, 50, 197-201.

Welte, John W., & Brenda A. Miller. 1987. Alcohol use by violent and property offenders. *Drug & Alcohol Dependence*, 19, 313-324.

Wenk, Ernst A., James O. Robison & Gerald W. Smith. 1972. Can violence be predicted? *Crime & Delinquency,* 18, 393-402.

West, Donald J., & Alexander Walk (eds.). 1977. *Daniel McNaughton: His Trial and the Aftermath.* Ashford, Kent: Royal College of Psychiatrists.

Westermeyer, Joe. 1993. Psychiatric disorders among American Indian vs. other patients with psychoactive substance use disorders. *American Journal on Addictions*, 2, 79-91.

Wettstein, Robert M. 1987. Legal aspects of neuropsychiatry, In Robert E. Hales & Stuart C. Yudofsky (eds.), *American Psychiatric Press Textbook of Neuropsychiatry.* Washington, DC: American Psychiatric Press. Pp. 451-463.

Wettstein, Robert M. 1988. Psychiatry and the law. In John A. Talbott, Robert E. Hales & Stuart C. Yudofsky (eds.), *American Psychiatric Press Textbook of Psychiatry.* Washington, DC: American Psychiatric Press. Pp. 1059-1084.

Wetzel, Hermann, Andreas Hillert, Gerhard Gründer & Otto Benkert. 1994. Roxindole, a dopamine autoreceptor agonist, in the treatment of positive and negative schizophrenic symptoms. *American Journal of Psychiatry*, 151, 1499-1502.

Wheeler, Stanton. 1976. Trends and problems in the sociological study of crime. *Social Problems,* 23, 525-534.

White, Garland F. 1989. Media and violence: The case of professional football championship games. *Aggressive Behavior*, 15, 423-433.

White, Helene Raskin, Erich W. Labouvie & Marsha E. Bates. 1985. The relationship between sensation seeking and delinquency: A longitudinal analysis. *Journal of Research in Crime & Delinquency*, 22, 198-211.

White, Ralph K. 1995. When does intervention make sense? *Peace & Conflict*, 1, 85-95.

Whitman, Steven, Tina E. Coleman, Cecil Patmon, Bindu T. Desai, Robert Cohen & Lambert N. King. 1984. Epilepsy in prison: Elevated prevalence and no relationship to violence. *Neurology*, 34, 775-782.

Widom, Cathy S. 1989—a. Does violence beget violence? A critical examination of the literature. *Psychological Bulletin*, 106, 3-28.

Widom, Cathy S. 1989-b. A tail on an untold tale: Response to "Biological and genetic contributors to violence: Widom's untold tail." *Psychological Bulletin*, 109, 130-132.

Widom, Cathy S. 1989-c. The cycle of violence. *Science*, 244, 160-166.

Widom, Cathy S., 1989-d. Child abuse, neglect, and violent criminal behavior. In David A. Brizer & Martha L. Crowner (eds.), *Current Approaches to the Prediction of Violence.* Washington, DC: American Psychiatric Press. Pp. 121-148.

Widom, Cathy S., 1995. Victims of childhood sexual abuse — Later criminal consequences, *National Institute of Justice Research Brief,* March. 1-8.

Widom, Cathy S., & M. Ashley Ames. 1994. Criminal consequences of childhood sexual victimization. *Child Abuse & Neglect*, 18, 303-317.

Widom, Cathy S., Timothy Ireland & Patricia J. Glynn. 1995. Alcohol abuse in abused and neglected children followed-up: Are they are at increased risk? *Journal of Studies on Alcohol*, 56, 207-217.

Wiens, Arthur N., & William H. Banaka. 1960. Estimating WAIS IQ from Hartford-Shipley scores. *Journal of Clinical Psychology*, 16, 452.

Wiggins, Jerry. 1973. *Personality and Prediction*. Reading, MA: Addison-Wesley.

Wilbanks, William. 1980. Relationships among victimization rates for accidents, suicide, and homicide. *Victimology, 7*, 213-217.

Wilbanks, William. 1982. Fatal accidents, suicide, and homicide: Are they related? *Victimology, 7*, 213-217.

Wilbanks, William. 1983. Female homicide offenders in the U.S. *International Journal of Women's Studies, 6*, 302-310.

Wilbanks, William. 1985. Is violent crime intraracial? *Crime & Delinquency, 31*, 117-128.

Wilcox, Rand R. 1995. ANOVA: A paradgim for low power and misleading measures of effect size. *Review of Educational Research, 65*, 51-77.

Wilkes, John. 1986. Murder in mind. *Psychology Today, 21*, 26-32.

Williams, Arhtur H. 1982. Adolescents, violence, and crime. *Journal of Adolescence, 5*, 125-134.

Williams, Denis. 1969. Neural factors related to habitual aggression: Consideration of differences between those habitual aggressives and others who have committed crimes of violence. *Brain, 92*, 501-520.

Williams, Euphemia G. 1983. Adolescent loneliness. *Adolescence, 18*, 51-66.

Williams, Frank P. 1985. Deterrence and social control: Rethinking the relationship. *Journal of Criminal Justice, 13*, 141-151.

Williams, Joyce F., & Karen A. Holmes. 1982. In judgment of victims: The social context of rape. *Journal of Sociology & Social Welfare, 9*, 154-169.

Williams, Kirk R. 1984. Economic sources of homicide: Re-estimating the effects of poverty and inequality. *American Sociological Review, 49*, 283-289.

Williams, Linda S. 1984. The classic rape: When do victims report? *Social Problems, 31*, 459-467.

Williams, Wright, & Kent S. Miller. 1977. The role of personal characteristics in perceptions of dangerousness. *Criminal Justice & Behavior, 4*, 241-252.

Wilson, G. Terence, & K. Daniel O'Leary. 1980. *Principles of Behavior Therapy*. Englewood Cliffs, NJ: Prentice-Hall.

Wilson, James Q., & Richard J. Herrnstein. 1985. *Crime & Human Nature: The Definitive Study of the Causes of Crime*. New York: Simon & Schuster.

Wilson, Margo, & Martin Daly. 1985. Competitiveness, risk taking, and violence: The young male syndrome. *Ethology & Sociobiology, 6*, 59-73.

Wilson, Paul R. 1987. "Stranger" child murder: Issues related to causes and controls. *International Journal of Offender Therapy & Comparative Criminology, 31*, 49-59.

Wineburg, Samuel S. 1987. The self-fulfillment of the self-fulfilling prophecy: A critical appraisal. *Educational Researcher, 16*, 28-37.

Wish, Eric D. 1990. Drug testing. In Larry J. Siegiegel (ed.), *American Justice: Research of the National Institute of Justice*. St. Paul, MN: West. Pp. 109-113.

Wish, Eric D., & Joyce Ann O'Neil. 1989. Drug use forecasting (DUF) research update. *Research in Action: Drug Use Forecasting*. National Institute of Justice, U.S. Department of Justice, September 1989.

Wish, Eric D., Elizabeth Brady & Mary Cuadrado. 1986. *Urine Testing of Arrestees: Findings from Manhattan*. New York: Narcotic and Drug Research, Inc.

Witkin, Herman A., Sarnoff A. Mednick, Fini Schulsinger, Eskild Bakkestrøm, Karl O. Christiansen, Donald R. Goodenough, Kurt Hirschhorn, Claes Lundsteen, David R. Owen, John Philip, David B. Rubin & Marth Stocking. 1976. Criminality in XYY and XXY men. *Science, 193*, 547-555.

Wolfe, David A. 1985. Child-abusive parents: An empirical review and analysis. *Psychological Bulletin, 97*, 462-482.

Wolfe, David A., John A. Fairbank, Jeffrey A. Kelly & Andrew S. Bradlyn. 1983. Child abusive parents' physiological responses to stressful and non-stressful behavior in children. *Behavioral Assessment, 5*, 363-371.

Wolfgang, Marvin E. 1958. *Patterns in Criminal Homicide*. Philadelphia: University of Pennsylvania Press.

Wolfgang, Marvin E., & Franco Ferracuti. 1967. *The Subculture of Violence*. London: Tavistock.

Wood, Nollie P. 1990. Black homicide: A public health crisis. *Journal of Interpersonal Violence,* 5, 147-150.

Wood, Nollie P., & James A. Mercy. 1990. Unintentional firearm-related fatalities, 1970-84. *Public Health Surveillance of 1990: Injury Control Objectives of the Nation,* 37, 47-52.

Wood, Rodger Llewellyn. 1987. *Brain Injury Rehabilitation: A Neurobehavioral Approach.* Rockville, MD: Aspen.

Wood, Wendy, Frank Y. Yong & J. Gregory Chachere. 1991. Effects of media violence on viewers' aggression in unconstrained social interaction. *Psychological Bulletin,* 109, 371-383.

Woods, Bryan T., Susan Brennan, Deborah Yurgelun-Todd, Tina Young & Peter Panzarino. 1995. MRI abnormalities in major psychiatric disorders: an exploratory comparative study. *Journal of Neuropsychiatry and Clinical Neurosciences,* 7, 49-53.

World Health Organization. 1992. *The ICD-10 Classification of Mental and Behavioural Disorders.* Geneva: The Organization.

Wright, Kevin N. 1991. The violent and the victimized in the male prison. *Journal of Offender Rehabilitation,* 16, 1-25.

Wright, Richard. 1957. *White Man, Listen!* Garden City, NY: Doubleday.

Wright, Robert. 1995. The biology of violence. *New Yorker,* March 13, 68-77.

Wyer, Robert S., Galen V. Bodenhausen & Theresa F. Gorman. 1985. Cognitive mediators of reactions to rape. *Journal of Personality & Social Psychology,* 48, 324-338.

Wynne, Edward, & Mary Hess. 1986. Long-term trends in youth conduct and the revival of traditonal value patterns. *Educational Evaluation & Policy Analysis,* 8, 294-308.

Wyricka, Wanda. 1996. *Imitation in Human and Animal Behavior.* New Brunswick, NJ: Transaction Publishers.

Yang, Bijou, & David Lester. 1988-*a*. The participation of females in the labor force and rates of personal violence (suicide and homicide). *Suicide & Life-Threatening Behavior,* 18, 270-278.

Yang, Bijou, & David Lester. 1988-*b*. Predicting execution rates in the U.S.A. *Psychological Reports,* 62, 305-306.

Yarmey, A. Daniel. 1985. Older and younger adults' attributions of responsibility toward rape victims and rapists. *Canadian Journal of Behavioural Science,* 17, 327-338.

Yeh, Shih-Rung, Russel A. Fricke & Donald H. Edwards. 1996. The effect of social experience on serotonergic modulation of the escape circuit of crayfish. *Science,* 271, 366- 369.

Yesavage, Jerome A., Michel Benezech, Roland Larrieu-Arguille & Marc Bourgeois. 1986. Recidivism of the criminally insane in France: A 22-year follow-up. *Journal of Clinical Psychiatry,* 47, 465-466.

Yeudall, Lorne T., & D. Fromm-Auch. 1979. Neuropsychological impairments in various psychopathological populations. In John Gruzelier & Pierre Flor-Henry (eds.), *Hemisphere Asymmetries of Function in Psychopathology.* Amsterdam: Elsevier/North Holland Biomedical Press. Pp. 401-428.

Yeudall, Lorne T., Orestes Fedora & DaLee Fromm. 1987. A neuropsychological theory of persistent criminality: Implications for assessment and treatment. *Advances in Forensic Psychology & Psychiatry,* 2, 119-191.

Yochelson, Samuel, & Stanton E. Samenow. 1976. *The Criminal Personality.* New York: Jason Aronson.

Yohman, J. Robert, Kim W. Schaeffer & Oscar A. A. Parsons. 1988. Cognitive retraining in alcoholic men. *Journal of Consulting & Clinical Psychology,* 56, 67-72.

Yudofsky, Stuart C., & Robert E. Hales. 1992. Introduction. *The American Psychiatric Press Textbook of Neuropsychiatry,* 2nd ed. Washington, DC: American Psychiatric Press.

Zachary, Robert A. 1990. *Shipley Institute of Living Scale — User's Guide to the Microcomputer Edition,* 2d ed., Version 2.000. Los Angeles: Western Psychological Services.

Zager, Lynne D. 1988. The MMPI-based criminal classification system: A review, current status, and future directions. *Criminal Justice & Behavior,* 15, 39-57-57.

Zaidi, L.Y., J.F. Knutson & J.G. Mehm. 1989. Transgenerational patterns of abuse parenting: Analog and clinical tests. *Aggressive Behavior,* 15, 137-152.

Zaleski, Zbigniew. 1984. Sensation-seeking and risk-taking behaviour. *Personality & Individual Differences,* 5, 607-608.

Zentall, Thomas R. 1993. *Animal Cognition.* Hillsdale, NJ: Erlbaum.

Zillman, Dolf, & Jennings Bryant. 1983. Pornography and social science research: Higher moralities. *Journal of Communication,* 33, 111-114.

Zimring, Franklin E. 1990. Gun control. In Larry J. Siegel (ed.), *American Justice: Research of the National Institute of Justice.* St. Paul, MN: West. Pp. 32-36.

Zimring, Franklin, & Gordon Hawkins. 1986. *Capital Punishment and the American Agenda.* New York: Cambridge University Press.

Zuckerman, Marvin. 1995. Good and bad humors: Biochemical bases of personality and its disorders. *Psychological Science,* 6, 325-332.

INDEX OF NAMES AND SENIOR AUTHORS

INDEX OF TOPICS

NATHANIEL J. PALLONE is University Distinguished Professor, Psychology & Criminal Justice, at Rutgers — The State University of New Jersey, where he previously served as dean and as academic vice president. On leave from Rutgers, he has served as a visiting professor at the University of Minnesota and the School of Public Health, Harvard University. A fellow of the American Psychological Association, the American Psychological Society, and the American College of Forensic Psychology and a diplomate of the American Board of Professional Psychology, since 1976 he has chaired the Classification Review Board for Sex Offenders in New Jersey's Department of Corrections, a statutory "dangerousness review" body charged with assessing the therapeutic progress of criminal sexual psychopaths confined for treatment under the state's habitual sex offender act. He has treated adjudicated heroin addicts at the New York State Narcotics Addiction Control Commission and has been a consultant to the Criminal Justice Research Center (Albany) and the Connecticut Department of Corrections. Pallone is executive editor of *Current Psychology* (Transaction Periodicals Consortium) and editor-in-chief of the *Journal of Offender Rehabilitation*. His most recent books include *Rehabilitating Criminal Sexual Psychopaths, Mental Disorder among Prisoners*, and, with James J. Hennessy, *Criminal Behavior: A Process Psychology Analysis* and *Fraud and Fallible Judgment*, each published by Transaction.

JAMES J. HENNESSY chairs the Division of Psychological & Educational Services in the Graduate School of Education at Fordham University, Lincoln Center, where he previously served as director of the PhD program in counseling psychology. Active in the scientific programs of the American Psychological Association, the American Psychological Society, and the American Educational Research Association, he has served as a research consultant to the Connecticut Department of Corrections and, between 1973-91, as consulting psychologist at a network of publicly funded day treatment centers in two New York counties that provide educational services for adjudicated delinquents and adolescents diagnosed with conduct and behavior disorders. An editor of *Current Psychology* (Transaction Periodicals Consortium) and of *Comprehensive Mental Health Care* and a member of the editorial board of the *Journal of Offender Rehabilitation*, Hennessy is a frequent contributor to scholarly and professional journals on psychometric methodology and advanced data analysis techniques. His most recent books, with Nathaniel J. Pallone, are *Criminal Behavior: A Process Psychology Analysis* and *Fraud and Fallible Judgment*, both published by Transaction.